ALSO BY MATTHEW J. BRUCCOLI

The Composition of *Tender Is the Night*

F. Scott Fitzgerald in His Own Time (editor, with Jackson Bryer)

As Ever, Scott Fitz— (editor, with Jennifer Atkinson)

F. Scott Fitzgerald: A Descriptive Bibliography; Revised Edition

The Great Gatsby: A Facsimile of the Manuscript (editor)

F. Scott Fitzgerald's Ledger: A Facsimile (editor)

Bits of Paradise (editor, with Scottie Fitzgerald Smith)

The Romantic Egoists (editor, with Scottie Fitzgerald Smith
    and Joan P. Kerr)

"The Last of the Novelists": F. Scott Fitzgerald and *The Last
    Tycoon*

The Notebooks of F. Scott Fitzgerald (editor)

Scott and Ernest: The Authority of Failure and the Authority
    of Success

F. Scott Fitzgerald's Screenplay for *Three Comrades* (editor)

The Price Was High: 50 Uncollected Stories by F. Scott Fitzgerald
    (editor)

Correspondence of F. Scott Fitzgerald (editor,
    with Margaret Duggan)

F. Scott Fitzgerald: Poems 1911–1940 (editor)

Some Sort of Epic Grandeur: The Life of F. Scott Fitzgerald;
    Revised Edition

New Essays on *The Great Gatsby* (editor)

The Short Stories of F. Scott Fitzgerald (editor)

F. Scott Fitzgerald Manuscripts, 18 vols. (editor)

The Cambridge Edition of the Works of F. Scott Fitzgerald
    (editor)—*The Great Gatsby* and *The Love of the Last Tycoon:
    A Western* published to date

Zelda Fitzgerald: The Collected Writings (editor)

The Yacht Club,
White Bear Lake.

Dear Mr. Perkins:

Glad you liked the addenda to the Table of Contents. I feel quite confident the book will go. How do you think The Far Legend will sell? You'll be glad to know that nothing has come of the movie idea + I'm rather glad myself. At present I'm working on my play — the same one. Trying to arrange for an Oct. production in New York. Bunny Wilson (Edmund Wilson Jr.) says that it's without doubt the best American comedy to date (that's just between you and me.)

Did you see that in that Literary Digest contest I stood 6th among the novelists? Not that it matters. I suspect you of having been one of the voters.

Will you see that the semi-yearly account is mailed to me by the 1st of the month — or before if it is ready? I want to see where I stand. I want to write something new — something extraordinary and beautiful and simple + intricately patterned.

As Usual
F Scott Fitzgerald

In the final paragraph of this letter to editor Maxwell Perkins (mid-July, 1922), Fitzgerald sets forth his vision of his masterpiece, the novel that was to become *The Great Gatsby* (Princeton University).

F. Scott Fitzgerald
A Life in Letters

❖

EDITED BY

MATTHEW J. BRUCCOLI

WITH THE ASSISTANCE OF
JUDITH S. BAUGHMAN

A TOUCHSTONE BOOK
Published by Simon & Schuster Inc.
New York   London   Toronto
Sydney   Tokyo   Singapore

TOUCHSTONE
Rockefeller Center
1230 Avenue of the Americas
New York, NY 10020

First Touchstone Edition 1995

TOUCHSTONE and colophon are registered trademarks
of Simon & Schuster Inc.

Manufactured in the United States of America

1   3   5   7   9   10   8   6   4   2

Library of Congress Cataloging-in-Publication Data
Fitzgerald, F. Scott (Francis Scott), 1896-1940.
A life in letters / F. Scott Fitzgerald : edited by Matthew J. Bruccoli : with the
assistance of Judith S. Baughman.
p.   cm.
Includes bibliographical references and index.
1. Fitzgerald, F. Scott (Francis Scott), 1896-1940—Correspondence.
2. Authors, American—20th century—Correspondence.
I. Bruccoli, Matthew Joseph, 1931-
II. Title.
PS3511.I9Z48   1995
813'.52—dc20

[B]   94-43901 CIP

ISBN 0-684-19570-4
0-684-80153-1 (Pbk)

The editor dedicates this volume to
CHARLES SCRIBNER III

The compensation of a very early success is a conviction that life is a romantic matter. In the best sense one stays young. When the primary objects of love and money could be taken for granted and a shaky eminence had lost its fascination, I had fair years to waste, years that I can't honestly regret, in seeking the eternal Carnival by the Sea. Once in the middle twenties I was driving along the High Corniche Road through the twilight with the whole French Riviera twinkling on the sea below. As far ahead as I could see was Monte Carlo, and though it was out of season and there were no Grand Dukes left to gamble and E. Phillips Oppenheim was a fat industrious man in my hotel, who lived in a bathrobe—the very name was so incorrigibly enchanting that I could only stop the car and like the Chinese whisper: "Ah me! Ah me!" It was not Monte Carlo I was looking at. It was back into the mind of the young man with cardboard soles who had walked the streets of New York. I was him again—for an instant I had the good fortune to share his dreams, I who had no more dreams of my own. And there are still times when I creep up on him, surprise him on an autumn morning in New York or a spring night in Carolina when it is so quiet that you can hear a dog barking in the next county. But never again as during that all too short period when he and I were one person, when the fulfilled future and the wistful past were mingled in a single gorgeous moment—when life was literally a dream.

—"Early Success" (1937)

CONTENTS

❖

ACKNOWLEDGMENTS

—————— ❖ ——————

Arlyn Bruccoli helped me to formulate the editorial plan for this volume. Eleanor Lanahan vetted the working draft and advised me on footnote policy. Kreg A. Abshire, Tracy S. Bitonti, Bruce A. Bowlin, Hoke Greiner, Merrill Horton, Jennifer A. Hynes, Cy League, Eric Roman, and Robert Trogdon, graduate research assistants in the University of South Carolina Department of English, performed their tasks splendidly. Prof. Bert Dillon, Chairman of the Department, and Prof. Paula Feldman, Director of the Graduate Program, provided all the help within their powers. Maurice and Marcia Neville made available letters from their collection, as did Douglas Wyman. Honoria Murphy Donnelly provided copies and answered questions. These librarians rendered crucial aid: Daniel Boice (University of South Carolina Libraries), William Cagle (Lilly Library, Indiana University), Vincent Fitzpatrick (Enoch Pratt Free Library), Sidney F. Huttner (University of Tulsa Library), Don Skemer and Alice Clark (Princeton University Library), Thomas F. Staley (Harry Ransom Humanities Research Center, University of Texas, Austin), and Patricia Willis (Yale University Library). Thanks are due to Paul Gitlin (Estate of Thomas Wolfe).

Judith S. Baughman liberally shared her good judgment and intelligence.

M.J.B.

Introduction

❖

Everything F. Scott Fitzgerald wrote was a form of autobiography. His fiction is transmuted autobiography. Characters start as self-portraits and turn into fiction, as did Amory Blaine in *This Side of Paradise*; they start as fiction and become Fitzgerald, as did Dick Diver in *Tender Is the Night*. Jay Gatsby is pure invention and pure Fitzgerald.

A culture hero who saw his life as characterized by "some sort of epic grandeur," Fitzgerald functioned as a self-historiographer, as the curator of the F. Scott Fitzgerald research center. His letters reveal this concern: they were written for the record—in contrast to Ernest Hemingway's letters, which were written for the legend. For a writer, Fitzgerald was remarkably truthful. Apart from the documentary evidence they provide, his letters are worth reading if only because he couldn't write badly: even in routine correspondence there are flashes of wit and combinations of words that bear the Fitzgerald stamp. Fitzgerald's wit is a defining quality of his mind.

This volume properly includes a high proportion of letters about writing. The most important thing about Fitzgerald—about any writer—is his witing. The playboy image that has attached itself like fungus to Fitzgerald's reputation obscures the proper assessment of his genius. Because Fitzgerald is regarded as "a natural"—a misleading claim made by civilians—his literary intelligence has been impugned. These letters amply demonstrate that when Fitzgerald wrote about literature, even informally, he wrote with the authority of a professional who had mastered his craft.

This volume is not a supplementary collection of F. Scott Fitzgerald letters. The publisher intends for it to serve as the standard one-volume edition of Fitzgerald letters meeting the requirements of a cross-section of his readership.

The first publication of F. Scott Fitzgerald's letters came in *The Crack-Up* (1945),[1] in which Edmund Wilson excerpted letters to Fitzgerald's daughter, Scottie. Andrew Turnbull's edition of *The Letters of F. Scott Fitzgerald* (1963)[2] selected many of Fitzgerald's best letters; but the organization by recipient restricted its usefulness as an autobiographical source. Moreover, the printed texts of these letters are not accurate; Turnbull silently corrected

---

[1] New York: New Directions.
[2] New York: Scribners.

and cut the documents. Important Fitzgerald letters have been discovered during the thirty years since the Turnbull collection. Two hundred and eleven letters printed here are not in Turnbull.

Fitzgerald's professional life as literary artist and commercial writer are covered in two volumes: *Dear Scott/Dear Max: The Fitzgerald-Perkins Correspondence* (1971),[1] edited by John Kuehl and Jackson Bryer, and *As Ever, Scott Fitz—Letters Between F. Scott Fitzgerald and His Literary Agent Harold Ober* (1972),[2] edited by Bruccoli with Jennifer Atkinson. These collections make Fitzgerald's authorial career the most thoroughly documented one among American writers.

In 1980 Bruccoli and Margaret M. Duggan edited *Correspondence of F. Scott Fitzgerald*,[3] which included previously uncollected letters from Fitzgerald, as well as letters he received. The four volumes of letters are supplemented by Fitzgerald's autobiographical and autobibliographical *Ledger* (1972),[4] and by *The Romantic Egoists* (1974),[5] compiled from the Fitzgeralds' scrapbooks and albums.

This abundance of evidence in the published collections of Fitzgerald's letters is inconvenient for general readers—those outside academia who have maintained the classic status of his work by reading it. Accordingly, Charles Scribner III proposed a single-volume collection that would organize the best of the collected and unpublished Fitzgerald letters in chronological order. The principle of selection recommended by Mr. Scribner was that letters be chosen on the basis of their autobiographical content: hence *A Life in Letters*. This editorial rationale is appropriate because Fitzgerald's life and work were inseparable. His writing, both fiction and nonfiction, was a form of historiography, for he regarded his career as emblematic of American life.

There are disappointing gaps in Fitzgerald's extant correspondence. Neither Ginevra King nor Zelda Sayre preserved his love letters. Only a few letters to his parents survive. His letters to Father Sigourney Fay have not been found.

EDITORIAL NOTE

A rule of publishing holds that volumes of letters sell poorly because they are hard to read. But it is an editor's task to make the letters usable. Fitzgerald's letters—particularly his humorous letters—have a density of topical and literary references; they require their own cultural literacy. The editor of this volume was initially advised to keep footnoting at a minimum because of anticipated reader resistance to footnotes: it is assumed that so-called

[1] New York: Scribners.
[2] Philadelphia & New York: Lippincott.
[3] New York: Random House.
[4] Washington, D.C.: Bruccoli Clark/NCR-Microcard Editions.
[5] Edited by Scottie Fitzgerald Smith, Bruccoli, and Joan P. Kerr. New York: Scribners.

general readers find footnotes distracting. Nevertheless, when sample letters were tested on a cross-section of readers, it became clear that reader puzzlement or frustration was a much stronger response than irritation at the footnote apparatus.

Accordingly, this volume footnotes literary references and figures who were Fitzgerald's friends or who influenced him. Jokes have not been explicated. Great authors and classic works of literature have not been identified. Lists of celebrities (see September 21, 1925, letter to John Peale Bishop) and passing mentions of public figures (see the letter to Bishop from Capri, late March 1925) have not been explained. There will be objections to this policy on the basis that Fitzgerald's writings, public and private, expressed his sense of social history; whatever he wrote was motivated by the instinct to record the way it was at a time and place. Yet full documentation of Fitzgerald's correspondence would require an additional volume. This *Life in Letters* provides what the editor and his advisers regard as necessary explanations and identifications. The brief account of F. Scott Fitzgerald's career and the chronologies assist readers to make necessary connections among the letters.

There are no silent deletions or revisions. The letters have been transcribed exactly as F. Scott Fitzgerald wrote them—with the exception of the few stipulated cases where words have been omitted. Unlocated letters published in the Turnbull volume have perforce been reprinted from these texts.

Fitzgerald was a bad speller—so were other major authors—but his alleged "illiteracy" has been grossly exaggerated. He wrote what he heard. His ear for sentence structure and his sense of paragraph development were close to perfect.

Each letter is provided with an identifying heading, thus:

Recipient   *Description and location of document*
Assigned date (if required)   *Assigned place of writing (if required)*

The return address and date are printed as they appear on the letter; but the address of the recipient has not been transcribed. Spaced hyphens in typed letters have been printed as dashes. Standard acronyms are used in the description rubric: ALS—Autograph Letter Signed (a letter written in Fitzgerald's hand and signed by him); TLS—Typed Letter Signed (a typed letter signed by Fitzgerald); TL—Typed Letter (unsigned); CC—Carbon Copy; R—Revised in Fitzgerald's hand (RTLS designates a typed letter with Fitzgerald's handwritten revisions and his signature). Fitzgerald did not type; the typed letters in this volume were secretarial.

M.J.B.
August 21, 1993

A Brief Life of Fitzgerald

❖

The dominant influences on F. Scott Fitzgerald were aspiration, literature, Princeton, Zelda Sayre Fitzgerald, and alcohol.

Francis Scott Key Fitzgerald was born in St. Paul, Minnesota, on September 24, 1896, the namesake and second cousin three times removed of the author of the National Anthem. Fitzgerald's given names indicate his parents' pride in his father's ancestry. His father, Edward, was from Maryland, with an allegiance to the Old South and its values. Fitzgerald's mother, Mary (Mollie) McQuillan, was the daughter of an Irish immigrant who became wealthy as a wholesale grocer in St. Paul. Both were Catholics.

Edward Fitzgerald failed as a manufacturer of wicker furniture in St. Paul, and he became a salesman for Procter & Gamble in upstate New York. After he was dismissed in 1908, when his son was twelve, the family returned to St. Paul and lived comfortably on Mollie Fitzgerald's inheritance. Fitzgerald attended the St. Paul Academy; his first writing to appear in print was a detective story in the school newspaper when he was thirteen.

During 1911–1913 he attended the Newman School, a Catholic prep school in New Jersey, where he met Father Sigourney Fay, who encouraged his ambitions for personal distinction and achievement. As a member of the Princeton Class of 1917, Fitzgerald neglected his studies for his literary apprenticeship. He wrote the scripts and lyrics for the Princeton Triangle Club musicals and was a contributor to the *Princeton Tiger* humor magazine and the *Nassau Literary Magazine*. His college friends included Edmund Wilson and John Peale Bishop. On academic probation and unlikely to graduate, Fitzgerald joined the army in 1917 and was commissioned a second lieutenant in the infantry. Convinced that he would die in the war, he rapidly wrote a novel, "The Romantic Egotist"; the letter of rejection from Charles Scribner's Sons praised the novel's originality and asked that it be resubmitted when revised.

In June 1918 Fitzgerald was assigned to Camp Sheridan, near Montgomery, Alabama. There he fell in love with a celebrated belle, eighteen-year-old Zelda Sayre, the youngest daughter of an Alabama Supreme Court judge. The romance intensified Fitzgerald's hopes for the success of his novel, but after revision it was rejected by Scribners a second time. The war ended just before he was to be sent overseas; after his discharge in 1919 he went to New York City to seek his fortune in order to marry. Unwilling to wait while Fitzgerald succeeded in the advertisement business and unwilling to live on his small salary, Zelda broke their engagement.

Fitzgerald quit his job in July 1919 and returned to St. Paul to rewrite his novel as *This Side of Paradise*; it was accepted by editor Maxwell Perkins of Scribners in September. Set mainly at Princeton and described by its author as "a quest novel," *This Side of Paradise* traces the career aspirations and love disappointments of Amory Blaine.

In the fall-winter of 1919 Fitzgerald commenced his career as a writer of stories for the mass-circulation magazines. Working through agent Harold Ober, Fitzgerald interrupted work on his novels to write moneymaking popular fiction for the rest of his life. *The Saturday Evening Post* became Fitzgerald's best story market, and he was regarded as a "*Post* writer." His early commercial stories about young love introduced a fresh character: the independent, determined young American woman who appeared in "The Offshore Pirate" and "Bernice Bobs Her Hair." Fitzgerald's more ambitious stories, such as "May Day" and "The Diamond as Big as the Ritz," were published in *The Smart Set*, which had a small circulation.

The publication of *This Side of Paradise* on March 26, 1920, made the twenty-four-year-old Fitzgerald famous almost overnight, and a week later he married Zelda in New York. They embarked on an extravagant life as young celebrities. Fitzgerald endeavored to earn a solid literary reputation, but his playboy image impeded the proper assessment of his work.

After a riotous summer in Westport, Connecticut, the Fitzgeralds took an apartment in New York City; there he wrote his second novel, *The Beautiful and Damned*, a naturalistic chronicle of the dissipation of Anthony and Gloria Patch. When Zelda became pregnant they took their first trip to Europe in 1921 and then settled in St. Paul for the birth of their only child; Frances Scott (Scottie) Fitzgerald was born in October 1921.

Fitzgerald expected to become affluent from his play, *The Vegetable*; in the fall of 1922 they moved to Great Neck, Long Island, in order to be near Broadway. The political satire—subtitled "From President to Postman"— failed at its tryout in November 1923, and Fitzgerald wrote his way out of debt with short stories. The distractions of Great Neck and New York prevented Fitzgerald from making progress on his third novel. During this time his drinking increased. Fitzgerald was an alcoholic, but he wrote sober. Zelda regularly got "tight," but she was not an alcoholic. There were frequent domestic rows, usually triggered by drinking bouts.

Literary opinion makers were reluctant to accord Fitzgerald full marks as a serious craftsman. His reputation as a drinker inspired the myth that he was an irresponsible writer; yet he was a painstaking reviser whose fiction went through layers of drafts. Fitzgerald's clear, lyrical, colorful, witty style evoked the emotions associated with time and place. When critics objected to Fitzgerald's concern with love and success, his response was: "But, my God! it was my material, and it was all I had to deal with." The chief theme of Fitzgerald's work is aspiration—the idealism he regarded as defining

American character. Another major theme was mutability or loss. As a social historian Fitzgerald became identified with "The Jazz Age": "It was an age of miracles, it was an age of art, it was an age of excess, and it was an age of satire."

The Fitzgeralds went to France in the spring of 1924 seeking tranquillity for his work. He wrote *The Great Gatsby* during the summer and fall in Valescure near St. Raphael, but the marriage was damaged by Zelda's involvement with a French naval aviator. The extent of the affair—if it was in fact consummated—is not known. On the Riviera the Fitzgeralds formed a close friendship with Gerald and Sara Murphy.

The Fitzgeralds spent the winter of 1924–1925 in Rome, where he revised *The Great Gatsby*; they were en route to Paris when the novel was published in April. *The Great Gatsby* marked a striking advance in Fitzgerald's technique, utilizing a complex structure and a controlled narrative point of view. Fitzgerald's achievement received critical praise, but sales of *Gatsby* were disappointing, though the stage and movie rights brought additional income.

In Paris Fitzgerald met Ernest Hemingway—then unknown outside the expatriate literary circle—with whom he formed a friendship based largely on his admiration for Hemingway's personality and genius. The Fitzgeralds remained in France until the end of 1926, alternating between Paris and the Riviera.

Fitzgerald made little progress on his fourth novel, a study of American expatriates in France provisionally titled "The Boy Who Killed His Mother," "Our Type," and "The World's Fair." During these years Zelda's unconventional behavior became increasingly eccentric.

The Fitzgeralds returned to America to escape the distractions of France. After a short, unsuccessful stint of screen writing in Hollywood, Fitzgerald rented "Ellerslie," a mansion near Wilmington, Delaware, in the spring of 1927. The family remained at "Ellerslie" for two years interrupted by a visit to Paris in the summer of 1928, but Fitzgerald was still unable to make significant progress on his novel. At this time Zelda commenced ballet training, intending to become a professional dancer. The Fitzgeralds returned to France in the spring of 1929, where Zelda's intense ballet work damaged her health and estranged them. In April 1930 she suffered her first breakdown. Zelda was treated at Prangins clinic in Switzerland until September 1931, while Fitzgerald lived in Swiss hotels. Work on the novel was again suspended as he wrote short stories to pay for psychiatric treatment.

Fitzgerald's peak story fee of $4,000 from *The Saturday Evening Post* may have had in 1929 the purchasing power of $40,000 in 1994 dollars. Nonetheless, the general view of his affluence is distorted. Fitzgerald was not among the highest-paid writers of his time; his novels earned comparatively little, and most of his income came from 160 magazine stories. During the 1920s his income from all sources averaged under $25,000 a year—good money at a time when a schoolteacher's average annual salary was $1,299, but not a fortune. Scott and Zelda Fitzgerald did spend money faster than he earned it; the author who wrote so eloquently about the effects of money on character was unable to manage his own finances.

The Fitzgeralds returned to America in the fall of 1931 and rented a house in Montgomery. Fitzgerald made a second unsuccessful trip to Hollywood in 1931. Zelda suffered a relapse in February 1932 and entered Johns Hopkins Hospital in Baltimore. She spent the rest of her life as a resident or outpatient of sanitariums.

In 1932, while a patient at Johns Hopkins, Zelda rapidly wrote *Save Me the Waltz*. Her autobiographical novel generated considerable bitterness between the Fitzgeralds, for he regarded it as pre-empting the material that he was using in his novel-in-progress. Fitzgerald rented "La Paix," a house outside Baltimore, where he completed his fourth novel, *Tender Is the Night*. Published in 1934, his most ambitious novel was a commercial failure, and its merits were matters of critical dispute. Set in France during the 1920s, *Tender Is the Night* examines the deterioration of Dick Diver, a brilliant American psychiatrist, during the course of his marriage to a wealthy mental patient.

The 1935–1937 period is known as "the crack-up" from the title of an essay Fitzgerald wrote in 1936. Ill, drunk, in debt, and unable to write commercial stories, he lived in hotels in the region near Asheville, North Carolina, where in 1936 Zelda entered Highland Hospital. After Baltimore Fitzgerald did not maintain a home for Scottie. When she was fourteen she went to boarding school, and the Obers became her surrogate family. Nonetheless, Fitzgerald functioned as a concerned father by mail, attempting to supervise Scottie's education and to shape her social values.

Fitzgerald went to Hollywood alone in the summer of 1937 with a six-month Metro-Goldwyn-Mayer contract at $1,000 a week. He received his only screen credit for adapting *Three Comrades* (1938), and his contract was renewed for a year at $1,250 a week. This $91,000 from MGM was a great deal of money during the late Depression years when a new Chevrolet coupé cost $619; although Fitzgerald paid off most of his debts, he was unable to save. His trips East to visit Zelda were disastrous. In California Fitzgerald fell in love with movie columnist Sheilah Graham. Their relationship endured despite his benders. After MGM dropped his option at the end of 1938, Fitzgerald worked as a freelance script writer and wrote short-short stories for *Esquire*. He began his Hollywood novel, *The Love of the Last Tycoon*, in 1939 and had written more than half of a working draft when he died of a heart attack in Graham's apartment on December 21, 1940. Zelda Fitzgerald perished in a fire in Highland Hospital in 1948.

F. Scott Fitzgerald died believing himself a failure. The obituaries were condescending, and he seemed destined for literary obscurity. The first phase of the Fitzgerald resurrection—"revival" does not properly describe the process—occurred between 1945 and 1950. By 1960 he had achieved a secure place among America's enduring writers: *The Great Gatsby*, a work that seriously examines the theme of aspiration in an American setting, defines the classic American novel.

F. Scott Fitzgerald
A Life in Letters

——— ❖ ———

YOUTH, PRINCETON, ZELDA
1896–1919

——— ❖ ———

September 24, 1896

 Birth of F. Scott Fitzgerald at 481 Laurel Avenue, St. Paul, Minnesota.

April 1898

 Fitzgerald family moves to Buffalo, New York.

July 24, 1900

 Birth of Zelda Sayre at Sayre home on South Street, Montgomery, Alabama.

January 1901

 Fitzgerald family moves to Syracuse, New York.

July 1901

 Birth of Annabel Fitzgerald, FSF's sister.

September 1903

 Fitzgerald family moves back to Buffalo.

1907

 The Sayre family moves into a house at 6 Pleasant Avenue, Zelda's home until her marriage.

July 1908

 Fitzgerald family returns to St. Paul. FSF enters St. Paul Academy in September.

1909

> Judge Sayre of the City Court is appointed an Associate Justice of the Supreme Court of Alabama.

October 1909

> Publication of "The Mystery of the Raymond Mortgage" in *The St. Paul Academy Now & Then*—FSF's first appearance in print.

August 1911

> Production of FSF's first play, *The Girl from Lazy J*, in St. Paul.

September 1911

> FSF enters Newman School, Hackensack, New Jersey, where he meets Father Sigourney Fay and writer Shane Leslie.

August 1912

> Production of *The Captured Shadow* in St. Paul.

August 1913

> Production of *The Coward* in St. Paul.

September 1913

> FSF enters Princeton University with Class of 1917. Meets Edmund Wilson '16, John Peale Bishop '17, and John Biggs, Jr. '17.

August 1914

> Production of *Assorted Spirits* in St. Paul.

December 1914

> Production of *Fie! Fie! Fi-Fi!*, FSF's first Princeton Triangle Club show.

December 1914

> First FSF appearance in *The Princeton Tiger*.

January 4, 1915

FSF meets Ginevra King, the model for several of his heroines, in St. Paul.

April 1915

"Shadow Laurels," first FSF appearance in *The Nassau Literary Magazine*.

December 1915

FSF drops out of Princeton for rest of year; though in academic difficulty, he is allowed to leave for health reasons.

December 1915

Production of *The Evil Eye* by the Triangle Club.

September 1916

FSF returns to Princeton as member of the class of 1918.

December 1916

Production of *Safety First* by the Triangle Club.

October 26, 1917

FSF receives commission as 2nd lieutenant.

November 20, 1917

FSF reports to Fort Leavenworth, Kansas; begins his novel "The Romantic Egotist" there.

March 1918

FSF completes first draft of novel while on leave in Princeton and staying at Cottage Club; submits novel to Scribners.

May 31, 1918

Zelda graduates from Sidney Lanier High School.

June 1918

FSF reports to Camp Sheridan near Montgomery, Alabama.

July 1918

FSF meets Zelda at a country club dance in Montgomery.

August 1918

Scribners returns "The Romantic Egotist." FSF revises it, but by the end of October it is finally rejected.

February 1919

FSF discharged from army and goes to New York to seek his fortune; finds employment at Barron Collier advertising agency; lives in a room at 200 Claremont Avenue. Informally engaged to Zelda.

June 1919

Zelda breaks engagement.

TO: *Edward Fitzgerald*　　　　*ALS, 1 p.*[1] *Scrapbook. Princeton University*
　　　　　　　　　　　　　　　　Camp Chatham stationery. Orillia, Ontario

July 15, 07

Dear Father,

I recieved the St Nickolas[2] today and I am ever so much obliged to you for it.

Your loving son.
Scott Fitzgerald

TO: *Mollie McQuillan Fitzgerald*　　　*Scrapbook. Princeton University*
Summer 1907　　　　　　　　　　　*Camp Chatham. Orillia, Ontario.*

Dear Mother,

I wish you would send me five dollars as all my money is used up. Yesterday I went in a running contest and won a knife for second prize. This is a picture of Tom Penney and I starting on a paper chase.

Your loving son
Scott Fitzgerald

TO: *Mollie McQuillan Fitzgerald*　　　*Scrapbook. Princeton University*

July 18, 07

Dear Mother, I recieved your letter this morning and though I would like very much to have you up here I dont think you would like it as you know no one hear except Mrs. Upton and she is busy most of the time I dont think you would like the accomadations as it is only a small town and no good hotels. There are some very nise boarding houses but about the only fare is lamb and beef. Please send me a dollar becaus there are a lot of little odds and ends i need. I will spend it causiusly. All the other boys have pocket money besides their regullar allowence.

Your loving son
Scott Fitzgerald.

[1] The earliest dated letter by Fitzgerald.
[2] *The St. Nicholas*, a popular children's magazine.

Dear Mother,
          I wish you would send
me five dollars as all my money
is used up. Yesterday I went in
an running contest and won
a knife for second prize.
This is a picture of Tom Penney
and I starting on a paper chase
          Your loving son
          Scott Fitsger

TO: *Annabel Fitzgerald*[1]
c. 1915

*AL, 10 pp. Princeton University
Princeton, New Jersey*

Written by me at 19 or so
Basis of Bernice[2]

The General Subject of Conversation

Conversation like grace is a cultivated art. Only to the very few does it come naturally. You are as you know, not a good conversationalist and you might very naturally ask, "What do boys like to talk about?'

(1) Boys like to talk about themselves—much more than girls. A girl once named Helen Walcott, told me (and she was the most popular debutante in Washington one winter) that as soon as she got a man talking about himself she had him cinched and harnessed—they give themself away. Here are some leading questions for a girl to use.

a) You dance so much better than you did last year.

b) How about giving me that sporty necktie when you're thru with it.

c) You've got the longest eyelashes! (This will embarrass him, but he likes it)

d) I hear you've got a "line"!

e) Well who's you're latest crush!

Avoid

a) When do you go back to school?

b) How long have you been home?

c) Its warm or the orchestras good or the floors good.

Also avoid any talk about relations or mutual friends. Its a sure sign you're hard up for talk if you ask Jack Allen about Harriette or Tuby about Martha. Dont be afraid of slang—use it, but be careful to use the most modern and sportiest like "line," camafluage etc. Never talk about a boy about about his school or college unless he's done something special or unless he starts the subject. In a conversation its always good to start by talking about nothing—just some fresh camafluage; but start it yourself—never let the boy start it: Dont talk about your school—no matter where you go. Never sing no matter how big the chorus.

2.

As you get a little old you'll find that boys like to talk about such things as smoking and drinking. Always be very liberal—boys hate a prig—tell them you dont object to a girl smoking but dont like cigarettes yourself. Tell them you smoke only cigars—kid them!—When you're old still you want always to have a line on the latest books plays and music. More men like that than you can imagine.

---

[1]Fitzgerald's sister was five years younger than he.
[2]"Bernice Bobs Her Hair," *The Saturday Evening Post* (May 1, 1920).

In your conversation always affect a complete frankness but really be only as frank as you wish to be. Never try to give a boy the affect that you're popular—Ginevra[1] always starts by saying shes a poor unpopular woman without any beause. Always pay close attention to the man. Look at him in his eyes if possible. Never effect boredom. Its terribly hard to do it gracefully   Learn to be worldly. Remember in all society nine girls out of ten marry for money and nine men out of ten are fools.

Poise: Carriage: Dancing: Expression

(1) Poise depends on carriage, expression and conversation and having discussed the last and most important I'll say a few words on the other two.
(2) A girl should hold herself straight. Margaret Armstrongs slouch has lost her more attention than her lack of beauty. Even Sandy is criticsized for stopping. When you cross a room before people nine out of ten look at you and if you're straight and self contained and have a graceful athletic carriage most of them will remark on it. In dancing it is very important to hold yourself well and remember to dance hard. Dancers like Betty and Grace and Alice <u>work hard</u>. Alice is an entirely self made dancer. At sixteen she was no better than you, but she practised and tried. A dancer like Elizabeth Clarkson looses partners. <u>You can not be lazy</u>. You should try not to trow a bit of weight on the man and keep your mind on it enough to follow well. If you'd spent the time on dancing with me as I've often asked you instead of playing the piano youd be a good dancer. Louis Ordway taught Kit to dance the Castle walk one summer and as long as it lasted she was almost rushed at dances. And dancing counts as nothing else does.
(3) Expression that is facial expression, is one of your weakest points. A girl of your good looks and at your age ought to have almost perfect control of her face. It ought to be almost like a mask so that she'd have perfect control of any expression or impression she might wish to use.
a) A good smile and one that could be assumed at will, is an absolute necesity. You smile on one side which is <u>absolutely wrong</u>. Get before a mirror and practise a smile and get a good one, a radiant smile ought to be in the facial vocabulary of every girl. Practise it—on girls, on the family. Practise doing it when you dont feel happy and when you're bored. When youre embarrassed, when you're at a disadvantage. Thats when you'll have to use it in society and when you've practised a thing in calm, then only are you sure of it as a good weapon in tight places.
(b) A laugh isn't as important but its well to have a good one on ice. You natural one is very good, but your artificial one is bum. Next time you laugh naturally remember it and practise so you can do it any time you want. <u>Practise anywhere</u>.
(c) A pathetic, appealing look is one every girl ought to have. Sandra and

---

[1]Ginevra King, celebrated beauty with whom Fitzgerald was in love when he was at Princeton; she provided a model for his debutante characters.

Ginevra are specialists at this: so is Ardita, Its best done by opening the eyes wide and drooping the mouth a little, looking upward (hanging the head a little) directly into the eyes of the man you're talking to. Ginevra and Sandra use this when getting of their "I'm so unpopular speeches and indeed they use it about half the time. Practise this.

(d) Dont bit or twist your lips—its sure death for any expression

(e) The two expressions you have control over now are no good. One is the side smile and the other is the thoughtful look with the eyes half closed.

I'm telling you this because mother and I have absolutely no control over our facial expressions and we miss it. Mothers worse than I am—you know how people take advantage of what ever mood her face is in and kid the life out of her. Well you're young enough to get over it—tho' you're worse than I am now. The value of this practise is that whenever you're at a disadvantage you dont show it and boys hate to see a girl at a disadvantage.

  Practise Now

Dress and Personality.

(A) No two people look alike in the same thing. but very few realize it. Shop keepers make money on the fact that the fat Mrs. Jones will buy the hat that looked well on the thin Mrs. Smith. You've got to find your type. To do so always look at girls about your size and coloring and notice what they look well in. Never buy so much as a sash without the most careful consideration   Study your type. That is get your good points and accentuate them. For instance you have very good features—you ought to be able to wear jaunty hats and so forth.

(B) Almost all neatness is gained in man or woman by the arrangement of the hair. You have beautiful hair—you ought to be able to do something with it. Go to the best groomed girl in school and ask her and then wear it that way—Dont get tired and changed unless you're sure the new way is better. Catherine Tie is dowdy about her hair lately   Dont I notice it? When Grace's hair looks well—She looks well   When its unkempt it looks like the devil. Sandy and Betty always look neat and its their hair that does it.

(2)

(C) I'll line up your good points against your bad physically.

Good	Bad
Hair	Teeth only fair
Good general size	Pale complexion
Good features	Only fair figure
	Large hands and feet.

  Now you see of the bad points only the last cannot be remedied. Now

9

while slimness is a fashion you can cultivate it by exercise—Find out now from some girl. Exercise would give you a healthier skin. You should never rub cold cream into your face because you have a slight tendency to grow hairs on it. I'd find out about this from some Dr. who'd tell you what you could use in place of a skin cream.

(D) A girl should always be careful about such things as underskirt show-ing, long drawers showing under stocking, bad breath, mussy eye-brows (with such splendid eyebrows as yours you should brush them or wet them and train them every morning and night as I advised you to do long ago. They oughtn't to have a hair out of place.

(E) Walk and general physical grace. The point about this is that you'll be up against situations when ever you go out which will call for you to be graceful—not to be physically clumsy. Now you can only attain this by practise because it no more comes naturally to you than it does to me. Take some stylish walk you like and imitate it. A girl should have a little class. Look what a stylish walk Eleanor and Grace and Betty have and what a homely walk Marie and Alice have. Just because the first three deliberately practised every where until now its so natural to them that they cant be ungraceful—This is true about every gesture. I noticed last Saturday that your gestures are awkward and so unnatural as to seem affected. Notice the way graceful girls hold their hands and feet. How they stoop, wave, run and then try because you cant practise those things when men are around. Its two late then. They ought to be incentive then

(F) General summing up.
   (1) dress scrupulously neatly and then forget your personal appearance. Every stocking should be pulled up to the last wrinkle.
   (2) Dont wear things like that fussy hat that aren't becoming to you— At least buy no more. Take someone who knows with you—some one who really knows.
   (3) Conform to your type no matter what looks well in the store
   (4) Cultivate deliberate physical grace. You'll never have it if you dont. I'll discuss dancing in a latter letter.

(G) You see if you get any where and feel you look alright then there's one worry over and one bolt shot for self-confidence—and the person you're with, man, boy, woman, whether its Aunt Millie or Jack Allen o myself likes to feel that the person they're sponsoring is at least externally a credit.

TO: Marie Hersey[1]   *ALS, 1 p. Scrapbook. Princeton University*
     Princeton, New Jersey

---

[1] St. Paul friend with whom Fitzgerald corresponded when they were both away at school.

<u>Thurs</u>

My Very Very Dear Marie:
I got your little note
For reasons very queer Marie
You're mad at me I fear Marie
You made it very clear Marie
    You cared not what you wrote

The letter that you sent Marie
    Was niether swift nor fair
I hoped that you'd repent Marie
Before the start of Lent Marie
But Lent could not prevent Marie
    From being debonaire

So write me what you will Marie
    Altho' I will it not
My love you can not kill Marie
And tho' you treat me ill Marie
Believe me I am still Marie
    Your fond admirer
                                        Scott

(Letter sent to Marie Jan 29, 1915)

TO: Edmund Wilson   *ALS, 6 pp. Yale University*
Fall 1917

                                        Cottage Club
                                        Princeton, N.J.
Dear Bunny:
    I've been intending to write you before but as you see I've had a change
of scene and the nessesary travail there-off has stolen time.
    Your poem came to John Biggs, my room mate, and we'll put in the
next number—however it was practically illegable so I'm sending you my
copy (hazarded) which you'll kindly correct and send back——
    I'm here starting senior year and still waiting for my commission. I'll
send you the Litt. or no—you've subscribed haven't you.
    Saw your friend Larry Noyes in St. Paul and got beautifully stewed after
a party he gave—He got beautifully full of canned wrath—I dont imagine
we'd agree on much——
    Do write John Bishop and tell him not to call his book "Green Fruit."

Alec is an ensign. I'm enclosing you a clever letter from Townsend Martin[1] which I wish you'd send back.

Princeton is stupid but Gauss + Gerrould[2] are here. I'm taking naught but Philosophy + English—I told Gauss you'd sailed (I'd heard as much) but I'll contradict the rumor.

The Litt is prosperous—Biggs + I do the prose——Creese and Keller (a junior who'll be chairman) and I the poetry. However any contributions would be ect. ect.

Have you read Well's "Boon; the mind of the race" (Doran—1916) Its marvellous! (Debutante expression. Young Benêt[3] (at New Haven) is getting out a book of verse before Xmas that I fear will obscure John Peale's. His subjects are less Precieuse + decadent. John is really an anachronism in this country at this time—people want ideas and not fabrics.

I'm rather bored here but I see Shane Leslie occassionally and read Wells and Rousseau. I read Mrs. Geroulds "British Novelists Limited[4] + think she underestimates Wells but is right in putting Mckenzie at the head of his school. She seems to disregard Barry and Chesterton whom I should put even above Bennet or in fact anyone except Wells.[5]

Do you realize that Shaw is 61, Wells 51, Chesterton 41 Leslie 31 and I 21. (Too bad I havn't a better man for 31. I can hear your addition to this remark).

Oh and that awful little Charlie Stuard (a sort of attenuated Super-Fruit) is still around (ex '16—now 17½). He belongs to a preceptorial where I am trying to demolish the Wordsworth legend—and contributes such elevating freshman-cultural generalities as "Why I'm suah that romantisism is only a cross-section of reality Dr. Murch."

Yes—Jack Newlin is dead—killed in ambulance service. He was, potentially a great artist

Here is a poem I just had accepted by "Poet Lore"[6]

The Way of Purgation

A fathom deep in sleep I lie
    With old desires, restrained before;
To clamor life-ward with a cry
    As dark flies out the greying door.
And so in quest of creeds to share
    I seek assertive day again;

[1] Wealthy Princeton classmate of Fitzgerald's later a movie writer and producer.
[2] Professors Christian Gauss and Gordon Hall Gerould.
[3] Poet Stephen Vincent Benét, then a Yale undergraduate.
[4] Katharine Fullerton Gerould, *Yale Review* (October 1917).
[5] Compton Mackenzie, James M. Barrie, G. K. Chesterton, Arnold Bennett, H. G. Wells—contemporary British novelists.
[6] This poem was not published by *Poet Lore*.

But old monotony is there—
   Long, long avenues of rain.

Oh might I rise again! Might I
   Throw off the throbs of that old wine—
See the new morning mass the sky
   With fairy towers, line on line—
Find each mirage in the high air
   A symbol, not a dream again!
But old monotony is there—
   Long, Long avenues of rain.

   No—I have no more stuff of Johns—I ask but never recieve

news   {   If Hillquit gets the mayorality of New York it meens a new
jottings   {   era—Twenty million Russians from South Russia have come
(unofficial) {   over to the Roman Church

   I can go to Italy if I like as private secretary of a man (a priest)[1] who is
going as Cardinal Gibbons representative to discuss the war with the Pope
(American Catholic point of view—which is most loyal—barring the Sien-
Fien—40% of Pershing's army are Irish Catholics. Do write.

                 Gaelicly Yours
                 Scott Fitzgerald

I remind myself lately of Pendennis, Sentimental Tommy (who was not
sentimental and whom Barry never understood) Michael Fanc, Maurice
Avery + Guy Hazelwood)[2]

TO: *Mollie McQuillan Fitzgerald*   *ALS, 4 pp. Princeton University*
                Cottage Club stationery. Princeton, New Jersey

                              Nov 14th
                              1917

Dear Mother:
   You were doubtless surprised to get my letter but I certainly was delighted
to get my commission.
   My pay started the day I signed the Oath of Allegiance and sent it back
which was yesterday—Went up to Brooke's Bros yesterday afternoon and
ordered some of my equipment.
   I havn't received any orders yet but I think I will be ordered to Fort
Leavanworth within a month— I'll be there three months and would have

---

[1] Father Cyril Sigourney Webster Fay had befriended Fitzgerald at the Newman School. He
was the model for Monsignor Darcy in *This Side of Paradise*.
   [2] Characters in novels by William Makepeace Thackeray, Barrie, and Mackenzie.

six additional months training in France before I was ordered with my regiment to the trenches.

I get $141 dollars a month ($1700 a year) with a 10% increase when I'm in France.

My uniforms are going to cost quite a bit so if you havn't sent me what you have of <u>my own money</u> please do so.

I'm continuing here going to classes until I get orders. I am a second Lieutenant in the <u>regular</u> infantry and <u>not</u> a reserve officer—I rank with a West Point graduate.

Things are stupid here—I hear from Marie and Catherine Tighe[1] occasionally + got a letter from Non two weeks ago—I hear he's been ordered to Texas.

Went down to see Ellen Stockton in Trenton the other night. She is a perfect beauty.

About the army please lets not have either tragedy or Heroics because they are equeally distastful to me. I went into this perfectly cold bloodedly and dont sympathize with the

"Give my son to country" ect
ect
ect

or
"Hero stuff"

because <u>I just went</u> and purely for <u>social reasons</u>. If you want to pray, pray for my soul and not that I wont get killed—the last doesn't seem to matter particularly and if you are a good Catholic the first ought to.

To a profound pessimist about life, being in danger is not depressing. I have never been more cheerful. Please be nice and respect my wishes

Love
Scott.

TO: Shane Leslie   *ALS, 3 pp. Bruccoli*

Dec 22nd, 1917

My Dear Mr. Leslie:

Your letter followed me here—

My novel isn't a novel in verse—it merly shifts rapidly from verse to prose—but its mostly in prose.

The reason I've abandoned my idea of a book of poems is that I've only about twenty poems and cant write any more in this atmosphere—while I can write prose so I'm sandwitching the poems between rheams of autobiography and fiction.

---

[1] Katherine Tighe, St. Paul friend of Fitzgerald; she became one of the dedicatees of Fitzgerald's *The Vegetable*.

It makes a pot-pouri especially as there are pages in dialogue and in vers libre but it reads as logically for the times as most public utterances of the prim and prominent. It is a tremendously concieted affair. The title page looks (will look) like this

The Romantic Egoist
by
F. Scott Fitzgerald

"The Best is over!
You may remember now and think and sigh
Oh silly lover!"

Rupert Brooke

"Ou me coucha banga loupa
Domalumba guna duma . . ."

Gilbert Chesterton

Some gibberish from "The Club of Queer Trades"

"Experience is the name Tubby gives to all his mistakes."
Oscar Wilde

I'll send you a chapter or two to look over if you would—Id like it a lot if you would.

I'm enclosing you a poem that "Poet Lore" a magazine of verse has just taken

Yours
F. Scott Fitzgerald
2nd Lt. U.S.
Co. Q P.O.Bn
Ft. Leavenworth
Kan.

TO: Edmund Wilson   ALS, 4 pp. Yale University
1918

Jan 10th, 1917.

Dear Bunny:
Your last refuge from the cool sophistries of the shattered world, is destroyed!—I have left Princeton. I am now Lieutenant F. Scott Fitzgerald

15

of the 45th Infantry (regulars.) My present adress is

Co Q   P.O.B.

Ft. Leavenworth

Kan.

After Feb 26th

593 Summit Ave

St. Paul

Minnesota

will always find me forwarded

    —So the short, swift chain of the Princeton intellectuals (Brooke's clothes, clean ears and, withall, a lack of mental prigishness . . . . Whipple,[1] Wilson, Bishop, Fitzgerald . . . . have passed along the path of the generation—leaving their shining crown apon the gloss and unworthiness of John Biggs head.

One of your poems I sent on to the Litt and I'll send the other when I've read it again. I wonder if you ever got the Litt I sent you . . . . so I enclosed you two pictures, well give one to some poor motherless Poilu fairy who has no dream. This is smutty and forced but in an atmosphere of cabbage . . . .

John's book came out in December and though I've written him rheams (Rhiems) of praise, I think he's made poor use of his material. It is a thin Green Book.

    <u>Green Fruit</u>   (One man here remarked that he didn't read it because Green Fruit always gave him a pain in the A——!)

by

John Peale Bishop

1st Lt. Inf. R.C.

Sherman French Co

    Boston.

In section one (Souls and Fabrics) are Boudoir, The Nassau Inn and, of all things, Fillipo's wife, a relic of his decadent sophmore days. Claudius and other documents in obscurity adorn this section.

Section two contains the Elspeth Poems—which I think are rotten. Section three is (Poems out of Jersey and Virginia) and has Cambell Hall, Mellville and much sacharine sentiment about how much white bodies pleased him and how, nevertheless he was about to take his turn with crushed brains (this slender thought done over in poem after poem). This is my confidential opinion, however; if he knew what a nut I considered him for leaving out Ganymede and Salem Water and Francis Thompson and Prayer and all the things that might have given some body to his work, he'd drop me from his writing list. The book closed with the dedication to

---

[1] T. K. Whipple became a literary critic.

Townsend Martin which is on the circular I enclose. I have seen no reviews of it yet.

~~~~~~

<div style="text-align:center">

The Romantic Egotist
by
F. Scott Fitzgerald

".... The Best is over
You may complain and sigh
Oh Silly Lover ...."
Rupert Brooke

"Experience is the name Tubby gives to his mistakes ..
Oscar Wilde

Chas. Scribners Sons (Maybe!)
MCMXVIII

</div>

~~~~~~

There are twenty three Chapters, all but five are written and it is in poetry, prose, vers libre and every mood of a tempermental temperature. It purports to be the picaresque ramble of one Stephen Palms from the San Francisco fire, thru School, Princeton to the end where at twenty one he writes his autobiography at the Princeton aviation school. It shows traces of Tarkington, Chesteron, Chambers Wells, Benson (Robert Hugh), Rupert Brooke[1] and includes Compton-Mckenzie like love-affairs and three psychic adventures including one encounter with the devil in a harlots apartment.

It rather damns much of Princeton but its nothing to what it thinks of men and human nature in general. I can most nearly describe it by calling it a prose, modernistic Childe Harolde[2] and really if Scribner takes it I know I'll wake some morning and find that the debutantes have made me famous over night. I really believe that no one else could have written so searchingly the story of the youth of our generation. ..

[1]Booth Tarkington, G. K. Chesterton, Robert W. Chambers, H. G. Wells, and Robert Hugh Benson were contemporary novelists; Rupert Brooke was a young British poet killed in World War I.

[2]*Childe Harold's Pilgrimage* (1812–1818) was a partially autobiographical heroic poem by George Gordon Byron, Lord Byron.

17

In my right hand bunk sleeps the editor of Contemporary Verse (ex) Devereux Joseph, Harvard '15 and a peach—on my left side is G. C. King a Harvard crazy man who is <u>dramatizing</u> "War and Peace"; but you see Im lucky in being well protected from the Philistines.

The Litt continues slowly but I havn't recieved the December issue yet so I cant pronounce on the quality.

This insolent war has carried off Stuart Walcott in France, as you may know and really is beginning to irritate me—but the maudlin sentiment of most people is still the spear in my side. In everything except my romantic Chestertonian orthodoxy I still agree with the early Wells on human nature and the "no hope for Tono Bungay"[1] theory.

God! How I miss my youth—thats only relative of course but already lines are beginning to coarsen <u>in other peop</u>le and thats the sure sign. I dont think you ever realized at Princeton the childlike simplicity that lay behind all my petty sophistication, selfishness and my lack of a real sense of honor. I'd be a wicked man if it wasn't for that and now thats dissapearing . . .

Well I'm over stepping and boring you and using up my novel's material so good bye. Do write and lets keep in touch if you like.

God Bless You
Celticly
F. Scott Fitzgerald

<u>Bishop's adress</u>

Lieut. John Peale Bishop   (He's a 1st Lt.)
334th Infantry
Camp Taylor
Kentucky

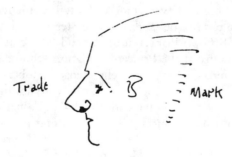

TO: Shane Leslie   *ALS, 1 p. Princeton University*

Co. Q. P.O. Bn.
Ft. Leavenworth, Kan

---

[1]H. G. Wells's novel *Tono-Bungay* (1909) portrayed the corruption of English society.

Dear Mr. Leslie:

This is just a note to inform you that the first draft of the "Romantic Egotist," will be ready for your inspection in three weeks altho' I'm sending you a chapter called "The Devil" next week.

Think of a romantic egotist writing about himself in a cold barracks on Sunday afternoons . . . yet that is the way this novel has been scattered into shape—for it has no form to speak of.

Dr. Fay told me to send my picture that he wants through you. Whether he meant for you to forward it to him or put it away until he returns I didn't comprehend.

I certainly appreciate your taking an interest in my book . . . By the way I join my regiment, the 45th Infantry, at Camp Taylor, Kentucky in three weeks.

> Faithfully
> F. Scott Fitzgerald

February 4th
1918

TO: *Shane Leslie*   *ALS, 1 p. Bruccoli*
February 1918   *Fort Leavenworth, Kansas*

Dear Mr. Leslie:

Here's Chapter XVI "The Devil" and Chapter XIII. I picked it out as a Chapter you could read without knowing the story. I wish you'd look it over and see what you think of it. It's semi-typical of the novel in its hastiness and scrubby style.

I have a weeks leave before joining my regiment and I'm going up to Princeton to rewrite. Now I can pass thru Washington and see you about this novel either on the seventh or eighth or ninth of February. Will you tell me which of these days you'd be liable to have an afternoon off. Any one of them are conveinent as far as I'm concerned. I could bring you half a dozen chapters to look at and I'd like to know whether you think it would have any chance with Scribner.

The novel begins nowhere as most things do and ends with the war as all things do. Chapter XIII will seem incoherent out of its setting. Well— I leave here Monday the 26th. After that my address will be Cottage Club— Princeton, N.J.

I'd be much obliged if you'd let me know which afternoon would be most convenient for you

> Faithfully,
> F. Scott Fitzgerald

Did you ever notice that remarkable coincidence.——Bernard Shaw is 61 yrs old, H. G. Wells is 51, G. K. Chesterton 41, you're 31 and I'm 21——All the great authors of the world in arithmetical progression

F.S.F.

TO: Shane Leslie   *RTLS, 1 p. Bruccoli*

45th Inf. Camp Gordon Ga.
May 8th 1918

Dear Mr. Leslie:

Your letter filled me with a variety of literary emotions. . . . You see yours is the first pronouncment of any kind that I've received apon my first born. . . . . .

That it is crude, incredibatly dull in place is too true to be pleasant. . . . I have no idea why I hashed in all that monotonous drivel about childhood in the first part and would see it hacked out like an errant apendicitus without a murmur. . . . There are too many characters and too much local social system in the Princeton section. . . . . and in places all through the verses are too obviusly lugged in. . . . . .

At any rate I'm tremendously obliged for taking an interest in it and writing that awfully decent letter to Scribner. . . . If he thinks that a revision would make it at all practicable I'd rather do it than not or if he dispairs of it I might try some less conservative publisher than Scribner is known to be. . .

We have no news except that we're probably going inside of two months—and, officers and men, we're wild to go. . . .

I wonder if you're working on the history of Martin Luther or are on another tack. . . . Do write a novel with young men in it, and kill the rancid taste that the semi-brilliant "Changing Winds"[1] left on so many tongues. Or write a thinly disguised autobiography. . . . or something. I'm wild for books and none are forthcoming. . . I wrote mine (as Stevenson wrote Treasure Island) to satisfy my own craving for a certain type of novel. Why are all the trueish novels written by the gloomy, half-twilight realists like Beresford and Walpole and St. John Irvine?[2] Even the Soul of a Bishop is colorless. . . . Where are the novels of five years ago: Tono Bungay, Youth's Encounter, Man Alive, The New Machiavelli[3]. . . . . Heavens

---

[1] *Changing Winds* (1917) was by St. John Greer Ervine.

[2] John Davys Beresford, Hugh Walpole, and Ervine were contemporary British novelists.

[3] *The Soul of a Bishop* (1917), *Tono-Bungay* (1909), and *The New Machiavelli* (1910) were by H. G. Wells; *Youth's Encounter* was the American title for the first volume of Compton Mackenzie's *Sinister Street* (1913); *Manalive* (1912) was by G. K. Chesterton.

has the war caught all literature in the crossed nets of Galesworthy and George Moore[1]. . .

Well. . . May St. Robert (Benson)[2] appear to Scribner in a dream. . .

Faithfully

F. Scott Fitzgerald

P. S. much obliged for mailing on Dr. Fay's letter

F.S.F.

TO: Shane Leslie   *ALS, 1 p. Bruccoli*

17thInf. Brig Hq
Camp Sheridan Ala.
Jan 13th 1919

Dear Mr. Leslie:

I can't tell you how I feel about Monsiegneur Fay's death—He was the best friend I had in the world and last night he seemed so close and so <u>good</u> that I was almost glad—because I think he wanted to die. Deep under it all he had a fear of that blending of the two worlds, that sudden change of values that sometimes happened to him and put a vague unhappiness into the stray corners of his life.

But selfishly I am sorry. Never more

"Will we drink with the sunlight for lamp
        Myself and the dead"[3]

I know how you feel too and Stephen Parrot + Mrs Leslie + Mrs Chandler and Father Hemmick and Delbos + OKelley + Sanderson and the fifty people that must somehow have felt a great security in him. He was such a <u>secure</u> man: one <u>knows</u> that he is happy now—oh God! I cant write—

I just wanted to talk to someone who knew him as I knew him

Sincerely

F. Scott Fitzgerald

---

[1] John Galsworthy and George Moore were realistic British novelists.
[2] Benson, son of an Archbishop of Canterbury, converted to Catholicism.
[3] Fitzgerald alludes to lines from Leslie's "The Dead Friend," *Verses in Peace & War* (1917): "And drunk with the sunset for lamp/—Myself and the dead."

TO: *Shane Leslie*
January–February 1919

ALS, 3 pp. Bruccoli
American Red Cross Base Hospital
stationery. Camp Sheridan,
Alabama

Dear Mr. Leslie.

Your letter seemed to start a new flow of sorrow in me. I've never wanted so much to die in my life—Father Fay always thought that if one of us died the others would and now how I've hoped so.

Oh it all seemed so easy, life I mean—with people who understood and satisfied needs. Even the philistines seemed very good and quiet always ready to be duped or influenced or something and now my little world made to order has been shattered by the death of one man.

I'm beginning to have a horror of <u>people</u>; I can quite sympathize with your desire to become a Carthusian.

This has made me nearly sure that I will become a priest—I feel as if in a way his mantle had descended apon me—a desire or more, to some day recreate the atmosphere of him—I think he was the sort of man St. Peter was, so damned human—

Think of the number of people who in a way looked to him and depended on him—His faith shining thru all the versatility and intellect.

I think I did feel him but I cant tell you of it in a letter. It was rather ghastly——

I'm coming to New York in Feb. or March to write or something.
I'll come and see you then.

If there's anything about him in any magazines I wish youd send them. I've been here in the hospital with influenza

As Ever
F Scott Fitzgerald

17thBrig. Hq.
Camp Sheridan
Ala

TO: *Zelda Sayre*
After February 22, 1919

Wire. Scrapbook. Princeton University
New York City

MISS SELDA SAYRE

DARLING HEART AMBITION ENTHUSIASM AND CONFIDENCE I DECLARE EVERY-THING GLORIOUS THIS WORLD IS A GAME AND WHITE I FEEL SURE OF YOU LOVE EVERYTHING IS POSSIBLE I AM IN THE LAND OF AMBITION AND SUCCESS AND MY ONLY HOPE AND FAITH IS THAT MY DARLING HEART WILL BE WITH ME SOON.[1]

[1] Fitzgerald was in New York trying to succeed in the advertising business in order to marry Zelda Sayre.

TO: Zelda Sayre   *Wire. Scrapbook. Princeton University*

NEWYORK NY   MAR 22 1919
  MISS LILDA SAYRE
DARLING I SENT YOU A LITTLE PRESENT FRIDAY THE RING[1] ARRIVED TONIGHT AND
I AM SENDING IT MONDAY I LOVE YOU AND I THOUGHT I WOULD TELL YOU HOW
MUCH ON THIS SATURDAY NIGHT WHEN WE OUGHT TO BE TOGETHER DONT LET
YOUR FAMILY BE SHOCKED AT MY PRESENT

  SCOTT

---

[1] An engagement ring.

THIS SIDE OF PARADISE,
MARRIAGE, EARLY SUCCESS
1919–1924

❖

July–August 1919

FSF quits New York job, returns to St. Paul, and rewrites novel at 599 Summit Avenue.

September 1919

"Babes in the Woods" published in *The Smart Set*, FSF's first commercial magazine appearance.

September 16, 1919

Maxwell Perkins of Scribners accepts *This Side of Paradise*.

November 1919

First sale to *The Saturday Evening Post*: "Head and Shoulders," published February 1920. FSF becomes client of Harold Ober at the Reynolds agency.

November 1919

FSF visits Zelda in Montgomery; engagement resumed.

November 1919–February 1920

The Smart Set publishes "The Debutante," "Porcelain and Pink," "Benediction," and "Dalyrimple Goes Wrong."

March–May 1920

The Saturday Evening Post publishes "Myra Meets His Family," "The

Camel's Back," "Bernice Bobs Her Hair," "The Ice Palace," and "The Offshore Pirate."

March 26, 1920

Publication of *This Side of Paradise*.

April 3, 1920

Marriage at rectory of St. Patrick's Cathedral in New York; honeymoon at the Biltmore and later at Commodore Hotel.

May–September 1920

Fitzgeralds rent house in Westport, Connecticut.

July 1920

"May Day" in *The Smart Set*.

September 10, 1920

Publication of *Flappers and Philosophers*, FSF's first short story collection.

1920

The Chorus Girl's Romance, first movie made from FSF work ("Head and Shoulders").

October 1920–April 1921

Apartment at 38 West 59th Street, New York City.

May–July 1921

First trip to Europe: England, France, and Italy.

Mid-August 1921–September 1922

St. Paul; rent a house at Dellwood, White Bear Lake; after birth of their daughter take a house at 646 Goodrich Avenue; in June 1922 move to White Bear Yacht Club for the summer.

October 26, 1921

Birth of Scottie.

March 4, 1922

Publication of *The Beautiful and Damned*.

June 1922

"The Diamond as Big as the Ritz" in *The Smart Set*.

1922

The Beautiful and Damned made into movie.

September 22, 1922

Publication of *Tales of the Jazz Age*, second collection of short stories.

Mid-October 1922–April 1924

Fitzgeralds rent house at 6 Gateway Drive in Great Neck, Long Island.

April 27, 1923

Publication of *The Vegetable*.

November 1923

The Vegetable fails at its tryout in Atlantic City, New Jersey.

Mid-April 1924

Fitzgeralds sail for France.

TO: *Maxwell Perkins*   *ALS, 2 pp. Princeton University*

599 Summit Ave
St. Paul, Minnesota
July 26th, 1919

Dear Mr. Perkins:

After four months attempt to write commercial copy by day and painful half-hearted imitations of popular literature by night I decided that it was one thing or another. So I gave up getting married and went home.

Yesterday I finished the first draft of a novel called

THE EDUCATION OF A PERSONAGE

It is in no sense a revision of the ill-fated <u>Romantic Egotist</u> but it contains some of the former material improved and worked over and bears a strong family resemblance besides.

But while the other was a tedius, disconnected casserole this is definate attempt at a big novel and I really believe I have hit it, as immediately I stopped disciplining the muse she trotted obediently around and became an erratic mistress if not a steady wife.

Now what I want to ask you is this—if I send you the book by August 20th and you decide you could risk its publication (I am blatantly confident that you will) would it be brought out in October, say, or just what would decide its date of publication?

This is an odd question I realize especially since you havn't even seen the book but you have been so kind in the past about my stuff that I venture to intrude once more apon your patience.

Sincerely
F Scott Fitzgerald

TO: *Edmund Wilson*   *ALS, 4 pp. Yale University*
1919

<u>599</u> Summit Ave
St. Paul, Minn
August 15th

Dear Bunny:

Delighted to get your letter. I am deep in the throes of a new novel. Which is the best title

(1) The Education of a Personage
(2) The Romantic Egotist
(3) This Side of Paradise

I am sending it to Scribner—They liked my first one. Am enclosing two letters from them that migh t'amuse you. Please return them.

I have just the story for your book. Its not written yet. An American girl falls in love with an officier Francais at a Southern camp.
Since I last saw you I've tried to get married + then tried to drink myself to death but foiled, as have been so many good men, by the sex and the state I have returned to literature

Have sold three or four cheap stories to Amurican magazines.

Will start on story for you about 25th d'Auout (as the French say or do not say). (which is about 10 days off)

I am ashamed to say that my Catholoscism is scarcely more than a mem—ory—no that's wrong its more than that; at any rate I go not to the church nor mumble stray nothings over chrystaline beads.

May be in N'York in Sept or early Oct.
Is John Bishop in hoc terrain?
Remember me to Larry Noyes. I'm afraid he's very much off me. I don't think he's seen me sober for many years.
For god's sake Bunny write a novel + don't waste your time editing collections. It'll get to be a habit.
That sounds crass + discordant but you know what I mean.

Yours in the Holder[1] group
F Scott Fitzgerald

TO: *Maxwell Perkins*   *ALS, 3 pp. Princeton University*

599 Summit Ave
St. Paul Minn
August 16th, 1919

Dear Mr. Perkins:
I appreciated both your letters and I'm sure you wont be dissapointed in the book when you get it. It is a well-considered, finished <u>whole</u> this time

[1] Holder Hall, Princeton University dormitory.

and I think its a more <u>crowded</u> (in the best sense) piece of work than has been published in this country for some years.

It is finished, except for one last revision or rather correction and the typewriting, so I think you'll get it before September 1st. As to sample chapters—it seems hardly worth while to send them to you now. The title has been changed to

This Side of Paradise

from those lines of Rupert Brookes

> . . . Well, this side of paradise
> There's little comfort in the wise.

About two chapters are from my old book, completly changed and re-written, the rest is new material
On the next page I've written the chapter names.

Book I
        The Romantic Egotist
Chapter I   Amory, son of Beatrice
     "   II   Spires and Gargoyles
     "   III The Egotist considers

Interlude
        March 1917 – February 1919

Book II
        The Education of a Personage
Chapter I   The Debutante
     "   II   Experiments in Convalescense
     "   III Young Irony
     "   IV The Supercillious Sacrifice
     "   V   The Egotist becomes a Personage

Book One contains about   35,000 words
The Interlude   "   "   4,000 words
Book Two   "   "   <u>47,000 words</u>
Total   "   "   86,000 words

about publication—I asked you the chances of an early publication (in case you take it) for two reasons: first—because I want to get started both in a literary and financial way; second—because it is to some extent a timely book and it seems to me that the public are wild for decent reading matter—"Dangerous Days" and "Ramsey Milholland"[1]—My God!

Thanking you again for past favors—I am

Sincerely
F. Scott Fitzgerald

TO: Maxwell Perkins   *ALS, 2 pp. Princeton University*

599 Summit Ave.
St. Paul, Minn.
Sept. 4th 1919.

Dear Mr. Perkins:

I sent the book today under a separate cover. I want to discuss a few things in connection with it.

You'll notice that it contains much material from the <u>Romantic Egotist</u>.

(1) Chapter II Bk I of the present book contains material from "Spires + Gargoyles, Ha-Ha Hortense, Babes in the Wood + Crecendo"—rewritten in third person, cut down and re-edited

(2) Chapter III Bk I contains material from "Second descent of the Egotist and the Devil." rewritten ect.

(3) Chapter IV Bk I contains material from "The Two Mystics, Clara + the End of Many Things"

(4) Chapter III Bk II is a revision of Eleanor in 3d person—with that fur incident left out.

Chap I Bk I, + Chaps I, II, IV + V of Bk II are entirely new.

You'll see that of the old material there is all new use, outside the revision in the 3d person. For instance the Princeton characters of the R.E.—Tom, Tump, Lorry, Lumpy, Fred, Dick, Jim, Burne, Judy, Mcintyre and Jesse have become in this book—Fred, Dick, Alec, Tom, Kerry + Burne. Isabelle + Rosalind of the R.E. have become just Isabelle while the new Rosalind is a different person.

Beatrice is a new character—Dr. Dudly becomes Monsignor Darcy; is much better done—in fact every character is in better perspective.

The preface I leave to your discretion—perhaps its a little too clever-clever; likewise you may object to the literary personalities in Chap II + Bk II and to the length of the socialistic discussion in the last chapter. The

[1] *Dangerous Days* (1919), by Mary Roberts Rinehart; *Ramsey Milholland* (1919), by Booth Tarkington.

book contains a little over ninety thousand words. I certainly think the hero gets somewhere.

I await anxiously your verdict

Sincerely
F Scott Fitzgerald

P.S. Thorton Hancock is Henry Adams[1]—I didn't do him thoroughly of course—but I knew him when I was a boy.

S.F.

TO: *Maxwell Perkins*   *ALS, 5 pp. Princeton University*

599 Summit Ave.
St. Paul, Minn
Sept 18th, 1919

Dear Mr. Perkins:

Of course I was delighted to get your letter and I've been in a sort of trance all day; not that I doubted you'd take it but at last I have something to show people. It has enough advertisement in St. Paul already to sell several thousand copies + I think Princeton will buy it (I've been a periodical, local Great-Expectations for some time in both places.)

Terms ect I leave to you but one thing I can't relinquish without at least a slight struggle. Would it be utterly impossible for you to publish the book Xmas—or say by February? I have so many things dependent on its success—including of course a girl—not that I expect it to make me a fortune but it will have a psychological effect on me and all my surroundings and besides open up new fields. I'm in that stage where every month counts frantically and seems a cudgel in a fight for happiness against time. Will you let me know more exactly how that difference in time of publication influences the sale + what you mean by "early Spring"?

Excuse this ghastly handwriting but I'm a bit nervous today. I'm beginning (last month) a very ambitious novel called "The Demon Lover" which will probably take a year also I'm writing short stories. I find that what I enjoy writing is always my best—Every young author ought to read Samuel Butler's Note Books.[2]

I'm writing quite a marvellous after-the-war story. Does Mr Bridges[3] think that they're a little passé or do you think he'd like to see it?

I'll fix up data for advertising + have a photo taken next week with the

---

[1] American man of letters to whom the sixteen-year-old Fitzgerald had been introduced by Father Fay and Shane Leslie.

[2] *The Note-Books of Samuel Butler,* ed. Henry Festing Jones (1912), which Fitzgerald once described as "The most interesting human document ever written."

[3] Robert Bridges, editor of *Scribner's Magazine.*

most gigantic enjoyment (I'm trying H.G. Well's use of vast garagantuan [sp.] words)

Well thank you for a very happy day and numerous other favors and let me know if I've any possible chance for earlier publication and give my thanks or whatever is in order to Mr. Scribner[1] or whoever else was on the deciding committee.

Probably be East next month or Nov.

(over for P.S.)

Sincerely

F Scott Fitzgerald

P.S. Who picks out the cover? I'd like something that could be a set—look cheerful + important like a Shaw Book. I notice Shaw, Galesworthy + Barrie do that. But Wells doesn't—. I wonder why. No need of illustrations is there? I knew a fellow at College who'd have been a wonder for books like mine—a mixture of Aubrey Beardsly, Hogarth + James Montgomery Flagg. But he got killed in the war.

Excuse this immoderately long and rambling letter but I think you'll have to allow me several days for recuperation.

Yrs.

F.S.F.

TO: *Alida Bigelow*[2]   *ALS, 4 pp. Princeton University*
Postmarked September 23, 1919

1st Epistle of St. Scott to the Smithsonian
Chapter the I
Verses the I to the last—

(599 Summit Ave.)

In a house below the average
Of a street above the average
In a room below the roof
With a lot above the ears
I shall write Alida Bigelow
Shall indite Alida Bigelow
As the worlds most famous gooph
(This line don't rhyme)

---

[1] Charles Scribner II, head of Charles Scribner's Sons at this time.
[2] St. Paul friend with whom Fitzgerald corresponded while she was at college.

(September 22, 1919)

What's a date!		Stop this rot.
Mr. Fate		Keep a date, What's a date,
Can't berate		Father time, Mr. Fate?
Mr. Scott.		Such a lot S'ever
He is not		To berate; Scott
Marking time:		Tho I hate
Its too late	To the dot!	
	So, in rhyme,	

Most beautiful, rather-too-virtuous-but-entirely-enchanting Alida:

Scribner has accepted my book. Ain't I Smart!

But hic jublilatio erat totam spoiled for meum par lisant une livre, une novellum (novum) nomine "Salt" par Herr C. G. Morris[1]—a most astounding piece of realism, it makes Fortitude[2] look like an antique mental ash-can and is quite as good as "The Old Wives Tale."[3]

Of course I think Walpole is a weak-wad anyhow.

Read Salt young girl so that you may know what life B.

In a few days I'll have lived one score and three days in this vale of tears. On I plod—always bored, often drunk, doing no penance for my faults—rather do I become more tolerant of myself from day to day, hardening my chrystal heart with blasphemous humor and shunning only toothpicks, pathos, and poverty as being the three unforgivable things in life.

Before we meet again I hope you will have tasted strong liquor to excess and kissed many emotional young men in red and yellow moonlights—these things being chasterners of those prejudices which are as gutta percha to the niblicks of the century.

I am frightfully unhappy, look like the devil, will be famous within 1 12 month and, I hope, dead within 2.

Hoping you are the same

I am

With Excruciating respect

F. Scott Fitzgerald

P.S. If you wish, you may auction off this letter to the gurls of your collidge—on condition that the proceeds go to the Society for the drownding of Armenian Airedales.

Bla!

F.S.F.

---

[1] Charles G. Norris; *Salt* appeared in 1918.
[2] 1913 novel by Hugh Walpole.
[3] 1908 novel by Arnold Bennett.

TO: *Robert Bridges*   *ALS, 2 pp. Princeton University*
1919

599 Summit Ave
St. Paul, Minn
Oct. twenty-5th

Dear Mr. Bridges:

This is a query. I have a project. It is a work of about 20,000 words and more on the order of my novel than like these stories I've been doing. But its the sort of thing that will require a full months work and as The New Republic, Scribners + possibly the Atlantic Monthly are the only magazines that would publish it I don't want to start until you assure me that there's nothing in the project which seems to bar it from Scribner's if it be suffiently interesting and well done.

It is a literary forgery purporting to be selections from the note-books of a man who is a complete literary radical from the time he's in college thru two years in New York—finally he goes to training camp, gets bored and enlists as a pvt. This is the end of the book—a note by me will say that he served in Companies E and G of the twenty-eighth Infantry and died of appenditis in Paris in 1918.

It will be in turns cynical, ingenious, life saturated, critical and bitter. It will be racy and startling with opinions and personalities. I have a journal I have kept for 3 ½ yrs. which my book didn't begin to exhaust, which I don't seem to be able to draw on for stories but which certainly is, I think, highly amusing. This thoroughly edited and revised, plus some imagination + ½ doz ingredients I have in mind will be the bulk of it. It would take 2 or possibly 3 parts to publish it.

The tremendous sucess of Butler's note books and of Barbellions (Wells?) Disappointed Man[1] makes me think that the public loves to find out the workings of active minds in their personal problems. It will be bound to have that streak of coarseness that both Wells + Butler have but there won't be any James Joyce flavor to it.

Of course you can't possibly commit yourself until you've seen it but as I say I'd want to know before I start if a work of that nature would be intrinsicly hostile to the policy of Scribner's Magazine. With apologies for intruding apon your patience once again I am

Sincerely
F. Scott Fitzgerald

---

[1] *The Journal of a Disappointed Man* (1919), by W. N. P. Barbellion.

TO: *Harold Ober*   ALS, 2 pp. Lilly Library
1920

Dear Mr. Ober—

You could have knocked me over with a feather when you told me you had sold Myra—I never was so heartily sick of a story before I finished it as I was of that one.

Enclosed is a new version of <u>Barbara</u>, called <u>Bernice Bobs Her Hair</u> to distinguish it from Mary Rineheart's "Bab" stories in the <u>Post</u>. I think I've managed to inject a snappy climax into it. Now this story went to several Magazines this summer—Scribners, Woman's H. Companion + the Post but it was in an entirely different, <u>absolutely unrecognizable</u> form, <u>single-spaced</u> and none of 'em kept it more than three days except Scribner, who wrote a personal letter on it.

Is there any money in collections of short stories?

This Post money comes in very handy—my idea is to go south—probably New Orleans and write my second novel. Now my novels, at least my first one, are not like my short stories at all, they are rather cynical and pessimistic—and therefore I doubt if as a whole they'd stand much chance of being published serially in any of the uplift magazines at least until my first novel + these Post stories appear and I get some sort of a reputation.

Now I published three incidents of my first novel in <u>Smart Set</u> last summer + my idea in the new one is to sell such parts as might go as units separately to different magazines, as I write them, because it'll take ten weeks to write it + I don't want to run out of money. There will be one long thing which might make a novellette for the Post called The <u>Diary of a Popular Girl</u>, half a dozen cynical incidents that might do for <u>Smart Set</u> + perhaps a story or two for <u>Scribners</u> or <u>Harpers</u>. How about it—do you think this is a wise plan—or do you think a story like C. G. Norris' <u>Salt</u> or Cabells <u>Jurgen</u> or Driesers <u>Jenny Gerhard</u>[1] would have one chance in a million to be sold serially? I'm asking you for an opinion about this beforehand because it will have an influence on my plans.

Hoping to hear from you I am

Sincerlerly
F. Scott Fitzgerald

P.S. The excellent story I told you of probably wont be along for two or three weeks. I'm stuck in the middle of it.

F S F.

599 Summit Ave.
St. Paul, Minn
Jan 8th 1919.

[1]Norris's *Salt*, James Branch Cabell's *Jurgen* (1919), and Theodore Dreiser's *Jennie Gerhardt* (1911) were controversial novels in their time.

TO: *Zelda Sayre*   *Wire. Scrapbook. Princeton University*
Before January 9, 1920   *New York City*

I FIND THAT I CANNOT GET A BERTH SOUTH UNTIL FRIDAY OR POSSIBLY SATURDAY
NIGHT WHICH MEANS I WONT ARRIVE UNTIL THE ELEVENTH OR TWELFTH PERIOD
AS SOON AS I KNOW I WILL WIRE YOU THE SATURDAY EVENING POST HAS JUST
TAKEN TWO MORE STORIES PERIOD ALL MY LOVE

TO: *Zelda Sayre*   *Wire. Scrapbook. Princeton University*

NEWYORK NY   FEB 24 1920
MISS LIDA SAYRE
I HAVE SOLD THE MOVIE RIGHTS OF HEAD AND SHOULDERS TO THE METRO
COMPANY FOR TWENTY FIVE HUNDRED DOLLARS[1] I LOVE YOU DEAREST GIRL

SCOTT

TO: *John Grier Hibben*[2]   *ALS, 3 pp. Princeton University*

Wakeman's, Westport, Conn, June 3d, 1920
My Dear President Hibben:
 I want to thank you very much for your letter and to confess that the
honor of a letter from you outweighed my real regret that my book gave
you concern. It was a book written with the bitterness of my discovery that
I had spent several years trying to fit in with a curriculum that is after all
made for the average student. After the curriculum had tied me up, taken
away the honors I'd wanted, bent my nose over a chemistry book and said
"No fun, no activities, no offices, no Triangle trips—no, not even a diploma" if you can't do chemistry"—after that I retired. It is easy for the
successful man in college, the man who has gotten what he wanted to say
 "It's all fine. It makes men. It made me, see"—
 —but it seems to me its like the Captain of a Company when he has his
men lined up at attention for inspection. He sees only the tightly buttoned
coat and the shaved faces. He doesn't know that perhaps a private in the
rear rank is half crazy because a pin is sticking in his back and he can't move,
or another private is thinking that his wife is dying and he can't get leave
because too many men in the company are gone already.
 I don't mean at all that Princeton is not the happiest time in most boys
lives. It is of course—I simply say it wasn't the happiest time in mine. I

---

[1]Made as *The Chorus Girl's Romance* by Metro Pictures (1920).
[2]President of Princeton University; Hibben's letter to Fitzgerald had expressed concern
about Fitzgerald's treatment of Princeton in *This Side of Paradise* and had praised his story "The
Four Fists," published in the June 1920 *Scribner's Magazine*.

> This "Exquisite burlesque
> of Compton McKenzie
> with the pastiche of
> Wells at the end" is
> presented
> <u>as toll</u>
>
> to
>
> Bunny Wilson
>
> F Scott Fitzgerald
> March 20th, 1920

Fitzgerald's description of This Side of Paradise *is quoted from a Wilson letter.*

As a matter of fact, Mr Mencken, I stuck your name in on Page 224 in the last proof— partly, I suppose, as a vague bootlick and partly because I have since adopted a great many of your views. But the other literary opinions, especial'y the disparagement of Cobb were written when you were little more than a name to me —

This is a bad book full of good things, a novel about flappers written for Philosophers, an exquisite burlesque of Compton McKenzie with a pastiche of Wells at the end —

F. Scott Fitzgerald
March 20th, 1920

Irvin S. Cobb was a Kentucky humorist on whom Fitzgerald commented in This Side of Paradise: *"This man Cobb—I don't think he's either clever or amusing—and what's more, I don't think very many people do, except the editors."*

love it now better than any place on earth. The men—the undergraduates of Yale + Princeton are cleaner, healthier, better looking, better dressed, wealthier and more attractive than any undergraduate body in the country. I have no fault to find with Princeton that I can't find with Oxford and Cambridge. I simply wrote out of my own impressions, wrote as honestly as I could a picture of its beauty. That the picture is cynical is the fault of my temperment.

My view of life, President Hibben, is the view of Theodore Driesers and Joseph Conrads—that life is too strong and remorseless for the sons of men. My idealism flickered out with Henry Strater's anticlub movement at Princeton.[1] "The Four Fists" latest of my stories to be published was the first to be written. I wrote it in desperation one evening because I had a three inch pile of rejection slips and it was financially nessesary for me to give the magazines what they wanted. The appreciation it has recieved has amazed me.

I must admit however that This Side of Paradise does over accentuate the gayiety + country club atmosphere of Princeton. For the sake of the readers interest that part was much over stressed, and of course the hero not being average reacted rather unhealthily I suppose to many perfectly normal phenomena. To that extent the book is inaccurate. It is the Princeton of Saturday night in May. Too many intelligent class mates of mine have failed to agree with it for me to consider it really photgraphic any more, as of course I did when I wrote it.

Next time I am in Princeton I will take the priveledge of coming to see you.

I am, sir,

Very Respectfully Yours
F Scott Fitzgerald

TO: *David Balch*[2]   ALS, 2 pp. Collection of Marcia and Maurice Neville

Westport, Conn
June 19th, 1920

Dear Mr. Balch:

I have unearthed so many esoteric facts about myself lately for magazines ect. that I blush to continue to send out colorful sentences about a rather colorless life. However here are some "human interest points".

(1.) I was always interested in prodigies because I almost became one— that is in the technical sense of going to college young. I finally decided to enter at the conventional age of 17. I went in on my 17th birthday and, I

---

[1] Strater had been one of the leaders of a movement during the spring 1917 term to abolish eating clubs at Princeton on the grounds that they were undemocratic.

[2] Editor of *Movie Weekly*.

think, was one of the ten youngest in my class at Princeton. Prodigies always interested me + it seemed to me that the Harvard prodigy, Boris Siddis, offerred grounds for a story. The original title of Head + Shoulders was "The prodigy" + I just brought in the chorus girl by way of a radical contrast. Before I'd finished she almost stole the story.

(2) I got four dozen letters from readers when it first appeared in the Post.

(3) It will be republished in my collection of short stories "Flappers + Philosophers" which The Scribners are publishing this fall.

(4) I'd rather watch a good shimmee dance than Ruth St. Dennis + Pavalowa combined. I see nothing at all disgusting in it.

(5) My story "The Camel's Back" in The S.E.P. (which you may be buying) was the fastest piece of writing I've ever heard of. It is twelve thousand words long and it was written in fourteen hours straight writing and sent to the S.E.P. in its original form.

I can't think of any thing else just now that hasn't been used before. And I have no good picture. I expect to have some soon though + will send you one

Sincerely
F Scott Fitzgerald

TO: Charles Scribner II   *ALS, 1 p. Princeton University*

Westport, Conn.
Aug. 12th 1920

Dear Mr. Scribner:

Again I am immensely obiged to you. I should certainly feel much more business-like and less profligate if you would tell your book-keeper when our reckoning comes this autumn to charge me full interest on the advances you've made me.

My new novel, called "The Flight of the Rocket,"[1] concerns the life of one Anthony Patch between his 25th and 33d years (1913–1921). He is one of those many with the tastes and weaknesses of an artist but with no actual creative inspiration. How he and his beautiful young wife are wrecked on the shoals of dissipation is told in the story. This sounds sordid but it's really a most sensational book + I hope won't dissapoint the critics who liked my first one. I hope it'll be in your hands by November 1st

Sincerely
F Scott Fitzgerald

---

[1] *The Beautiful and Damned.*

Dear Mr. Mencken:

Worth reading

The Ice Palace
The Cut Glass Bowl
Benediction
Dalyrimple goes wrong

Amusing

The Off Shore Pirate

Trash

Head & Shoulders
The Four Fists
Bernice Bobs her Hair

With profound bows
F. Scott Fitzgerald

Chere Bunnay:

Ici est la ms. (le parte remainant)

Sincserlely

Francois Don Scotus Fitz

Family Tree of F. Scott Fitzgerald

Duns Scotus — m. — Mary, Queen of Scotts   Edward Fitzgerald — m. — Sir Walter Scott
(philos)   (Queen)   (The Rubra)   (Ivanhoe)

Francis Scott Key   m   Duke Fitzgerald
(hymnalist)   (Earl of Leinster)

F. Scott Fitzgerald
(drunkard)

TO: *Maxwell Perkins*   ALS, 1 p. *Princeton University*

> 38 W 59th St.
> New York City
> Dec 31st, 1920

Dear Mr. Perkins:

The bank this afternoon refused to lend me anything on the security of stock I hold—and I have been pacing the floor for an hour trying to decide what to do. Here, with the novel within two weeks of completion, am I with six hundred dollars worth of bills and owing Reynolds[1] $650 for an advance on a story that I'm utterly unable to write. I've made half a dozen starts yesterday and today and I'll go mad if I have to do another debutante which is what they want.

I hoped that at last being square with Scribner's I could remain so. But I'm at my wit's end. Isn't there some way you could regard this as an advance on the new novel rather than on the Xmas sale which won't be due me till July? And at the same interest that it costs Scribner's to borrow? Or could you make it a month's loan from Scribner + Co. with my next ten books as security? I need $1600.00

> Anxiously
> F Scott Fitzgerald

TO: *John Biggs, Jr.*   ALS, 1 p. *Bruccoli*
Winter 1921

> 38 W. 59th St.
> New York City

Dear Jawn:

Wired you today for your adress which I've mislaid. The enclosure explains why I want it.

Glad you liked my suggestion. When Perkins comes to see you I shouldn't tell him your plot but <u>for God's sake</u> tell him the novel's damn good! No decent workman belittles his own work unless, and until, its been over-praised.

When you finish it I have a brilliant scene for you. Let me hear from you soon

> Scott F.

P.S. Perkins is one hell of a good fellow. He's the one who stuck out for my 1st novel almost 3 years ago. He's the editorial brain of The Scribner Co.

> S.

[1] Paul Revere Reynolds literary agency, of which Harold Ober was a partner.

P.S.[2] Am writing a movie for Dorothy Gish by request of Griffith[1] for which I hope to get ten thousand.

TO: *Robert D. Clark*[2]   *ALS, 4 pp. Bruccoli*
1921

38 W 59th St.
New York City
Feb 9th 1920

Dear Bob:

Your letter riled me to such an extent that I'm answering immediatly. Who are all these "real people" who "create business and politics"? and of whose approval I should be so covetous? Do you mean grafters who keep sugar in their ware houses so that people have to go without or the cheapjacks who by bribery and high-school sentiment manage to controll elections. I can't pick up a paper here without finding that some of these "real people" who will not be satisfied only with "a brilliant mind" (I quote you) have just gone up to Sing Sing for a stay—Brindell and Hegerman, two pillars of society, went this morning.

Who in hell ever respected Shelley, Whitman, Poe, O. Henry, Verlaine, Swinburne, Villon, Shakespeare ect when they were alive. Shelley + Swinburne were fired from college; Verlaine + O Henry were in jail. The rest were drunkards or wasters and told generally by the merchants and petty politicians and jitney messiahs of their day that real people wouldn't stand it   And the merchants and messiahs, the shrewd + the dull, are dust—and the others live on.

Just occasionally a man like Shaw who was called an immoralist 50 times worse than me back in the 90ties, lives on long enough so that the world grows up to him. What he believed in 1890 was heresy then—by by now its almost respectable. It seems to me I've let myself be dominated by "authorities" for too long—the headmaster of Newman, S.P.A, Princeton, my regiment, my business boss—who knew no more than me, in fact I should say these 5 were all distinctly my mental inferiors. And that's all that counts! The Rosseaus, Marxes, Tolstois—men of thought, mind you, "impractical" men, "idealist" have done more to decide the food you eat and the things you think + do than all the millions of Roosevelts and Rockerfellars that strut for 20 yrs. or so mouthing such phrases as 100% American (which means 99% village idiot), and die with a little pleasing flattery to the silly and cruel old God they've set up in their hearts.

---

[1]Dorothy Gish, sister of Lillian Gish, was a silent-movie actress; D. W. Griffith was a legendary director. Fitzgerald's scenario for Gish was rejected.

[2]Boyhood friend of Fitzgerald's in St. Paul.

A letter

Stratford-on-Avon
June 8th 1595

Dear Will:

Your family here are much ashamed that you could write such a bawdy play as Troilius and Cressida. All the real people here (Mr. Beef, the butcher and Mr. Skunk, the village undertaker) say they will not be satisfied with a brilliant mind and a pleasant manner. If you really want to ammount to something you've got be respected for yourself as well as your work

Affectionately
Your Mother, Mrs. Shakespeare

Concieted Ass! says Bob.

And I don't blame you for saying so, neither do I blame anybody much for anything. The only lesson to be learned from life is that there's no lesson to be learned from life.

Have you read Main Street?[1] Its a great book. Had a letter from Sinclaire Lewis telling me we must not expect our books to sell in St. Paul. I expect my new one, just completed, "The Beautiful and Damned" to be barred from the St. Paul library—by the wives of Mr. Frost and Mr. Rietsky— and Mr. Severance.

Don Stuart[2] vowing he can stand business no longer has come to N.Y. to take up writing. He's a knock-out, I think.

But really Bob, fond as I am of you, I do think that was a silly letter to write me.

Come on east + look us up when you do.

Faithfully
F Scott Fitzg—

<table>
<tr><td>TO: Edmund Wilson</td><td align="right">ALS, 6 pp. Yale University</td></tr>
<tr><td>July 1921</td><td align="right">Hotel Cecil stationery. London</td></tr>
</table>

Dear Bunny:

Of course I'm wild with jealousy! Do you think you can indecently parade this obscene success[3] before my envious desposition, with <u>equanaminity</u>, you are mistaken.

God damn the continent of Europe. It is of merely antiquarian interest. Rome is only a few years behind Tyre + Babylon. The negroid streak

---

[1] Sinclair Lewis's *Main Street* (1920) satirized small-town, midwestern values.
[2] Donald Ogden Stewart became a successful humorist and screenwriter.
[3] Wilson's *New Republic* article on Mencken, which Mencken had commended.

creeps northward to defile the nordic race. Already the Italians have the souls of blackamoors. Raise the bars of immigration and permit only Scandinavians, Teutons, Anglo Saxons + Celts to enter. France made me sick. It's silly pose as the thing the world has to save. I think its a shame that England + America didn't let Germany conquor Europe. Its the only thing that would have saved the fleet of tottering old wrecks. My reactions were all philistine, anti-socialistic, provincial + racially snobbish. I believe at last in the white man's burden. We are as far above the modern frenchman as he is above the negro. Even in art! Italy has no one. When Antole France dies French literature will be a silly jealous rehashing of technical quarrels. They're thru + done. You may have spoken in jest about N.Y. as the capitol of culture but in 25 years it will be just as London is now. Culture follows money + all the refinements of aesthetescism can't stave off its change of seat (Christ! what a metaphor). We will be the Romans in the next generation as the English are now.

Alec[1] sent me your article. I read it half a dozen times and think it is magnificent. I can't tell you how I hate you. I don't hate Don Stuart half as much (tho I find that I am suddenly + curiously irritated by him) because I don't really dread him. But you! Keep out of my sight. I want no more of your articles!

Enclosed is 2 francs with which you will please find a french slave to make me a typed copy of your letter from Mencken. Send here at once, if it please you. I will destroy it on reading it. Please! I'd do as much for you. I haven't gotten hold of a bookman.

Paradise is out here. Of 20 reviews about half are mildly favorable, a quarter of them imply that I've read "Sinister Street once too often" + the other five (including the Times) damn it summarily as artificial. I doubt if it sells 1,500 copies.

Menckens 1st series of Predjudices is attracting wide attention here. Wonderful review in the Times.

I'm delighted to hear about The Undertaker.[2] Alec wrote describing how John "goes to see Mrs. Knopf and rubs himself against her passionately hoping for early fall publication." Edna[3] has no doubt told you how we scoured Paris for you. Idiot! The American Express mail dept has my adress. Why didn't you register. We came back to Paris especially to see you. Needless to say our idea of a year in Italy was well shattered + we sail for America on the 9th + thence to The "Sahara of Bozart" (Montgomery) for life.

With envious curses + hopes of an immediate responce

F. Scott Fitzgerald (author of Flappers + Philosophers [juvenile])

[1] Alexander McKaig, Princeton '17.
[2] *The Undertaker's Garland* (1922), a collection of verse and prose by Wilson and Bishop.
[3] Poet Edna St. Vincent Millay.

TO: Maxwell Perkins   ALS, 2 pp. Princeton University

Dellwood, White Bear Lake
Minn, Aug 25th 1921

Dear Mr. Perkins—

Excuse the pencil but I'm feeling rather tired and discouraged with life tonight and I havn't the energy to use ink—ink the ineffable destroyer of thought, that fades an emotion into that slatternly thing, a written down mental excretion. What ill-spelled rot!

About the novel—which after my letters I should think you'd be so bored with you'd wish it had never existed: I'd like very much if it came out in England simultaneously with America. You have the rights to it have you not? If you do not intend to place it would you be willing to turn them over to me on the same 10% basis as <u>Paradise</u>. So I could place it either with Collins[1] or thru Reynolds?

Hope you're enjoying New Hampshire—you probably are. I'm having a hell of a time because I've loafed for 5 months + I want to get to work. Loafing puts me in this particularly obnoxious and abominable gloom. My 3d novel, if I ever write another, will I am sure be black as death with gloom. I should like to sit down with ½ dozen chosen companions + drink myself to death but I am sick alike of life, liquor and literature. If it wasn't for Zelda I think I'd dissapear out of sight for three years. Ship as a sailor or something + get hard—I'm sick of the flabby semi-intellectual softness in which I flounder with my generation.

Scott Fitz

TO: Edmund Wilson   ALS, 5 pp. Yale University
Postmarked November 25, 1921

626 Goodrich Ave.
St. Paul, Minn.

Dear Bunny—

Thank you for your congratulations.[2] I'm glad the damn thing's over. Zelda came through without a scratch + I have awarded her the croix-de-guerre with palm. Speaking of France, the great general with the suggestive name is in town today.

I agree with you about Mencken—Weaver + Dell[3] are both something awful. I like some of John's critisism but Christ! he is utterly dishonest. Why does he tell us how rotten he thinks Mooncalf is and then give it a

---

[1] W. Collins Sons, British publisher of Fitzgerald's first two novels and first two story collections.

[2] On the birth of the Fitzgeralds' daughter, Scottie.

[3] John V. A. Weaver, poet and reviewer; Floyd Dell, novelist best known for *Moon-Calf* (1920).

"polite bow" in his column. Likewise he told me personally that my "book just missed being a great book" + how I was the most hopeful ect ect + then damned me with faint praise in two papers six months before I'm published. I am sat with a condescending bow "halfway between the posts of Compton Mckenzie and Booth Tarkington." So much for that!

I have almost completely rewritten my book. Do you remember you told me that in my midnight symposium scene I had sort of set the stage for a play that never came off—in other words when they all began to talk none of them had anything important to say. I've interpolated some recent ideas of my own and (possibly) of others. See enclosure at end of letter.

Having desposed of myself I turn to you. I am glad you + Ted Paramore[1] are together. I was never crazy over the oboist nor the accepter of invitations and I imagine they must have been small consolation to live with. I like Ted immensely. He is a little too much the successful Eli to live comfortably in his mind's bed-chamber but I like him immensely.

What in hell does this mean? My controll must have dictated it. His name is Mr. Ikki and he is an Alaskan orange-grower.

Nathan[2] and me have become reconciled by letter. If the baby is ugly she can retire into the shelter of her full name Frances Scott.

I hear strange stories about you and your private life. Are they all true? What are you going to do? Free lance? I'm delighted about the undertaker's garland. Why not have a preface by that famous undertaker in New York. Say justa blurb on the cover. He might do it if he had a sense of humor

St. Paul is dull as hell. Have written two good short stories + three cheap ones.

I liked Three Soldiers[3] immensely + reviewed it for the St. Paul Daily News. I am tired of modern novels + have just finished Paine's biography of Clemens.[4] It's excellent. Do let me see if if you do me for the Bookman. Isn't The Triumph of the Egg[5] a wonderful title. I liked both John's + Don's[6] articles in Smart Set. I am lonesome for N.Y. May get there next fall + may go to England to live. Yours in this hell-hole of life & time,

the world.
F Scott Fitz—

<hr>

[1]E. E. Paramore, friend of Wilson, and, later, Fitzgerald's collaborator on *Three Comrades*.

[2]George Jean Nathan, co-editor with Mencken of *The Smart Set*; he was the model for Maury Noble in *The Beautiful and Damned*.

[3]1921 novel by John Dos Passos.

[4]*Mark Twain: A Biography*, 3 vols. (1912), by Albert Bigelow Paine.

[5]1921 story collection by Sherwood Anderson.

[6]Bishop and Stewart.

TO: *Harold Ober*   ALS, *1 p. Lilly Library*
c. November–December 1921

626 Goodrich Ave. St. Paul
Dear Mr. Ober:

Am enclosing The Diamond in the Sky[1] cut to 15,000 words from the original 20,000—from 87 pages to 66. I don't feel that I can cut it any farther without ruining the story. I think this much cutting has improved it.

If the better priced markets won't have it I suggest Scribners or even Smart Set tho I doubt if they'd pay more than $200. or $250. or possibly $300 for it as a novellette.

Thank you for depositing the money for me. I am concieving a play which is to make my fortune

Sincerely
F Scott Fitzgerald

TO: *Edmund Wilson*   ALS, *7 pp. Yale University*
January 1922

626 Goodrich Ave.
St. Paul, Minn
Dear Bunny—

Needless to say I have never read anything with quite the uncanny facination with which I read your article.[2] It is, of course, the only intelligible and intelligent thing of any length which has been written about me and my stuff—and like every thing you write it seems to me pretty generally true. I am guilty of its every stricture and I take an extraordinary delight in its considered approbation. I don't see how I could possibly be offended at anything in it—on the contrary it pleases me more to be compared to "standards out of time", than to merely the usual scapegoats of contemporary critisism. Of course I'm going to carp at it a little but merely to conform to convention. I like it, I think its an unpredjudiced diagnosis and I am considerably in your debt for the interest which impelled you to write it.

Now as to the liquor thing—its true, but nevertheless I'm going to ask you take it out. It leaves a loophole through which I can be attacked and discredited by every moralist who reads the article. Wasn't it Bernard Shaw who said that you've either got to be conventional in your work or in your private life or get into trouble? Anyway the legend about my liquoring is terribly widespread and this thing would hurt me more than you could imagine—both in my contact with the people with whom I'm thrown—

[1] "The Diamond as Big as the Ritz."
[2] Wilson's "F. Scott Fitzgerald," *The Bookman* (March 1922).

50

relatives + respectable friends—and, what is much more important, financially.

So I'm asking you to cut:

1. "when sober" on page one. I have indicated it. If you want to substitute "when not unduly celebrating" or some innuendo no more definite than that, all right.

2. From "This quotation indicates . . ." to ". . . sets down the facts" would be awfully bad for me. I'd much rather have you cut it or at least leave out the personal implication if you must indicate that my characters drink. As a matter of fact I have never written a line of any kind while I was under the glow of so much as a single cocktail + tho my parties have been many its been their spectacularity rather than their frequency which has built up the usual "dope-fiend" story. Judge + Mrs. Sayre would be crazy! and they never miss The Bookman.

Now your three influences, St. Paul, Irish (incidently, though it doesn't matter, I'm not Irish on Father's side—that's where Francis Scott Key comes in) and liquor are all important I grant. But I feel less hesitancy asking you to remove the liquor because your catalogue is not complete anyhow—the most enormous influence on me in the four + ½ yrs since I met her has been the complete fine and full hearted selfishness and chill-mindedness of Zelda.

Both Zelda and I roared over the Anthony-Maury incident.[1] You've improved mine (which was to have Muriel go blind) by 100%—we were utterly convulsed.

But Bunny, and this I hate to ask you, please take out the soldier incident.[2] I am afraid of it. It will not only utterly spoil the effect of the incident in the book but will give rise to the most unpleasant series of events imaginable. Ever since Three Soldiers, the New York Times has been itching for a chance to get at the critics of the war. If they got hold of this I would be assailed with the most violent vituperation in the press of the entire country (and you know what the press can do, how they can present an incident to make a man upholding an unpopular cause into the likeness of a monster— vide Upton Sinclair[3]). And, by God, they would! Besides the incident is not correct. I didn't apologize. I told the Col. about it very proudly. I wasn't sorry for months afterwards and then it was only a novelist's remorse.

So for God's sake cut that paragraph. I'd be wild if it appeared! And it would without doubt do me serious harm.

[1] Wilson's burlesque of the final meeting of Anthony Patch and Maury Noble reads: "It seemed to Anthony that Maury's eyes had a fixed glassy stare; his legs moved stiffly as he walked and when he spoke his voice had no life in it. When Anthony came nearer, he saw that Maury was dead!"

[2] Unidentified incident during Fitzgerald's army service.

[3] Sinclair, whose novels and nonfiction books treated controversial subjects, was frequently attacked in the press.

I note from the quotation from Head and Shoulders + from reference to Bernice that you have plowed through Flappers for which conscientious labor I thank you. When the strain has abated I will send you two exquisite stories in what Professor Lemuel Ozuk in his definative biography will call my "second" or "neo-flapper" manner.

But one more carp before I close. Gloria and Anthony are representative. They are two of the great army of the rootless who float around New York. There must be thousands. Still I didn't bring it out.

With these two cuts, Bunny, the article ought to be in my favor. At any rate I enjoyed it enormously and shall try to reciprocate in some way on The Undertaker's Garland though I doubt whether you'd trust it to my palsied hands for review. Don't change the Irish thing—its much better as it is—besides the quotation hints at the whiskey motif.

Forever,

Benjamin Disraeli

I am consoled for asking you to cut the soldier and alcoholic paragraphs by the fact that if you hadn't known me you couldn't or wouldn't have put them in. They have a critical value but are really personal gossip.

F. S. F.

I'm glad about the novellette in Smart Set. I am about to send them one. I am writing a comedy—or a burlesque or something. The "romantic stories" about you are none of my business. They will keep until I see you.

S.

Hersesassery—Quelque mot!

How do you like echolalia for "meaningless chatter?"

Glad you like the title motto— Zelda sends best— Remember me to Ted. Did he say I was "old woman with jewel?"[1]

TO: *John Peale Bishop* ALS, *3 pp. Princeton University*
February 1922 *St. Paul, Minnesota*

626 Goodrich Ave

Dear John:

I'll tell you frankly what I'd rather you'd do.[2] Tell specifically what you like about the book + don't—the characters—Anthony, Gloria, Adam Patch, Maury, Bloeckman, Muriel Dick, Rachael, Tana ect ect ect. Exactly whether they're good or bad, convincing or not. What you think of the style, too ornate (if so quote) good (also quote) rotten (also quote). What emotion (if any) the book gave you. What you think of its humor. What you think of its ideas. If ideas are bogus hold them up specifically and laugh

---

[1] Edna St. Vincent Millay had compared Fitzgerald to a stupid old woman with whom someone had left a diamond.

[2] Bishop reviewed *The Beautiful and Damned* in the March 5, 1922 *New York Herald*.

at them. Is it boring or interesting. How interesting. What recent American books are more so. If you think my "Flash Back in Paradise" in Chap I is like the elevated moments of D. W. Griffith say so. Also do you think its imitative and of whom. What I'm angling for is a specific definate review. I'm tickled both that they've asked for such a lengthy thing and that your going to do. You cannot hurt my feelings about the book—tho I did resent in your Baltimore article[1] being definately limited at 25 years old to a place between Mckenzie who wrote 2 ½ good (but not wonderful) novels + then died—and Tarkington who if he has a great talent has the mind of a school boy. I mean, at my age they'd done nothing.

As I say I'm delighted that you're going to do it and as you wrote asking me to suggest a general mode of attack I am telling you frankly what I would like. I'm so afraid of all the reviews being general + I devoted so much more care myself to the detail of the book than I did to thinking out the general sceme that I would appreciate a detailed review. If it is to be that length article it could scarcely be all general anyway

I'm awfully sorry you've had the flue. We arrive east on the 9th. I enjoy your book page in Vanity Fair and think it is excellent—
The baby is beautiful.

As Ever
Scott

TO: Harold Ober   ALS, 3 pp. Lilly Library

626 Goodrich Ave
St. Paul
Feb 5th, 1922

Dear Mr. Ober—
I have your letter of Jan 30th. There are several things I want to speak to you about
(1.) My play will be done in about 10 days—two weeks. It is a wonder, I think, and should make a great deal of money.
(2.) A well-known author who came through here last week said he thought The Metropolitan was on the verge of failure.[2] As I understand they have finally paid you for my novel[3] but have not paid for my last short story (though you have paid me for it—advanced it, I mean). If this is true do you think Benjamin Button should go to them until they have paid for

---

[1] Bishop had reviewed the serialization in the *Baltimore Evening Sun* (October 8, 1921).
[2] The "well-known author" was probably Joseph Hergesheimer.
[3] *The Beautiful and Damned* was serialized in *Metropolitan Magazine* (September 1921–March 1922).

Two for a Cent? I think that Benjamin Button, tho, like The Diamond in the Sky, satirical, would sell, because it does not "blaspheme" like the latter—which leads to my third point:

(3.) I should much prefer that The Diamond in the Sky be sent to Smart Set as soon as it can be re-typed with "Chap I" substituted for "I" ect. If Rascoe of Mccauls[1] wouldn't risk it then Bridges of Scribners wouldn't. Besides he would hack it all to pieces—I once had reams of correspondence with him over a "God damn" in a story called The Cut Glass Bowl. Besides they would pay little more than Scribner—possibly four hundred or five hundred I should guess at most for a two part short story—while Smart Set, though they pay only $35–$80 for short stories, once gave me $200.00 for a novellette when I was unknown, and I feel sure they'd give me $250.00 now.

In short I realize I can't get a real good price for the three weeks work that story represents—so I'd much rather get no price but reap the subtle, and nowadays oh-so-valuble dividend that comes from Mencken's good graces. Besides, in the Smart Set it will be featured.

Again, I'm anxious to get it published soon so it can go in a collection I plan for next fall. I think if you offer it to them as a novellette without mentioning that its been the rounds but simply saying that I asked you to send it to them, they will take it. Of course if you'd rather not deal with Smart Set send it to me.

I suppose that I have been more trouble to you with less profit than any writer whose work you have yet handled but I have every confidence that when my play comes out we will square the whole thing. You have advanced me everything so far sold in America and I imagine the few pounds earned in England have been used up in type writing bills ect.

But I am going to call on you again to advance me, if you will, five hundred dollars on Benjamin Button. Don't bother to telegraph unless you can't.

I am rather discouraged that a cheap story like The Popular Girl written in one week while the baby was being born brings $1500.00 + a genuinely imaginative thing into which I put three weeks real enthusiasm like The Diamond in the Sky brings not a thing. But, by God + Lorimer,[2] I'm going to make a fortune yet.

F Scott Fitzgerald

I note what you say about my "travel stories" I start on them in two weeks when I finish my play====F.S.F.

TO: Edmund Wilson   ALS, 2 pp. Yale University
1922

[1] Columnist and critic Burton Rascoe.
[2] George Horace Lorimer, editor of *The Saturday Evening Post.*

626 Goodrich Ave, St. Paul, Minn
Feb 6th 1921

Dear Bunny—

I read your letter in a chastened mood. My whole point was that you read the book a long time ago in its informal condition, before its final revision and before your own critisisms had strained out some of the broken cork—that, therefore, while as a critic seeing the book for the first time you would, of course, have to speak the truth whether it hurt me financially or not, still that this case was somewhat different and that a pre-publication review which contained private information destined (in my opinion) to hurt the sale of my book, was something of which I had a legitimate right to complain. My specification of "financial" injury is simply a private remark to you—it would be absurd for me to pretend to be indifferent to money, and very few men with a family they care for can be. Besides, you know that in these two novels I have not suppressed anything with the idea of making money by the suppression but I think I am quite justified in asking you to suppress a detail of my private life—and it seems to me that a financial reason is as good as any, rather better in fact, according to Samuel Butler, than to spare my family.

I had forgotten, as a matter of fact, that those Spotlight things are supposed to be personal. Please don't think that I minded the Maury thing. I was simply congratulating you on inventing a more witty parody than I thought I had made. Still I was tight that night and may have said it. The actual quotation from my first draft is quite correct—I didn't say it wasn't.

This is a quibbling letter and I hope it doesn't sound ill natured. It isn't. I simply felt that your letter put me in a bad light and I hasten to explain my objections.

As a matter of fact I am immensely grateful to you for the article and tried to tell you so in my letter. Despite the fact that I am not quite insane about "What Maisie Knew"[1] as you prophecied I would be I admire your judgements in almost every way more than those of anyone else I know, and I value your opinion on my stuff. In your first letter you said yourself that it was O.K. to object to the booze thing and your quarrel with me seems to be that I gave you a perfectly unaffected and honest answer when I told you I feared financial injury.[2]

As you have a 1st edition of the book I won't send you another but will give it my invaluable autograph when I reach New York. I had intended that Perkins should send me the novel to autograph first.

I think its too bad that you have gone to all this trouble over the article and I'm afraid I have put you to it. Anyway its a complicated subject + I can excuse myself better when I see you sometime next month. But I feel quite sure that if Mencken in doing a Literary Spotlight on Drieser had

[1] 1897 novel by Henry James.
[2] Wilson's published Bookman article did not mention Fitzgerald's drinking.

remarked in dead earnest that Drieser's having four wives had had considerable influence on his work, Drieser would have raised a slight howl. And if he had remarked that Drieser was really the hero of all the seductions mentioned in The Titan I think Drieser would have torn his hair—and complained, at least, that he wanted to save such data for his privately printed editions.

> As Ever
>
> F. Scott Fitz-Hardy

TO: *Charles Scribner II*   *TLS, 4 pp. Princeton University*

> 626 Goodrich Avenue,
> St. Paul, Minnesota,
> April 19th, 1922.

Dear Mr. Scribner:

I am consumed by an idea and I can't resist asking you about it. It's probably a chestnut, but it might not have occurred to you before in just this form.

No doubt you know of the success that Boni and Liveright have made of their "Modern Library". Within the last month Doubleday Page & Company have withdrawn the titles that were theirs from Boni's modern library, and gone in on their own hook with a "Lambskin Library". For this they have chosen so far about 18 titles from their past publications—some of them books of merit (Frank Norris and Conrad, for instance) and some of them trashy, but all books that at one time or another have been sensational either as popular successes or as possible contributions to American literature. The Lambskin Library is cheap, bound uniformly in red leather (or imitation leather), and makes, I believe, a larger appeal to the buyer than the A. L. Burt reprints, for its uniformity gives it a sort of permanence, a place of honor in the scraggly library that adorns every small home. Besides that, it is a much easier thing for a bookseller to display and keep up. The titles are numbered and it gives people a chance to sample writers by one book in this edition. Also it keeps before the public such books as have once been popular and have since been forgotten.

Now my idea is this: the Scribner Company have many more distinguished years of publishing behind them than Doubleday Page. They could produce a list twice as long of distinguished and memorable fiction and use no more than one book by each author—and it need not be the book by that author most in demand.

Take for instance <u>Predestined</u> and <u>The House of Mirth</u>. I do not know, but I imagine that those books are kept upstairs in most bookstores, and only obtained when some one is told of the work of Edith Wharton and Stephen French Whitman. They are almost as forgotten as the books of

Frank Norris and Stephen Crane were five years ago, before Boni's library began its career.

To be specific, I can imagine that a Scribner library containing the following titles and selling for something under a dollar would be an enormous success:

1.	The House of Mirth (or Ethan Frome)	Edith Wharton
2.	Predestined	Stephen French Whitman
3.	This Side of Paradise	F. Scott Fitzgerald
4.	The Little Shepherd of Kingdom Come	John Fox, Jr.
5.	In Ole Kentucky	Thomas Nelson Page
6.	Sentimental Tommy	J. M. Barrie
7.	Some Civil War book by	George Barr Cable
8.	Some novel by	Henry Van Dyke
9.	Some novel by	Jackson Gregory
10.	Saint's Progress	John Galsworthy
11.	The Ordeal of Richard Feverel	George Meredith
12.	Treasure Island	Robert Louis Stevenson
13.	The Turn of the Screw	Henry James
14.	The Stolen Story (or The Frederic Carrolls)	Jesse Lynch Williams
15.	The Damnation of Theron Ware (I think Stone used to own this)	Harold Frederick
16.	Soldiers of Fortune	Richard Harding Davis
17.	Some book by	Mary Raymond Shipman Andrews
18.	Simple Souls	John Hastings Turner

Doubtless a glance at your old catalogues would suggest two dozen others. I have not even mentioned less popular writers such as Burt and Katherine Gerould. Nor have I gone into the possibilities of such non-fiction as a volume of Roosevelt, a volume of Huneker, or a volume of Shane Leslie.

As I say, this is quite possibly an idea which has occurred to you before and been dismissed for reasons which would not appear to me, an outsider. I am moved to the suggestion by the success of the experiments I have mentioned. They have been made possible, I believe, by the recent American strain for "culture" which expresses itself in such things as uniformity of bindings to make a library. Also the selective function of this library would appeal to many people in search of good reading matter, new or old.

One more thing and this interminably long letter is done. It may seem to you that in many cases I have chosen novels whose sale still nets a steady revenue at $1.75—and that it would be unprofitable to use such property in this way. But I have used such titles only to indicate my idea—<u>Gallegher</u> (which I believe is not in your subscription sets of Davis) could be substituted for <u>Soldiers of Fortune</u>, <u>The Wrong Box</u> for <u>Treasure Island</u>, and so on in the case of Fox, Page and Barrie. The main idea is that the known titles in the series should "carry" the little known or forgotten. That is: from the little known writer you use his best novel, such as <u>Predestined</u>— from the well-known writer you use his more obscure, such as <u>Gallegher</u>.

I apologize for imposing so upon your time, Mr. Scribner. I am merely mourning that so many good or lively books are dead so soon, or only imperfectly kept alive in the cheap and severe impermanency of the A. L. Burt editions.

I am, sir,

Most sincerely,
F. Scott Fitzgerald

TO: *Edmund Wilson*   *ALS, 3 pp. Yale University*
Postmarked May 30, 1922

F. SCOTT FITZGERALD
HACK WRITER AND PLAGIARIST
SAINT PAUL, MINNESOTA[1]

626 Goodrich Avenue

Dear Bunny:

Your delightful letter, of which I hope you have kept a copy, arrived this a.m. + the Fitzgeralds perused it ferociously, commending especially your hope that Don gets a good screw in France.

I am so discouraged about the play that it has cheered me to know its still under consideration.[2] I thot they'd burned it up.

I think you overestimate the play—tho Act I is a gem. Also I think you're wrong about the soldier scene. Zelda, Geo. Nathan, Miller, Townsend and I think John all thot it should come out. Still I should not object to it being reinserted. Do you like my letterhead? I have jazzed up the millionaire scene in the revised version. I have not read Ulysses but I'm wild to—especially now that you mention some coincidence. Do you know where I can get it at any price? Sorry about your Smart Set novelette. I agree with you that John's marriage is a calamity—rather—and, having the money, she'll hold

---

[1] Printed letterhead.
[2] Wilson had submitted Fitzgerald's play to the Theatre Guild and to actor/producer Frank Craven. Neither produced the play.

a high hand over him. Still I don't think he's happy and it may release him to do more creative work.

I am enormously interested in your play. Send me a copy when you can.

I'd like to meet Dos Passos— God this is a dull letter. I didn't read your Double Dealer poem tho I heard about it and it seems to have achieved fame. The magazine is unprocurable out here.

We're going to the country for the summer, but write me here immediately. I wish I could close in a rapsody like yours but the fire is out for the night. Harris[1] sent back the play to Reynolds without comment. If you can think of a title for it jot it down + let me know.

Yield to your country complex. Zelda says how-de-do.

Ever Thine
F Scott F——

TO: Maxwell Perkins   ALS, 3 pp. Princeton University
c. June 20, 1922

The Yatch Club, White Bear Lake, Minn

Dear Mr. Perkins:

The first four stories, those that will comprise the section "My Last Flappers" left here several days ago. The second four, "Fantasies" leave either this afternoon or tomorrow morning. And the last three "And So Forth" will leave here on the 24th (Sat.) + should reach you Tuesday without fail. I'm sorry I've been so slow on this—there's no particular excuse except liquor and of course that isn't any. But I vowed I'd finish a travel article + thank God its done at last.

Don't forget that I want another proof of the Table of Contents. There's been one addition to the first section and one substitution in the 3d. Its damn good now, far superior to Flappers + the title, jacket + other books ought to sell at least 10,000 copies and I hope 15,000. You can see from the ms. how I've changed the stories. I cut out my last Metropolitan story not because it wasn't technically excellent but simply because it lacked vitality. The only story about which I'm in doubt is The Camel's Back. But I've decided to use it—it has some excellent comedy + was in one O. Henry Collection—though of course that's against it. Here are some suggested blurbs.

1.   Contains the famous "Porcelain and Pink Story"—the bath-tub classic—as well as "The Curious Case of Benjamin Button" and nine other tales. In this book Mr. F. has developed his gifts as a satiric humorist to a point rivalled by few

---

[1] Broadway producer William Harris.

if any living American writers. The lazy meanderings of a brilliant and powerful imagination.

2. TALES OF THE JAZZ AGE
    Satyre upon a Saxaphone by the most brilliant of the younger novelists. He sets down "My Last Flappers" and then proceeds in section two to fresher and more fantastic fields. You may like or dislike his work but it will never bore you.

3. TALES OF THE JAZZ AGE
    Have you met "Mr. Icky" and followed the ghastly car-reer of "Benjamin Button"? A medly of Bath-tubs, dia-mond mountains, Fitzgerald Flappers and Jellybeans.
    Ten acts of lustrous farce—and one other.

That's probably pretty much bunk but I'm all for advertising it as a cheerful book and not as "eleven of Mr. Fitzgerald's best stories by the y.a. of T.S.O.P."

Thank you immensely for the $1000.00. and also for the Phila. Ledger picture. Has the book gone over 40,000 yet? I'm delighted you like Boyd.[1] He hasn't a very original mind—that is: he's too young to be qiute his own man intellectually but he's on the right track + if he can read much more of the 18th century—and the middle ages and ease up on the moderns he'll grow at an amazing rate. When I send on this last bunch of stories I may start my novel[2] and I may not. Its locale will be the middle west and New York of 1885 I think. It will concern less superlative beauties than I run to usually + will be centered on a smaller period of time. It will have a catholic element. I'm not quite sure whether I'm ready to start it quite yet or not. I'll write next week + tell you more definate plans.

> As Ever
> F Scott Fitzgerald

TO: *Edmund Wilson*   ALS, 3 pp. *Yale University*
                                       White Bear Lake, Minnesota

June 25th 1922

Dear Bunny:
    Thank you for giving the play to Craven—and again for your interest in it in general. I'm afraid I think you overestimate it—because I have just

---

[1] Thomas Boyd, whose first novel, *Through the Wheat*, was published by Scribners in 1923 at Fitzgerald's recommendation.

[2] This projected novel became *The Great Gatsby*.

been fixing up "Mr. Icky" for my fall book and it does not seem very good to me. I am about to start a revision of the play—also to find a name. I'll send it to Hopkins[1] next So far it has only been to Miller, Harris + The Theatre Guild. I'd give anything if Craven would play that part. I wrote it, as the text says, with him in mind. I agree with you that Anna Christie[2] was vastly overestimated.

Your description of the wedding amused us violently. I'm writing a Dunciad[3] on the critics to the tune of the Princton faculty song.

Here is one verse.

Whatever Umpty Dumpty damns
His errors sound like epigrams
He tidies up his mental turds
By neat arrangement of the words.

Am going to write another play whatever becomes of this one. The Beautiful + Damned has had a very satisfactory but not inspiring sale. We thought it'd go far beyond Paradise but it hasn't. It was a dire mistake to serialize it. Three Soldiers and Cytherea[4] took the edge off it by the time it was published.

I wonder if John's insatiable penis has drunk its fill at last. He probably never left his bed during the trip. Did you like The Diamond as Big as the Ritz or did you read it. Its in my new book anyhow.

What do you think of Rascoe's page. Its excellent of course compared to The Times or Herald but I think your critisism of his Frank-Harrassment[5] of his conversations hit the mark. There is something faintly repellant in his manner—in writing I mean. Who is this professionally quaint Kenhelm Digby.[6] He is kittenish beyond credibility + I hate his guts. Is it Morley or Benêt? I have Ullyses from the Brick Row Bookshop + am starting it. I wish it was layed in America—there is something about middle-class Ireland, that depresses me inordinately—I mean gives me a sort of hollow, cheerless pain. Half of my ancestors came from just such an Irish strata or perhaps a lower one. The book makes me feel appallingly naked. Expect to go either south

or to New York in October for the winter.

Ever Thine   F. Scott Fitz.

---

[1] Arthur Hopkins, Broadway producer.
[2] 1921 play by Eugene O'Neill.
[3] Alexander Pope's satirical poem (1728) on literary figures.
[4] 1922 novel by Joseph Hergesheimer.
[5] Fitzgerald is punning on Frank Harris, author of self-aggrandizing autobiographical works.
[6] Pseudonym used in *The Saturday Review of Literature*.

TO: *Maxwell Perkins*   ALS, 2 pp. *Princeton University*
c. August 12, 1922

The Yatch Club
White Bear Lake
Minn

Dear Mr. Perkins—

I've labored over these proofs for a week and feel as if I never want to see a short story again. Thanks the information about Canadian + Australian publishers. You ought to penalize the lighted-match-girl twenty yards.

Now as to Tarquin of Cheapside. It first appeared in the Nassau Literary Magazine at Princeton and Katherine Fullerton Gerrould reviewing the issue for the Daily Princetonian gave it high praise, called it "beautifully written" and tickled me with the first public praise my writing has ever had. When Mencken printed it in the Smart set it drew letters of praise from George O'Niell, the poet and Zoe Akins.[1] Structurally it is almost perfect and next to The Off-Shore Pirate I like it better than any story I have ever written.

If you insist I will cut it out though very much against my better judgement and Zelda's. It was even starred by O'Brien in his year book of the short story and mentioned by Blanche Colton Williams[2] in the preface to the last O Henry Memorial Collection. Please tell me what you think.

As to another matter. My play, Gabriel's Trombone[3] is now in the hands of Arthur Hopkins. It is, I think, the best American comedy to date + undoubtedly the best thing I have ever written. Noting that Harpers are serializing "The Intimate Strangers", a play by Booth Tarkington I wonder if Scribners Magazine would be interested in serializing Gabriel's Trombone that is, of course, on condition that it is to be produced this fall. Will you let me know about this or shall I write Bridges.

Also, last but not least, I have not yet recieved a statement from you. I am awfully hard up. I imagine there's something over $1000.00 still in my favor. Anyways will you deposit a $1000.00 for me when you recieve this letter. If there's not that much due me will you charge off the rest as advance on Tales of the Jazz Age? After my play is produced I'll be rich forever and never have to bother you again.

Also let me know about the Tarquin matter + about Gabriel's Trombone.

As Ever
F Scott Fitzgerald

P.S. Thanks for the Fair + Co. check.

[1] Zoë Akins, dramatist.
[2] Edward J. O'Brien produced an annual collection of best stories originally published in magazines; he also rated with stars other good stories appearing that year. Williams was an anthologist who specialized in the short story.
[3] Retitled *The Vegetable* before it was produced.

TO: Cecilia Delihant Taylor   *ALS, 2 pp. Princeton University*
After October 1922

Great Neck, Long Island

Dear Cousin Cecie:

The pictures are wonderful—also you are a very sweet person (as always) to write me about Tales of the Jazz Age. We are established in the above town very comfortably and having a winter of hard work. I'm writing a play which I hope will go on about the 1st of Jan. I wish you could arrange to come up for the opening.

Great Neck is a great place for celebrities—it being the habitat of Mae Murray, Frank Craven, Herbert Swope, Arthur Hopkins, Jane Cowl, Joseph Santley, Samuel Goldwyn, Ring Lardner, Fontayne Fox, "Tad," Gene Buck, Donald Bryan, Tom Wise, Jack Hazard, General Pershing. It is most amusing after the dull healthy middle west. For instance at a party last night where we went were John McCormick, Hugh Walpole, F.P.A, Neysa Mcmien, Arthur William Brown, Rudolph Frimll + Deems Taylor. They have no mock-modesty + all perform their various stunts apon the faintest request so its like a sustained concert. I

don't know when we're going to have a chance to see you again. Zelda hasn't seen her mother now for almost two years and it doesn't look as tho we'll be able to get south till Spring.

> Our Love to All of you
> Yr. Devoted Cousin
> Scott

TO: Edmund Wilson   *ALS, 1 p. Yale University*
Before March 1923

Great Neck, L.I.

Dear Bunny:

Nominating Ring Lardner as America's most popular humorist,[1]

Because he is really inimitable, as is shown by the lamentable failure of his many imitators,

Because he does not subscribe to a press-clipping bureau and is quite unaware of the critical approval he is recieving in recondite circles,

Because he is frequently covered with bruises from being the Yale football team against his four Harvard-bound boys.

---

[1]"We Nominate for the Hall of Fame," *Vanity Fair* (March 1923). The published caption reads: "Because he is quite unaware of the approval he is receiving in erudite circles; because he is covered with bruises from representing the Yale football team against his Harvard-bound boys; and finally, because with a rare true ear he has set down for postcrity the accents of the American language."

And finally because with a rare, true ear he has set down for the enlightenment of posterity the American language as it is talked today

---

Dear Bunny: Chop this up if you want. See you soon.

F. S. Fitzgerald

TO: *Maxwell Perkins* ALS, 2 pp. Princeton University
c. March 1923

6 Pleasant Ave.
Montgomery, Ala

Dear Mr. Perkins:

I'm awfully curious to hear any new opinions on the book[1] so when Whitney Darrow[2] or anyone else who hasn't read it, reads it, do let me know. I expect to be here about a week or 10 days longer. I'm working on the "treatment"[3] of <u>This Side of Paradise</u>. They've paid me $1000. and are to pay $9000. more on delivery of this so I'm anxious to get it done by the first.

I'll want two extra galley proofs of the play if its convenient, to send to the managers.

I have a few changes for Act III, bits of polyphonic prose that I'm going to insert. Its good weather here but I'm rather miserable and depressed about life in general. Being in this town where the emotions of my youth culminated in one emotion makes me feel old and tired. I doubt if, after all, I'll ever write anything again worth putting in print.

As Ever
F Scott Fitzgerald

TO: *C. O. Kalman*[4] ALS, 2 pp. Princeton University
After November 17, 1923

---

[1]Presumably *The Vegetable*, which was published by Scribners in April 1923.
[2]Scribners advertising manager.
[3]The movie of *This Side of Paradise* was not produced.
[4]St. Paul friend of the Fitzgeralds.

Great Neck   Long Island
5.30 A.M.
(not so much up already
as up still)

Dear Kaly;—

I hear that you have given two seats to this nonsensical game between the Yale blues vs. the Princeton Elis, to F. Scott Fitzgerald. For what reason, is what I want to know.

Ring W. Lardner

Dear Kaly:

This is a letter from your two favorite authors. Ring + I got stewed together the other night + sat up till the next night without what he would laughingly refer to as a wink of sleep. About 5.30 I told him he should write you a letter. The above is his maudlin extacy.

The tickets arrived and I am enclosing check for same. I'm sorry as the devil you didn't come. We could have had a wonderful time even tho the game was punk.

We took Mr + Mrs Gene Buck (the man who writes the Follies + Frolics.) This is a very drunken town full of intoxicated people and retired debauchés + actresses so I know that you and she to who you laughingly refer to as the missus would enjoy it.

I hope St Paul is cold + raw

I discover this tell tale evidence on the paper[1]

so that you'll be driven east before Xmas.
Everything is in its usual muddle. Zelda says ect, asks, ect, sends ect.

Your Happy but Lazy friend
F Scott Fitzgerald

TO: *Maxwell Perkins*　　　　　　*ALS, 2 pp. Princeton University*
c. April 10, 1924　　　　　　　　　　*Long Island, New York*

Great Neck.

Dear Max:

A few words more relative to our conversation this afternoon. While I have every hope + plan of finishing my novel in June you know how those things often come out. And even it takes me 10 times that long I cannot let it go out unless it has the very best I'm capable of in it or even as I feel sometimes, something better than I'm capable of. Much of what I wrote last summer was good but it was so interrupted that it was ragged + in

---

[1] A ring from a wet glass.

Ernest Truex
"The best postman in the world"
Atlantic City
Nov 19th, 1923
F Scott Fitzgerald

Truex was the leading man in the theatrical production of The Vegetable. *This copy was inscribed during the tryout of the play.*

approaching it from a new angle I've had to discard a lot of it—in one case 18,000 words (part of which will appear in the Mercury as a short story). It is only in the last four months that I've realized how much I've—well, almost <u>deteriorated</u> in the three years since I finished the Beautiful and Damned. The last four months of course I've worked but in the two years— over two years—before that, I produced exactly <u>one</u> play, <u>half a dozen</u> short stories and three or four articles—an average of about <u>one hundred</u> words a day. If I'd spent this time reading or travelling or doing anything—even staying healthy—it'd be different but I spent it uselessly, niether in study nor in contemplation but only in drinking and raising hell generally. If I'd written the B. & D. at the rate of 100 words a day it would have taken me <u>4 years</u> so you can imagine the moral effect the whole chasm had on me.

What I'm trying to say is just that I'll have to ask you to have patience about the book and trust me that at last, or at least for the 1st time in years, I'm doing the best I can. I've gotten in dozens of bad habits that I'm trying to get rid of

1. Laziness

2. Referring everything to Zelda—a terrible habit, nothing ought to be referred to anybody until its finished

3. Word consciousness—self doubt

ect. ect. ect. ect.

I feel I have an enormous power in me now, more than I've ever had in a way but it works so fitfully and with so many bogeys because I've <u>talked so much</u> and not lived enough within myself to delelop the nessessary self reliance. Also I don't know anyone who has used up so [torn]sonel experience as I have at 27. Copperfield + Pendennis were written at past forty while This Side of Paradise was three books + the B. + D. was two. So in my new novel I'm thrown directly on purely creative work—not trashy imaginings as in my stories but the sustained imagination of a sincere and yet radiant world. So I tread slowly and carefully + at times in considerable distress. This book will be a consciously artistic achievment + must depend on that as the 1st books did not.

If I ever win the right to any liesure again I will assuredly not waste it as I wasted this past time. Please believe me when I say that now I'm doing the best I can.

Yours Ever
Scott F———

TO: Thomas Boyd   ALS, 6 pp. Princeton University
May 1924   Grimm's Park Hotel stationery. Hyères, France

Dear Tom:

Your letter was the first to reach me after I arrived here. This is the lovliest piece of earth I've ever seen without excepting Oxford or Venice or Princeton or anywhere. Zelda and I are sitting in the café l'Universe writing letters (it is 10.30. P.M.) and the moon is an absolutely <u>au fait</u> Mediteraenean moon with a blurred silver linnen cap + we're both a a little tight and very happily drunk if you can use that term for the less nervous, less violent reactions of this side.

We found a wonderful English nurse in Paris for <u>$26.00 a month</u> (My God! We paid $90.00 in New York) and tomorrow we're going to look at a villa that has a butler + cook with it for the summer + fall. I have 100 feet of copper screen against the mosquitoes (we brought 17 pieces of baggage) + on the whole it looks like a gorgeous working summer.

We missed Edith Wharton by one day—she left yesterday for Paris + won't return until next season. Not that I care, except that I met her in New York + she's a very distinguished grande dame who fought the good fight with bronze age weapons when there were very few people in the line at all.

I'm going to read nothing but Homer + Homeric literature—and history 540–1200 A.D. until I finish my novel + I hope to God I don't see a soul for six months. My novel grows more + more extraordinary; I feel absolutely self-sufficient + I have a perfect hollow craving for lonliness, that has increased for three years in some arithmetical progression + I'm going to satisfy it at last.

I agree with you about Bunny + Mencken—though with qualifications as to both. Bunny appreciates feeling after its been filtered through a temperment but his soul is a bit <u>sec</u>—and in beginning the Joyce cult on such an exalted scale he has probably debauched the taste of a lot of people—(who of course don't matter anyhow)—but these unqualified admirations! Poor Waldo Frank![1]

My God! Do you know you once (its been a year) thought that <u>Middleton Murray</u>[2] was an important man!

Paul Rosenfeld[3] is quite a person—(he admires Sandburg though!)— + the "Port of New York" is quite an adventure in our nervous critical entheusiasm; its nicer tho to be sitting here, to watch slow dogs inspect old posts. (I don't kid myself Ive got away from anything except <u>people</u> in the most corporeal sense.)

---

[1] Novelist and critic.
[2] British critic.
[3] Rosenfeld's *Port of New York: Essays on Fourteen American Moderns* (1924) treated writers, artists, and musicians.

Well, I shall write a novel better than any novel ever written in America and become par excellence the best second-rater in the world.

> Good night old kid
> F Scott Fitz—

P.S. Brentano's (Paris) seems to have had some <u>Thru the Wheat</u> but are sold out—Max is entheusiastic about The Dark Cloud[1] + promised to send it to me. I made a suggestion about brighter color in the jacket. Between you + me the background of the first proof suggested a story of the steel mills. It should be rather rich, I think, like Melvilles Moby Dick jacket. This is <u>entre nous</u>

For Christs sake don't blame Scribners because of that ass Bridges. Perkins + Old Charles would make 20 Bridges bearable. What do you mean you lost $1200.00.

The Jellybean is junk! I've written a fine story called The Baby Party (a bit soft but good stuff) that will appear in Hearsts for July or August.

> F.S.F

Message from Zelda ⟶ (Hello <u>Tom</u> + <u>Peggy</u>)

---

[1] 1924 novel by Boyd.

EUROPE, *THE GREAT GATSBY,* DETERIORATION 1924–1930

❖

June 1924

Settle at Villa Marie, Valescure, St. Raphael. ZF becomes involved with French aviator Edouard Jozan. FSF writes *The Great Gatsby* during summer–fall 1924.

June 1924

"Absolution" in the *American Mercury.*

Winter 1924–1925

Rome, at Hotel des Princes, where FSF revises *The Great Gatsby.*

February 1925

Capri, stay at Hotel Tiberio.

April 10, 1925

Publication of *The Great Gatsby.*

May–December 1925

Apartment at 14, rue de Tilsitt, in Paris on Right Bank.

May 1925

FSF meets Ernest Hemingway in the Dingo Bar, Paris.

August 1925

Leave Paris for a month at Antibes.

January 1926

ZF takes "cure" at Salies-de-Bearn.

January and February 1926

"The Rich Boy" in *Red Book* magazine.

February 1926

Play version of *The Great Gatsby*, by Owen Davis, produced on Broadway.

February 26, 1926

Publication of *All the Sad Young Men*, third short story collection.

Early March 1926

Return to Riviera and rent Villa Paquita, Juan-les-Pins.

May 1926

Hemingways join Murphys and Fitzgeralds on Riviera. The Fitzgeralds turn their villa over to the Hemingways and move to the Villa St. Louis, Juan-les-Pins, where they remain until the end of 1926.

1926

First movie version of *The Great Gatsby*.

December 1926

Return to America.

January 1927

First trip to Hollywood to work on "Lipstick" (unproduced) for United Artists; stay at Ambassador Hotel.

March 1927–March 1928

The Fitzgeralds rent "Ellerslie," near Wilmington, Delaware.

April 1928

Return to Paris for the summer.

April–August 1928

Apartment at 58, rue Vaugirard, on the Left Bank.

April 1928

Publication of the first Basil Duke Lee story, "The Scandal Detectives," in *The Saturday Evening Post*. This eight-story series about FSF's youth appears in the *Post* from April 1928 to April 1929.

Midsummer 1928

ZF commences dancing lessons with Lubov Egorova in Paris.

September 1928

Return to America.

September 1928–March 1929

At "Ellerslie."

Winter 1928–1929

ZF begins writing the series of short stories dealing with the lives of six young women for *College Humor*.

March 1929

"The Last of the Belles" in *The Saturday Evening Post*.

March 1929

Return to France, traveling from Genoa along the Riviera and then to Paris.

June 1929

Leave Paris for Riviera, renting the Villa Fleur des Bois, Cannes.

October 1929

Return to Paris; take apartment at 10, rue Pergolese on Left Bank.

February 1930

FSF and ZF travel to North Africa.

TO: *Robert Kerr*[1]   *ALS, 1 p. Doris K. Brown*
June 1924

Great Neck—I mean
St. Raphael, France
Villa Marie.

Dear Bob:

Thanks for your letter + for selling the membership many thanks indeed. One hundred and fifty is more than I expected. I hope some time that I may be able to return the favor.

The part of what you told me which I am including in my novel is the ship, yatch I mean, + the mysterious yatchsman whose mistress was Nellie Bly[2]   I have my hero occupy the same position you did + obtain it in the same way.[3] I am calling him Robert B. Kerr instead of Robert C. Kerr to conceal his identity (this is a joke—I wanted to give you a scare. His name is Gatsby).

Best to you all from all of us and again thanks enormously for your courtesy + your trouble

Sincerely
Scott Fitzg—

TO: *Maxwell Perkins*   *ALS, 1 p. Princeton University*

Villa Marie, Valescure
St. Raphael, France
June 18th, 1924

Dear Max:

Thanks for your nice long letter. I'm glad that Ring's had good reviews[4] but I'm sorry both that he's off the wagon + that the books not selling. I had counted on a sale of 15 to 25 thousand right away for it.

Shelley was a God to me once. What a good man he is compared to that collosal egotist Browning! Havn't you read <u>Ariel</u>[5] yet? For heaven's sake read it if you like Shelley. Its one of the best biographies I've ever read of anyone + its by a Frenchman. I think Harcourt publishes it. And who "thinks <u>badly</u>" of Shelley now?

---

[1]Great Neck friend of the Fitzgeralds.

[2]Muckraking journalist who wrote sensational "inside" stories about such institutions as asylums and prisons; she is primarily remembered for her 1890 account of her successful attempt to travel around the world within eighty days.

[3]As a boy Kerr had been befriended by yachtsman Edward Gilman, and Fitzgerald drew upon Kerr's experiences for Gatsby's association with Dan Cody.

[4]For *How to Write Short Stories* (1924); Fitzgerald had convinced Lardner and Perkins to assemble this collection of Lardner's stories and had provided its title.

[5]*Ariel: The Life of Shelley* (1924), by André Maurois.

We are idyllicly settled here + the novel is going fine—it ought to be done in a month—though I'm not sure as I'm contemplating another 16,000 words which would make it about the length of Paradise—not quite though even then.

I'm glad you liked <u>Absolution</u>. As you know it was to have been the prologue of the novel but it interfered with the neatness of the plan. Two Catholics have already protested by letter. Be sure + read "The Baby Party" in Hearsts + my article in the Woman's Home Companion.

Tom Boyd wrote me that Bridges had been a dodo about some Y.M.C.A. man—I wrote him that he oughtn't to fuss with such a silly old man. I hope he hasn't—you don't mention him in your letter. I enjoyed Arthur Trains[1] story in the Post but he made three steals on the 1st page—one from Shaw (the Arabs remark about Christianity) one from Stendahl + one I've forgotten. It was most ingeniously worked out. I never could have handled such an intricate plot in a thousand years. War + Peace came—many thanks + for the inscription too. Don't forget the clippings. I will have to reduce my tax in Sept.

As Ever, Yours
F Scott Fitzgerald

P.S. If Struthers Burt[2] comes over give me his address.

TO: Edmund Wilson   *ALS, 3 pp. Yale University*
Summer 1924

Villa Marie, Valescure, St Raphael France

Dear Bunny:
The above will tell you where we are as you proclaim yourself unable to find it on the map. We enjoyed your letter enormously, collossally, stupendously. It was epochal, acrocryptical, categorical. I have begun life anew since getting it and Zelda has gone into a nunnery on the Pelleponesus.

---

[1] Arthur Train, Scribners author of extremely popular stories and novels about a lawyer named Ephraim Tutt.
[2] Poet and novelist published by Scribners.

Yes, John seemed to us a beaten man—with his tiny frail mustache—but perhaps only morally. Whether or not he still echoes the opinions of others I don't know—to me he said nothing at all. In fact I remember not a line (I was drunk + voluble myself though).

The news about the play is grand + the ballet too. I gather from your letter that O'Niell + Mary had a great success.[1] But you are wrong about Ring's book. My title was the best possible. You are always wrong—but always with the most correct possible reasons. (This statement is merely acrocrytical, hypothetical, diabolical, metaphorical)

You speak of John's wife. I didn't see her—but stay there was a woman there, but what she said + did + looked like I can not tell. Is she an elderly, gross woman with hair growing in her ears and and a red porous forehead? If so I remember her. Or stay—there was a rumor that he had married an Ethiope and took her to bleach beside the ffjiords. Or was that John, Or Eb Gaines. . . . .

I had a short curious note from the latter yesterday, calling me to account for my Mercury Story.[2] At first I couldn't understand this communication after seven blessedly silent years—behold: he was a catholic. I had broken his heart.

This is a dumb letter but I have just been reading the advertisements of whore-houses in the French magazines. I seethe with passion for a "bains-massage" with volupté oriental delights (tout nu) in a Hotel Particular or else I long to go with a young man (intell. bon famile. affecteux) for a paid amorous week end to the coast of Guine. Deep calling to deep. I will give you now the Fitzg touch without which this letter would fail to conform to your conception of my character;

Sinclair Lewis sold his new novel to The Designer for $50,000 (950,000.00 francs) + I never did like that fellow. (I do really).

My book is wonderful, so is the air + the sea. I have got my health back—I no longer cough and itch and roll from one side of the bed to the other all night and have a hollow ache in my stomach after two cups of black coffee. I really worked hard as hell last winter—but it was all trash and it nearly broke my heart as well as my iron constitution.

Write me of all data, gossip, event, accident, scandal, sensation, deterioration, new reputation,—and of yourself.

Our Love
Scott

---

[1] Wilson's wife Mary Blair had played the female lead in Eugene O'Neill's *All God's Chillun Got Wings* (1924).
[2] "Absolution," *American Mercury* (June 1924).

TO: Ludlow Fowler[1]   ALS, 2 pp. Princeton University
August 1924

Villa Marie, Valescure
St Raphael, France

Dear Lud: I knew there wasn't a chance of seeing you when your trip was so short but I wrote a note to Sap[2] asking him to drop in on us if he stayed over and got down this far. I sent it care of Eleanor Maurice, American Express. I wonder if he ever got it.

My novel is finished and I'm doing the last revision of it. We've had a quiet summer and are moving on in the fall either to Paris or Italy. I'm going to write another play and I hope it'll be less disastrous than the last.

The real purpose of this letter is sordid + material is this. The field glasses you gave me were out of whack—they showed two ships instead of one and made the Olympic look as if it had 8 smokestacks which can't be true according to the papers.

So I'm going to ask you to send mine to Ring Lardner, Steamship <u>Paris</u>, sailing Sept. 10th + he'll bring them to me. And will you wrap a newspaper around them so the Captain won't appropriate them for himself. About yours I'll do just as you say—send them home by somebody or have them fixed in Paris and leave them at some definate place there so you can call for them on your annual jaunt last summer.

I remember our last conversation and it makes me sad. I feel old too, this summer—I have ever since the failure of my play a year ago. Thats the whole burden of this novel—the loss of those illusions that give such color to the world so that you don't care whether things are true or false as long as they partake of the magical glory.

We both send our best love to you, Lud.

Scott

PS. Don't forget the glasses—I'm awfully anxious to get them. I'm sorry I've been such a bother about it.

TO: Maxwell Perkins   ALS, 1 p. Princeton University
After August 8, 1924

[1]Fowler, a Newman School and Princeton classmate of Fitzgerald, was the model for Anson Hunter in "The Rich Boy."
[2]Charles W. Donahoe, Newman School and Princeton classmate of Fitzgerald.

Villa Marie
Valescure, St Raphael
France.

Dear Max:

Thanks for your long + most interesting letter. I wrote you yesterday so this is just a note. I feel like saying "I told you so" about the Bobbs-Merril + Doran books of Rings but I know that it is mostly Bobbs-Merrils fault and a good deal Ring's.[1] The ad was great—especially the Barrie. I imagine that Mr. Scribner was pleased—and a little surprised. Poor Ring—its discouraging that he keeps on drinking—how bored with life the man must be. I certainly think his collection for 1925 should include all <u>fantasies</u>. Certain marvellous syndicate articles such as the "fur coat + the worlds series" + the "celebrities day-book" should be saved for the "My Life and Loves" volume.[2] Do read Seldes[3] on Ring in "The Seven Lively Arts." Be sure to. I'll really pay you to do it before making the selections.

As Ever
Scott

TO: *Maxwell Perkins*
c. August 27, 1924

ALS, 2 pp. Princeton University

Villa Marie, Valescure
St Raphael, France

Dear Max:

(1) The novel will be done next week. That doesn't mean however that it'll reach America before October 1st. as Zelda + I are contemplating a careful revision after a weeks complete rest.

(2) The clippings have never arrived.

(3) Seldes has been with me and he thinks "For the Grimalkins" is a wonderful title for Rings book. Also I've got great ideas about "My Life and Loves" which I'll tell Ring when comes over in September.

(4) How many copies has his short stories sold?

(5) Your bookkeeper never did send me my royalty report for Aug 1st.

(6) For Christs sake don't give anyone that jacket you're saving for me. I've written it into the book.[4]

[1] Scribners was negotiating for the Lardner volumes previously published by Bobbs-Merrill and Doran.

[2] *What of It?* (Scribners, 1925).

[3] Critic Gilbert Seldes.

[4] This remark has generated disagreement. The published jacket art by Francis Cugat depicts a woman's face above an amusement park night scene. It is not known whether Fitzgerald saw the final art or an earlier version. See "Appendix 3: Note on the Dust Jacket," *The Great Gatsby*, ed. Bruccoli (Cambridge & New York: Cambridge University Press, 1991), pp. 209–10.

(7) I think my novel is about the best American novel ever written. It is rough stuff in places, runs only to about 50,000 words, and I hope you won't shy at it

(8) Its been a fair summer. I've been unhappy but my work hasn't suffered from it. I am grown at last.

(9) What books are being talked about? I don't mean best sellers. Hergeshiemers novel[1] in the Post seems vile to me.

(10) I hope you're reading Gertrude Stiens novel[2] in The <u>Transatlantic Review</u>.

(11) Raymond Radiguets last book (he is the young man who wrote "<u>Le deable au Corps</u>" at sixteen [untranslatable]) is a great hit here. He wrote it at 18. Its called "<u>Le Bal de Compte Orgel</u>" + though I'm only half through it I'd get an opinion on it if I were you. Its cosmopolitan rather than French and my instinct tells me that in a good translation it might make an enormous hit in America where everyone is yearning for Paris. Do look it up + get at least one opinion of it. The preface is by the da-dist Jean Cocteau but the book is not da-da at all.

(12) Did you get hold of Rings other books?

(13) We're liable to leave here by Oct 1st so after the 15th of Sept I wish you'd send everything care of Guarantee Trust Co. Paris

(14) Please ask the bookstore, if you have time, to send me Havelock Ellis "Dance of Life" + charge to my account

(15) I asked Struthers Burt to dinner but his baby was sick.

(16) Be <u>sure</u> and answer <u>every</u> question, Max.

I miss seeing you like the devil.

Scott

TO: *Hazel McCormack*[3]   *ALS, 2 pp. Princeton University*
September 1924

Villa Marie, Valescure
St Raphael, France

Dear Patsy:

We've been here on the Medeteraenean since May and my novel is finished at last. The stories you objected to were nessessary—they arose from a complicated situation between the Post, Hearsts and me. Besides, some of them—"Absolution" (in the Mercury) "The Baby Party" (in Hearsts) are awfully good. So were "Rags Martin-Jones" and "The Sensible Thing"

---

[1] *Balisand* (1924).
[2] *The Making of Americans* (1925).
[3] Young aspiring St. Louis writer whose fan letter initiated an extended correspondence.

before two editors cut them to pieces. The Post stuff was pretty raw, I'll admit.

My novel is wonderful. I've read to everyone within hearing (Seldes [the critic] Donald Stuart, Maxwell Struthers Burt, John Dos Passos + other literary gents who have done time with us and I hope it'll be out in the Spring. We are waiting for the Ring Lardners to take a jaunt through Spain, largely so we can see a bullfight. Then I think we'll spend the winter in Sorrento (where Shelley wrote the "West Wind" + "Lines written in dejection"); and Spring in Paris and perhaps next summer.

"In Granchester—in Grantchester"[1]

(By all means read The Life of Shelley, or rather, <u>Ariel</u> if the English translation is good. I hear there is one. You'll love it.) I went to school with Cyril Hume[2]—I remember him as a little prig, son of the headmaster. But he's turned out to be a nice fellow + I liked his book which he sent me— all except the rotten passages of polyphonic prose.

Zelda sends her very best + thanks you for the sweet compliment.

Thine   F Scott Fitzgerald

Arn't you the big swell with the typewriter!

TO: Harold Ober   *ALS, 1 p. Lilly Library*

Villa Marie, Valescure
St Raphael, France
Sept 20th, 1924

Dear Mr. Ober:

The situation is as follows. I have finished my novel and will send it to you within 10 days or two weeks. It may or may not serialize—certainly it'd never get in the Post. Artisticly its head + shoulders over everything I've done. When I send it I'll send a letter about terms ect.

I'm about broke and as soon as the novel gets off I will write a story immediately, either for the Post or for Wheeler[3] who has been dunning me for one violently. That story will be followed within a month by two more. The first one should reach you by October 20th or a little over two weeks after you recieve this letter—and as you have no doubt already guessed I'm going to ask you for an advance on it.

Now as I understand it I'm about $90.00 in your debt—$180.00 advanced on the Screenland article that got in too late as against $90 or so due me

---

[1]Village near Cambridge; setting for Rupert Brooke's poem "The Old Vicarage, Grant-chester."

[2]Author of the 1923 novel *Wife of the Centaur*.

[3]John N. Wheeler, editor of *Liberty*.

from the English rights of the "3d casket." Here's what I fondly hope you can do:

deposit $600.00 for me on Oct 5th

" 800.00 for me on Reciept of the Story which will be about the 20th of the month. However I will write you again about the 2nd deposit when I mail the story. If this is inconvenient please drop me a cable.

Considering the fact that of the eleven stories I've written this year 4 of the 7 that have been published were run 1st in their issues I think I've had hard luck with the movies. I must try some love stories with more action this time. I'm going to try to write three that'll do for Famous-Players[1] as well as for the Post. We are leaving for Rome about the 1st of November to spend the winter.

Sincerely
F Scott Fitzgerald

TO: *Maxwell Perkins*   *ALS, 2 pp. Princeton University*
c. October 10, 1924

Villa Marie,
Valescure
St Raphael, France

Dear Max:

The royalty was better than I'd expected. This is to tell you about a young man named Ernest Hemmingway, who lives in Paris, (an American) writes for the transatlantic Review + has a brilliant future. Ezra Pount published a a collection of his short pieces in Paris, at some place like the Egotist Press.[2] I haven't it hear now but its remarkable + I'd look him up right away. He's the real thing.

My novel goes to you with a long letter within five days. Ring arrives in a week. This is just a hurried scrawl as I'm working like a dog. I thought Stalling's book[3] was disappointingly rotten. It takes a genius to whine appealingly. Have tried to see Struthers Burt but he's been on the move. More later.

Scott

P.S. Important. What chance has a smart young frenchman with an intimate knowledge of French literature in the bookselling business in New York. Is a clerk paid much and is there any opening for one specializing in French literature? Do tell me as there's a young friend of mine here just out of the army who is anxious to know

Sincerely
Scott

[1] Movie studio.

[2] Probably *in our time*, published by the Three Mountains Press in the spring of 1924. Ezra Pound had encouraged Hemingway in his work.

[3] *Plumes* (1924), a World War I novel by Laurence Stallings.

TO: *Harold Ober*   *ALS, 2 pp. Lilly Library*

<u>St. Raphael</u>, Oct 25th
(After Nov. 3d, Care of the
American Express Co.
Rome Italy)

Dear Mr. Ober:

I am sending you today under separate cover the manuscript of my new novel <u>The Great Gatsby</u> for serialization. Whether it will serialize you will be a better judge than I. There is some pretty frank stuff in it and I wouldn't want it to be chopped as Hovey chopped the <u>Beautiful + Damned</u>. Now here are my ideas:

(1.) I think the best bet by all odds is <u>Liberty</u>. It is a love story and it is sensational. Also it is only 50,000 words long which would give them ten installments of 5000 words each, just what they're looking for. And moreover if they started it by February 1st it could be over in time for spring publication. I havn't had a book for almost three years now and I want Scribners to bring this out in April. I wish you would specify to John Wheeler that it must be run through by then.

(2.) Of course Ray Long[1] will have to have first look at it according to our contract of 1923. But I don't want him to have it (small chance of his wanting it) because in his magazines it would drag on forever + book publication would be postponed. So I'd like to ask him $25,000 for it—a prohibitive price. But it wouldn't be worth my while to give it to him for less. For <u>Liberty</u> I would take $15,000 + I'm against asking more because of a peculiar situation between John + me. He told me he'd never bargain for a thing of mine again—he'd take it at the price offered or refuse it. Ring Lardner told him I was annoyed at him—anyhow its a sort of personal question as you see. So I don't think I'd want to ask him more than $15,000. When I was getting $900 a story I got $7000 or a serial, so now that I'm getting $1750, $15000 for a serial seems a fair price. Especially as its very short.

(3.) The Post I don't want to offer it to. Its not their kind of thing + I don't want to have it in there anyhow as it kills the book sale at one blow. So that's out.

(4.) In fact I think <u>Liberty</u> is far and away the best bet—I don't see who else could squeeze it in before April. The third chapter bars it from the womens magazines and that leaves nothing except the Red Book which would drag it out till Fall.

(5.) I've sent Scribners their copy. When you get a definate decision from Hearsts and Jack Wheeler will you phone Max Perkins and tell him as he'll be anxious to know and letters take so long. Also will you cable me.

(6.) Needless to say whether it serializes or not I will refer any and all

---

[1] Editor of *Hearst's International*; *The Great Gatsby* was not serialized before book publication.

moving picture bids on the book to you and will tell Scribners to let you know about any moving picture bids that come through them. Of course this is looking pretty far ahead.

(7.) In any case I would much appreciate your own frank opinion of the novel.

(8.) My story is now at the typist. It should reach you within the week.

As Ever

F Scott Fitzgerald

TO: Maxwell Perkins   *ALS, 2 pp. Princeton University*

October 27th, 1924

Villa Marie, Valescure

St. Raphael, France

(After Nov. 3d Care of

American Express Co, Rome Italy)

Dear Max:

Under separate cover I'm sending you my third novel:

The Great Gatsby

(I think that at last I've done something really my own), but how good "my own" is remains to be seen.

I should suggest the following contract.

15% up to 50,000

20% after 50,000

The book is only a little over fifty thousand words long but I believe, as you know, that Whitney Darrow has the wrong psychology about prices (and about what class constitute the bookbuying public now that the low-brows go to the movies) and I'm anxious to charge two dollars for it and have it a full size book.

Of course I want the binding to be absolutely uniform with my other books—the stamping too—and the jacket we discussed before. This time I don't want any signed blurbs on the jacket—not Mencken's or Lewis' or Howard's[1] or anyone's. I'm tired of being the author of This Side of Paradise and I want to start over.

About serialization. I am bound under contract to show it to Hearsts but I am asking a prohibitive price, Long hates me and its not a very serialized book. If they should take it—they won't—it would put of publication in the fall. Otherwise you can publish it in the spring. When Hearst turns it down I'm going to offer it to Liberty for $15,000 on condition that they'll

[1]Sidney Howard, playwright whose *They Knew What They Wanted* opened on Broadway in 1924 and won a Pulitzer Prize for drama.

publish it in ten weekly installments before April 15th. If they don't want it I shan't serialize. <u>I am absolutely positive Long won't want it</u>.
I have an alternative title:

Gold-hatted Gatsby

After you've read the book let me know what you think about the title. Naturally I won't get a nights sleep until I hear from you but do tell me the absolute truth, <u>your first impression of the book</u> + tell me anything that bothers you in it.

As Ever
Scott

I'd rather you wouldn't call Reynolds as he might try to act as my agent. Would you send me the N.Y. World with accounts of Harvard-Princeton and Yale-Princeton games?

TO: Maxwell Perkins *ALS, 1 p. Princeton University*
c. November 7, 1924

Hotel Continental, St. Raphael, Sun.
(Leaving Tuesday)

Dear Max:
By now you've recieved the novel. There are things in it I'm not satisfied with in the middle of the book—Chapters 6 + 7. And I may write in a complete new scene in proof. I hope you got my telegram.

Trimalchio[1] in West Egg

The only other titles that seem to fit it are <u>Trimalchio</u> and <u>On the Road to West Egg</u>. I had two others <u>Gold-hatted Gatsby</u> and <u>The High-bouncing Lover</u> but they seemed too light.
We leave for Rome as soon as I finish the short story I'm working on.

As Ever
Scott

I was interested that you've moved to New Canaan. It sounds wonderful. Sometimes I'm awfully anxious to be home.
But I am confused at what you say about Gertrude Stien. I thought it was one purpose of critics + publishers to educate the public up to original work. The first people who risked Conrad certainly didn't do it as a commercial venture. Did the evolution of startling work into accepted work cease twenty years ago?

---

[1]Trimalchio was an ostentatious party giver in Petronius' *Satyricon*.

Do send me Boyds (Ernest's) book[1] when it comes out. I think the Lardner ads are wonderful. Did the Dark Cloud flop?

Would you ask the people down stairs to keep sending me my monthly bill for the encyclopedia?

FROM: *Maxwell Perkins*[2]   *CC, 2 pp. Princeton University*
New York City

Nov. 18, 1924

Dear Scott:

I think the novel is a wonder. I'm taking it home to read again and shall then write my impressions in full;—but it has vitality to an extraordinary degree, and <u>glamour</u>, and a great deal of underlying thought of unusual quality. It has a kind of mystic atmosphere at times that you infused into parts of "Paradise" and have not since used. It is a marvelous fusion, into a unity of presentation, of the extraordinary incongruities of life today. And as for sheer writing, it's astonishing.

Now deal with this question: various gentlemen here don't like the title,—in fact none like it but me. To me, the strange incongruity of the words in it sound the note of the book. But the objectors are more practical men than I. Consider as quickly as you can the question of a change.

But if you do not change, you will have to leave that note off the wrap. Its presence would injure it too much;—and good as the wrap always seemed, it now seems a masterpiece for this book. So judge of the value of the title when it stands alone and write or cable your decision the instant you can.

With congratulations, I am,
Yours,

FROM: *Maxwell Perkins*   *CC, 4 pp. Princeton University*
New York City

November 20, 1924

Dear Scott:

I think you have every kind of right to be proud of this book. It is an extraordinary book, suggestive of all sorts of thoughts and moods. You adopted exactly the right method of telling it, that of employing a narrator who is more of a spectator than an actor: this puts the reader upon a point of observation on a higher level than that on which the characters stand and

---

[1] Boyd's *Portraits: Real and Imaginary* (1924) contained an article on Fitzgerald.
[2] Perkins's November 18 and November 20 letters reporting his responses to the typescript of *The Great Gatsby* are included to document the editor's role in the revision of the novel.

at a distance that gives perspective. In no other way could your irony have been so immensely effective, nor the reader have been enabled so strongly to feel at times the strangeness of human circumstance in a vast heedless universe. In the eyes of Dr. Eckleberg various readers will see different significances; but their presence gives a superb touch to the whole thing: great unblinking eyes, expressionless, looking down upon the human scene. It's magnificent!

I could go on praising the book and speculating on its various elements, and meanings, but points of criticism are more important now. I think you are right in feeling a certain slight sagging in chapters six and seven, and I don't know how to suggest a remedy. I hardly doubt that you will find one and I am only writing to say that I think it does need something to hold up here to the pace set, and ensuing. I have only two actual criticisms:—

One is that among a set of characters marvelously palpable and vital—I would know Tom Buchanan if I met him on the street and would avoid him—Gatsby is somewhat vague. The reader's eyes can never quite focus upon him, his outlines are dim. Now everything about Gatsby is more or less a mystery i.e. more or less vague, and this may be somewhat of an artistic intention, but I think it is mistaken. Couldn't _he_ be physically described as distinctly as the others, and couldn't you add one or two characteristics like the use of that phrase "old sport",—not verbal, but physical ones, perhaps. I think that for some reason or other a reader—this was true of Mr. Scribner and of Louise[1]—gets an idea that Gatsby is a much older man than he is, although you have the writer say that he is little older than himself. But this would be avoided if on his first appearance he was seen as vividly as Daisy and Tom are, for instance;—and I do not think your scheme would be impaired if you made him so.

The other point is also about Gatsby: his career must remain mysterious, of course. But in the end you make it pretty clear that his wealth came through his connection with Wolfsheim. You also suggest this much earlier. Now almost all readers numerically are going to be puzzled by his having all this wealth and are going to feel entitled to an explanation. To give a distinct and definite one would be, of course, utterly absurd. It did occur to me though, that you might here and there interpolate some phrases, and possibly incidents, little touches of various kinds, that would suggest that he was in some active way mysteriously engaged. You do have him called on the telephone, but couldn't he be seen once or twice consulting at his parties with people of some sort of mysterious significance, from the political, the gambling, the sporting world, or whatever it may be. I know I am floundering, but that fact may help you to see what I mean. The _total_ lack of an explanation through so large a part of the story does seem to me a defect;—or not of an explanation, but of the suggestion of an explanation. I wish you were here so I could talk about it to you for then I know I could

---

[1]Louise Perkins, Maxwell Perkins's wife.

at least make you understand what I mean. What Gatsby did ought never to be definitely imparted, even if it could be. Whether he was an innocent tool in the hands of somebody else, or to what degree he was this, ought not to be explained. But if some sort of business activity of his were simply adumbrated, it would lend further probability to that part of the story.

There is one other point: in giving deliberately Gatsby's biography when he gives it to the narrator you do depart from the method of the narrative in some degree, for otherwise almost everything is told, and beautifully told, in the regular flow of it,—in the succession of events or in accompaniment with them. But you can't avoid the biography altogether. I thought you might find ways to let the truth of some of his claims like "Oxford" and his army career come out bit by bit in the course of actual narrative. I mention the point anyway for consideration in this interval before I send the proofs.

The general brilliant quality of the book makes me ashamed to make even these criticisms. The amount of meaning you get into a sentence, the dimensions and intensity of the impression you make a paragraph carry, are most extraordinary. The manuscript is full of phrases which make a scene blaze with life. If one enjoyed a rapid railroad journey I would compare the number and vividness of pictures your living words suggest, to the living scenes disclosed in that way. It seems in reading a much shorter book than it is, but it carries the mind through a series of experiences that one would think would require a book of three times its length.

The presentation of Tom, his place, Daisy and Jordan, and the unfolding of their characters is unequalled so far as I know. The description of the valley of ashes adjacent to the lovely country, the conversation and the action in Myrtle's apartment, the marvelous catalogue of those who came to Gatsby's house,—these are such things as make a man famous. And all these things, the whole pathetic episode, you have given a place in time and space, for with the help of T. J. Eckleberg and by an occasional glance at the sky, or the sea, or the city, you have imparted a sort of sense of eternity. You once told me you were not a <u>natural</u> writer—my God! You have plainly mastered the craft, of course; but you needed far more than craftsmanship for this.

As ever,

P.S. Why do you ask for a lower royalty on this than you had on the last book where it changed from 15% to 17½% after 20,000 and to 20% after 40,000? Did you do it in order to give us a better margin for advertising? We shall advertise very energetically anyhow and if you stick to the old terms you will sooner overcome the advance. Naturally we should like the ones you suggest better, but there is no reason you should get less on this than you did on the other.

TO: *Maxwell Perkins*   *ALS, 3 pp. Princeton University*
c. December 1, 1924

> Hotel des Princes
> Piazza di Spagna
> Rome, Italy

Dear Max:

Your wire + your letters made me feel like a million dollars—I'm sorry I could make no better response than a telegram whining for money. But the long siege of the novel winded me a little + I've been slow on starting the stories on which I must live.

I think all your critisisms are true

(a) About the title. I'll try my best but I don't know what I can do. Maybe simply "Trimalchio" or "Gatsby." In the former case I don't see why the note shouldn't go on the back.

(b) Chapters VI + VII I know how to fix

(c) Gatsby's business affairs I can fix. I get your point about them.

(d) His vagueness I can repair by <u>making more pointed</u>—this doesn't sound good but wait and see. It'll make him clear

(e) But his long narrative in Chap VIII will be difficult to split up. Zelda also thought I was a little out of key but it is good writing and I don't think I could bear to sacrifice any of it

(f) I have 1000 minor corrections which I will make on the proof + several more large ones which you didn't mention.

Your critisisms were excellent + most helpful + you picked out all my favorite spots in the book to praise as high spots. Except you didn't mention my favorite of all—the chapter where Gatsby + Daisy meet.

Two more things. Zelda's been reading me the cowboy book[1] aloud to spare my mind + I love it—tho I think he learned the American language from Ring rather than from his own ear.

Another point—in Chap. II of my book when Tom + Myrte go into the bedroom while Carraway reads Simon called Peter[2]—is that raw? Let me know. I think its pretty nessessary.

I made the royalty smaller because I wanted to make up for all the money you've advanced these two years by letting it pay a sort of interest on it. But I see by calculating I made it too small—a difference of 2000 dollars. Let us call it 15% up to 40,000 and 20% after that. That's a good fair contract all around.

---

[1] *Cowboys North and South* (1924), by Will James.
[2] Fitzgerald regarded this popular 1921 novel by Robert Keable as immoral; the protagonist is an army chaplain who becomes involved in passionate episodes.

By now you have heard from a smart young french woman who wants to translate the book. She's equeal to it intellectually + linguisticly I think—had read all my others—If you'll tell her how to go about it as to royalty demands ect.

Anyhow thanks + thanks + thanks for your letters. I'd rather have you + Bunny like it than anyone I know. And I'd rather have you like it than Bunny. If its as good as you say, when I finish with the proof it'll be perfect.

Remember, by the way, to put by some cloth for the cover uniform with my other books.

As soon as I can think about the title I'll write or wire a decision. Thank Louise for me, for liking it. Best Regards to Mr. Scribner. Tell him Galsworthy is here in Rome.

> As Ever,
> Scott

TO: *Maxwell Perkins*   *ALS, 5pp. Princeton University*
c. December 20, 1924

Hotel des Princes, Piazza de Spagna, Rome.
Dear Max:

I'm a bit (not very—not dangerously) stewed tonight + I'll probably write you a long letter. We're living in a small, unfashionable but most comfortable hotel at $525.00 a month including tips, meals ect. Rome does not particularly interest me but its a big year here, and early in the spring we're going to Paris. There's no use telling you my plans because they're usually just about as unsuccessful as to work as a religious prognosticaters are as to the End of the World. I've got a new novel to write—title and all, that'll take about a year. Meanwhile, I don't want to start it until this is out + meanwhile I'll do short stories for money (I now get $2000.00 a story but I hate worse than hell to do them) and there's the never dying lure of another play.

Now! Thanks enormously for making up the $5000.00. I know I don't technically deserve it considering I've had $3000.00 or $4000.00 for as long as I can remember. But since you force it on me (inexecrable [or is it execrable] joke) I will accept it. I hope to Christ you get 10 times it back on Gatsby——and I think perhaps you will.

For:

I can now make it perfect but the proof (I will soon get the immemorial letter with the statement "We now have the book in hand and will soon begin to send you proof" [what is 'in hand'—I have a vague picture of everyone in the office holding the book in the right and and reading it]) will be one of the most expensive affairs since Madame Bovary. Please charge it to my account. If its possible to send a second proof over here I'd love to have it. Count on 12 days each way—four days here on first proof + two on the second. I hope there are other good books in the spring because I think now the public interest in <u>books</u> per se rises when there seems to be a group of them as in 1920 (spring + fall), 1921 (fall), 1922 (spring). Ring's + Tom's (first) books, Willa Cathers <u>Lost Lady</u> + in an inferior, cheap way Edna Ferber's are the only American fiction in over two years that had a really excellent press (say, since Babbit).[1]

With the aid you've given me I can make "Gatsby" perfect. The chapter VII (the hotel scene) will never quite be up to mark—I've worried about it too long + I can't quite place Daisy's reaction. But I can improve it a lot. It isn't imaginative energy thats lacking—its because I'm automaticly prevented from thinking it out over again <u>because I must get all those characters to New York</u> in order to have the catastrophe on the road going back + I must have it pretty much that way. So there's no chance of bringing the freshness to it that a new free conception sometimes gives.

The rest is easy and I see my way so clear that I even see the mental quirks that queered it before. Strange to say my notion of Gatsby's vagueness was O.K. What you and Louise + Mr. Charles Scribner found wanting was that: <u>I myself didn't know what Gatsby looked like or was engaged in</u> + you felt it. If I'd known + kept it from you you'd have been <u>too impressed with my knowledge to protest</u>. This is a complicated idea but I'm sure you'll understand. But I know now—and as a penalty for not having known first, in other words to make sure I'm going to tell more.

It seems of almost mystical significance to me that you thot he was older—the man I had in mind, half unconsciously, <u>was</u> older (a specific individual) and evidently, without so much as a definate word, I conveyed the fact.—or rather, I must qualify this Shaw-Desmond-trash by saying, that I conveyed it without a word that I can at present and for the life of me, trace. (I think Shaw Desmond[2] was one of your bad bets—I was the other)

Anyhow after careful searching of the files (of a man's mind here) for the Fuller Magee case[3] + after having had Zelda draw pictures until her fingers ache I know Gatsby better than I know my own child. My first instinct after your letter was to let him go + have Tom Buchanan dominate the book (I suppose he's the best character I've ever done—I think he and the brother in "Salt" + Hurstwood in "Sister Carrie" are the three best characters in American fiction in the last twenty years, perhaps and perhaps not) but Gatsby sticks in my heart. I had him for awhile then lost him + now I know I have him again. I'm sorry Myrtle is better than Daisy. Jordan of course was a great idea (perhaps you know its Edith Cummings)[4] but she

---

[1] Ferber's *So Big* (1924) and Sinclair Lewis's *Babbitt* (1922).

[2] Writer published by Scribners.

[3] Edward M. Fuller and William F. McGee, partners in a stock brokerage firm, were convicted of embezzlement; Arnold Rothstein—the model for Meyer Wolfshiem in *The Great Gatsby*—was allegedly involved in their peculations.

[4] Golfer who had been a school friend of Ginevra King.

fades out. Its Chap VII thats the trouble with Daisy + it may hurt the book's popularity that its <u>a man's book</u>.

Anyhow I think (for the first time since The Vegetable failed) that I'm a wonderful writer + its your always wonderful letters that help me to go on believing in myself.

Now some practical, very important questions. Please answer every one.

①. Montenegro has an order called <u>The Order of Danilo</u>. Is there any possible way you could find out for me there what it would look like—whether a courtesy decoration given to an American would bear an English inscription—or anything to give versimilitude to the medal which sounds horribly amateurish.

② Please have <u>no blurbs of any kind on the jacket</u>!!! No Mencken or Lewis or Sid Howard or anything. I don't believe in them <u>one bit</u> any more.

③ Don't forget to change name of book in list of works

④ Please shift exclamation point from end of 3d line to end of 4th line in title page. <u>Please!</u> Important!

⑤ I thought that the whole episode (2 paragraphs) about their playing the Jazz History of the world at Gatsby's first party was rotten. Did you? Tell me frank <u>reaction</u>—<u>personal</u>. Don't <u>think</u>! We can all think!

Got a sweet letter from Sid Howard—rather touching, I wrote him first. I thought <u>Transatlantic</u> was great stuff—a really gorgeous surprise. Up to that I never believed in him 'specially + I was sorry because he did in me. Now I'm tickled silly to find he has power, and his own power. It seemed tragic too to see <u>Mrs. Viectch</u> wasted in a novelette when, despite Anderson the short story is at its lowest ebb as an art form. (Despite Ruth Suckow, Gertrude Stien, Ring there is a horrible impermanence on it <u>because</u> the overwhelming number of short stories are impermanent.[1]

Poor Tom Boyd! His cycle sounded so sad to me—perhaps it'll be wonderful but it sounds to me like ploughing in a field (whose) first freshness has gone.

See that word?[2] The ambition of my life is to make that use of it correct. The temptation to use it as a neuter is one of the vile fevers in my still insecure prose.

Tell me about Ring! About Tom—is he poor? He seems to be counting on his short story book, frail cane! About Biggs—did he ever finish the novel? About Peggy Boyd,[3] I think Louise might have sent us her book!

I thot the <u>White Monkey</u> was stinko. On second thoughts I didn't like

---

[1] Howard's stories "Transatlantic" and "Mrs. Vietch" had been collected in his *Three Flights Up* (1924); Ruth Suckow was known for her stories and novels of midwestern life.

[2] "whose" in the previous paragraph.

[3] Peggy Boyd, wife of Thomas Boyd, wrote under the name Woodward Boyd.

Cowboys, West + South either. What about Bal de Compte Orget? and Ring's set? and his new book? + Gertrude Stien? and Hemmingway?[1]

I still owe the store almost $700 on my Encyclopedia but I'll pay them on about Jan 10th—all in a lump as I expect my finances will then be on a firm footing. Will you ask them to send me Ernest Boyd's book? Unless it has about my drinking in it that would reach my family. However, I guess it'd worry me more if I hadn't seen it than if I had. If my book is a big success or a great failure (financial—no other sort can be imagined, I hope) I don't want to publish stories in the fall. If it goes between 25,000 and 50,000 I have an excellent collection for you. This is the longest letter I've written in three or four years. Please thank Mr. Scribner for me for his exceeding kindness.

Always yours

Scott Fitz——

TO: *Harold Ober*   *ALS, 2 pp. Lilly Library*
Received January 23, 1925

I'd rather use this {American Express Co.
for an adress {Rome, Italy

Dear Ober:

(After all these years I agree with you that it is high time to drop honorifics) 1st Thanks very much for the money, which eats well into the second story. I'm sure that the third story ("Not in The Guide Book") will sell much easier than the other two. The Adjuster may seem too gloomy. However, time will tell.

I am starting a fourth story (really a sixth, for one I tore up and Love in the Night I rewrote completely, as you see. I'm a little disappointed about the novel but I suppose it did seem raw to Wheeler. He immediately wrote me the inevitable letter asking for a story.

If the novel is a big success I'm hoping my price will go up to $2000 regular. It's a neat sum and while I don't feel my stuff is worth anything like that its as good as a lot that gets much more.

I feel very old this winter. I'm twenty eight. I was twenty-two when I came to New York and found that you'd sold Head and Shoulders to the Post. I'd like to get a thrill like that again but I suppose its only once in a lifetime.

You've been awfully kind about this money. I don't know what I could have done without it. I've owed Scribner the advance on this novel for

---

[1] *The White Monkey* (1924), by John Galsworthy, was published by Scribners, as was Will James's *Cowboys North and South*. Neither Raymond Radiguet nor Gertrude Stein was published by Scribners.

almost two years. Did Warner Bros. ever render a definate account on the
B. + D. movie?

I hate Italy and the Italiens so violently that I can't bring myself to write
about them for the <u>Post</u>.—unless they'd like an article called "Pope Siphilis
the Sixth and his Morons" or something like that. But we're resolutely
trying to econemize, so we wouldn't move back to France till March even
if we could afford it.

Scott Fitz.

TO: Maxwell Perkins   *TLS, 3 pp—with holograph postscript*
Princeton University

Hotel des Princes
Rome, Italy
January 24.-1925
(But address the American Express
Co. because its damn cold here
and we may leave any day.

Dear Max:

This is a most important letter so I'm having it typed. Guard it as your
life.

1) Under a separate cover I'm sending the first part of the proof. While I
agreed with the general suggestions in your first letters I differ with you in
others. I <u>want</u> Myrtle Wilson's breast ripped off—its exactly the thing, I
think, and I don't want to chop up the good scenes by too much tinkering.
When Wolfshiem says "sid" for "said", it's deliberate. "Orgastic" is the
adjective from "orgasm" and it expresses exactly the intended ecstasy. It's
not a bit dirty. I'm much more worried about the disappearance of Tom
and Myrtle on galley 9—I think it's all right but I'm not sure. If it isn't
please wire and I'll send correction.

2) Now about the page proof—under certain conditions never mind sending them (unless, of course, there's loads of time, which I suppose there
isn't. I'm keen for late March or early April publication)
<u>The conditions are two</u>.

a) That someone reads it <u>very carefully twice</u> to see that every one of my
inserts are put in correctly. There are so many of them that I'm in terror of
a mistake.

b) That no changes <u>whatsoever</u> are made in it except in the case of a misprint
so glaring as to be certain, and that only by you.

If there's some time left but not enough for the double mail send them
to me and I'll simply wire O.K. which will save two weeks. However don't
postpone for that. In any case send me the page proof as usual just to see.

3) Now, many thanks for the deposit. Two days after wiring you I had a
cable from Reynolds that he'd sold two stories of mine for a total of $3,750.

but before that I was in debt to him and after turning down the ten thousand dollars from College Humor[1] I was afraid to borrow more from him until he'd made a sale. I won't ask for any more from you until the book has earned it. My guess is that it will sell about 80,000 copies but I may be wrong. Please thank Mr. Charles Scribner for me. I bet he thinks he's caught another John Fox[2] now for sure. Thank God for John Fox. It would have been awful to have had no predecessor.

4) This is very important. Be sure not to give away <u>any</u> of my plot in the blurb. Don't give away that Gatsby <u>dies</u> or is a <u>parvenu</u> or <u>crook</u> or anything. It's a part of the suspense of the book that all these things are in doubt until the end. You'll watch this won't you? And remember about having no quotations from critics on the jacket—<u>not even about my other books</u>!

5) This is just a list of small things.

a) What's Ring's title for his spring book?

b) Did O'Brien star my story <u>Absolution</u> or any of my others on his trash-album?

c) I wish your bookkeeping department would send me an account on Feb. 1st. Not that it gives me pleasure to see how much in debt I am but that I like to keep a yearly record of the sales of all my books.

Do answer every question and keep this letter until the proof comes. Let me know how you like the changes. I miss seeing you, Max, more than I can say.

As ever,
Scott

P.S. I'm returning the proof of the title page ect. It's O.K. but my heart tells me I should have named it <u>Trimalchio</u>. However against all the advice I suppose it would have been stupid and stubborn of me. <u>Trimalchio in West Egg</u> was only a compromise. <u>Gatsby</u> is too much like Babbit and <u>The Great Gatsby</u> is weak because there's no emphasis even ironically on his greatness or lack of it. However let it pass.

TO: *Maxwell Perkins*	*ALS, 1 p. Princeton University*
c. February 18, 1925	

New Address {Hotel Tiberio / Capri

Dear Max:

After six weeks of uninterrupted work the proof is finished and the last of it goes to you this afternoon. On the whole its been very successful labor

---

[1] For serialization of *The Great Gatsby*.

[2] John Fox, Jr. (1863?–1919), the author of *The Trail of the Lonesome Pine* (1908) and other popular novels, borrowed heavily from Scribners.

(1.) I've brought Gatsby to life

(2.) I've accounted for his money

(3.) I've fixed up the two weak chapers (VI and VII)

(4.) I've improved his first party

(5.) I've broken up his long narrative in Chap. VIII

This morning I wired you to <u>hold up the galley of Chap 40</u>. The correction—and God! its important because in my other revision I made Gatsby look too mean—is enclosed herewith. Also some corrections for the page proof.

We're moving to Capri. We hate Rome, I'm behind financially and have to write three short stories. Then I try another play, and by June, I hope, begin my new novel.

Had long interesting letters from Ring and John Bishop. Do tell me if all corrections have been recieved. I'm worried

Scott

I hope you're setting publication date at first possible moment.

TO: Harold Ober   *ALS, 1 p. Lilly Library*
March 1925

Hotel Tiberio, Capri

Dear Ober:

We've had a hell of a time here. My wifes been sick in bed three weeks + there isn't a typist nearer than Naples—the farmer who did this kept it for 10 days at the other end of the Island. I have another ready too if he ever brings it back.

Good stories write themselves—bad ones have to be written so this took up about three weeks. And look at it. I'd rather not offer it to the Post because everybody sees the <u>Post</u> but I know its saleable and I need the money. I leave it to you.

The Red Book story will be along shortly. For God's sake don't give them this. Thank you for the deposits. I don't know whats the matter with me. I can't seem to keep out of debt. Whenever I get ahead things like this sickness happen. Such is life. However two other stories will follow this thick and fast

As Ever
F Scott Fitzgerald

TO: *Maxwell Perkins*   *ALS, 2 pp. Princeton University*
c. March 12, 1925

Hotel Tiberio, Capri

Dear Max:

Thanks many times for your nice letter. You answered all questions (except about the account) I wired you on a chance about the title—I wanted to change back to <u>Gold-hatted Gatsby</u> but I don't suppose it would matter. That's the one flaw in the book—I feel <u>Trimalchio</u> might have been best after all.

Don't forget to send Ring's book. Hemmingway could be reached, I'm sure, through the Transatlantic review. I'm going to look him up when we get to Paris. I think its amusing about Sherman and Mencken[1]—however Sherman's such a louse that it doesn't matter. He wouldn't have shaken Mencken's hand during the war—he's only been bullied into servility and all the Tribune appointments in the world wouldn't make him more than 10th rate. Poor Sherwood Anderson. What a mess his life is—almost like Driesers. Are you going to do "Le Bal de Compte Orgel"—I think you're losing a big opportunity if you dont. The success of <u>The Little French Girl</u>[2] is a pointer of taste—and this is really French, and sensational and meritorious besides.

I hope you're sending <u>page proofs</u> to that French woman who wants to translate Gatsby! I'm sending in two other envelopes.

(1.) Cards to go in books to go to critics
(2)   "   " " "   "   "   " " friends

Also, I'm enclosing herewith a note I wish you'd send down to the retail dept.

They won't forget to send copies to all the liberal papers—Freeman, Liberator, Transatlantic, Dial ect?
Can't you send me
a jacket now?   Scott

While, on the contrary these 16 are all personal. Like wise I wish they'd tear off the adress and send each message in a book charged to my account.

For myself in Europe 6 books will be enough—one post haste and five at liesure.

Fitzg.

---

[1] In his February 24, 1925, letter Perkins had reported on a confrontation between New York *Herald Tribune Books* editor Stuart P. Sherman and H. L. Mencken.
[2] Popular 1924 novel by Anne Douglas Sedgwick.

TO: *Charles Scribner's Sons*   *Wire. Princeton University*

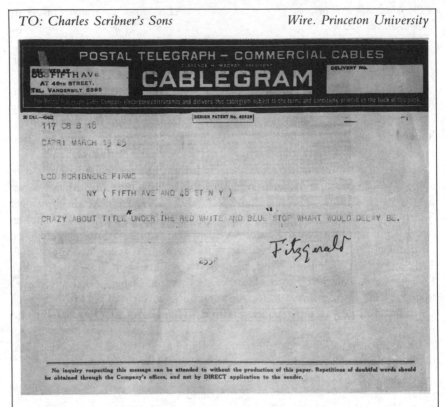

Fitzgerald never felt confident about "The Great Gatsby" as a title and tried to change it shortly before publication. Perkins wired that changing the title would delay publication and that he preferred "The Great Gatsby." On March 22 Fitzgerald wired: YOURE RIGHT.

TO: *John Peale Bishop*   *ALS, 3 pp. Princeton University*
Late March 1925

> I am quite drunk
> I am told that this is Capri, though
> as I remember Capri was quieter.

Dear John:

As the literary wits might say, your letter recieved and contents quoted. Let us have more of the same—I think it showed a great deal of power and the last scene—the dinner at the young Bishops—was handled with admirable restraint. I am glad that at last Americans are producing letters of their own. The climax was wonderful and the exquisite irony of the "sincerely yours" has only been equealed in the work of those two masters Flaubert and Ferber.

Norman Douglas is not here now and anyway I have piles.

I will now have two copies of Wescotts "Apple"[1] as in despair I ordered one—a regular orchard. I shall give one to Brooks, here whom I like. Do you know Brooks? He's just a fellow here . . .

Excuse the delay. I have just been working on the envelope . . .

That was a caller. His name was Musselini, I think, and he says he is in politics here. And besides I have lost my pen so I will have to continue in pencil . . . It turned up—I was writing with it all the time and hadn't noticed. That is because I am full of my new work, a historical play based on the life of Woodrow Wilson

Act I. At Princeton

Woodrow seen teaching philosophy. Enter Pyne. Quarrel scene—Wilson refuses to recognize clubs. Enter woman with Bastard from Trenton. Pyne reenters with glee club and trustees. Noise outside "We have won—Princeton 12 - Layfayette 3." Cheers. Football team enter and group around Wilson. Old Nassau. Curtain

Act II. Gubernatorial Mansion at Patterson

Wilson seen signing papers. Tasker Bliss and Marc Connelly come in with proposition to let bosses get controll. "I have important papers to sign—and none of them legalize corruption." Triangle Club begins to sing out side window. Enter woman with Bastard from Trenton. President continues to sign papers. Enter Mrs. Galt, John Grier Hibben, Al Jolsen and Grantland Rice. Song "The call to Larger Duty." Tableau. Coughdrop.

Act III. (optional)

The Battle front 1918.

Act IV

The peace congress. Clemenceau, Wilson and Jolsen at table. The Bastard from Trenton now grown up but still a baby, in the uniform of the Prussian Guard is mewling and pewking in Wilson's lap. Orlando is fucking Mrs. Galt in a corner. The junior prom committee comes in through the skylight. Clemenceau: "We want the Sarre." Wilson: "No, sarre, I wont hear of it." Laughter Orlando grunts at a passing orgasm. Enter Marylyn Miller, Gilbert Seldes and Irish Meusel. Tasker Bliss falls into the cuspidor . . .

Oh Christ! I'm sobering up! Write me the opinion you may be pleased to form of my chef d'oevre + others opinion. Please! I think its great but because it deals with much debauched materials, quick-deciders like Rascoe may mistake it for Chambers. To me its facinating. I never get tired of it.

"Dodo" Benson is here. I think he is (or was) probably a fairy.

[1]Glenway Wescott, *The Apple of the Eye* (1924).

Zelda's been sick in bed for five weeks, poor child, and is only now looking up. No news except I now get 2000 a story and they grow worse and worse and my ambition is to get where I need write no more but only novels. Is Lewis' book any good. I imagine that mine is infinitely better—what else is well-reviewed this spring? Maybe my book is rotten but I don't think so.

What are you writing? Please tell me something about your novel. And if I like the idea maybe I'll make it into a short story for the Post to appear just before your novel and steal the thunder. Who's going to do it? Bebé Daniels? She's a wow!

How was Townsends first picture. Good reviews? What's Alec doing? And Ludlow? And Bunny? Did you read Ernest Boyd's account of what I might ironicly call our "private" life in his "Portraits?" Did you like it? I rather did.

Scott

I am quite drunk again and enclose a postage stamp.

TO: *Willa Cather*   *ALS, 1 p. Princeton University*
Late March/early April 1925

Hotel Tiberio, Capri, Italy

My Dear Miss Cather:

As one of your greatest admirers—an admirer particularly of My Antonia, A Lost Lady, Paul's Case and Scandal I want to write to explain an instance of apparent plagiarism which some suspicious person may presently bring to your attention.

To begin with, my new book The Great Gatsby will appear about the time you recieve this letter (I am sending you the book besides). When I was in the middle of the first draft A Lost Lady was published and I read it with the greatest delight. One of the finest passages is the often-quoted one toward the end which includes the phrases "she seemed to promise a wild delight that he has not found in life . . . "I could show you" . . . ect (all misquoted here as I have no copy by me).[1]

Well, a month or two before I had written into my own book a parallel and almost similar idea in the description of a woman's charm—an idea that I'd had for several years. Now my expression of this was neither so clear, nor so beautiful, nor so moving as yours but the essential similarity was undoubtedly there. I was worried because I hated the devil to cut mine out so I went to Ring Lardner and several other people and showed them mine and yours and finally decided to retain it. Also Ive kept the pages from my first draft to show you and am enclosing them here. The passage as finally

[1] See *A Lost Lady* (New York: Knopf, 1923), pp. 171–72.

worked out is in my Chapter One. Hoping you will understand my motive in communicating this to you I am[1]

> With Best Wishes and Most Sincere Admiration
> F. Scott Fitzgerald

TO: *John Peale Bishop* ALS, 5 pp. *Princeton University*
April 1925

> American Express Co.
> Rome, Italy.

Dear John:

Your letter was perfect. It told us everything we wanted to know and the same day I read your article (very nice too) in Van. Fair about cherching the past. But you disappointed me with the quality of some of it (the news)—for instance that Bunnys play failed, that Townsend has got the swelled-head and that you + Margaret find life dull and depressing there. We want to come back but we want to come back with money saved and so far we havn't saved any—tho I'm one novel ahead and book of pretty good (seven) short stories. I've done about 10 pieces of horrible junk in the last year tho that I can never republish or bear to look at—cheap and without the spontaneity of my first work. But the novel Im sure of. Its marvellous

We're just back from Capri where I sat up (tell Bunny) half the night talking to my old idol Compton Mackenzie. Perhaps you met him. I found him cordial, attractive and pleasantly mundane. You get no sense from him that feels his work has gone to pieces. He's not pompous about his present output. I think he's just tired. The war wrecked him as it did Wells and many of that generation.

To show how well you geussed the gossip I wanted we were wondering where The Seldes got the money for Havana, whether The Film Guild finally collapsed (Christ! You should have seen their last two pictures—one from my story.[2]) But I don't doubt that Frank Tuttle[3] + Townsend will talk themselves into the Cabinet eventually. I do it myself if I could but I'm too much of an egotist + not enough of a diplomat ever to succeed in the movies. You must begin by placing the tongue flat against the posteriors of such worthys as Gloria Swanson + Allan Dwan and commence a slow carressing movement. Say what they may of Cruze—Famous Players is the product of two great ideas Demille[4] + Gloria Swansons and it stands or falls not their "conference methods" but on those two + the stock pictures that imitate them. The Cruze winnings are usually lost on such expensive

[1] On April 28 Cather wrote Fitzgerald that she had enjoyed reading *The Great Gatsby* before receiving his letter and had detected no duplication of *A Lost Lady*.
[2] *Grit* (1924).
[3] Actor who was a partner with Townsend Martin in the Film Guild.
[4] Allan Dwan, James Cruze, and Cecil B. De Mille were movie directors.

TO: *Robert Kerr*
April 1925

Inscription pasted in The Great Gatsby.[1]
Doris Kerr Brown
Capri, Italy

Dear Bob:
Keep reading and you'll finally come to your own adventures which you told to me one not-forgotten summer night. As your friend
F. Scott Fitzgerald

TO: *Van Wyck Brooks*[2]
April 1925

Inscription pasted in The Great Gatsby.
Bruccoli

Dear Brooks: I'm taking the liberty of sending you this, after having run across a copy of *America's Coming of Age* in a book store here and bought and read it with enormous pleasure.
Capri, Italy.
F. Scott Fitzgerald

[1]Fitzgerald sent Scribners inscriptions on slips of paper to be pasted in presentation copies.
[2]Literary historian and critic.

Dear Sinclair Lewis: I've just sent for Arrowsmith. My hope is that then The Great Gatsby will be the second best American book of the Spring.

F Scott Fitzgerald

Dear Menck: This is a grand book. I see you don't review fiction any more. If you like this well you write me a ~~~~ line about it? If not — just say you received it and will read & preserve it. Always Sincerely

F Scott Fitzgerald

experiments as Frank Tuttle. (Needless to say this letter is not for T. M. or Alec, but for your ears alone.)

Is Dos Passos novel any good?[1] And what's become of Cummings work. I havn't read <u>Some do Not</u>[2] but Zelda was crazy about. I glanced though it + kept wondering why it was written backward. At first I thought they'd sewn the cover on upside down. Well—these people <u>will</u> collaborate with Conrad.

Do you still think Dos Passos is a genius? My faith in him is somehow weakened. Theres so little time for faith these days.

Pinna Cruger is a damned attractive woman + while the husbands a haberdasher he's at least a Groton Haberdasher (he went there, I mean, to school) + almost as gentile as Cupie Simon. Is Harlock (no connection) dead, or was that Leopold and Loeb.

The Wescott book will be eagerly devoured. A personable young man of that name from Atlantic introduced himself to me after the failure of the <u>Vegetable</u>. I wonder if he's the same. At any rate your Wescott, so Harrison Rhodes tells me is coming here to Rome.

I've given up Nathan's books. I liked the 4th series of predjudices. Is Lewis new book good. Hergeshiemers was awful. He's all done.

Merrit Hemminway—I have a dim memory that he + I admired Ginevra King at the same time once in those palmy days.

The cheerfulest things in my life are first Zelda and second the hope that my book has something extradordinary about it. I want to be extravagantly admired again. Zelda and I sometimes indulge in terrible four day rows that always start with a drinking party but we're still enormously in love and about the only truly happily married people I know.

Our Very Best To Margaret
Please Write!
Scott

In the Villa d'Este at Tivoli all that ran in my brain was:

> An alley of dark cypresses
>> Hides an enrondured pool of light
> And there the young musicians come
>> With instruments for her delight
>>>> . . . . . locks are bowed
> Over dim lutes that sigh aloud
>> Or else with heads thrown back
>>>>> they tease
> Reverberate <u>echoes</u> from the drum
> The stiff folds <u><u>ect</u></u>[3]

[1] *Manhattan Transfer* (1925).
[2] 1924 novel by Ford Madox Ford.
[3] Lines from Bishop's poem "Plato in Italy."

It was wonderful that when you wrote that you'd never seen Italy—or, by God, now that I think of it never lived in the 15th Century.

But then I wrote T. S. of P. without ever having been to Oxford.

TO: *Maxwell Perkins*   *ALS, 5 pp. Princeton University*
1925   *En route to Paris*

April 10th

Dear Max:

The book comes out today and I am overcome with fears and forebodings. Supposing women didn't like the book because it has no important woman in it, and critics didn't like it because it dealt with the rich and contained no peasants borrowed out of <u>Tess</u> in it and set to work in Idaho? Suppose it didn't even wipe out my debt to you—why it will have to sell 20,000 copies even to do that! In fact all my confidence is gone—I wouldn't tell you this except for the fact that by the this reaches you the worst will be known. I'm sick of the book myself—I wrote it over at least five times and I still feel that what should be the strong scene (in the Hotel) is hurried and ineffective. Also the last chapter, the burial, Gatsby's father ect is faulty. Its too bad because the first five chapters and parts of the 7th and 8th are the best things I've ever done.

"The best since Paradise". God! If you you knew how discouraging that was. That was what Ring said in his letter together with some very complementary remarks. In strictest confidence I'll admit that I was disappointed in <u>Haircut</u>[1]—in fact I thought it was pretty lousy stuff—the crazy boy as the instrument of providence is many hundreds of years old. However please don't tell him I didn't like it.

Now as to the changes I don't think I'll make any more for the present. Ring suggested the correction of certain errata—if you made the changes all right—if not let them go. Except on Page 209 old dim La Salle Street Station should be <u>Union</u> old dim Union Station and should be changed in the second edition. Transit will do fine though of course I really meant compass. The page proofs arrived and seemed to be O.K. though I don't know how the printer found his way through those 70,000 corrections. The cover (jacket) came too and is a delight. Zelda is mad about it (incidently she is quite well again).

When you get this letter address me % Guaranty Trust Co. 1 Rue Des Italennes, Paris.

Another thing—I'm convinced that Myers[2] is all right but have him be sure and keep all such trite phrases as "Surely the book of the Spring!" out of

---

[1] Lardner's story had appeared in the March 28, 1925 *Liberty* and would be collected in *The Love Nest* (1926).

[2] Wallace Meyer of the Scribners advertising department.

the advertiseing. That one is my pet abomination. Also to use no quotations except those of unqualified and exceptionally entheusiastic praise from emminent individuals. Such phrases as

"Should be on everyone's summer list"
Boston Transcript
"Not a dull moment . . . a thoroughly sound solid piece of work"

havn't sold a copy of any book in three years. I thought your advertising for Ring was great. I'm sorry you didn't get Wescotts new book. Several people have written me that The Apple of the Eye is the best novel of the year.

Life in New Cannan sounds more interesting than life in Plainfield. I'm sure anyhow that at least two critics Benet + Mary Column[1] will have heard about the book. I'd like her to like it—Benet's opinion is of no value whatsoever.

And thanks mightily for the $750.00 which swells my debt to over $6000.00.

When should my book of short stories be in?

Scott

P. S.

I had, or rather saw, a letter from my uncle who had seen a preliminary announcement of the book. He said:

"it sounded as if it were very much like his others."

This is only a vague impression, of course, but I wondered if we could think of some way to advertise it so that people who are perhaps weary of assertive jazz and society novels might not dismiss it as "just another book like his others". I confess that today the problem baffles me—all I can think of is to say in general to avoid such phrases as "a picture of New York life" or "modern society"—though as that is exactly what the book is its hard to avoid them. The trouble is so much superficial trash has sailed under those banners. Let me know what you think

Scott

TO: *Maxwell Perkins*   *ALS, 2 pp. Princeton University*
c. April 24, 1925

Marseille, en route to Paris

Dear Max:

Your telegram[2] depressed me—I hope I'll find better news in Paris and am wiring you from Lyons. There's nothing to say until I hear more. If the book fails commercially it will be from one of two reasons or both

---

[1] William Rose Benét and Mary Colum.
[2] Perkins cabled Fitzgerald on April 20: "Sales situation doubtful. Excellent reviews."

1st The title is only fair, rather bad than good.

2nd <u>And most important</u>—the book contains no important woman character and women controll the fiction market at present. I don't think the unhappy end matters particularly.

It will have to sell 20,000 copies to wipe out my debt to you. I think it will do that all right—but my hope was it would do 75,000. This week will tell.

Zelda is well, or almost but the expense of her illness and of bringing this wretched little car of ours back to France which has to be done, by law, has wiped out what small progress I'd made in getting straight financially.

In all events I have a book of good stories for the fall. Now I shall write some cheap ones until I've accumulated enough for my my next novel. When that is finished and published I'll wait and see. If it will support me with no more intervals of trash I'll go on as a novelist. If not I'm going to quit, come home, go to Hollywood and learn the movie business. I can't reduce our scale of living and I can't stand this financial insecurity. Anyhow there's no point in trying to be an artist if you can't do your best. I had my chance back in 1920 to start my life on a sensible scale and I lost it and so I'll have to pay the penalty. Then perhaps at 40 I can start writing again without this constant worry and interruption

<u>Yours in great depression</u>
Scott

P.S. Let me know about Ring's Book. Did I tell you that I thought <u>Haircut</u> was mediochre?

P.S. (2) Please refer any movie offers to Reynolds.

TO: Maxwell Perkins   *ALS, 2 pp. Princeton University*
1925

Guaranty Trust Co.
Paris. May 1st

Dear Max:

There's no use for indignation against the long suffering public when even a critic who likes the book fails to be fundamentally held—that is Stallings who has written the only intelligent review so far[1]— but its been depressing to find how quick one is forgotten, especially unless you repeat yourself <u>ad nauseam</u>. Most of the reviewers floundered around in a piece of work that obviously they completely failed to understand and tried to give it reviews that committed them neither <u>pro</u> or <u>con</u> until some one of culture

---

[1]Laurence Stallings reviewed *The Great Gatsby* in the *New York World* on April 22.

had spoken. Of course I've only seen the <u>Times</u> and the <u>Tribune</u>—and, thank God, Stallings, for I had begun to believe no one was even glancing at the book.

Now about money. With the $1000. for which I asked yesterday (and thank you for your answer) I owe you about $7200, or if the book sells 12,000 about $4000.00. If there is a movie right I will pay you all I owe— if not, all I can offer you at present is an excellent collection of stories for the fall entitled "All the Sad Young Men"—none of the stories appeared in the <u>Post</u>—I think <u>Absolution</u> is the only one you've read. Thank you for all your advertising and all the advances and all your good will. When I get ahead again on trash I'll begin the new novel.

I'm glad Ring is getting such a press and hope he's selling. The boob critics have taken him up and always take a poke at the "intelligentia" who patronize him. But the "intelligentsia"—Seldes + Mencken discovered him (after the people) while the boob critics let <u>The Big Town</u> and <u>Gullibles Travels</u> come out in dead silence. Let me know the sale.

A profound bow to my successor Arlen[1]—when I read <u>The London Venture</u> I knew he was a comer and was going to tell you but I saw the next day that Doran had already published <u>Piracy</u>. That was just before I left New York.

Which reminds me—it seems terrible that all the best of the young Englishmen have been snapped up. I tried to get Louis Golding[2] for you in Capri but he'd signed a rotten cash contract with Knopf a week before. Also they've just signed Brett Young who might have been had any time in the last two years and who'll be a big seller and now I see <u>The Constant Nymph</u>[3] is taken. Wouldn't it pay you to have some live young Londoner watch the new English books. I imagine Kingsley[4] gets his information a month late out of the <u>London Times Supplement</u>. This sounds ill-natured but I am really sorry to see you loose so many new talents when they are appearing as fast now in England as they did here in 1920. Liverite[5] has got Hemminway! How about Radiguet?

We have taken an appartment here from May 12th to Jan 12th, eight months, where I shall do my best. What a six months in Italy! Christ!

I'm hoping that by some miracle the book will go up to 23,000 and wipe off my debt to you. I haven't been out of debt now for three years and with the years it grows heavy on my ageing back. The happiest thought I have is of my new novel—it is something really NEW in form, idea, structure— the model for the age that Joyce and Stien are searching for, that Conrad didn't find.

---

[1] Michael Arlen, author of English society novels; his best-known work was *The Green Hat* (1924).

[2] British novelist and critic.

[3] By British novelist Margaret Kennedy.

[4] Charles Kingsley ran the London office of Scribners.

[5] American publisher Horace Liveright.

Write me any news—I havn't had a written line since publication except a pleasant but not thrilling note from the perennial youth, Johnny Weaver.[1] I am bulging with plans for—however that's later. Was Rings skit which was in Mencken's <u>American Language</u> incorporated into <u>What of It</u>? If not it should have been—its one of his best shorter things. And doesn't it contain his famous world's series articles about Ellis Lardners Coat? If not they'd be a nucleous for another book of nonsense. Also his day at home in imitation of F.P.A.'s[2] diary.

My adress after the 12th is <u>14 Rue de Tilsitt</u>. If you have my <u>Three Lives</u> by Gertrude Stien don't let anybody steal it.

Many thanks to Mr. Scribner and to all the others and to you for all you've done for me and for the book. The jacket was a hit anyhow.

Scott

P.S. And Tom Boyd's Book?

TO: Edmund Wilson   *ALS, 2 pp. Yale University*
May 1925

14 Rue de Tillsit
Paris, France

Dear Bunny:

Thanks for your letter about the book. I was awfully happy that you liked it and that you approved of its design. The worst fault in it, I think is a Big Fault: I gave no account (and had no feeling about or knowledge of) the emotional relations between Gatsby and Daisy from the time of their reunion to the catastrophe. However the lack is so astutely concealed by the retrospect of Gatsby's past and by blankets of excellent prose that no one has noticed it—tho everyone has felt the lack and called it by another name. Mencken said (in a most enthusiastic letter received today) that the only fault was that the central story was trivial and a sort of anecdote (that is because he has forgotten his admiration for Conrad and adjusted himself to the sprawling novel.) and I felt that what he really missed was the lack of any emotional backbone at the very height of it.

Without makeing any invidious comparisons between Class A. and Class C., if my novel is an anectdote so is <u>The Brothers Karamazoff</u>. From one angle the latter could be reduced into a detective story. However the letters from you and Mencken have compensated me for the fact that of all the reviews, even the most enthusiastic, not one had the slightest idea what the book was about and for the even more depressing fact that it was, in comparison with the others, a financial failure (after I'd turned down fifteen thousand for the serial rights!). I wonder what Rosenfeld[3] thought of it?

[1] Poet John V. A. Weaver.
[2] Franklin Pierce Adams, newspaper columnist who signed his work "F.P.A."
[3] Paul Rosenfeld.

I looked up Hemminway. He is taking me to see Gertrude Stien tomorrow. This city is full of Americans—most of them former friends—whom we spend most of our time dodgeing, not because we don't want to see them but because Zelda's only just well and I've got to work; and they seem to be incapable of any sort of conversation not composed of semi-malicious gossip about New York courtesy celebrities. I've gotten to like France. We've taken a swell appartment until January. I'm filled with disgust for Americans in general after two weeks sight of the ones in Paris—these preposterous, pushing women and girls who assume that you have any personal interest in them, who have all (so they say) read James Joyce and who simply adore Mencken. I suppose we're no worse than any one else, only contact with other races brings out all our worst qualities. If I had anything to do with creating the manners of the contemporary American girl I certainly made a botch of the job.

I'd love to see you. God, I could give you some laughs. There's no news except that Zelda and I think we're pretty good, as usual, only more so.

Scott

Thanks again for your cheering letter.

TO: *H. L. Mencken*   *ALS, 2 pp. Enoch Pratt Free Library*

14 Rue de Tilsitt
Paris, France
May 4th, 1925

Dear Menk—

Your letter was the first outside word that reached me about my book. I was tremendously moved both by the fact that you liked it and by your kindness in writing me about it. By the next mail came a letter from Edmund Wilson and a clipping from Stallings, both bulging with interest and approval, but as you know I'd rather have you like a book of mine than anyone in America.

There is a tremendous fault in the book—the lack of an emotional presentment of Daisy's attitude toward Gatsby after their reunion (and the consequent lack of logic or importance in her throwing him over). Everyone has felt this but no one has spotted it because its concealed beneath elaborate and overlapping blankets of prose. Wilson complained: "The characters are so uniformly unpleasant," Stallings: "a sheaf of gorgeous notes for a novel" and you say: "The story is fundamentally trivial." I think the smooth, almost unbroken pattern makes you feel that. Despite your admiration for Conrad you have lately—perhaps in reaction against the merely well-made novels of James' imitators—become used to the formless. It is in protest against my own formless two novels, and Lewis' and Dos Passos' that this was written. I admit that in comparison to <u>My Antonia</u> and <u>The Lost Lady</u>

it is a failure in what it tries to do but I think in comparison to <u>Cytherea</u> or <u>Linda Condon</u>[1] it is a success. At any rate I have learned a lot from writing it and the influence on it has been the masculine one of <u>The Brothers Karamazov</u>, a thing of incomparable form, rather than the feminine one of <u>The Portrait of a Lady</u>. If it seems trivial or "anecdotal" (sp) it is because of an aesthetic fault, a failure in one very important episode and not a frailty in the theme—at least I don't think so. Did you ever know a writer to calmly take a just critisism and shut up?

Incidently, I had hoped it would amuse the Mencken who wrote the essay on New York in the last book of <u>Prejudices</u>—tho I know nothing in the new Paris streets that I like better than Park Avenue at twilight.

I think the book is so far a commercial failure—at least it was two weeks after publication—hadn't reached 20,000 yet. So I rather regret (but not violently) the fact that I turned down $15,000.00 for the serial rights. However I have all the money I need and was growing rather tired of being a popular author. My trash for the Post grows worse and worse as there is less and less heart in it—strange to say my whole heart was in my first trash. I thought that the <u>Offshore Pirate</u> was quite as good as <u>Benediction</u>. I never really "wrote down" until after the failure of the <u>Vegetable</u> and that was to make this book possible. I would have written down long ago if it had been profitable—I tried it unsuccessfully for the movies. People don't seem to realize that for an intelligent man writing down is about the hardest thing in the world. When people like Hughes and Stephen Whitman[2] go wrong after one tragic book it is because they never had any real egos or attitudes but only empty bellies and cross nerves. The bellies full and the nerves soothed with vanity they see life rosily and would be violently insincere in writing anything but the happy trash they do. The others, like Owen Johnson,[3] just get tired—there's nothing the matter with some of Johnson's later books—they're just rotten that's all. He was tired and his work is no more writing in the sense that the work—Thomas Hardy and Gene Stratton Porter[4] is writing than were Driesers dime novels.

However I won't bore you any longer. I expect to spend about two years on my next novel and it ought to be more successful critically. Its about myself—not what I thought of myself in <u>This Side of Paradise</u>. Moreover it will have the most amazing form ever invented.

With many, many thanks

F. Scott Fitzg——

P.S. This is simply an acknowledgment and expects no answer.

[1] Novels by Joseph Hergesheimer.

[2] Rupert Hughes, *The Thirteenth Commandment* (1916), and Stephen French Whitman, *Predestined* (1910).

[3] Author of stories about Lawrenceville School and *Stover at Yale* (1912), Johnson also wrote adult novels about the privileged classes.

[4] Porter wrote popular fiction.

P.S. Italy (but not France) is full of Pilsen and Munich beer of fine quality.
There is less than there was when I got there.

TO: *Hazel McCormack*   *ALS, 2 pp. Princeton University*
Postmarked May 15, 1925

> 14 Rue de Tilsitt
> Paris, France

Dear Patsy—Thanks enormously for your kind note—One from Mencken
and a handful of fairly intelligent reviews arrived in the same mail and did
a lot to lift me up from the wearying fact that it isn't going to sell. Not like
the others, I mean, which automaticly condemns me to 6 months of canned
rubbish for the popular magazines. Thank you for likeing Love in the Night
too. I didn't like it.

Gatsby was far from perfect in many ways but all in all it contains such
prose as has never been written in America before. From that I take heart.
From that I take heart and hope that some day I can combine the verve of
Paradise, the unity of the Beautiful + Damned and the lyric quality of
Gatsby, its aesthetic soundness, into something worthy of the admiration
of those few——God, I am inextricably intangled in that sentence, and the
only thing to do is to start a new one. Anyhow, thanks.

We have taken an appartment in the Rue de Tillsit near the Etoile for 8
months and I have taken a studio near by to write in. We're glad to leave
Italy and Paris in the Spring is no easy place to settle down to work. In fact
most of our time is taken up in dodging our friends, most of whom seem
to be over here. About July I'm starting a new novel.

About my life in general I can refer you to the following gems of biography.

F. Scott Fitzgerald—by Edmund Wilson—In "The Literary
Spotlight" (Doran)
" — " Paul Rosenfeld—In "Men Seen" (Dial
Press)
" — " Ernest Boyd—In "Portraits Real +
Imaginary" (Appleton)
I think
" — " Bee Wilson—In "Smart Set" early in 1924
" — " Himself—In Who's Who in Sat. Eve. Post
late in 1920
or early " 1921

And such articles of my own as you've seen like "How to Live on 36,000
a year", its sequeal, "What I Think + Feel at 25" ect. not to mention a
book called This Side of Paradise which is what a most egotistic young man
thought of himself at twenty-two (or was it sixteen).

I enclose you a picture of a naked woman—who, much to my shame is not a member of the Folies Bergere but my own daughter.

Please send me any stories ect. that you publish and thanks again for the letter.

As Ever Your Friend
F Scott Fitzg——

TO: *Maxwell Perkins*   *ALS, 1 p. Princeton University*
c. May 22, 1925

14 Rue de Tillsit
Paris
(Permanent adress)

Dear Max:

I suppose you've sent the book to Collins. If not please do and let me know right away. If he won't take it because of its flop we might try Capes.[1] I'm miserable at owing you all that money—if I'd taken the serial money I could at least have squared up with you.

I've had enthusiastic letters from Mencken and Wilson—the latter says he's reviewing it for that <u>Chicago Tribune</u> syndicate he writes for. I think all the reviews I've seen, except two, have been absolutely stupid and lowsy. Some day they'll eat grass, by God! This thing, both the effort and the result have hardened me and I think now that I'm much better than any of the young Americans <u>without exception</u>.

Hemminway is a fine, charming fellow and he appreciated your letter and the tone of it enormously. If Liveright doesn't please him he'll come to you, and he has a future. He's 27.

Bishop sent me <u>The Apple of the Eye</u> and it seemed pretty much the old stuff that D. H. Lawrence, Anderson, Suckow and Cather did long ago and Hardy before them. I don't think such a peasantry exists in America—Ring is much closer to the truth. I suspect tragedy in the American country side because all the people capable of it move to the big towns at twenty. All the rest is pathos. However maybe its good; a lot of people seem to think so.

I will send <u>All The Sad Young Men</u> about June 1st or 10th. Perhaps the deferred press on Gatsby will help it but I think now there's no use even sending it to that crowd Broun, F.P.A., Ruth Hale ect.[2] Incidently my being over here + the consequent delay in the proofs and review copies undoubtedly hurt the effect of the books appearance. Thanks again for your kind letters and all you've done. Let me know about Collins.

Scott

Please let me know how many copies sold + whether the sale is now dead.

[1] Chatto & Windus published *The Great Gatsby* in England (1926).

[2] Heywood Broun, influential New York newspaper columnist; his wife, journalist Ruth Hale, gave *The Great Gatsby* a bad review in the *Brooklyn Eagle*.

TO: *Harold Ober*   *ALS, 1 p. Lilly Library*
Received May 28, 1925

14 Rue de Tilsitt   }   Permanent
Paris, France   }   Adress

Dear Ober:

Thank you for selling those two stories and for the deposits and for the extra five hundred—it came in handy. We have decided that travelling saves no money, and taken an appartment here for eight months.

"What Price Macaroni?" and "The Rich Boy" (second and third versions respectively) are at the typist. Commercially the book has fallen so flat that I'm afraid there'll be no movie rights. However a book always has a chance value as a movie property. I imagine that if one movie makes a strike they buy the rights of all the other books you've written. However I'm not depressed and intend to do about five short stories this summer.

As Ever, Yours
F Scott Fitz—

TO: *T. R. Smith*[1]   *ALS, 1 p. Collection of Marcia*
Late May 1925   *and Maurice Neville*

14 Rue de Tilsitt
Paris, France

Dear Tom:

Thank you many times for your kind letter about <u>Gatsby</u>. I'm afraid its not going to sell like the others but I'm delighted at the response from the people who care about writing.

Now as to the publishing business. Max Perkins is one of my closest friends + my relations with the Scribners in general have always been so cordial and so pleasant that I couldn't imagine breaking them. But as I told you once before if anything should happen to make our relations impossible I should certainly come to your firm, and I know we'd get along.

But it would be a monopoly in restraint of trade. You already have the only other two Americans under thirty who promise a great deal— Hemminway + Cummings. I hope the former's book succeeds + will be glad to review it for any paper you might select.

We'll be here in Paris the rest of 1925 and, we sometimes hope, forever.

Best regards to Horace

As Ever, Your Friend
Scott Fitzg—

But please don't quote this about them; I don't want to step on the toes of two other particular friends.

[1] Boni & Liveright editor.

114

TO: *Gertrude Stein*   *ALS, 1 p. Yale University*

14 Rue de Tilsitt
June 1925.

Dear Miss Gertrude Stien:

Thank you. None of your letter was "a bad compliment" and all of it "was a comfort."[1] Thank you very much. My wife and I think you a very handsome, very gallant, very kind lady and thought so as soon as we saw you, and were telling Hemminway so when you passed us searching your car on the street. Hemminway and I went to Lyons shortly after to get my car and had a slick drive through Burgundy. He's a peach of a fellow and absolutely first rate.

I am so anxious to get <u>The Makeings of Americans</u> + learn something from it and imitate things out of it which I shall doubtless do. That future debt I tried so hard to repay by making the Scribners read it in the <u>Transatlantic</u> + convinced one, but the old man's mind was too old.

You see, I am content to let you, and the one or two like you who are accutely sensitive, think or fail to think for me and my kind artisticly (their name is not legend but the word like it), much as the man of 1901, say, would let Nietche (sp.) think for him intellectually. I am a very second rate person compared to first rate people—I have indignation as well as most of the other major faults—and it honestly makes me shiver to know that such a writer as you attributes such a significance to my factitious, meritricous (metricious?) <u>This Side of Paradise</u>. Like Gatsby I have only hope. It puts me in a false position, I feel.

Thank you cnormously for writing me

Scott Fitzg——

TO: *Maxwell Perkins*   *ALS, 8 pp. Princeton University*
c. *June 1, 1925*

14 Rue de Tilsitt, Paris, France

Dear Max:

This is the second letter I've written you today—I tore my first up when the letter in longhand from New Cannan telling me about Liveright arrived. I'm wiring you today as to that rumor—but also it makes it nessessary to tell you something I didn't intend to tell you.

Yesterday arrived a letter from T. R. Smith asking for my next book— saying nothing against the Scribners but just asking for it: "if I happened to be dissatisfied they would be delighted" ect. ect. I answered at once saying

---

[1] Stein's May 22, 1925, letter to Fitzgerald had praised his sensibility and prose style in *The Great Gatsby* ("that is a comfort") and had compared the novel to Thackeray's *Pendennis* and *Vanity Fair* in "creating the contemporary world" ("and this isn't a bad compliment").

that you were one of my closest friends and that my relations with Scribners had always been so cordial and pleasant that I wouldn't think of changeing publishers. That letter will reach him at about the time this reaches you. I have never had any other communication <u>of any sort</u> with Liveright or any other publisher except the <u>very definate and explicit letter</u> with which I answered their letter yesterday.

So much for that rumor. I am both angry at Tom who must have been in some way responsible for starting it and depressed at the fact that you could have believed it enough to mention it to me. Rumors start like this.

Smith: (<u>a born gossip</u>) "I hear Fitzgerald's book isn't selling. I think we can get him, as he's probably blaming it on Scribners.

The Next Man: It seems Fitzgerald is disatisfied with Scribners and Liveright is after him.

The Third Man: I hear Fitzgerald has gone over to Liverite

Now, Max, I have told you many times that you are my publisher, and permanently, as far as one can fling about the word in this too mutable world. If you like I will sign a contract with you immediately for my next three books. The idea of leaving you has never for <u>one single moment</u> entered my head.

<u>First</u>.   Tho, as a younger man, I have not always been in sympathy with some of your publishing ideas, (which were evolved under the pre-movie, pre-high-literacy-rate conditions of twenty to forty years ago), the personality of you and of Mr. Scribner, the tremendous squareness, courtesy, generosity and open-mindedness I have always met there and, if I may say it, the special consideration you have all had for me and my work, much more than make up the difference.

<u>Second</u>   You know my own idea on the advantages of one publisher who backs you and not your work. And my feeling about uniform books in the matter of house and binding.

<u>Third</u>   The curious advantage to a rather radical writer in being published by what is now an ultra-conservative house.

<u>Fourth</u>   (and least need of saying) Do you think I could treat with another publisher while I have a debt, which is both actual and a matter of honor, of over $3000.00?

If Mr. Scribner has heard this rumor please show him this letter. So much for Mr. Liveright + Co.

Your letters are catching up with me. Curtis in <u>Town + Country</u> + Van Vetchten in <u>The Nation</u> pleased me.[1] The personal letters: Cabell, Wilson, Van Wyke Brooks etc. have been the best of all. Among people over here Ernest Hemminway + Gertrude Stien are quite entheusiastic. Except for Rascoe it has been, critically only a clean sweep—and his little tribute is a result of our having snubbed his quite common and cheaply promiscuous wife.

Ring's book has been a terrible disappointment to everyone here. He didn't even bother to cut out the connecting tags at the end of his travel articles and each of the five plays contain the same joke about "his mother—afterwards his wife." I shouldn't press him about his new collection, if I were you, because if you just took the first nine stories he writes, they couldn't be up to the others <u>and you know how reviewers are quick to turn on anyone in whom they have believed and who now disappoints them</u>. Of course I've only read <u>Haircut</u> and I may be wrong. I do want him to believe in his work + not have any blows to take away his confidence. The reviews I have seen of <u>What of It?</u> were sorry imitations of Seldes stuff and all of them went out of their way to stab Seldes in the back. God, cheap reviewers are low swine—but one must live.

As I write word has just come by cable that Brady has made an offer[2] for the dramatic rights of <u>Gatsby</u>, with Owen Davis, king of proffessional play doctors, to do the dramatization. I am, needless to say, accepting, but please keep it confidential until the actual contract is signed.

As you know, despite my admiration for <u>Through the Wheat</u>, I haven't an enormous faith in Tom Boyd either as a personality or an artist—as I have, say, in E. E. Cummings and Hemminway. His ignorance, his presumptious intolerance and his careless grossness which he cultivates for vitality as a man might nurse along a dandelion with the hope that it would turn out to be an onion, have always annoyed me. Like Rascoe he has never been known to refuse an invitation from his social superiors—or to fail to pan them with all the venom of a James-Oliver-Curwood[3]-He-Man when no invitations were forthcoming.

All this is preparatory to saying that his new book sounds utterly lowsy—Shiela Kaye-Smith[4] has used the stuff about the farmer having girls instead of boys and being broken up about it. The characters you mention have every one, become stock-props in the last ten years—"Christy, the quaint old hired man" after a season in such stuff as Owen Davis' <u>Ice Bound</u> must be almost ready for the burlesque circuit.

[1] Reviews of *The Great Gatsby* by William Curtis and Carl Van Vechten.
[2] Broadway impresario William A. Brady and playwright Owen Davis; the play version of *The Great Gatsby* opened on Broadway on February 2, 1926, and ran for 112 performances.
[3] James Oliver Curwood, author of western adventure fiction.
[4] British novelist.

History of the Simple Inarticulate Farmer and his Hired Man Christy

(Both guaranteed to be utterly full of the Feel of the Soil)

1st Period

1855— English Peasant discovered by Geo. Elliot in <u>Mill on the Floss,</u>
<u>Silas Marner</u> ect.

1888—Given intellectual interpretation by Hardy in <u>Jude</u> and <u>Tess</u>

1890—Found in France by Zola in <u>Germinal</u>

1900—Crowds of Scandanavians, Hamsun, Bojer[1] ect, tear him bodily
from the Russian, and after a peep at Hardy, Hamlin Garland[2]
finds him in the middle west.

———————

Most of that, however, was literature. It was something pulled
by the individual out of life and only partly with the aid of
models in other literatures.

2nd Period

1914— Shiela Kaye-Smith frankly imitates Hardy, produces two good
books + then begins to imitate herself.

1915—Brett Young[3] discovers him in the coal country

1916—Robert Frost discovers him in New England

1917—Sherwood Anderson discovers him in Ohio

1918—Willa Cather turns him Swede

1920—Eugene O'Niell puts him on the boards in <u>Different</u> + <u>Beyond</u>
<u>Horizon</u>

1922—Ruth Suckow <u>gets</u> in before the door closes
These people were all good second raters (except Anderson)
Each of them brought something to the business—but they
exhausted the ground, the type was set. All was over.

———————

3rd Period

The Cheapskates discover him—Bad critics and novelists ect.

1923   Homer Croy[4] writes <u>West of the Water Tower</u>

1924   Edna Ferber turns from her flip jewish saleswoman for a strong

[1]Knut Hamsun and Johan Bojer, Norwegian novelists.
[2]American naturalistic writer.
[3]Francis Brett Young, British novelist.
[4]Midwestern novelist and humorist.

silent earthy carrot grower and—the Great Soul of Charley Towne[1] thrills to her passionately. Real and Earthy Struggle

1924 Ice Bound[2] by the author of <u>Nellie the Beautiful Cloak Model</u> wins Pulitzer Prize
The Able Mcgloughlins[3] wins $10,000 prize + is forgotten the following wk.

1925 <u>The Apple of the Eye</u> pronounced a masterpiece

<u>1926</u>—TOM, BOYD, WRITES, NOVEL, ABOUT, IN-ARTICULATE, FARMER WHO, IS, CLOSE, TO SOIL, AND, HIS, HIRED, MAN CHRISTY! "STRONG! VITAL! REAL!"

As a matter of fact the American peasant as "real" material scarcely exists. He is scarcely 10% of the population, isn't bound to the soil at all as the English + Russian peasants were—and, if has any sensitivity whatsoever (except a most sentimental conception of himself, which our writers persistently shut their eyes to) he is in the towns before he's twenty. Either Lewis, Lardner and myself have been badly fooled, or else using him as typical American material is simply <u>a stubborn seeking for the static in a world that for almost a hundred years has simply not been static</u>. Isn't it a 4th rate imagination that can find only that old property farmer in all this amazing time and land? And anything that ten people a year can do well enough to pass muster has become so easy that it isn't worth the doing.

I can not disassociate a man from his work.—That this Wescott (who is an effeminate Oxford fairy) and Tom Boyd and Burton Rascoe (whose real ambition is to lock themselves into a stinking little appartment and screw each others' wives) are going to tell us mere superficial "craftsmen" like Hergeshiemer, Wharton, Tarkington and me about the Great Beautiful Appreciation they have of the Great Beautiful life of the Manure Widder—rather turns my stomach. The real people like Gertrude Stien (with whom I've talked) and Conrad (see his essay on James) have a respect for people whose materials may not touch theirs <u>at a single point</u>. But the fourth rate + highly derivative people like Tom are loud in their outcry against any subject matter that doesn't come out of the old, old bag which their betters have used and thrown away.

For example there is an impression among the thoughtless (including Tom) that Sherwood Anderson is a man of profound ideas who is "handicapped by his inarticulateness". As a matter of fact Anderson is a man of practically no ideas—but he is one of the very best and finest writers in the

---

[1] Ferber's *So Big* won the 1925 Pulitzer Prize for fiction; Charles H. Towne was a journalist and editor.

[2] *Icebound*, a play by Owen Davis, won the 1923 Pulitzer Prize for drama.

[3] *The Able McLaughlins*, by Margaret Wilson, won the 1924 Pulitzer Prize for fiction.

English language today. God, he can write! Tom could never get such rythms in his life as there are on the pages of Winesburg, Ohio—. Simple! The words on the lips of critics makes me hilarious: Anderson's style is about as simple as an engine room full of dynamoes. But Tom flatters himself that he can sit down for five months and by dressing up a few heart throbs in overalls produce literature.

It amazes me, Max, to see you with your discernment and your fine intelligence, fall for that whole complicated fake. Your chief critical flaw is to confuse mere earnestness with artistic sincerity. On two of Ring's jackets have been statements that he never wrote a dishonest word (maybe it's one jacket). But Ring and many of the very greatest artists have written thousands of words in plays, poems and novels which weren't even faintly sincere or ernest and were yet artisticly sincere. The latter term is not a synonym for plodding ernestness. Zola did not say the last word about literature; nor the first.

I append all the data on my fall book, and in closing I apologize for seeming impassioned about Tom and his work when niether the man or what he writes has ever been personally inimical to me. He is simply the scapegoat for the mood Rascoe has put me in and, tho I mean every word of it, I probably wouldn't have wasted all this paper on a book that won't sell + will be dead in a month + an imitative school that will be dead by its own weight in a year or so, if the news about Liveright hadn't come on top of the Rascoe review and ruined my disposition. Good luck to Drummond.[1] I'm sure one or two critics will mistake it for profound stuff— maybe even Mencken who has a weakness in that direction. But I think you should look closer.

With best wishes as always, Max,

Your Friend

DATA ON NEW FITZGERALD BOOK.

Title

ALL THE SAD YOUNG MEN

(9 short stories)

Print list of previous books as before with addition of this title under "Stories". Binding uniform with others.

Jacket plain (,as you suggest,) with text instead of picture

Dedication: To Ring and Ellis Lardner

The Stories (now under revision) will reach you by July 15th. No proofs need be sent over here.

It will be fully up to the other collections and will contain only one of those Post stories that people were so snooty about. (You have read only one

---

[1] *Samuel Drummond* (1925), by Boyd.

of the stories ("Absolution")—all the others were so good that I had difficulty in selling them, except two.

They are, in approximate order to be used in book:

1. The Rich Boy (Just finished. Serious story and very
   good)   13,000 wds.

2. Absolution (From Mercury)   6,500 "

3. Winter Dreams (A sort of 1st draft of the Gatsby
   idea from Metropolitan 1923)   9,000 "

4. Rags Martin-Jones and the Pr-nce of Wales
   (Fantastic Jazz, so good that Lorimer + Long
   refused it. From McCalls)   5,000 "

5. The Baby Party (From Hearsts. A fine story)   5,000 "

6. Dice, Brass Knuckles and Guitar (From Hearsts.
   Exuberant Jazz in my early manner)   8,000 "

7. The Sensible Thing (Story about Zelda + me.
   All true. From Liberty)   5,000 "

8. Hot + Cold Blood (good story, from Hearsts)   6,000 "

9. Gretchen's Forty Winks (from Post. Farrar,
   Christian Gauss and Jesse Williams[1] thought
   it my best. It isn't.)   7,000 "

Total – about   – – – – – – – – – – – – – – –   64,500

(And possibly one other short one)

This title is because seven stories deal with young men of my generation in rather unhappy moods. The ones to mention on the outside wrap are the 1st five or the 1st three stories.

————

Rather not use advertising appropriation in Times—people who read Times Book Review won't be interested in me. Recommend Mercury, the F. P. A. page of the World, Literary Review and Fanny Bucher[2] page of Chicago Tribune.

No blurbs in ad. as I think the blurb doesn't help any more. Suggestion.

> Charles Scribners Sons
> Announce a new book of short stories
> by
> F. Scott Fitzgerald

[1] Jesse Lynch Williams, playwright and short-story writer.
[2] Butcher, book reviewer for the *Chicago Tribune*.

Advertising Notes

Suggested line for jacket: "Show transition from his early exuberant stories of youth which created a new type of American girl and the later and more serious mood which produced <u>The Great Gatsby</u> and marked him as one of the half dozen masters of English prose now writing in America. . . . What other writer has shown such unexpected developments, such versatility, changes of pace"

ect – ect – ect – I think that, toned down as you see fit, is the general line. Don't say "Fitzgerald has done it!" + then in the next sentence that I am an artist. People who are interested in artists aren't interested in people who have "done it." Both are O.K. but don't belong in the same ad. This is an author's quibble. All authors have one quibble.

However, you have always done well by me (Except for Black's[1] memorable excretion in the <u>Allumni Weekly</u>: do you remember "Make it a Fitzgerald Christmas!") and I leave it to you. If 100,000 copies are not sold I shall shift to Mitchell Kennerley.[2]

By the way what has become of Black? I hear he has written a very original and profound novel. It is said to be about an inarticulate farmer and his struggles with the "soil" and his sexual waverings between his inarticulate wife and an inarticulate sheep. He finally chooses his old pioneering grandmother as the most inarticulate of all but finds her in bed with none other than our old friend THE HIRED MAN CHRISTY!

CHRISTY HAD DONE IT!

[In 1962 Fitzgerald's famous letter to Perkins was sold at auction at Chrystie's (not old man Christy's) for £7000.][3]

TO: *Van Wyck Brooks*   ALS, 1 p. Bruccoli
Postmarked June 13, 1925

Paris, France

Dear Brooks:

I read the James book,[4] so did Zelda + Ernest Hemminway + everyone I've been able to lend it to and I think it rises high above either Bunny's carping or Seldes tag on it. I like it even better than the Mark Twain.[5] It is exquisitely done + entirely facinating

One reason it is of particular interest to us over here is obvious. In my own case I have no such delicate doubts—nor does anyone need to have

---

[1] John Black of the advertising department at Scribners.
[2] Publisher known for his parsimonious dealings with authors.
[3] Fitzgerald's marginal note.
[4] *The Pilgrimage of Henry James* (1925).
[5] *The Ordeal of Mark Twain* (1920).

them now since the American scene has become so complicated + ramified but the question of freshening material always exists. I shall come back after one more novel.

Why didn't you touch more on James impotence (physical) and its influence? I think if hadn't had at least one poignant emotional love affair with an American girl on American soil he might have lived there twice as long, tried twice as hard, had the picaresque past of Huck Finn + yet never struck roots. Novelists like he (him) + in a sense (to descend a good bit) me, have to have love as a main concern since our interest lies outside the economic struggle or the life of violence, as conditioned to some extent by our lives from 16–21.

However this is just shooting in the dark at a target on which you have expended your fine talent in full daylight. It was a really thrilling pleasure for a writer to read. Thanking you for writing me about my book so kindly + for sending me yours.

Scott Fitzgerald

TO: *Gilbert Seldes*   *ALS, 1 p. Glenn Horowitz*
June–July 1925

14 Rue de Tilsitt
Paris, France

Dear Gilbert:

Thank you a thousand times for your entheusiasm about Gatsby. I believe I'd rather stir your discriminating entheusiasm than anyone's in America, (did I tell you this before?), and to be really believed-in again, to feel "exciting", is tremendously satisfactory. My new novel may be my last for ten years or so—that is if it sells no better than <u>Gatsby</u> (which has only gone a little over 20,000 copies) for I may go to Hollywood + try to learn the moving picture business from the bottom up.

We leave for Antibes on August 4th—Zelda and I in our car (the same one) and nurse + baby by train. There we shall spend one month growing brown and healthy—then return here for the fall. Beyond January our plans are vague Nice followed by Oxford or Cambridge for the summer perhaps. Don Stuart has been here—he seemed horribly pretentious to me and more than usually wrong—in fact it was a shock to see the change in him. I see Hemminway a great deal and before he left, something of Gerald—both of them[1] are thoroughly charming.

If you + Amanda come over in the Spring we may have a villa big enough for you to visit us in Nice. God, I'm wild for the Rivierra. Love from us to you both

Scott

[1]Gerald and Sara Murphy.

TO: *Maxwell Perkins*   ALS, 3 pp. *Princeton University*
c. July 8, 1925

14 Rue de Tilsitt
Paris, France

Dear Max:

This is another one of those letters with a thousand details in them, so I'll number the details + thus feel I'm getting them out of the way.

(1.) Will you have an account (bi-yearly statement) sent me as soon as you can. I don't know how much I owe you but it must be between 3 and 4 thousand dollars. I want to see how much chance <u>All The Sad Young Men</u> has of making up this difference. Thanks many times for the 700.00. It will enable me to go ahead next month with <u>Our Type</u>[1] which is getting shaped up both in paper and in my head. I'd rather not tell about it just yet.

② Is Gatsby to be published in England. I'm awfully anxious to have it published there. If Collins won't have it can't you try Jonathan Cape? Do let me know about this.

(3) Will you tell me the figures on Ring's books? Also on <u>Through the Wheat</u>. I re-read the latter the other day + think its marvellous. Together with the Enormous Room[2] and, I think, Gatsby, its much the best thing that has come out of American fiction since the war. I exclude Anderson because since reading <u>Three Lives</u> and his silly autobiography my feeling about him has entirely changed. He is a short story writer only.

④ I spent $48.00 having a sketch of me done by Ivan Opfer. It was lousy and he says he'll try another. If its no good I'll send a photo. The stories for the book leave here day after tomorrow.

⑤ I think the number of Americans in Europe has hurt the book market. <u>Gatsby</u> is the last principle book of mine that I want to publish in the spring. I believe that from now on fall will be much the best season.

⑥.) I'm sorry about that outburst at Tom. But I am among those who suffer from the preoccupation of literary America with the drab as subject matter. Seldes points this out in a great review of <u>Gatsby</u> for the <u>London Criterion</u>.[3] Also he says "Fitzgerald has certainly the best chance at present of becoming our finest artist in fiction". Quite a bit from Gilbert who only likes Ring, Edith Wharton Joyce and Charlie Chaplin. Please get Myer to put it on the cover of the new book and delete the man who says I "deserve the huzza's of those who want to further a worthy American Literature." Perhaps I deserve their huzzas but I'd rather they'd express their appreciation in some less boisterous way.

⑦.) I'm sending back the questionairre.

⑧ I suppose that by now Gatsby is over 18,000. I hope to God it reaches 20,000. It sounds so much better. Shane Leslie thought it was fine.

---

[1] Working title for novel in progress.
[2] 1922 novel by e. e. cummings.
[3] *New Criterion* (January 1926).

No news, Max. I was drinking hard in May but for the last month I've been working like a dog. I still think Count Orget's Ball by Radiguet would sell like wildfire. If I had the time I'd translate it myself.

Scott

TO: *Maxwell Perkins*   *ALS, 1 p. Princeton University*
c. *July 10, 1925*

14 Rue de Tilsitt.
Paris, France

Dear Max:

(1.) I'm afraid in sending the book I forgot the dedication, which should read

TO RING AND ELLIS LARDNER

will you see to this?

(2.) I've asked The Red Book to let you know the first possible date on "The Rich Boy"

(3.) I'm terribly sorry about the whooping cough but I'll have to admit it did give me a laugh.

(4.) Max, it amuses me when praise comes in on the "structure" of the book—because it was you who fixed up the structure, not me. And don't think I'm not grateful for all that sane and helpful advice about it.

(5) The novel has begun. I'd rather tell you nothing about it quite yet. No news. We had a great time in Antibes and got very brown + healthy. In case you don't place it its the penninsula between Cannes + Nice on the Rivierra where Napoeleon landed on his return from Elba.

As Ever
Scott.

TO: *John Peale Bishop*   *ALS, 1 p. Princeton University*
c. *August 9, 1925*

14 Rue de Tilsitt
Paris, France

Dear John:

Thank you for your most pleasant, full, discerning and helpful letter about The Great Gatsby. It is about the only critisism that the book has had which has been intelligable, save a letter from Mrs. Wharton.[1] I shall duly ponder, or rather I have pondered, what you say about accuracy—I'm afraid I haven't quite reached the ruthless artistry which would let me cut out an

---

[1] Edith Wharton's letter was published in *The Crack-Up* (1945).

exquisite bit that had no place in the context. I can cut out the almost exquisite, the adequate, even the brilliant—but a true accuracy is, as you say, still in the offing. Also you are right about Gatsby being blurred and patchy. I never at any one time saw him clear myself—for he started as one man I knew and then changed into myself—the amalgam was never complete in my mind.

Your novel sounds facinating and I'm crazy to see it. I am beginning a new novel next month on the Rivierra. I understand that MacLiesh[1] is there, among other people (at Antibes where we are going). Paris has been a madhouse this spring and, as you can imagine, we were in the thick of it. I don't know when we're coming back—maybe never. We'll be here till Jan. (except for a month in Antibes, and then we go Nice for the Spring, with Oxford for next summer. Love to Margaret and many thanks for the kind letter.

Scott

TO: John Peale Bishop   *CC, 1 p. Princeton University*
Postmarked September 21, 1925   *Paris*

Dear Sir:

The enclosed explains itself. Meanwhile I went to Antibes and liked Archie Macliesh enormously. Also his poem, though it seems strange to like anything so outrageously derivative. T. S. of P. was an original in comparison.

I'm crazy to see your novel. I'm starting a new one myself. There was no one at Antibes this summer except me, Zelda, the Valentino, the Murphy's, Mistinguet, Rex Ingram, Dos Passos, Alice Terry, the Mclieshes, Charlie Bracket, Maude Kahn, Esther Murphy, Marguerite Namara, E. Phillips Openhiem, Mannes the violinist, Floyd Dell, Max and Chrystal Eastman, ex-Premier Orlando, Etienne de Beaumont—just a real place to rough it, an escape from all the world. But we had a great time. I don't know when we're coming home—

The Hemmingways are coming to dinner so I close with best wishes.

Scott

TO: Deems Taylor[2]   *ALS, 1 p. Collection of Marcia and*
September–October 1925   *Maurice Neville*

14 Rue de Tilsitt, Paris, France

Dear Deems:

Your letter followed me all around Europe with that elusive circularity peculiar to correspondence. I was deeply touched by your entheusiasm by

---

[1] Poet Archibald MacLeish.
[2] Composer and critic.

your writing to tell me of it. At first, you know, I thought Gatsby must be a terrible failure—nothing came in but a snotty (and withal ungrammatical) paragraph by Ruth Hale, another paragraph in the World headed "Fitzgerald's latest is a dud" and some faint praise from, God help us, The Times! It took things like your letter and Seldes' and Menckens' cordial reviews to make me sit up and take nourishment. I was for ending it all at Hollywood in the movies. Thank you more than I can say both for the thought and, especially, the act.

Sincerely
F Scott Fitzgerald

TO: *Maxwell Perkins*   *ALS, 2 pp. Princeton University*
c. October 20, 1925

14 Rue de Tilsitt

Dear Max:

Thanks for your letters of 6th, 7th, + 12th. I'm delighted that you like the 1st four stories. The reason I want to get proof on The Rich Boy is that the original of the hero wants something changed—something that would identify him.

I'm relieved that Gatsby is coming out this Spring in England—your first letter implied the Fall of 1927! But I'm disappointed that its only reached 19,640 copies. I hoped that it had reached nearer 25,000.

I was interested in the figures on Tom Boyd + Ring—needless to say I won't mention them, but I thought Through the Wheat had sold much more. Considering the success of "What Price Glory?"[1] I don't understand it. And Points of Honor[2] only 1545! I'm astonished, and appalled. I see the New Yorker and The Nation (or New Republic) mention Samuel Drummond favorably.

There is no news. The novel progresses slowly + carefully with much destroying + revision. If you hear anything about the Gatsby dramatization—cast, date, ect. do let me know.

I wired you yesterday for $100.00 which brings me up to $3171.66 again—depressing thought! Will I ever be square. The short stories probably won't sell 5,000

Somewhat Mournfully
Scott

P.S. Did the Gatsby syndication with Bell Syndicate fall through?

P.S. A year + ½ ago Knopf published a book (novel) by Ruth Suckow

---

[1] 1924 play by Laurence Stallings and Maxwell Anderson.
[2] 1925 collection of stories by Boyd.

In a letter to Fitzgerald, Eliot declared that The Great Gatsby *was "the first step American fiction has taken since Henry James." Eliot's letter was published in* The Crack-Up *(1945).*

called <u>Country People</u>. So he didn't risk her short stories. It didn't go. But Mencken + I + many others think her stories wonderful. They're in the Smart Set (years 1921, 1922, 1923) and the American Mercury (1924, 1925), just enough to make about an 80,000 word book. A great press assured— she could be the American Katherine Mansfield.[1] This fine book The Perrenial Bachelor by Miss Parrish[2] derives from her I think. (She's the best woman writer in American under 50)

Why not approach her? Knopf seems to be letting her ride. You could probably get the next novel if she isn't signed up + you tried the stories first. I think this is an A.1. tip.

Scott

TO: *Marya Mannes*[3]   *ALS, 3 pp. Collection of Marcia*
Postmarked October 21, 1925   *and Maurice Neville*

14 Rue de Tilsitt
Paris, France

Dear Marya:

Thank you for writing me about <u>Gatsby</u>—I especially appreciate your letter because women, and even intelligent women, haven't generally cared much for it. They do not like women to be presented as <u>emotionally</u> passive—as a matter of fact I think most women are, that their minds are taken up with a sort of second rate and inessential bookkeeping which their apologists call "practicallity"—like the French they are centime-savers in the business of magic. (You see I am a Schopenhaurian, not a Shavian).

You are thrilled by New York—I doubt you will be after five more years when you are more fully nourished from within. I carry the place around the world in my heart but sometimes I try to shake it off in my dreams. America's greatest promise is that something is going to happen, and after awhile you get tired of waiting because nothing happens to people except that they grow old and nothing happens to American art because America is the story of the moon that never rose. Nor does the "minute itself" ever come in life either, the minute not of unrest + hope but of a glowing peace—such as when the moon rose that night on Gerald + Sara's garden + you said you were happy to be there. No one ever makes things in America with that vast, magnificent, cynical disillusion with which Gerald + Sara make things like their parties.

(They were here, last week, + we spent six or seven happy days together.)

My new novel is marvellous. I'm in the first chapter. You may recognize certain things and people in it.

[1] British short-story writer.

[2] *The Perennial Bachelor* (1925), by Anne Parrish.

[3] Mannes, later a journalist, was the daughter of conductor and violinist David Mannes, whom Fitzgerald met on the Riviera.

The young people in America are brilliant with 2nd hand sophistication inherited from their betters of the war generation who to some extent worked things out for themselves. They are brave, shallow, cynical, impatient, turbulent and empty. I like them not. The "fresh, strong river of America,"! My God, Marya, where are your eyes—Or are they too fresh and strong to see anything but their own color + contour in the glass. America is so decadent that its brilliant children are damned almost before they are born—Can you name a single American artist except James + Whisler (who lived in England) who didn't die of drink? If it is fresh + strong to be unable to endure or tolerate things-as-they-are, to shutor eyes or to distort and lie—then you're right Marya Mannes and no one has ever so misinterpeted the flowers of civilization, the Greek + Gallic idea, as

Your Sincere Admirer

F Scott Fitzgerald

TO: *Ernest Hemingway*   ALS, *2 pp. John F. Kennedy Library*
Postmarked November 30, 1925

Dear Ernest: I was quite ashamed of the other morning. Not only in disturbing Hadly,[1] but in foistering that "Juda Lincoln" alias George Morgenthau apon you. However it is only fair to say that the deplorable man who entered your appartment Sat. morning <u>was not</u> me but a man named Johnston who has often been mistaken for me.

Zelda, evidences to the contrary, was not suffering from lack of care but from a nervous hysteria which is only releived by a doctor bearing morphine. We both went to Bellau Wood next day to recuperate.

For some reason I told you a silly lie—or rather an exageration, silly because the truth itself was enough to make me sufficiently jubilant. The Sat. Eve. Post. raised me to $2750.00 and not $3000. which is a jump of $750. in one month. It was probably in my mind that I could now get $3000. from the smaller magazines. The <u>Post</u> merely met the Hearst offer, but that is something they seldom do.

What garbled versions of the Mcalmon episode or the English orgy we lately participated in, I told you, I don't know. It is true that I saved Mcalmon[2] from a beating he probably deserved and that we went on some wild parties in London with a certain Marchioness of Milford Haven whom we first met with Telulah Bankhead. She was about half royalty, I think. Anyhow she was very nice—anything else I may have added about the relations between the Fitzgeralds and the house of Windsor is pure fiction.

---

[1]Hadley Richardson Hemingway, Hemingway's first wife.

[2]Robert McAlmon, American writer and publisher in Paris. He had spread gossip that Fitzgerald and Hemingway were homosexuals.

I'm crazy to read the comic novel.[1] Are you going to the Mclieshe's Tuesday? I hope Hadly is well now. Please believe that we send our

Best Wishes to

Ernest M. Hemminway

TO: *Maxwell Perkins*   ALS, *3 pp. Princeton University*
c. *December 27, 1925*

14 Rue de Tilsitt

Paris, France

Dear Max:

I write to you from the depths of one of my unholy depressions. The book is wonderful—I honestly think that when its published I shall be the best American novelist (which isn't saying a lot) but the end seems far away. When its finished I'm coming home for awhile anyhow though the thought revolts me as much as the thought of remaining in France. I wish I were twenty-two again with only my dramatic and feverishly enjoyed miseries. You remember I used to say I wanted to die at thirty—well, I'm now twenty-nine and the prospect is still welcome. My work is the only thing that makes me happy—except to be a little tight—and for those two indulgences I pay a big price in mental and physical hangovers.

I thank you for your newsy letter—by the way we got and hugely enjoyed Louise's beautiful book[2] and I wrote and thanked her care of Scribners. I liked too your idea about Representative Men[3] but it seems remote to me. Let me know if it comes to something and I'll contribute.

That was a sweet slam from Ellen Mackey. Is it true that she and Irving Berlin have signed up to play a permanent engagement in Abie's Irish Rose?[4]

I hope the short stories sell seven or eight thousand or so. Is Gatsby dead? You don't mention it. Has it reached 25,000? I hardly dare to hope so. Also I deduce from your silence that Tom Boyd's book was a flop. If so I hope he isn't in financial difficulties. Also I gather from reviews that the penciled frown[5] came a croper. I wish Liveright would lose faith in Ernest. Through the whole year only the following American novels have seemed worth a damn to me.

The Spring Flight[6]

---

[1] *The Torrents of Spring* (Scribners, 1926).

[2] *The Knave of Hearts* (1925), by Louise Saunders, Mrs. Maxwell Perkins.

[3] A burlesque biographical dictionary proposed by Perkins.

[4] The marriage of society writer Ellen Mackay and Irving Berlin was a sensation; *Abie's Irish Rose* was a sentimental play by Anne Nichols about the marriage of an Irish Catholic girl to a Jew.

[5] *The Penciled Frown* (1926), by James Gray.

[6] By Lee J. Smits (1925).

Perrenial Bachelor

In Our Time

The Great Gatsby

I thought the books by <u>Lewis</u>, <u>Van Vechten</u>, <u>Edith Wharton</u>, <u>Floyd Dell</u>, <u>Tom Boyd</u> and <u>Sherwood Anderson</u> were just <u>lowsy</u>![1]

And the ones by <u>Willa Cather</u> and <u>Cyril Hume</u> almost as bad.[2]

<u>Dos Passos</u> + <u>Ruth Suckow</u> I havn't yet read.[3]

The press Anderson got on <u>Dark Laughter</u> filled me with a much brighter shade of hilarity. You notice it wasn't from those of us who waited for the Winesburg stories one by one in the <u>Little Review</u> but by Harry Hansen, Stallings ect + the other boys who find a new genius once a week and at all cost follow the fashions.

Its good you didn't take my advice about looking up Gertrude Stien's new book (The Making of Americans). Its bigger than Ullyses and only the first parts, the parts published in the Transatlantic are intelligable at all. Its published privately here.

The best English books of the fall are <u>The Sailor's Return</u> by David Garnett and <u>No More Parades</u> by Ford Maddox Ford (a sequeal to <u>Some do Not</u>)

(Speaking of Gertrude Stien I hope you are keeping my precious <u>Three Lives</u> safe for me. Ring's book sounds good. Send me a copy—also the wrap of mine.

I told Ober to send you half a dozen seats for the <u>Gatsby</u> opening to distribute to the Scribners as you think best. If you want more phone him.

No, Zelda's not entirely well yet. We're going south next month to Salies-les–Bains to see if we can cure her there. <u>So from the time of recieving this letter adress all mail to me care of</u>

<u>The Guaranty Trust Co.</u>
<u>1 Rue des Italiens</u>
<u>Paris, France</u>

Why was Jack Wheeler kicked out of Liberty?

My novel should be finished next fall.

Tell me all the gossip that isn't in <u>The New Yorker</u> or the <u>World</u>—isn't there any regular dirt?

I called on <u>Chatto and Windus</u> in London last month + had a nice talk with Swinnerton,[4] their reader (It was he, it seems, who was strong for the book. Saw Leslie also + went on some very high tone parties with Mount-

---

[1]Lewis's *Arrowsmith*, Van Vechten's *Firecrackers*, Wharton's *The Mother's Recompense*, Dell's *This Mad Ideal*, Boyd's *Points of Honor*, and Anderson's *Dark Laughter*.

[2]Cather's *The Professor's House* and Hume's *Cruel Fellowship*.

[3]Dos Passos's *Manhattan Transfer* and Suckow's *The Odyssey of a Nice Girl*.

[4]Frank Swinnerton, British novelist who was an editor at Chatto & Windus.

battens and all that sort of thing. Very impressed, but not very, as I furnished most of the amusement myself. <u>Please write</u>! Best to Louise.

<u>Your Friend</u>

Scott Fitz—

Has story book had good advance sale? Or hasn't it been the rounds yet. Whats its date?

TO: *Maxwell Perkins*   *ALS, 3 pp. Princeton University*
c. December 30, 1925   *Paris*

14 Rue de Tilsitt

[New adress

Guaranty Trust Co.

1 Rue des Italiennes]

Dear Max:

(1.) To begin with many thanks for all deposits, to you and to the Scribners in general. I have no idea now how I stand with you. To set me straight will you send me my account <u>now</u> instead of waiting till February 1<u>st</u>. It must be huge, and I'm miserable about it. The more I get for my tra<u>sh</u> the less I can bring myself to write. However this year is going to be different.

②. Hemmingways book (not his novel) is a 28,000 word satire on Sherwood Anderson and his imitators called The <u>Torrents of Spring</u>. I loved it, but believe it wouldn't be popular, ɪ Liveright have refused it—<u>they are backing Anderson</u> and the book is almost a vicious parody on him. You see I agree with Ernest that Anderson's last two books have let everybody down who believed in him—I think they're cheap, faked, obscurantic and awful. Hemmingway thinks, but isn't yet sure to my satisfaction, that their refusal sets him free from his three book (letter) agreement with them. In that case I think he'll give you his novel (on condition you'll publish satire first—probable sale 1000 copies) which he is now revising in Austria. Harcourt has just written Louie Bromfield[1] that to get the novel they'll publish satire, sight unseen (utterly confidential) and Knopf is after him via Aspinwall Bradley.[2]

He and I are very thick + he's marking time until he finds out how much he's bound to Liveright. If he's free I'm almost sure I can get satire to you first + then if you see your way clear you can contract for the novel <u>tout ensemble</u>. He's anxious too to get a foothold in your magazine—one story I've sent you—the other, to my horror he'd given for about $40 to an "arty" publication called <u>This Quarter</u>, over here.

---

[1] Alfred Harcourt, a founder of the Harcourt, Brace publishing company; novelist Louis Bromfield, who lived in France.

[2] William Aspinwall Bradley, American literary agent in Paris.

He's <u>dead set</u> on having the satire published first. His idea has always been to come to you + his only hesitation has been that Harcourt might be less conservative in regard to certain somewhat broad scenes. His adress is:

Herr Ernest Hemmingway
Hotel Taube   Don't even tell him I've discussed
Schrunns   his Liveright + Harcourt relations
Vorarlburg   with you
Austria

As soon as he has definate dope I'll pass it on to you I wanted a strong wire to show you were as interested, and more, than Harcourt. Did you know your letter just missed by two weeks getting <u>In Our Time</u>. It had no sale of course but I think the novel may be something extraordinary—Tom Boyd and E. E. Cummings + Biggs combined.

Wasn't Dos Passos' book[1] astonishingly good. I'm very fond of him but I had lost faith in his work.

(3.) Tell me all about my play.

(4.) I can't wait to see the book your sending me. Zelda says it might be <u>Gatsby</u> but I don't think so.

(5) Poor Eleanor Wylie! Poor Bill Benet![2] Poor everybody!

(6) My novel is wonderful.

(7) The translation of Gatsby sounds wonderful.

⑧ Will you ask the bookstore to send The Beautiful and Damned to <u>M. Victor Llona, 106 Rue de La Tour, Paris</u> Thanks. Charge to my account, of course.

⑨ I thought Dunns[3] remark about Biggs book was wonderful. Tell me about it. Also about Tom Boyd's work and Ring's. You never do.

As Ever
Scott

TO: Blanche Knopf[4] ALS, 2 pp. Harry Ransom Humanities Research Center,
January 1926? *University of Texas, Austin*

c/o Guaranty Trust
1 Rue des Italiennes

Dear Blanche:
I hate like hell to have to decline all those invitations but as this is three days too late I've no choice. As "cocktail", so I gather, has become a verb,

[1] *Manhattan Transfer.*
[2] Poet and novelist Elinor Wylie had separated from her husband, critic William Rose Benét.
[3] Charles Dunn, editor at Scribners.
[4] Wife of Alfred A. Knopf and vice president of the Knopf publishing firm.

it ought to be be conjugated at least once, so here goes

Present	I cocktail	We cocktail
	Thou cocktail	You cocktail
	It cocktails	They cocktail
Imperfect	I was cocktailing	
Perfect	I cocktailed	

(past definate)

Pastperfect	I have cocktailed
Conditional	I might have cocktailed
Pluperfect	I had cocktailed
Subjunctive	I would have cocktailed
Voluntary Sub.	I should have cocktailed
Preterite	I did cocktail
Imperative	Cocktail!
Interrogtive	Cocktailest thou? (Dos't Cocktail?)
	(or Wilt Cocktail?)
Subjunctive Conditional	I would have had to have cocktailed
Conditional Subjunctive	I might have had to have cocktailed
Participle	Cocktailing

I find this getting dull, and would much rather talk to you, about turbans. Please come back to Paris, as I would be glad to set you up in the publishing business here. A new addition of <u>The Memoirs of Fanny Hill</u>[1] is need at once and I'm collecting material

So be sure to come back in early August. We are moving around impulsively so I'm giving the bank as adress, but I'm sure to be here in Paris

Undying Devotion
from
Scott Fitzg

TO: Harold Ober　　　　　　　　　　　*ALS, 2 pp. Lilly Library*
Received February 4, 1926

c/o Guaranty Trust Co.
1 Rue des Italiens

Dear Ober:

We have come to a lost little village called Salies-de-Béarn in the Pyrenes where my wife is to take a special treatment of baths for eleven months for an illness that has run now for almost a year.[2] Here they have the strongest salt springs in the world—and out of season nothing much else—we are two of seven guests in the only open hotel.

---

[1] Eighteenth-century pornographic novel by John Cleland.
[2] Zelda Fitzgerald had colitis.

We'll be here until March 1st but you'd better adress any letters to me at Paris—that's just as quick for letters. Cables about the play had better come to Fitzgerald, Bellevue

Salies-de-Bearn, France.

One Word

About the story <u>The Dance</u>, the first detective story I've ever tried, I'm afraid its no good—(if it ever reaches you—I'm beginning to think that nothing I send ever does. That one I had registered. Did both copies of <u>Adolescent Marrige</u> come—or either) to continue—please don't offer the dance to the <u>Post</u> or <u>Red Book</u>. Why not <u>College Humor</u> for $1500. or <u>Women's Home Companion</u> (?). Tell me what you think?

I must owe you thousands—three at least—maybe more. I am forever under obligations to you for your kindness. From now till March 1st will be a steady stream of $2500. stories—five more of them. And I hope by then the play will begin to yield something on the side. I honestly think I cause you more trouble and bring you less business than any of your clients. How you tolerate it I don't know—but thank God you do. And 1926 is going to be a different story.

Did I tell you McCalls wrote again asking me about the novel. Will you talk to them? Its begun but I'm putting it aside for a month or so like I did <u>Gatsby</u> and it won't be done before the end of the year.

Someone told me Mr. Reynolds had been sick. Is that so? I hope not.

Thank you for the thousandth thousand for the thousandth time.

Scott Fitzg—

Story sent yesterday which was to have been 4th of series but was so much revised that I didn't send it from Paris after all. Have sent in all <u>seven</u> manuscripts of <u>four</u> different stories.

TO: Maxwell Perkins   ALS, 3 pp. *Princeton University*

South of France
Feb 20th, 1926

Dear Max:

Two things have just occurred to me—or rather three.

(1.) You'll get this letter about the 3d of March. My book of stories may, at that time have been out three weeks or three days—you've not told me the date. Will you in any case write me immediately forcasting roughly the approximate sale? I know it can be only guesswork and you'll be afraid of over estimating but I'd like to know <u>at least</u> the sale to that date. It has something to do with my income tax which must leave here the 14th. Also, would you send me an income tax blank?

My God! If it should sell 10,000 copies I'd be out of debt to you for the 1st time since 1922. Isn't that a disgrace, when I get $2500. for a story as my regular price. But trash doesn't come as easily as it used to and I've grown to hate the poor old debauched form itself.

How about Tom Boyd? Is he still going to be one of the barnyard boys? Or has he got sense and decided to write about the war, or seducing married women in St. Paul, or life in a bum Kentucky military school, or something he knows about. He has no touch of genius like Hemmingway and Cummings but like Dos Passos he has a strong, valuable talent. He must write about the external world, as vividly and accutely and even brilliantly as he can, but let him stop there. He is almost without the power of clear ratiocination and he has no emotional depths whatsoever. His hide is so thick that only battle itself could really make an impression on him—playing with the almost evanescent spiritual material of Anderson he becomes an ox to public view. I wish to God I could see him + talk to him. For heavens sake, Max, curb your usual (and, generally, sagacious) open-mindedness and don't help him to ruin his future by encouraging his stupidest ambitions. He'll turn bitter with failure.

(2.) Has the play's success helped the book Gatsby. My theory, you know, is that nowadays theres not the faintest connection. That's why I wouldn't allow a movie addition of the Beautiful + Damned. By the way I don't imagine those little 75 cent books sell any more. They shouldn't. Do they? I mean did the Jesse William's, Arthur Train's, Wilson's adresses, ect, sell like The Perfect Tribute[1] + The Third Wise Man.[2]

Now, confidential. T.S. Eliot for whom you know my profound admiration—I think he's the greatest living poet in any language—wrote me he'd read Gatsby three times + thought it was the 1st step forward American fiction had taken since Henry James.

Wait till they see the new novel!

Did you get Hemmingway?

There was something else I wanted to ask you. What was it? damn it!

We're coming home in the fall, but I don't want to. I'd like to live and die on the French Rivierra

What's the inside dope on the Countess Cathcart case?[3]

I can't remember my other question and its driving me frantic. Frantic! (Half an hour later) Frantic!

[1]By Mary Raymond Shipman Andrews (1906).

[2]Unidentified; perhaps *The Story of the Other Wise Man* (1899 and 1923), by Henry Van Dyke.

[3]In a sensational 1921 British court case, Vera, Countess Cathcart, daughter of a South African diamond magnate, had been divorced by the Earl of Cathcart on grounds of adultery. In February 1926, when Countess Cathcart attempted to enter New York to stage a production of her autobiographical play *Ashes*, she was detained by immigration officials who contended that she should be barred from the United States because of her "moral turpitude." The countess was admitted to the country, where she remained for only a few weeks; but her case stirred controversy over the nature and intent of American immigration laws.

FRANTIC!!!

If you see anybody I know tell 'em I hate 'em all, him especially. Never want to see 'em again.

Why shouldn't I go crazy? My father is a moron and my mother is a neurotic, half insane with pathological nervous worry. Between them they havn't and never have had the brains of Calvin Coolidge.

If I knew anything I'd be the best writer in America.

Scott Fitzg——

Eureka! Remembered! Refer my movie offers to Reynolds.

TO: Maxwell Perkins   *ALS, 2 pp. Princeton University*
c. March 1, 1926

Hotel Bellevue
Saliés-de-Béarn

Dear Max:

Ernest will reach N.Y. as soon as this. Apparently he's free so its between you and Harcourt. He'll get in touch with you.

There are several rather but not very Rabelaisian touches in Torrents of Spring (the satire) <u>No worse than Don Stuart</u> or Benchley's Anderson parody.[1] Also Harcourt <u>is said</u> to have offerred $500. advance <u>Torrents</u> and $1000. on almost completed novel. (Strictly confidential.) If Bridges takes <u>50 Grand</u> I don't think Ernest would ask you to meet those advances but here I'm getting involved in a diplomacy you can handle better. I don't say hold <u>50 Grand</u> over him but in a way he's holding it over you—one of the reasons he verges toward you is the magazine.

In any case he is tempermental in business made so by these bogus publishers over here. If you take the other two things <u>get a signed contract</u> for The <u>Sun Also Rises</u> (novel) Anyhow this is my last word on the subject—confidential between you + me. Please destroy this letter.

Zelda liked Biggs wrapper[2]—I didn't, much.

I   "   Ring's   " [3]—Zelda didn't much.

Niether of us thought mine was a success[4]—a fair idea but drab and undistinguished—the figure might be a woman. I think it would have been much wiser to have just printing as I suggested. In fact its much the least satisfactory jacket I've had. However, after <u>Gatsby</u> I dont believe people buy jackets any more.

---

[1] Both Donald Ogden Stewart and Robert Benchley wrote popular literary parodies.
[2] For Biggs's first novel, *Demigods* (1926).
[3] For *The Love Nest and Other Stories* (1926).
[4] For *All the Sad Young Men* (1926).

Will you send me a sample copy of this McNaughts magazine some time?

You havn't mentioned Bigg's book—is it the migrations of the Dunkards or something new. And is it good?

As Ever

Scott Fitzg—

How about Tom and Peggy?

TO: *Harold Ober*   *ALS, 1 p. Lilly Library*
Received March 15, 1926

Salies . de . Béarn

God knows where

Dear Ober:

This[1] is one of the lowsiest stories I've ever written. Just terrible! I lost interest in the middle (by the way the last part is typed triple space because I thought I could fix it—but I couldn't)

Please—and I mean this—don't offer it to the Post. I think that as things are now it would be wretched policy. Nor to the Red Book. It hasn't one redeeming touch of my usual spirit in it. I was desperate to begin a story + invented a business plot—the kind I can't handle. I'd rather have $1000, for it from some obscure place than twice that + have it seen. I feel very strongly about this!

Am writing two of the best stories I've ever done in my life.

As Ever—Scott Fitz—

TO: *Maxwell Perkins*   *ALS, 1 p. Princeton University*
c. March 15, 1926

Villa Paquita	}	adress
Juan-les-Pins		till
Alpes Maritime	}	June
France		15th

Dear Max:

Thanks very much for your nice letter + the income blank. Im delighted about the short story book. In fact with the play going well + my new novel growing absorbing + with our being back in a nice villa on my beloved Rivierra (between Cannes and Nice) I'm happier than I've been for years. Its one of those strange, precious and all too transitory moments when everything in one's life seems to be going well.

[1]"Your Way and Mine," *Woman's Home Companion* (May 1927), for which Fitzgerald received $1,750.

Thanks for the Arthur Train legal advice.[1]

I'm glad you got Hemmingway—I saw him for a day in Paris on his return + he thought you were great. I've brought you two successes (Ring + Tom Boyd) and two failures (Biggs + Woodward Boyd)—Ernest will decide whether my opinions are more of a hindrance or a help.

Why not try College Humor for his story. They published one thing of mine.

Poor Tom Boyd! First I was off him for his boneheadedness. Now I'm sorry for him.

Your Friend Scott

I am out of debt to you for the first time in four years.

Think of that horse's ass F.P.A. coming around to my work after six years of neglect. I'd like to stick his praise up his behind. God knows its no use to me now.

Will you get the enclosure for me, open it + write me what it is.

TO: *Harold Ober*   *ALS, 3 pp. Lilly Library*
Received May 3, 1926

Villa Paquita
Juan-les-Pins
Alpes Maritime
(After May 3d adress me
Villa St. Louis
Juan-les-Pins
Alpes Maritime

Dear Ober:

Naturally I was very excited about the movie opportunity. As I've heard no more I fear its fallen through—I'm anxiously awaiting news.[2]

I have your two letters in regard to Liberty. Now as to the short story business alone I would rather, without qualification, stay with the Post at $2500. than go to Liberty at $3500. Not only that but I shall probably write no short stories of any kind until next autumn.

But there is another element which might force me to leave the Post and that is the novel serialization. The novel is about one fourth done and will be delivered for possible serialization about January 1st. It will be about 75,000 words long, divided into 12 chapters, concerning tho this is absolutely confidential such a case as that girl who shot her mother on the Pacific

[1] Perkins had asked Train about the rights of Americans who commit murder on French soil—a plot element in Fitzgerald's projected novel.
[2] A silent movie of *The Great Gatsby* was made by Famous Players in 1926.

coast last year.[1] In other words, like <u>Gatsby</u> it is highly sensational. Not only would this bar it from the <u>Post</u> but also they are hostile, as you know, to the general cast of thought that permeates my serious work.

On the other hand <u>Liberty</u> is evidently very much in my favor at the moment. And if they would give between $25,000 and $40,000 for the serial I'd be an idiot to throw it away. In other words with say about 30,000 for the serial + assurance that Liberty will have a stable editorial policy at least till Jan 1st 1927, I'd better swing over there. Frankly I'm at sea. Perhaps it had better depend on whether they would really contract for the novel in advance. I hope to bring it home completed next December.

Wire me your advice. The trouble is that if <u>McCalls</u> or <u>Red Book</u> ran it it would take a solid year and I hate that while <u>Liberty</u> would run it in 3 mos.

Oh, hell—I hate to leave the <u>Post</u>. What is <u>Liberty</u> like anyhow? Prosperous or just subsidized?

Anxiously
F Scott Fitzgerald

TO: *Harold Ober*   *ALS, 1 p. Lilly Library*
Received June 3, 1926

Adress →   Villa St. Louis
till Oct 1st   Juan-les-Pins, Alpes Maritime
                 France

Dear Ober—

Well, its rather melancholy to hear that the run[2] was over. However as it was something of a <u>succés d'estime</u> and put in my pocket seventeen or eighteen thousand without a stroke of work on my part I should be, and am, well content.

A thousand thanks for your courtesy to my father. You went out of your way to be nice to him and he wrote me a most pleased and entheusiastic letter. He misses me, I think, and at his age such an outing as that was an exceptional pleasure. I am, as usual, deeply in your debt, and now for a most pleasant + personal reason. His own life after a rather brilliant start back in the seventies has been a "failure"—he's lived always in mother's shadow and he takes an immense vicarious pleasure in any success of mine. Thank you.

Yours Always
Scott Fitzgerald

No stories sent since your way and mine.

---

[1] In January 1925 Dorothy Ellingson murdered her mother in San Francisco.
[2] Of the *Great Gatsby* play.

TO: *Ernest Hemingway*[1]
June 1926

AL, 10 pp. John F. Kennedy Library
Juan-les-Pins, France

Dear Ernest: Nowdays when almost everyone is a genius, at least for awhile, the temptation for the bogus to profit is no greater than the temptation for the good man to relax (in one mysterious way or another)—not realizing the transitory quality of his glory because he forgets that it rests on the frail shoulders of professional entheusiasts. This should frighten all of us into a lust for anything honest that people have to say about our work. I've taken what proved to be excellent advice (On The B. + Damned) from Bunny Wilson who never wrote a novel, (on Gatsby—change of many thousand wds) from Max Perkins who never considered writing one, and on T. S. of Paradise from Katherine Tighe (you don't know her) who had probably never read a novel before.

[This is beginning to sound like my own current work which resolves itself into laborious + sententious preliminaries].[2]

Anyhow I think parts of <u>Sun Also</u> are careless + ineffectual. As I said yestiday (and, as I recollect, in trying to get you to cut the 1st part of 50 Grand)[3] I find in you the same tendency to envelope or (and as it usually turns out) to <u>embalm</u> in mere wordiness an anecdote or joke thats casually appealed to you, that I find in myself in trying to preserve a piece of "fine writing." Your first chapter contains about 10 such things and it gives a feeling of condescending <u>casuallness</u>[4]

P. 1. "highly moral story"

"Brett said" (O. Henry stuff)

"much too expensive

"something or other" (if you don't want to tell, why waste 3 wds. saying it. See P. 23—"<u>9 or 14</u>" and "or how many years it was since 19XX" when it would take two words to say   That's what youd kid in anyone else as mere "style"—mere horse-shit   I can't find this latter but anyhow you've not only got to write well yourself but you've also got to scorn <u>not-do</u> what anyone can do and I think that there are about 24 sneers, superiorities, and nose-thumbings-at-nothing that mar the whole narrative up to p. 29 where (after a false start on the introduction of Cohn) it really gets going. And to preserve these perverse and willfull non-essentials you've done a lot of writing that <u>honestly</u> reminded me of Michael Arlen.

[You know the very fact that people have committed themselves to you

---

[1] Hemingway and Fitzgerald were both on the Riviera, where Fitzgerald read the typescript of *The Sun Also Rises* for the first time.

[2] Fitzgerald's brackets.

[3] Fitzgerald had persuaded Hemingway to cut an anecdote about Jack Brennan and Benny Leonard from "Fifty Grand."

[4] The first chapter included a series of comments and anecdotes about the Paris Latin Quarter; Hemingway cut these in proof.

will make them watch you like a cat. + if they don't like it creap away like one][1]

For example.

Pps. 1 + 2. Snobbish (not in itself but because the history of English Aristocrats in the war, set down so verbosely so uncritically, so exteriorly and yet so obviously inspired from within, is shopworn.) You had the same problem that I had with my Rich Boy, previously debauched by Chambers ect. Either bring more thot to it with the realization that that ground has already raised its wheat + weeds or cut it down to seven sentences. It hasn't even your rythym and the fact that may be "true" is utterly immaterial.

That biography from you, who allways believed in the superiority (the preferability) of the imagined to the seen   not to say to the merely re-counted.

P.   3.   "Beautifully engraved shares" (Beautifully engraved 1886 irony) All this is O.K. but so glib when its glib + so profuse.

P.   5   Painters are no longer real in prose. They must be minimized. [This is not done by making them schlptors, backhouse wall-experts or miniature painters][2]

P.   8.   "highly moral urges" "because I believe its a good story" If this paragraph isn't maladroit then I'm a rewrite man for Dr. Cadman.[3]

P.   9.   Somehow its not good. I can't quite put my hand on it—it has a ring of "This is a true story ect."

P. 10.   "Quarter being a state of mind ect." This is in all guide books. I havn't read Basil Swoon's[4] but I have fifty francs to lose.

[5][About this time I can hear you say "Jesus this guy thinks I'm lousy, + he can stick it up his ass for all I give a Gd Dm for his 'critisism.'" But remember this is a new departure for you, and that I think your stuff is great. You were the first American I wanted to meet in Europe—and the last. (This latter clause is simply to balance the sentence. It doesn't seem to make sense tho I have pawed at it for several minutes. Its like the age of the French women.[6]

P. 14.   (+ therabout) as I said yesterday I think this anecdote is flat as hell without naming Ford[7] which would be cheap.

It's flat because you end with mention of Allister Crowly.[8] If he's nobody

---

[1]Fitzgerald's brackets.
[2]Fitzgerald's brackets.
[3]Samuel Parkes Cadman, inspirational preacher.
[4]Basil Woon, author of *The Paris That's Not in the Guidebooks.*
[5]Fitzgerald's bracket.
[6]A reference to the epigraph for Hemingway's *in our time* (1924).
[7]An anecdote about Ford Madox Ford, which Hemingway later used in *A Moveable Feast.*
[8]Aleister Crowley, English diabolist; Hemingway later salvaged the anecdote about him in *A Moveable Feast.*

its nothing. If he's somebody its cheap. This is a novel. Also I'd cut out actual mention of H. Stearns[1] earlier.

———————

Why not cut the inessentials in Cohens biography?[2] His first marriage is of no importance. When so many people can write well + the competition is so heavy I can't imagine how you could have done these first 20 pps. so casually. You can't <u>play</u> with peoples attention—a good man who has the power of arresting attention at will must be especially careful.

From here   Or rather from p. 30 I began to like the novel but Ernest I can't tell you the sense of disappointment that beginning with its elephantine facetiousness gave me. Please do what you can about it in proof. Its 7500 words—you could reduce it to 5000. And my advice is not to do it by mere pareing but to take out the worst of the <u>scenes</u>.

I've decided not to pick at anything else, because I wasn't at all inspired to pick when reading it. I was much too excited. Besides this is probably a heavy dose. The novel's damn good. The central theme is marred somewhere but hell! unless you're writing your life history where you have an inevitable pendulum to swing you true (Harding[3] metaphor), who can bring it entirely off? And what critic can trace whether the fault lies in a possible insufficient thinking out, in the biteing off of more than you eventually cared to chew in the impotent theme or in the elusiveness of the lady character herself.[4] My theory always was that she dramatized herself in terms of Arlens dramatatization of somebody's dramatizatatg of Stephen McKenna's[5] dramatization of Diana Manner's[6] dramatization of the last girl in Well's <u>Tono Bungay</u>—who's original probably liked more things about Beatrix Esmond than about Jane Austin's Elizibeth[7] (to whom we owe the manners of so many of our wives.)

Appropos of your foreward about the Latin quarter—suppose you had begun your stories with phrases like: "Spain is a peculiar place—ect" or "Michigan is interesting to two classes—the fisherman + the drummer."

Pps 64 + 65[8] with a bit of work should tell all that need be known about <u>Brett's</u> past.

(Small point) "Dysemtry" instead of "killed" is a clichês to avoid a cliché. It stands out. I suppose it can't be helped. I suppose all the 75,000000

———

[1] Harold Stearns, alcoholic American journalist in Paris; model for Harvey Stone in *The Sun Also Rises*.

[2] Hemingway made this cut.

[3] President Warren G. Harding, who often had trouble with his rhetoric.

[4] Duff Twysden, an alcoholic and promiscuous English woman; model for Brett Ashley.

[5] English society novelist.

[6] English actress Diana Manners.

[7] Beatrix Esmond, a worldly character in Thackeray's *The History of Henry Esmond* and *The Virginians*; Elizabeth Bennet, spirited heroine of Jane Austen's *Pride and Prejudice*.

[8] Ch. 5 scene in which Jake tells Cohn about Brett.

Europeans who died between 1914–1918 will always be among the 10,000,000 who were killed in the war.

God! The bottom of p. 77 Jusque the top p. 78 are wonderful,[1] I go crazy when people aren't always at their best. This isn't picked out—I just happened on it.

The heart of my critisim beats somewhere apon p. 87.[2] I think you can't change it, though. I felt the lack of some crazy torturing tentativeness or insecurity—horror, all at once, that she'd feel—and he'd feel—maybe I'm crazy. He isn't <u>like an impotent man. He's like a man in a sort of moral chastity belt</u>.

Oh, well. It's fine, from Chap V on, anyhow, in spite of that—which fact is merely a proof of its brilliance.

Station Z.W.X. square says good night. Good night all.

TO: Maxwell Perkins   *ALS, 2 pp. Princeton University*
c. June 25, 1926

Villa St. Louis
Juan-les-Pins
A-M.

Dear Max:

Thanks for both letters. We were in Paris having Zelda's appendix neatly but firmly removed or I would have answered before.

First as to Ernests book. I liked it but with certain qualifications. The fiesta, the fishing trip, the minor characters were fine. The lady I didn't like, perhaps because I don't like the original. In the mutilated man I thought Ernest bit off more than can yet be chewn between the covers of a book, then lost his nerve a little and edited the more vitalizing details out. He has since told me that something like this happened. Do ask him for the absolute minimum of nessessary changes, Max—he's so discouraged about the previous reception of his work by publishers and magazine editors. (Tho he loved your letter) From the latter he has had a lot of words and until Bridges offer for the short story (from which he had even before cut out a thousand words on my recommendation) scarcely a single dollar. From the <u>Torrents</u> I expect you'll have little response. Do you think the Bookman article did him any good?[3]

I roared at the idea of you and the fish in the tree.

O.K. as to Haldeman-Julius.

Will you ask them (your accounts dept.) to send me an account the 1st

---

[1]Ch. 6 scene in which Frances Clyne, Cohn's mistress, berates him for abandoning her.
[2]Ch. 7 scene in which Brett comes to Jake's flat.
[3]Fitzgerald had written an essay-review of *In Our Time* for *The Bookman* (May 1926).

of August. I'd love to see what a positive statement looks like for the first time in three years.

I am writing Bridges today. I have an offer now for a story at $3,500.00 (rather for six stories). To sell one for $1,000.00 would mean a dead loss of $2,500 and as I average only six stories a year I don't see how I can do it. I hope he'll understand

The novel, in abeyance during Zelda's operation now goes on apace. This is confidential but Liberty, with certain conditions, has offered me $35,000. sight unseen. I hope to have it done in January.

Do send out a picture to everyone that got that terrible one.

Ever Your Friend
Scott

TO: *Ernest Hemingway*   ALS, 1 p. *John F. Kennedy Library*
September 1926   *Juan-les-Pins, France*

Dear Ernest—Sorry we missed you + Hadley. No news. I'm on the wagon + working like hell. Expect to sail for N.Y Dec 10th from Genoa on the Conte Biancamo. Will be here till then. Saw Bullfight in Frejus. Bull was euneuch (sp.). House barred + dark. Front door chained. Have made no new enemies for a week. Hamilton domestic row ended in riot. Have new war books by Pierrefeu.[1] God is love.

Signed
Ernestine
Murphy.

Did you read in the N.Y Herald about—
". . . Henry Carpenter, banker, and Willie Stevens, halfwit, . . ."
S

TO: *Ernest Hemingway*   ALS, 2 pp. *John F. Kennedy Library*
Fall 1926   *Juan-les-Pins, France*

We were in a back-house in Juan-les-Pins. Bill had lost controll of his splincter muscles. There were wet Matins in the rack beside the door. There were wet Eclairers de Nice in the rack over his head. When the King of Bulgaria came in Bill was just firing a burst that struck the old limeshit twenty feet down with a splat-tap. All the rest came just like that. The King of Bulgaria began to whirl round and round.

"The great thing in these affairs—" he said.

Soon he was whirling faster and faster. Then he was dead.

---

[1] Jean de Pierrefeu, author of works about the Great War.

At this point in my letter my 30th birthday came and I got tight for a week in the company of such facinating gents as Mr. Theodore Rousseau + other ornaments of what is now a barren shore.

Ernest of little faith I hope the sale of The Killers[1] will teach you to send every story either to Scribners or an agent. Can't you get "Today is Friday" back? Your letter depressed and rather baffled me. Have you and Hadley permanently busted up, and was the nessessity of that what was on your soul this summer. Don't answer this unless you feel like it. Anyhow I'm sorry everything's such a mess and I do want to see you if you come to Marseitte in October.

We saw the Murphys before they left, got stewed with them (at their party)—that is we got stewed—and I believe there was some sort of mawkish reconciliation. However they've grown dim to me and I don't like them much any more. Mclieshes too have grown shadowy—he's <u>so</u> nice but she's a club woman at heart and made a great lot of trouble in subtle ways this summer. We saw Marice the day she left + the huge Garoupe standing desolate, and her face, and the pathetic bales of <u>chiclets</u> for the Garoupe beach in her bedroom are the strongest impression I have left of a futile and petty summer. It might all have happened at Roslynn Long Island.

Swimmings almost over now. We have our tickets for America Dec. 10th on the Conte Biancamo—we'll spend the winter in New York. Bishop was here with his unspeakably awful wife. He seems aenemic and washed out, a memory of the past so far as I'm concerned.

Im glad as hell about the story and I hope its the first of many. I feel too much at loose ends to write any more tonight. Remember—if I can give you any financial help let me know.

Always Your Friend
Scott—

I had a lot more to say but its 3.30 A.M. and Ive been working since 11 this morning and its very hazy. Have you read

<u>The Spanish Farm</u>
+
<u>Sixty four—ninety four</u> } by Mottram ?

<u>Wonderful</u> war books. Much better than Ford Maddox Ford. In fact the best thing I've read this summer. Met your cousin from Princeton!

---

[1] *Scribner's Magazine* (March 1927).

TO: *Ernest Hemingway*
December 1926

ALS, 2 pp. John F. Kennedy Library
SS Conte Biancamano *stationery—*
mailed from Washington, D.C.

Dear Ernest =

Your letter depressed me—illogicly because I knew more or less what was coming. I wish I could have seen you + heard you, if you wished, give some sort of version of what happened to you. Anyhow I'm sorry for you and for Hadley + for Bumby[1] and I hope some way you'll all be content and things will not seem so hard and bad.

I can't tell you how much your friendship has meant to me during this year and a half—it is the brightest thing in our trip to Europe for me. I will try to look out for your interests with Scribner in America, but I gather that the need of that is past now and that soon you'll be financially more than on your feet.

I'm sorry you didn't come to Marseille. I go back with my novel still unfinished and with less health + not much more money than when I came, but somehow content, for the moment, with motion and New York ahead and Zelda's entire recovery—and happy about the amount of my book that I've already written.

I'm delighted with what press I've already seen of The Sun ect. Did not realize you had stolen it all from me but am prepared to believe that its true + shall tell everyone. By the way I liked it in print even better than in manuscript.

1st Printing was probably 5000. 2nd Printing may mean that they've sold 4,500 so have ordered up 3000 more. It may mean any sale from 2500 to 5000, tho.

College Humor pays fine. No movie in Sun Also unless book is big success of scandal. That's just a guess.

We all enjoyed "la vie est beau avec Papa". We agree with Bumby.

Always Yours Affectionately,

Scott

Write me care of Scribners.

TO: *Harold Ober*
January 2, 1927

Wire. Lilly Library
Montgomery, Alabama

I CAN FINISH NOVEL BY MAY FIRST BUT WOULD LIKE UNTIL JUNE FIRST IF POSSIBLE PLEASE CONSULT LIBERTY AND WIRE REPLY IMMEDIATELY CARE JUDGE SAYRE SIX PLEASANT AVENUE MONTGOMERY ALA HAPPY NEW YEAR.
SCOTT FITZGERALD

[1] The Hemingways' son, John Hadley Nicanor.

148

TO: *Harold Ober* ALS, *1 p. Lilly Library*
Received January 24, 1927 *Ambassador Hotel stationery.*
Los Angeles, California

Dear Ober:
   Will see you in 3 weeks. Am here trying to write an original story for
Constance Talmadge.[1] Was only 12 hrs in New York. Expect to finish
novel before April 1st.

As Ever
Scott Fitzg—

TO: *Ernest Hemingway* ALS, *1 p. John F. Kennedy Library*
April 18, 1927 *"Ellerslie," Edgemoor, Delaware*

   God! Those terrible Bromfields! I recognized the parsimonious dinner
Dear Ernest:
   Your stories were great (in April Scribner). But like me you must beware
Conrad rythyms in direct quotation from characters especially if you're
pointing a single phrase + making a man live by it.
   "In the fall the war was always there but we did not go to it any more"[2]
is one of the most beautiful prose sentences I've ever read.
   So much has happened to me lately that I despair of ever assimilating it—
or for forgetting it which is the same thing.
   I hate to think of your being hard up. Please use this if it would help.[3]
The Atlantic will pay about $200, I suppose. I'll get in touch with Perkins
about it when he returns from vacation (1 wk.). Won't they advance you
all you need on the bk of stories? Your title is fine by the way. What chance
of yr. crossing this summer?

   Adress for a year
Ellerslie Mansion ⎤ Huge old house ⎞ My novel to be
Edge Moor [drawing ⎬ on Delaware ⎠ finished July 1st
Delaware of house] ⎦ River With eager + anxious good wishes
   Pillars ect. I am called "Colonel." Zelda "de old Missus" —— Scott

[1]Fitzgerald's flapper comedy "Lipstick," for this silent screen actress, was rejected.
[2]First line of "In Another Country," one of the two Hemingway stories published in the
April 1927 *Scribner's Magazine*.
[3]One hundred dollars loan.

TO: Harold Ober
September 1, 1927

Wire. Lilly Library
Wilmington, Delaware

ARTICLE ROTTEN WORKING ON A TWO PART SOPHISTICATED FOOTBALL STORY[1]
ASK POST IF IT IS FINISHED IN ONE WEEK WILL IT BE TOO LATE FOR SCHEDULE
THIS FALL CAN YOU DEPOSIT FIVE HUNDRED.
   SCOTT FITZGERALD.

TO: Harold Ober
September 9, 1927

Wire. Lilly Library
Wilmington, Delaware

STORY ALMOST FINISHED CALL YOU DEPOSIT FIVE HUNDRED.
   FITZGERALD.

TO: Harold Ober
September 14, 1927

Wire. Lilly Library
Wilmington, Delaware

STORY FINISHED CAN YOU DEPOSIT FIVE HUNDRED MORE.
   FITZGERALD

TO: Harold Ober
September 22, 1927

Wire. Lilly Library
Philadelphia, Pennsylvania

CAN YOU DEPOSIT 300 THIS MORNING SOMEWHAT URGENT WILL BE IN TO SEE
YOU AT 215.
   FITZGERALD.

TO: Harold Ober
September 30, 1927

Wire. Lilly Library
Wilmington, Delaware

WAS CALLED UNAVOIDABLE TO NEWYORK AND STOPPED OFF IN PRINCETON TWO
DAYS TO WATCH FOOTBALL PRACTICE AND SEE IF I COULD GET A LITTLE LIFE
INTO THAT WHICH IS THE WEAK PART OF MY STORY SO I JUST GOT YOUR
TELEGRAM AND LETTER LAST NIGHT WORKING AS FAST AS I CAN BUT HATE IDEA
OF SENDING PRT IS IT ESSENTIAL HOPE TO BE THROUGH MON OR TUES TERRIBLY
SORRY
   SCOTT FITZGERALD.

---

[1]This story was not published, but was rewritten as "The Bowl," *The Saturday Evening Post*, January 21, 1928.

TO: *Harold Ober*   *Wire. Lilly Library*
October 3, 1927   *Wilmington, Delaware*

THE STORY IS JUST AN AWFUL MESS AND I CANT FINISH IT BY TOMMORROW FEEL
TERRIBLY AT LETTING YOU AND POST DOWN ABOUT IT BUT ALSO FEEL THAT I
HAVE DONE MY BEST PERHAPS I HAD BETTER TACKLE SOMETHING ELSE FOR IMME-
DIATE PROFIT THAT IS DO A STORY THIS WEEK AND THEN RETURN TO THE
FOOTBALL STORY WITH HOPES THAT THEY WILL BUY IT FOR PUBLICATION NEXT
SEPTEMBER.
  SCOTT FITZGERLA.

TO: *Harold Ober*   *Wire. Lilly Library*
October 18, 1927   *Wilmington, Delaware*

AM GOING TO TAKE ONE MORE DAY WILL BE UP TOMORROW INSTEAD CAN YOU
STILL HAVE LUNCH WITH ME PLEASE FORGIVE ME.
  SCOTT FITZGERALD.

TO: *Harold Ober*   *Wire. Lilly Library*
October 27, 1927   *Wilmington, Delaware*

CAN YOU DEPOSIT ONE HUNDRED EMERGENCY BRINGING NEW STORY MONDAY.
  FITZGERALD.

TO: *Ernest Hemingway*   *ALS, 3 pp. John F. Kennedy Library*
October 1927   *"Ellerslie" stationery. Edgemoor, Delaware*

Dear Ernest:
  Thousands will send you this clipping.[1] I should think it would make you
quite conscious of your public existence. Its well meant—he praised your
book a few days before.
  The book is fine. I like it quite as well as The Sun, which doesn't begin
to express my enthusiasm. In spite of all its geographical + emotional
rambling its a unit, as much as Conrad's books of Contes were. Zelda read
it with facination, liking it better than anything you've written. Her favorite
was Hills like White Elephants, mine, barring The Killers was Now I Lay
Me. The one about the Indians was the only one that left me cold and I'm
glad you left out Up in Michigan. They probably belong to an earlier +
almost exhaused vein.

[1]Parody of Hemingway by F.P.A.

"In the fall the war was always there but we did not go to it anymore." God, what a beautiful line. And the waking dreams in <u>Now I Lay me</u> and the whole mood of <u>Hills Like</u>.

Did you see the pre-review by that cocksucker Rascoe who obviously had read only three stories but wanted to be up to the minute?

Max says its almost exhausted 7500—however that was five days ago. I like your title—<u>All the Sad Young Men Without Women</u>—and I feel my influence is beginning to tell. Manuel Garcia is obviously Gatsby. What you havn't learned from me you'll get from Good Woman Bromfield and soon you'll be Marching in the Van of the Younger Generation.

No work this summer but lots this fall. Hope to finish the novel by 1st December. Have got nervous as hell lately—purely physical but scared me somewhat—to the point of putting me on the wagon and smoking denicotinized cigarettes. Zelda is ballet dancing three times a week with the Phila symphony—painting also. I think you were wise not jumping at Hearsts offer. I had a contract with them that, as it turned out, did me unspeakable damage in one way or another. Long is a sentimental scavenger with no ghost of taste or individuality, not nearly so much as Lorimer for example. However, why not send your stories to Paul Reynolds? He'll be glad to handle them + will get you good prices. The <u>Post</u> now pays me $3500.—this detail so you'll be sure who's writing this letter.

I can't tell you how I miss you. May cross for 6 wks in March or April. <u>The Grandmothers</u>[1] was respectable but undistinguished, and are you coming home. Best to Pauline.[2] With good wishes + Affection Scott

TO: Harold Ober
November 9, 1927

Wire. Lilly Library
Wilmington, Delaware

CAN YOU DEPOSIT ONE HUNDRED STOP I WILL BE UP WITH THE STORY THURSDAY SURE AND PERHAPS WEDNESDAY.

SCOTT FITZGERALD.

TO: Harold Ober
November 12, 1927

Wire. Lilly Library
Wilmington, Delaware

CAN YOU DEPOSIT FOUR HUNDRED THIS MORNING THAT MAKES ALMOST TWO THOUSAND AND MY STORY HAS COLLAPSED BUT I HAVE ANOTHER ALMOST FINISHED AND WILL BRING IT UP MONDAY.

SCOTT FITZGERALD

[1] 1927 novel by Glenway Wescott.
[2] Pauline Pfeiffer Hemingway, Hemingway's second wife.

TO: *Harold Ober*   *Wire. Lilly Library*
November 18, 1927   *Wilmington, Delaware*

CAN YOU DEPOSIT TWO HUNDRED TODAY COMING IN TOMORROW MORNING BUT WITHOUT STORY.
    SCOTT FITZGERALD.

TO: *Harold Ober*   *Wire. Lilly Library*
December 2, 1927   *Wilmington, Delaware*

CAN YOU DEPOSIT TWO HUNDRED AND FIFTY I WILL BE IN TOMORROW MORNING WITH FOOTBALL STORY WITHOUT FAIL.
    FITZGERALD.

TO: *Ring and Ellis Lardner*   *TL, 1 p. Scrapbook. Princeton University*
December 1927?   *"Ellerslie," Edgemoor, Delaware*

To the Ring Lardners[1]

You combed Third Avenue last year
  For some small gift that was not too dear
—Like a candy cane or a worn out truss—
  To give to a loving friend like us
You'd found gold eggs for such wealthy hicks
  As the Edsell Fords and the Pittsburgh Fricks
The Andy Mellons, the Teddy Shonts
  The Coleman T. and Pierre duPonts
But not one gift to brighten our hoem
  —So I'm sending you back your God damn poem.

TO: *Ernest Hemingway*   *ALS, 4 pp. John F. Kennedy Library*
December 1927

Ellerslie
Edgemoor
Delaware

Dear Ernest:
    Perkins send me the check for 800 bits (as we westerners say), indicating I hope, that you are now comfortably off in your own ascetic way. I am

---

[1] Written in response to the Lardners' printed poem about their inability to find suitable Christmas gifts.

almost through my novel, got short and had to do three Post stories but as I am now their pet exhibit and go down on them to the tune of 32,000 bits per felony it didn't take long to come to the surface.

(This tough talk is not really characteristic of me—its the influence of <u>All the Sad Young Men Without Women in Love</u>.) Louis Golding stepped off the boat + said you and I were the hope of American Letters (if you can find them) but aside from that things look black, "old pard"—Brommy[1] is sweeping the west, Edna Ferber is sweeping the east and Paul Rosenfeld is sweeping what's left into a large ornate wastebasket, a gift which any Real Man would like, to be published in November under the title: <u>The Real Liesure Class</u>, containing the work of one-story Balzacs and poets so thin-skinned as to be moved by everything to exactly the same degree of mild remarking.

Lately I've enjoyed <u>Some People</u>,[2] <u>Bismark</u> (Ludwig's), <u>Him</u>[3] (in parts) and the <u>Memoirs</u> of Ludendorff. I have a new German war book, <u>Die Krieg against Krieg</u>, which shows men who mislaid their faces in Picardy and the Caucasus—you can imagine how I thumb it over, my mouth fairly slithering with facination.

If you write anything in the line of an "athletic" story please try the <u>Post</u> or let me try them for you, or Reynolds. You were wise not to tie up with Hearsts. They are absolute bitches who feed on contracts like vultures, if I may coin a neat simile.

I've tasted no alcohol for a month but Xmas is coming.

Please write me at length about your adventures—I hear you were seen running through Portugal in used B.V.Ds, chewing ground glass and collecting material for a story about Boule players; that you were publicity man for Lindberg; that you have finished a novel a hundred thousand words long consisting entirely of the word "balls" used in new groupings; that you have been naturalized a Spaniard, dress always in a wine-skin with "zipper" vent and are engaged in bootlegging Spanish Fly between St. Sebastian and Biaritz where your agents sprinkle it on the floor of the Casino. I hope I have been misformed but, alas! it all has too true a ring. For your own good I should be back there, with both of us trying to be good fellows at a terrible rate. Just before you pass out next time think of me.

This is a wowsy country but France is swehw and I hope to spend March and April, or April and May, there and elsewhere on the continent.

How are you, physically and mentally? Do you sleep? <u>Now I Lay Me</u> was a fine story—you ought to write a companion piece, <u>Now I Lay Her</u>. Excuse my bawdiness but I'm oversexed and am having saltpetre put in my <u>Pâté de Foie Gras au Truffles Provêncal</u>.

[1]Louis Bromfield.
[2]Volume of biographical essays by Harold Nicolson (1927).
[3]Play by e. e. cummings (1927).

Please write news. My best to Pauline—Zelda's also to you both. God will forgive everybody—even Robert McAlmon and Burton Rascoe.

                                        Always afftly
                                                Scott

TO: *Edmund Wilson*   *ALS, 2 pp. Yale University*
Early February 1928?   *"Ellerslie" stationery. Edgemoor, Delaware*

Dear Bunny:
    (Such a quaint nickname. It reminds me of a—oh, you know, a sort of a—oh, a rabbit, you know.)
    All is prepared for February 25th. The stomach pumps are polished and set out in rows, stale old entheusiasms are being burnished with that zeal peculiar only to the Brittish Tommy. My God, how we felt when the long slaughter of Paschendale had begun. Why were the generals all so old? Why were The Fabian society discriminated against when positions on the general staff went to Dukes and sons of profiteers. Agitators were actually hooted at in Hyde Park and Anglican divines actually didn't become humanitarian internationalists over night. What is Briton coming to—where is Milton, Cromwell, Oates, Monk? Where are Shaftsbury, Athelstane, Thomas a Becket, Margot Asquith, Iris March, Where are Blackstone, Touchstone, Clapham-Hopewellton, Stoke-Poges? Somewhere back at G.H.Q. handsome men with grey whiskers murmured "We will charge them with the cavalry" and meanwhile boys from Bovril and the black country sat shivering in the lagoons of Ypres writing memoirs for liberal novels about the war. What about the tanks? Why did not Douglas Haig or Sir John French (the big smarties) (Look what they did to General Merccr) invent tanks the day the war broke out, like Sir Phillip Gibbs the weeping baronet, did or would, had he thought of it.
    This is just a sample of what you will get on the 25th of Feb. There will be small but select company, coals, blankets, "something for the inner man".
    Please don't say you can't come the 25th but would like to come the 29th. We never recieve people the 29th. It is the anniversary of the 2nd Council of Nicea when our Blessed Lord, our Blessed Lord, our Blessed Lord, our Blessed Lord——
    It always gets stuck in that place. Put on "Old Man River," or something of Louis Bromfields.
    Pray gravity to move your bowels. Its little we get done for us in this world. Answer.
                            Scott

Enjoyed your Wilson article enormously. Not so Thompson affair.

TO: *Harold Ober*   *Wire. Lilly Library*
April 8, 1928   *Wilmington, Delaware*

HAVE DECIDED TO GO TO FRANCE FOR THREE MONTHS AS I TOLD YOU IN OUR
TALK FRIDAY CAN YOU DEPOSIT FOUR HUNDRED DOLLARS CASH MONDAY MORN-
ING HAVE THE FIRST STORY AT THE TYPISTS NOW AND SHOULD BE OFF BY TUESDAY
AFTERNOON AND I SHALL DO AT LEAST ONE MORE BEFORE WE SAIL WHICH
ACCORDING TO PRESENT PLANS WILL BE THE TWENTY FIRST THIS MONTH
    SCOTT FITZGERALD.

TO: *Harold Ober*   *Wire. Lilly Library*
June 3, 1928   *Paris*

TWO MORE CHAPTERS FINISHED ALL COMPLETED AUGUST[1] CAN YOU DEPOSIT
ONEFIFTY AT ONCE AND ONETHOUSAND WHEN STORY IS PAID

TO: *Sylvia Beach*[2]   *ALS, 1 p. and inscription in*
                                  The Great Gatsby. Princeton University

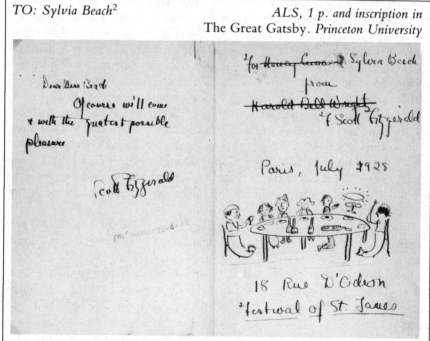

Left to right: Adrienne Monnier, Lucie Chamson, André Chamson, Zelda Fitzgerald, Fitzgerald, James Joyce, Sylvia Beach.

---

[1]Refers to progress on the novel that became *Tender Is the Night*.
[2]Proprietor of Shakespeare & Company bookshop, a gathering place for expatriate writers in Paris. Beach published Joyce's *Ulysses* in 1922.

TO: *Ernest Hemingway*   *ALS, 2 pp. John F. Kennedy Library*
c. July 1928   *Paris*

Teenie-weenie Corner
Sunshineville.

Precious Papa, Bull-fighter, Gourmand ect.

It has come to my ears

ⓐ That you have been bycycling through Kansas, chewing +
spitting a mixture of goat's meat + chicory which the natives collect + sell
for artery-softener and market-glut

ⓑ That Bumby has won the Benjamin Altman scholarship at Cundle
School + taken first prizes in <u>Comparitive Epistomology</u>, <u>Diseases of Cor-
morants</u> + <u>Small Vultures</u>, <u>Amateur Gyncology</u> + <u>Intestinal Hysterics</u>

ⓒ That you are going to fight Jim Tully[1] in Washdog Wisconsin on
Decoration Day in a chastity belt with your hair cut á la garconne.

————————

Is it all true?

————————

We are friends with the Murphys again. Talked about you a great deal
+ while we <u>tried</u> to say only kind things we managed to get in a few good
cracks that would amuse you—about anybody else—which is what you get
for being so far away. Incidently called twice on Hadley—she was both
times out but saw Bumby once + think he's the best kid I ever saw by 1000
miles.

Well, old Mackerel Snatcher,[2] wolf a Wafer + + a Beaker of blood for
me,—and when you come Shadowboxing into my life again with your new
similes for "swewa" and "wousy" (which, as you doubtless notice, you've
given to the world) no one will be glader than your

Devoted Friend
Scott Fitzg—

While in America don't cast any doubt on my statement that you held a
bridgehead (or was it a hophead) at Caporetto for three days + utterly
baffled the 2nd Austrian Army Corps. In 50 yrs all the people that could
have denied it will be dead or busy holding their own bridgeheads—like
Lawrence Stallings, who is slowly taking to himself the communal exploits
of the 5th + 6th Marines. "Hebuterne—of course I know it—I took that
village."

Do send Lorimer a story. I read Mencken's public apology.[3] Not bad for

[1] Hobo writer.
[2] Hemingway became a practicing Catholic at the time of his marriage to Pauline Pfeiffer.
[3] Possibly a reference to Mencken's review of *Men Without Women* in the *American Mercury*
(May 1928).

an old man who has had his troubles. God help us all! Have seen a good deal of Joyce. Please come back—will be here till Aug 20$\underline{\text{th}}$ 58 Rue de Vaugirard. Then back to America for a few months.

Best to Pauline!

TO: Maxwell Perkins   *ALS, 2 pp. Princeton University*
c. July 21, 1928   *Paris*

Dear Max

(1) The novel goes fine. I think its quite wonderful + I think those who've seen it (for I've read it around a little) have been quite excited. I was encouraged the other day, when James Joyce came to dinner, when he said "Yes, I expect to finish my novel in three or four years more at the latest" + he works 11 hrs a day to my intermittent 8. Mine will be done sure in September.

(2) Did you get my letter about André Chamson?[1] Really Max, you're missing a great opportunity if you don't take that up. Radiguet was perhaps obscene—Chamson is absolutely not—he's head over heals the best young man here, like Ernest + Thornton Wilder rolled into one. This Hommes de la Route (Road Menders) is his 2nd novel + all but won the Prix Goncourt—the story of men building a road, with all the force of K. Hamsun's Growth of the Soil—not a bit like Tom Boyds bogus American husbandmen. Moreover, tho I know him only slightly and have no axe to grind, I have every faith in him as an extraordinary personality like France + Proust. Incidently King Vidor[2] (who made The Crowd + The Big Parade) is making a picture of it next summer. If you have any confidence in my judgement do at least get a report on it + let me know what you decide. Ten years from now he'll be beyond price.

(3) I plan to publish a book of those Basil Lee Stories after the novel. Perhaps one or two more serious ones to be published in the Mercury or with Scribners if you'd want them, combined with the total of about six in the Post Series, would make a nice light novel, almost, to follow my novel in the season immediately after, so as not to seem in the direct line of my so-called "work". It would run to perhaps 50 or 60 thousand words.

(4) Do let me know any plans of ⓐ Ernest ⓑ Ring ⓒ Tom (reviews poor, I notice) ⓓ John Biggs

(5) Did you like Bishops story? I thought it was grand.

(6) Home Sept 15th I think. Best to Louise

(7) About Cape—won't you arrange it for me + take the 10% commission? That is if Im not committed morally to Chatto + Windus who did,

---

[1] The only French writer with whom Fitzgerald formed a friendship, Chamson became a Scribners author.

[2] American movie director.

so to speak, pick me up out of the English gutter. I'd <u>rather</u> be with Cape. Please decide + act accordingly if you will. If you don't I'll just ask Reynolds. As you like. Let me know

Ever yr Devoted + Grateful Friend
Scott

TO: *Maxwell Perkins*   *ALS, 1 p. Princeton University*
October/November 1928   *"Ellerslie," Edgemoor, Delaware*

Dear Max:

Am going to send you two chapters a month of the final version of book beginning next week + ending in Feb.[1] Strictly confidential. Don't tell Reynolds! I think this will help me get it straight in my own mind—I've been alone with it too long.

I think Stearns will be delighted + hereby accept for him.[2] Send me a check made out <u>to him</u>—he hasn't had that much money since I gave him $50 in '25—the poor bastard. If you leave out his name leave out mine too—or as you like.

Ever Yrs
Scott

Sending chapters Tues or Wed or Thurs.

TO: *Maxwell Perkins*   *ALS, 2 pp. Princeton University*

Edgemoor
Nov. '28

Dear Max:

It seems fine to be sending you something again, even though its only the first fourth of the book (2 chapters, 18,000 words). Now comes another short story, then I'll patch up Chaps. 3 + 4 the same way, and send them, I hope, about the 1st of December.

Chap I. here is good.

Chap II. has caused me more trouble than anything in the book. You'll realize this when I tell you it was once 27,000 words long! It started its career as Chap I. I am far from satisfied with it even now, but won't go into its obvious faults. I would appreciate it if you jotted down any criticisms—and <u>saved them until</u> I've sent you the whole book, because I want to <u>feel</u> that each part is finished and not worry about it any longer, even though I may change it enormously at the very last minute. All I want to

---

[1] Fitzgerald sent only one installment of the novel.
[2] Harold Stearns, "Apology of an Expatriate," *Scribner's Magazine* (March 1929)—written in the form of a letter to Fitzgerald.

know now is if, in general, you like it + this will have to wait, I suppose, until you've seen the next batch which finishes the first half. (My God its good to see those chapters lying in an envelope!

I think I have found you a new prospect of really extraordinary talent in a Carl Van Vechten way. I have his first novel at hand—unfortunately its about Lesbians. More of this later.

I think Bunny's title[1] is <u>wonderful!</u>

Remember novel is confidential, even to Ernest.

Always Yrs.
Scott

TO: *Adelaide Neall*[2]　　　　　　*ALS, 1 p. Historical Society of Pennsylvania*
"Ellerslie" stationery. Edgemoor, Delaware

Dec 12th 1928

Dear Miss Neale:

Many thanks for the really beautiful medal. I shall use it, a little irreverendly, to weigh down many future manuscripts.

Your asking me for a picture reminds me that with my new story I will have appeared thirty times in the <u>Post</u>—beginning just nine years ago. This averages one story every three or four months—and a little over sixty-three thousand dollars (which I am sending back in the next mail as I don't think they were really worth it, and anyhow the medal is more than enough.)

And herewith the photo.

Sincerely
F Scott Fitzgerald

TO: *Ernest Hemingway*　　　　　　*ALS, 2 pp. John F. Kennedy Library*
December 28, 1928

Dear Ernest:

I'm terribly sorry about your trouble.[3] I guess losing parents is just one of the things that happens to one in the thirties—every time I see my father now I think its the last time.

Thank Pauline for the really beautiful Xmas card. It was great to have you both here, even when I was intermittently unconscious.

I send you what may be news, and what a nice precedent for beating up Mencken.[4] Saw the Murphys for an hour in New York. We're sailing March

---

[1] *I Thought of Daisy* (1929).
[2] Fiction editor at *The Saturday Evening Post*.
[3] Hemingway's father had committed suicide.
[4] A newspaper clipping, "Toreador Is Barred for Beating Up Critic."

1st + I hope to have the novel here. (Confidential about sailing though until I'm sure—won't go unless novel's finished.) Ring thought you were fine—he was uncharacteristicly entheusiastic.

I'm bored + somewhat depressed tonight so I won't continue. Oh, yes— I met old H. Stearns just before leaving Paris and feeling drunk and Christ- like suggested a title to him: "Why I go on being poor in Paris", told him to write it as an informal letter to me and I'd sell it. In a burst of energy he did + I sent it to Max who wrote a check for $100.00 for it. Now Harold writes me that $100 isn't very much (as a matter of fact, it isn't much of a letter either) and exhibits such general dissatisfaction that I think he thinks I held out on him. You've got to be careful who you do favors for—within a year you'll probably hear a story that what started him on his downward path was my conscienceless theft of his royaties.

Spengler's second volume[1] is marvellous. Nothing else is any good— when will you save me from the risk of memorizing your works from over- reading them by finishing another? Remember, Proust is dead—to the great envy of

Your Crony and Gossip
Scott

Edgemoor
Delaware

TO: *Maxwell Perkins*   *ALS, 3 pp. Princeton University*
c. March 1, 1929   *"Ellerslie," Edgemoor, Delaware*

Dear Max: I am sneaking away like a thief without leaving the chapters— there is a weeks work to straighten them out + in the confusion of influenza + leaving, I havn't been able to do it. I'll do it on the boat + send it from Genoa. A thousand thanks for your patience—just trust me a few months longer, Max—its been a discouraging time for me too but I will never forget your kindness and the fact that you've never reproached me.

I'm delighted about Ernest's book—I bow to your decision on the modern library without agreeing at all. $100 or $50 advance is better than ⅛ of $40 for a years royalty, + the Scribner collection sounds vague + arbitrary to me. But its a trifle + I'll give them a new + much inferior story instead as I want to be represented with those men, i e Forster, Conrad, Mansfield ect.

Herewith an ms I promised to bring you—I think it needs cutting but it just might sell with a decent title + no forward. I don't feel certain tho at all—

Will you watch for some stories from a young Holger Lundberg who has appeared in the Mercury; he is a man of some promise + I headed him your way.

---

[1] *The Decline of the West.*

I hate to leave without seeing you—and I hate to see you without the ability to put the finished ms in your hands. So for a few months good bye + my affection + gratitude always

Scott.

TO: *Harold Ober*   ALS, *1 p. Lilly Library*

TO: *Harold Ober*
March/April 1929

Hotel Beau Rivage. Nice
(After Sun. c/o Guaranty)

Dear Harold:

We arrive in Paris April 1st, have no appartment yet so will be care of the bank. It will be fine to see you if you can get over. <u>The Rough Crossing</u> has been sent + I've almost finished another. I hope to God the novel will be done this summer.

$400. seems OK. for the sketch. My wife has too more nearly finished—both longer.[1]

No news—I'm happy to be back here + if you cross the channel will take pleasure in buying you the best dinner procurable in France + I've become somewhat of a connessieur.

Ever Yours
F Scott Fitzg

TO: *John Peale Bishop*   ALS, *8 pp. Princeton University*
March/April 1929?   *Paris*

<u>c/o Guaranty Trust</u>

Dear John:

My depression over the badness of the novel[2] as novel had just about sunk me, when I began the novellette[3]—John, it's like two different men writing. The novellette is one of the best war things I've ever read—right up with the very best of Crane and Bierce—intelligent, beautifully organized + written—oh, it moved me and delighted me—the Charlestown country, the night in town, the old lady—but most of all, the position I was in at 4 this afternoon when I was in agony about the novel, the really fine dramatic handling of the old-lady-and-silver episode + the butchery scene. The preparation for the latter was adroit and delicate and just enough.

Now, to be practical—Scribners Magazine will, I'm sure, publish the novellette, if you wish, + pay you from $250–$400 therefore This price is a guess but probably accurate, I'd be glad to act as your amateur agent in the case. It is <u>almost impossible</u> without a big popular name to sell a two-

---

[1] Zelda Fitzgerald's series of "girl" stories for *College Humor*.
[2] Unpublished work by Bishop.
[3] Bishop's story "The Cellar."

part story to any higher priced magazine than that, as I know from my experience with Diamond Big as Ritz, Rich Boy ect. Advise me as to whether I may go ahead—of course authority confined only to American serial rights.

The novel is just something you've learned from + profited by. It has occasional spurts—like the conversations frequently of Brakespeare, but it is terribly tepid—I refrain—rather I don't refrain but here set down certain facts which you are undoubtedly quite as aware of as I am

① Pps 1–28. Elaborate preparation. Baby born without a scene—. Only announcement. Monsignor feeble A Catholic Bishop does not rank above Monsignor—his ambition to be a bishop is as incomprehensible as the idea of a staff captain to have a company.

② You have now all but lost the reader. He will not face the mass of detail 28 et sequitur. Italian theme strained—your ignorance of the catholic church facinates me. Did you ever meet Mrs. Winthrop Chanler? Madden good idea but observed thinly.

Your combination of leaning on a great thing for your color + simultaneously trying to patronize it—!

At end something happens—child cries—feeble—has no significance except the strained one of making the reader think—"Well, after all that climb it must mean more than I think it does!"
Pps 48. et sequitur

1st really fine page—my novel has same idea (shorter) about an English whore. However, when this 6th Who's Who commences all interest finally vanishes. No life is that dull. Did you ever see those mid-western books of the eighties + nineties "Our pioneers", or "Mid-western Military Men— a compilation"? Even lists of dates, with their suggestion, are more alive.

(I'm taking you for a beating, but do you remember your letter to me about Gatsby. I suffered but I got something—like I did out of your friendly tutelage in English poetry.

You ought never to use an unfamiliar word unless you've had to search for it to express a delicate shade—where in effect you have recreated it. This is a damn good prose rule I think. (c.f. "andrognous" ect
   exceptions:
   ⓐ need to avoid repetition
   ⓑ need of rythm, ect.
   ⓒ ect
P. 62 Story interest again begins
p. 71 Gone again. Reader's effort like writers was too much.
P 79 ect. (Incidently in this novel you have ⓐ suggestion that Gettysburg was fought before Chancellorsville ⓑ that retreat from Gettysburg + from Antietam was in same campaign ⓒ that Colonels were often locally elected in Southern armies—which contrasts sharply with your profound knowledge of The Civil War in story.

A big person can make a much bigger mess than a little person and your impressive stature converted a lot of pottery into pebbles during the three years or so you were in the works. Luckily the pottery was never very dear to you. Novels are not written, or at least begun, with the idea of making an ultimate philosphical system—you tried to attone for your lack of confidence by a lack of humility before the form.

The main thing is: no one in our language possibly accepting Wilder has your talent for "the world", your culture, + accuteness of social critisism as implied in the story, there the approach (2nd + 3d person ect.) is considered, full scope for your special talents (descriptive power, sense of "le pays", ramifications of your special virtues such as loyalty, concealment of the sensuality, that is your <u>bête noir</u> to such an extent that you can no longer see it black, like me my drunkeness.

Anyhow it's (the story) marvellous. Don't be mad at this letter. I have the horrors tonight + perhaps am taking it out on you. Write me when I could see you here in Paris in the afternoon between 2.30— +6.30 + talk— + name a day and a cafe at your convenience—I have no dates save on Sunday so any day will suit me. Meanwhile I'll make one more stab at your novel to see if I can think of any way by a miracle of cutting it could be made presentable. But I fear there's neither honor nor money in it for you

Your Old + Always
Affectionate Friend
Scott

Excuse Christ-like tone of letter. Began tippling at page 2 and am now positively holy (like Dostioeveffskis non-stinking monk)

TO: Ernest Hemingway[1]   *AL, 9 pp. John F. Kennedy Library*
June 1929   *Paris*

114–121 is slow + needs cutting—[2] it hasn't the incisiveness of other short portraits in this book or in yr. other books. The characters too numerous + too much nailed down by gags. <u>Please</u> cut! There's absolutely no psycholical justification in introducing those singers—its not even bizarre—if he got stewed with them + in consequence thrown from hospital it would be O.K. At least reduce it to a sharp + self sufficient vignette. It's just rather gassy as it is, I think.

---

[1] In June 1929 Fitzgerald and Hemingway were in Paris when Fitzgerald read a typescript of *A Farewell to Arms* while the novel was being serialized in *Scribner's Magazine*. The nine unnumbered pages of this memo are printed here as units in the order of the references to Hemingway's typescript—except for the pages on which Fitzgerald departed from numerical order.

[2] Ch. 19, pp. 126–29, of *A Farewell to Arms* (New York: Scribners, 1929): the meeting with Meyers and his wife through the conversation with the opera singers and Ettore Moretti. This material is crossed out on Hemingway's typescript, perhaps indicating that he considered cutting it.

For example—your Englishman on the fishing trip in T.S.A.R. contributes to the tautness of waiting for Brett. You seem to have written this to
try to "round out the picture of Milan during the war" during a less inspired
moment.

(Arn't the Croats Orthodox Greeks?[1] or some Byzantine Christian Sect—
Surely they're not predominantly Mohamedens + you can't say their not
Christans

122ect[2]

In "Cat in the rain" + in the story about "That's all we do isn't it, go +
try new drinks ect,"[3] you were really listening to women—here you re only
listening to yourself, to your own mind beating out facily a sort of sense
that isn't really interesting, Ernest, nor really much except a sort of literary
exercise—it seems to me that this ought to be <u>thoroughly</u> cut, even rewritten.

(Our poor old friendship probably won't survive this but there you are—
better me than some nobody in the Literary Review that doesn't care about
you + your future.)

P. 124 <u>et sequitur</u>[4]
This is definately <u>dull</u>—it's all right to say it was meant all the time +
that a novel can't have the finesse of a short story but this has got to. This
scene as it is seems to me a shame.
<u>Later</u> I was astonished to find it was only about 750 wds. which only
goes to show the pace you set yourself up to that point. Its dull because the
war goes further + further out of sight every minute. "That's the way it
was" is no answer—this triumphant proof that races were fixed!
—I should put it as <u>400</u> word beginning to Chap XXI
<u>Still later</u>   Read by itself it has points, but coming on it in the novel I
still believe its dull + slow

Seems to me a last echo of the war very faint when Catherine is dying
and he's drinking beer in the Café.

---

[1]Ch. 26, p. 189: possibly a reference to the priest's statement "The Austrians are Christians—
except for the Bosnians."
[2]Ch. 19, pp. 134–35: Frederic and Catherine's conversation about the rain: "I'm afraid of
the rain because sometimes I see me dead in it."
[3]"Hills Like White Elephants."
[4]Ch. 20, pp. 136ff.: the account of Frederic and Catherine's day at the races.

Look over Switzerland stuff for cutting
        (ie. 2nd page numbered 129)[1]
129 (NW)   Now here's a great scene—your comedy used as part of you
+ not as mere roll-up-my-sleeves- + pull-off a-tour-de-force as on pages
114–121

P. 130—[2]
This is a comedy scene that really becomes offensive for you've trained
everyone to read every word—now you make them read the word cooked
(+ fucked would be as bad) <u>one dozen times</u>. It has ceased to become
amusing by the 5th, for they're too packed, + yet the scene has possibilities.
Reduced to five or six <u>cooked</u> it might have rythm like the word "wops"
in one of your early sketches. You're a little hypnotized by yourself here.

133–138[3]
This could stand a good cutting. Sometimes these conversations with her
take on a naive quality that wouldn't please you in anyone else's work.
Have you read Noel Coward?
    Some of its wonderful—about brave man 1000 deaths ect. Couldn't you
cut a little?

134[4]
Remember the brave expectant illegitimmate mother is an <u>old situation</u>
+ has been exploited by all sorts of people you won't lower yourself to
read—so be sure every line rings <u>new</u> + has some claim to being incarnated
+ inspired truth or you'll have the boys apon you with scorn.

By the way—that buying the pistol is a <u>wonderful</u> scene.[5]

Catherine is too glib, talks too much physically. In cutting their conversations cut some of her speeches rather than his. She is too glib—
    I mean—you're seeing him in a sophisticated way as now you see yourself
then—but you're still seeing her as you did in 1917 thru nineteen yr. old
eyes. In consequence unless you make her a bit fatuous occasionally the
contrast jars—either the writer is a simple fellow or she's Eleanora Duse
disguised as a Red Cross nurse. In one moment you expect her to prophecy
the 2nd battle of the Marne—as you probably did then. Where's that desper-

---

[1]Ch. 22, pp. 152–55: Miss Van Campen's discovery of the empty bottles in Frederic Henry's
hospital room.
    [2]Ch. 21, pp. 142–43: Henry's report of the British major's analysis of the war. "Wops"
refers to the Ch. VIII vignette of *In Our Time* or Ch. 9 of *in our time*.
    [3]Ch. 21, pp. 146–51: the scene in which Catherine announces she is pregnant.
    [4]Ch. 21, p. 147: "I'm going to have a baby, darling."
    [5]Ch. 23, pp. 158–59.

ate, half-childish dont-make-me-think V.A.D. feeling you spoke to me about? It's there—here—but cut <u>to</u> it! Don't try to make her make sense— she probably didn't!

The book, by the way is between 80,000 + 100,000 wds—not 160,000 as you thought

P. 241[1] is one of the best pages you've ever written, I think

P 209– + 219[2] I think if you use the word cocksuckers here the book will be suppressed + confiscated within two days of publication.

———————

All this retreat is marvellous the confusion ect.
The scene from 218[3] on is the best in recent fiction

I think 293–294[4] need cutting but perhaps not to be cut altogether.

Why not end the book with that wonderful paragraph on P. 241.[5] It is the most eloquent in the book + could end it rather gently + well.

A beautiful book it is!

Kiss my ass
EH[6]

TO: *Harold Ober*   *ALS, 2 pp. Lilly Library*
Received June 26, 1929   *Cannes*

Dear Harold: Did the B. + Damned Talkie come thru? Have asked for money as if it had.

I'm calling on you heavily this month (Insurance, income tax, child's adenoid + tonsil operation car, Cannes villa in advance to pay) + last American bills but am sending another story in three days which I hope will more than square us. Adress after 30th June [for emergencies]

> [Fleur des Bois]
> 12 (Boulevard) Gazagnaire
>
> unnessessary (GAZAGNAIR)
> in cables   Cannes

[1] Ch. 34, pp. 266–67: Frederic Henry's night soliloquy after his reunion with Catherine at Stresa: "If people bring so much courage to this world the world has to kill them to break them, so of course it kills them." Fitzgerald wrote in the margin of the typescript: "This is one of the most beautiful pages in all English literature." The note was erased but is still readable.

[2] Ch. 30, pp. 228, 238. The word was replaced with dashes in print.

[3] Ch. 30, pp. 237–41: Frederic Henry's arrest by the *carabinieri* and his escape.

[4] Opening of Ch. 40. This passage was cut by Hemingway.

[5] Ch. 34. See note 1.

[6] Added by Hemingway.

Excuse this scrawl but its four + I've been correcting since ten + have grown hazy with exactitude—I'd like to write this upside down. With 2nd story will have more than 2 clear mos. on Rivierra where we will have a really inexpensive menage, for I'm damn tired of this delay about novel. for novel + if end is in sight in Sept. won't hesitate to borrow from Perkins.

My wife's 4th sketch along shortly. No news. Sorry you didn't get over

Scott Fitzg—

TO: *Harold Ober*   *ALS, 1 p. Lilly Library*
Received July 15, 1929   *Cannes*

Dear Harold:

Of course I was delighted with the news about the raise—which makes actually 900% in 10 yrs., you've made for me.[1] Probably in this case by your own entheusiasm for the story. For that I thank you also. For the enormous loans you've made me I don't even dare begin.

About the Lit. Digest. I'm enclosing Outside the Cabinet Makers with the proof sent me too late for correction but which I'd like to be followed if they use the story. I'll leave it to you to decide whether they use

(1) This enclosed (Outside the ect)
(2) Southern Girl
(3) At Your Age (since you seem to like it so much)

Let me know which you decide to use.

Ever Yrs.
Scott

If you don't use this please return.

TO: *Ernest Hemingway*   *ALS, 2 pp. John F. Kennedy Library*

Villa Fleur des Bois
Cannes. Sept 9th 1929

Dear Ernest:

I'm glad you decided my letter wasn't snooty—it was merely hurried (incidently I thought you wanted a word said to Ruth G.[2] if it came about naturally—I merely remarked that you'd be disappointed if you lost your appartment—never a word that you'd been exasperated.) But enough of

---

[1] *The Saturday Evening Post* had raised Fitzgerald's story price to $4,000 for "At Your Age."
[2] The Hemingways were subletting a Paris apartment from Ruth Obre-Goldbeck-de Vallombrosa.

pretty dismal matters—let us proceed to the really dismal ones. First tho let me say that from Perkins last your book like Pickwick has become a classic while still in serial form. Everything looks bright as day for it and I envy you like hell but would rather have it happen to you than to anyone else.

Just taken another chapter to typists + its left me in a terrible mood of depression as to whether its any good or not. In 2 ½ mos. I've been here I've written 20,000 words on it + one short story, which is suberb for me of late years. I've paid for it with the usual nervous depressions and such drinking manners as the lowest bistrop (bistrot?) boy would scorn. My latest tendency is to collapse about 11.00 and with the tears flowing from my eyes or the gin rising to their level and leaking over, + tell interested friends or acquaintances that I havn't a friend in the world and likewise care for nobody, generally including Zelda and often implying current company—after which the current company tend to become less current and I wake up in strange rooms in strange palaces. The rest of the time I stay alone working or trying to work or brooding or reading detective stories—and realizing that anyone in my state of mind who has in addition never been able to hold his tongue is pretty poor company. But when drunk I make them all pay and pay and pay.

Among them has been Dotty Parker.[1] Naturally she having been in an equivalent state lacks patience—(this isn't snooty—no one likes to see people in moods of despair they themselves have survived.) incidently the Murphys have given their whole performance for her this summer and I think, tho she would be the last to admit it, she's had the time of her life.

We're coming to Paris for 2 mos the 1st of October.

Your analysis of my inability to get my serious work done is too kind in that it leaves out dissipation, but among acts of God it is possible that the 5 yrs between my leaving the army + finishing Gatsby 1919–1924 which included 3 novels, about 50 popular stories + a play + numerous articles + movies may have taken all I had to say too early, adding that all the time we were living at top speed in the gayest worlds we could find. This au fond is what really worries me—tho the trouble may be my inability to leave anything once started—I have worked for 2 months over a popular short story that was foredoomed to being torn up when completed. Perhaps the house will burn down with this ms + preferably me in it

Always Your Stinking Old Friend
Scott

I have no possible right to send you this gloomy letter. Really if I didn't feel rather better with one thing or another I couldn't have written it. Here's a last flicker of the old cheap pride:—the Post now pay the old whore $4000. a screw. But now its because she's mastered the 40 positions—in her youth one was enough.

[1] Writer Dorothy Parker.

TO: *Harold Ober*   *Wire. Lilly Library*
September 24, 1929   *Cannes*

FOLLOWING YOU NATURALLY[1]
  FITZGERALD

TO: *Harold Ober*   *ALS, 1 p. Lilly Library*
Received October 8, 1929   *Cannes*

Dear Harold:

It seems to me this is worth a thousand.[2] Perhaps not from Swanson's[3] point of view though he's running them pretty far forward in his issue—but from the point of view that most of them have been pretty strong draughts on Zelda's and my common store of material. This is Mary Hay for instance + the "Girl the Prince Liked" was Josephine Ordway both of whom I had in my notebook to use. Also they've been coming along pretty faithfully + have a culminative value.

Mailing story of my own Monday. Adress after 1st Paris.

As Ever
Scott

If he can only pay $500 it seems to me Zelda's name should stand alone.

TO: *Harold Ober*   *ALS, 1 p. Lilly Library*
Received October 23, 1929   *Paris*

Adress Guaranty Trust

Dear Harold:

Of course I was sorry to see the firm of Reynolds + Ober broken up, because it had become a part of my life. I hope it was settled + will turn out to your advantage + I'm sure it will.

About Hemmingway—he had recieved several offers from America thru Reynolds and while I have told him that I much preferred to remain with you, I don't know what his intentions are. I think it was foolish to let him slide so long as he was so obviously a comer. I will write you at length about this later.

We are taking an appartment here for the winter + I've sworn not to

---

[1] Ober had left the Reynolds agency to form his own agency, Harold Ober Associates.
[2] "The Girl with Talent," *College Humor* (April 1930). Published as "by F. Scott and Zelda Fitzgerald."
[3] H. N. Swanson, editor of *College Humor*.

come back without the novel which is really drawing to a close. Does Swanson's new price include the Mary Hay sketch?

Ever Yours
Scott Fitzg

I think only the last page of the enclosed need be typed.

TO: *Maxwell Perkins*   *ALS, 2 pp. Princeton University*
c. November 15, 1929   *Paris*

10 Rue Pergolèse
Dear Max:

For the first time since August I see my way clear to a long stretch on the novel, so I'm writing you as I can't bear to do when its in one of its states of postponement + seems so in the air. We are not coming home for Xmas, because of expense + because it'd be an awful interruption now. Both our families are raising hell but I can't compromise the remains of my future for that.

I'm glad of Ring's success tho—at least its for something new + will make him think he's still alive + not a defunct semi-classic. Also Ernest's press has been marvellous + I hope it sells.[1] By the way, McAlmon is a bitter rat and I'm not surprised at anything he does or says. He's failed as a writer and tries to fortify himself by tieing up to the big boys like Joyce and Stien and despising everything else. Part of his quarrel with Ernest some years ago was because he assured Ernest that I was a fairy—God knows he shows more creative imagination in his malice than in his work. Next he told Callaghan[2] that Ernest was a fairy. He's a pretty good person to avoid

Sorry Bunny's book didn't go—I thought it was fine, + more interesting than better or at least more achieved novels.

Congratulations to Louis.

Oh, and what the <u>hell</u> is this book I keep getting clippings about with me and Struthers Burt and Ernest ect.[3] As I remember you refused to let <u>The Rich Boy</u> be published in the <u>Modern Library</u> in a representative collection where it would have helped me + here it is in a book obviously fordoomed to oblivion that can serve no purpose than to fatigue reviewers with the stories. I know its a small matter but I am disturbed by the fact that you didn't see fit to discuss it with me.

However that's a rather disagreeable note to close on when I am forever in your debt for countless favors and valuable advice. It is because so little has happened to me lately that it seems magnified. Will you, by the way,

---

[1] *A Farewell to Arms.*
[2] Canadian novelist Morley Callaghan was published by Scribners.
[3] *Present-Day American Stories* (Scribners, 1929).

send me the Princeton book by Edgar[1]—its not available here. Did Tom
Boyd elope? And what about Biggs play.

Ever Yr. Afft Friend
Scott

TO: *Harold Ober*   *ALS, 2 pp. Lilly Library*
Received November 16, 1929

Adress	10 Rue Pergolèse
till February 15th	Paris
at least	

Dear Harold:

Sorry this has been so delayed. I had another called <u>The Barnaby Family</u>
that I worked on to the point of madness + may yet finish, but simply lost
interest. The enclosed is heavy but, I think, good. Is it too heavy?

Now to answer questions ect

(1) As to Hemmingway. You (I speak of you personally, not the old
firm) made a mistake not to help sell his stuff personally 2 yrs ago—if any
success was more clearly prognosticated I don't know it. I told him the
present situation + I know from several remarks of his that he thought at
first he was being approached by the same agents as mine—but he is being
fought over a lot now + is confused + I think the wisest thing is to do
nothing at present. If any offer for moving pictures of his book for $20,000
or more came to you however don't hesitate to wire him as he's not satisfied
with present picture offers. Simply wire him Garritus—he knows quite well
who you are, ect. <u>Please</u> don't in any correspondence with him use my
name—you see my relations with him are entirely friendly + not business
+ he'd merely lose confidence in me if he felt he was being hemmed in by
any coalition. My guess is, and I'm not sure, that he is pretty much deferring
definate action for the present on stories + serials but this may not be true
by the time this reaches you and may not be at this moment)

(2) I note cable formula + will save $25 or $50 a year thereby.

(3) Post stories all available here—don't send Post.

(4) <u>World</u> offer seems small ($300.). Will answer refusing it politely myself.

(5) Of new authors this Richard Douglass[2] author of <u>The Innocent Voyage</u>
(called <u>High Wind in Bermuda</u>) in England is much the best bet. Will try
to keep you informed at the same time I usually do Scribners of anybody
new I hear of, as, if he interests me I like to give him a chance for a hearing;
but there's nobody now—but may write about that later! America will from
now on give about ½ its book-buying ear to <u>serious</u> people or at any rate
to people who have a backing from the sophisticated minority

---

[1] *In Princeton Town* (1929), by Day Edgar.
[2] Richard Hughes, author of *High Wind in Jamaica* (1929).

(6) <u>New Yorker</u> offers O.K. but uninteresting—as for Mrs. Angell[1] (who-ever she is) I will gladly modify my style and subject matter for her but she will have to give me her beautiful body first and I dare say the price is too high.

(7) Did <u>McCalls</u> like the article "Girls believe in Girls"?

(8) Now I have two uninterrupted months on the novel and will do my best. There is no question of my not trying for the serial right + never has been.

(9) About The <u>Womans Home Companion</u>, you know.

Yours Ever in Masonry and Concubinage
Scott Fitzg—

TO: Maxwell Perkins　　　　　　　　　*ALS, 7 pp. Princeton University*

10 Rue Pergolèse
Paris, France
Jan 21st 1930

This has run to seven long close-written pages so you better not read it when you're in a hurry.

Dear Max: There is so much to write you—or rather so many small things that I'll write 1st the personal things and then on another sheet a series of suggestions about books and authors that have accumulated in me in the last six months.

(1.) To begin with, because I don't mention my novel it isn't because it isn't finishing up or that I'm neglecting it—but only that I'm weary of setting dates for it till the moment when it is in the Post Office Box.

(2) I was very grateful for the money—it won't happen again but I'd man-aged to get horribly into debt + I hated to call on Ober, who's just getting started, for another cent

(3.) Thank you for the documents in the Callaghan case.[2] I'd rather not discuss it except to say that I don't like him and that I wrote him a formal letter of apology. I never thought he started the rumor + never said nor implied such a thing to Ernest.

(4.) Delighted with the success of Ernest's book. I took the responsibility of telling him that McAlmon was at his old dirty work around New York. McAlmon, by the way, didn't have anything to do with founding <u>Transi-</u>

---

[1] Katharine Angell, an editor at the *New Yorker*.

[2] During the summer of 1929, Fitzgerald, acting as timekeeper for a sparring match between Hemingway and Callaghan, inadvertently allowed a round to run long, during which Callaghan knocked down Hemingway. This event was publicized and placed a strain on the Hemingway-Fitzgerald friendship. See Callaghan, *That Summer in Paris* (1963).

tion. He published Ernest's first book over here + some books of his own + did found some little magazine but of no importance.

(5) Thank you for getting Gatsby for me in foreign languages

(6) Sorry about John Biggs but it will probably do him good in the end. The Stranger in Soul Country had something + the Seven Days Whipping was respectable but colorless. Demigods was simply oratorical twirp. How is his play going?

(7.) Tom Boyd seems far away. I'll tell you one awful thing tho. Lawrence Stallings was in the West with King Vidor at a <u>huge</u> salary to write an equivalent of What Price Glory. King Vidor told me that Stallings in despair of showing Vidor what the war was about gave him a copy of Through the Wheat. And that's how Vidor so he told me made the big scenes of the Big Parade. Tom Boyd's profits were a few thousand—Stallings were a few hundred thousands. Please don't connect my name with this story but it is the truth and it seems to me rather horrible.

(8) Lastly + most important. For the English rights of my next book Knopf made me an offer so much better than any in England (advance $500.00; royalies sliding from ten to fifteen + twenty; guaranty to publish next book of short stories at same rate) that I accepted of course.[1] My previous talk with Cape was encouraging on my part but conditional. As to Chatto + Windus—since they made no overtures at my All the Sad Young Men I feel free to take any advantage of a technicality to have my short stories published in England, especially as they answered a letter of mine on the publication of the book with the signature (Chatto + Windus, per Q), undoubtedly an English method of showing real interest in one's work.

I must tell you (+ privately) for your own amusement that the first treaty Knopf sent me contained a clause that would have required me to give him $10,000 on date of publication—that is: 25% of <u>all</u> serial rights (no specifying only English ones,) for which Liberty have contracted, as you know, for $40,000. This was pretty Jewish, or maybe an error in his office, but later I went over the contract with a fine tooth comb + he was very decent. Confidential! Incidently he said to me as Harcourt once did to Ernest that you were the best publishers in America. I told him he was wrong—that you were just a lot of royalty-doctorers + short changers.

No more for the moment. I liked Bunny's book + am sorry it didn't go. I thot those Day Edgar stories made a nice book, didn't you?

Ever Your Devoted Friend
Scott

I append the sheet of brilliant ideas of which you may find one or two worth considering. Congratulations on the Eddy Book

(Suggestion list)

(1.) Certainly if the ubiquitous and ruined McAlmon deserves a hearing

---

[1]Knopf did not publish *Tender Is the Night* in England.

then John Bishop, a poet and a man of really great talents and intelligence does. I am sending you under another cover a sister story[1] of the novelette you refused, which together with the first one and three shorter ones will form his Civil-War-civilian-in-invaded-Virginia-book, a simply grand idea + a new, rich field. The enclosed is the best thing he has ever done and the best thing about the non-combatant or rather behind-the-lines war I've ever read. I hope to God you can use this in the magazine—couldn't it be run into small type carried over like Sew Collins did with Boston + you Farewell to Arms? He needs the encouragement + is so worth it.

(2) In the new American Caravan amid much sandwiching of Joyce and Co is the first work of a 21 year old named Robert Cantwell. Mark it well, for my guess is that he's learned a better lesson from Proust than Thornton Wilder did and has a destiny of no mean star.

(3.) Another young man therein named Gerald Sykes has an extraordinary talent in the line of heaven knows what, but very memorable and distinguished.

(4) Thirdly (and these three are all in the whole damn book) there is a man named Erskine Caldwell, who interested me less than the others because of the usual derivations from Hemmingway and even Callaghan—still read him. He + Sykes are 26 yrs old. I don't know any of them.

If you decide to act in any of these last three cases I'd do it within a few weeks. I know none of the men but Cantwell will go quick with his next stuff if he hasn't gone already. For some reason young writers come in groups—Cummings, Dos Passos + me in 1920–21; Hemmingway, Callaghan + Wilder in 1926–27 and no one in between and no one since. This looks to me like a really new generation

(5) Now a personal friend (but he knows not that I'm you)—Cary Ross (Yale 1925)—poorly represented in this American Caravan, but rather brilliantly by poems in the Mercury + Transition, studying medicine at Johns Hopkins + one who at the price of publication or at least examination of his poems might prove a valuable man. Distincly younger that post war, later than my generation, sure to turn to fiction + worth corresponding with. I believe these are the cream of the young people

(6) [general] Dos Passos wrote me about the ms. of some protegée of his but as I didn't see the ms. or know the man the letter seemed meaningless. Did you do anything about Murray Godwin (or Goodwin?). Shortly I'm sending you some memoirs by an ex-marine, doorman at my bank here. They might have some documentary value as true stories of the Nicaraguan expedition ect.

---

[1]Bishop's "The Cellar" had been rejected by *Scribner's Magazine*, which then accepted "Many Thousands Gone" (September 1930). The novelette won the *Scribner's Magazine* prize for 1930 and became the title story for Bishop's first Charles Scribner's Sons book in 1931.

(7.) In the foreign (French) field there is besides Chamson one man, and at the opposite pole, of great great talent. It is not Cocteau nor Arragon but young <u>René Crevel</u>. I am opposed to him for being a fairy but in the last <u>Transition</u> (number 18.) there is a <u>translation</u> of the beginning of his current novel which simply knocked me cold with its beauty. The part in <u>Transition</u> is called <u>Mr. Knife and Miss Fork</u> and I wish to God you'd read it immediately. Incedently the novel is a great current success here. I know its not yet placed in America + if you're interested <u>please</u> communicate with me <u>before</u> you write Bradley.

(8) Now, one last, much more elaborate idea. In France any military book of real tactical or strategical importance, theoretical or fully documented (+ usually the latter) (and I'm not referring to the one-company battles between "<u>Red</u>" + "<u>Blue</u>" taught us in the army under the name of Small Problems for Infantry). They are mostly published by Payots here + include such works as <u>Ludendorf's Memoirs</u>; and the <u>Documentary Preparations for the German break-thru in 1918</u>—how the men were massed, trained, brought up to the line in 12 hours in 150 different technical groups from flame throwers to field kitchens, the whole inside story <u>from captured orders</u> of the greatest <u>tactical</u> attack in history; a study of <u>Tannenburg</u> (German); several, both French + German of the 1st Marne; a thorough study of gas warfare, another of Tanks, no dogmatic distillations compiled by some old dotart, but original documents.

 <u>Now</u>—believing that so long as we have service schools and not much preparation (I am a political cynic and a big-navy-man, like all Europeans) English Translations should be available in all academies, army service schools, staff schools ect (I'll bet there are American army officers with the rank of Captain that don't know what "infiltration in depth" is or what Colonel Bruckmüller's idea of artillery employment was.) It seems to me that it would be a great patriotic service to consult the war-department bookbuyers on some subsidy plan to bring out a tentative dozen of the most important as "an original scource tactical library of the lessons of the great war." It would be a parallel, but <u>more</u> essentially <u>military</u> rather than <u>politics-military</u>, to the enclosed list of Payot's collection. I underline some of my proposed inclusions. This, in view of some millions of amateurs of battle now in America might be an enormous popular success as well as a patriotic service. Let me know about this because if you shouldn't be interested I'd like to for my own satisfaction make the suggestion to someone else. Some that I've underlined may be already published.

 My God—this is 7 pages + you're asleep + I want to catch the Olympic with this so I'll close. Please tell me your response to <u>each</u> idea.

 Does Chamson sell at all? Oh, for my income tax will you have the usual statement of lack of royalties sent me—+ for my curiosity to see if I've sold a book this year except to myself.

DISASTER, *TENDER IS THE NIGHT*, "CRACK-UP" *1930–1937*

April 1930

 ZF has first breakdown in Paris, enters Malmaison clinic outside Paris, then Valmont clinic in Switzerland. Publication of the first Josephine story, "First Blood," in *The Saturday Evening Post*; the five-story series appears in the *Post* from April 1930 to August 1931.

June 5, 1930

 ZF enters Prangins clinic near Geneva, Switzerland.

Summer and fall 1930

 FSF in Geneva, Lausanne, and Montreux.

Late January 1931

 FSF's father dies. FSF returns alone to America to attend the funeral and for a brief trip to Montgomery to report to the Sayres about ZF.

February 1931

 "Babylon Revisited" in *The Saturday Evening Post*.

September 15, 1931

 ZF is discharged from Prangins; Fitzgeralds return to America permanently.

September 1931–spring 1932

 Rent house at 819 Felder Avenue in Montgomery. FSF goes to Hollywood alone to work on *Red-Headed Woman* for Metro-Goldwyn-Mayer.

November 17, 1931

> Death of Judge A. D. Sayre.

February 1932

> ZF's second breakdown; she enters Phipps Psychiatric Clinic of Johns Hopkins Hospital in Baltimore.

March 1932

> ZF completes the first draft of her novel, *Save Me the Waltz*, while at Phipps Clinic.

May 20, 1932–November 1933

> FSF rents "La Paix" on the outskirts of Baltimore.

June 26, 1932

> ZF discharged from Phipps; joins family at "La Paix."

October 7, 1932

> Publication of *Save Me the Waltz*.

December 1933

> FSF rents house at 1307 Park Avenue, Baltimore.

January 1934

> ZF's third breakdown; enters Sheppard-Pratt Hospital, outside Baltimore.

January–April 1934

> Serialization of *Tender Is the Night* in *Scribner's Magazine*.

March 1934

> ZF enters Craig House clinic in Beacon, New York.

March 29–April 30, 1934

> ZF art exhibit in New York.

April 12, 1934

Publication of *Tender Is the Night*.

May 19, 1934

ZF is transferred back to Sheppard-Pratt Hospital.

February 3, 1935

FSF, convinced he has tuberculosis, goes to Oak Hall Hotel in Tryon, North Carolina.

March 20, 1935

Publication of *Taps at Reveille*, fourth short-story collection.

Summer 1935

FSF at the Grove Park Inn, Asheville, North Carolina.

September 1935

FSF takes apartment at Cambridge Arms, Baltimore.

November 1935

FSF at the Skyland Hotel in Hendersonville, North Carolina, where he begins writing "The Crack-Up" essays.

April 8, 1936

ZF enters Highland Hospital in Asheville.

July–December 1936

FSF at the Grove Park Inn.

September 1936

Death of Mollie McQuillan Fitzgerald in Washington.

January–June 1937

FSF at Oak Hall Hotel in Tryon.

TO: Maxwell Perkins
May 1930

ALS, 2 pp. Princeton University
Paris

Dear Max

First let me tell you how shocked I was by Mr. Scribner's death. It was in due time of course but nevertheless his fairness toward things that were of another generation, his general tolerance and simply his being there as titular head of a great business.

Please tell me how this effects you—if at all.

The letter enclosed[1] has been in my desk for three weeks as I wasn't sure whether to send it when I wrote it. Then Powell Fowler[2] + his wedding party arrived + I got unfortunately involved in dinners + night clubs + drinking; then Zelda got a sort of nervous breakdown from overwork + consequently I havn't done a line of work or written a letter for twenty one days.

Have you read <u>The Building of St. Michele</u>[3] + D. H. Lawrences <u>Fantasia of the Unconscious</u>? Don't miss either of them.

Always Yours
Scott

Adress till July 1<u>st</u>
<u>4 Rue Herran</u>

What news of Ernest?
Please don't mention the enclosed letter to Ober as I've written him already.

TO: Maxwell Perkins
May 1930

ALS, 1 p. Princeton University
Paris

Dear Max:

I was delighted about the Bishop story—the acceptance has done wonders for him. The other night I read him a good deal of my novel + I think he liked it. Harold Ober wrote me that if it couldn't be published this fall I should publish the Basil Lee stories, but I know too well by whom reputations are made + broken to ruin myself completely by such a move—I've seen Tom Boyd, Michael Arlen + too many others fall through the eternal trapdoor of trying cheat the public, no matter what their public is, with substitutes—better to let four years go by. I wrote young + I wrote a lot + the pot takes longer to fill up now but the novel, my novel, is a different matter than if I'd hurriedly finished it up a year and a half ago. If you

---

[1] The following letter in this collection.
[2] Brother of Ludlow Fowler.
[3] *The Story of San Michele* (1929), by Axel Munthe.

think Callahgan hasn't completely blown himself up with this death house masterpiece[1] just wait and see the pieces fall. I don't know why I'm saying this to you who have never been anything but my most loyal and confident encourager and friend but Ober's letter annoyed me today + put me in a wretched humor. I know what I'm doing—honestly, Max. How much time between The Cabala + The Bridge of St Lois Rey, between The Genius + The American Tragedy between The Wisdom Tooth + Green Pastures.[2] I think time seems to go by quicker there in America but time put in is time eventually taken out—and whatever this thing of mine is its certainly not a mediocrity like The Woman of Andros + The Forty Second Parallel.[3] "He through" is an easy cry to raise but its safer for the critics to raise it at the evidence in print than at a long silence.

Ever yours
Scott

TO: *Harold Ober*   *ALS, 4 pp. Lilly Library*
Received May 13, 1930   *Paris*

Dear Harold:

(1st) I will be mailing a new story about the 25th. Glad you liked A Nice Quiet Place. Did you ask about the corrected proof of First Blood—I do so want to have it. Glad you put up a kick about the illustrations—they were awful, with all the youthful suggestion of a G.A.R. congress

Thanks for the statements. I'm about where I feared I was.

Zelda was delighted with your compliments about the Millionaire's Girl.

Now—about the novel—the other night I read one great hunk of it to John Peale Bishop, and we both agreed that it would be ruinous to let Liberty start it uncompleted. Here's a hypothetical possibility. Suppose (as may happen in such cases) they didn't like the end + we quarreled about it—then what the hell! I'd have lost the Post, gained an enemy in Liberty— who would we turn to—Ray Long? Suppose Liberty didn't like even the first part + went around saying it was rotten before it was even finished. I want to be in New York if possible when they accept it for there's that element of cutting, never yet discussed—are they going to cut it? Are they going to cut my stories to 5000 words or not? Are they going to pay $3500. or $4000. At one time I was about to send four chapters out of eight done to you. Then I cut one of those chapters absolutely to pieces. I know you're losing faith in me + Max too but God knows one has to rely in the end on one's own judgement. I could have published four lowsy, half baked books

---

[1] Callaghan, *Strange Fugitive* (1928).

[2] *The Cabala* (1926) and *The Bridge of San Luis Rey* (1927), by Thornton Wilder; *The "Genius"* (1915) and *An American Tragedy* (1925), by Theodore Dreiser; *The Wisdom Tooth* (1926) and *The Green Pastures* (1929), by Marc Connelly.

[3] *The Woman of Andros* (1930), by Wilder; *The 42nd Parallel* (1930), by John Dos Passos.

in the last five years + people would have thought I was at least a worthy young man not drinking myself to pieces in the south seas—but I'd be dead as Michael Arlen, Bromfield, Tom Boyd, Callaghan + the others who think they can trick the world with the hurried and the second rate. These Post stories in the Post are at least not any spot on me—they're honest and if their form is stereotyped people know what to expect when they pick up the Post. The novel is another thing—if, after four years I published the Basil Lee stories as a book I might as well get tickets for Hollywood immediately.

Well, that's how things are. If you'll have confidence in me I think you'll shortly see I knew what I was doing

Ever Yours
Scott Fitz—

This letter sounds cross but I'm stupid-got with work today + too tired to rewrite it. Please forgive it—it has to get tomorrow's boat.

Addenda

Zelda's been sick + not dangerously but seriously, + then I got involved in a wedding party + after 2 weeks just got to work on new story yesterday but 3000 words already done—about as many as I must owe you dollars.

Meanwhile I acknowledge

(1) The account
(2) News about "the Beautiful + D——"
(3) Costain's[1] suggestion (incidently he can go to hell). The only way I can write a decent story is to imagine no one's going to accept it + who cares. Self-consciousness about editors is ruinous to me. They can make their critisisms afterwards. I'm not doing to do another Josephine thing until I can get that out of my head. I tore up the beginning of one. You might tell him pleasantly, of course, that I just can't work that way—Still there's no use telling him—the harms done but if he has any other ideas about writing stories please don't tell me.
(4) I'm sorry the proofs destroyed on First Blood. Could you get me a copy of the magazine its in—I've lost mine. I want to fix it while I remember. By the way I don't mind not having when I'm here on my own stories— but when I've worked on a proof its like losing a whole draft of a thing.

Yours Always
Scott

Last Word

I understand the movies are buying short stories again. Do you know a good agent in Hollywood you might persuade to interest himself in Majesty.

---

[1]Thomas B. Costain, *Saturday Evening Post* editor, who later became a popular historical novelist.

Its constructed dramaticly like a play + has some damn good dramatic scenes in it

FSF

Address till July 1st
4 Rue Herran

TO: *Mollie McQuillan Fitzgerald*   *ALS, 2 pp. Princeton University*
June 1930   *Beau-Rivage Palace stationery.*
                                                    Ouchy-Lausanne, Switzerland

Adress Paris

Dear Mother:

My delay in writing is due to the fact that Zelda has been desperately ill with a complete nervous breakdown and is in a sanitarium near here. She is better now but recovery will take a long time I did not tell her parents the seriousness of it so say nothing—the danger was to her sanity rather than her life.

Scotty is in the appartment in Paris with her governess. She loved the picture of her cousins. Tell Father I visited the

"—seven pillars of Gothic mould
in Chillon's dungeons deep and old,"[1]

+ thought of the first poem I ever heard, or was "The Raven." Thank you for the Chesterton.

Love
Scott

TO: *Mollie McQuillan Fitzgerald*   *ALS, 1 p. Princeton University*
June 1930   *Montreux, Switzerland*

Dear Mother:

I've thought of you both a lot lately and I hope Father is better after his indigestion. Zelda's recovery is slow. Now she has terrible ecxema—one of those mild but terrible diseases that don't worry relations but are a living hell for the patient. If all goes as well as it did up to a fortnight ago we will be home by Thanksgiving.

According to your poem I am destined to be a failure. I re-enclose it

(1) All big men have spent money freely. I hate avarice or even caution

(2) I have never forgiven or forgotten an injury

---

[1] From "The Prisoner of Chillon," by Byron.

(3) This is the only one that makes sense.

(4) If its worth doing. Otherwise it should be thrown over immediately

(5) No man's critisism has ever been worth a damn to me.

These would be good rules for a man who wanted to be a chief clerk at 50.

Thanks for the check but really you mustn't. I re-enclose it. The snap I'll send to Scotty. The children are charming. Adress me care of my Paris Bank though I'm still by father's Castle of Chillon. Have you read Maurois' Life of Byron?[1] And Thomas Wolfe's <u>Look Homeward, Angel?</u>[2]

> Much love to you both
>
> Scott

TO: Madame Lubov Egorova[3]   *CC, 2 pp.*[4] *Princeton University*

HOTEL RIGHI VAUDOIS,
GLION

June 22, 1930

Dear Madame Egarowa,

Zelda is still very ill. From time to time there is some improvement and then all of a sudden she commits some insane act. Unfortunately, complete recovery seems to be still far away.

As you know, one of the things which prevents her from getting better, and goes against all of the doctors' efforts, is her continuous fear that she is wasting time required for her dancing class and that she has no time to lose. This fear makes her nervous and unsettled, and it postpones her recovery every time she thinks about it. It is for this reason that she left Malmaison much too soon.

It is doubtful—though she is unaware of it—that she could ever return to her dancing school; in any event, she will never be able to work with the same intensity, even though to my mind her appearing on stage could do her a lot of good.

Moreover, doctors would like to know what her chances were, what her future was like as a dancer, when she fell ill. She does not know it herself: one minute she says one thing, the next another. Her situation being critical, it is rather necessary that she should know the answer, despite all the disappointment it could cause her. That is why, knowing the affection you bear her and all the interest that you take in her ambitions I have come to ask you for a frank opinion.

---

[1] André Maurois, *Byron* (1930).

[2] *Look Homeward, Angel* had been published by Scribners in 1929.

[3] Zelda Fitzgerald's ballet teacher in Paris.

[4] Fitzgerald sent Egorova a French translation of his letter; the text printed here was translated by Eric Roman.

It may be that in answering the following questions we would succeed in finding a solution.

1.- Could she ever reach the level of a first-rate dancer?

2.- Will she ever be a dancer like Nikitina, Danilowa etc.?

3.- If the answer to question number 2 is yes, then how many years would be required for her to achieve this goal, based on the progress she was making?

4.- If the answer to question number 2 is no, then do you believe that through the charm of her face and that of her beautiful body she could manage to get important roles in ballets such as Massine, for example, produces in New York?

5.- Are there things such as balance, etc. that she will never achieve because of her age and because she started too late?

6.- Is she as good a dancer as "Galla," for example? To give me an idea of her position in your school, are there many students who are better than she?

7.- On the whole, do you believe that if she had not taken ill, she could have achieved a level as a dancer that would have satisfied both her ideal and her ambitions?

Have you ever thought that, lately, Zelda was working too much for someone her age?

I understand that all these questions are importunate but the goal of this is to save her sanity, and the truth about her career is necessary. You are the only person whom I can ask because you have always been very good to my wife, and you have always been interested in her work.

With all my apologies for the bother I may cause you, please rest assured of my admiration and of my respectful feelings.[1]

TO: Maxwell Perkins   *ALS, 1 p. Princeton University*
c. July 20, 1930   *Switzerland*

Dear Max:

Zelda is still sick as hell, and the psychiatrist who is devoting almost his entire time to her is an expensive proposition. I was so upset in June when hopes for her recovery were black that I could practically do no work + got behind—then arrived a wire from Ober that for the first time he couldn't make me the usual advance up to the price of a story. So then I called on you. I am having him turn over to you 3000. from the proceeds of the story I am sending off this week, as its terrible to be so in debt. A thousand thanks + apologies

Yours As Ever (if somewhat harrassed and anxious about life)

Scott

---

[1] On July 9, 1930, Egorova replied that Zelda would never be a first-rate dancer because she had started too late. Egorova added that Zelda could become a good to very good dancer and that she would be capable of dancing important roles in the Massine Ballet Company.

TO: *Zelda Fitzgerald*   *AL, 7 pp.*[1] *Princeton University*
Summer? 1930   *Paris or Lausanne*

Written with Zelda gone to the Clinique

I know this then—that those days when we came up from the south, from Capri, were among my happiest—but you were sick and the happiness was not in the home.

I had been unhappy for a long time then—When my play failed a year and a half before, when I worked so hard for a year, twelve stories and novel and four articles in that time with no one believing in me and no one to see except you + before the end your heart betraying me and then I was really alone with no one I liked   In Rome we were dismal and was still working proof and three more stories and in Capri you were sick and there seemed to be nothing left of happiness in the world anywhere I looked.

Then we came to Paris and suddenly I realized that it hadn't all been in vain. I was a success—the biggest man in my profession everybody admired me and I was proud I'd done such a good thing. I met Gerald and Sara who took us for friends now and Ernest who was an equeal and my kind of an idealist. I got drunk with him on the Left Bank in careless cafés and drank with Sara and Gerald in their garden in St Cloud but you were endlessly sick and at home everything was unhappy. We went to Antibes and I was happy but you were sick still and all that fall and that winter and spring at the cure and I was alone all the time and I had to get drunk before I could leave you so sick and not care and I was only happy a little while before I got too drunk. Afterwards there were all the usuall penalties for being drunk.

Finally you got well in Juan-les-Pins and a lot of money came in and I made of those mistakes literary men make—I thought I was "a man of the world—that everybody liked me and admired me for myself but I only liked a few people like Ernest and Charlie McArthur[2] and Gerald and Sara who were my peers. Time goes bye fast in those moods and nothing is ever done. I thought then that things came easily—I forgot how I'd dragged the great Gatsby out of the pit of my stomach in a time of misery. I woke up in Hollywood no longer my egotistic, certain self but a mixture of Ernest in fine clothes and Gerald with a career—and Charlie McArthur with a past. Anybody that could make me believe that, like Lois Moran[3] did, was precious to me.

Ellerslie, the polo people, Mrs. Chanler[4] the party for Cecelia[5] were all attempts to make up from without for being undernourished now from

---

[1] Draft for a letter that may not have been sent.
[2] Charles MacArthur, playwright and screenwriter; married to actress Helen Hayes.
[3] Young movie actress whom Fitzgerald had met in Hollywood in 1927; she provided the model for Rosemary Hoyt in *Tender Is the Night*.
[4] Probably Mrs. Winthrop Chanler, a wealthy friend of Father Fay's.
[5] Daughter of Fitzgerald's cousin Cecilia Taylor.

within. Anything to be liked, to be reassured not that I was a man of a little genius but that I was a great man of the world. At the same time I knew it was nonsense—the part of me that knew it was nonsense brought us to the Rue Vaugirard.

But now you had gone into yourself just as I had four years before in St. Raphael—And there were all the consequences of bad appartments through your lack of patience ("Well, if you were [   ] why don't you make some money") bad servants, through your indifference ("Well, if you don't like her why don't you send Scotty away to school") Your dislike for Vidor, your indifference to Joyce I understood—share your incessant entheusisam and absorbtion in the ballet I could not. Somewhere in there I had a sense of being exploited, not by you but by something I resented terribly no happiness. Certainly less than there had ever been at home—you were a phantom washing clothes, talking French bromides with Lucien or Del Plangue[1]—I remember desolate trips to Versaille to Rhiems, to La Baule undertaken in sheer weariness of home. I remember wondering why I kept working to pay the bills of this desolate menage. I had evolved. In despair I went from the extreme of isolation, which is to say isolation with Mlle Delplangue, or the Ritz Bar where I got back my self esteem for half an hour, often with someone I had hardly ever seen before. In the evenings sometimes you and I rode to the Bois in a cab—after awhile I preferred to go to Cafe de Lilas and sit there alone remembering what a happy time I had had there with Ernest, Hadley, Dorothy Parker + Benchley two years before. During all this time, remember I didn't blame anyone but myself. I complained when the house got unbearable but after all I was not John Peale Bishop—I was paying for it with work, that I passionately hated and found more and more difficult to do. The novel was like a dream, daily farther and farther away.

Ellerslie was better and worse. Unhappiness is less accute when one lives with a certain sober dignity but the financial strain was too much. Between Sept when we left Paris and March when we reached Nice we were living at the rate of forty thousand a year.

But somehow I felt happier. Another spring—I would see Ernest whom I had launched, Gerald + Sarah who through my agency had been able to try the movies.[2] At least life would less drab; there would be parties with people who offered something, conversations with people with something to say. Later swimming and getting tanned and young and being near the sea.

It worked out beautifully didn't it. Gerald and Sara didn't see us. Ernest and I met but it was a more irritable Ernest, apprehensively telling me his whereabouts lest I come in on them tight and endanger his lease. The discovery that half a dozen people were familiars there didn't help my self

---

[1]Scottie's governess.
[2]Gerald Murphy had worked with movie director King Vidor on *Hallelujah*.

esteem. By the time we reached the beautiful Rivierra I had developed such an inferiority complex that I couldn't fase anyone unless I was tight. I worked there too, though, and the unusual combination exploded my lungs.

You were gone now—I scarcely remember you that summer. You were simply one of all the people who disliked me or were indifferent to me. I didn't like to think of you—You didn't need me and it was easier to talk to or rather at Madame Bellois and keep full of wine. I was grateful when you came with me to the Doctors one afternoon but after we'd been a week in Paris and I didn't try any more about living or dieing. Things were always the same. The appartments that were rotten, the maids that stank—the ballet before my eyes, spoiling a story to take the Troubetskoys to dinner, poisoning a trip to Africa. You were going crazy and calling it genius—I was going to ruin and calling it anything that came to hand. And I think everyone far enough away to see us outside of our glib presentation of ourselves guessed at your almost meglomaniacal selfishness and my insane indulgence in drink. Toward the end nothing much mattered. The nearest I ever came to leaving you was when you told me you thot I was a fairy in the Rue Palatine but now whatever you said aroused a sort of detached pity for you. For all your superior observation and your harder intelligence I have a faculty of guessing right, without evidence even with a certain wonder as to why and whence that mental short cut came. I wish the Beautiful and Damned had been a maturely written book because it was all true. We ruined ourselves—I have never honestly thought that we ruined each other.

FROM: Zelda Fitzgerald[1]　　　　　　*AL, 42 pp. Princeton University*
Late summer/early fall 1930　　　　　*Prangins Clinic, Nyon, Switzerland*

Dear Scott:

I have just written to Newman[2] to come here to me. You say that you have been thinking of the past. The weeks since I haven't slept more than three or four hours, swathed in bandages sick and unable to read so have I.

There was:

The strangeness and excitement of New York, of reporters and furry smothered hotel lobbies, the brightness of the sun on the window panes and the prickly dust of late spring: the impressiveness of the Fowlers and much tea-dancing and my eccentric behavior at Princeton. There were Townsend's[3] blue eyes and Ludlow's[4] rubbers and a trunk that exhuded sachet and the marshmallow odor of the Biltmore. There were always

---

[1] This letter by Zelda Fitzgerald provides her history of the Fitzgeralds' marriage up to the time of her hospitalization in Switzerland.

[2] Newman Smith, Zelda Fitzgerald's brother-in-law.

[3] Townsend Martin.

[4] Ludlow Fowler.

Ludow and Townsend and Alex and Bill Mackey[1] and you and me. We did not like women and we were happy. There was Georges[2] appartment and his absinth cock-tails and Ruth Findleys gold hair in his comb, and visits to the "Smart Set" and "Vanity Fair"—a collegiate literary world puffed into wide proportions by the New York papers. There were flowers and night clubs and Ludlow's advice that moved us to the country. At West Port, we quarrelled over morals once, walking beside a colonial wall under the freshness of lilacs. We sat up all night over "Brass Knuckles and Guitar." There was the road house where we bought gin, and Kate Hicks and the Maurices and the bright harness of the Rye Beach Club. We swam in the depth of the night with George before we quarrelled with him and went to John Williams parties where there were actresses who spoke French when they were drunk. George played "Cuddle up a Little Closer" on the piano. There were my white knickers that startled the Connecticut hills, and the swim in the sandaled lady's bird-pool. The beach, and dozens of men, mad rides along the Post Road and trips to New York. We never could have a room at a hotel at night we looked so young, so once we filled an empty suit case with the telephone directory and spoons and a pin-cushion at The Manhattan—I was romanticly attached to Townsend and he went away to Tahatii—and there were your episodes of Gene Bankhead and Miriam. We bought the Marmon with Harvey Firestone and went south through the haunted swamps of Virginiia, the red clay hills of Georgia, the sweet rutted creek-bottoms of Alabama. We drank corn on the wings of an aeroplane in the moon-light and danced at the country-club and came back. I had a pink dress that floated and a very theatrical silver one that I bought with Don Stewart.

We moved to 59th Street. We quarrelled and you broke the bathroom door and hurt my eye. We went so much to the theatre that you took it off the income tax. We trailed through Central Park in the snow after a ball at the Plaza, I quarrelled with Zoë about Bottecelli[3] at the Brevoort and went with her to buy a coat for David Belasco.[4] We had Bourbon and Deviled Ham and Christmas at the Overmans[5] and ate lots at the Lafayette. There was Tom Smith and his wall-paper and Mencken and our Valentine party and the time I danced all night with Alex and meals at Mollats with John[6] and I skated, and was pregnant and you wrote the "Beautiful and Damned." We came to Europe and I was sick and complained always. There was London, and Wopping with Shane Leslie and strawberries as big as tomatoes at Lady Randolph Churchills. There was St. Johns Ervines wooden leg and Bob Handley in the gloom of the Cecil—There was Paris and the heat and

[1] Alexander McKaig and possibly William Mackie.
[2] George Jean Nathan, co-editor of *The Smart Set*.
[3] Playwright Zoë Akins; Botticelli is a parlor game.
[4] Theatrical producer.
[5] Lynne Overman, stage and screen actor.
[6] John Peale Bishop.

the ice-cream that did not melt and buying clothes—and Rome and your friends from the British Embassy and your drinking, drinking. We came home. There was "Dog"[1] and lunch at the St. Regis with Townsend and Alex and John: Alabama and the unbearable heat and our almost buying a house. Then we went to St. Paul and hundreds of people came to call. There were the Indian forests and the moon on the sleeping porch and I was heavy and afraid of the storms. Then Scottie was born and we went to all the Christmas parties and a man asked Sandy[2] "who is your fat friend?" Snow covered everything. We had the Flu and went lots to the Kalmans and Scottie grew strong. Joseph Hergesheimer came and Saturdays we went to the university Club. We went to the Yacht Club and we both had minor flirtatons. Joe began to dislike me, and I played so much golf that I had Tetena.[3] Kollie[4] almost died. We both adored him. We came to New York and rented a house when we were tight. There was Val Engelicheff and Ted Paramour[5] and dinner with Bunny in Washington Square and pills and Doctor Lackin   And we had a violent quarrell on the train going back, I don't remember why. Then I brought Scottie to New York. She was round and funny in a pink coat and bonnet and you met us at the station. In Great Neck there was always disorder and quarrels: about the Golf Club, about the Foxes, about Peggy Weber, about Helen Buck, about everything. We went to the Rumseys,[6] and that awful night at the Mackeys[7] when Ring sat in the cloak-room. We saw Esther and Glen Hunter[8] and Gilbert Seldes. We gave lots of parties: the biggest one for Rebecca West. We drank Bass Pale Ale and went always to the Bucks or the Lardners or the Swopes when they weren't at our house. We saw lots of Sydney Howard and fought the week-end that Bill Motter was with us. We drank always and finally came to France because there were always too many people in the house. On the boat there was almost a scandal about Bunny Burgess. We found Nanny and went to Hyeres—Scottie and I were both sick there in the dusty garden full of Spanish Bayonet and Bourgainvilla. We went to St. Raphael. You wrote, and we went sometimes to Nice or Monte Carlo. We were alone, and gave big parties for the French aviators. Then there was Josen[9] and you were justifiably angry. We went to Rome. We ate at the Castelli dei Cesari.

[1] A comic song Fitzgerald had written.

[2] Xandra Kalman.

[3] Possibly tetany, a condition resembling tetanus.

[4] Oscar Kalman.

[5] Prince Vladimir N. Engalitcheff, son of the former Russian vice consul in Chicago and a wealthy American mother; E. E. Paramore.

[6] Charles Cary Rumsey, sculptor and polo player who had an estate at Westbury, Long Island.

[7] Probably financier Clarence MacKay.

[8] Actor Glenn Hunter appeared in *Grit* (1924), a silent movie for which Fitzgerald wrote the scenario.

[9] Edouard Jozan, French naval aviator with whom Zelda Fitzgerald was romantically involved in the summer of 1924.

The sheets were always damp. There was Christmas in the echoes, and eternal walks. We cried when we saw the Pope. There were the luminous shadows of the Pinco and the officer's shining boots. We went to Frascati and Tivoli. There was the jail,[1] and Hal Rhodes at the Hotel de Russie and my not wanting to go to the moving-picture ball[2] at the Excelsior and asking Hungary Cox[3] to take me home. Then I was horribly sick, from trying to have a baby and you didn't care much and when I was well we came back to Paris. We sat to-gether in Marseilles and thought how good France was. We lived in the rue Tilsitt, in red plush and Teddy[4] came for tea and we went to the markets with the Murphies. There were the Wimans[5] and Mary Hay and Eva La Galliene and rides in the Bois at dawn and the night we all played puss-in-the-corner at the Ritz. There was Tunti and nights in Mont Matre. We went to Antibes, and I was sick always and took too much Dial.[6] The Murphy's were at the Hotel du Cap and we saw them constantly. Back in Paris I began dancing lessons because I had nothing to do. I was sick again at Christmas when the Mac Leishes came and Doctor Gros said there was no use trying to save my ovaries. I was always sick and having picqures[7] and things and you were naturally more and more away. You found Ernest and the Cafe des Lilas and you were unhappy when Dr. Gros sent me to Salies-de Bearn.[8] At the Villa Paquita I was always sick. Sara brought me things and we gave a lunch for Geralds father. We went to Cannes and and listned to Raquel Miller[9] and dined under the rain of fire-works. You couldn't work because your room was damp and you quarrelled with the Murphys. We moved to a bigger villa and I went to Paris and had my appendix out. You drank all the time and some man called up the hospital about a row you had had. We went home, and I wanted you to swim with me at Juan-les-Pins but you liked it better where it was gayer: at the Garoupe[10] with Marice Hamilton and the Murphys and the Mac Leishes. Then you found Grace Moore[11] and Ruth and Charlie[12] and the summer passed, one party after another. We quarrelled about Dwight Wiman and you left me lots alone. There were too many people and too many things to do: every-day there was something and our house was always full. There was Gerald and Ernest and you often did not come home. There were the English sleepers that I found downstairs one morning and Bob

---

[1]In the fall of 1924 Fitzgerald was jailed in Rome after a drunken brawl.
[2]A Christmas party for the cast of *Ben-Hur*.
[3]Howard Coxe, journalist and novelist.
[4]Possibly composer Theodore Chanler.
[5]Producer Dwight Wiman.
[6]Preparation containing alcohol; used as a sedative.
[7]Probably *piqûres* ("injections").
[8]Spa in the Pyrenees where Zelda Fitzgerald took a "cure" in January 1926.
[9]Raquel Meller, internationally known Spanish singer.
[10]A beach at Cap d'Antibes.
[11]Opera singer and actress whom the Fitzgeralds knew on the Riviera.
[12]Ruth Ober-Goldbeck-de Vallombrosa; Charles MacArthur.

and Muriel and Walker[1] and Anita Loos, always somebody—Alice Delamar and Ted Rousseau and our trips to St. Paul[2] and the note from Isadora Duncan and the countryside slipping by through the haze of Chamberry-fraises and Graves—That was your summer. I swam with Scottie except when I followed you, mostly unwillingly. Then I had asthma and almost died in Genoa. And we were back in America—further apart than ever before. In California, though you would not allow me to go anywhere without you, you yourself engaged in flagrantly sentimental relations with a child.[3] You said you wanted nothing more from me in all your life, though you made a scene when Carl[4] suggested that I go to dinner with him and Betty Compson. We came east: I worked over Ellerslie incessantly and made it function. There was our first house-party and you and Lois—and when there was nothing more to do on the house I began dancing lessons. You did not like it when you saw it made me happy. You were angry about rehearsals and insistent about trains. You went to New York to see Lois and I met Dick Knight[5] the night of that party for Paul Morand.[6] Again, though you were by then thoroughly entangled sentimentally, you forbade my seeing Dick and were furious about a letter he wrote me. On the boat coming over you paid absolutely no attention of any kind to me except to refuse me the permission to stay to a concert with whatever-his-name-was. I think the most humiliating and bestial thing that ever happenned to me in my life is a scene that you probably don't remember even in Genoa. We lived in the rue Vaugirard. You were constantly drunk. You didn't work and were dragged home at night by taxi-drivers when you came home at all. You said it was my fault for dancing all day. What was I to do? You got up for lunch. You made no advances toward me and complained that I was un-responsive. You were literally eternally drunk the whole summer. I got so I couldn't sleep and I had asthma again. You were angry when I wouldn't go with you to Mont Matre. You brought drunken under-graduates in to meals when you came home for them, and it made you angry that I didn't care any more. I began to like Egorowa—On the boat going back I told you I was afraid that there was something abnormal in the relationship and you laughed. There was more or less of a scandal about Philipson, but you did not even try to help me. You brought Philippe[7] back and I couldn't manage the house any more; he was insubordinate and disrespectful to me and you wouldn't let him go. I began to work harder

[1] Walker Ellis, Princetonian with whom Fitzgerald had worked on *Fie! Fie! Fi-Fi!*

[2] St.-Paul-de-Vence, a town in the mountains above the Riviera where Zelda was angered one night by Fitzgerald's attentions to Isadora Duncan.

[3] Zelda resented Fitzgerald's friendship with Lois Moran.

[4] Carl Van Vechten.

[5] New York lawyer Richard Knight.

[6] French diplomat and author; best known for *Open All Night* (1923) and *Closed All Night* (1924).

[7] Paris taxi driver whom Fitzgerald brought to "Ellerslie" in 1928 to serve as chauffeur.

at dancing—I thought of nothing else but that. You were far away by then and I was alone. We came back to rue Palantine and you, in a drunken stupor told me a lot of things that I only half understood[1]: but I understood the dinner we had at Ernests'. Only I didn't understand that it matterred. You left me more and more alone, and though you complained that it was the appartment or the servants or me, you know the real reason you couldn't work was because you were always out half the night and you were sick and you drank constantly. We went to Cannes. I kept up my lessons and we quarrelled   You wouldn't let me fire the nurse that both Scottie and I hated. You disgraced yourself at the Barry's[2] party, on the yacht at Monte Carlo, at the casino with Gerald and Dotty.[3] Many nights you didn't come home. You came into my room once the whole summer, but I didn't care because I went to the beach in the morning, I had my lesson in the afternoon and I walked at night. I was nervous and half-sick but I didn't know what was the matter. I only knew that I had difficulty standing lots of people, like the party at Wm J. Locke's and that I wanted to get back to Paris. We had lunch at the Murphy's and Gerald said to me very pointedly several times that Nemchinova[4] was at Antibes. Still I didn't understand. We came back to Paris. You were miserable about your lung,[5] and because you had wasted the summer, but you didn't stop drinking   I worked all the time and I became dependent on Egorowa. I couldn't walk in the street unless I had been to my lesson. I couldn't manage the appartment because I couldn't speak to the servants. I couldn't go into stores to buy clothes and my emotions became blindly involved. In February, when I was so sick with bronchitis that I had ventouses[6] every day and fever for two weeks, I had to work because I couldn't exist in the world without it, and still I didn't understand what I was doing. I didn't even know what I wanted. Then we went to Africa and when we came back I began to realize because I could feel what was happenning in others. You did not want me. Twice you left my bed saying "I can't. Don't you understand"—I didn't. Then there was the Harvard man who lost his direction, and when I wanted you to come home with me you told me to sleep with the coal man. At Nancy Hoyt's[7] dinner she offered her services but there was nothing the matter with my head then, though I was half dead, so I turned back to the studio. Lucienne[8]

---

[1]Fitzgerald had come home after a drinking session with Hemingway and passed out. In his sleep he said "No more baby," which Zelda interpreted as evidence that Fitzgerald and Hemingway were engaged in a homosexual affair.

[2]Playwright Philip Barry.

[3]Dorothy Parker.

[4]Prima ballerina Nemtchinova.

[5]Fitzgerald believed he had tuberculosis.

[6]French medical term for cupping.

[7]Novelist; sister of Elinor Wylie.

[8]Ballerina in Madame Egorova's studio.

was sent away but since I knew nothing about the situation, I didn't know why there was something wrong. I just kept on going. Lucienne came back and later went away again and then the end happenned   I went to Malmaison. You wouldn't help me—I don't blame you by now, but if you had explained I would have understood because all I wanted was to go on working. You had other things: drink and tennis, and we did not care about each other. You hated me for asking you not to drink. A girl came to work with me but I didn't want her to. I still believed in love and I thought suddenly of Scottie and that you supported me. So at Valmont I was in tortue, and my head closed to-gether. You gave me a flower and said it was "plus petite et moins etendue"—[1] We were friends—Then you took it away and I grew sicker, and there was nobody to teach me, so here I am, after five months of misery and agony and desperation. I'm glad you have found that the material for a Josepine story[2] and I'm glad that you take such an interest in sports. Now that I can't sleep any more I have lots to think about, and since I have gone so far alone I suppose I can go the rest of the way— but if it were Scottie I would not ask that she go through the same hell and if I were God I could not justify or find a reason for imposing it—except that it was wrong, of cource, to love my teacher when I should have loved you. But I didn't have you to love—not since long before I loved her.

I have just begun to realize that sex and sentiment have little to do with each other. When I came to you twice last winter and asked you to start over it was because I thought I was becoming seriously involved sentimentally and preparing situations for which I was morally and practicly unfitted. You had a song about Gigolos: if that had ever entered my head there was, besides the whole studio, 3 other solutions in Paris.

I came to you half-sick after a difficult lunch at Armonville and you kept me waiting until it was too late in front of the Guaranty Trust.

Sandy's[3] tiny candle was not much of a strain, but it required something better than your week of drunkenness to put it out. You didn't care: so I went on and on—dancing alone, and, no matter what happens, I still know in my heart that it is a Godless, dirty game; that love is bitter and all there is, and that the rest is for the emotional beggars of the earth and is about the equivalent of people who stimulate themselves with dirty post-cards—

[1]Fitzgerald used this phrase in one of Nicole's letters from the sanitarium in *Tender Is the Night*.

[2]In 1930 Fitzgerald began a series of five stories for *The Saturday Evening Post* about Josephine Perry, a teenage girl who undergoes a process of "emotional bankruptcy."

[3]The Kalmans were in Paris at the time of Zelda Fitzgerald's breakdown in the spring of 1930.

TO: Dr. Oscar Forel[1] AL (draft), 6 pp. Princeton University
Summer? 1930 Switzerland

For translation with carbon. But
not on hotel stationary.

This letter is about a matter that had best be considered frankly now than
six months or a year from now. When I last saw you I was almost as broken
as my wife by months of horror. The only important thing in my life was
that she should be saved from madness or death. Now that, due to your
tireless intelligence and interest, there is a time in sight where Zelda and I
may renew our life together on a decent basis, a thing which I desire with
all my heart, there are other considerations due to my nessessities as a
worker and to my very existence that I must put before you.

   During my young manhood for seven years I worked extremely hard, in
six years bringing myself by tireless literary self-discipline to a position
of unquestioned preeminence among younger American writers, also by
additional "hack-work" for the cinema ect. I gave my wife a comfortable
and luxurious life such as few European writers ever achieve. My work is
done on coffee, coffee and more coffee, never on alcohol. At the end of five
or six hours I get up from my desk white and trembling and with a steady
burn in my stomach, to go to dinner. Doubtless a certain irritability developed in those years, an inability to be gay which my wife—who had never
tried to use her talents and intelligence—was not inclined to condone. It
was on our coming to Europe in 1924 and apon her urging that I began to
look forward to wine at dinner—she took it at lunch, I did not. We went
on hard drinking parties together sometimes but the regular use of wine
and apperatives was something that I dreaded but she encouraged because
she found I was more cheerful then and allowed her to drink more. The
ballet idea was something I inaugurated in 1927 to stop her idle drinking
after she had already so lost herself in it as to make suicidal attempts. Since
then I have drunk more, from unhappiness, and she less, because of her
physical work—that is another story.

   Two years ago in America I noticed that when we stopped all drinking
for three weeks or so, which happened many times, I immediately had dark
circles under my eyes, was listless and disinclined to work.

   I gave up strong cigarettes and, in a panic that perhaps I was just giving
out, applied for a large insurance policy. The one trouble was low blood-
pressure, a matter which they finally condoned, and they issued me the
policy. I found that a moderate amount of wine, a pint at each meal made
all the difference in how I felt. When that was available the dark circles
disappeared, the coffee didn't give me excema or beat in my head all night,
I looked forward to my dinner instead of staring at it, and life didn't seem

[1] Head psychiatrist at Les Rives de Prangins clinic.

196

a hopeless grind to support a woman whose tastes were daily diverging from mine. She no longer read or thought or knew anything or liked anyone except dancers and their cheap satellites   People respected her because I concealed her weaknesses, and because of a certain complete fearlessness and honesty that she has never lost, but she was becoming more and more an egotist and a bore. Wine was almost a nessessity for me to be able to stand her long monalogues about ballet steps, alternating with a glazed eye toward any civilized conversation whatsoever

Now when that old question comes up again as to which of two people is worth preserving, I, thinking of my ambitions once so nearly achieved of being part of English literature, of my child, even of Zelda in the matter of providing for her—must perforce consider myself first. I say that without defiance but simply knowing the limits of what I can do. To stop drinking entirely for six months and see what happens, even to continue the experiment thereafter if successful—only a pig would refuse to do that. Give up strong drink permanently I will. Bind myself to forswear wine forever I cannot. My vision of the world at its brightest is such that life without the use of its amentities is impossible. I have lived hard and ruined the essential innocense in myself that could make it that possible, <u>and the fact that I have abused liquor</u> is something <u>to be paid for with suffering and death perhaps but not with renunciation</u>. For me <u>it would be as illogical as permanently giving up sex because I caught a disease</u> (which I hasten to assure you I never have)   I cannot consider one pint of wine at the days end as anything but one of the rights of man.

Docs this sound like a long polemic composed of childish stubborness and ingratitude? If it were that it would be so much easier to make promises. What I gave up for Zelda was women and it wasn't easy in the position my success gave me—what pleasure I got from comradeship she has pretty well ruined by dragging me of all people into her homosexual obsession. Is there not a certain disingenuousness in her wanting me to give up all alcohol? Would not that <u>justify her</u> conduct completely to herself and prove to <u>her relatives, and our friends that it was my drinking that had caused this calamity, and that I thereby admitted it? Wouldn't she finally get to believe herself that she had consented to "take me back" only if I stopped drinking? I could only be silent</u>. And any human value I might have would disappear <u>if I condemned myself to a life long ascetisim to which I am not adapted either by habit, temperment</u> or the circumstances of my metier.

That is my case about the future, a case which I have never stated to you before when her problem needed your entire consideration. I want very much to see you before I see her. And please disassociate this letter from what I shall always feel in signing myself

Yours with Eternal Gratitude and Admiration

FIN

TO: *Zelda Fitzgerald*   AL *(draft), 4 pp. Princeton University*
Summer? 1930   *Switzerland*

When I saw the sadness of your face in that passport picture I felt as you can imagine. But after going through what you can imagine I did then and looking at it and looking at it, I saw that it was the face I knew and loved and not the mettalic superimposition of our last two years in France. . . .[1]

The photograph is all I have: it is with me from the morning when I wake up with a frantic half dream about you to the last moment when I think of you and of death at night. The rotten letters you write me I simply put away under Z in my file. My instinct is to write a public letter to the Paris Herald to see if any human being except yourself and Robert McAlmon has ever thought I was a homosexual. The three weeks after the horror of Valmont when I could not lift my eyes to meet the eyes of other men in the street after your stinking allegations and insinuations will not be repeated. If you choose to keep up your wrestling match with a pillar of air I would prefer to be not even in the audience.

I am hardened to write you so brutally by thinking of the ceaseless wave of love that surrounds you and envelopes you always, that you have the power to evoke at a whim—when I know that for the mere counterfiet of it I would perjure the best of my heart and mind. Do you think the solitude in which I live has a more amusing decor than any other solitude? Do you think it is any nicer for remembering that there were times very late at night when you and I shared our aloneness?

I will take my full share of responsibility for all this tragedy but I cannot spread beyond the limits of my reach and grasp. I can only bring you the little bit of hope I have and I don't know any other hope except my own. I have the terrible misfortune to be a gentleman in the sort of struggle with incalculable elements to which people should bring centuries of inexperience; if I have failed you is it just barely possible that you have failed me (I can't even write you any more because I see you poring over every line like Mr. Sumner[2] trying to wring some slant or suggestion of homosexuality out of it)

I love you with all my heart because you are my own girl and that is all I know.

TO: *Edmund Wilson*   ALS, *2 pp. Yale University*
Summer 1930

[1]Sixty-two words omitted.
[2]John S. Sumner, secretary of the New York Society for the Suppression of Vice.

c/o Guaranty Trust
4 Place de la Concorde
Paris

Dear Bunny:

Congratulations on your marriage[1] and all real hopes for your happiness. We heard through Mary,[2] long after the event of your collapse[3] and the thought that you'd survived it helped me through some dispairing moments in Zelda's case. She is now almost "well", which is to say the psychosis element is gone. We must live quietly for a year now and to some extent forever. She almost went permanently crazy—four hours work a day at the ballet for two years, and she 27 and too old when she began. I'm relieved that the ballet was over anyhow as our domestic life was cracking under the strain and I hadn't touched my novel for a year. She was drunk with music that seemed a crazy opiate to her and her whole cerebral tradition was something locked in such an absolutely unpregnable safe inside her that it was months after the break before the doctors could reach her at all. We hope to get home for Christmas.

I have seen no one for months save John in Paris—he is now more in prison than ever + the brief spell of work I nagged him into during Margaret's pregnancy has now given way to interminable talk about a well on their property. What an awful woman. Also a man named Thomas Wolfe, a fine man and a fine writer. Paris swarms with fairies and I've grown to loathe it and prefer the hospital-like air of Switzerland where nuts are nuts and coughs are coughs. Met your friend Allen Tate,[4] liked him + pitied him his wife

Salute the new Mrs. Wilson for me (my God, I just noticed this accidental justaposition—forgive me) and remember you're never long absent from the sollicitudes of

Your Old Friend
Scott

It was nice of you, + like you, to write Zelda.

TO: *Maxwell Perkins*
c. September 1, 1930

ALS, 2 pp. Princeton University

Geneva, Switzerland

Dear Max:

All the world seems to end up in this flat and antiseptic smelling land—with an overlay of flowers. Tom Wolfe is the only man I've met here who isn't sick or hasn't sickness to deal with. You have a great find in him—

[1] To Margaret Canby.
[2] Wilson's first wife, actress Mary Blair.
[3] Wilson had suffered a nervous breakdown in the spring of 1929.
[4] Poet and critic married to fiction writer Caroline Gordon.

what he'll do is incalculable. He has a deeper culture than Ernest and more vitality, if he is slightly less of a poet that goes with the immense surface he wants to cover. Also he lacks Ernests quality of a stick hardened in the fire—he is more susceptible to the world. John Bishop told me he needed advice about cutting ect, but after reading his book I thought that was nonsense. He strikes me as a man who should be let alone as to length, if he has to be published in five volumes. I liked him enormously.

I was sorry of course about Zelda's stories—possibly they mean more to me than is implicit to the reader who doesn't know from what depths of misery and effort they sprang. One of them, I think now, would be incomprehensible without a Waste-Land footnote. She has those series of eight portraits that attracted so much attention in <u>College Humor</u> and I think in view of the success of Dotty Parkers <u>Laments</u>[1] (25,000 copies) I think a book might be got together for next Spring if Zelda can add a few more during the winter.

Wasn't that a nice tribute to C.S.[2] from Mencken in the Mercury?

The royalty advance or the national debt as it might be called shocked me. The usual vicious circle is here—I am now exactly $3000. ahead which means 2 months on the Encyclopedia. I'd prefer to have all above the $10,000 paid back to you off my next story (in October). You've been so damn nice to me.

Zelda is almost well. The doctor says she can never drink again (not that drink in any way contributed to her collapse), and that I must not drink anything, not even wine, for a year, because drinking in the past was one of the things that haunted her in her delerium.

Do please send me things like Wolfe's book when they appear. Is Ernest's book a history of bull-fighting? I'm sending you a curious illiterate ms written by a chasseur at my bank here. Will you skim it + see if any parts, like the marines in Central America, are interesting as pure data? And return it, if not, directly to him? You were absolutely right about the dollar books—its a preposterous idea and I think the author's league went crazy

Always Yours
Scott

This illness has cost me a fortune—hence that telegram in July. The biggest man in Switzerland gave all his time to her— + saved her reason by a split second.

---

[1] *Laments for the Living* (1930).
[2] Charles Scribner II.

TO: *Harold Ober*   *ALS, 1 p. Lilly Library*
Received November 11, 1930   *Paris*

Dear Harold:

I havn't written for so long to you because I've been swamped with worries + anxieties here. Zelda has been in a hell of a mess, still in the sanitarium—she came within an ace of losing her mind + isn't out of the woods yet. We had a frantic time last spring + in midsummer from the combination of worry + work my lungs sprang a leak. That's all right now thank heaven—I went up to Caux + rested for a month. All this is between you + me—even Max doesn't know. Then Scotty fell ill + I left at midnight by plane for Paris to decide about an immediate appendix operation. In short its been one of those periods that come to all men I suppose when life is so complicated that with the best will in the world work is hard as hell to do. Things are better, but no end in sight yet. I figure I've written about 40,000 words to Forel (the psychiatrist) on the subject of Zelda trying to get to the root of things, + keeping worried families tranquil in their old age + trying to be a nice thoughtful female mother to Scotty—well, I've simply replaced letters by wires wherever possible.

About Zelda's sketches, have you tried Century? They printed my little skit on Scotty. But better still—send them to the New Republic, attention of Edmund Wilson, under the blanket title of Stories from a Swiss Clinique. Failing that I'll try This Quarter here in Paris. Unfortunately Transition has quit. Sorry about the Enerson thing.

About money. Having wired you last week that The Hotel Child was sent, I found on its return from the typist that it needed revision + amputation. That is done + it is back there but won't be ready till day after tomorrow. I'm sure you'll like it. I thought the last Josephine was feeble. If I press you too hard about money please try to arrange advance[1] from Lorimor, telling him frankly I've never worked under such conditions of expense + pressure in my life, for when I wire you it means trouble for me if deposit isn't made. What this seems to amount too is that I am an average outstanding loan of yours of about $2000. I hope to God things will be better soon. How are things going with you. Write me

                                             Ever Yours Gratefully
                                             Scott Fitzg—

Thought very little of Swanson offer. Havn't touched novel for four months, save for one week.

---

[1]Line drawn to the top margin indicates the words: "I mean cash advance, not price advance."

Paris, the 1st December 1930.

My dear Judge Sayre and Mrs. Sayre,

Herewith a summary of the current situation shortly after I wrote you: at length I became dissatisfied with the progress of the treatment—not from any actual reason but from a sort of American hunch that something could be done, and maybe wasn't being done to expedite the cure.

The situation was briefly that Zelda was acting badly and had to be transferred again to the house at Praugras reserved for people under restraint—the form in her case being that if she could go to Geneva alone she would "see people that would get her out of her difficulties."

When Forel told me this I was terribly perturbed and had the wires humming to see where we stood. I wrote Gros who is the head of the American hospital in Paris and the dean of American medecine here. Through the agency of friends I got opinions from medical specialists of all sorts and the sum and substance of the matter was as follows:

1°—That Forel's clinique is as I thought the best in Europe, his father having had an extraordinary reputation as a pioneer in the field of psychiatry, and the son being universally regarded as a man of intelligence and character.

2°—That the final rescourse in such cases are two men of Zürich—Dr. Jung and Dr. Blenler,[1] the first dealing primarily with neurosis and the second with psychosis, which is to say, that one is a psychoanalist and the other a specialist in insanity, with no essential difference in their approach.

With this data in hand and after careful consideration I approached Dr. Forel on the grounds, that I was not satisfied with Zelda's progress and that I had always at the back of my mind the idea of taking her home, and asked for a consultation. I think he had guessed at my anxiety and he greeted the suggestion with a certain relief and thereupon suggested the same two men I had already decided to call in—so that it made a complete unit. I mean to say there was nothing left undone to prove that I was dealing with final authorities.

After much, much talk I decided on Blenler rather than Jung—this was important because these consultations cost about five hundred dollars and one can't be complicated by questions of medical etiquette. He came down a fortnight ago, spent the afternoon with Zelda and then the evening with Forel and me. Here is the total result.

1°—He agreed absolutely in principle with the current treatment.

2°—He recognized the case (in complete agreement with Forel) as a case of what is known as skideophranie, a sort of borderline insanity, that takes the form of double personality. It presented to him no feature that was unfamiliar and no characteristic that puzzled him.

[1] Dr. Paul Eugen Bleuler.

3°—He said in answer to my questions that over a field of many thousands of such cases three out of four were discharged, perhaps one of those three to resume perfect functioning in the world, and the other two to be delicate and slightly eccentric through life—and the fourth case to go right down hill into total insanity.

4°—He said it would take a whole year before the case could be judged as to its direction in this regard but he gave me hope.

5°—He discussed at length the possibility of an eventual discovery of a brain tumor for the moment unlikely and the question of any glandular change being responsible. Also the state of American medical thought on such matters. (Forel incidently was at the Congress of Psychiatrists at Johns Hopkins last spring). But he insisted on seeing the case as a case and to my questioning answered that he did not know and no one knew what were the causes and what was the cure. The principles that he believes in from his experience are those that he and the older Forel, the father, (and followed by Myers[1] of John Hopkins) evolved are rest and "re-education," which seems to me a vague phrase when applied to a mind as highly organized as Zelda's. I mean to say that it is somewhat difficult to teach a person who is capable now of understanding the Einstein theory of space, that 2 and 2 actually make four. But he was hardboiled, regarded Zelda as an invalid person and that was the burden of his remarks in this direction.

6°—The question of going home. He said it wasn't even a question. That even with a day and night nurse and the best suite on the Bremen, I would be taking a chance not justified by the situation,— that a crisis, a strain at this moment might make the difference between recovery and insanity, and this question I put to him in various forms i.e. the "man to man" way and "if it were your own wife"—and he firmly and resolutely said "NO"—not for the moment. "I realize all the possible benefits but no, not for the moment."

7°—He changed in certain details her regime. In particular he felt that Forel was perhaps pushing her too much in contact with the world, expediting a little her connection with me and Scotty, her shopping expeditions to Geneva, her going to the opera and the theatre, her seeing the other people in the sanitarium (which is somewhat like a hotel).

8°—He not only confirmed my faith in Forel but I think confirmed Forel's own faith in himself on this matter. I mean an affair of this kind needs to be dealt with every subtle element of character. Humpty Dumpty fell off a wall and we are hoping that all the king's horses will be able to put the delicate eggshell together.

9°—This is of minor importance and I put it in only because I know you despise certain weaknesses in my character and I do not want during this tragedy that fact to blur or confuse your belief in me as a man of integrity.

[1]Dr. Adolf Meyer, psychiatrist at the Phipps Clinic of Johns Hopkins Hospital, who later treated Zelda Fitzgerald.

Without any leading questions and somewhat to my embarrassment Blenler said "This is something that began about five years ago. Let us hope it is only a process of re-adjustment. Stop blaming yourself. You might have retarded it but you couldn't have prevented it.

My plans are as follows. I'm staying here on Lake Geneva indefinately because even if I can only see Zelda once a fortnight, I think the fact of my being near is important to her. Scotty I see once a month for four or five days,—it's all unsatisfactory but she is a real person with a life of her own which for the moment consists of leading a school of twenty two French children which is a problem she set herself and was not arbitarily

TO: *Dr. Oscar Forel*   *CC, 7 pp. Princeton University*
Paris

29th January, 1931.

Dear Dr. Forel,

After this afternoon I am all the more interested in my own theory.

I hope you will be patient about this letter. A first year medical student could phrase it better than I, who am not sure what a nerve or a gland looks like. But despite my terminological ignorance I think you'll see I'm really not just guessing.

I am assuming with you and with Dr. Bleuler that the homosexuality is merely a symbol—something she invented to fill her slowly developing schizophenie. Now let me plot the course of her illness according to my current idea.

Youth & early womanhood Age 15–25	She has a nervous habit of biting to the bleeding point the inside of her mouth. With all her talents she is without ambition. She has been brought up in a climate not unlike the French Riviera but even there she is considered a lazy girl. A lovely but faulty complexion with blemishes accentuated by her picking at them.
Age 26–28	First appearance of definitely irrational acts (burning her old clothes in bath-tub in February 1927, age 26 years, 7 months). At this time she began to go into deep long silences and husband felt he has lost her confidence. Began dancing at age 27 <u>and had two severe attacks of facial eczema cured by electric ray treatment</u>. A feeling that she wasn't well provoked tests for metabolism. Results normal.
Age 28–29½	First mention of homosexual fears August 1928. This coincides with complete and never entirely renewed break of confidence with husband. From

204

	this time on work is intensive every day <u>with extraordinary sweating, so much so that in the summers of '28 and '29 I have seen literal wet pools on the floor when watching her lessons.</u>
April 29th, 1930	<u>Collapse</u>—and quick physical recovery. After two weeks' rest at Malmaison she <u>seemed</u> better than she does now.
April–June	A confused period about which my own judgment is not reliable. Then comes
June–July	Hysteria, madness with moments of brilliance (her short stories etc.) Schizophrania well divided so that her Doctor finds her charming at one moment and yet is forced to confine her to the Eglantine[1] the next. The good effect of this last measure. This period culminates with the visit of her daughter. Two very stirring experiences which have a marked effect on accentuating her best side—until—
August	Finding her to be ripe the doctor intensifies the process of reeducation, aiming at, for one thing, reconciliation with the husband. Things apparently progress. She writes nice and pleasant letters. She has good will again and hope and your interest in her case and hope for her is at its strongest. Suddenly as things reach a point where the meeting with husband and the resumption of serious life is a week off, when she has reached the point when the doctor has been able to try, though unsuccessfully, psycho-<u>analysis she breaks out with virulent eczema</u>. In this eczema she becomes necessarily more the invalid, the weakling, more self-indulgent. Her will power decreases. When the postponed meeting with the husband occurs she
September	brings to it only enough balance in favor of normality to last an hour <u>and a renewed attack of eczema succeeds it.</u>

Now I want to interrupt the sequence here to insert my idea. The original nervous biting, followed by the need to sweat might indicate some lack of normal elimination of poison. This uneliminated poison attacks the nerves.

When I used to drink hard for several days and then stopped I had a tendency toward mild eczema—of elimination of toxins through the skin. (Isn't there an especially intimate connection between the skin and the nerves, so that they share together the distinction of being the things we

---

[1]House at Prangins clinic for the most severely disturbed patients.

know least about?) Suppose the skin by sweating eliminated as much as possible of this poison, the nerves took on the excess—then the breakdown came, and due to the exhaustion of the sweat glands the nerves had to take it all, but at the price of a gradual change in their structure as a unit.

Now (I know you're regarding this as the wildest mysticism but please read on)—now just as the mind of the confirmed alcoholic accepts a certain poisoned condition of the nerves as the one to which he is the most at home and in which, therefore, he is the most comfortable, Mrs. F. encourages her nervous system to absorb the continually distilled poison. Then the exterior world, represented by your personal influence, by the shock of Eglantine, by the sight of her daughter causes an effort of the will toward reality, she is able to force this poison out of the nerve cells and the process of elimination is taken over again by her skin.

In brief my idea is this. That the eczema is not relative but is the clue to the whole business. I believe that the eczema is a definite concurrent product of every struggle back toward the normal, just as an alcoholic has to struggle back through a period of depression.

	To resume the calendar for a moment:
October	She is obviously making an effort. But at the same time comes the infatuation for the red-haired girl. At first I thought that caused the third attack of eczema but now I don't. Isn't it possible that it was her resistance, her initial shame at the infatuation and the consequent struggle that brought on the third eczema? This is supported by the fact that the infatuation continued after the eczema had gone. The eczema may have proceeded from the struggle toward reality rather than from the excitation itself.

The whole system is trying to live in equilibrium. When her will dominates her she doesn't find it. I can't help clinging to the idea that some essential physical thing like salt or iron or semen or some unguessed at holy water is either missing or is present in too great quantity. But to continue

November	Physical health fine but more in the hallucination. Growing vagueness and almost complete lack of effort. No eczema—but no effort. Her second infatuation does not cause eczema and neither does the
December	First visit of child. Because she behaves badly at my behest she makes an effort to think before the second visit and there is immediate eczema.

One more note and then I'll draw my conclusions.

When she was discharged as cured from Malmaison she had facial eczema which we attributed to drugs. But it did not appear at Valmont or in early days at Prangins in spite of drugs at Valmont and disintoxication at Prangins for she was sunk safely in her insane self on both occasions.

My conclusions.

(a) The nature of any such poison would, of course, be too subtle for us. I believe she needs
(1) Naturally all you include under the term reeducation.

(b) Renewal of full physical relations with husband, a thing to be enormously aided by an actual timing of the visits to the periods just before and just after menstruation, and avoiding visits in the middle of such times or in the exact centre of the interval.

(c) To disintoxicate artificially in exact accord with the intensity of the reeducation. I can not believe that with her bad eyes that give her headaches and her many highly developed artistic appreciations, that embroidery, carpentry or book-binding are, in her case, any substitute for real sweating. She has a desire to sweat—for many summers she cooked all the pigments out of her skin tanning herself. I know this is difficult now but couldn't she take intensive tennis lessons in the spring or couldn't we think of something? Golf perhaps?

(d) Failing this I believe artificial eliminations should be absolutely concurrent with every effort at mental cure. I believe that constipation or delayed menstruations or lack of real exercise at such a time should be foreseen and forestalled as, in my opinion, eczema will always be the result.

I suppose the only new thing in all this is that I connect the eczema with one only sort of agitation the good sort and not with all agitation. Will you write me whether you agree at all while this is still fresh in your mind. I left my American addresses at the desk. Is her physical health good in general? Have her eyes been examined—she complains that her lorgnettes no longer work. The doctoress told me she had no warm underwear and I recommended some very light angora wool and silk stuff but Telda wouldn't listen to me.

She was enormously moved by my father's death or by my grief at it and literally clung to me for an hour. Then she went into the other personality and was awful to me at lunch. After lunch she returned to the affectionate tender mood, utterly normal, so that with pressure I could have manoeuvred her into intercourse but the eczema was almost visibly increasing so I left early. Toward the very end she was back in the schizophrania.

I was encouraged by our talk to-day. I am having this typed and translated and sent you from Paris. I shall be back in three or four weeks. Would you kindly cable me five or six words at about the middle of every week to the address LITOBER NEW YORK (my name not required).

Always gratefully yours,

207

TO: *Maxwell Perkins*   ALS, 2 pp. Princeton University
c. January 15, 1932   Don Ce-Sar Hotel stationery.
                                                   St. Petersburg, Florida

For three days only
Dear Max:

At last for the first time in two years + ½ I am going to spend five consecutive months on my novel. I am actually six thousand dollars ahead Am replanning it to include what's good in what I have, adding 41,000 new words + publishing. Don't tell Ernest or anyone—let them think what they want—you're the only one whose ever consistently felt faith in me anyhow.

Your letters still sound sad. For God's sake take your vacation this winter. Nobody could quite ruin the house in your absence, or would dare to take any important steps. Give them a chance to see how much they depend on you + when you come back cut off an empty head or two. Thalberg[1] did that with Metro-Goldwyn-Mayer.

Which reminds me that I'm doing that "Hollywood Revisited" in the evenings + it will be along in, I think, six days—maybe ten.

Have Nunnally Johnston's humorous stories from the Post been collected? Everybody reads them. Please at least look into this. Ask Myers—he ought to search back at least a year which is as long as I've been meaning to write you about it.

Where in hell are my Scandanavian copies of The Great Gatsby?

You couldn't have sent me anything I enjoyed more than the Churchill book.[2]

Always Yours Devotedly
Scott Fitz

TO: *Dr. Mildred Squires*[3]   CC of retyped letter, 2 pp.
                                          Alan Mason Chesney Medical Archives,
                                                      Johns Hopkins Hospital
                                                      Montgomery, Alabama

Zelda Fitzgerald   3.14.32
#6408   Letter from husband.

---

[1]Irving Thalberg, legendary movie producer; he became the model for Monroe Stahr, protagonist of Fitzgerald's unfinished novel, *The Love of the Last Tycoon: A Western*.

[2]Probably the one-volume abridgment of Winston Churchill's *The World Crisis*, published by Scribners in 1931.

[3]Of the Phipps Clinic of Johns Hopkins University; Zelda Fitzgerald dedicated *Save Me the Waltz* to Dr. Squires.

Dear Dr. Squires:

Zelda's novel,[1] or rather her intention of publishing it without any discussion, has upset me considerably. First, because it is such a mixture of good and bad in its present form that it has no chance of artistic success, and, second, because of some of the material within the novel.

As you may know I have been working intermittently for four years on a novel which covers the life we led in Europe. Since the spring of 1930 I have been unable to proceed <u>because</u> of the necessity of keeping Zelda in sanitariums. However, about fifty thousand words exist and this Zelda has heard, and literally one whole section of her novel is an imitation of it, of its rythym, materials, even statements and speeches. Now you may say that the experience which two people have undergone is common is common property—one transmutes the same scene through different temperments and it "comes out different" As you will see from my letter to her there are only two episodes, both of which <u>she</u> has reduced to anecdotes <u>but upon which whole sections of my book turn</u>, that I have asked her to cut. Her own material—her youth, her love for Josaune, her dancing, her observation of Americans in Paris, the fine passages about the death of her father—my critisisms of that will be simply impersonal and professional. But do you realize that "Amory Blaine" was the name of the character in my first novel to which I attached my adventures and opinions, in effect my autobiography? Do you think that his turning up in a novel signed by my wife as a somewhat aenemic portrait painter with a few ideas lifted from Clive Bell, Leger,[2] ect. could pass unnoticed? In short it puts me in an absurd and Zelda in a rediculous position. If she should choose to examine our life together from an inimacable attitude & print her conclusions I could do nothing but answer in kind or be silent, as I chose—but this mixture of fact and fiction is simply calculated to ruin us both, or what is left of us, and I can't let it stand. Using the name of a character I invented to put intimate facts in the hands of the friends and enemics we have accumulated <u>enroute</u>—My God, my books made her a legend and her single intention in this somewhat thin portrait is to make me a non-entity. That's why she sent the book directly to New York.

Of course were she not sick I would have to regard the matter as an act of disloyalty or else as something to turn over to a lawyer. Now I don't know how to regard it. I know however that this is pretty near the end. Her mother thinks she is an abused angel incarcerated there by my bad judgement or ill intention. In the whole family there is just a bare competence save what I dredge up out of my talent and work to pay for such luxuries as insanity. But Scotty and I must live and it is getting more and

---

[1] The original draft of *Save Me the Waltz*, written while Zelda Fitzgerald was in the Phipps Clinic, has not survived.

[2] Bell was a British art critic; Fernand Léger was a French painter.

more difficult in this atmosphere of suspicion to turn out the convinced and well-decorated sopiusous for which Mr. Lorimer pays me my bribe.

My suggestion is this—that you try to find <u>why</u> Zelda sent to the novel north without getting my advice, which, as I have given her her entire literary education, all her encouragement and all her opportunity, was the natural thing to do.

Secondly that you tell Mrs. Sayre that I am any kind of a villain you want, and that you have private information on the fact, but htat her daughter is sick, sick, sick, and that there is no possibility of being mistaken on that.

Third—keep the novel out of circulation until Zelda reads my detailed criticism & appeal to reason which will take two days more to prepare.

Meanwhile I will live here in a state of mild masturbation and a couple of whiskys to go to sleep on, until my lease expires April 15th when I will come north. I appreciate your letters and understand the difficulties of prognosis in this case. My sister-in-law will be north this week. She is a trivial, charming woman and we dislike each other deeply. Her observation or analysis of any given series of facts is open to the same skeptesism as that of any member of the Sayre family—they left the habit of thinking to the judge for so long that it practically has become a parlor game with them.

I enclose Zelda a check for fifty dollars.

> Yours Sincerely & Gratefully
> F. Scott Fitzgerald

TO: *Maxwell Perkins*   *Wire. Princeton University*

MONTGOMERY ALA   1932 MAR 16   PM 10 21
PLEASE DO NOT JUDGE OR IF NOT ALREADY DONE EVEN CONSIDER ZELDAS BOOK
UNTIL YOU GET REVISED VERSION LETTER FOLLOWS
    SCOTT FITZGERALD.

TO: *Dr. Mildred Squires*   *CC of retyped letter, 1 p.*
Alan Mason Chesney Medical Archives,
Johns Hopkins Hospital
Montgomery, Alabama

Zelda Fitzgerald   no date (I think 3.20.32)
#6408   Letter from husband.

Dear Dr. Squires:

On the advice of a doctor here I sent Zelda a very much shortened version of the letter here inclosed which incorporate my ideas on the subject of her self expression. I am simply unable to depart from my professional atti-tude—if you think that in any way I have departed from it please tell me—

but I think that what further speculation we indulge in are in the realms of the most highly experimental ethics. I feel helpless and alone in the face of the situation; nevertheless I feel myself a personality, and if the situation continues to shape itself as one in which only one of us two can survive, perhaps you would doing a kindness to us both by recommending a separation. My whole stomach hurts when I contemplate such an eventuality—it would be throwing her broken upon a world which she despises; I would be a ruined man for years—but, alternatively, I have reached the point of submersion if I must continue to rationalize the irrational, stand always between Zelda and the world and see her build this dubitable career of hers with morsels of living matter chipped out of my mind, my belly, my nervous system and my loins. Perhaps fifty percent of our friends and relatives would tell you in all honest conviction that my drinking drove Zelda insane—the other half would assure you that her insanity drove me to drink. Niether judgement would mean anything: The former class would be composed of those who had seen me unpleasantly drunk and the latter of those who had seen Zelda unpleasantly psychotic. These two classes would be equally unanimous in saying that each of us would be well rid of the other—in full face of the irony that we have never been so desperately in love with each other in our lives. Liquor on my mouth is sweet to her; I cherish her most extravagant hallucination.

So you see I beg you not to pass the buck to me. Please, when I come north, remember that I have exhausted my intelligence on the subject—I have become a patient in the face of it. Her affair with Edward Josaune in 1925 (and mine with Lois Moran in 1927, which was a sort of regenge) shook something out of us, but we can't both go on paying and paying forever. And yet I feel that that's the whole trouble back of all this.

I will see you Thursday or Friday—I wish you'd tell me then what I ought to do—I mean I wish that you and Doctor Myers would re-examine the affair,

Sincerely
F. Scott Fitzgerald

TO: *Maxwell Perkins*   *Wire. Princeton University*

MONTGOMERY ALA   1932 MAR 25   PM 11 52
THINK NOVEL CAN SAFELY BE PLACED ON YOUR LIST FOR SPRING IT IS ONLY A QUESTION OF CERTAIN SMALL BUT NONE THE LESS NECESSARY REVISIONS MY DISCOURAGEMENT WAS CAUSED BY THE FACT THAT MYSELF AND DAUGHTER WERE SICK WHEN ZELDA SAW FIT TO SEND MANUSCRIPT TO YOU YOU CAN HELP ME BY RETURNING MANUSCRIPT TO HER UPON HER REQUEST GIVING SOME PRETEXT FOR NOT HAVING AS YET TIME READ IT AM NOW BETTER AND WILL WRITE LETTER TOMORROW IN MY OPINION IT IS A FINE NOVEL STOP WILL TAKE

UP ARTICLE AS SOON AS I HAVE FINISHED CURRENT POST STORY WHICH WILL BE
ON ARRIVAL BALTIMORE WEDNESDAY BEST REGARDS FAITHFULLY
  SCOTT FITZGERALD.

TO: Maxwell Perkins   *Wire. Princeton University*

MONTGOMERY ALA   1150A 1932 MAR 28   PM 1 41
READ MANUSCRIPT BUT IF YOU HAVE ALREADY RETURNED IT WIRE AND ILL SEND
MY COPY STOP IF YOU LIKE IT AND WANT TO USE IMMEDIATELY REMEMBER ALL
MIDDLE SECTION MUST BE RADICALLY REWRITTEN STOP TITLE AND NAME OF
AMORY BLAINE CHANGED[1] STOP ARRIVING BALTIMORE THURSDAY TO CONFER
WITH ZELDA WILL IMMEDIATELY DECIDE ON NEW TITLE AND NAME CHANGES
REVISING SHOULD TAKE FORTNIGHT
  SCOTT FITZGERALD.

TO: Dr. Mildred Squires   *CC of retyped letter, 2 pp.*
Spring 1932   *Alan Mason Chesney Medical Archives,*
                   Johns Hopkins Hospital
                   Baltimore, Maryland

                 FITZGERALD, Zelda
Letter from husband.   # 6408

                 Saturday Evening

Dear Dr. Squires:
    The whole current lay-out is somewhat discouraging. I seem to be bring-
ing nothing to its solution except money and good will—and Zelda brings
nothing at all, except a power of arousing sumpathy. She has perhaps
achieved something fairly good, at everybodys cost all around, including
especially mine. She thinks she has done a munificent thing in changing the
novel at all—she has become as hard and coldly egotistic as she was when
she was in the ballet and I would no more think of living with her as she
now than I would repeat those days. The one ray of hope is this—that once
the novel is sent off (it has almost torn down all the relations patiently built
up for a year) she <u>must not</u> write any more <u>personal stuff</u> while she is under
treatment. What has happened is the worst possible thing that could have
happened—it has put her through a detailed recapituation of all the worldly
events that first led up to the trouble, embittering her in retrospect, and

---

[1]The original title of *Save Me the Waltz* is not known. The male protagonist was renamed
David Knight.

then been passed back through me, so that I've been in an intolerable position. Through no fault of yours her stay at the clinic has resolved itself into a very expensive chance to satisfy her desire for self-expression. We are farther apart than we have been since she first got sick two years ago and this time I have no sense of guilt what soever.

Now some particular points (alas, unrelated!)

First: In regard to our phone conversation. Our sexual relations have been good or less good from time to time but they have always been normal. She had her first orgasm about ten days after we were married, and from that time to this there haven't been a dozen times in twelve years , when she hasn't had an orgasm. And since the renewal of our relations last spring that accident has never occurred and our relations, in that regard up to the day she entered Johns Hopkins were more satisfactory than ever before (Also O. K. here in Balt. as explained)

The difficulty in 1928–1930 was tempermental—it led to long periods of complete lack of desire. During 1929 we were probably together only two dozen times and always it was purely physical, but in so far as the purely physical goes it was mutually satisfactory. I have had experience & read all available literature, including that book by the Dutchman I saw on your shelves and I know whereof I speak.[1]

On the other hand I think it is unfortunate she has had no more children; also she's probably a rather polygamus type; and possibly she has, when not herself, a touch of mental lesbianism. The first and third things I can't do anything about—the second thing I simply I couldn't stand for and stillfeel any nessessity to preserve the family.

Second She weighed 110 on a slot machine today, dressed, and told me she'd been losing weight. She eats, when she's with me, two packs of mints, tho sugar has always caused her acne. I asked her if she'd like to go down the valley (Shenendoah) & spend a night next Saturday. Else, I said, I'd like to go to New York for a day or so, wanting a change. She had no interest in the valley trip, but asked why didn't I go to New York? There is a vague form in her mind of "go on—do what you want—All I want is a chance to work." The only essential that she leaves out is that I also want a chance to work, to cease this ceaseless hack work that her sickness compells me to. You will see that some blind unfairness in the novel. The girl's love affair is an idyll—the man's is sordid—the girl's drinking is glossed over (when I think of the two dozen doctors called in to give her 1/5 grain of morphine or a raging morning!), while the man's is accentuated. However there's no use going over that again. It's all been somewhat modified. The point is that there's no working basis between us and less all the time—unless this novel finishes a phase in her life & it all grows dim with having been written. That's the best hope at present. But she musn't start another personal piece of work—she spoke today of a novel "on our personal quarrel & her insanity."

[1]There is a note in the margin beside this paragraph: "(as relations are now)."

Should she begin such a work at present I would withdraw my backing from her immediately because the sands are running out again on my powers of indurance—I can't pay for the smithy where she forges a weapon to bring down on mine and Scottys &, eventually, her own head, for all the pleasant exercise it may give her mental muscles.

Also she spoke of a play again. That would do no harm because its more cold & impersonal—it might overlay the memory of the novel & all that the novel evoked. Ironically enough I gave her the plan for the novel, recommended autobiography ect, with no idea that <u>this</u> would happen.

<u>Third</u> I have vague ideas of (a) tennis lessons for her (I still think of the ski-ing & her nessessity of being superior at <u>something</u>.) (b) A few spring clothes—to encourage minor vanities in place of this repellant & devastating pride (c) trying her <u>without</u> nurses to see how she will do her stuff there. <u>Or, for a week: Apparently without nurses.</u>

We have been nessessarily marking time till the novel was finished but something must now be done about taking a definate decision, I feel. It is not healthy for me to brood in such facts as these: that I have one terrible ace-in-the-hole which is to take her out, give her her head and simply wait the fortnight until she gave the evidence nessessary to commit her. She has not the faintest Idea how much she depends on me, and if the only salvation for us all will be for her to thus see the withdrawal of my support (as she saw it in miniature in the shortage of money) then it shall be done.

I have still another plan, but one which depends on some additional sacrifice on my part & I'm not sure I can make it. Of that more later. In any case I'd like very much to see you & Doctor Myers early this week; but, <u>please</u> I want to be told what <u>you've</u> considered & decided. I have exhausted my own original impetus & laid all my cards on the table. I need advice for myself as the essentially responsible party. I feel that, practically, you would be helping me swaying either toward the idea that Zelda is essentially sick and therefore giving me the right to ask you to insulate me from the attendant evils. <u>Or</u> by swaying toward the idea that she is <u>well</u>, that <u>our</u> marriage is at fault, letting the problem become a worldly one where I can consult my own interest as to dealing with it. At present our collaboration is too vague. I don't know my rôle and count on you to point it out to me.

Ever yours gratefully
F. Scott Fitzgerald

TO: *Harold Ober*　　　　　　　　　　　　　　　　*ALS, 3 pp. Lilly Library*
Received April 23, 1932　　　　　　　　　　　　　　*Baltimore, Maryland*

Dear Harold:

The <u>Post</u> story is mailed tomorrow reaches you Mon.

Here are a whole lot of points

214

(1.) Are you sure my letter reached Van Cortland Enerson? It was a reference to a story idea of his I wanted to buy, + its rather important
(2.) My alternative idea for the next is to revise <u>Crazy Sunday</u>, so if you have any advice send it

---

<u>Nightmare</u>[1] will never, never sell for money, in <u>any</u> times. I note there are two Clayton Magazines called "Strange Tales" + "Astounding Stories." Would either of them pay $250.00? Their rates are 2 cents a word + up.

Last + most important.
Will you write a letter to the Collector of Internal Revenue, St Paul, Minn (but send it to McNiell Seymore, Pioneer Bldg. St Paul) embodying the following points.
(1.) Who you are—long time in business ect.
(2.) Surprise at hearing that my earnings from Post ect were not accepted as earned income.
(3.) That you had never considered me a free lance author but that on the contrary my sales were arranged long in advance and that it has been understood for years among editors that my stories were written specificly for the Post by definate arrangement and that I was what is known as a "Post Author".
(4.) Moreover that they conform to Post specifications as to length and avoidance of certain themes so that for instance they could not have been published in <u>Liberty</u> which insisted on stories not over 5000 words, + would have been inacceptable to womens magazines since they were told from the male angle. That when I contracted with another magazine such as <u>College Humor</u> the stories were different in tone + theme, half as long, signed in conjunction with my wife. That the <u>Post</u> made it plain that they wanted to be offered all my work of the kind agreed apon; that they always specified that no work of mine should appear in several competing magazines. That during the years 1929 and 1930 no story of mine was rejected by the Post (The first was in February 1931, but as that year isn't in question don't mention it)
(5.) That had not the possibility you have just been informed of (i.e. of treating short story money as unearned income under G.C.M. 236) come as a completely new attitude all the magazines would assuredly have substituted written contracts in such cases as this where the author is in fact the employee of the magazine, and should his story appear in rival journals the arrangment would be broken. It is as much a contract as a telephone conversation between two brokers. And And no story order would be accepted even from a non-competing magazine without discussing it with the Post.

[1] The story was never published.

That's a hell of a lot to ask. Can you Send it off as soon as possible. It means a lot of money to me, as I'll explain when I see you. (Otherwise I get a reduction for having worked in Europe + paid taxes there—but this only applies to <u>earned</u> income)

> In Haste
> Ever Yours
> Scott

Also that letters + conversation were almost always substituted for contracts when arranging for short stories—the contrary being true as to play + picture contracts where the buyer is often a less stable party.

TO: Gertrude Stein *TLS, 1 p. Yale University*
Hotel Rennert stationery.
Baltimore, Maryland

April 28, 1932.

Dear Gertrude Stien:

You were so nice to think of me so far off and send me your book.[1] Whenever I sit down to write I think of the line that you drew for me and told me that my next book should be that thick. So many of your memorable remarks come often to my head, and they seem to survive in a way that very little current wisdom does.

I read the book, of course, immediately, and was half through it for the second time (learning a lot as we all do from you) when my plans were upset by my wife's illness, and by an accident it was consigned to temporary storage.

I hope to be in Europe this summer and to see you. I have never seen nearly as much of you as I would like.

Yours always, admiringly and cordially,

> F. Scott Fitzgerald

Miss Gertrude Stien,
c/o Shakespearre & Co. Librarie,
Pres de la Theatre de l' odeon, Paris.

TO: Maxwell Perkins *ALS, 3 pp. Princeton University*
c. April 30, 1932

<u>Personal and Confidential</u> from F. Scott Fitzgerald

> Hotel Rennert
> Baltimore, Maryland

---

[1] *How to Write* (1931). The inscription reads: "To Fitzgerald and I hope you did not mind my putting you in from Gtde Stn." Bruccoli.

216

Dear Max:

I was shocked to hear of your daughter's illness. If it is anything mental I can deeply sympathize for there is nothing so "terrifying + mysterious", as you say. I am somewhat of an amateur expert on the subject + if at any time things don't go well let us meet in New York and talk about it. I mean there were times Zelda's illness when I needed a <u>layman's</u> advice. If she is in good hands <u>do not make the criminal mistake of trying to hurry things</u>, for reasons of family affection or family pride.

———————————

Zelda's novel is now good, improved in every way. It is new. She has largely eliminated the speakeasy-nights-and-our-trip-to-Paris atmosphere. You'll like it. It should reach you in ten days. I am too close to it to judge it but it may be even better than I think. <u>But</u> I must urge you two things

(1.) If you like it please <u>don't</u> wire her congratulations, and please keep whatever praise you may see fit to give <u>on the staid side</u>—I mean, <u>as you naturally would</u>, rather than yield to a tendency one has with invalids to be extra nice to cheer them up. This seems a nuance but it is rather important at present to the doctors that Zelda does not feel that the acceptance (always granted you like it) means immediate fame and money. I'm afraid all our critical tendencies in the last decade got bullish; we discovered one Hemmingway to a dozen Callaghans and Caldwells (I think the latter is a washout) + probably created a lot of spoiled geniuses who might have been good workmen. Not that I regret it—if the last five years uncovered Ernest, Tom Wolfe + Faulkner it would have been worth while, but I'm not certain enough of Zelda's present stability of character to expose her to any superlatives. If she has a success coming she must associate it with work done in a workmanlike manner for its own sake, + part of it done fatigued and uninspired, and part of it done when even to remember the original inspiration and impetus is a psychological trick. She is not twenty-one and she is not strong, and she must not try to follow the pattern of my trail which is of course blazed distinctly on her mind.

(2.) Don't discuss contract with her until I have talked to you.

———————————

Ring's last story in the <u>Post</u> was pathetic, a shade of himself, but I'm glad they ran it first and I hope it'll stir up his professional pride to repeat.

Beginning the article for you on Monday. You can count on it for the end of next week.

Now <u>very important</u>.

(1.) I must have a royalty report for 1931 for my income tax—they insist.

(2.) I borrowed $600 in 1931. $500 of this was redeemed by my article. The other hundred should show in royalty report.

③ Since <u>Gatsby</u> was not placed with <u>Grosset</u> or <u>Burt</u> I'd like to have it in the <u>Modern Library</u>. This is my own idea + have had no approach but imagine I can negotiate it. Once they are interested would of course turn negotiations over to you. But I feel, should you put obstacles in the way you would be doing me a great harm and injustice. <u>Gatsby</u> is constantly mentioned among memorable books but the man who asks for it in a store on the basis of such mention does not ask twice. Booksellers do not keep such an item in stock + there is a whole new generation who cannot obtain it. This has been on my mind for two years and I must insist that you you give me an answer that doesn't keep me awake nights wondering why it possibly benefited the Scribners to have me represented in such an impersonal short story collection as that of <u>The Modern Library</u> by a weak story + Ring ect by none at all. That "they would almost all have been Scribner authors" was a most curious perversion of what should have been a matter of pride into an attitude of dog-in-the-manger.

Excuse that outburst, Max. Please write, answering all questions. Tell Louise I liked her story + hope she's better. Things go all right with me now. What news of Ernest? And his book?

Ever Your Friend
Scott

TO: *Maxwell Perkins*   ALS, 3 pp. *Princeton University*
c. *May 14, 1932*   *Hotel Rennert stationery. Baltimore, Maryland*

Dear Max:

Here is Zelda's novel. It is a good novel now, perhaps a very good novel—I am too close to it to tell. It has the faults + virtues of a first novel. It is more the expression of a powerful personality, like <u>Look Homeward Angel</u> than the work of a finished artist like Ernest Hemmingway. It should interest the many thousands interested in dancing. It is <u>about something</u> + absolutely new, + should sell.

Now, about its reception. If you refuse it, which I don't think you will, all communication should come through me. If you accept it write her directly and I withdraw all restraints on whatever meed of praise you may see fit to give. The strain of writing it was bad for her but it had to be written—she needed relaxation afterwards and I was afraid that praise might encourage the incipient egomania the doctors noticed, but she has taken such a sane common sense view lately (at first she refused to revise—then she revised completely, added on her own suggestion + has changed what was a rather flashy and self-justifying "true confessions" that wasn't worthy of her into an honest piece of work. She can do more with the galley but I cant ask her to do more now.)—but now praise will do her good within reason. But she musn't write anything more on the <u>personal</u> side for six months or so until she is stronger.

Now a second thing, more important than you think. You havn't been in the publishing business over twenty years without noticing the streaks of smallness in very large personalities. Ernest told me once he would "never publish a book in the same season with me", meaning it would lead to ill-feeling. I advise you, if he is in New York, (and always granting you like Zelda's book) do not praise it, or even talk about it to him! The finer the thing he has written, the more he'll expect your entire allegiance to it as this is one of the few pleasures, rich + full + new, he'll get out of it. I know this, + I think you do too + probably there's no use warning you. There is no possible conflict between the books but there has always been a subtle struggle between Ernest + Zelda, + any apposition might have curiously grave consequences—curious, that is, to un-jealous men like you and me.

One more thing. Please, in your letter to Zelda (if of acceptance) do not mention contracts or terms. I will take it up immediately on hearing from you.

Thanks about the Modern Library. I don't know exactly what I shall do. Five years have rolled away from me and I can't decide exactly who I am, if anyone.

Tell me if anything further happens in the family matter—actually I am such a blend of the scientific + the laymans attitude on such subjects that I could be more help than anyone you could think of. I could come to New York, + intend to soon anyhow.

Ever your Friend
Scott

TO: Dr. Thomas Rennie[1]

CC of retyped letter, 4 pp.
Alan Mason Chesney Medical
Archives, Johns Hopkins Hospital
"La Paix." Towson, Maryland

LETTER FROM HUSBAND TO PHYSICIAN: October, 1932

The situation has reduced itself in my mind to a rather clear-cut struggle of egos between Zelda and myself. Last night, after a most affectionate day, a day in which at home, at the theatre, in the car, she would literally not move an inch from me nor talk of anything save how she loved me and admired me—a situation which I dread for it almost always precedes a reaction of some kind—after such a day, she suddenly announced in the evening what sounded to me like an ultimatum, a threat to go crazy. She wrote out some notes to Dr. Meyer, which as you will see are all aimed at rather vague persecuting forces and in which I am not named but am suggested.

[1] Psychiatrist at Phipps Clinic of Johns Hopkins Hospital.

I think I know what is underneath and it parallels what happened last February. Here it is:

As I told you, I got ahead at last financially in August and since then I have written 30,000 words on my novel. She knows this and one side of her is glad. She knows my plans, to break off presently for a week and then resume, completing the whole task, which is the fruit of four years of preparation and note taking and experiment in such time as I could afford to give to it. She knows it is serious and that it naturally rests to some degree upon my life.

Now for the last five years—the two and a half of ballet and the two and a half of sickness, she has come to regard me as the work horse and herself as the artist—the producer of the finer things such as painting, uncommercial literature, ballet, etc., such as I have not been able to mix with the damn Post story writing. Consciously she knows that her Literary work is founded upon mine and that she is still a long way from turning out work as the best of mine. Nevertheless she is damn well going to try and naturally I've helped and encouraged her. But regard this:

It is significant that last February her breakdown was associated with my outlining to her a frame for what was then a new approach to my work which was a story of our eight years in Europe. I read her a chapter. What did she do immediately on her arrival in the clinic but <u>sit down and try to write it herself</u>, including what she must have known was some of the best material in my notebook, stuff I had often discussed with her and that she knew I hadn't touched for short stories because it belonged in a more important medium. Together with this were a great mass of my ideas, my remarks, comments on my failings, my personal habits, fragments of my style and bits of all my stock in trade. This was sent off to a publisher before I could see it. What happened you know—I protested vehemently and what was for me an unsatisfactory compromise, was reached—she cut out the most offensive of the material and on my advice worked up the best parts so that the book assumed a certain artistic coherence.

But the fundamental struggle continued, shown indirectly by her unwillingness to let me help her with her stories coupled with a study of my books so profound that she is saturated with them, whole fragments of my scenes and cadences come out in her work, which she admits. One is flattered—it is only when she aims to use the materials of our common life, the only fact material that I have (heaven knows there's no possible harm in her using her own youth, her dancing, etc.) that she becomes a danger to my life and to us. She knows that my novel is almost entirely concerned with the Riviera and the two years we spent there, and I have continually asked her to keep away from it and she agrees in theory, yet she has just blandly completed a play about it, laid on the very beach where my novel begins. Her agitation to begin another novel increases in intensity—I know there will be whole sections of it that are simply muddy transcriptions of things in my current novel—things we both observed and have a right to, but that under the present circumstances I have all rights to. Imagine a painter trying to paint on canvasses each of which has a sketchy vulgarization, in his own manner, lined across it, by the companion within whose company he first observed the subject—at the painter's expense.

Now Zelda is a fine person and she sees this. The arrangement is that I am to finish and publish my novel before she tries another extended piece of work. This is absolutely all right with me. But in her subconscious there is a deathly terror that I may make something very fine in the use of this material of "ours", that I may preclude her making something very fine. She knows that her book is not an achieved artistic whole, but she wants to hurry through a lot more material in the same way—incidentally leaving me literally nothing.

The conflict is bothering her. The nearer I come to completion, that is to artistic satisfaction, and announce it to her, the more restless she becomes, though outwardly rejoicing. The fact that her undertaking a long piece of work of a deeply personal order would be a serious menace to her health is apparent to her. And it is an equal menace—this subconscious competing with me.

"Why can't I sell my short stories?" she says.

"Because you're not putting yourself in them. Do you think the Post pays me for nothing?"

(She wants to make money but she wants to save her good stuff for books so her stories are simply casually observed, unfelt phenomena, while mine are sections, debased, over-simplified, if you like, of my own soul. That is our bread and butter and her health and Scotty's education).

And, I added, foolishly but truly, "Besides, a lot of visual emotion has been going into this current series of pictures, so that your description, that is your emotional description, not the merely casual observation, has suffered."

Bang! She abandons pictures. She writes, writes, writes, and goes backward and has been going backward for over a fortnight.

The conflict is at the root of it. She feels that my success has got to be, otherwise we all collapse—she feels also that it is a menace to her. "Why should it be him—why shouldn't it be me?" "I'm as good or better than he is." If she thought she would again be permitted to write in a clinic, I believe she would have "conflicted" herself into one long ago and sat down at a big piece of direct self-justification.

And I believe she is considering making an attempt at such an idea. If her book goes well it may reinforce the idea and all my effort be reduced to a scrap of paper. So far as my own novel is concerned I am absolutely desperate and determined to finish it without interference from Zelda, sane or insane. Can't we do something to forestall the dangers on the horizon?

Sincerely,

F. Scott Fitzgerald.

Talked over main ideas with Zelda. Didn't read it to her.

F.

TO: *Thomas Rennie*
1933

Inscription in Rene Fülöp-Miller's
The Mind and Face of Bolshevism
(1929).[1] Bruccoli

[1]Zelda Fitzgerald inscribed this book to her psychiatrist; F. Scott Fitzgerald added an inscription listing prominent psychiatrists.

TO: Zelda Fitzgerald   AL (draft)[1], 11 pp. Princeton University
After 1932   "La Paix." Towson, Maryland

Do you feel that you are now able to be your own doctor—to judge what is good for you?

If no—do you know what should be done?

Should you be in a clinic do you think?

Would a trained nurse help?

An experienced one?

An inexperienced one?

If you were really not yourself and in a fit of temper or depression would you ask the judgement of such of woman or would you come to me?

Are these bursts of temper part of the derangement you mentioned?

Or are they something that is in your surroundings?

If they are in your sickness how can you accept another's opinion when the nature of your attack has taken away your power of reasoning?

If they are in your home surroundings in what practical ways would you like your home surroundings changed?

Must there big changes which seriously affect the life of husband and children?

———————

If you feel that you are now able to be your own doctor—to judge what is good for you.

Of what use would a nurse be?

Would she be a sort of clock to remind you it was time for this and that?

If that function in your husband is annoying would it not be more annoying in the case of a stranger in your own house?

———————

Is there not an idea in your head sometimes that you must live close to the borders of mental trouble in order to create at your best?

Which comes first your health or your work?

Are you in delicate health?

If a person sacrificed some of their health to their work is that within their human rights?

If a sick person sacrificed some of their health to their work is that within their human rights?

If a sick person sacrificed some of their health to their work and sacrificed others also would that be within their rights

If the other people felt that they would not willingly be sacrificed could they refuse?

[1]It is not known whether any version of this document was sent.

What recourse would the determined worker have if <u>well</u>?

What recourse if sick?

Must he not wait until he is well bringing such matters to a decision, because being sick he will be inevitably worsted in trying to infringe on the rights of others?

———————

Is there any enlightened opinion which considers that you are liable to be strong for another year?

Can you make yourself strong by any means except the usual ones?

Are you an exceptional person who will be cured differently from anyone else

———————

Will you make the usual return to society for its protection of you during your sickness and convalescence

Is the return usually the virtues of patience and submissiveness in certain important regards?

In case the ill person (suppose a man with small pox) runs around hurting and infecting others will society tend to take stern measures to protect itself?

Are you ill?

———————

Are your husband and child, in their larger aspects, society?

If one of them were contagiously sick and wanted to return to the home during convalescence would you let him infect the other and yourself?

Who would be your natural guides in determining what was the end of convalescence?

———————

Did "good" behavior in the clinic preceed your previous recovery?

Was it better behavior than any other?

Did not furious activity and bad behavior preceed the previous denoument at Valmont and Prangins?

Are you or have you been ill?

Does furious activity lead often to consequent irritability even in well persons?

Would not this be terribly accentuated by an ill person?

Does a person recovering from heart trouble start by moving boulders

———————

Is "I have no time" an answer to the previous questions?"

What is the order of importance of everything in your mind—

Is your health first?

Is it always first?

Is it first in the midst of artistic creation when the two are in conflict?

If it is not, and you should be well, should society coerce you into putting health first?

If you should be ill should society so act apon you?

Does your child have the same priviledges when ill as when well?

Are not lessons stopped?

Is this logical?

What does logic mean?

Is it important to be logical?

If not, is it important to be dramatic?

Is it important to have been dramatic?

If an illness becomes a nuisance to society does society act sternly?

Is it important to be dramatic or logical in the future?

Is an ill person or a well person more capable of being logical or dramatic?

Can a very ill person try to be only a little ill?

Why does madness not enlarge the artistic range?

What is disaccociation of ideas?

How does it differ in an artistic person and in a mentally ill person?

Who pays for illness?

Who pays in suffering?

Does only the ill person suffer?

When you left Prangins would you have taken any patient there into your home if they came in a refractory way

Would you constitute yourself a doctor for them?

Suppose the choice was between two patients and one patient would accept your judgement while the other one said he would not   Which would you choose

---

When doctors recommend a normal sexual life do you agree with them?

Are you normal sexually?

Are you retiscent about sex?

Are you satisfied sexually with your husband?

TO: *Maxwell Perkins*   *TLS, 1 p. Princeton University*

"La Paix," Rodgers' Forge,
Towson, Maryland,
January 19, 1933.

Dear Max:

I was in New York for three days last week on a terrible bat. I was about to call you up when I completely collapsed and laid in bed for twenty-four hours groaning. Without a doubt the boy is getting too old for such tricks. Ernest told me he concealed from you the fact that I was in such rotten shape. I send you this, less to write you a Rousseau's Confession than to let you know why I came to town without calling you, thus violating a custom of many years standing.

Thanks for the books that you have had sent to me from time to time. They comprise most of the reading I do because like everybody else I gradually cut down on expenses. When you have a line on the sale of Zelda's book let us know.

Found New York in a high state of neurosis, as does everybody else, and met no one who didn't convey the fact to me: it possibly proves that the neurosis is in me. All goes serenely down here. Am going on the water-wagon from the first of February to the first of April but don't tell Ernest because he has long convinced himself that I am an incurable alcoholic, due to the fact that we almost always meet on parties. I am his alcoholic just like Ring is mine and do not want to disillusion him, tho even Post stories must be done in a state of sobriety. I thought he seemed in good shape, Bunny less so, rather gloomy. A decision to adopt Communism definitely, no matter how good for the soul, must of necessity be a saddening process for anyone who has ever tasted the intellectual pleasures of the world we live in.

For God's sake can't you lighten that pall of gloom which has settled over Scribner's?—Erskine Caldwell's imitations of Morley Callaghan's imitations of Ernest, and Stuart Chase's imitations of Earl Browder imitating Lenine.[1] Maybe Ring would lighten your volume with a monthly article. I see he has perked up a little in the New Yorker.

All goes acceptably in Maryland, at least from the window of my study, with distant gun flashes on the horizon if you walk far out of the door.

Ever your old friend,
F Scott Fitzgerald

TO: *Edmund Wilson*   *ALS, 3 pp. Yale University*
c. February 1933

---

[1]Chase was a political writer; Browder was the head of the Communist Party in America; Lenin was the founder of Bolshevism and a leader of the Communist revolution in Russia.

La Paix (My God!)
Towson Md 1933

Dear Bunny

Your letter with the head of Vladimir Ulianov[1] just recieved. Please come here the night of the inauguration + stay at least the next day. I want to know with what resignation you look forward to your rôle of Lunafcharsky[2] + whether you decided you had nothing further worth saying in prose fiction or whether there was nothing further to say. Perhaps I should draw the answer to the last question from <u>Axel's Castle</u> yet I remember stories of yours that anticipated so much that was later said that it seems a pity. (Not that I don't admire your recent stuff—particularly I liked Hull House.

We had a most unfortunate meeting. I came to New York to get drunk + swinish and I shouldn't have looked up you and Ernest in such a humor of impotent desperation. I assume full responsibility for all unpleasantness—with Ernest I seem to have reached a state where when we drink together I half bait, half truckle to him; and as for bringing up the butcher boy matter—my God! making trouble between friends is the last thing I had ever thought myself capable of. Anyhow, plenty of egotism for the moment.

Dos was here, + we had a nice evening—we never quite understand each other + perhaps that's the best basis for an enduring friendship. Alec came up to see me at the Plaza the day I left (still in awful shape but not conspicuously so). He told me to my amazment that you had explained the fundamentals of Leninism, even Marxism the night before, + Dos tells me that it was only recently made plain thru the same agency to the editors to The New Republic. I little thought when I left politics to you + your gang in 1920 you would devote your time to cutting up Wilson's shroud into blinders! Back to Mallarmé.

—Which reminds me that T. S. Eliot and I had an afternoon + evening together last week. I read him some of his poems and he seemed to think they were pretty good. I liked him fine. Very broken and sad + shrunk inside.

However come in March. Don't know what time the inauguration takes place but you find out + tell us the approximate time of your arrival here. Find out <u>in advance</u> for we may go to it too + we might all get lost in the shuffle.

Always Your Friend
Scott

P.S. Please not a word to Zelda about anything I may have done or said in New York. She can stand literally nothing of that nature. I'm on the water-wagon but there'll be lots of liquor for you

---

[1] Wilson had put a stamp with the head of Lenin on his letter to Fitzgerald.

[2] Anatoly Lunacharsky had directed arts and education in the Soviet Union from 1917 to 1921.

TO: *Dr. Adolf Meyer*   CC, 7 pp. Princeton University

"La Paix"
Roger's Forge, Md.
April 10th, 1933

Dear Dr. Myer:

Taking Zelda Fitzgerald's case as it existed in a purer form—last October, say, when I was standing up under the thing—I would like to submit you some questions which might clarify things for me. I've had the feeling of a certain futility in our conversations with you and Dr. Rennie, though at first they did much good because she was still close to the threat of force and more acutely under the spell of your personality. Certain questions never really came to a head—no doubt you saw the thing in flux. And I know also that you were trying to consider as a whole the millieu in which she is immersed, including my contributions to it—nevertheless in one way or another our discussions have gotten so wide in scope that they would properly have to include the whole fields of philosophy, sociology and art to lead anywhere.

This is my fault. In my own broodings about the case, I have gone through the same experience—arriving at the gate of such questions as to whether Zelda isn't more worth saving than I am. I compromised on the purely utilitarian standpoint that I was the wage-earner, that I took care of wife and child, financially and practically, and beyond that that I was integrated—integrated in spite of everything, in spite of the fact that I might have two counts against me to her one.

That fact has stood up for the last three years (save for her mother's little diversion to the effect that I wanted to spirit away her daughter to a madhouse.) It began to collapse, bit by bit, six months ago—that is to say the picture of Zelda painting things that show a distinct talent, of Zelda trying faithfully to learn how to write is much more sympathetic and, superficially, more solid than the vision of me making myself iller with drink as I finish up the work of four years.

But when I began to compromise my case by loss of self-control and outbreaks of temper, my own compensation was to believe in it more and more. I will probably be carried off eventually by four strong guards shrieking manicly that after all I was right and she was wrong, while Zelda is followed home by an adoring crowd in an automobile banked with flowers, and offered a vaudeville contract. But to return to last October, may I ask my first categorical question.

Does Dr. Meyer suspect, or did Dr. Squires lead him to suspect that there were elements in the case that were being deliberately concealed? I ask this because for a month Zelda had Dr. Forel convinced that I was a notorious Parisien homo-sexual.

The second question also requires a certain introduction. It goes back to something we've talked about before and if I restate it in detail it is chiefly to clarify it in my own mind.

All I ever meant by asking authority over her was the power of an ordinary nurse in any continental country over a child; to be able to say "If you don't do this I shall punish you." All I have had has been the power of the nurse-girl in America who can only say, "I'll tell your Mama."

It seems to me that one must either have

(1) A mutual bond between equals

(2) Direct authority

(3) Delegated authority

To give responsibility without authority seems to me impossible. If a nurse can and does punish, or instead of "punish" let me say "enforce"—there is a certain healthy action and reaction set up between nurse and child, perhaps from the nurse's remorse at her strictness or the child's sense that the punishment was just—at the very worst, in the case of real injustice or over-punishment, the child has recourse to the parents. We once had a nurse of that sort—we were aware of it before the child was.

Naturally I can't rush in and turn out Zelda's lights when its her bedtime. I can't snatch strong cigarettes away from her, or countermand orders for a third cup of strong coffee given to a servant. Through moral suasion I might but more of that later.

Here is my second question:

Will Doctor Meyer give me the authority to ask Zelda when she is persistently refactory to pack her bag and spend a week under people who can take care of her, such as in the clinic?

If Doctor Meyer is in doubt about my ability to decide when such force is necessary, then hasn't the case reached such a point of confusion psychologically that I had better resort to legal means to save myself, my child and the three of us in toto.

My third question:

I have noted throughout our conversations a reluctance on your part to impose any ideas of morality upon her, save ideas of moderation in various directions. It has seemed to me that she has taken advantage of this difference of attitude from that of the continental physicians with whom she was most in contact to draw a false inference. Because Dr. Forel believes in the strictly teutonic idea of marriage and Dr. Meyer does not she imagines that the latter's attitude is nihilistic and that it somehow negates all mutual duty between husband and wife except the most casual profession of it.

Now this idea of mutual duty was, from Zelda's youth, the thing most lacking in her personality, much more lacking than in the average spoiled American girl. So that it shocked other women, even gay society women and theatrical women, again and again. At the same time she is the type who most clearly needs a guiding hand. There is the predisposition of her family to mental troubles, and in addition her mother tried hard to make everlasting babies of her children. Zelda played the baby with me always except when an important thing came up, when she was like a fire-horse in her determination and on the principal occasion she ended in Switzerland. In that moral atmosphere—which I admit can't be transported entire to the U.S.A.—she changed very much, became less dependent and more mature in smaller things and more dependent on my advise on a few main issues.

The nine months before her second breakdown were the happiest of my life and I think, save for the agonies of her father's death, the happiest of hers. Now all that is disappearing week by week and we are going back to the agonizing cat and dog fight of four or five years ago.

To recapitulate—since her personality began to split about 1928, the two main tendencies have been:

(1) Self-expression, extreme neglect of home, child and husband, exageration of physical and mental powers . . .[1] bullheadedness (Beautiful psychiatric term!).

(2) Conservatism, almost Victorianism, dread of any extremes or excess, real domesticity, absorbtion in child, husband, family and close friends, quick amenity to moral suasion.

One of her reasons for gravitating toward the first state is that her work is perhaps at its best in the passage from the conservative to the self-expressive phase, just before and just after it crosses the line—which, of course, could be the equivalent of the period of creative excitement in an integrated person. Just before crossing it is better—over the line she brings that demonaic intensity to it that achieves much in bulk with more consequent waste. I could make you a list in parallel lines but refrain out of respect for your patience.

Creatively she does not seem able to keep herself around that line. A healthful approach with all that implies, and a limited work time never to be exceeded, gives the best results but seems to be impossible outside of the dicipline of a clinic. We came nearest to this last August and September. With much pushing and prodding she lived well, wrote well and painted well.

But the question of her work I must perforce regard from a wider attitude. I make these efforts possible and do my own work besides. Possibly she would have been a genius if we had never met. In actuality she is now hurting me and through me hurting all of us.

First, by the ill-will with which she regards any control of her hours.

Second, by the unbalanced egotism which contributes to the above, and which takes the form of an abnormal illusion cherished from her ballet days: that her work's success will give her some sort of divine irresponsibility backed by unlimited gold. It is still the idea of an Iowa high-school girl who would like to be an author with an author's beautiful care-free life. It drives her to a terrible pressing hurry.

[1]Two words omitted by the editor.

Third, by her inferiority complex caused by a lack of adaptation to the fact that she is working under a greenhouse which is my money and my name and my love. This is my fault—years ago I reproached her for doing nothing and she never got over it. So she is mixed up—she is willing to use the greenhouse to protect her in every way, to nourish every sprout of talent and to exhibit it—and at the same time she feels no responsibility about the greenhouse and feels that she can reach up and knock a piece of glass out of the roof at any moment, yet she is shrewd to cringe when I open the door of the greenhouse and tell her to behave or go.

Fourth, by her idea that because some of us in our generation with the effort and courage of youth battered a nitch in an old wall, she can make the same kind of crashing approach to the literary life with the frail equipment of a sick mind and a berserk determination.

With one more apology for this—my God, it amounts to a booklet!—I arrive at my last question.

Doesn't Dr. Meyer think it might be wise to let Zelda have the feeling for a minute of being alone, of having exhausted everyone's patience—to let her know that he is not essentially behind her in any way for she interprets his scientific impersonality as a benevolent neutrality?

Otherwise the Fitzgerald's seem to be going out in the storm, each one for himself, and I'm afraid Scotty and I will weather it better than she.

Yours gratefully always, and in extremis

TO: Dr. Adolf Meyer   *AL (draft), 6 pp. Princeton University*
Spring 1933   *"La Paix," Towson, Maryland*

Dear Dr. Myer:

Thanks for your answer to my letter—it was kind of you to take time to reply to such an unscientific discussion of the case. I felt that from the difference between my instinctive-emotional knowledge of Zelda, extending over 15 years, and your objective-clinical knowledge of her, and also from the difference between the Zelda that everyone who lives a hundred consecutive hours in this house sees and the Zelda who, as a consumate actress, shows herself to you—from these differences we might see where the true center of her should lie, around what point its rallying ground should be. When you qualify or disqualify my judgement on the case, or put it on a level very little above hers on the grounds that I have frequently abused liquor I can only think of Lincoln's remark about a greater man and heavier drinker than I have ever been—that he wished he knew what sort of liquor Grant drank so he could send a barrel to all his other generals.

This is not said in any childish or churlish spirit of defying you on your opinions on alcohol—during the last six days I have drunk altogether slightly less than a quart and a half of weak gin, at wide intervals. But if there is no essential difference between an overextended, imaginative, functioning man using alcohol as a stimulus or a temporary <u>aisment</u> and a schitzophrene I am naturally alarmed about my ability to collaborate in this cure at all.

Again I must admit that you are compelled to make your judgements apon the basis of observed behavior but my claim is that a true synthesis of the totality of the behavior elements in this case has not yet been presented to you.

If you should for example be in a position to interview an indefinate number of observers—let me say at random my family as opposed to hers, my particular friends as opposed to hers, or even my instinctive protection of Zelda as opposed to her instinctive protection of me—you could formulate simply nothing—you would have to guess, rather like a jury sitting on the case of a pretty girl and a plausible man. Or if as you say (and I must disagree) that this is a dual "case" in any sense further than that it involves the marriage of two artistic temperments, you should interview Dr. Squires or any of Zelda's nurses while she was in Phipps—there would be the fault of Zelda being the subject and me becoming the abstraction so that there would be real play of subjective forces between us to be observed.

But if, to follow out my (fable) there should be another series of people to be examined to whom our life bares a nearer relation in its more basic and more complex terms, I mean terms that are outside "acting" and personal charm because they are in each case qualified by a hard an objective reality—you might be confronted with my child and what she thinks; by any professional writer of the first rank (say Dos Passos, Lewis, Mencken, Hemmingway, any real professional) on being told that their amateur wives were trying to cash in secretly on their lust for "self expression" by publishing a book about your private life with a casual survey of the material apon which you were currently engaged; by my business associates a publisher each of fourteen years standing; by every employee, secretaries, nurses, tennis-instructors, governesses; and by every servant almost without exception—if you could meet an indefinate series of these people extending back long before Zelda broke down I think there would be less doubt in your mind as to whence this family derives what mental and moral stamina it possesses. There would be a good percentage who liked her better than me and probably a majority who found her more attractive (as it should be); but on the question of integrity, responsibility, conscience, sense of duty, judgment, will-power, whatever you want to call it—well, I think that 95% of this group of ghosts; their judgment would be as decided as Solomon pronouncing apon the two mothers.

This beautiful essay (I find that manic-depressives go in for such lengthy expositions and I suspect myself + all authors of being incipient manic-depressives) is another form of my old plea to let me sit apon the bench with you instead of being kept down with the potential accomplices—largely on the charge of criminal associations.

The witness is weary of strong drink and until very recently He had had the matter well in hand for four years and has it in hand at the moment, and needs no help on the matter being normally frightened by the purely physical consequences of it. He does work and is not to be confused with the local Hunt-Club-Alcoholic and asks that his testimony be considered as of prior validity to any other.

Sincerely

P.S. Please don't bother to answer the above—its simply a restatement anyhow. In answer to your points—I can concieve of giving up all liquor but only under conditions that seem improbable—Zelda suddenly a helpmate or even divorced and insane. Or, if one can think of some way of doing it, Zelda marrying some man of some caliber who would take care of her, really take care of her   This is a possibility   Her will to power must be broken without that—the only alternative would be to break me and I am forwarned + forearmed against that

    P.S. ② All I meant by the difference between the Teutonic + American ideas of marriage is expressed in the differences between the terms Herr + Frau and the terms Mr + Mrs

TO: John O'Hara[1]   RCC, 1 p.(fragment). Princeton University

La Paix, Rodgers' Forge,
Towson, Maryland,
July 18, 1933.

Dear O'Hara:

    I am especially grateful for your letter. I am half black Irish and half old American stock with the usual exaggerated ancestral pretensions. The black Irish half of the family had the money and looked down upon the Maryland side of the family who had, and really had, that certain series of reticences and obligations that go under the poor old shattered word "breeding" (modern form "inhibitions"). So being born in that atmosphere of crack, wisecrack and countercrack I developed a two cylinder inferiority complex. So if I were elected King of Scotland tomorrow after graduating from Eton, Magdalene to the Guards with an embryonic history which tied me to the Plantagonets,[2] I would still be a parvenue. I spent my youth in alternately crawling in front of the kitchen maids and insulting the great.

    I suppose this is just a confession of being a Gael though I have known many Irish who have not been afflicted by this intense social self-consciousness. If you are interested in colleges, a typical gesture on my part would have been, for being at Princeton and belonging to one of its snootiest clubs, I

---

[1] O'Hara, whose first novel, *Appointment in Samarra*, would be published in 1934, had written Fitzgerald a fan letter about one of his *Saturday Evening Post* stories.

[2] Eton, prestigious English school; Magdalen, a college of Oxford University; The Guards, a socially prominent British regiment; Plantagenets, English royal house from 1154 to 1399.

233

would be capable of going to Podunk on a visit and being absolutely booed and over-awed by its social system, not from timidity but simply because of an inner necessity of starting my life and my self justification over again at scratch in whatever new environment I may be thrown.

The only excuse for that burst of egotism is that you asked forrit. I am sorry things are breaking

TO: Scottie Fitzgerald   *CC, 3 pp. Princeton University*

La Paix, Rodgers' Forge,
Towson, Maryland,
August 8, 1933.

Dear Pie:

I feel very strongly about you doing duty. Would you give me a little more documentation about your reading in French? I am glad you are happy—but I never believe much in happiness. I never believe in misery either. Those are things you see on the stage or the screen or the printed page, they never really happen to you in life.

All I believe in in life is the rewards for virtue (according to your talents) and the <u>punishments</u> for not fulfilling your duties, which are doubly costly. If there is such a volume in the camp library, will you ask Mrs. Tyson to let you look up a sonnet of Shakespeare's in which the line occurs "<u>Lilies that fester smell far worse than weeds.</u>"

Have had no thoughts today, life seems composed of getting up a <u>Saturday Evening Post</u> story. I think of you, and always pleasantly; but if you call me "Pappy" again I am going to take the White Cat out and beat his bottom <u>hard, six times for every time you are impertinent.</u> Do you react to that?

I will arrange the camp bill.

Halfwit, I will conclude. Things to worry about:

Worry about courage
Worry about cleanliness
Worry about efficiency
Worry about horsemanship
Worry about . . .

Things not to worry about:

Don't worry about popular opinion
Don't worry about dolls
Don't worry about the past
Don't worry about the future
Don't worry about growing up
Don't worry about anybody getting ahead of you
Don't worry about triumph
Don't worry about failure unless it comes through your own fault

Don't worry about mosquitoes
Don't worry about flies
Don't worry about insects in general
Don't worry about parents
Don't worry about boys
Don't worry about disappointments
Don't worry about pleasures
Don't worry about satisfactions
Things to think about:
What am I really aiming at?
How good am I really in comparison to my contemporaries in regard to:
(a) Scholarship
(b) Do I really understand about people and am I able to get along with them?
(c) Am I trying to make my body a useful instrument or am I neglecting it?

With dearest love,

P.S. My come-back to your calling me Pappy is christening you by the word Egg, which implies that you belong to a very rudimentary state of life and that I could break you up and crack you open at my will and I think it would be a word that would hang on if I ever told it to your contemporaries. "Egg Fitzgerald." How would you like that to go through life with "Eggie Fitzgerald" or "Bad Egg Fitzgerald" or any form that might occur to fertile minds? Try it once more and I swear to God I will hang it on you and it will be up to you to shake it off. Why borrow trouble?

Love anyhow.

TO: *Maxwell Perkins*   *TLS, 4 pp. Princeton University*

La Paix, Rodgers' Forge,
Towson, Maryland,
September 25, 1933.
Dear Max:
The novel has gone ahead faster than I thought. There was a little set back when I went to the hospital for four days[1] but since then things have gone ahead of my schedule, which you will remember, promised you the whole manuscript for reading November 1, with the first one-fourth ready to shoot into the magazine (in case you can use it) and the other three-fourths to undergo further revision. I now figure that this can be achieved by about the 25th of October. I will appear in person carrying the manuscript and wearing a spiked helmet.

[1] Between September 1933 and January 1937 Fitzgerald checked into Johns Hopkins Hospital eight times to taper off from alcohol and receive treatment for tubercular fevers.

235

There are several points and I wish you would answer them categorically.

1. Did you mean that you could get the first fourth of the story into the copy of the magazine appearing late in December and therefore that the book could appear early in April?[1] I gathered that on the phone but want to be sure. I don't know what the ocean travel statistics promise for the spring but it seems to me that a May publication would be too late if there was a great exodus and I should miss being a proper gift book for it. The story, as you know, is laid entirely in Europe—I wish I could have gotten as far as China but Europe was the best I could do, Max (to get into Ernest's rhythm).

2. I would not want a magazine proof of the first part, though of course I would expect your own proof readers to check up on blatant errors, but would want to talk over with you any small changes that would have to be made for magazine publication—in any case, to make them myself.

3. Will publication with you absolutely preclude that the book will be chosen by the Literary Guild[2] or the Book of the Month? Whatever the answer the serial will serve the purpose of bringing my book to the memory and attention of my old public and of getting straight financially with you. On the other hand, it is to both our advantages to capitalize if possible such facts as that the editors of those book leagues might take a fancy to such a curious idea that the author, Fitzgerald, actually wrote a book after all these years (this is all said with the reservation that the book is good.) Please answer this as it is of importance to me to know whether I must expect my big returns from serial and possibly theatrical and picture rights or whether I have as good a chance at a book sale, launched by one of those organizations, as any other best seller.

Ober is advancing me the money to go through with it (it will probably not need more than $2,000 though he has promised to go as far as $4,000) and in return I am giving him 10% of the serial rights. I plan to raise the money to repay him (if I have not already paid him by <u>Post</u> stories) by asking a further advance on the book royalties or on my next book which might be an omnibus collection of short stories or those two long serial stories about young people that I published some time ago in the <u>Post</u> as the Basil stories and the Josephine stories—this to be published in the fall.

You are the only person who knows how near the novel is to being finished, <u>please don't say a word to anyone</u>.

4. How will you give a month's advance notice of the story—slip a band on the jacket of the December issue? I want to talk to you about advertising when I see you in late October so please don't put even the publicity man at any work yet. As to the photographs I have a snap-shot negative of the three of us with a surf board, which enlarges to a nice 6 × 10 glossy suitable for rotogravures and also have a fine double profile of Zelda and me in

---

[1] *Tender Is the Night* was serialized in *Scribner's Magazine* (January–April 1934).
[2] The novel was a Literary Guild alternate for June 1934.

regular cabinet photograph size and have just gotten figures from the photographer. He wants $18.00 for twelve, $24.00 for twenty-four and $35.00 for fifty and says he does not sell the plates, though I imagine he could be prevailed upon if we give him a "take it or leave it" offer. How many would you need? These two photographs are modern I don't want any of the old ones sent out and I don't want any horrors to be dug up out of newspaper morgues.

Tell me how many you would need to cover all the press? Would it be cheaper if I sat when I came up there—the trouble is that in only one out of any three pictures is my pan of any interest.

5. My plan, and I think it is very important, is to prevail upon the <u>Modern Library</u>, even with a subsidy, to bring out <u>Gatsby</u> a few weeks after the book publication of this novel.[1] Please don't say that anybody would possibly have the psychology of saying to themselves "One of his is in the <u>Modern Library</u> therefore I will not buy another", or that the two books could be confused. The people who buy the <u>Modern Library</u> are not at all the people who buy the new books. <u>Gatsby</u>—in its present form, not actually available in sight to book buyers, will only get a scattering sale as a result of the success of this book. I feel that every time your business department has taken a short-sighted view of our community of interest in this matter, which is my reputation, there has been no profit on your part and something less than that on mine. As for example, a novel of Ernest's in the <u>Modern Library</u> and no novel of mine, a good short story of Ernest's in their collection of the Great Modern Short Stories and a purely commercial story of mine. I want to do this almost as much as I want to publish this novel and will cooperate to the extent of sharing the cost.

There will be other points when I see you in October, but I will be greatly reassured to have some sort of idea about these points so that I can make my plans accordingly. I will let you know two or three days in advance when you may expect me.

One last point: Unlike Ernest I am perfectly agreeable to making any necessary cuts <u>for serial publication</u> but naturally insist that I shall do them myself.

You can imagine the pride with which I will enter your office a month from now. <u>Please do not have a band as I do not care for music.</u>

Ever yours,
F. Scott Fitzgerald

---

[1] *The Great Gatsby*, with a new introduction by Fitzgerald, was published by Modern Library in September 1934.

I would like my novel in its unfinished form to be sent to John Peale Bishop, c/o Guarantee Trust Company, Paris, who I appoint as my literary executor in case of misfortune. What necessary work Mr. Bishop conceives should be done on it before publication he should award himself as seems just on a percentage basis, the rest going to my heirs and assigns.

Signed *F. Scott Fitzgerald*
Witness *Essie Jackson*
Witness *Isabel W. Owens*

August 9, 1933

This document refers to Tender Is the Night. *Jackson was the Fitzgeralds' cook; Owens was Fitzgerald's secretary at "La Paix" and in Baltimore.*

TO: *Maxwell Perkins*   TLS, 2 pp. *Princeton University*

La Paix, Rodgers' Forge,
Towson, Maryland,
September 29, 1933.

Dear Max:

Since talking to you and getting your letter another angle has come up. Ober tells me that Burton[1] of Cosmopolitan is very interested in the novel and if he took it would, in Ober's opinion, pay between $30,00 and $40,000 for it. Now against that there are the following factors:

1. The fact that though Burton professes great lust for my work the one case in which I wrote a story specifically for him, that movie story that you turned down and that Mencken published,[2] he showed that he really can't put his taste into action; in that case the Hearst policy man smeared it.

2. The tremendous pleasure I would get from appearing in Scribners.

3. The spring publication.

4. My old standby, the Post, would not be too pleased to have my work running serially all spring and summer in the Cosmopolitan.

On the other hand, the reasons why it must be considered are between thirty and forty thousand, and all of them backed by the credit of the U.S. Treasury. It is a purely hypothetical sum I admit and certainly no serial is

[1]Harry Burton, editor of Hearst magazines.
[2]"Crazy Sunday" appeared in the October 1932 *American Mercury.*

238

worth it, yet if Willie Hearst[1] is still pouring gold back into the desert in the manner of 1929 would I be stupid not to take some or would I be stupid not to take some? My own opinion is that if the thing is offered to Burton, he will read it, be enthusiastic, and immediately an Obstacle will appear. On the other hand, should I even offer it to them? Should I give him a copy on the same day I give you a copy asking an answer from him within three days? Would the fact that he refused it diminish your interest in the book or influence it? Or, even, considering my relations with you would it be a dirty trick to show it to him at all? What worries me is the possibility of being condemned to go back to the Saturday Evening Post grind at the exact moment when the book is finished. I suppose I could and probably will need a damn good month's rest outdoors or traveling before I can even do that.

Can you give me any estimate as to how much I could expect from you as to payment for the serial and how much of that will be in actual cash? It seems terrible to ask you this when it is not even decided yet whether or not you want it; but what I want to do is to see if I can not offer it at all to Burton; I wish to God I had never talked to Harold about it and got these upsetting commercial ideas in my head.

I am taking care of the picture matter. I certainly would like to be on your cover and stare down Greta Garbo on the news stands. I figure now that it should reach you, at the latest, on the 25th, though I am trying for the 23rd.

Ring's death was a terrible blow. Have written a short appreciation of him for the New Republic.[2]

Please answer.

Ever yours,
Scott

TO: *Maxwell Perkins*   *TLS, 4 pp. Princeton University*

La Paix, Rodgers' Forge,
Towson, Maryland,
October 19, 1933.

Dear Max:

All goes well here. The first two chapters are in shape and am starting the third one this afternoon. So the first section comprising about 26,000 words will be mailed to you Friday night or Saturday morning.

Naturally I was delighted by your gesture of coming up two thousand. I hope to God results will show in the circulation of the magazine and I have an idea they will. Negotiations with Cosmopolitan were of course

---

[1] William Randolph Hearst, magazine and newspaper publisher.
[2] "Ring," *New Republic* (October 11, 1933).

stopped and Ober is sure that getting the release from <u>Liberty</u> is merely a matter of form which he is attending to. I think I will need the money a little quicker than by the month, say $1000 on delivery of the first section and then the other 3 $1000s every fortnight after that. This may not be necessary but the first $2000 will. As you know, I now owe Ober two or three thousand and he should be reimbursed so he can advance me more to carry me through the second section and a <u>Post</u> story. Naturally, payments on the serial should be made to him.

I am saying this now and will remind you later. My idea is that the <u>book</u> form of the novel should be set up <u>from the corrected proof of the serial,</u>— in that I will reinsert the excisions which I am making for the serial.

If you have any way of getting French or Swiss railroad posters it would be well for you to try to. Now as to the blurbs: I think there should not be too many; I am sending you nine.[1]

> "The Great Gatsby is undoubtedly a work of art."
> London Times

———————

As to T. S. Eliot: what he said was in a letter to me—that he'd read it several times, it had interested and excited him more than any novel he had seen, either English or American, for a number of years, and he also said that it seemed to him that it was the first step forward in the American novel since Henry James.

I know him slightly but I would not dare ask him for an endorsement. If it can be managed in any way without getting a rebuff, even some more qualified statement would be the next best thing to an endorsement by Joyce or Gertrude Stein.

Of course I think blurbs have gotten to be pretty much the bunk, but maybe that is a writer's point of view and the lay reader does not understand the back-scratching that is at the root of most of them. However, I leave it in your hands. Don't quote all of these unless you think it is advisable.

We can talk over the matter of <u>Gatsby</u> in the Modern Library after your announcement has appeared.

Again thanks for the boost in price and remember the title is a secret to the last.

Ever your friend,
Scott Fitzgerald

I should say to be careful in saying it's my first book in seven years <u>not to imply that it contains seven years</u> work. People would expect too much in bulk + scope.

This novel, my 4th, completes my story of the boom years. It might be

———

[1] The one and one-half pages that contained the first eight blurbs are missing from this letter.

wise to accentuate the fact that it does <u>not</u> deal with the depression. <u>Don't</u> accentuate that it deals with Americans abroad—there's been too much trash under that banner.

No exclamatory "At last, the long awaited ect." That merely creates the "Oh yeah" mood in people.

TO: *Maxwell Perkins*   *TLS, 2 pp. Princeton University*

La Paix, Rodgers' Forge,
Towson, Maryland,
October 20, 1933.

Dear Max:

Made not only the changes agreed upon but also cut out several other small indelicacies that I happened upon.[1] I think this is now damn good.

How is this for an advertising approach:

"For several years the impression has prevailed that Scott Fitzgerald had abandoned the writing of novels and in the future would continue to write only popular short stories. His publishers knew different and they are very glad now to be able to present a book which is in line with his three other highly successful and highly esteemed novels, thus demonstrating that Scott Fitzgerald is anything but through as a serious novelist."

I don't mean necessarily these exact words but something on that general line, I mean something politic enough not to disparage the <u>Post</u> stories but saying quite definitely that this is a horse of another color.

If Dashiell[2] likes this section of the book ask him to drop me a line. Am starting the revision of the second section Monday.

Ever your friend,
F Scott Fitzgerald

[1] For the *Tender Is the Night* serial.
[2] Alfred Dashiell was managing editor of *Scribner's Magazine*.

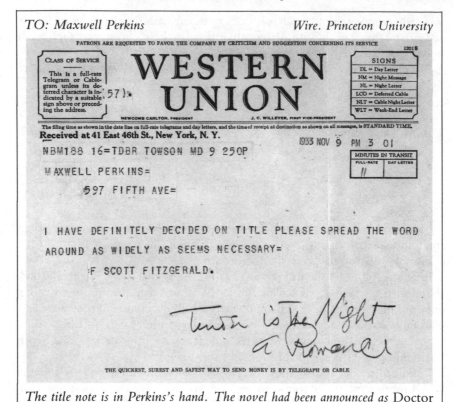

TO: Maxwell Perkins   *Wire. Princeton University*

The title note is in Perkins's hand. The novel had been announced as Doctor Diver's Holiday.

TO: Maxwell Perkins   *TLS, 2 pp. Princeton University*

La Paix, Rodgers' Forge,
Towson, Maryland,
November 13, 1933.

Dear Max:

I was too sanguine in estimating the natural divisions of the novel. As it turns out in the reworking the line up is as follows:

I. The first triangle story, which you have

(26,000 words)

II. Completion of that story, plus the throw-back to courtship of doctor and his wife (19,000 words)

III. The doctor's struggles with his problem, concluding with his debacle in Rome.

IV. The doctor's decline after he has given up.

These two last parts are going to be <u>long as hell</u>, especially IV. Section III, as you may remember, includes the part about his journeying around Europe, which we agreed could be considerably cut, but Section IV could not be cut much without omission of such key incidents as would cripple the timing of the whole plan. That Section is liable to amount to as much as forty thousand words—could you handle it? Or must I divide it, and lose a month on spring publication?

By that time reader interest in the serial will be thoroughly aroused (or thoroughly killed) so I think the idea of the book publication should be paramount if you can arrange the material factor of such a long installment.

Ever yours
Scott Fitz——

P.S. By the way: where in hell is the proof? And will you have two struck off? This is important for Section II where the medical part begins, but how can I ask a doctor to judge fairly upon Section II unless he can read Section I?

TO: Egbert S. Oliver[1]   *TLS, 2 pp. Original unlocated*

1307 Park Avenue
Baltimore, Maryland,
January 7, 1934.

Dear Mr. Oliver:

The first help I ever had in writing in my life was from my father who read an utterly imitative Sherlock Holmes story of mine and pretended to like it.[2]

But after that I received the most invaluable aid from one Mr. C. N. B. Wheeler then headmaster of the St. Paul Academy now the St. Paul Country Day School in St. Paul, Minnesota. 2. From Mr. Hume, then co-headmaster of the Newman School and now headmaster of the Canterbury School. 3. From Courtland Van Winkle in freshman year at Princeton—now professor of literature at Yale (he gave us the book of Job to read and I don't think any of our preceptorial group ever quite recovered from it.) After that comes a lapse. Most of the professors seemed to me old and uninspired, or perhaps it was just that I was getting under way in my own field.

I think this answers your question. This is also my permission to make full

---

[1] Of Willamette University, Salem, Oregon.
[2] Probably "The Mystery of the Raymond Mortgage," *St. Paul Academy Now and Then* (February 1910).

use of it with or without my name. Sorry I am unable from circumstances of time and pressure to go into it further.

Sincerely,
F. Scott Fitzgerald

TO: Maxwell Perkins   *TLS, 3 pp. Princeton University*

1307 Park Avenue,
Baltimore, Maryland,
January 13, 1934.

Dear Max:

What do you think of the idea of using twenty-four of those wood-cuts, which illustrate the serial, as head and tail pieces for chapters in the book or, alternatively, interspersing them through the novel? I think it is comparatively an innovation in recent fiction and might give the book a certain distinction. I've gotten very fond of the illustrations. Who the hell is the illustrator? If it is too expensive a process let me know, but since the cuts are already made I thought it might not be.[1]

Please do not send me any book galley for the present, just hold it there. I am already confused by the multiplicity of the irons I have in the fire and as far as possible would prefer to do the book galley in one or two long stretches.

I did not thank you over the phone for the further advance, which does not mean that I did not appreciate it, but only that I have so much to thank you for.

Tell Dashiell that I cannot promise not to make changes in Section III, but under no conditions will it be lengthened. Section IV is taking longer than I thought and it may be the middle of next week before you get it.

Ever Yours
Scott Fitz, —

P.S. 1. Will you ask Dashiell to strike off as many as half a dozen additional proofs because I have always a use for them in passing them around for technical advice. Again, this request is condition by not wanting it to be exhorbitantly expensive.

P.S. 2. Don't forget my suggestion that the jacket flap should carry an implication that though the book starts in a lyrical way, heavy drama will presently develop.

P.S. 3. Any contract you suggest will probably be O.K. You might bring one with you when you come down, an event to which I look forward eagerly.

---

[1] Edward Shenton's pen-and-ink illustrations were retained in the book.

P.S. 4. Also remember that upon due consideration I would prefer the binding to be uniform with my other books. If these were prosperous times and there were any prospect of a superior reissue of my whole tribe I'd say "let it begin here" to quote the famous commander of the Minute men, but there isn't, so I prefer to stick to my undistinguished green uniform—I mean even to the point of the guilt stampings being uniform to the others.

P.S. 5. I don't want to bore you by reiterating but I do think the matter of Gatsby in the Modern Library should be taken up as shortly as possible after the appearance of installment II.

P.S. 6. Am getting responses only from a few writers and from the movies. The novel will certainly have success d'estime but it may be slow in coming—alas, I may again have written a novel for novelists with little chance of its lining anybody's pockets with gold. The thing is perhaps too crowded for story reachers to search it through for the story but it can't be helped, there are times when you have to get every edge of your finger-nails on paper. Anyhow I think this serial publication will give it the best chance it can possibly have because it is a book that only gives its full effect on its second reading. Almost every part of it now has been revised and thought out from three to six times.

P.S. 7 What is the name of a functioning Press Clipping Bureau?

TO: Maxwell Perkins   *TLS, 2 pp. Princeton University*

1307 Park Avenue
Baltimore, Maryland
January 18, 1934

Dear Max:
   You letter covers everything except the English publication. Since the old Chatto & Windus idea I came to practically an understanding with Cape, came to a real one with Knopf, which was broken when they dissolved their London house. What would you do about Faber & Faber? Advise me.[1]
   Much as I value your advice, by which I profited in the revision of Gatsby, I can't see cutting out the "shooting at the train-side." It serves all sorts of subtle purposes and since I have decided that the plan of the book is best as originally conceived, the small paring away would be very little help and I think would do more harm than good. I intend to think over this question once more but at the moment I am satisfied with the book as it stands, as well as being pretty dead on it. I want to hear some reactions on Section II, but I like the slow approach, which I think has a psychological significance

---

[1] *Tender Is the Night* was published in Great Britain by Chatto & Windus in 1934.

affecting not only the work in question, but also having a bearing on my career in general. Is that too damn egotistical an association?

Ever yours,

F. Scott Fitz——

TO: *Maxwell Perkins*   *TLS, 4 pp. Princeton University*

1307 Park Avenue,
Baltimore, Maryland,
February 5, 1934.

Dear Max:

Isn't there any mechanical means by which you can arrange to include the 1400 words of the arrest in Cannes?[1] The more I think of it the more I think that it is absolutely necessary for the unity of the book and the effectiveness of the finale to show Dick in the dignified and responsible aspect toward the world and his neighbors that was implied so strongly in the first half of the book. It is all very well to say that this can be remedied in book publication but it has transpired that at least two dozen important writers and newspaper men are reading the book in the serial and will form their impressions from that. I have made cuts in Section IV—a good bit of the last scene between Dick and Tommy but also the proof has swollen somewhat in revision which counteracts that, nor can I reduce the 1250 words of that scene to 800. I am saying 1400 because I know there will be a slight expansion. Couldn't you take out some short piece from the number? Surely it hasn't crystallized at this early date. Even with this addition the installment is shorter than the others, as I promised Fritz.[2]

If I do not hold these two characters to the end of the book it might as well never have been written. It is legitimate to ruin Dick but it is by no means legitimate to make him an ineffectual. In the proof I am pointing up the fact that his intention dominated all this last part but it is not enough and the foreshortening without the use of this scene, which was a part of the book structure from the first, does not contain enough of him for the reader to reconstruct his whole personality as viewed as a unit throughout— and the reason for this is my attempt to tell the last part entirely through Nicole's eyes. I was even going to have her in on the Cannes episode but decided against it because of the necessity of seeing Dick alone.

My feeling about this was precipitated by the remarks of the young psychiatrist who is the only person who had read all the magazine proof and only the magazine proof. He felt a sharp lesion at the end which those who had read the whole novel did not feel.

While I am writing you I may as well cover some other points:

[1]Perkins had asked Fitzgerald whether the scene could be condensed for the magazine installment.
[2]Alfred Dashiell.

1. Please don't forget the indentation of title and author on the front cover as in previous books. There are other Fitzgeralds writing and I would like my whole name on the outside of the book, and also I would prefer uniformity.

2. Would you please strike off at least three book proofs for me, all to be used for revisions such as medical, linguistic, etc? Also, I would like an extra galley of book proof Section IV when you have it, for Ober to pass on to Davis[1] in order to supply the missing material.

3. In advertising the book some important points are: Please do not use the phrase "Riviera" or "gay resorts." Not only does it sound like the triviality of which I am so often accused, but also the Riviera has been thoroughly exploited by E. Phillips Oppenheim[2] and a whole generation of writers and its very mention invokes a feeling of unreality and unsubstantiality. So I think it would be best to watch this and reduce it only to the statement that the scenes of the book are laid in Europe. If it could be done, a suggestion that, after a romantic start, a serious story unfolds, would not be amiss; also it might be mentionable that for exigencies of serialization, a scene or two was cut. In general, as you know, I don't approve of great ballyhoo advertisements, even of much quoted praise. The public is very, very, very weary of being sold bogus goods and this inevitably reacts on solider manufactures.

I find that revising in this case is pulling up the weakest section of the book and then the next weakest, etc. First, Section III was the weakest and Section IV the strongest, so I bucked up III, then IV was the weakest and is still but when I have fixed that Section I will be the weakest. The section that has best held up is Section II.

I was tremendously impressed with "South Moon Under"[3] until I read her prize short story, "Gal Young Un." I suddenly saw the face of Ethan Fromme peering out from under a palmetto hat. The heroine is even called Matt in tribute to the power of the subconscious.[4] Well, well, well, I often think of Picasso's remark "You do it first then other people can come along and do it pretty and get off with a big proportion of the spoils. When you do it first you can't do it pretty." So I guess Miss Rawlings is just another writer after all, just when I was prepared to welcome her to the class of 1896 with Ernest, Dos Passos and myself.

Please wire about the inclusion of the Cannes episode,[5] and <u>don't</u> sidetrack these advertising points.

Ever yours,
Scott

[1] Playwright Owen Davis.
[2] Popular British espionage novelist.
[3] Marjorie Kinnan Rawlings's novel was published by Scribners in 1933.
[4] Ethan Frome and Mattie Silver are central figures in Edith Wharton's *Ethan Frome* (1911).
[5] The scene was printed in its entirety in the magazine installment.

TO: *Harold Ober*
February 21, 1934

Wire. Lilly Library
Baltimore, Maryland

WANT TO DECIDE NOW HOW TO RAISE MONEY TO TIDE ME OVER THE MONTH
BEFORE FINISHING FINAL BOOK REVISION WITHOUT CONSULTING MAX CAN YOU
GET OPINION OF ONE PROMINENT PLAYWRIGHT ABOUT POSSIBILITIES OF DRAMA-
TIZATION OTHERWISE I WOULD RATHER SHOOT THE WORKS AND SELL TO THE
PICTURES TO GET OUT OF THIS FINANCIAL HOLE IT MUST BE DECIDED IMMEDI-
ATELY LUNCHING WITH CLARK GABLE TOMORROW AND WANT TO KNOW PRESENT
STATUS OF GATSDY AS HE WOULD LIKE TO PLAY IT PLEASE WIRE IMMEDIATELY
    F SCOTT FITZGERALD

TO: *Maxwell Perkins*

TLS, 2 pp. Princeton University

1307 Park Avenue
Baltimore, Maryland
March 4, 1934

Dear Max:

Confirming our conversation on the phone this morning, I wish you
could get some word to the printers that they should not interfere with my
use of italics. If I had made a mess of a type face, that would be another
matter. I know exactly what I am doing, and I want to use italics for
emphasis, and not waste them on the newspaper convention laid down by
Mr. Munsey[1] in 1858. Of course, always you have been damned nice in
having your printers follow my specifications, but in this case, and under
the very pressing conditions under which we are working, it worries me
that the book galleys came back with exactly the same queries that the
magazine galleys had. Could you tip them the wink some way so that they
would please follow my copy exactly as they used to, as this is my last
chance at the book? Whoever has been in charge of it must be very patient
because I know at the ninth revision that the very sight of any part of it fills
me with nausea. However, I have to go on in this particular case while they
don't, and so are liable to get careless.

Going over the other points, I hope both (1) that the review copies will
go out in plenty of time, and (2) that they will get the version of the novel
as it will be published because there is no doubt that each revision makes a
tremendous difference in the impression that the book will leave. After all,
Max, I am a plodder. One time I had a talk with Ernest Hemingway, and
I told him, against all the logic that was then current, that I was the tortoise
and he was the hare, and that's the truth of the matter, that everything that
I have ever attained has been through long and persistent struggle while it
is Ernest who has a touch of genius which enables him to bring off extraordi-

[1]Frank A. Munsey, American publisher.

nary things with facility. I have no facility. I have a facility for being cheap, if I wanted to indulge that. I can do cheap things. I changed Clark Gable's act at the moving picture theatre here the other day. I can do that kind of thing as quickly as anybody but when I decided to be a serious man, I tried to struggle over every point until I have made myself into a slow-moving behemoth (if that is the correct spelling), and so there I am for the rest of my life. Anyhow, these points of proofreading, etc., are of tremendous importance to me, and you can charge it all to my account, and I will realize all the work you have had on it.

As I told you on the phone, I enjoyed Marjory Rawlin's praise, but it was somewhat qualified by her calling my people trivial people. Other stuff has drifted in from writers from all over America, some of it by telegram, which has been complimentary.

Now, about advertising. Again I want to tell you my theory that everybody is absolutely dead on ballyhoo of any kind, and for your advertising department to take up any interest that the intellectuals have so far shown toward the book and exploit that, would be absolutely disastrous. The reputation of a book must grow from within upward, must be a natural growth. I don't think there is a comparison between this book and The Great Gatsby as a seller. The Great Gatsby had against it its length and its purely masculine interest. This book, on the contrary, is a woman's book. I think, given a decent chance, it will make its own way insofar as fiction is selling under present conditions.

Excuse me if this letter has a dogmatic ring. I have lived so long within the circle of this book and with these characters that often it seems to me that the real world does not exist but that only these characters exist, and, however pretentious that remark sounds (and my God, that I should have to be pretentious about my work), it is an absolute fact—so much so that their glees and woes are just exactly as important to me as what happens in life.

Zelda is better. There is even a chance of her getting up for the exhibition of her paintings[1] at Easter, but nothing certain. Do you still think that idea of piling the accumulated manuscript in the window[2] is a valid one? My instinct does not quite solve the problem. What do you think? Would it seem a little phony?

With best wishes,

Scott

---

[1] Held at Cary Ross's gallery in New York City, March 29 to April 30, 1934.
[2] The Scribners bookstore display window at 597 Fifth Avenue.

TO: *Edmund Wilson*   *Wilson's retyped copy, 2 pp. Yale University*
Postmarked March 12, 1934

1307 Park Avenue
Baltimore, Maryland

Dear Bunny:

Despite your intention of mild criticism in our conversation, I felt more elated than otherwise—if the characters got real enough so that you disagreed with what I chose for their manifest destiny the main purpose was accomplished (by the way, your notion that Dick should have faded out as a shyster alienist was in my original design, but I thot of him, in reconsideration, as an "homme epuisé," not only an "homme manqué". I thought that, since his choice of a profession had accidentally wrecked him, he might plausibly have walked out on the profession itself.)

Any attempt by an author to explain away a partial failure in a work is of course doomed to absurdity—yet I could wish that you, and others, had read the book version rather than the mag. version which in spots was hastily put together. The last half for example has a <u>much</u> more polished facade now. Oddly enough several people have felt that the surface of the first chapters was <u>too</u> ornate. One man even advised me to "coarsen the texture", as being remote from the speed of the main narrative!

In any case when it appears I hope you'll find time to look it over again. Such irrevelancies as Morton Hoyt's nosedive and Dick's affair in Ohnsbruck are out, together with the scene of calling on the retired bootlegger at Beaulieu, & innumerable minor details. I have driven the Scribner proofreaders half nuts but I think I've made it incomparably smoother.

Zelda's pictures go on display in a few weeks & I'll be meeting her in N.Y. for a day at least. Wouldn't it be a good time for a reunion?

It was good seeing you & good to think that our squabble, or whatever it was, is ironed out.

With affection always,
Scott Fitzgerald

for Phil Lenhart
from F. Scott
        Fitzgerald

Let me make a
comment — this is an
attempt at the "tour
de jorce" — to promote
myself momentarily, the
Henry Esmond type of
thing.
    If you like my stuff
        (over)

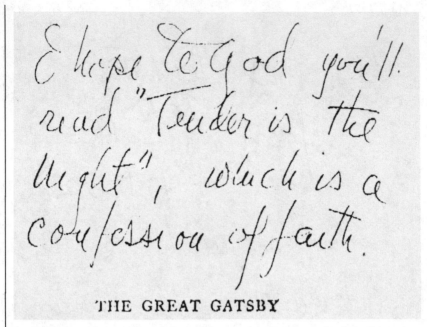

THE GREAT GATSBY

Lenhart was a former Harvard tennis star and a newspaper book reviewer.

TO: *John Peale Bishop*   TLS, *2 pp. Princeton University*

1307 Park Avenue,
Baltimore, Maryland,
April 2, 1934.

Dear John:

Somebody (I've forgotten who after an overcrowded and hectic twenty-four hours in New York) quoted you to me as saying that this current work[1] is "no advance on what he's done before." That's a legitimate criticism, but I can't take it as a slam. I keep thinking of Conrad's Nigger of the Narcissus Preface[2]—and I believe that the important thing about a work of fiction is that the essential reaction shall be profound and enduring. And if the ending

[1] *Tender Is the Night.*

[2] Conrad wrote: "My task which I am trying to achieve is, by the power of the written word, to make you hear, to make you feel—it is, before all, to make you *see.* That—and no more, and it is everything. If I succeed, you shall find there according to your deserts: encouragement, consolation, fear, charm—all you demand; and, perhaps, also that glimpse of truth for which you have forgotten to ask."

of this one is not effectual I should be gladder to think that the effect came back long afterwards, long after one had forgotten the name of the author.

All this makes it more necessary to see you and do some doping on the practise of the novel while you're in process of revision. I'll be up in New York toward the beginning of next week. Will you keep that in mind and if your plans change suddenly let me know.

Pleasant thoughts to you all.

As ever,

Scott

Two things I forgot to say—

1. There's a deliberate choice in my avoidance of a dramatic ending—I deliberately did not want it.

2. Without making apologies, I'd prefer to fade off my book, like the last of The Brothers Karanzoff, or Time Regained, and let the belly carry my story, than to resort the arbitrary blood-letting of Flaubert, Stendahl and the Elizabethans.

You see we must talk—no room in a letter.

F.S F.

TO: Thomas Wolfe   TLS, 2 pp. Harvard University

1307 Park Avenue,
Baltimore, Maryland,
April 2, 1934

Dear Arthur, Garfield, Harrison & Hayes[1]:

Thanks a hell of a lot for your letter which came at a rather sunken moment and was the more welcome. It is hard to believe that it was in the summer of 1930 we went up the mountainside together—some of our experiences have become legendary to me and I am not sure even if they happened at all. One story, (a lie or a truth), which I am in the habit of telling, is how you put out the lights of Lake Geneva with a Gargantuan gesture,[2] so that I don't know any more whether I was with you when it happened, or whether it ever happened at all!

I am so glad to hear from our common parent, Max, that you are about to publish. Again thanks for your generous appreciation.

Ever yours,

F. Scott Fitzgerald + Arthur, Garfield, Harrison & Hayes

---

[1]American Presidents treated in Wolfe's story "The Four Lost Men," Scribner's Magazine (February 1934).

[2]Fitzgerald claimed that the tall Wolfe broke power lines in Switzerland while gesticulating.

Dear Dotty
This is better
than the Magazine
Love Always
Scott

Dorothy Parker
c/o The New Yorker

TO: *John Peale Bishop*   *RTLS, 2 pp. Princeton University*

1307 Park Avenue
Baltimore, Maryland,
April 7, 1934

Dear John:

On receiving your first letter with its' handsome tribute and generous praise I realized that I had been hasty in crediting that you would make such a criticism as "this book is no advance on Gatsby." You would be the first to feel that the intention in the two books was entirely different, that (to promote myself momentarily) Gatsby was shooting at something like Henry Esmond while this was shooting at something like Vanity Fair. The dramatic novel has cannons quite different from the philosophical, now called psychological novel. One is a kind of tour de force and the other a confession of faith. It would be like comparing a sonnet sequence with an epic.

The point of my letter which survives is that there were moments all through the book where I could have pointed up dramatic scenes, and I deliberately refrained from doing so because the material itself was so harrowing and highly charged that I did not want to subject the reader to a series of nervous shocks in a novel that was inevitably close to whoever read it in my generation

—contrariwise, in dealing with figures as remote as are a bootlegger-crook to most of us, I was not afraid of heightening and melodramatizing any scenes; and I was thinking that in your novel I would like to pass on this theory to you for what it is worth. Such advice from fellow-craftsmen has been a great help to me in the past, indeed, I believe it was Ernest Hemingway who developed to me, in conversation, that the dying fall was preferable to the dramatic ending under certain conditions, and I think we both got the germ of the idea from Conrad.

With affection always,
Scott

TO: *H. L. Mencken*   *TLS, 2 pp. Enoch Pratt Free Library*

1307 Park Avenue,
Baltimore, Maryland,
April 23, 1934.

Dear Menck:

I am afraid that I am going to have to violate your favorite code of morals—the breaking of engagements—because I've got to go to New York about trying to capitalize on my novel in the movies.

Without wanting to add to your mass of accumulated correspondence just as you've cleared it away, I would like to say in regard to my book that there was a deliberate intention in every part of it except the first. The first part, the romantic introduction, was too long and too elaborated, largely because of the fact that it had been written over a series of years with varying plans, but everything else in the book conformed to a definite intention and if I had to start to write it again tomorrow I would adopt the same plan, irrespective of the fact of whether I had, in this case, brought it off or not brought it off. That is what most of the critics fail to understand (outside of the fact that they fail to recognize and identify anything in the book) that the motif of the "dying fall" was absolutely deliberate and did not come from any diminuition of vitality, but from a definite plan.

That particular trick is one that Ernest Hemmingway and I worked out—probably from Conrad's preface to "The Nigger"—and it has been the greatest "credo" in my life, ever since I decided that I would rather be an artist than a careerist. I would rather impress my image (even though an image the size of a nickel) upon the soul of a people than be known, except in so far as I have my natural obligation to my family—to provide for them. I would as soon be as anonymous as Rimbaud,[1] if I could feel that I had accomplished that purpose—and that is no sentimental yapping about being disinterested. It is simply that having once found the intensity of art, nothing else that can happen in life can ever again seem as important as the creative process.

With terrific regrets that I probably wont be back in time to hear your harrowing African adventures, and compare them with my own, and with best regards always to my favorite Venus, Sara, I am

As ever,

F. Scott Fitzgerald

TO: Zelda Fitzgerald   *CC, 3 pp. Princeton University*

1307 Park Avenue,
Baltimore, Maryland,
April 26, 1934.

Forgive me for dictating this letter instead of writing it directly, but if you could see my desk at the moment and the amount of stuff that has come in you would understand.

The thing that you have to fight against is defeatism of any kind. You have no reason for it. You have never had really a melancholy temperament, but, as your mother said: you have always been known for a bright, cheerful, extraverting attitude upon life. I mean especially that you share none of the melancholy point of view which seems to have been the lot of Anthony and

---

[1]French Symbolist poet Arthur Rimbaud (1854–1891).

Marjorie.[1] You and I have had wonderful times in the past, and the future is still brilliant with possibilities if you will keep up your morale, and try to think that way. The outside world, the political situation, etc., is still gloomy and it <u>does</u> effect everybody directly, and will inevitably reach you indirectly, but try to separate yourself from it by some form of mental hygiene—if necessary, a self-invented one.

Let me reiterate that I don't want you to have too much traffic with my book, which is a melancholy work and seems to have haunted most of the reviewers. <u>I feel very strongly about your re-reading it</u>. It represents certain phases of life that are now over. We are certainly on some upsurging wave, even if we don't yet know exactly where it's heading.

There is no feeling of gloom on your part that has the <u>slightest</u> legitimacy. Your pictures have been a success, your heath has been very much better, according to the doctors—and the only sadness is the living without you, without hearing the notes of your voice with its particular intimacies of inflection.

You and I have been happy; we haven't been happy just once, we've been happy a thousand times. The chances that the spring, that's for everyone, like in the popular songs, may belong to us too—the chances are pretty bright at this time because as usual, I can carry most of contemporary literary opinion, liquidated, in the hollow of my hand—and when I do, I see the swan floating on it and—I find it to be you and you only. But, Swan, float lightly because you are a swan, because by the exquisite curve of your neck the gods gave you some special favor, and even though you fractured it running against some man-made bridge, it healed and you sailed onward. Forget the past—what you can of it, and turn about and swim back home to me, to your haven for ever and ever—even though it may seem a dark cave at times and lit with torches of fury; it is the best refuge for you—turn gently in the waters through which you move and sail back.

This sounds allegorical but is <u>very</u> real. I want you here. The sadness of the past is with me always. The things that we have done together and the awful splits that have broken us into war survivals in the past stay like a sort of atmosphere around any house that I inhabit. The good things and the first years together, and the good months that we had two years ago in Montgomery will stay with me forever, and you should feel like I do that they can be renewed, if not in a new spring, then in a new summer. I love you my darling, darling.

P.S. Did I tell you that, among others, Adele Lovett came in and bought a picture and so did Louise Perkins and the Tommy Daniels from St. Paul? Will see that the Dick Myers get one free.

---

[1] Brother and sister of Zelda Fitzgerald.

TO: *Mabel Dodge Luhan*[1]   *CC, 3 pp. Princeton University*

1307 Park Avenue
Baltimore, Maryland,
May 10, 1934

Dear Mrs. Luhan:

I was tremendously pleased and touched by your letter and by your communication to the <u>Tribune</u>.[2] It always strikes me as very strange when I find new people in the world, because I always crystallize any immediate group in which I move as being an all-sufficient, all-inclusive cross-section of the world, at the time I know it (the group)—this all the more because a man with the mobility of the writing profession and a certain notoriety thinks that he has a good deal of choice as to whom he will know. That from the outer bleakness, where you were only a name to me, you should have felt a necessity of communicating an emotion felt about a stranger, gave me again the feeling that Conrad expresses as "the solidarity of innumerable human hearts," at times a pretty good feeling, and your letter came to me at one of those times. Having been compared to Homer and Harold Bell Wright for fifteen years, I get a pretty highly developed delirium tremens at the professional reviewers: the light men who bubble at the mouth with enthusiasm because they see other bubbles floating around, the dumb men who regularly mistake your worst stuff for your best and your best for your worst, and, most of all, the cowards who straddle and the leeches who review your books in terms that they have cribbed out of the book itself, like scholars under some extraordinary dispensation which allows them to heckle the teacher. With every book I have ever published there have always been two or three people, as often as not strangers, who have seen the intention, appreciated it, and allowed me whatever percentage I rated on the achievement of that intention. In the case of this book your appreciation has given me more pleasure than any other, not excepting Gilbert Seldes who seemed to think that I had done completely what I started out to do and that it was worth doing.

With gratitude for that necessity in you which made you take the special trouble, the extra steps, which reassured me that even at the moment of popping out something new I was reaching someone by air mail—and with the added declaration that I want to see you,

I am

Yours most cordially,

P.S. My excuse for dictating this is a sprained arm.

---

[1] Wealthy patroness of the arts.
[2] Luhan's letter to the editor (May 6, 1934) praised *Tender Is the Night*.

TO: Ernest Hemingway　　　　　*TLS & AL, 1 p. John F. Kennedy Library*

1307 Park Avenue,
Baltimore, Maryland,
May 10, 1934.

Dear Ernest:

Did you like the book? For God's sake drop me a line and tell me one way or another. You can't hurt my feelings. I just want to get a few intelligent slants at it to get some of the reviewers jargon out of my head.

Ever Your Friend
Scott

All I meant about the editing was that if I'd been in Max's place I'd have urged you to hold the book for more material.[1] It had neither the surprise of I.O.T (nessessessarily) nor its unity. And it did not have <u>as large a proportion</u> of 1st flight stories as M.W.W. I think in a "general presentation" way this could have been attoned for by sheer bulk. Take that opinion for what it's worth.

On the other hand: you can thank God you missed this publishing season! I am 5th best seller in the country + havn't broken 12,000.

TO: Maxwell Perkins　　　　　*RTLS, 6 pp. Princeton University*

1307 Park Avenue,
Baltimore, Maryland,
May 15, 1934.

Dear Max:

In reference to our conversation: I have roughly about four plans for a book to be published this autumn.[2] Now I think that we must, to some extent, set aside the idea that a diffuse collection stands much chance of a decent sale, no matter what previous records Ernest and I have made. Of course I shall make every attempt to unify what I prepare by an inclusive and definitive title, which is even more important with short stories than with a novel, for it is necessary to bind them together and appeal to one mood in a buyer. Moreover, with so much material to choose from I think the collection should have some real inner unity, even in preference to having it include selected stories of many types. Roughly here are my ideas:

Plan 1. The idea of a big omnibus including both new stories and the pick of the other three collections. You must tell me what luck you've had with the omnibus volumes of Lardner, Galsworthy, etc.

---

[1] Fitzgerald is referring to Hemingway's story collection *Winner Take Nothing* (1933), which he compares to Hemingway's earlier collections *In Our Time* and *Men Without Women*.

[2] *Taps at Reveille* was published in March 1935.

Plan 2. The Basil Lee stories, about 60,000 words, and the Josephine stories, 37,500—with one or two stories added, the last of which will bring Basil and Josephine together—making a book of about 120,000 words under some simple title such as "Basil and Josephine." This would in some ways look like the best commercial bet because it might be taken like Tarkington's "Gentle Julia," "Penrod," etc. almost as a novel, and the most dangerous artistically for the same reason—for the people who buy my books might think that I was stringing them by selling them watered goods under a false name.

Plan 3. A collection of new short stories. Of these there are about forty, of which about twenty-nine are possible and say fifteen might be chosen, with the addition of one or two very serious non-commercial stories, which I have long planned but have yet to write, to heighten the tone of the volume. This might be unified under some title which would express that they are tales of the golden twenties, or even specifically, "More Tales of the Jazz Age." The table of contents would be something like this:

The dates are not the dates written but the period each story might represent.

1918 – The Last of the Belles or else
    The Love Boat
1919 – Presumption
1920 – The Adolescent Marriage or else
    One Trip Abroad
1921 – Outside the Cabinet Makers or else
    A Short Trip Home
1922 – Two Wrongs or else
    A Freeze-out
1923 – At Your Age or else
    In a Little Town
1924 – Crazy Sunday or else
    Jacob's Ladder
1925 – Rough Crossing or else
    Family in the Wind
1926 – The Bowl or else
    Interne
1927 – Swimmers or else
    A New Leaf
1928 – Hotel Child or else
1929 – Change of Class
    Majesty or else
1930 – The Bridal Party
    I Got Shoes
1931 – Babylon Revisited or else
    More Than Just a House
1932 – Between Three and Four

and three others, <u>Two for a Cent, The Pusher-in-the-Face</u> and <u>One of My Oldest Friends</u> which makes up the twenty-nine, excluding the Basil and Josephine stories, the unwritten ones and a couple of new ones I have just finished + can't judge.

I don't know how many of these you remember but of course I would ask you and perhaps a few other people to read over a selection and give some opinions, though among these twenty-nine there is scarcely one which <u>everybody</u> has enjoyed and scarcely one which <u>nobody</u> has enjoyed.

<u>Plan 4</u>. This is an idea founded on the success of such books as Alexander Woollcott's "While Rome Burns." As you know I have never published any personal stuff between covers because I have needed it all for my fiction; nevertheless, a good many of my articles and random pieces have attracted a really quite wide attention, and might again if we could get a tie-up of title and matter, which should contain wit and a soupçon of wisdom and not look like a collection of what the cat brought in, or be haunted by the bogey of all articles in a changing world, of being hilariously dated. It might be the best idea of all. Let me give you a rough idea as to what I have in that line:

There are my two articles for the <u>Post</u> which attracted such wide attention in their day that I have yet to hear the last of them, "How to Live on $36,000 a Year" and "How to Live on Practically Nothing a Year." There are "Echoes of the Jazz Age" from <u>Scribner's</u> and "My Lost City" which the <u>Cosmopolitan</u> has been holding up but wouldn't sell back to me to publish in the <u>American</u>. Other articles which have attracted attention are "Princeton" in <u>College Humor</u>, "One Hundred False Starts" in the <u>Post</u>, "The Cruise of the Rolling Junk," a long, supposedly humorous account of an automobile journey that appeared in <u>Motor</u>, an article called "Girls Believe in Girls" in <u>Liberty</u>, and two articles called "Making Monagomy Work" and "Are Irresponsible Rich?" published by the Metropolitan Syndicate in the early twenties, and an article called "On Being Twenty-five" in the <u>American</u>. And these also from the early twenties, "Wait till you have children of your own" (Woman's Home Companion), "Imagination" and "A Few Mothers" in the <u>Ladies Home Journal</u> and "The Little Brother of the Flapper" in <u>McCalls</u>.

This, or a good part of it, would have to comprise the backbone of the book and would be about 57,000 words. In addition there are some literary reviews, etc. of which nothing should be preserved except the elegy on Ring and an article in the <u>Bookman</u> on "How to Waste Material" welcoming Ernest's arrival. Beyond this there are a few hors d'oeuvres such as "A Short Autobiography" and "Salesmanship in the Champs Elysees" both in the <u>New Yorker</u> and a few other short sketches from <u>Vanity Fair</u>, <u>College Humor</u>, etc. and some light verse. There are also a couple of articles in which Zelda and I collaborated—idea, editing and padding being mine and most of the writing being hers—but I am not sure I would be justified in using it. Also I have some of my very first stories written at twelve and thirteen, some of which are funny enough to be reprinted.

Looking this over it doesn't seem very voluminous. I haven't seen Woollcott's book (by the way, did he get a copy of the novel?) and don't know how thick it is, but there seems to be some audience somewhere for collections (Dorothy Parker, etc.) as didn't exist in the 1920s.

The above all that I could count on getting ready for next fall. The "dark age" novel could not possibly be ready inside of a year, that is to say, for the autumn of 1935.

Would you please think over this line-up carefully and let me hear your advice, also I will ask Zelda's, which is often pretty good in what does not concern herself and which is always, strangely enough, conservative. A fifth idea of sandwiching some of my stuff in with hers, her old sketches of girls in College Humor, her short phantasies, etc. has occurred to me but I don't know that I think it's advisable.

I may come up but probably not. Thanks a lot for the money.

Ever yours,
Scott

TO: *Ernest Hemingway* TLS, 6 pp. *John F. Kennedy Library*

1307 Park Avenue,
Baltimore, Maryland,
June 1, 1934.

Dear Ernest:

Your letter crossed, or almost crossed, one of mine which I am glad now I didn't send, because the old charming frankness of your letter cleared up the foggy atmosphere through which I felt it was difficult for us to talk any more.

Because I'm going egoist on you in a moment, I want to say that just exactly what you suggested, that the edition of that Chinamen-running story in the Cosmopolitan[1] would have given Winner Take Nothing the weight that it needed was in my head too. Allow me one more criticism, that while I admire your use of purely abstract titles I do not think that one was a particularly fortunate choice.

Next to go to the mat with you on a couple of technical points. The reason I had written you a letter was that Dos[2] dropped in in passing through and said you had brought up about my book what we talked about once in a cafe on the Avenue de Neuilly about composite characters. Now, I don't entirely dissent from the theory but I don't believe you can try to prove your point on such a case as Bunny using his own father as the sire of John Dos Passos, or in the case of this book that covers ground that you personally

[1] "One Trip Across."
[2] Dos Passos.

paced off about the same time I was doing it. In either of those cases how could you trust your own detachment? If you had never met any of the originals then your opinion would be more convincing.

Following this out a little farther, when does the proper and logical combination of events, cause and effect, etc. end and the field of imagination begin? Again you may be entirely right because I suppose you were applying the idea particularly to the handling of the creative faculty in one's mind rather than to the effect upon the stranger reading it. Nevertheless, I am not sold on the subject, and especially to account for the big flaws of Tender on that ground doesn't convince me. Think of the case of the Renaissance artists, and of the Elizabethan dramatists, the first having to superimpose a medieval conception of science and archeology, etc. upon the bible story; and in the second, of Shakespeare's trying to interpret the results of his own observation of the life around him on the basis of Plutarch's Lives and Hollinshed's Chronicles. There you must admit that the feat of building a monument out of three kinds of marble was brought off. You can accuse me justly of not having the power to bring it off, but a theory that it can't be done is highly questionable. I make this point with such persistence because such a conception, if you stick to it, might limit your own choice of materials. The idea can be reduced simply to: you can't say accurately that composite characterization hurt my book, but that it only hurt it for you.

To take a case specifically, that of Gerald and Sara. I don't know how much you think you know about my relations with them over a long time, but from certain remarks that you let drop, such as one "Gerald threw you over," I guess that you didn't even know the beginning of our relations. In that case you hit on the exact opposite of the truth.

I think it is obvious that my respect for your artistic life is absolutely unqualified, that save for a few of the dead or dying old men you are the only man writing fiction in America that I look up to very much. There are pieces and paragraphs of your work that I read over and over—in fact, I stopped myself doing it for a year and a half because I was afraid that your particular rhythms were going to creep in on mine by process of infiltration. Perhaps you will recognize some of your remarks in Tender, but I did every damn thing I could to avoid that. (By the way, I didn't read the Wescott story of Villefranche sailors[1] till I'd done my own version. Think that was the wisest course, for me anyhow, and got a pleasant letter from him in regard to the matter.)

To go back to my theme song, the second technical point that might be of interest to you concerns direct steals from an idea of yours, an idea of Conrad's and a few lines out of David-into-Fox-Garnett.[2] The theory back of it I got from Conrad's preface to The Nigger, that the purpose of a work

[1]"The Sailor," Good-bye Wisconsin (1928).
[2]British novelist David Garnett, whose best-known work was Lady into Fox (1922).

of fiction is to appeal to the lingering after-effects in the reader's mind as differing from, say, the purpose of oratory or philosophy which leave respectively leave people in a fighting or thoughtful mood. The second contribution to the burglary was your trying to work out some such theory in your troubles with the very end of A Farewell to Arms. I remember that your first draft—or at least the first one I saw—gave a sort of old-fashioned Alger book summary of the future lives of the characters: "The priest became a priest under Fascism," etc., and you may remember my suggestion to take a burst of eloquence from anywhere in the book that you could find it and tag off with that; you were against this idea because you felt that the true line of a work of fiction was to take a reader up to a high emotional pitch but then let him down or ease him off. You gave no aesthetic reason for this—nevertheless, you convinced me. The third piece of burglary contributing to this symposing was my admiration of the dying fall in the aforesaid Garnett's book and I imitated it as accurately as it is humanly decent in my own ending of Tender, telling the reader in the last pages that, after all, this is just a casual event, and trying to let him come to bat for me rather than going out to shake his nerves, whoop him up, then leaving him rather in a condition of a frustrated woman in bed. (Did that ever happen to you in your days with MacCallagan or McKisco,[1] Sweetie?)

Thanks again for your letter which was damned nice, and my absolute best wishes to all of you (by the way, where did you ever get the idea that I didn't like Pauline, or that I didn't like her as much as I should? Of all that time of life the only temperamental coolness that I ever felt toward any of the people we ran around with was toward Ada MacLeish, and even in that case it was never any more than that. I have honestly never gone in for hating. My temporary bitternesses toward people have all been ended by what Freud called an inferiority complex and Christ called "Let him without sin—" I remember the day he said it. We were justlikethat then; we tossed up for who was going to go through with it—and he lost.

I am now asking only $5,000 for letters. Make out the check to Malcolm Republic, c/o The New Cowlick.[2]

Ever your friend,
Scott

P.S. Did you ever see my piece about Ring in the New Cowlick—I think you'd have liked it.
P.S.S. This letter and questions require no answers. You are "write" that I no longer listen, but my case histories seem to go in largely for the same magazines, and with simple people I get polite. But I listen to you and would like damn well to hear your voice again.

---

[1]Fitzgerald is punning on McAlmon and Callaghan; McKisco is a character in *Tender Is the Night*.
[2]Malcolm Cowley was the book-review editor of *The New Republic*.

TO: *Cecilia Delihant Taylor*   *ALS, 2 pp. Princeton University*
c. August 1934   *Baltimore, Maryland*

Dearest Ceci

Mrs. Owens says you asked her about the picture—I did get it. Didn't you get yours? Let me know.

Everything here goes rather badly. Zelda no better—your correspondent in rotten health + two movie ventures gone to pot—one for Gracie Allen + Geo. Burns that damn near went over + took 2 wks' work + they liked + wanted to buy—+ Paramount stepped on. It's like a tailor left with a made-to-order suit—no one to sell it to. So back to the Post.

(By the way I have a new series in the Red Bk.)

Hope to hell the whoopies are well, + all the kids.

Love Always

Scott

P.S. Appropos of our conversation it will interest you to know that I've given up politics. For two years I've gone half haywire trying to reconcile my double allegiance to the class I am part of, and the Great Change I believe in—considering at last such crazy solutions as the one I had in mind in Norfolk. I have become disgusted with the party leadership + have only health enough left for my literary work, so I'm on the sidelines. It had become a strain making speeches at "Leagues against Imperialistic War,"[1] + their treatment of the negro question finished me. This is confidential, of course

TO: *Rosalind Sayre Smith*[2]   *CC, 8 pp. Princeton University*

1307 Park Avenue,

Baltimore, Maryland,

August 8, 1934.

Dear Rosalind:

Your letter unsettled my intentions, or rather my idea of the means by which to put them into effect. I was trying to do so many things in New York that I must have been confused in leaving with the idea that you approved of the governess business. I had foreseen the difficulties attendant upon such a radical step as this but had determined to overcome them somehow. The problem of Scottie was so adequately solved during Zelda's sickness in Switzerland by the combination of the Cours Dieterlen and Mlle. Sereze[3] that I hoped to repeat it on a larger scale this winter.

---

[1] According to an undated newspaper clipping in the Fitzgerald Papers at Princeton University, Fitzgerald spoke at a Johns Hopkins University Liberal Club antiwar rally on the subject "How the War Came to Princeton."

[2] Zelda Fitzgerald's sister.

[3] The Cours Dieterlin was a Paris school that Scottie Fitzgerald attended; Mlle. Sereze was one of her governesses.

Let me list first what is impractical about the present regime and about alternatives:

1. There is no probability (let alone certainty) that Zelda and I will be able to make a place for her in the east beyond that of bearing a well known name.

2. I would not want to deliberately make of her a middle-westerner, or a southerner.

3. So the purely social education that she is now getting is essentially directionless.

4. All indications point to the fact that in the next generation there ain't going to be any young millionaires to snatch off.

5. Scottie has an essentially artistic temperament; though at present she is at the most conventional of all ages; I can't see her settling down at eighteen into a conventional marriage.

6. The actual objections to her going to day-school here are that either she would be living alone with me—with unending work ahead of me and not too much good time to give to a child—or else with Zelda and me in case it is recommended that Zelda spend the fall and winter in a new attempt to brave the world. In either case the atmosphere will not be conducive to the even tenor advisable for a child at that important age.

7. Such social alternatives as a straight country boarding school, or semi-boarding school in New York (such as you suggest) or else Spence or Brierly—all these lead into the same blank alley. Scottie has no talent such as a musical one that could be developed locally at the Peabody here or the Boston Conservatory.

To isolate Scottie with a governess wasn't my idea. The governess would serve as chaperone, teacher, and general guide, to a planned regime which I would constantly oversee; Scottie would go to a "social" dancing class in New York, and also to some sort of gymnastic association or club where she could have swimming and basket-ball. She would pass the week-ends either here or with friends in New York—I have friends there who have children exactly her age and if she managed to find so many friends in Paris among foreign people the question of her being lonely in New York is absolutely non-existent.

Now let me list what is in favor of my plan as conceived:

1. Scottie seems to have a varied talent which may express itself in any one of a number of ways. The theatre is the great universal of <u>all</u> talents. In the modern theatre every single bent is represented and by starting in early she would be learning the fundamentals not of one career but of half a dozen.

2. One of the reasons that the world shows little practical achievement by sons and daughters of talented people—with notable exceptions, of course—is that the son or daughter of a man who has sung an opera, written a book, or painted a picture, is inclined to think that that achievement will stand in place of any effort of his own. It is much easier for Scottie to play

being the daughter of a writer than to get down and write something herself, and I have noticed increasing tendencies toward that under present conditions. She used to write, with real pleasure and pride, little poems or stories for our Christmases and anniversaries. Now she's inclined to say, "What's the use? Daddy will do my writing for me"—Beyond that, Rosalind, she accepts the idea of most American children that Constance Bennett will do her acting for her and Bing Crosby her crooning. If I didn't see Scottie grimacing, posing, practising in front of mirrors and dressing herself up to the gills on all possible occasions, I would conclude that she had no desire for a public existence, but the contrary is true. She wants a lime-light and the question is whether it will be a healthy one of effort, or else one of these half-botched careers like Zelda's—of running yourself ragged for purely social ends and then trying to give the broken remnants to people and getting melancholia because people won't snap at it.

My point here is, that, as far as I can judge, Scottie is by nature and destiny a potential artist.

3. Broke off here for a moment to discuss the question with Mrs. Owens and was reminded of the fact that Scottie can always change from an artistic to a social career but the reverse is very difficult. (My God, Rosalind! if you would see the manuscripts that come my way from idle lawyers and bored housewives, who decided that they would take up literature in their "spare time"! It's as if I rushed into Johns Hopkins this afternoon, asking for a scalpel and an appendicitis patient, on the basis that I had an uncle who was a doctor, and people told me in my youth that I would make a good surgeon.) The pith of this is that only professionals function—capably within a profession—just as the time to begin ballet is about eleven years old, so the age to get used to the stage is at about thirteen or fourteen.

4. New York is the only possible center for Show Business (the boys and girls of Broadway persist in leaving the definite article out of that phrase.) The position of amateur teachers in society schools is less than nothing. To put Scottie with some defeated actress teaching for Miss This-Or-Thats would be to devitalize the whole idea. The moment Zelda entered Eglarova's ballet school she saw the difference between amateur and professional training. The fact that the shift from play to work led to disaster in Zelda's case has no bearing on this situation; if at any moment I find that Scottie has not the physical or nervous vitality to stand the rigors of real work, I shall snatch her out as quick as a blink.

But in the case of Miss Duff-Robinson[1] I think of how the Renaissance artists trained men in their studios and trained them well because the pupils did a great portion of their work for them—the system of apprenticing in the middle ages derives its value from that fact. Her whole livelyhood depends not on any fake "diplomas" but on the actual accomplishments of

---

[1] Drama teacher.

her pupils. As for the amateur teachers—well, I could teach Scottie as much about the stage here in our own parlor.

5. Having gone this far with the French I want to keep it up, and with a few more years of this part-time tutoring she will inevitably lose her bilinguality that I spent thousands of dollars sustaining by importing governess, etc. Even the private tutoring here has started to slip, insofar as her accent and vocabulary are concerned, though her constructions are still holding up well enough.

And now to discuss such factors as might militate against this plan:

1. Child snatched from healthy home influences, neighborhood activities, etc. thrown immature into the great world. But where are these healthy home influences, neighborhood activities, etc? Though I forbid a radio in the house she can go around the corner at any moment and sit in with other innocents on "Oh You Nasty Man" and other bucolic classics.

2. As to friends: with every move we make Scottie has kicked about leaving tried and true friends behind her. In the upshot, however, it is a struggle to get her to so much as answer the letters of her late pals. She makes friends so easily and has so much curiosity about people that she is not essentially a loyal child or one who is ever liable to be very lonely. She has been to two camps from here without any untoward sense of pining away. Only once in her life have I seen her actively miss anyone for more than a few days and that was in the case of Mlle. Sereze.

3. She will be less outdoors but she will have compensatory indoor exercise. One can't have everything.

———

I wish you would read this letter a couple of times, because I have written it partly to help me make up my own mind about Scottie's year, and I've spent a conscientious morning at it. If you see any loop-holes in my reasoning, please let me know. I am always ready to reconsider and there is a whole month before I will get to the actual engaging of a governess. (By the way she will have to be an actual native born Frenchwoman.) Miss Duff-Robinson, in tentatively agreeing to take her, made a point of her advantage in having that language. Zelda, in a clear-thinking moment was enthusiastic about the idea (though of course she would rather have had ballet for which Scottie is totally unfitted both physically and rhythmically.)

Best wishes to you both and hopes that your annoying uncertainty of domicile will be shortly liquidated.

TO: Christian Gauss   *Original unlocated. Text reprinted from Turnbull*

1307 Park Avenue
Baltimore, Maryland
September 7, 1934

Dear Dean Gauss:

This is a wild idea of mine, conditioned by the fact that my physician thinks I am in a solitary rut and that I ought to have outside interests. Well, outside interests generally mean for me women, liquor or some form of exhibitionism. The third seems to be most practical at the present moment, wherefore I would like to give a series of lectures at Princeton, say eight, on the actual business of creating fiction. There would be no charge and I would consider it a favor if I were allowed to do this in a University lecture hall. (Incidentally, to safeguard you from my elaborate reputation, I would pledge my word to do no drinking in Princeton save what might be served at your table if you should provide me with luncheon before one of these attempts.)

The lectures I've not planned but they would be, in general, the history of say:

1. What Constitutes the Creative Temperament.
2. What Creative Material Is.
3. Its Organization.

And so forth and so on.

This would be absolutely first-hand stuff and there might be a barrier to crash in regard to the English Department, and if you don't think this is the time to do it don't hesitate to let me know frankly. So many bogus characters have shown up in Princeton trying to preach what they have never been able to practice, that I think even if I reach only half a dozen incipient talents the thing might be worthwhile from the scholastic point of view, and will be selfishly worthwhile to me—I would like to time these lectures so that they would come on the afternoon or eve of athletic events that I would like to see.

You will know best how to sound out the powers-that-be in the English Department. I have a hunch that Gerould rather likes me and I like Root[1] whether he likes me or not. . . .

This is an arrow in the dark. I feel I never knew so much about my stuff as I now know, about the technique concerned, and I can't think of anywhere I would like to disseminate this egotistic feeling more than at Princeton.

This all might come to something, you know!

Hope you had a fine summer abroad. With my respects to Mrs. Gauss.

Ever yours,
F. Scott Fitzg

P.S. Naturally, after my wretched performance at the Cottage Club[2] you might be cynical about my ability to handle an audience, but my suggestion is that the first lecture should be announced as a single, and if there is further demand we could go from thence to thither.

[1]Robert K. Root, Princeton English professor.
[2]Fitzgerald had previously gotten drunk when invited to speak at the Cottage Club.

TO: *Christian Gauss*   *Original unlocated. Text reprinted from Turnbull*

1307 Park Avenue
Baltimore, Maryland
September 26, 1934

Dear Dean Gauss:

I know about "The Club" and they asked me last year to come and lecture. What I have against that is that it is sponsored by undergraduates which detracts from speaking under the authoritative aegis of the University, and second, because my plan was a series of lectures and not one that I could develop in a single evening. Also they were meant to be pretty serious stuff, that is, written out rather than spoken from notes, straight lectures rather than preceptorials. However, if the powers-that-be feel it inadvisable I can only yield the point and postpone the idea until a more favorable year.[1]

Glad you enjoyed your rest abroad and escaped Miriam Hopkins' jumping out of the second-story window onto your shoulders. But I suppose you've been kidded to death about that already and I know you took it with your usual sense of humor.

Best wishes always,
F. Scott Fitzgerald

TO: *Marie Hersey Hamm*   *TLS, 3 pp. Princeton University*

1307 Park Avenue,
Baltimore, Maryland,
October 4, 1934.

Dear Marie:

It seems late to answer your letter as at the time it was written you were in heavy marital difficulties about your two children and were still sailing under the name of Carroll. Since then I hear sensational news _about_ you, but not _from_ you, and worry sometimes if the kidnappers will get you, as you seem to move largely in an atmosphere of kidnappers, both of children and adults. I suppose that you are settled down in St. Paul for good. For a long time I have wanted to come back to spend a few weeks but life seems to get crowded in the late thirties and I don't know when the chance will come.

Scottie has become acclimated to Baltimore but I'd like to have her pull a sort of Gertrude Harris a little later to the extent of having a debut out there. So a few years may see us settled there for at least a summer. This in spite of the fact that, having rambled so much, I no longer regard St. Paul as my home any more than the Eastern seaboard or the Riviera. This is said

---

[1]Fitzgerald was not invited to give lectures.

with no disloyalty but simply because after all my father was an Easterner and I went East to college and I never did quite adjust myself to those damn Minnesota winters. It was always freezing my cheeks, being a rotten skater etc.—though many events there will always fill me with a tremendous nostalgia. Anyhow all recent reports paint it as a city of gloom and certainly the ones from the remnants of the McQuillan family are anything but cheerful. Baltimore is very nice, and with plenty of cousins and Princetonians if I were in a social mood, and I can look out the window and see a statue of the great, great uncle,[1] and all three of us like it here. There, have I rambled on long enough?

I send you this letter as a desperate bid for some news of St. Paul and the following people: the Kalmans, Flandraus, Jacksons, Clarks and Kid Ordway. I suppose Dud and Grace are now completely expatriated to Chicago and I know that Joe and Lou will most likely never return. Who runs things now? So many of us have emigrated, Katharine Tighe, etc. and so many new names keep popping up whenever I get hold of a St. Paul paper that I cling in spirit to the few friends I still have there.

With affection from Zelda and love always from me,

Scott

P.S. Don't omit to add news mostly about yourself.

TO: *Maxwell Perkins*   *TLS, 5 pp. Princeton University*

1307 Park Avenue,
Baltimore, Mayland,
November 8, 1934.

Dear Max:

In further reference to my telegram of Tuesday night: first, I am sending you the third story in its proper place ready to go into the book. The thing that worried me when I did it was whether the proofreader is going to be able to release a lot of type, because due to the fact that the end of one and the beginning of another were run on one galley, he will have to scrap half the type in the galley and yet retain the other half—this because the stories were not set up in proper order. I know this is a terrible and costly mess and I take full responsibility, nevertheless, I did think the stories would be set up separately and getting at them is as if the chapters of a book were set up any-which-way like I, VII, II, V, III, VI, and it all has to be straightened out each time. As you know that is fatiguing work and can best be done when one is fresh, and is hard to do at night.

My big mistake was in thinking I could possibly deliver this collection for this fall. I should have known perfectly well that, in debt as I was to the

[1] Francis Scott Key.

tune of about $12,000 on finishing "Tender," I should have to devote the summer and most of the fall to getting out of it. My plan was to do my regular work in the daytime and do one story every night, but as it works out, after a good day's work I am so exhausted that I drag out the work on a story to two hours when it should be done in one and go to bed so tired and wrought up, toss around sleepless, and am good for nothing next morning except dictating letters, signing checks, tending to business matters ect; but to work up a creative mood there is nothing doing until about four o'clock in the afternoon. Part of this is because of ill health. It would not have seemed so difficult for me ten years, or even five years ago, but now just one more straw would break the camel's back.

I have about half a dozen of these done but I am determined this time to send them in only in the proper order and not add further confusion either in my own mind or that of the printer's. The trouble began when I sent you two stories to be set up which were nowhere near each other in the book. If I told a story about a boy of sixteen years old and sixty pages on the reader came upon a story of the same boy at thirteen it would make no sense to him and look like careless presentation, and which, as you know, I dislike nothing more.

As you may have seen I took out "A New Leaf" and put in "Her Last Case." You didn't tell me whether or not you read it or liked it.

I know you have the sense that I have loafed lately but that is absolutely not so. I have drunk too much and that is certainly slowing me up. On the other hand, without drink I do not know whether I could have survived this time. In actual work since I finished the last proof of the novel in the middle of March, eight months ago, I have written and sold three stories for the Post, written another which was refused, written two and a half stories for the Redbook, rewritten three articles of Zelda's for Esquire and one original for them to get emergency money, collaborated on a 10,000 word treatment of "Tender Is the Night," which was no go, written an 8,000 word story for Gracie Allen, which was also no go, and made about five false starts on stories which went from 1,000 to 5,000 words, and a preface to the Modern Library edition of "The Great Gatsby," which equalizes very well what I have done in other years. I am good for just about one good story a month or two articles. I took no vacation this summer except three or four one-night trips to Virginia and two business trips to New York, each of which lasted about four or five days. Of course this is no excuse for not making more money, because in harder times you've got to work harder, but as it happens I am in a condition at the moment where to work extra hard means inevitably that I am laid up for a compensatory time either here or in the hospital. All I can say is that I will try to do two or three of these all at once after finishing each piece of work, and as I am now working at the rate of a story each ten days for the Redbook series I should finish up the ten I have left to do in about one hundred days and deliver the last of them in mid-February. Perhaps if things break better it may be a month sooner.

Thanks immensely for the Henry James which I thought was wonderful and which is difficult reading as it must have been to write and for "At Sea."[1]

The London press on my book has been spotty but the <u>London Times</u> gave it a good review as did G. B. Stern in <u>The Daily Telegraph</u> and so did <u>The Manchester Guardian</u> and <u>The Spectator</u> and those I guess are the four most important ones in England and I got a column in each of them. A letter says that it hasn't reached a thousand copies yet.

I hope you'll be down here soon. It was rather melancholy to think of "Welbourne"[2] being closed for the winter, but the last time I saw Elizabeth she seemed quite reconciled at visiting here and there, though such a prospect would drive me nuts. Hope you have sent off the carbon of the Table of Contents.

Best ever,
Scott

TO: Harold Ober   *CC—incomplete letter. Princeton University*

1307 Park Avenue,
Baltimore, Maryland,
December 8, 1934.

Dear Harold:

After rereading your letter there were some things I felt hadn't been sufficiently answered. The first is that I have a deep suspicion that you and Max got together at some point and decided I needed disciplining. Now I know of my fondness for you both and assume that it is reciprocated and I know also that when one man is in debt to another he is rather helpless in such matters. Nevertheless, the assumption that all my troubles are due to drink is a little too easy. Gliding over my domestic difficulties and my self indulgence on that score and not deciding which one has caused the trouble—whether the hen preceeded the egg or the egg preceeded the hen—I want to get down to a few facts: a compact "apologia pro sua vita" after all the horrors in Montgomery and the winter of '30 and '31, the return of Zelda's trouble, attacked by the family, etc (and you will find that this coincides almost exactly with my remissness in getting out MSS on specification. It became apparent to me that my literary reputation, except with the <u>Post</u> readers, was at its very lowest ebb. I was completely forgotten and this fact was rubbed in by Zelda's inadvertently written book. From that

---

[1] *The Art of the Novel*, by Henry James, and *At Sea*, by Arthur Calder-Marshall, were both published by Scribners in 1934.

[2] Perkins's cousin Elizabeth Lemmon lived at "Welbourne" in northern Virginia.

time on until early this spring my chief absorption was to get my book published at any cost to myself and still manage to keep the ball rolling. With yours and Max's help and some assistance from mother the thing was accomplished but at the end it left me in the black hole of Calcutta, mentally exhausted, physically exhausted, emotionally exhausted, and perhaps, morally exhausted. There seemed no time or space for recuperation. My expedition to Bermuda was a wash-out because of the pleurisy; Zelda collapsed again shortly after the holidays. The necessary "filling up" that a writer should be able to do after great struggles was impossible. No sooner did I finish the last galley on the last version of the last proof of the book proof of "Tender is the Night" than it was necessary to sit down and write a <u>Post</u> story.

Of course any <u>apologia</u> is necessarily a whine to some extent, a man digs his own grave and should, presumably, lie on it, and I know that the fault for this goes back to those years, which were really years of self-in-

TO: *Gertrude Stein*   *TLS, 1 p. Yale University*

1307 Park Avenue,
Baltimore, Maryland,
December 29, 1934.

Dearest Gertrude Stein:

It was a disappointment to think that you would not be here for another meeting. I was somewhat stupid-got with the Christmas spirit, but I enjoyed the one idea that you <u>did</u> develop and, like everything else you say, it will sing in my ears long after everything else about that afternoon is dust and ashes. You were the same fine fire to everyone who sat upon your hearth—for it was your hearth, because you carry home with you wherever you are—a home before which we have all always warmed ourselves.

It meant so much to Zelda, giving her a tangible sense of her own existence, for you to have liked two of her pictures enough to want to own them. For the other people there, the impression was perhaps more vague, but everyone felt their Christmas eve was well spent in the company of your handsome face and wise mind—and sentences "that never leak."[1]

All affection to you and Alice,

F. Scott Fitzgerald

TO: *John Peale Bishop*   *RTLS, 6 pp. Princeton University*

[1] Stein had remarked that sentences must not have bad plumbing and must not leak.

1307 Park Avenue

Baltimore, Maryland,

January 30, 1935

Dear John:

Your book[1] had an extraordinary effect on me. Let me be frank to say that I took it up with some misgivings due to the fact that I felt that you had decided to deal with somewhat drab material, and that to make it colorful you might be inclined to lean over into melodrama—but more of that later. From the first I got completely under the spell of the exquisite prose, the descriptions of the Shenandoah country and, as one by one, the characters began to unfold, the whole scene became tense and exciting. I think the way that you built up the character of Marston on the foundation of old Mason was fine—contrary to Ernest's dictum as to synthetic characters not being plausible.

Charlie emerges as an almost heroic figure early in the book, your young narrator is sympathetic but suffers insomuch as he partakes of the vague artist-as-a-young-man quality that distinguishes our time from the Werther-Byron-Stendahl character of a hundred years ago.

Virginia is the least achieved character to me. There are the fine passages describing her bedroom hysteria after the event, but, because it was never clear in your own mind exactly how she was, the courtroom scene in which she appeared did not hang fire with the intensity of similar scenes in High Wind in Jamaica or An American Tragedy or Sanctuary.

Your minor characters were fine, the comic aunt, the nigger pansy, the decayed Job's counsellor (female), the ghost of the poetic judge—all in all, the book is packed full of beauty and wisdom and richness of perception. I read through the first half in one night and was so excited that I had to call up somebody (it turned out to be Elizabeth Lemmon) to tell them how much I liked it, how good it was, and how delighted I was that it was good!

Yet when I finished the book there was a certain sense of unfulfillment and now I am going to permit myself to play papa for a moment:

When your heart was in poetry your inclination was to regard prose fiction as merely a stop-gap, a necessary nuisance. Time showed you the error of that early evaluation and it cost you a pretty penny in years. There are things in this book which are still typical of one who cannot light his way around and who has got to, for these are the years for you during which the best amunition has to be fired off. Let me list, not too categorically, what I consider the faults of execution in the opus:

First, conscientiously you must try to cut all traces of other people out of yourself. If you were twenty-one it wouldn't matter; it was all right for Tom Wolfe in Look Homeward Angel to make one chapter practically a parody of a chapter in Ulysses. It was forgivable for me to have done an equivalent thing half a dozen times in This Side of Paradise, but for anybody

[1]Bishop's novel *Act of Darkness* (Scribners, 1935).

over forty to do it is simply not in the picture of one who has to make himself a personality. Vide: Page 148.

Frank Norris, speaking of Kipling, said "the little colonial, to whose pipe we must all dance"—but by that general admission of the tremendous power of certain stylists he announced that he, for one, would fight shy of any effect that he might gain by using their rhythms to cradle his ideas or to fill gaps with reminiscent echolalia. Several times I saw patterns in this book which derived background and drama from Faulkner, or cadence from Hemingway and each time you might have produced something much stronger by having more of a conscience, by fighting against that tendency, cutting out the passage no matter how satisfactory it may have been in itself, and building up the structure with something that is yourself. In any case, that has been my experience, and I pass it on to you for what it's worth.

Let's call that the first point— there are only two. The second is a matter of purely structure. You once wrote me about Conrad's ability to build his characters into such a reality, commonplace reality, that any melodrama that afterwards occurred would be palatable. The first half of your book is so heavy with stimuli and promises, that the later catastrophe of the rape is minimized—both in itself and in its consequences. Charlie's whole wild day should have been telescoped and much cut, insofar as the intervening episodes are concerned, such as the bathers hearing the shots. The title should not have given away so much of the plot. You had put out so many leads by that time that the reader was practically expecting the world war and the actual fact that Charlie violated a spinster is anticlimatical as is her ensuing denunciation of him. When you plant a scene in a book the importance of the scene cannot be taken as a measure of the space it should occupy, for it is entirely a special + particular artistic problem. If Dreiser, in The American Tragedy; plans to linger over the drowning in upper New York well and good, but I could tell you plenty books in which the main episode, around which swings the entire drama, is over and accomplished in four or five sentences.

There is, after all, a third point. I think the book is a little too rough. The insistence on sex-in-the-raw occupies more space than the phenomenun usually does in life. Insofar as this is the story of a boy's awakening to the world of passion, it is justified, but when you launch yourself into an account of the brutal fate that haunts us the balance is not what it should be. Much of the testimony in the trial seemed to be arbitrarily introduced from Krafft Ebing.[1]

Now as a peroration let me congratulate you again. It is beautifully made, beautifully written and one of your three characters emerges as a creation. I liked Charlie, and would like to have met him, and he will stay with me

---

[1] Richard Krafft-Ebing, German psychiatrist who was an authority on sexual behavior.

when most of the fictional history of many years is forgotten. I congratulate you will all my heart.

With best to you both,

Scott

P.S. Aside from the fun of the above strictures it gives me great pleasure to tell you that the word "demean" does not mean "debase." The phrase "to demean" means only "to conduct one's self" and does not imply that the conduct is either good or bad. It is a common error. Other quibbles: On the jacket the Shenandoah Valley is placed in tidewater Virginia and the story in the 90s. When did people roll around so casually in cars in the late 90s? It seems to me that you would be justified in asking Max to correct these errors in further printings.

TO: Maxwell Perkins   *TLS, 4 pp. Princeton University*

1307 Park Avenue,
Baltimore, Maryland,
March 11, 1935.

Dear Max:

The second annoyance to you in two days—pretty soon I'm going to be your most popular author. (By the way we had sort of a Scribner congerie here last night. Jim Boyd[1] and Elizabeth[2] came to supper and George Calverton[3] dropped in afterwards. Your name came up frequently and you would have probably wriggled more than at Wolfe's dedication.[4] To prolong this parenthesis unduly I am sorry I mentioned Tom's book. I hope to God I won't be set up as the opposition for there are fine things in it, and I loved reading it, and I am delighted that it's a wow, and it may be a bridge for something finer. I simply feel a certain disappointment which I would, on no account, want Tom to know about, for, responding as he does to criticism, I know it would make us life long enemies and we might do untold needless damage to each other, so please be careful how you quote me. This is in view of Calverton's saying he heard from you that I didn't like it. It has become increasingly plain to me that the very excellent organization of a long book or the finest perceptions and judgment in time of revision do not go well with liquor. A short story can be written on a bottle, but for a novel you need the mental speed that enables you to keep the whole pattern in your head and ruthlessly sacrifice the sideshows as Ernest

[1] James Boyd, historical novelist published by Scribners.
[2] Elizabeth Lemmon.
[3] V. F. Calverton, born George Goetz, wrote and edited books on political and sociological subjects.
[4] Wolfe's eloquently grateful dedication of *Of Time and the River* (Scribners, 1935) to Maxwell Perkins had attracted considerable notice.

did in "A Farewell to Arms." If a mind is slowed up ever so little it lives in the individual part of a book rather than in a book as a whole; memory is dulled. I would give anything if I hadn't had to write Part III of "Tender is the Night" entirely on stimulant. If I had one more crack at it cold sober I believe it might have made a great difference. Even Ernest commented on sections that were needlessly included and as an artist he is as near as I know for a final reference. Of course, having struggled with Tom Wolfe as you did this is old hat to you. I will conclude this enormous parenthesis with the news that Elizabeth has gone to Middleburg to help Mrs. White open up her newly acquired house.)

This letter is a case of the tail (the parenthesis) wagging the dog. Here is the dog. A man named John S. Martens writes me wanting to translate "Tender is the Night" or "This Side of Paradise" or "The Great Gatsby" into Norwegian. He has written Scribner's and met the same blank wall of silence that has greeted me about all publishing of my books in other countries. I am quite willing to handle continental rights directly but I cannot do it when I do not know even the name of the publisher of my books, having never had copies of them or any information on that subject. Isn't there somebody in your office who is especially delegated to seeing to such things? It is really important to me and if I should write a book that had an international appeal it would be of great advantage to have a foothold with translators and publishers in those countries. All I want from you is the status of "The Great Gatsby" in Scandanavia, Germany, etc. and a word as to whether I shall go ahead and make arrangements myself for the future in that regard.

I'd be glad to get a dozen or so copies of "Taps at Reveille" as soon as available.

Ever yours,
Scott

P.S. I haven't had a drink for almost six weeks and haven't had the faintest temptation as yet. Feel fine in spite of the fact that business affairs and Zelda's health have never been worse.

TO: Maxwell Perkins   *TLS, 3 pp. Princeton University*

1307 Park Avenue,
Baltimore, Maryland,
April 15, 1935.

Dear Max:

You don't say anything about "Taps" so I gather it hasn't caught on at all. I hope at least it will pay for itself and its corrections. There was a swell review in <u>The Nation</u>[1]; did you see it?

[1] By William Troy (April 17, 1935).

I went away for another week but history didn't repeat itself and the trip was rather a waste. Thanks for the message from Ernest. I'd like to see him too and I always think of my friendship with him as being one of the high spots of life. But I still believe that such things have a mortality, perhaps in reaction to their very excessive life, and that we will never again see very much of each other. I appreciate what he said about "Tender is the Night." Things happen all the time which make me think that it is not destined to die quite as easily as the boys-in-a-hurry prophesied. However, I made many mistakes about it from its delay onward, the biggest of which was to refuse the Literary Guild subsidy.

Haven't seen Beth[1] since I got back and am calling her up today to see if she's here. I am waiting eagerly for a first installment of Ernest's book.[2] When are you coming south? Zelda, after a terrible crisis, is somewhat better. I am, of course, on the wagon as always, but life moves at an uninspiring gait and there is less progress than I could wish on the Mediaeval series[3]—all in all an annoying situation as these should be my most productive years. I've simply got to arrange something for this summer that will bring me to life again, but what it should be is by no means apparent.

About 1929 I wrote a story called "Outside the Cabinet Maker's" which ran in the <u>Century Magazine</u>. I either lost it here or else sent it to you with the first batch of selected stories for "Taps" and it was not returned. Will you (a) see if you've got it? or (b) tell me what and where the <u>Century</u> company is now and whom I should address to get a copy of the magazine?

I've had a swell portrait painted at practically no charge and next time I come to New York I am going to spend a morning tearing out of your files all those preposterous masks with which you have been libeling me for the last decade.

Just found another whole paragraph in "Taps," top of page 384, which appears in "Tender is the Night." I'd carefully elided it and written the paragraph beneath it to replace it, but the proof readers slipped and put them both in.

Ever yours,
Scott

---

[1] Elizabeth Lemmon.

[2] *Green Hills of Africa* was serialized in *Scribner's Magazine* (May–November 1935).

[3] Fitzgerald was working on a cycle of stories set in ninth-century France. He intended to combine them into a novel, but only three of the "Philippe, Count of Darkness" stories were published in his lifetime.

TO: *Maxwell Perkins*

TLS, 4 pp.—with holograph postscript. Princeton University

1307 Park Avenue,
Baltimore, Maryland,
April 17, 1935.

Dear Max:

Reading Tom Wolfe's story[1] in the current <u>Modern Monthly</u> makes me wish he was the sort of person you could talk to about his stuff. It has all his faults and virtues. It seems to me that with any sense of humor he could see the Dreiserian absurdities of how the circus people "ate the cod, bass, mackerel, halibut, clams and oysters of the New England coast, the terrapin of Maryland, the fat beeves, porks and cereals of the middle west" etc. etc. down to "the pink meated lobsters that grope their way along the sea-floors of America." And then (after one of his fine paragraphs which sounds a note to be expanded later) he remarks that they leave nothing behind except "the droppings of the camel and the elephant in Illinois." A few pages further on his redundance ruined some paragraphs (see the last complete paragraph on page 103) that might have been gorgeous. I sympathize with his use of repetition, of Joyce-like words, endless metaphor, but I wish he could have seen the disgust in Edmund Wilson's face when I once tried to interpolate part of a rhymed sonnet in the middle of a novel, disguised as prose. How he can put side by side such a mess as "With chitterling tricker fast-fluttering skirrs of sound the palmy honied birderies came" and such fine phrases as "tongue-trilling chirrs, plum-bellied smoothness, sweet lucidity" I don't know. He who has such infinite power of suggestion and delicacy has absolutely no right to glut people on whole meals of caviar. I hope to Christ he isn't taking all these emasculated paeans to his vitality very seriously. I'd hate to see such an exquisite talent turn into one of those muscle-bound and useless giants seen in a circus. Athletes have got to learn their games; they shouldn't just be content to tense their muscles, and if they do they suddenly find when called upon to bring off a necessary effect they are simply liable to hurl the shot into the crowd and not break any records at all. The metaphor is mixed but I think you will understand what I mean, and that he would too—save for his tendency to almost feminine horror if he thinks anyone is going to lay hands on his precious talent. I think his lack of humility is his most difficult characteristic, a lack oddly enough which I associate only with second or third rate writers. He was badly taught by bad teachers and now he hates learning.

There is another side of him that I find myself doubting, but this is something that no one could ever teach or tell him. His lack of feeling other people's passions, the lyrical value of Eugene Gant's love affair with the

[1] "Circus at Dawn."

universe—is that going to last through a whole saga? God, I wish he could discipline himself and really plan a novel.

I wrote you the other day and the only other point of this letter is that I've now made a careful plan of the Mediaeval novel as a whole (tentatively called "Philippe, Count of Darkness" confidential) including the planning of the parts which I can sell and the parts which I can't. I think you could publish it either late in the spring of '36 or early in the fall of the same year. This depends entirely on how the money question goes this year. It will run to about 90,000 words and will be a novel in every sense with the episodes unrecognizable as such. That is my only plan. I wish I had these great masses of manuscripts stored away like Wolfe and Hemingway but this goose is beginning to be pretty thoroughly plucked I am afraid.

A young man has dramatized "Tender is the Night" and I am hoping something may come of it.[1] I may be in New York for a day and a night within the next fortnight.

Ever yours,
Scott

Later—Went to N.Y. as you know, but one day only. Didn't think I would like Cape that day.[2] Sorry you + Nora Flynn[3] didn't meet. No news here— I think Beth is leaving soon.

TO: *John Peale Bishop*   *ALS 6 pp. Princeton University*
May 1935   *Asheville, North Carolina*

Dear John:

Here's a letter of uncalled for advice. I think though it's good. All right— into the lions mouth.

Act of Darkness must be written off. It was a good novel—it had high points (I'm coming back to that), it showed that your long phase of being self-conscious in prose is over. You've got ten good years—two or three fine novels left. Now, here's my inventory.

From the wildest fantasy (which you did not + could not handle through lack of readiness + incisiveness of wit + profuseness of it and through other reasons like Hergeshiemeric tendency to take it easy doing still-lifes) you went (+ I was all for it) to the most complete realism, taking in passing the civil war. The part taken in passing came closest to being your natural field. You jumped over it too quickly—I don't mean the war in particular— I mean the blend. Because you're two people—you are not yet your work as in a sense I am mine

---

[1] Baltimore writer Robert Spofford seems not to have completed his play.

[2] Perkins had invited Fitzgerald to meet British publisher Jonathan Cape.

[3] Nora Langhorne Flynn, who with her husband, former Yale football star Lefty Flynn, entertained Fitzgerald and Scottie in Tryon, North Carolina, during February of 1935.

You are

(a.) a person of conventional background + conduct with tendency almost to drabness, non-resistance, uxoriousness, bourgeoise-respectable ect ect ect ect.

(b.) a poet with sense of wonder and color of life expressed in men, women + words; + grand gestures, grand faits accomplis, parades.

(1) Setting. I should use a sensational set, probably costume set using some such character as the Lost Dauphin—I mean it—not a fulfilled rennaissanse character or you'll just make a picture book; Something enormous, gross obvious, untouched by fine hands. Some great stone the schulptors have rejected. Your background had better shimmer, not be static or peaceful

(2) Plot Advice on this is no good. You handle it well but I advise a change of pace—I find so many good enough books are in the same key i.e. appointment in Sammara. Life is not so smooth that it can't go over suddenly into melodrama. That's the other face of much worry about inevitability Everything's too beautifully caused—one can guess ahead. Even the movies know this + condemn a story as "too straight." My own best solution to date is the to-and-fro, keep facts back mystery stuff, but its difficult. Of course its the Dickins Dostoieffski thing. Act of Darkness was much too straight, + tempo too even. Only a very short piece wants complete tempo, one breath, Ethan Fromme. It's short story technique. Even Pride + Predjudice walks + runs like life

(3) Try and find more "bright" characters, if the women are plain make them millionairesses or nymphomaniacs, if they're scrub women give them hot sex attraction + charm. This is such a good trick I don't see why its not more used—I always use it just as I like to balance a beautiful word with a barbed one.

There is tremendous comedy inherent in your relations with Hurlock + Feustman. You can do more with minor characters—your perverted negroes ect are good enough but you're rich with stuff. You dredge yourself with difficulty.

I'd like to see some gayiety in your next book to help sell it. Can't you find some somewhere?

Anyhow all this care for shimmering set, active plot, bright characters, change of pace + gayiety should all show in the plan. Leave out any two, + your novel is weaker, any three or four + you're running a department store with only half the countirs open.

All this is presumption. Max Perkins told me the book hadn't gone + while I know it had a good press + the season was bad still I do worry about you + would hate to see you either discouraged or apathetic about your future as a novelist

Best to Yr. Huge Clan
Scott

282

Adress as on envelope
  till about June 25th.

P.S. Havn't had a drink this year—not even wine or beer—are you surprised?

TO: *Harold Ober*   *ALS, 5 pp. Lilly Library*
Received July 2, 1935

                        Adress Hotel Stafford <u>not</u> c/o Mrs Owens.[1]

Dear Harold:
  I'm still here—at the last moment it appears that there is a suggestion
about Zelda (three days ago was a most discouraged time) and it means
finding a very special nurse. So I wont leave till tomorrow. On an impulse
I'm sending you a letter from Zelda that came to day—a letter from which
you can guage the awful strangling heart-rending quality of this tragedy
that has gone on now more than six years, with two brief intervals of hope.
I know you'll understand the intrusion of sending it to you—please mail it
back to me, with things so black I hang on to every scrap that is like things
used to be.

                        ————————

  And with it's precise irony life continues—I went to N. Y. after all
Saturday afternoon to meet a girl—stayed 20 hrs. + got back here Sunday
night to put Scotty on the train to camp.
  Now as to business—or rather finances. I owe you still somewhere around
$6500. (?) + should be paying you back at the rate of $1500 per story. But
this has been a slow 6 wks—1st illness, then unsuccessful attempt at revise
of mediaval IV, then a false start, then <u>What You Don't Know</u>.[2] Considering
that story alone for a minute + supposing it sold for $3000. You've given
me

         $500   advance
         $500   "
  + $300   Commission
         ————
         1300
         1700
         ————
         3000

----

[1]Isabel Owens.
[2]Probably published as "Fate in Her Hands," *American Magazine* (April 1936).

Normally that would leave me $1700. And I need $1000 for bills due (that doesn't solve them but is "on account") + I'll need $700 on the 12th for Life Insurance. Of course I hope to have a new story in your hands by the 15th but I hope you can see your way clear to letting me have the whole sum this time—with the understanding that on the next story I will surely be able to reimburse you $1500. (Wont need the the 700 till the 12th but need the 1000 this week, by Friday, say, if the Post accepts + will put a check through.)

All this raises the ugly head of Mediaval IV. Granted that Post pays 3000.00 + you can complete paying me the whole sum this time—that is $1700. more—

Then shall I do Red Book revise IV first! (it's, alas, paid for!) + make Balmer[1] believe in me again? (He's already published III + it reads well), or shall I do a Post story + begin to square things with you? Only you can decide this. I told you: Red Bk IV can't be revised but must be rewritten, + that and a new Post story will take to the end of July. I can survive till then but will it be too much of a drain on you to wait till then for further payments.

There is no use of me trying to rush things. Even in years like '24, '28, '29, '30 all devoted to short stories I could not turn out more than 8–9 top price stories a year. It simply is impossible—all my stories are concieved like novels, require a special emotion, a special experience—so that my readers, if such there be, know that each time it'll be something new, not in form but in substance (it'd be far better for me if I could do pattern stories but the pencil just goes dead on me. I wish I could think of a line of stories like the Josephine or Basil ones which could go faster + pay $3000. But no luck yet. If I ever get out of debt I want to try a second play. It's just possible I could knock them cold if I let go the vulgar side of my talent.)

So that covers everything. Will you let me know by straight wire as soon as you've read this if I can count on these advances ($1000 this wk—$700 on the 12th) if the Post buys.

Then I can sign the checks + get off south with a clear conscience.

I want to see you + have a long talk with you under better conditions than we've found of late. You havn't seen me since I've been on my no-liquor regime.

Yrs Ever
Scott Fitzg—

Hotel Stafford
Baltimore
Mail Zelda's letter to Asheville. Thanks for yr. nice wire about story. It set me up.

[1] Edwin Balmer of *Red Book*.

FROM: *Zelda Fitzgerald*
June 1935

ALS, 4 pp. Princeton University
Sheppard and Enoch Pratt Hospital
Towson, Maryland

Dearest and always
Dearest Scott:

I am sorry too that there should be nothing to greet you but an empty shell. The thought of the effort you have made over me, the suffering this <u>nothing</u> has cost would be unendurable to any save a completely vacuous mechanism. Had I any feelings they would all be bent in gratitude to you and in sorrow that of all my life there should not even be the smallest relic of the love and beauty that we started with to offer you at the end.

You have been so good to me—and all I can say is that there was always that deeper current running through my heart: my life—you.

You remember the roses in Kinneys yard—you were so gracious and I thought "he is the sweetest person in the world" and you said "darling." You still are. The wall was damp and mossy when we crossed the street and said we loved the south. I thought of the south and a happy past I'd never had and I thought I was part of the south. You said you loved this lovely land. The wistaria along the fence was green and the shade was cool and life was old.

—I wish I had thought something else—but it was a confederate, a romantic and nostalgic thought. My hair was damp when I took off my hat and I was safe and home and you were glad that I felt that way and you were reverent. We were gold and happy all the way home.

Now that there isn't any more happiness and home is gone and there isn't even any past and no emotions but those that were yours where there could be any comfort—it is a shame that we should have met in harshness and coldness where there was once so much tenderness and so many dreams. Your song.

I wish you had a little house with hollyhocks and a sycamore tree and the afternoon sun imbedding itself in a silver tea-pot. Scottie would be running about somewhere in white, in Renoir, and you will be writing books in dozens of volumes. And there will be honey still for tea, though the house should not be in Granchester—[1]

I want you to be happy—if there were justice you would be happy—maybe you will be anyway—

Oh, Do-Do
Do-Do—

Zelda.

I love you anyway—even if there isn't any me or any love or even any life—

I love you.

[1] From Rupert Brooke's "The Old Vicarage, Grantchester."

TO: *Scottie Fitzgerald*   ALS, *4 pp. Princeton University*
Summer 1935   *Grove Park Inn stationery.*
                                             Asheville, North Carolina

Scottina:

It was fine seeing you, + I liked you a lot (this is aside from loving you which I always do). You are nicer, to adults—you are emerging from that rather difficult time in girls 12–15 usually, but you are emerging I think rather early—probably at 14 or so. You have one good crack coming but—well:

"Daddy the prophet!" I can hear you say in scorn. I wish to God I wasn't so right usually about you. When I wrote that "news-sheet" with events left out, you know: the letter that puzzled you, + headed it "Scottie Loses Head", it was because I saw it coming. I knew that your popularity with two or three dazed adolescent boys would convince you that you were at least the Queen of Sheba, + that you would "lose your head." What shape this haywire excursion would take I didn't know—I couldn't have guessed it would be writing a series of indiscreet letters to a gossipy + indiscreet boy who would show them to the persons for whom they were <u>not</u> meant (understand: I don't blame Andrew too much—the fault was yours—he didn't, will you notice, put into writing an analysis of his best friends of his own sex!)

However, that's of no seriousness. But I think that the next kick will be a bad one—but you will survive, and after that you will manage your affairs better. To avoid such blows you almost <u>have</u> to have them yourself so you can begin to think of others as valuing themselves, possibly, quite as much as you do yourself. So I'm not afraid of it for you. I don't want it to be so bad that it will break your self-confidence, which is attractive + is fine is founded on positive virtues, work, courage ect. but if you are selfish it had better be broken early. If you are unselfish you can keep it always—and it is a nice thing to have. I didn't know till 15 that there was anyone in the world except me, + it cost me <u>plenty</u>.

Signs + portents of your persistant conciet: Mrs. Owens said to me (+ Mrs. Owens loves you)

"For the 1st time in a long while Scottie was <u>nice</u>, + not a burden as I expected. It was really nice to be with her."

Because, I guess, for the 1st time you entered into <u>their</u> lives, humble lives of struggling people, instead of insisting that they enter into yours—a chance they never had, of belonging to "high society." Before, you had let them be aware of what <u>you</u> were doing, (not in any snobbish sense, because heaven knows I'd have checked you on that)—but because you never considered or pretended to consider their lives, their world at all—your own activities seemed of so much more overwhelming importance to you! <u>You did not use one bit of your mind, one little spot!</u> to think what <u>they</u> were thinking, or help <u>them</u>!

You went to Norfolk + gave out the information (<u>via</u> the Taylors, <u>via</u> Annabel, <u>via</u> mother that you were going to Dobbs. That doesn't matter save as indicative of a show-off frame of mind. You knew it was highly tentative. It was a case, again, of boasting, of "promoting yourself." But those signs of one big catastrophe (it'll come—I want to minimize it for you, but it cant be prevented because only experience can teach) are less important than your failure to realize that you are <u>a young member of the human race</u>, who has not proved itself in any but the most superficial manner. (I have seen "popular girls" of 15 become utterly déclassé in six months because they were essentially selfish. You + Peaches[1] (who isn't selfish, I think) had a superficial head-start with prettiness, but you will find more + more that less pretty girls will be attracting the soldier, more substantial boys as the next two years will show. Both you + Peaches are intelligent, but both of you will be warped by this early attention, <u>+ something tells me she wont lose her head</u>, she hasn't the "gift of gab" as you have—her laughter + her silence takes the place of much. That's why I wish to God you would write something when you have time—if only a one act play about how girls act in the bath house, in a tent, on a train going to camp.

I grow weary, but I probably won't write again for a month. Don't answer this, justifying yourself—of <u>course</u> I know you're doing the best you "can."
The points of the letter are.
1<u>st</u> You did spill over, rashly!
2<u>nd</u> You are getting over the selfish period—thank God!
3<u>d</u> But it'll take one more big kick, + I want it to be mild, so your backside won't suffer too much.
4<u>th</u> I wish you'd get your mind off your precious self enough to write me a one act play about other people—what they say + how they behave.
With <u>dearest</u> love,
Your Simply So-perfect Too, too Daddy

<u>Please</u>, turn back + read this letter over! It is too packed with considered thought to digest the first time. Like Milton—oh yeah!

TO: Sara Murphy   *ALS, 4 pp. Honoria Murphy Donnelly*
August 15, 1935   *Asheville, North Carolina*

Dearest Sara
Today a letter from Gerald, a week old, telling me this + that about the awful organ music around us, made me think of you, and I mean <u>think</u> of

---

[1] Scottie's close friend Peaches Finney.

you (of all people in the world you know the distinction). In my theory, utterly opposite to Ernest's, about fiction i.e. that it takes half a dozen people to make a synthesis strong enough to create a fiction character—in that theory, or rather in despite of it, I used you again and again in <u>Tender</u>:

"Her face was hard + lovely + pitiful"

and again

"He had been heavy, belly-frightened with love of her for years"

—in those and in a hundred other places I tried to evoke not <u>you</u> but the effect that you produce on men—the echoes and reverberations—a poor return for what you have given by your living presence, but nevertheless an artist's (what a word!) sincere attempt to preserve a true fragment rather than a "portrait" by Mr. Sargent. And someday in spite of all the affectionate skepticism you felt toward the brash young man you met on the Riviera eleven years ago, you'll let me have my little corner of you where I know you better than anybody—yes, even better than Gerald. And if it should perhaps be your left ear (you hate anyone to examine any single part of your person, no matter how appreciatively—that's why you wore bright clothes) on June evenings on Thursday from 11:00 to 11:15 here's what I'd say.

That not one thing you've done is for nothing. If you lost everything you brought into the world—if your works were burnt in the public square the law of compensation would still act (I am too moved by what I am saying to write it as well as I'd like). You are part of our times, part of the history of our race. The people whose lives you've touched directly or indirectly have reacted to the corporate bundle of atoms that's you in a <u>good</u> way. <u>I have seen you again + again at a time of confusion take the <u>hard</u> course almost blindly because long after your powers of ratiocination were exhausted you clung to the idea of dauntless courage</u>. You were the one who said:

"All right, I'll take the black checker men."

I know that you + Gerald are one + it is hard to separate one of you from the other, in such a matter for example as the love + encouragement you chose to give to people who were full of life rather than to others, equally interesting and less exigent, who were frozen into rigid names. I don't praise you for <u>this</u>—it was the little more, the little immeasurable portion of a millimeter, the thing at the absolute top that makes the difference between a World's Champion and an also-ran, the little glance when you were sitting with Archie on the sofa that you threw at me and said:

"And—Scott!"

taking me in too, and with a heart so milked of compassion by your dearest ones that no person in the world but you would have that little more to spare.

Well—I got somewhat excited there. The point is: I rather like you, + I <u>think</u> that perhaps you have the makings of a good woman.

Gerald had invited me to come up for a weekend in the fall, probably Sept.

288

It's odd that when I read over this letter it seems to convey no particular point, yet I'm going to send it. Like Cole's eloquent little song.
"I think it'll tell you how <u>great</u> you are."[1]

From your everlasting friend,

Scott

TO: Harold Ober
c. September 5, 1935

ALS, 4 pp. Lilly Library
Asheville, North Carolina

Personal
+
Confidential

Dear Harold:

This letter is about several things.

1st Story: I had made 3 false starts and only now am I satisfied with what I've got (about 4,200 words). I dont want to break it off again (broke it off once to do <u>Red Bk</u> + once to do radio sketch, now being typed so I think I'd better count on staying here till 12th instead of 9th as I'd planned. The story should reach you on Thurs 12th.

So if you can count on putting Scotty on the <u>Penn.</u> train for Baltimore on Fri 13th I'll meet her at the station. In Baltimore I'll go to <u>Hotel Stafford</u> as my plan is to move + I dont want to open up the house for only a week.

You have been a life-saver about Scotty—you may have guessed that things have gone less well here—just one day after the lung was pronounced completely well the heart went nutsey again + they sent me back to bed and I was only able to work about one day in three. I am up and around again but I dont like to allow less than five days to finish story, pack ect.

About shopping with Scotty (Mrs Ober's suggestion I mean) since I cant decide about schools, that had better wait because a child's equipment depends on that of course + I cant decide anything until I see how I stand the trip to Baltimore. If I would only die, at least she and Zelda would have the Life Insurance + it would be a general good riddance, but it seems as if life has been playing some long joke with me for the past eight months and cant decide when to leave off.

However for the moment I seem out of danger—they mean it too. I didn't want any kidding about it.

I like the radio skit—its original + quite powerful I think.[2] The little corrections to be done on it wont take a day.

It goes without saying that I'll be begging for money about the 12th or 13th when you have the story in your hands. I think I can get along all right till then.

[1]Fitzgerald is referring to the last line of the verse in Cole Porter's "You're the Top."

[2]"Let's Go Out and Play," an antiwar drama broadcast on the "World Peaceways" program, October 3, 1935.

About Spafford—I promised him some money if + when the play payed anything; he seemed to think that this included the option but I wrote advising him differently—I had meant from the 1st actual royalties. Some clippings told me that the contract was signed but I dont suppose they paid more than a few hundred, did they? Spafford said you were still afraid Kirkland would be slow on the delivery. Anyhow I told Spafford I couldn't help him now—it was a gratuitous offer merely between him + me to compensate him for his lost time + effort.[1]

Glad you liked the Red Bk story. Hated to do all that work for no reward but it was my fault, and it makes the Phillipe series 30,000 words long, almost half enough for a book. The next step I dont know in that line. Certainly I've got to shoot at the bigger money till Im out of debt.

Ever Yours
Scott Fitzg—

TO: *Laura Guthrie*[2]   *ALS, 6 pp. Princeton University*
                          Hotel Stafford stationery. Baltimore, Maryland

[pm Sept. 23, 1935]

Sweet Laura:

This can't be more than a note to answer your nice letter.

The news from the West is pretty terrible—I have seen plenty people disappointed in love from old maids who thought they had lost their only chance to Dorothy Parker who tried to kill herself when Charlie MacArthur threw her over—but I never saw a girl[3] who had so much, take it all so hard. She knew from the beginning there would be nothing more so it could scarcely be classed even as a dissapointment—merely one of those semi-tragic facts that must be faced. Its very strange, and sad. I have nothing from her except the wire.

For myself all goes well. I woke up on the train after a fine sleep, came to the hotel + went to work with Mrs Owens before noon. We discussed all the "ifs" and will decide nothing before a week. Scottie arrived like a sun goddess at 5.00 o'clock, all radiant + glowing. We had a happy evening walking and walking the dark streets. The next morning she was invited to visit in the country for the wk end + I continued my picking up of lose ends. First Zelda—she was fine, almost herself, has only one nurse now + has no more intention of doing away with herself. It was wonderful to sit with her head on my shoulder for hours and feel as I always have, even

---

[1] Broadway producer Sam H. Grisham took an option on the dramatization of *Tender Is the Night* and wanted Jack Kirkland and Austin Parker approved as dramatists for the project.

[2] Mrs. Guthrie served as confidante of and typist for Fitzgerald in Asheville.

[3] Beatrice Dance, a married woman with whom Fitzgerald had a brief affair during the summer of 1935.

now, closer to her than to any other human being. This is not a denial of other emotions—oh, you understand.

The bank matter was all straight—<u>yours</u> were the only checks that suffered. I'm sorry as hell for the inconvenience.

<u>Send me the page of notes with the stuff about the Ashville flower carnival</u>—I'm going to write one story here—I mapped it out today. I want to see how well I can stand this climate under working conditions. <u>Though</u> I still think I will be back in Ashville in two weeks. Also better tell Post Office my adress is here; they probably have hospital or Inn.

I have heard of Col. Bryan. Young Page, by the way, is not the boy I took him for. He was <u>not</u> head of the Princetonian but only copy editor, + no great sensation. I was thinking of another man. Have ordered the Wm. Boyce Thompson[1] book for you.

My story is about Carolina ¶I have stopped all connections with M. Barleycorn ¶The exema is almost gone but not quite ¶Baltimore is warm but pleasant—I love it more than I thought—it is so rich with memories— it is nice to look up the street + see the statue of my great uncle, + to know Poe is buried here and that many ancestors of mine have walked in the old town by the bay. I belong here, where everything is civilized and gay and rotted and polite. And I wouldn't mind a bit if in a few years Zelda + I could snuggle up together under a stone in some old graveyard here. That is really a happy thought + not melancholy at all.

Tell me <u>your</u> news.

Lovingly + gratefully
Scott

TO: *Harold Ober*　　　　　　　　　　　　　*ALS, 2 pp. Lilly Library*
c. November 18, 1935

Skylands Hotel
Hendersonville. N.C.

Dear Harold:

Things rather crashed again. Since Aug 20th I have written

(1.) Practically new Red Bk Story (pd. already)[2]
(2.) 1st Version <u>Provençe</u> Story
(3) Radio Broadcast (Sold)
(4) 1st version <u>Suicice</u> Story[3]
(5) 2nd Version <u>Provençe</u> Story (Sold)[4]
(6) 2nd Version <u>Suicice</u> Story

---

[1] *The Magnate: William Boyce Thompson and His Time* (1935), by Hermann Hagedorn.
[2] "Gods of Darkness."
[3] "I'd Die for You," unpublished.
[4] Probably "Image on the Heart."

(7)   Emergency <u>Esquire</u> article for $200 (finished today)[1]
(8)   Most of a radio broadcast. Finish tomorrow.

Certainly a good 3 months work—but total yield has been just short of $2000. so far—of course if <u>I'd Die for You</u> sells, it will change the face of the situation.

I worked one day with Spafford on the play, gave him a new 3d act which was his weakness. He has no great talent but he works hard + has common sense + he can find the talent in the book. Sorry Kirkland didn't kick thru.

I am here till I finish a <u>Post</u> story something young + joyful. I was beginning to cough again in Baltimore with the multiplicity of events, also to drink + get irrasticable with everybody around me. Scotty is there now with Mrs. Owens.

I am living here at a $2.00 a day hotel, utterly alone, thank God! and unless something happens to upset me again should finish the story by the 27th + reach Baltimore by 28th I hope for the winter this time.

Meanwhile you'll get the broadcast.

Typical of my confusion was my telling Constance Smith story should go to <u>Post</u>. It's already been there in it's first form and should have gone to <u>American</u>. Hope you overruled my suggestion.

Ever Yrs.
Scott Fitzg

The decision to leave Baltimore came when I found, after being all moved in, that a super salesman had rented me an appartment <u>next to a pianist</u>, + with clapboard walls!
Did you see Cormack?[2]

TO: *Harold Ober*   *ALS, 2 pp. Lilly Library*
Received December 12, 1935   *Hendersonville, North Carolina*

Dear Harold:

This story is the fruit of my desire to write about children of Scotty's age.[3] (it doesn't cross the radio idea, which I gather is a dud. Will you write me about it? Also the history of the <u>I'd Die for You</u>) But to return to this story.

I want it to be a series <u>if</u> the <u>Post</u> likes it. Now if they do please tell them that I'd like them to hold it for another one which should preceed it, like they did once in the <u>Basil</u> series. I am not going to wait for their answer to start a second one about Gwen but I am going to wait for a wire of encourag-

---

[1] Possibly "The Crack-Up," *Esquire* (March 1936).

[2] Bartlett Cormack, Hollywood agent, was trying to sell film rights for "Head and Shoulders."

[3] "Too Cute for Words," *The Saturday Evening Post* (April 18, 1936); the first story in an unsuccessful series about Gwen Bowers, a thirteen-year-old girl.

ment or discouragment on the idea from you. I'm getting this off Wed. It should reach you Thurs. noon. I'm going to rest Thurs. anyhow so if I hear from you Thurs night or Fri morning that you like it I'll start the other. Even if the <u>Post</u> didn't like the series the names could be changed + the two sold as separate stories.

But I do think it should be offered them <u>individually</u> before the series idea is broached to them

Money again rears its ugly head. I am getting accustomed to poverty and bankrupcy (In fact for myself I rather enjoy washing my own clothes + eating 20 cent meals twice a day, after so many years in the flesh pots— don't worry, this is only half true though I did do it for the 1st wk here to penalize myself for the expense of the journey) <u>but</u> I do object to the jails and I have almost $300 due on income tax the 15th (what a typically modern joke this is—me, with $11 in the bank at the moment.) Now can you let me have that and $200 to go with on the strength of this story? Read it first. If you can or can't please include the information in yr. telegram of Thurs. or Fri. I need $150 for Zelda + Scotty + $50 for myself—for I intend to finish the 2nd <u>Gwen</u> story + then go north for what Xmas is to be found there. If you <u>can</u> will you wire it to Baltimore to be there by <u>Sat.</u> morning?

If your report is favorable I shall move to Ashville Sat. + have the doctor go over me while I write. I arrived here weak as hell, got the grippe + spat blood again (1st time in 9 months) + took to bed for six days. I didn't dare see the Ashville doctor till I got this story off + wrote a $200 article for Gingrich[1] on which I've been living. I'm grateful I came south when I did though—I made a wretched mistake in coming north in Sept + taking that appartment + trying 1000 things at once, + am only grateful that I got out before the blizzard, + got grippe instead of pneumonia How that part (I mean living in Balt.) is going to work out I dont know. I'm going to let Scotty finish her term anyhow. For the rest things depend on health + money + its very difficult. I use up my health making money + then my money in recovering health. I got <u>well</u> last summer—but what was the use when I was broke in the fall. Dont answer—there isn't any answer If there was I'd have thought of it long ago. I am really not discouraged—I <u>enjoyed</u> writing this story which is the second time that's happened to me this year, + that's a good sign

Ever Yrs.
Scott Fitzg.

P. S. This is story number 7 for the year.

---

[1] Arnold Gingrich, editor of *Esquire*. The article was "The Crack-Up."

TO: Harold Ober   Wire. Lilly Library
December 28, 1935   *Baltimore, Maryland*

HAVE TRIED LIFE ON SUBSISTANCE LEVEL AND IT DOESNT WORK STOP I THOUGHT
IF I COULD HAVE THIS MONEY I COULD HOLD MY HEAD UP AND GO ON STOP
WHAT YOU SUGGEST POSTPONES BY HALF A YEAR THE LIQUIDATION WE BOTH
WANT STOP PLEASE CARRY ME OVER THE SECOND GWEN STORY AND GIVE ME
TWENTY SEVEN HUNDRED[1]
    FITZGERALD.

TO: Harold Ober   *TLS, 3 pp. Lilly Library*

Cambridge Arms Apartments,
Charles & 34th Streets,
Baltimore, Maryland,
December 31, 1935.

Dear Harold:

I'd have gone to Hollywood a year ago last spring. I don't think I could do it now but I might. Especially if there was no choice. Twice I have worked out there on other people's stories—on an "original" with John Considine telling me the plot twice a week and on the Katherine Brush story—it simply fails to use what qualities I have. I don't blame you for lecturing me since I have seriously inconvenienced you, but it would be hard to change my temperament in middle-life. No single man with a serious literary reputation has made good there. If I could form a partnership with some technical expert it might be done. (That's very different from having a supervisor who couldn't fit either the technical or creative role but is simply a weigher of completed values.) I'd need a man who knew the game, knew the people, but would help me tell and sell my story—<u>not his</u>. This man would be hard to find, because a <u>smart</u> technician doesn't want or need a partner, and an uninspired one is inclined to have a dread of ever touching tops. I could work best with a woman, because they haven't any false pride about yielding a point. I could have worked with old Bess Meredith if we hadn't been in constant committees of five. I'm afraid unless some such break occurs I'd be no good in the industry.

The matter will probably solve itself—I'll either pull out of this in the next few months or else go under—in which case I might start again in some entirely new way of my own.

I know what you would do now in my situation and what the Ideal Way would be, but it simply isn't in me to do my duty blindly. I have to follow my fate with my eyes wide open.

---

[1]On December 26 and 27 Ober proposed that a portion of the $3,000 *Saturday Evening Post* check for "Too Cute for Words" be used to reduce Fitzgerald's debts.

Scotty is so well and happy. She has such faith in me and doesn't know what's happening. Tonight she and two of her admirers decorated a tree. I hope Dick[1] is better and has a happy Christmas even out there away from his family.

Yours,
F Scott Fitzgerald

P. S. Do you think the <u>New Yorker</u> could use poem attached?[2]

TO: Harold Ober   *TLS, 7 pp. Lilly Library*

The Cambridge Arms,
Charles & 34th Streets,
Baltimore, Maryland,
February 8, 1936.

Dear Harold:

The man Braun[3] is a plain, simple man with a true instinct toward the arts. He is of complete financial integrity and we were awfully nice to him once during a journey through North Africa and I think he is honestly fond of both Zelda and me.

I start with this because I don't want to mess up this chance with any of the inadvertencies and lack of foresight that lost me the sale of "Tender is the Night" and ruined the Gracie Allen venture.[4] You are now in touch with Hollywood in a way that you were not several years ago. This is obviously a job that I can do expertly—but it is also obviously a job that a whole lot of other people can do fairly well. Now it seems to me that the point can be sold that I am equipped to do this treatment which is the whole gist of this letter.

He has gone out to Hollywood and they will put some hack on the thing and in two minutes will have a poor imitation of Lily Pons[5] deserting the stage for a poor country boy or a poor country girl named Lily Pons astounding the world in ten minutes. A hack will do exactly that with it, thinking first what previous stories dealing with the ballet and theatre have been about, and he will try to write a reasonable imitation about it. As you know Zelda and I have been through hell about the whole subject and you'll know, too, that I should be able to deliver something entirely authentic in the matter full of invention and feeling.

---

[1]Richard Ober, Harold Ober's son.

[2]"Thousand and First Ship," first published in *The Crack-Up* (1945).

[3]L. G. Braun, manager of ballerina Olga Spessivtzewa, asked Fitzgerald to write a movie for her. Fitzgerald's treatment for the ballet movie was entitled "Ballet Shoes" or "Ballet Slippers."

[4]Fitzgerald collaborated with Robert Spafford on a treatment for a George Burns and Gracie Allen movie, "Gracie at Sea," which was never made.

[5]French-American opera singer and movie star.

It seems odd having to sell you such a suggestion when once you would have taken it at my own valuation, but after these three years of reverses it seems necessary to reassure you that I have the stuff to do this job and not let this opportunity slide away with the rumor that "Scott is drinking" or "Scott is through."

You know that the merest discussion of ideas [three words omitted by the editor] would mean that they were public property. You know also as in the case of radio, (Columbia) that they want a sample. Now how on earth you can both sell the idea that I can do this job, that is, write a 5,000 word story with cash in advance, and yet be sure that the plot won't leak out, I don't know. That seems to be your problem. You remember that I lost the whole month of October on that false radio come-on where they were obviously kidding. Isn't there some way to determine whether these people are kidding or not? This man has, in a sense, come to me and I think the idea ought to be caught and trapped right now because as you may well imagine I have little energy to dissipate.

A list of suggestions follows:

First I enclose something which I wish you would read last because it has nothing to do with the present offer, but it is something that I wrote gratuitously for a Russian dancer some years ago. Please consider that last and featuring, as it does, a male dancer rather than a female, it would certainly not fit Spessivtzewa's requirements. The other ideas which follow are the basis of a moving picture while that was for an actual ballet.

1. Zleda's awful experience of trying a difficult art too late in life to culminate with the irony that just before she cracked up she had been hoping to get little "bits" in Diaghelief's[1] ballet and that people kept coming to the studio who she thought were emissaries of his and who turned out to be from the Folies Bergere and who thought they might make her into an American shimmy dancer. This was about like a person hoping to lead the Philadelphia Symphony being asked to be assistant conductor of Ben Bernie's band.

Please don't have anybody read Zelda's book because it is a bad book! But by glancing over it yourself you will see that it contains all the material that a tragedy should have, though she was incapable as a writer of realizing where tragedy lay as she was incapable of facing it as a person. Of course the tragic ending of Zelda's story need not be repeated in the picture. One could concede to the picture people the fact that the girl might become a popular dancer in the Folies Bergere. One could conceive of a pathetic ending a la Hepburn in which because of her idealism she went on being a fifth rate "figurine" in ballets all over Europe—this to be balanced by a compensatory love story which would make up for her the failure of her work. This would seem to me to be much the best treatment of this story.

2. This idea has to do with an episode of some memoirs of Pavlova. It

[1]Director of the Ballets Russes.

begins with a little girl briefly glimpsed and dancing in the Imperial ballet before the war. A scene later in Paris at the height of the flurry over the ballet and stranded finally with a ballet company in either Australia or Brazil for lack of funds. The climax would hinge on the catastrophe of the death of Diaghelief. The sorrow of it that Zelda felt, as did many others, who seemed to feel also that the ballet was ended; the old Imperial school was dead and now Diaghelief who had personally kept it alive in Paris had gone to his grave. There seemed to them no future and I know how strong that feeling was among the ballet people in '31 and '31, a sort of utter despair, a sense that they had once been under patronage of the Czar and later of an entrepreneur and that now nobody was taking care of them. They are like children to a ridiculous extent and have less practical ideas than the wildest musician imaginable. This story would end up in New York or in Hollywood, the ballet having a new renaissance under an American growing delight in that particular art as is practically true with Masine's[1] ballet in New York and with Trudy Schoop's[2] successful little trek around the country. That's idea number 2.

The third idea is more difficult in its selling aspects. In 1920 I tried to sell to D. W. Griffith the idea that people were so interested in Hollywood that there was money in a picture about that and romance in the studio. He was immediately contemptuous of it, but of course, a year later Merton of the Movies mopped up the country. The movies seem willing always to romanticize anything from a radio broadcasting room to a newspaper office as far as the entertainment world is concerned, but are so shy about themselves that another picture can be got out of Hollywood, which is certainly one of the most romantic cities in the world. A sort of mental paralysis came over them. Do you remember how the Hearst publicity men killed my story "Crazy Sunday" for Cosmopolitan. That was in case someone should get hurt, that it might offend Norma Shearer, Thalberg, John Gilbert or Marion Davies,[3] etc. etc. As a matter of fact I had mixed up those characters so thoroughly that there was no character who could have been identified except possibly King Vidor and he would have been very amused by the story.

Let me repeat that this is the most difficult idea to sell but in some ways the most interesting of the three. A Russian ballet dancer finds herself in the extra line in Hollywood; they pick her out of the crowd for her good looks, gave her bits of one kind or another but always on some other basis than the fact that she is a ballet dancer. This treatment of the general subject would have to close with a crash, at least I haven't thought any further

[1]Leonide Massine was a choreographer and ballet dancer, and director of the National Ballet Theatre.

[2]The Trudi Schoop Comic Ballet was organized in 1931.

[3]Norma Shearer, movie actress at MGM, was the wife of Irving Thalberg, executive producer with MGM. John Gilbert was a silent-screen star. Marion Davies, an actress with MGM, was William Randolph Hearst's mistress.

than that. It would turn entirely on the essential tonal background of the adventures of Europeans who develop their metier in a Yiddish world (only you don't use that word except in Germany) that would be interesting to the people in the same rococo sense that the demand for pictures about places like Shanghai and the Trans-Siberian Railroad have in the American people. Combined with it is the always fascinating Hollywood story.

I've spent the morning writing this letter because I am naturally disappointed about the Post's not liking the Gwen story and must rest and go to work this afternoon to try to raise some money somehow though I don't know where to turn.

Scott

TO: *Sara Murphy*   ALS, 2 pp. *Honoria Murphy Donnelly*
March 30, 1936

Dearest Sara (and Gerald too, if he's not in London)
I want news of you. The winter has presented too many problems here for me to come north, even as far as New York + my last word of you was by kindness of Archie—and not too encouraging.

If you read the little trilogy I wrote for Esquire you know I went through a sort of "dark night of the soul" last autumn, and again and again my thoughts reverted to you and Gerald, and I reminded myself that nothing had happened to me with the awful suddenness of your tragedy of a year ago,[1] nothing so utterly conclusive and irreparable. I saw your face, Sara, as I saw it a year ago this month, and Gerald's face last fall when I met him in the Ritz Bar, and I felt very close to you—and correspondingly detached from Ernest, who has managed to escape the great thunderbolts, and Nora Flinn whom the Gods haven't even shot at with much seriousness. She would probably deny that and she helped me over one black week when I thought this was probably as good a time to quit as any, but as I said to her the love of life is essentially as incommunicable as grief.

I am moving Zelda to a sanitarium in Ashville—she is no better, though the suicidal cloud was lifted—I thought over your Christian Science idea + finally decided to try it but the practitioner I hit on wanted to begin with "absent treatments," which seemed about as effectual to me as the candles my mother keeps constantly burning to bring me back to Holy Church— so I abandoned it. Especially as Zelda now claims to be in direct contact with Christ, William the Conqueror, Mary Stuart, Appollo and all the stock paraphanalea of insane asylum jokes. Of course it isn't a bit funny but after the awful strangulation episode of last spring I sometimes take refuge in an unsmiling irony about the present exterior phases of her illness. For what she has really suffered there is never a sober night that I do not pay a stark

---

[1]The Murphys' son Baoth had died in March 1935 of meningitis.

tribute of an hour to in the darkness. In an odd way, perhaps incredible to you, she was always my child (it was not reciprocal as it often is in marriages), my child in a sense that Scotty isn't, because I've brought Scotty up hard as nails (Perhaps that's fatuous, but I <u>think</u> I have.) Outside of the realm of what you called Zelda's "terribly dangerous secret thoughts" I was her great reality, often the only liason agent who could make the world tangible to her—

The only way to show me you forgive this great outpouring is to write me about yourselves. Some night when you're not too tired, take yourself a glass of sherry and write me as lovely and revealing letter as you did before. Willy-nilly we are still in the midst of life and all true correspondence is nessessarily sporadic but a letter from you or Gerald always pulls at something awfully deep in me. I want the best news, but in any case I want to know

With Dearest Affection to You All
Scott

Cambridge Arms Appts. Baltimore Md

TO: Harold Ober　　　　　　　　　*ALS, 3 pp. Collection of Douglas Wyman*
Received May 9, 1936　　　　　　　　　　　　　　　　*Baltimore, Maryland*

Dear Harold:

Here's for The <u>Pictorial</u>. (3d draft, 3d correction.) Every single story since <u>Phillipe</u> I in the Spring of 1934 two years ago I've had to write over. Save the 1st Mccalls + The Fortune Telling.

All three last Phillipe stories, Her last case, New Types, the Esquimo, the Image on the Heart, 1st Gwen, 2nd Gwen, 3d Gwen + now 4th Gwen.

Eleven stories! It simply doubles my work + keeps me in my room all the time so save when I was 1st sick last summer there is no break ever—ones finished I plan to rest, its no good so I must revise it so there's no rest for debts press + I start another. This business of debt is awful. It has made me lose confidence to an appalling extent. I used to write for myself—now I write for editors because I never have time to really think what I <u>do</u> like or find anything to like. Its like a man drawing out water in drops because he's too thirsty to wait for the well to fill. Oh, for one lucky break.

I sent off those Paramount things some days ago. Maybe they went to Paramount—I cant seem to remember. I can find out I think Do they want to use <u>The Gold Hat</u> as a title. I thought of calling Gatsby that at first.

Well, now I need two hundred pretty badly. So badly that there are collecting agencies at the door every day—rent unpaid, school unpaid, sanitarum unpaid + not a vestige of credit left in Baltimore.

I haven't had even a glass of beer for a month + shall try it again for a few months as I did last year + see if that'll help my morale, but I havn't

299

much faith. There seems to be too much to contend with to get any piece of mind. Where there were once two or three things there are now dozens. It will take a windfall

All well, everyone has troubles now. Except the rich, damn them.

Ever Yours

Scott

Please tell me about the money. I will start another <u>Post</u> story tomorrow. No more Gwen at present.

P. S. This story is really all smoothed out at last. I wish the <u>Post</u> had seen it this way, but I was sick in bed last wk. + not at my best. However I wouldn't want to try them again.

Just got word that I am being sued for debt by Zelda's last sanitarium. Could you make it 300 instead of two hundred It is impossible to write or even exist under these circumstances. I have even used the loan companies.

P.S One last thing. I realize that I am at the end of my rescources physically + financially. After getting rid of this house next month + storing furniture I am cutting expenses to the bone, taking Scotty to Carolina instead of camp + going to a boarding house for the summer, I have got to do that and get a sense of proportion and give her one. The doctors tell me at this rate of work I wont last two years, Zelda + I did that twice when I was making more than I am now + had less expenses.

This way I work all day + worry all night.

This copy looks mixed but it really isn't. Its only my hand sticks to the paper its so hot here. But put someone very careful on it to unravel the bad pages

TO: Bennett Cerf   *Wire. Columbia University*

BALTIMORE MD 402A   1936 MAY 16   AM 5 17
WOULD YOU CONSIDER PUBLISHING TENDER IS THE NIGHT IN THE MODERN LIBRARY[1] IF I MADE CERTAIN CHANGES TOWARD THE END WHICH I SEE NOW ARE ESSENTIAL COMMA IT WOULD MAKE ALL THE DIFFERENCE IN THE SPLIT UP OF THE TWO PRINCIPAL CHARACTERS STOP OR DO YOU THINK THAT ONCE PUBLISHED A

---

[1] The novel was not included in the Modern Library.

BOOK IS FOREVER CRYSTALIZED PLEASE ANSWER CAMBRIDGE ARMS CHARLES
STREET BALTIMORE MARYLAND
  SCOTT FITZGERALD.

TO: Adelaide Neall   *RTLS, 2 pp.—with holograph last line*
                                          and postscript. Historical Society
                                                      of Pennsylvania

                                          The Cambridge Arms,
                                              Baltimore, Maryland,
                                                  June 5, 1936.
Dear Miss Neale:
  I appreciated your interest yesterday. I think that if one cares about a
metiér (sp.) it is almost necessary to learn it over again every few years.
Somewhere about the middle of "Tender is the Night" I seemed to have
lost my touch on the short story—by touch I mean the exact balance, how
much plot, how much character, how much background you can crowd
into a limited number of words. It is a nice adjustment and essentially
depends upon the enthusiasm with which you approach a given subject. In
the last two years I've only too often realized that many of my stories were
built rather than written.
  Still and however, one is limited by one's experience and I've decided to
go with the series of medical stories[1] hoping to unearth something new—
and as a beginning have decided to rewrite this story with the original as a
skeleton.
  With best wishes to all of you and many thanks for your personal interest
in the prospected series
                                          F Scott Fitzgerald

(On re-reading this, it sounds somewhat stilted but I trust you'll understand
that I dont mind critisism a bit—the critics are always wrong (including
you!) but they are always right in the sense that they make one re-examine
one's artistic conscience.
                                          F.S.F.

[1]The projected series featured a nurse named Trouble. After rejecting the first story in the
series, *The Saturday Evening Post* reluctantly accepted the second—"Trouble"—which it did
not publish until March 1937. "Trouble" was the last of Fitzgerald's sixty-five *Post* stories.

TO: *Ernest Hemingway*   *ALS, 1 p. John F. Kennedy Library*
July 16, 1936   *Asheville, North Carolina*

Dear Ernest:

Please lay off me in print.[1] If I choose to write de profundis sometimes it doesn't mean I want friends praying aloud over my corpse. No doubt you meant it kindly but it cost me a night's sleep. And when you incorporate it (the story) in a book would you mind cutting my name?[2]

It's a fine story—one of your best—even though the "Poor Scott Fitzgerald ect" rather spoiled it for me

Ever Your Friend
Scott

Riches have <u>never</u> facinated me, unless combined with the greatest charm or distinction.

TO: *John O'Hara*   *TL, 2 pp. Princeton University*

Grove Park Inn
Asheville, N.C.
July 25, 1936

Dear John:

Your letter got side-tracked in moving and has just turned up. Possibly I may have answered it before and if I did everything I said was true and if what I say now contradicts everything I said before that is all true too. Before I tell you how to write your new novel let me tell you about affairs here.

There are no affairs here.

We will now turn to your new novel. You quoted in your letter a very cryptic passage from the wonderful advice that I give to people. It sounds exactly like the advice that Ernest and I used to throw back and forth at

[1] In "The Snows of Kilimanjaro" (*Esquire*, August 1936), Hemingway wrote: "The rich were dull and they drank too much or they played too much backgammon. They were dull and they were repetitious. He remembered poor Scott Fitzgerald and his romantic awe of them and how he had started a story once that began, 'The very rich are different from you and me.' And how someone had said to Scott, Yes, they have more money. But that was not humorous to Scott. He thought they were a special glamorous race and when he found they weren't it wrecked him just as much as any other thing that wrecked him." This passage inspired the most widely repeated apocryphal anecdote about Fitzgerald and Hemingway. But no such exchange between the two writers has been established. The source for this squelch— as documented by Maxwell Perkins—was a luncheon meeting of Hemingway, Perkins, and critic Mary Colum at which Hemingway remarked, "I am getting to know the rich." Mrs. Colum replied, "The only difference between the rich and other people is that the rich have more money." See Matthew J. Bruccoli, *Some Sort of Epic Grandeur*, pp. 485–88.

[2] When the story was collected in *The Fifth Column and the First Forty-Nine Stories* (Scribners, 1938), the name was changed to "Julian" at Perkins's insistence.

each other, none of which ever had any effect—the only effect I ever had on Ernest was to get him in a receptive mood and say let's cut everything that goes before this. The the pieces got mislaid and he caould never find the part that I said to cut out. And so he published it without that and later we agreed that it was a very wise cut. This is not literally true and I don't want it established as part of the Hemingway Legend, but it's just about as far as one writer can go in helping another. Years later when Ernest was writing <u>Farewell to Arms</u> he was in doubt about the ending and marketed around to half a dozen people for their advice. I worked like hell on the idea and only succeeded in evolving a philosophy in his mind utterly contrary to everything that he thought an ending should be and later convinced me that he was right and made me end <u>Tender Is the Night</u> on a fade away instead of a staccato. Didn't we talk about this once before—I seem to see your large ear in the way of my voice.

There is some element that can as well as not be expressed by the dietitian's word roughage or up-stream by which you can judge yourself as a novelist or as a personality (the fact recently quated by Middleton Murray)[1] that John Keats felt that creative talent is essentially without character is empiric: the acceptance of disorganization is another matter because it eventually implies a lesion of vitality. I have just written a long letter to an admirer or mourner as to why I do not believe in Psychoanalysis for the disintegration of that thing, that judgment, the extinction of that light is much more to be dreaded than any material loss.

We are creatures bounding from each other's shoulders, feeling already the feet of new creatures upon our backs bounding again toward an invisible and illusory trapeze (at present played by the shortwinded Saroyans).[2] If the calf no longer flexes the bound will not be so high. In any case the out-stretched arms will never reach that swinging thing because when life has been well lived one can make an adjustment and become the second man in the pyramid. It is when life has been ill lived one is the third man; the first man always falls to his death, a fact that has haunted Ernest all his life.

This is all rather poor metaphysics expressed in ineffectual images, Again and again in my books I have tried to imagize my regret that I have never been as good as I intended to be (and you must know that what I mean by good is the modern don't-hurt-a-hair-of-anybody's-head-and-kill-a-hundred-thousand-people-if-necessary—in other words a personal con-science and meaning by the personal conscience yourself stripped in white midnight before your own God).

To take off with my whole weight (Charlie MacArthur continually urges me) if my suggestion about the bucolic background for a novel makes any sense it is embraced in the paragraph you requoted to me. I certainly think you should undertake something more ambitious and I know to my own

[1]Critic and editor John Middleton Murry wrote several studies of Keats.
[2]William Saroyan's story collection *The Daring Young Man on the Flying Trapeze* had appeared in 1934.

sorrow that to contemplate and project a long work is often an excuse for laziness. But let me pass along a suggestion:

Invent a system Zolawsque (see the appendix to Josephson's Life of Zola[1] in which he gives Zola's plan for the first Rougon-Macquart book), but buy a file. On the first page of the file put down the outline of a novel of your times enormous in scale (don't worry, it will contract by itself) and work on the plan for two months. Take the central point of the file as your big climax and follow your plan backward and forward from that for another three months. Then draw up somthing as complicated as a continuity from what you have and set yourself a schedule.

After all who am I to be giving you advice? I dare to do so only because I know that you are at heat a humble man and not resentful of anything said by one who wishes you well.

(This is being taken down by a young man from Brown University who is wilting visibly as he writes after a session with the many concerns that seem to surround a man of forty and the hieroglyphics of a half-done Post story to decipher tomorrow. He sends his regards or does he? Do you? No answer. He says he wonders what would happen if he would write a post-script to this thing.)

So much for tonight. If this seems toilet paper you can also use it to wipe Dr. Daniel Ogden Stewart's mouth when he finally gets the kick in the ass that he has been asking for so long. I want one lens of his double monocle to set up here in Carolina in an astronomical station to be able to see human life as cheaply as he has seen it.[2]

Ever your friend,

Ernest Hemingway's note in the margin of the first page: This is all nonsense. He is referring to my cutting the first paragraphs of a story called Fifty Grand. It is a funny story which I would be glad to give you if you like

E. H.

TO: Annabel Fitzgerald Sprague   Unlocated fragment—reprinted from Turnbull
August 1936?   *Baltimore, Maryland*

Dear Annabel:

It has been a rather terrible day and tomorrow promises to be no better, but after that I'm going to—got to—put Mother out of my mind for a day or so. I'll summarize what happened.

It was sad taking her from the hotel, the only home she knew for fifteen years, to die—and to go thru her things. The slippers and corset she was married in, Louisa's dolls in tissue paper, old letters and souvenirs, and collected scrap paper, and diaries that began and got nowhere, all her prides

---

[1] Matthew Josephson's *Zola and His Time* (1929).

[2] Donald Ogden Stewart had become an active radical spokesman after many years of associating with the very rich.

Grove Park Inn,
Asheville, N. C.,
July 31, 1936.

Darling,

       I am enclosing in this some pictures that tell a sad
story. I had a terrific accident and broke my shoulder.
I thought I would be very smart and do some diving and
after a year and a half of inactivity I stretched my muscles too much in the air and broke my shoulder. It has
all been very troublesome and expensive but I have tried
to be as cheerful as possible
about it and everyone has been
very kind; the people here
have rigged up a curious writing board for me so that I work
with my hand over my head rather
like this.

       I enclose money for your
present small needs. It may
be that that the expenses of
this injury will preclude your
going to an expensive school
this fall but life sometimes
does those things to you and I know you are brave and
able to adjust yourself to changing conditions and to
know that all the effort that I have will be thrown into
your education and the care of your mother. If I had
not had this operation on my shoulder the doctor tells
me I would never have been able to raise my arm above
my shoulder again. It is still an open bet as to whether
or not I will ever be able to raise it above my shoulder.

       I am proud of you and I am only a little angered
by the fact that you have not managed to read more than
one of the French books.

       Sunday night I leave for Baltimore and you can
write me either there care of Mrs. Owens or here where
I am returning. Isn't it lucky I did not go to Spain
after all! Or maybe it would have been rather fun.

                         Your loving Daddy

and sorrows and disappointments all come to nothing, and her lugged away like so much useless flesh the world had got thru with—

Mother and I never had anything in common except a relentless stubborn quality, but when I saw all this it turned me inside out realizing how unhappy her temperament made her and how she clung, to the end, to all things that would remind her of moments of snatched happiness. So I couldn't bear to throw out anything, even that rug, and it all goes to storage.

TO: Bennett Cerf   CC, 1 p. Princeton University

Grove Park Inn,
Asheville, N.C.,
August 13, 1936.

Dear Bennett:

The revision job[1] would take the form, to a large extent, of a certain new alignment of the scenes—without changing their order in any case. Some such line as this:

That the parts instead of being one, two, and three (they were one, two, three and four in the magazine serial) would include in several cases sudden stops and part headings which would be to some extent explanatory; certain pages would have to be inserted bearing merely headings. Part two, for example, should say in a terse and graceful way that the scene is now back on the Riviera in the fall after these events have taken place, or that, This brings us up to where Rosemary first encounters the Divers. Those examples are not accurate to my intention nor are they at all couched as I would have them, but that's the general idea. (Do you remember the number of sub-heads I used in "This Side of Paradise"—at that time a rather novel experiment, the germ of which I borrowed from Bernard Shaw's preface headings to his plays; indeed that was one of the few consciously original things in "This Side of Paradise".)

There would be certain changes but I would supply the equivalent line lengths. I have not my plan with me; it seems to be in Baltimore. But I know how printing costs are. It was evolved to have a very minimum of replacement. There is not more than one complete sentence that I want to eliminate, one that has offended many people and that I admit is out of Dick's character: "I never did go in for making love to dry loins." It is a strong line but definitely offensive. These are all the changes I contemplated with in addition some minor spelling corrections such as would disturb nothing but what was within a printed line. There will be no pushing over of paragraphs or disorganization of the present set-up except in the aforesaid inserted pages. I don't want to change anything in the book but sometimes

---

[1] On the proposed Modern Library edition of *Tender Is the Night*.

by a single word change one can throw a new emphasis or give a new value
to the exact same scene or setting.

Ever yours,

TO: *Maxwell Perkins*   *TLS, 2 pp.—with holograph revisions*
                                         Princeton University

Asheville, N.C.,
Sept. 19th, 1936

Dear Max:

This is my second day of having a minute to catch up with correspondence. Probably Harold Ober has kept you in general touch with what has
happened to me but I will summarize:

I broke the clavicle of my shoulder, diving—nothing heroic, but a little
too high for the muscles to tie up the efforts of a simple swan dive—At first
the Doctors thought that I must have tuberculosis of the bone, but x-ray
showed nothing of the sort, so (like occasional pitchers who throw their
arm out of joint with some unprepared for effort) it was left to dangle for
twenty-four hours with a bad diagnosis by a young Intern; then an x-ray
and found broken and set in an elaborate plaster cast.

I had almost adapted myself to the thing when I fell in the bath-room
reaching for the light, and lay on the floor until I caught a mild form of
arthritis called "Miotoosis," which popped me in the bed for five weeks
more. During this time there were domestic crises: Mother sickened and
then died and I tried my best to be there but couldn't. I have been within a
mile and a half of my wife all summer and have seen her about half dozen
times. Total accomplished for one summer has been one story—not very
good, two Esquire articles, neither of them very good.

You have probably seen Harold Ober and he may have told you that
Scottie got a remission of tuition at a very expensive school where I wanted
her to go (Miss Edith Walker's School in Connecticut).[1] Outside of that I
have no good news, except that I came into some money from my Mother,
not as much as I had hoped, but at least $20,000. in cash and bonds at the
materilization in six months—for some reason, I do not know the why or
wherefore of it, it requires this time. I am going to use some of it, with the
products of the last story and the one in process of completion, to pay off
my bills and to take two or three months rest in a big way. I have to admit
to myself that I haven't the vitality that I had five years ago.

I feel that I must tell you something which at first seemed better to leave
alone: I wrote Ernest about that story of his, asking him in the most mea-

---

[1]Ethel Walker School, Simsbury, Connecticut.

sured terms not to use my name in future pieces of fiction. He wrote me back a crazy letter, telling me about what a great Writer he was and how much he loved his children, but yielding the point—"If I should out live him—" which he doubted. To have answered it would have been like fooling with a lit firecracker.

Somehow I love that man, no matter what he says or does, but just one more crack and I think I would have to throw my weight with the gang and lay him. No one could ever hurt him in his first books but he has completely lost his head and the duller he gets about it, the more he is like a punch-drunk pug fighting himself in the movies.

No particular news except the dreary routine of illness.

As ever yours,
Scott Fitz

Scotty excited about the wedding.

TO: Harold Ober   *ALS, 3 pp. Lilly Library*
Received October 5, 1936   *Asheville, North Carolina*

(personal: Mr Ober only)

Dear Harold: I'll try to summarize all that's happened in the last two weeks. 1st about the story[1]:

It is all corrected except one part but I'm in a quandary about getting it typed because I can't send it off as is without having even the original that being in shorthand as the arm was just a broken mess one week (before last) + I had to dictate again. The two available stenographers I found between jobs. + both are engaged but I'll think of something + shoot to get it off tomorrow night its about a cartoonist + I like it + so do the people who've heard parts of it.

2nd About the article about Michael Muck.[2] I was in bed with temp about 102 when the [obliterated] phone rang and a voice said that this party had come all the way from N. Y to interview me. I fell for this like a damn fool, got him up, gave him a drink + accepted his exterior good manners. He had some relative with mental trouble (wife or mother) so I talked to him freely about treatments symtoms ect, about being depressed at advancing age and a little desperate about the wasted summer with this shoulder and arm—perhaps more freely than if had been well. I hadn't the faintest suspicion what would happen + I've never been a publicity seeker + never gotten a rotten deal before. When that thing came it seemed about the end and I got hold of a morphine file and swallowed four grains enough to kill

---

[1] Possibly "They Never Grow Older," unpublished.

[2] The September 25, 1936, issue of the *New York Post* printed an interview with Fitzgerald by Michel Mok; the interview depicted Fitzgerald as ruined and pitiful on his fortieth birthday.

a horse. It happened to be an overdose and almost before I could get to the bed I vomited the whole thing and the nurse came in + saw the empty phial + there was hell to pay. for awhile + afterwards I felt like a fool. And if I ever see, Mr Mock what will happen will be very swift and sudden. Dont tell Perkins.

As to Scotty there's nothing I can say to thank you;[1] when I'm straight there will be expenses you've undertaken for her we can allocate.

For the financial angle: I wait from day to day—unable now to buy medicines even, or to leave to the hotel because I couldn't pay a r.r fare—and twenty thousand of mine lies idle in a Baltimore Bank. Edgar Allen Poe Jr. the exector says he can advance me $2000 to $5000 (perhaps that much) but I wire him again and there is no news up to noon today. The hotel, doctors, Zelda's clinic ect clamor for money but there is none. By Maryland law I cant get the whole sum for six months but the other I cant understand. I want this to catch the only mail. I'll write the rest this afternoon.

> Ever
> Scott

TO: C. O. Kalman   *Wire, 2 pp. Princeton University*

ASHEVILLE NCAR   442P   1936 OCT 5   PM 5 20

    OSCAR KALMAN, BROKER WELL KNOWN
    PHONE AND DLR OFFICE OR REISDENCE TONIGHT
MOTHER LEFT ME SECURITIES OF MARKET VALUE OF ABOUT TWENTY THOUSAND DOLLARS AND AN ADMINISTRATOR HAS ONLY JUST BEEN APPOINTED WHO TELLS ME THAT BY MARYLAND LAW I CANT HAVE THEM FOR SIX MONTHS AND NO BALTIMORE BANK WILL ADVISE[2] MONEY ON THEM UNDER THOSE CONDITIONS STOP I HAVE BEEN IN BED TEN WEEKS WITH BROKEN SHOULDER AND CONSEQUENT ARTHRITIES INCAPACITATING ME FOR WORK UNTIL THIS WEEK AND AM HEAD OVER HEELS IN DEBT TO PUBLISHER AND INSURANCE COMPANY ANDSOFORTH WITH PERSONAL OBLIGATIONS EMBARRASSING TO STATE IN TELEGRAM STOP CANNOT EVEN PAY TYPISTS OR BUY MEDICINE STOP I NEED ONE THOUSAND IMMEDIATELY AND FIVE THOUSAND WITHIN THE WEEK STOP[3] CAN YOU CONSULT WITH ANNABEL MCQUILLAN[4] HOW I CAN RAISE THIS AS PERSONAL LOAN SECURED BY NOTE OF HAND OR LIEN DUE ON LIQUIDATION OF LEGACY AT ANY INTEREST AND WIRE ME TONIGHT IF POSSIBLE AT GROVEPARK INN ASHEVILLE AS TO WHAT MIGHT BE DONE STOP THIS IS ABSOLUTELY LAST RECOURSE

    SCOTT FITZGERALD.

[1] Beginning in the fall of 1936 Harold and Anne Ober acted as surrogate parents to Scottie Fitzgerald.
[2] ADVISE was crossed out and ADVANCE written in.
[3] Kalman arranged the loan.
[4] Fitzgerald's aunt.

TO: Maxwell Perkins   *Wire. Princeton University*

ASHEVILLE NCAR   1936 OCT 6   AM 2 23

EVEN THOUGH ADMINISTRATOR HAS BEEN APPOINTED BALTIMORE BANK WILL
NOT ADVANCE MONEY ON MY SECURITIES OF TWENTY THOUSAND I MARKET
VALUE AT THEIR ESTIMATE UNTIL SIX WEEKS BY WHICH TIME I WILL BE IN JAIL
STOP WHAT DO YOU DO WHEN YOU CANT PAY TYPIST OR BUY MEDICINES OR
CIGARETTS STOP ANY LOANS FROM SCRIBNERS CAN BE SECURED BY LIEN PAYABLE
ON LIQUIDATION CANT SOMETHING BE DONE I AM UP AND PRETTY STRONG BUT
THESE ARE IMPOSSIBLE WRITING CONDITIONS I NEED THREE HUNDRED DOLLARS
WIRED TO FIRST NATIONAL BALTIMORE AND TWO THOUSAND MORE THIS WEEK
WIRE ANSWER

F. SCOTT FITZGERALD.

TO: C. O. Kalman   *TLS, 2 pp. Princeton University*

Asheville, N.C.,
Grove Park Inn,
October 10, 1936.

Dear Kallie

Above and beyond the egotism that seems to descend upon a sick man,
like a dark cloud, I have been able to appreciate the kindness and friendliness
with which you have come to my assistance. I do not know very many rich
people well, in spite of the fact that my life has been cast among rich
people—certainly only two well enough to have called upon in this emergency, the first personal loan I have ever asked for—though I have made
heavy drains on my publishers and agents at times.

I was just about up to the breaking point financially when I came down
here to Asheville. I had been seriously sick for a year and just barely recovered and tried to set up a household in Baltimore which I was ill equipped
to sustain. I was planning to spend a fairly leisurely summer, keeping my
debt in abeyance on money I had borrowed on my life insurance, when I
went over with Zelda (who is in a sanitarium near here, better, but still a
mental patient, as perhaps she always will be) to a pool near here and tried
a high dive with muscles that had not been exercised, by the doctors' orders,
for two years; and split my shoulder and tore the arm from its moorings,
so that the ball of the ball-and-socket joint hung two and one-half inches
below the socket joint. It started to heal after two weeks and I fell on it
when it was soaked with sweat inside the plaster cast, and got a thing called
"Miotosis" which is a form of arthritis. To make a long story short, I was
on my back for ten weeks, with whole days in which I was out of bed
trying to write or dictate, and then a return to the impotency of the trouble.
The more I worried, the less I could write. Being one mile from Zelda, I

saw her twice all summer, and was unable to go North when my Mother had a stroke and died, and later was unable to go North to put my daughter in school. (She earned a scholarship to a very expensive school—Miss Walker's, do you know it? She is now in school and apparently very happy).

The nervous system is pretty well shot. You have probably guessed that I have been doing a good deal of drinking to keep up what morale has been necessary—think of it any way you want to; I know, thank God, you are no moralist. I know you have lent this money on the ask-me-no-question basis, but I feel I owe you this explanation.

For Heaven's sake, please try to expedite the loan. The first time in my life I have known what it is to be hog-tied by lack of money, as you know how casually I have always dealt with it.

I want to bring Scottie West at Easter and, seeing her, you will see how much I still have to live for, in spite of a year in a slough of despond.

Ever afftly yours,
Scott Fitzg—

TO: *Maxwell Perkins*   *TLS, 3 pp.—with holograph revisions*
                                         and postscript. Princeton University

Grove Park Inn
Asheville, N.C.
October 16, 1936

Dear Max:

As I wired you, an advance on my Mother's estate from a friend makes it unnecessary to impose on you further.

I do not like the idea of the biographical book. I have a novel planned, or rather I should say conceived, which fits much better into the circumstances, but neither by this inheritance nor in view of the general financial situation do I see clear to undertake it. It is a novel certainly as long as Tender Is The Night, and knowing my habit of endless corrections and revisions, you will understand that I figure it at two years. Except for a lucky break you see how difficult it would be for me to master the leisure of the two years to finish it. For a whole year I have been counting on such a break in the shape of either Hollywood buying Tender or else of Grisman getting Kirkland or someone else to do an efficient dramatization. (I know I would not like the job and I know that Davis[1] who had every reason to undertake it after the success of Gatsby simply turned thumbs down from his dramatist's instinct that the story was not constructed as dramatically as Gatsby and did not readily lend itself to dramatization.) So let us say that all accidental, good breaks can not be considered. I can not think up any practical way of undertaking this work. If you have any suggestions they

[1]Owen Davis.

will be welcomed, but there is no likelihood that my expenses will be reduced below $18,000 a year in the next two years, with Zelda's hospital bills, insurance payments to keep, etc. And there is no likelihood that after the comparative financial failure of Tender Is The Night that I should be advanced such a sum as $36,000. The present plan, as near as I have formulated it, seems to be to go on with this endless Post writing or else go to Hollywood again. Each time I have gone to Hollywood, in spite of the enormous salary, has really set me back financially and artistically. My feelings against the autobiographical book are:

First: that certain people have thought that those Esquire articles did me definite damage and certainly they would have to form part of the fabric of a book so projected. My feeling last winter that I could put together the articles I had written vanished in the light of your disapproval, and certainly when so many books have been made up out of miscellaneous material and exploited material, as it would be in my case, there is no considerable sale to be expected. If I were Negly Farson[1] and had been through the revolutions and panics of the last fifteen years it would be another story, or if I were prepared at this moment to "tell all" it would have a chance at success, but now it would seem to be a measure adopted in extremis, a sort of period to my whole career.

In relation to all this, I enjoyed reading General Grant's Last Stand,[2] and was conscious of your particular reasons for sending it to me. It is needless to compare the force of character between myself and General Grant, the number of words that he could write in a year, and the absolutely virgin field which he exploited with the experiences of a four-year life under the most dramatic of circumstances. What attitude on life I have been able to put into my books is dependent upon entirely different field of reference with the predominant themes based on problems of personal psychology. While you may sit down and write 3,000 words one day, it inevitably means that you write 500 words the next.

I certainly have this one more novel, but it may have to remain among the unwritten books of this world. Such stray ideas as sending my daughter to a public school, putting my wife in a public insane asylum, have been proposed to me by intimate friends, but it would break something in me that would shatter the very delicate pencil end of a point of view. I have got myself completely on the spot and what the next step is I don't know.

I am going to New York around Thanksgiving for a day or so and we might discuss ways and means. This general eclipse of ambition and determination and fortitude, all of the very qualities on which I have prided myself, is ridiculous, and, I must admit, somewhat obscene.

Anyhow, that you for your willingness to help me. Thank Charlie for

[1] American journalist known for his autobiographical adventure books.
[2] By Horace Green (Scribners, 1936).

me and tell him that the assignments he mentioned have only been waiting on a general straightening up of my affairs. My God, debt is an awful thing!

Yours,

F Scott Fitzgerald

Heard from Mrs Rawlins + will see her.

TO: *Scottie Fitzgerald*   *TLS, 2 pp. Princeton University*

Grove Park Inn
Asheville, N.C.
October 20, 1936

Dearest Scottina:

I had already decided to go up Thanksgiving which I will do, God willing, and so on your own suggestion I have killed the idea of going up on your birthday. You seem to understand the fact that I cannot afford at the moment to make two trips within the same month; so I know you won't be unduly disappointed.

To finish up news of me, the arm is really definitely out of danger and I am going to be able to use it again, which I doubted for three or four weeks. Went out to football game with the Flynns last Saturday, the same sort of game exactly that we went to last fall at very much the same time. Lefty was his usual handsome self and Nora was charming as always. They asked about you repeatedly, and not because they thought they ought to but because they have a real affection for you, and I mean both of them. They were so happy to know that you are getting along so well at your school.

Confirming my Christmas plans, they are, briefly: that we shall have a party for you in Baltimore at the Belvedere or the Stafford, if we can afford it! Then the actual Christmas day will be spent either here with your mother (it won't be like that awful Christmas in Switzerland), or else you and your mother and the trained nurse will go to Montgomery and spend Christmas with your grandmother; perhaps with a little time afterwards in Baltimore before you go back to school.

Don't be a bit discouraged about your story not being tops. At the same time, I am not going to encourage you about it, because, after all, if you want to get into the big time, you have to have your own fences to jump and learn from experience. Nobody ever became a writer just by wanting to be one. If you have anything to say, anything you feel nobody has ever said before, you have got to feel it so desperately that you will find some way to say it that nobody has ever found before, so that the thing you have to say and the way of saying it blend as one matter—as indissolubly as if they were conceived together.

Let me preach again for a moment: I mean that what you have felt and thought will by itself invent a new style, so that when people talk about

313

style they are always a little astonished at the newness of it, because they think that it is only <u>style</u> that they are talking about, when what they are talking about is the attempt to express a new idea with such force that it will have the originality of the thought. It is an awfully lonesome business, and as you know, I never wanted you to go into it, but if you are going into it at all I want you to go into it knowing the sort of things that took me years to learn.

Why are you whining about such matters as study hall, etc., when you deliberately picked this school as the place you wanted to go above all places? Of course it is hard. Nothing any good isn't hard, and you know you have never been brought up soft, or are you quitting on me suddenly? Darling, you know I love you, and I expect you to live up absolutely to what I laid out for you in the beginning.

Scott

TO: Scottie Fitzgerald   *TLS, 2 pp. Princeton University*

GROVE PARK INN
Asheville, N.C.

November 17, 1936

Dearest Pie:

I got a School Letter saying that Thanksgiving Day is best, and it is better for me that way. There is no particular advantage in going out two or three times rather than one, without particular objectives; the idea is to go out once and have a good time. I'll be delighted to meet whoever you want, and our engagement is on Thanksgiving Day.

(This is a parenthesis: I got the little charms that you sent me for my birthday: the bells dangling and the mule, and appreciated your thought of me—you little donkey!)

Park Avenue girls are hard, aren't they? Usually the daughters of "up-and-coming" men and, in a way, the inevitable offspring of that type. It's the "Yankee push" to its last degree, a sublimation of the sort of Jay Gould who began by peddling bad buttons to a county and ended, with the same system of peddler's morals, by peddling five dollar railroads to a nation.

Don't mistake me. I think of myself always as a Northerner—and I think of you the same way. Nevertheless, we are all of one nation and you will find all the lassitude and laziness there that you despise, enough to fill Savannah and Charleston, just as down here you will find the same "go getter" principle in the Carolinas.

I don't know whether you will stay there another year—it all depends on your marks and your work, and I can't give you the particular view of life that I have, (which as you know is a tragic one,) without dulling your enthusiasm. A whole lot of people have found life a whole lot of fun. I have not found it so. But, I had a hell of a lot of fun when I was in my twenties and thirties; and I feel that it is your duty to accept the sadness, the tragedy of the world we live, in with a certain <u>esprit</u>.

Now, insofar as your course is concerned, there is no question of your dropping mathematics and taking the easiest way to go into Vassar, and being one of the girls fitted for nothing except to reflect other people without having any particular character of your own. I want you to take mathematics up to the limit of what the school offers. I want you to take physics and I want you to take chemistry. I don't care about your English courses or your French courses at present. If you don't know two languages and the ways that men chose to express their thoughts in those languages by this time, then you don't sound like my daughter. You are an only child, but that doesn't give you any right to impose on that fact.

<u>I want you to know certain basic scientific principles</u>, and I feel that it is impossible to learn them unless you have gone as far into mathematics as coordinate geometry. <u>I don't want you to give up mathematics next year</u>. I learned about writing from doing something that I didn't have any taste for. If you don't carry your mathematics such as coordinate geometry (conic sections), you will have strayed far afield from what I had planned for you. I don't insist on the calculus, but it is certainly nothing to be decided by what is easiest. You are going into Vassar with mathematical credits and a certain side of your life there is going to be scientific.

Honey, I wish I could see you. It would be so much easier to go over these important matters without friction, but at a distance it seems rather tough that you are inclined to slide into the subjects that are easy for you, like modern languages.

No more until I see you Thanksgiving.

With dearest love,

F. Scott Fitz——

P.S. Sorry you are on bounds—feel as if I had been the same for six months. However I have bought an ancient Packard roadster and get out more now. I always allow for your exuberance but I hope this doesn't come from a feud with any special teacher, or from any indiscretion of speech, a fault you should be beginning to control.

TO: Maxwell Perkins   *Wire. Princeton University*

ASHEVILLE NCAR   1936 DEC 3   PM 7 44
CANT EVEN GET OUT OF HERE UNLESS YOU DEPOSIT THE REMAINING THOUSAND STOP IT IS ONLY FOR A COUPLE OF MONTHS STOP I HAVE COUNTED ON IT SO THAT I HAVE CHECKS OUT AGAINST IT ALREADY STOP PLEASE WIRE ME IF YOU

HAVE WIRED IT TO THE BALTIMORE BANK STOP THE DOCTORS THINK THAT THIS
SESSION OF COMPARATIVE PROSTRATION IS ABOUT OVER

SCOTT FITZGERALD.

TO: *Harold Ober*   *ALS, 2 pp. Lilly Library*
1937

Jan 2nd   Johns Hopkins Hospital
                                           Baltimore.
                                           <u>But</u> Stafford Hotel after
                                           tomorrow.

Dear Harold:
    I've owed you a letter a long time.
    1st as to money. I arranged another loan but I hope to God this new
story[1] (last version now at typists) will sell quick as I have enough for a
fortnight only + am at the end of borrowing on mother's little estate until
it's settled in April.
    2nd I can do no more with <u>Thumbs Up</u>. I think I told you that it's shifting
around was due to my poor judgement in founding it arbitrarily on two
unrelated events in father's family—the Thumbs Up and the Empresses
Escape. I dont think I ever put more work on a story with less return. Its
early diffuseness was due, of course, to my inability to measure the length
of dictated prose during the time my right arm was helpless—that's why it
strung out so long.
    I suggest this—send it to <u>Esquire</u>—I owe them $500. See if they'll accept
this in full payment—maybe something more. They paid me 200–250 for
a mere appearance (1000 to 2000 wds of any sort in any genre)—but at least
twice they've published Hemmingway long stories—one of 6000 + one
that must have been 9000 or over. At least it would clear up that debt + in
dire emergency I could get a couple of hundred there instead of having to
go to mechanics loan offices as has been the case this last terrible year.
3d <u>Scottie</u> I'd promised to give Scotty a little tea dance + arranged it should
cost $60. Every child in Baltimore came, it seemed to me + brought their
friends. Immediately afterwards she went to the country with her friend
Peaches—and I came to the hospital with 104° + raging flu to spend Xmas
to New Years.
    I'm all right now—(back on the absolute wagon by the way) + could
have gone out today except that it's sleety. My plan is have Scottie join me
at The Stafford tomorrow for a day or so—I've seen nothing of her + in
any case the Baltimore schools open Monday so her friends can't keep her

---

[1] "They Never Grow Older."

or rather they would but none of the adults are close enough to me so that she would feel quite at home there.

The alternative arises—either she comes south with me at extra expense of time + money for a week (My God why do they open these schools <u>the 11th</u>!) or she visits you or Max—I couldn't send her to what would for her be strangers just now unless it were urgent. But I know how Xmas leaves anyone, you + Anne included + be frank with me. Her aunt, Mrs Smith, is under the surgeons knife + that's out + I'm so out of touch with all other New York friends that I don't know who to ask. She has one standing invitation—but it is to a tuberculosis Chateau! (Gerald + Sara Murphy of whom you've heard me speak.

Anyhow I'll be at the Stafford all Monday anyhow finishing the last infinitismal details of mother's affairs. Let me know what. Then I've <u>got</u> to go see Zelda.

This last is general: I can live cheaper at a hotel I know in Tryon N.C. (Oak Hall), than at Grove Park (Ashville). As far as I can plan ahead it seems better to go to the former place for a few months. It is warmer and I am still in such wretched health that such a fact means a lot. The arm has healed right + I should be thankful. Perhaps I shall be pushing you along more hopeful indications before the first grass pushes up. Anyhow wire me (Stafford) about Scottie

F.S.F.

TO: Maxwell Perkins ALS, *2 pp. Princeton University*
Late February 1937 *Tryon, North Carolina*

Dear Max:

Thanks for your note and the appalling statement. Odd how enormous sums of $10,000 have come to seem lately—I can remember turning down that for the serialization of <u>The Great Gatsby</u>—from College Humor.

Well, my least productive + lowest general year since 1926 is over. In that year I did 1 short story + 2 chaps. of a novel—that is two chaps. that I afterwards used. And it was a terrible story. Last year, even though laid up 4 mos. I sold 4 stories + 8 Esq. pieces, a poor showing God knows. This year has started slowly also, some damn lack of interest, staleness, when I have every reason to want to work if only to keep from thinking. Havn't had a drink since I left the north (about six weeks, not even beer) but while I feel a little better nervously it doesn't bring back the old exuberance. I honestly think that all the prizefighters, actors, writers who live by their own personal performances ought to have managers in their best years. The ephemeral part of the talent seems, when it is in hiding so apart from one, so "otherwise," that it seems it ought to have some better custodian than the poor individual with whom it lodges and who is left with the bill. My chief achievement lately has been in cutting down my and Zelda's expenses to rock bottom; my chief failure is my inability to see a workable future. Hollywood for money has much against it, the stories are somehow mostly out of me unless some new $\left\{ \begin{array}{l} \text{scourse} \\ \text{source} \end{array} \right\}$ of material springs up, a novel takes money + time—I am thinking of putting aside certain hours and digging out a play, the ever-appealing mirage. At 40 one counts carefully one's remaining vitality and rescources and a play ought to be within both of them. The novel + the autobiography have got to wait till this load of debt is lifted.

So much, + too much, for my affairs. Write me of Ernest + Tom + who's new + does Ring still sell + John Fox + The House of Mirth. Or am I the only best seller who doesn't sell?

The account, I know, doesn't include my personal debt to you. How much is it please?

I don't know at all about Brookfield. Never have heard of it but there are so many schools there. Someone asked me about Oldfields where Mrs. Simpson went + Id never heard of that. Please write me—you are about the only friend who does not see fit to incorporate a moral lesson, especially since the <u>Crack Up</u> stuff. Actually I hear from people in Sing Sing + Joliet all comforting + advising me.

Ever Your Friend
Scott

TO: *Maxwell Perkins*   *ALS, 1 p. Princeton University*
c. March 19, 1937   *Tryon, North Carolina*

Dear Max:

Thanks for the book—I don't think it was very good but then I didn't go for Sheean[1] or Negley Farson either. Ernest ought to write a swell book now about Spain—real Richard Harding Davis reporting or better. (I mean not the sad jocosity of P.O.M.[2] passages or the mere callender of slaughter.) And speaking of Ernest, did I tell you that when I wrote asking him to cut me out of his story he answered, with ill grace, that he would—in fact he answered with such unpleasantness that it is hard to think he has any friendly feeling to me any more. Anyhow please remember that he agreed to do this if the story should come in with me still in it.

At the moment it appears that I may go to Hollywood for awhile, and I hope it works out. I was glad to get news of Tom Wolfe though I don't understand about his landlady. What?[3]

Ever yours
Scott

[1]Foreign correspondent Vincent Sheean.
[2]In *Green Hills of Africa* (Scribners, 1935), Hemingway referred to his wife Pauline as "Poor Old Mama" or "P.O.M."
[3]Wolfe's landlady had brought a libel suit against him.

Write me again—I hear no news. On the wagon since January + in good shape physically.

TO: *Harold Ober*   *ALS, 2 pp. Lilly Library*
Received March 23, 1937   *Tryon, North Carolina*

Going to country dog shows isn't my daily occupation—it was my single appearance of that kind. I wanted you to see how different I look from Xmas.[1]

Dear Harold:

Here, or herewith is the revision of <u>Thumbs Up</u>. Maybe it'll go. It's an odd story—one editor says cut the thumbs episode, another says cut everything else—I've done the latter and shortened it to about 5500 words (from 8000) <u>+</u> revised it thoroughly + written a new scene.

Thanks for the money—as time passes my position becomes more + more ludicrous, I mean generally. I just got a book (Books + Battles of the Twenties)[2] in which I am practically a leading character, my birthday is two column front page news as if I were 80 instead of 40—and I sit worrying about next weeks $35.00 hotel bill! I really mean it that I'd like to go to Hollywood + let them <u>see</u> me. I wish you could see me. Weight 160 instead of 143 which was it last Xmas. And the dullest dogs making 1000 a week in Hollywood. Something has got to be done—this will end in slow ruination. Anyhow I've begun the football story but God knows where the next two weeks rent come from. I will owe $105 by Thurs. + will need cash—all in all $150. I was going to Max as a last rescource but you have tapped that. What in hell shall I do? I want to write the football story unworried + uninterrupted. Since going on the wagon I will have written two originals, rewritten two stories (<u>Thumbs</u> + the cartoon story) and written 3 little Esquire pieces (two of them mediochre) to live on. That will be a hard two ½ mos work. But reward there is none.

In fatalistic optimism,

                                                                 Scott

Look at this Margaret Banning[3] next to me—covered with rings, lives in a mansion + owns it. Ah me—well, perhaps I've learned wisdom at forty at last. If I ever get out of this mess!

---

[1] Fitzgerald enclosed a newspaper photo of himself with other writers at a Tryon, North Carolina, dog show.

[2] By Irene and Allen Cleaton (1937).

[3] Popular novelist Margaret Culkin Banning.

To: Corey Ford[1]   ALS, 1 p. Princeton University

That always reminds me of you + your ———→   Oak Hall
Rover Boys—didn't you read Dave   Tryon, N.C.
Porter too?[2]   April 1937

Dear Corey:

I think you have read or heard that I've been in a somewhat bitter temper for a year, and that led you to say to yourself "It might cheer the poor bastard up to think he's not forgotten." Whatever was the impulse that made you write it <u>did</u> cheer me up and the idea that people have such thoughts + do something so concrete about it is the most cheering thought of all.

I had been sick as hell for a year and took an extra one to get over it morally for as a child of the bitch goddess I began trying to fight it with 2 quarts a day + got into an awful psychological jam. However I came back to life last January after the newspapers began cracking at me (it was rather a shock—nobody ever tried to interfere with Ring Lardner's utterly private life, but I had myself to blame with those indiscreet <u>Esquire</u> articles) and decided to be an example to myself. I now admire myself almost as much as Wm Seabrook, Mary McLane[3] and Casanova.

Maybe this has nothing to do with why you wrote me. Anyhow thank you more than I can say. Im sorry our meetings have been so brief—the last at Marice Hamilton's in February, 1931. My God, where have these six years gone—whole months go by and nothing seems to happen. Is that just middle-age? I'd like to do a lot of liesurely things now but there seems to be no time. Yours F. Scott Fitzgerald

TO: Harold Ober   ALS, 1 p. Lilly Library
Received April 6, 1937   Tryon, North Carolina

Dear Harold:

The Hollywood affair was a blow of course.[4] It might have meant everything. Of course one cannot do justice to purely imaginative work when in rotten health + extreme worry. But since the health is good + the worry would be alleviated by the pay check it would have been ideal. My biggest loss is confidence.

---

[1] American humorist.

[2] "Rover Boys," a series of books for boys by Edward Stratemeyer; David Dixon Porter, naval historian and novelist.

[3] William Seabrook wrote *Asylum* (1935), about his treatment for alcoholism; Mary MacLane was the author of *The Story of Mary MacLane* (1902). Both books were regarded as shocking when they were published.

[4] H. N. Swanson, Hollywood agent, had tried to get Fitzgerald a screenwriting assignment at MGM on a movie called *The Duke Steps Out*.

So I hope that you'll bend all your efforts for me apon bringing about a chance in Hollywood. Week by week Things get worse financially and of course this <u>can't</u> go on much longer if I have to go out there + sell myself for a few hundred a week. I am finishing the football story + will start another but it would be twice as possible to work well if I could see any way out of this morass. If Swanson can't sell me how about Leland Hayward—he used to be a great friend + admirer.

Perhaps tomorrow I wont feel as low as today but at the moment things look very black. You might send me the cartoon story to look over. I hope to God you sell <u>Thumbs</u>—wire me if you do.

Ever Yours
Scott Fitzg

TO: *Harold Ober*   *ALS, 2 pp. Lilly Library*
Received April 13, 1937   *Tryon, North Carolina*

Dear Harold:

With this you will recieve the story

  Athletic Interview[1]

and a plea for another $100.00. The situation is terrible. One check has just come back to the hotel. Threats of suits come in daily from all over hell—not big sums but enormous now. Some matters as buying razor blades + even cigarettes have grown serious. There ought to be a little left from mother's estate this month but I dont know when or whether itll be a hundred or a thousand, all the rest being mortgaged away.

I am revamping <u>The Vanished Girl</u>[2] for Esquire and can't get any money for it until it gets there which won't be before next Monday. The $100 is for the hotel bill—I had to give them another check and if it comes back I'll be in the street.

At least I have taken my time on this story as I should have started doing two years ago. My rate is never more than one a month—why I kept thinking I could do more with the added burden of illness and anxiety I don't know.

For God's sake wire me you have been able to do something.

Scott

---

[1] The story variously titled "Offside Play," "Athletic Interview," or "Athletic Interval" was not published.

[2] The revised story remained unpublished until it appeared under the title "A Full Life" in the *Princeton University Library Chronicle* (Winter 1988).

TO: *Harold Ober*   *Wire. Lilly Library*
May 2, 1937   *Tryon, North Carolina*

PLEASE TAKE ANY PRICE FOR INTERLUDE OVERDRAWN 150 AND WHOLE SITUATION
TENSE NO HELP FROM ESTATE FOR ANOTHER WEEK STORY ALMOST FINISHED BY
CONDITIONS OF WORK IMPOSSIBLE
     FITZGERALD

TO: *Mrs. Richard Taylor*   *ALS, 1 p. Princeton University*
Spring 1937

Dearest Ceci:
     Zelda is at
     Highland's Hospital
     Ashville, N.C.
She is much much better. So am I. I stopped drinking in January and
have been concentrating on other mischief, such as work, which is even
duller, or seems so to me at present. But Scottie must be educated + Zelda
can't starve. As for me I'd had enough of the whole wretched mess some
years ago + seen thru a sober eye find it more appalling than ever.
                     With Dearest Love Always
                             Scott

Oak Hall
     Tryon, N.C.

TO: *Harold Ober*   *Wire. Lilly Library*
May 11, 1937   *Tryon, North Carolina*

TO REMAIN HERE AND EAT MUST HAVE ONE HUNDRED AND THIRTY TODAY PLEASE
ASK PERKINS
     FITZGERALD

TO: *Harold Ober*   *ALS, 3 pp. Lilly Library*
Received May 13, 1937   *Tryon, North Carolina*

Dear Harold:
     Life had me going there for a little while. A check came back from the
bank + then another + then the 1st over again. Hadn't tipped servants for
6 wks, paid typist, druggist, old doctors bills ect—every mail a threat of
suite. All in all the short + simple annals of the poor. It has been entirely
a charity year—almost a year mind you <u>since I've sold a story</u>, tho I've

only written five + two may yet sell. In fact if these two dont I am immediately on a worse spot than before. I have a balance of six dollars after immediately putting forth what you sent.

All that can save me now is that there may be a few hundred in the estate which will be settled in two weeks. What I need is a substantial sum 1st to pay a percentage on bills, 2nd for a full months security + 3d to take Zelda for a 3 day trip to Myrtle Beach which I've been promising for two month + which the sanitarum want her to take. She hasn't been out of hospital for 3½ years + they feel that she's well enough for a trip.

These two stories seem to me in the old line. I feel the stuff coming back as my health improves. I told you that since stopping drinking I've gained from just over 140 to over 160. I sleep at last and tho my hair's grey I feel younger than for four years. I am surprisingly not depressed by all these bad breaks but I am exceedingly hampered—just sheerly finding it difficult to function. I tried to give up smoking from pure economy + did give up expensive medicines and treatments. Such matters as four abcessed teeth and a growth that ought to be removed honestly dont bother me—two years of fainting + spitting blood cured me physical worry, but the money difficulty if not solved soon will have more and more psycholigal influence on my work, undermining confidence and wrecking what's left of my market.

Why Littaur?[1] I don't think the Post have been unreasonable. They've turned down some good stories from Crazy Sunday and Phillipe to Intimate Strangers but most of what they saw wasn't good. I didn't like their cutting my price but I'd like to wait till they turned down a good story for no reason at all before deciding that Stout[2] just don't like me.

Well, I hope you'll have good news about a story by the time you get this.

Ever Yours Scott Fitz

It was a shame to sell the little story in this months Esq for $200, wasn't it. That's a sheer result of debt.

TO: C. O. Kalman   ALS, 2 pp. Princeton University
June 1937   Tryon, North Carolina

Dear Kaly:

Well, you certainly gave me a generous helping hand out of a nightmare and now that it is paid up—as far as such an 'obligation' can be paid—I want to tell you that I've been constantly thinking of what you did with gratitude and appreciation. What got me into the two years mess that

[1] Kenneth Littauer, fiction editor of Collier's magazine.
[2] Wesley Winans Stout succeeded George Horace Lorimer as editor of The Saturday Evening Post in 1937.

reached its lowest point in the fall of 1936 was the usual combination of circumstances. A predjudiced enemy might say it was all drink, a fond mama might say it was a run of ill-luck, a banker might say it was 'not providing' for the future in better days, a psychiatrist might say it was a nervous collapse—it was perhaps partly all these things—the effect was to fantastic prevent me from doing any work at the very age when presumably one is at the height of one's powers. My life looked like a hopeless mess there for awhile and the point was I didn't <u>want</u> it to be better. I had completely ceased to give a good Goddamn.

Luckily a few people had faith in me, or perhaps only kindliness—there was a doctor that was interested and some old friends who simply couldn't believe it was me. I hurt myself professionally no end but did no great damage to private relations—Scottie being away at school, Zelda in a sanitarium + myself in North Carolina where I saw no people at all. And for six months (I went on the complete wagon, not even beer, in January) I have been steadily coming back, first physically + finally financially, tho that's only just begun and I'm afraid I'll have to go to Hollywood before accumulating any surplus.

So much for me and I don't think it will ever happen again. I want to come to St Paul sometime this summer, probably on my way to or from the coast, + I want to be sure you're there, so write me if + when you + Sandy will be gone to Europe to fight with Gen. Franco for the rights of labor and the 20 hr. day. Scribners, 597 5th Ave is a permanent address for me, though in person I am usually in Carolina near Zelda. I took her out swimming yesterday + we talked of you. Again my deepest gratitude

With Affection Always

Scott Fitzg—

TO: Ernest Hemingway
Postmarked June 5, 1937

ALS, 1 p. John F. Kennedy Library
Pennsylvania Railroad stationery

It was fine to see you so well + full of life, Ernest. I hope you'll make your book fat—I know some of that <u>Esquire</u> work is too good to leave out.[1] All best wishes to your Spanish trip—I wish we could meet more often. I don't feel I know you at all.

Ever Yours

Scott

Going South always seems to me rather desolate + fatal and uneasy. This is no exception. Going North is a safe dull feeling.

[1]Fitzgerald had attended a meeting of the American Writers' Congress in New York City where Hemingway had denounced fascism. Following the meeting Fitzgerald had advised Hemingway to include stories with his forthcoming novel *To Have and Have Not* (Scribners, 1937).

HOLLYWOOD
1937–1940

———— ❖ ————

July 1937

FSF goes to Hollywood for third and last time with six-month MGM contract at $1,000 a week; lives at Garden of Allah, where he meets Sheilah Graham.

September 1937–January 1938

FSF works on *Three Comrades* script, his only screen credit.

December 1937

MGM contract is renewed for one year at $1,250 a week; works on unproduced scripts for "Infidelity," *Marie Antoinette*, *The Women*, and *Madame Curie*.

April 1938

FSF rents bungalow at Malibu Beach, California.

September 1938

Scottie enters Vassar.

October 1938

FSF moves to cottage on the Edward Everett Horton estate, "Belly Acres," at Encino in the San Fernando Valley.

December 1938

MGM contract is not renewed; money problems recur.

February 1939

> FSF travels to Dartmouth College with Budd Schulberg to work on *Winter Carnival*; fired for drunkenness.

March 1939–October 1940

> FSF has freelance assignments with Paramount, Universal, Fox, Goldwyn, and Columbia.

October 1939

> FSF begins work on *The Love of the Last Tycoon: A Western*.

January 1940

> Publication of the first Pat Hobby story, "Pat Hobby's Christmas Wish," in *Esquire*; the seventeen-story series runs in *Esquire* from January 1940 to May 1941.

April 15, 1940

> ZF leaves Highland Hospital to live with her mother at 322 Sayre Street in Montgomery.

May 1940

> FSF moves to 1403 North Laurel Avenue, Hollywood.

May–August 1940

> FSF works on "Cosmopolitan" ("Babylon Revisited") script.

December 21, 1940

> FSF dies of heart attack at Graham's apartment, 1443 North Hayworth Avenue, Hollywood.

December 27, 1940

> FSF is buried in the Rockville Union Cemetery, Rockville, Maryland. ZF is not able to attend.

October 27, 1941

> Publication of *The Last Tycoon*.

August 12, 1945

Publication of *The Crack-Up*.

Early 1946

ZF returns to Highland, as she does intermittently, from Montgomery.

March 10, 1948

ZF dies in fire at Highland, Asheville, North Carolina.

March 17, 1948

Zelda is buried with Scott in Rockville Union Cemetery, Rockville, Maryland.

TO: *Harold Ober*   *ALS, 1 p. Lilly Library*
Received July 6, 1937   *Battery Park Hotel stationery.*
                                     Asheville, North Carolina

The item * better not start for two or three weeks as I'll need a second hand car.
So for that time add it to my expense check.

Dear Harold:
Here's the way I'd like to divide my pay check for the moment.
Per week
       100   to you—commission
       150   "   "   on debt
        50   " Scribners on debt, as follows
               <u>1st</u> to paid against Perkins loan
               <u>2nd</u> to be paid against insurance assignment held by Charles
                   Scribner
               <u>3d</u> to be paid against their movie loan on <u>Tender</u>
*   200   4th to be paid against my retail bill there
            to be banked by you against taxes somewhere where I can get
            compound interest. Perhaps you make a suggestion where
       100   to be banked at 1st National Baltimore for "vacation money" for
            I will be taking six to 8 weeks off a year.
       400   to be put to my account out of which I pay expenses + $100
            insurance. For the present we will call this one the expense check
            + when I find a bank in California will deposit it there.
  $1000

(Do you like this arrangement? With those stories it should clear you and me within a year)—all percentages to go up after six months of course
                     Scott

TO: *Carl Van Vechten*[1]   *ALS, 3 pp. Yale University*
Postmarked July 5, 1937   *Argonaut/Southern Pacific stationery*

Dear Carl: Being on this train "getting away from it all" makes me think of you + your occasional postcards, even if the splended pictures hadn't done so.
    Zelda + Scottie (do you remember her squabbled for them + got the two best to remember me by while I am on this buccaneering expedition— the first since—I am wrong, the second since we were out there together.

---

[1] Novelist, music critic, photographer, and student of black culture; he and the Fitzgeralds had been friends during the 1920s.

But nothing will ever be like that 1st trip and I have formed my Californian cosmology from that.

It was kind and generous of you to send them—do you remember the inadequacy in the Fitzgerald household you repaired with a beautiful shaker.

I miss both your work + our meetings but I hope you are obtaining what measure of happiness is allowed in this world.

Ever Devotedly Yours
Scott

I will remember you not to anyone in particular but to what ghosts of our former selves I may encounter under Pacific Skies.

TO: Scottie Fitzgerald   *ALS, 3 pp. Princeton University*
July 1937   *Argonaut/Southern Pacific stationery*

1937 (on the way to Hollywood)

Dearest Pie:

This may be the last letter for a time, though I won't forget the check when I get at my check book.

I feel a certain excitement. The third Hollywood venture. Two failures behind me though one no fault of mine. The first one was just ten years ago. At that time I had been generally acknowledged for several years as the top American writer both seriously and, as far as prices went, popularly. I had been loafing for six months for the first time in my life and was confidant to the point of conciet. Hollywood made a big fuss over us and the ladies all looked very beautiful to a man of thirty. I honestly believed that <u>with no effort on my part</u> I was a sort of magician with words—an odd delusion on my part when I had worked so desperately hard to develop a hard, colorful prose style.

Total result—a great time + no work. I was to be paid only a small amount unless they made my picture—they didn't.

The second time I went was five years ago. Life had gotten in some hard socks and while all was serene on top, with your mother apparently recovered in Montgomery, I was jittery underneath and beginning to drink more than I ought to. Far from approaching it too confidently I was far too humble. I ran afoul of a bastard named de Sano, since a suicide, and let myself be gyped out of command. I wrote the picture + he changed as I wrote. I tried to get at Thalberg but was erroneously warned against it as "bad taste." Result—a bad script. I left with the money, for this was a contract for weekly payments, but disillusioned and disgusted, vowing never to go back, tho they said it wasn't my fault + asked me to stay. I wanted to get east when the contract expired to see how your mother was. This was later interpreted as "running out on them" + held against me.

(The train has left El Paso since I began this letter—hence the writing—Rocky Mountain writing.)

I want to profit by these two experiences—I must be very tactful but keep my hand on the wheel from the start—find out the key man among the bosses + the most malleable among the collaborators—then fight the rest tooth + nail until, in fact or in effect, I'm alone on the picture. That's the only way I can do my best work. Given a break I can make them double this contract in less than two years. You can help us all best by keeping out of trouble—it will make a great difference to your important years. Take care of yourself mentally (study when you're fresh), physically (don't pluck your eyebrows) morally (don't get where you have to lie) + I'll give you more scope than Peaches

Daddy

TO: *Harold Ober*　　　　　　　　　　　*ALS, 3 pp. Lilly Library*
Received July 8, 1937　　　　*Argonaut/Southern Pacific stationery*

Dear Harold: This is written on a rocky train—I hope its decipherable.

1st When you figure what I owe you you better figure interest too for the past four years at some percentage you think proper. When I made from 25–35 thousand a year with so little negotiation I didn't mind being a story in debt to you—in fact I was rather upset when the Reynolds office made me pay a double commission on the Gatsby movie—almost 20%, remember? But this big debt is entirely another matter from those days + represents a loss for you in years of smaller profit + more expense on my account. So figure something you consider fair.

2nd When the pay off begins I think that you should send me a witnessed note somewhat as follows—that you will accept from the insurance assignment only such a sum as I may be in debt to you on your books at the time of my demise. This protects my estate as I pay back the money—I will file it with my will.

Nothing more at present. I suppose Scottie will be with you. Let me know if she arrives on that 11.30 train Thursday morning. Best to Anne + all of you. Wire me if stories sell.

Ever Yours
Scott

TO: *Thomas Wolfe*   ALS, 1 p. Harvard University
Mid-July 1937

                                      Pure Impulse
                                      U.S.A.
                                      1937

Dear Tom: I think I could make out a good case for your nessessity to cultivate an alter ego, a more conscious artist in you. Hasn't it occurred to you that such qualities as pleasantness or grief, exuberance or cyniscism can become a plague in others? That often people who live at a high pitch often don't get their way emotionally at the important moment because it doesn't stand out in relief?

Now the more that the stronger man's inner tendencies are defined, the more he can be sure they will show, the more nessessity to rarify them, to use them sparingly. The novel of selected incidents has this to be said that the great writer like Flaubert has consciously left out the stuff that Bill or Joe, (in his case Zola) will come along and say presently. He will say only the things that he alone see. So Mme Bovary becomes eternal while Zola already rocks with age. Repression itself has a value, as with a poet who struggles for a nessessary ryme achieves accidently a new word association that would not have come by any mental or even flow-of-consciousness process. The Nightengale is full of that.

To a talent like mine of narrow scope there is not that problem. I must put everything in to have enough + even then I often havn't got enough.

That in brief is my case against you, if it can be called that when I admire you so much and think your talent is unmatchable in this or any other country

                    Ever your Friend
                                      Scott Fitzg

TO: *Ernest Hemingway*   Wire.[1] John F. Kennedy Library
July 13, 1937   Los Angeles

THE PICTURE WAS BEYOND PRAISE AND SO WAS YOUR ATTITUDE
    scott.

TO: *Edwin Knopf* [2]   CC, 2 pp. Princeton University
                                      Hollywood, California

[1] Shortly after Fitzgerald moved to Hollywood, Hemingway showed *The Spanish Earth* there to raise money for the Spanish Loyalists.
[2] MGM producer.

July 19, 1937

Dear Eddie:

A sight of me is Zelda's (my wife's) life line, as the doctor told me before I left. And I'm afraid the little flying trips would just be for emergencies.

I hate to ask for time off. I've always enjoyed being a hard worker, and you'll find that when I don't work through a Saturday afternoon, it's because there's not a thing to do. So just in case you blew off your head, (as David Belasco so tactfully put it), I'd like to put the six weeks a year, one week every two months, into the contract.

It will include everything such as the work left over from outside, as indicated below.

First here is a memo of things that might come up later.

Stories sold but not yet published

The Pearl and the Fur ⎫
Make Yourself at Home ⎬ —Pictorial Review[1]

Gods of the Darkness —Red Book

In the Holidays ⎫
Pub Room 32[2] ⎬ —Esquire
Oubliette[3] ⎭

New York (article)[4] —Cosmopolitan

Early Success Cavalcade

Unsold but in the Possession of my Agent in June, 1937

Financing Finnegan

Dentist's Appointment[5]

Offside Play[6]

   (All the above belongs to the past)

In Possession

One play (small part of last act to do.)[7]

To write sometime during the next two years

2 Sat. Eve Post Stories

   (I've never missed a year in the Post in seventeen years)[8]

1 Colliers Story (advance paid)[9]

3 Short Esquire pieces (advance paid)

So the total time I should ask for over two years would be twelve weeks to write these things while near my wife. It could be allotted as two weeks

---

[1]"The Pearl and the Fur" was not published; "Make Yourself at Home" appears to have been published as "Strange Sanctuary," Liberty (December 9, 1939).

[2]Published as "The Guest in Room Nineteen."

[3]Published as "The Long Way Out."

[4]"My Lost City" was first published in The Crack-Up.

[5]Published as "The End of Hate," Collier's (June 22, 1940).

[6]Unpublished.

[7]This play had the working title "Institutional Humanitarianism"; it was never published or produced.

[8]Fitzgerald did not appear in the Post after 1937.

[9]Collier's accepted "The End of Hate" for this advance.

apiece for the stories, a week apiece for the articles, three weeks for finishing Act III of the play. Though if convenient, I shall in practice, use the weeks singly.[1]

Sincerely,

FROM/TO: *F. Scott Fitzgerald*　　　　　　　　*Postcard (not mailed)*
Summer 1937?　　　　　　　　　　　　　　　*Princeton University*

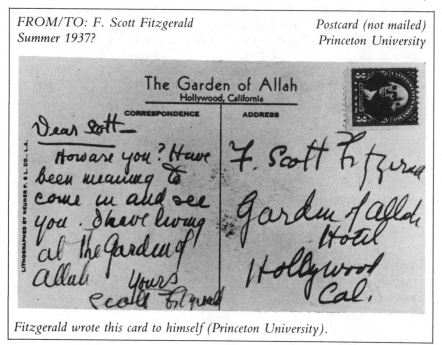

Fitzgerald wrote this card to himself (Princeton University).

TO: *Anne Ober*　　　　　　　　　　　　　*ALS, 2 pp. Bruccoli*
July 26, 1937　　　　　　　　　　　　　*Hollywood, California*

Dear Anne:

This letter is long overdue. Suffice to summarize: I have seen Hollywood[2]—talked with Taylor, dined with March, danced with Ginger Rogers (this will burn Scottie up but its true) been in Rosalind Russel's dressing room, wise-cracked with Montgomery, drunk (gingerale) with Zukor and Lasky, lunched alone with Maureen OSullivan, watched Crawford act and lost my heart to a beautiful half caste Chinese girl whos name I've forgotten. So far I've bought my own breakfasts.

And this is to say Im through. From now on I go nowhere and see no one because the work is hard as hell, at least for me and I've lost ten pounds.

---

[1] Fitzgerald's MGM contract stipulated that he had the right to work on his own writing during layoff periods.

[2] The Hollywood figures mentioned by their last names in this letter are actors Robert Taylor, Fredric March, and Robert Montgomery; studio executives Adolph Zukor and Jesse Lasky; and actresses Joan Crawford and Marlene Dietrich.

So farewell Miriam Hopkins who leans so close when she talks, so long Claudette Clobert as yet unencountered, mysterious Garbo, glamourous Dietrich, exotic Shirley Temple—you will never know me. Except Miriam who promised to call up but hasn't. There is nothing left, girls but to believe in reincarnation and carry on.

Tell my daughter she is a vile daughter of Babylon who does not write letters but can charge $25. worth of wash dresses at Franklin Simons but nowhere else. Or if she wants Harold will advance her $25 from a check sent today to go to Saks.

Im glad she is playing tennis. I do want to see the wretched little harpy and don't let her make a mess of it. Helen[1] will be in Nyack after the 29th— and is leaving the 2nd. No Long Island date should prevent Scottie from getting in touch with her and coming with her. All Metro could find for chaperones were the Ritz Brothers[2] and I can't see it. They might vanish her as a practical joke.

> Yours with Gratitude + De-
> votion
> Scott

TO: Maxwell Perkins   *TLS, 1 p.—with holograph postscript*
Princeton University.
MGM stationery. Culver City, California

Sept. 3, 1937.

Dear Max:

Thanks for your long, full letter. I will guard the secrets as my life.

I was thoroughly amused by your descriptions, but what transpires is that Ernest did exactly the same asinine thing that I knew he had in him to do when he was out here.[3] The fact that he lost his temper only for a minute does not minimize the fact that he picked the exact wrong minute to do it. His discretion must have been at low ebb or he would not have again trusted the reporters at the boat.

He is living at the present in a world so entirely his own that it is impossible to help him, even if I felt close to him at the moment, which I don't. I like him so much, though, that I wince when anything happens to him, and I feel rather personally ashamed that it has been possible for imbeciles to dig at him and hurt him. After all, you would think that a man who has arrived at the position of being practically his country's most imminent writer, could be spared that yelping.

---

[1] Scottie traveled to California with actress Helen Hayes.
[2] The Ritz Brothers were a comedy team.
[3] Hemingway had brawled with critic Max Eastman in Perkins's office.

All goes well—no writing at all except on pictures.

Ever your friend,
Scott

The Schulberg book[1] is in all the windows here.

TO: *Anne Ober*   *TLS, 1 p. Lilly Library*
MGM stationery. Culver City, California

September 18, 1937.

Dear Ann:

I am enclosing a letter from the Walker School. I hope the note about tutoring reached you.

I don't know whether Scottie is with you or with her Aunt Rosalyn. She hasn't bothered to write me. She really behaved herself beautifully out here and made a great hit with everyone, though I am quite sure she will be the school nuisance this term with her tales of the great and the near-great.

My holiday wasn't much of a holiday as you can imagine, but I think Zelda enjoyed it. Things had gone beautifully out here up to then, but this week it has been very hard to pick up the thread of work, and I see next week a horror trying to make up for five wasted days.

I have your letter and notice that you mentioned something else beside the smoking (I wrote you about that). I still don't believe that she should go out unchaperoned with a boy at night and have never allowed it. As for going alone somewhere after the theatre—my God! is that anywhere allowed at fifteen, or am I Rip Van Winkle? I once let her go with two boys to a dinner dance place here on condition that they would be home before midnight, but I think she understands that was an exception.

She was much too precocious in the things she did at fourteen, but after this year at Walkers, she seems much more appropriately her age, capable of amusing herself usefully and rationally without constant stimulation. I really think she's going to be all right now, though there was a time about a year and a half ago when I thought she was going to become an awful empty head. Thank God for boarding schools.

Something else I wanted to say has eluded me. I am your forever grateful and devoted henchman

Scott F.

TO: *Scottie Fitzgerald*   *TLS, 3 pp. Princeton University*
MGM stationery. Culver City, California

---

[1] *They Cried a Little* (Scribners, 1937), by Sonja Schulberg.

October 8, 1937

Darling Pie:

I'm awfully sorry about that telegram. I got a letter from Bill Warren,[1] saying that it was all around Baltimore that I was making twenty-five hundred a week out here, and it disturbed and upset me. I suppose it was one of Rita Swann's[2] ideas. I don't know why I suspected you—I should have known you would be more discrete and would at least name some believable figure. You see what a reputation you've made with your romantic tales!

As to the missing three days, I really don't blame you for that either. The trouble was that Harold Ober didn't know where you were either. If you had wired him instead of Aunt Rosalind, it would have been all right. However it gave me only one bad hour, as I really don't fret about you as much as I used to. I did worry about your smoking this Summer, but you gave me your word that you wouldn't smoke at Peaches' so that was all right; and I don't care much who you go out with so long as you are in at a decent hour and don't get the practice on your mind. From next Summer on, you can find you'll have more privileges, but I don't want them to become habits that will turn and devour you. You have got to devote the best and freshest part of your energies to things that will give you a happy and profitable life. There is no other time but now.

No special news—things have been quiet. Had the questionable honor meeting Walter Winchell, a shifty-eyed fellow surrounded by huge body-guards. Norma Shearer invited me to dinner three times but I couldn't go, unfortunately as I like her. Maybe she will ask me again. Also have seen something of Buff Cobb, Irving Cobb's daughter, who is an old friend; and Shielah who, by the way, has broken her engagement to the Marquess of Donnegal. (The poor man was about to get on a boat, but it was a sort of foolish marriage in many ways.) Also have been to much tennis and saw Helen Wills come back in company with Von Cramm to defeat Budge and his partner. Took Beatrice Lily,[3] Charley MacArthur and Shielah to the Tennis Club the other night, and Errol Flynn joined us—he seemed very nice though rather silly and fatuous. Don't see why Peaches is so fascinated. Frank Morgan[4] came over and talked to me, telling me that we had a fight in the cloak room at Gloria Swanson's seventeen years ago, but I had no recollection of the incident except that I had a scuffle with somebody. But in those days there so many scraps that this one doesn't stand out in my memory.

I hope you thought over my analysis as to how to deal with the neatness habit, and if for one week you put each thing away individually _from the_

[1] Charles Marquis Warren, Baltimore protégé of Fitzgerald.
[2] Baltimore friend.
[3] Lillie was a British comedienne.
[4] Character actor; Morgan later played the wizard in _The Wizard of Oz_.

moment of touching it to the moment of its final disposal—instead of putting away three things at a time—I think that you would lick it in a month and life would be easier for you in one more way. Please tell me about this when you write.

Looking over your letters and answering them in turn—it was nice of Peaches to give a party for you, and I'm glad Stanley is divine looking; sorry Andrew is repulsive. I'm glad that you went out with that great heart-throb, Bob-theBaker. Was Bob Haas nice? Your next letter comes from Exeter. Sorry you can't go to Annapolis—you'll be invited there again. Here I have a postcard and by God, I'm awfully sore at you about that tutoring. I don't understand how on earth the letter could have been mislaid. I posted it from the airport in Spartansburg that night. So you are still dwelling on the Fisher's Island party in retrospect!

Another letter tells of visiting Mary Earl on Long Island. It sounds fine, but you are right that romantic things really happen in roachy kitchens and back yards. Moonlight is vastly over-estimated. It was all right what you borrowed from Harold. He will put it on my account. So Merdith called from Baltimore! Aren't you afraid of stirring up those old embers? Your disloyalty to Princeton breaks my heart. I sent Andrew football tickets. Your dress sounds fine, Scottie my bonnie lass.

Lastly, the letter with the Yale postmark—I bet you bought that stationery. It reminds me of something that happened yesterday. On such paper but with the Princeton seal, I used to write endless letters throughout Sophomore and Junior years to Genevra King of Chicago and Westover, who later figured in THIS SIDE OF PARADISE. Then I didn't see her for twenty-one years, though I telephoned her in 1933 to entertain your mother at the World's Fair, which she did. Yesterday I get a wire that she is in Santa Barbara and will I come down there immediately. She was the first girl I ever loved and I have faithfully avoided seeing her up to this moment to keep that illusion perfect, because she ended up by throwing me over with the most supreme boredom and indifference. I don't know whether I should go or not. It would be very, very strange. These great beauties are often something else at thirty-eight, but Genevra had a great deal beside beauty.

I was hoping that they'd get up a "Higher French" course for you. Was nothing done about that? Miss Walker mentioned it in her letter. Your learning German seems to me rather pointless but don't construe this into any tendency to loaf on it. Knowing just a little bit would be a foundation—especially if we go abroad for a few weeks next Summer.

I sent the thirteen dollars to Rosalind.

What do you want for your birthday? You might make a suggestion.

I think of you a lot. I was very proud of you all summer and I do think that we had a good time together. Your life seemed gaited with much more moderation and I'm not sorry that you had rather a taste of misfortune during my long sickness, but now we can do more things together—when we can't find anybody better. There—that will take you down! I do adore you and will see you Christmas.

Your loving
Daddy

TO: Scottie Fitzgerald　　　　　　　　　*RTL, 2 pp. Princeton University*
　　　　　　　　　　　　　　　　　MGM stationery. Culver City, California

Nov. 4, 1937.

Dearest Pie:

I admit I'm a terrible correspondent but I hope it isn't the pot calling the kettle black—i.e. do you write your mother regularly once a week? As I assured you before, it is of the greatest importance, even if Bob-the-Butcher or Bill-the-Baker doesn't get the weekly hook in his gills.

News about the picture: The cast is tentatively settled. Joan Crawford had her teeth in the leed for a while but was convinced that it was a man's picture; and Loretta Young[1] not being available, the decision rests at present on Margaret Sullivan. Certainly she will be much better than Joan Crawford in the role. Tracy and Taylor will be reinforced by Franchot Tone at present writing,[2] and the cameras will presumably roll sometime in December. An old friend, Ted Paramore,[3] has joined me on the picture in fixing up much of the movie construction, at which I am still a semi-amateur, though I won't be that much longer.

Plans about Christmas depend on whether I will be held here for changes through the shooting. I don't think that's probable, and if it weren't my first picture that I'm anxious to get as perfect as can be, I wouldn't let it be possible, because I can always have a vacation on three weeks notice—but I want to mention it as a very faint chance. However, let us suppose I come East, as I will nine chances out of ten—I will expect to spend the time with you and your mother, perhaps a little in Baltimore, some in Ashville. Maybe I can take your mother to Montgomery, though that is very faint indeed and should not be mentioned to her. Also I want to spend a couple of days in New York and I have no doubt that you will want to be with me then.

Have you any plans of what you'd like to do? Would you like another party in Baltimore? I mean just an afternoon affair like the last? It might become a sort of an institution, a yearly round up of your Baltimore friends. Write me immediately what you thought you wanted to do—of course you also will go to see your mother sometime during the holidays.

---

[1] Actress who specialized in sympathetic roles.

[2] Robert Taylor, Margaret Sullavan, Franchot Tone, and Robert Young appeared in *Three Comrades*.

[3] Fitzgerald quarreled with E. E. Paramore about responsibility for the screenplay of *Three Comrades*.

By ill chance the Harvard game tickets for Andrew went astray and were sent me here. I'm sorry. He must have been disappointed—save that he missed the worst drubbing Princeton has had in many years.

My social life is in definite slow motion. I refused a good many parties and am now in the comfortable position of not being invited much any more. I had dinner at Gladys Swarthout's last week with John McCormick and some of the musical crowd.[1] I have taken in some football games with Sheilah Graham, and met the love of my youth, Genevra King (Mitchell), after an interval of twenty-one years. She is still a charming woman and I'm sorry I didn't see more of her.

How much do the ads cost for your year book? Please let me know.

I have a small apartment now at the Garden of Allah, but have done nothing about the house situation, as there seems no chance of your mother coming out here at the present.

I am anxiously awaiting your first report and will be more inclined to go Christmas if it give rest of the col [letter torn]

Congratulations on Cheerleader ect. Can you turn a cartwheel?

TO: Harold Ober   *ALS, 2 pp. Lilly Library*
Received December 14, 1937   *Garden of Allah stationery.*
                                                            Hollywood, California

Dear Harold:

Im glad too that they renewed the contract. Well, I've worked hard as hell—in a world where it seems to me the majority are loafers + incompetents.

If they'll let me work alone all the time, which I think they will when they have a little more confidence I think I can turn out four pictures a year by myself with months off included. Then I'll ask for some big money.

It is nervous work but I like it, save for the damn waiting + the time-killing conferences.

Im going to try to bring the Colliers story East at Xmas. I will come to N. Y. for at least a day + let you know my whereabouts in the meanwhile. Scottie has managed to work out some system for what looks like a good share of Baltimore dancing. Thanks for wanting her—She'll write you or I will to arrange a visit to you when its convenient of you to have her. I hope to have my scattered family together Xmas day somewhere More later

                                                                    Scott

[1]Swarthout was an opera soprano who appeared in movies; McCormack was a celebrated Irish tenor.

TO: *Anne Ober*   *ALS, 2 pp. Lilly Library*
c. Christmas 1937   *Hollywood, California*

Dear Anne:

Thanks for your note. Scottie will be north again before school opens. As she is obviously destined to be a perpetual guest I do try to split her visits with such easily-imposed-on yaps as the Finneys and Obers into reasonable bits lest the golden gooses cease to lay—wait a minute, this metaphor has gotten entirely out of hand. Any how all I can think of is for you and Harold to spend your old age with me—and even that wont square things.

These letters or cards for Scottie come to hand—better hold them. I have high hopes of getting East <u>before</u> she goes back to school—if not I'll go to her school in January. I love it here. It's nice work if you can get it and you can get it if you try about three years. The point is once you've got it— Screen Credit 1st, a Hit 2nd and the Academy Award 3d—you can count on it forever—like Laurence Stallings does—and know there's one place you'll be fed, without being asked to even wash the dishes. But till we get those three accolades we Hollywood boys keep trying.

That's cynical but I'm not a bit cynical. I'm delighed with screen credit and really hopeful of a hit—the line up is good, depending on whether or not one of our principals has to have an operation. I hope none of you need even an extraction

Ever Affectionately
Scott Fitzg—

P.S. I recognized the dogs individually in your Christmas card. I'm going to have my suite photographed with the mice in the hall for next Xmas. (Im getting old and un-fertile so will put this crack in my note-book)

TO: *Scottie Fitzgerald*   *AL, 1 p. Princeton University*
1938?   *Hollywood, California*

Instruction   .

Read carefully Keat's Ode to a Nightingale

In this poem is a phrase which will immediately remind you of my work.[1]

---

[1]"Already with thee! tender is the night,
    And haply the Queen-Moon is on her throne,
        Cluster'd around by all her starry Fays;
            But here there is no light,
    Save what from heaven is with the breezes blown
        Through verdurous glooms and winding mossy ways."

First find this. In the <u>same</u> stanza is another phrase which I rather guiltily adapted to prose in the 2nd paragraph on p. 115 of <u>The Great Gatsby</u>.[1]

The question

When you have found what I refer to have you learned anything about the power of the verb in description?

TO: *Joseph Mankiewicz*[2]   *CC, 3 pp. Princeton University*
New York City

January 17, 1938.

Dear Joe:

I read the third batch (to page 51) with mixed feelings. Competent it certainly is, and in many ways tighter knit than before. But my own type of writing doesn't survive being written over so thoroughly and there are certain pages out of which the rhythm has vanished. I know you don't believe the Hollywood theory that the actors will somehow "play it into shape," but I think that sometimes you've changed without improving.

<u>P. 32</u>   The shortening is good.

<u>P. 33</u>   "Tough but sentimental." Isn't it rather elementary to have one character describe another? No audience heeds it unless it's a false plant.

<u>P. 33</u>   Pat's line "I would etc.," isn't good. The thing isn't supposed to provoke a sneer at Alons. The pleasant amusement of the other is much more to our purpose. In the other she was natural and quick. Here she's a kidder from Park Avenue. And Erich's "We're in for it etc.," carries the joke to its death. I think those two lines about it in midpage should be cut. Also the repeat on next page.

<u>P. 36</u>   Original form of "threw it away like an old shoe" has humor and a reaction from Pat. Why lose it? For the rest I like your cuts here.

<u>P. 37</u>   The war remark from Pat is as a chestnut to those who were in it—and meaningless to the younger people. In 8 years in Europe I found few people who talked that way. The war became rather like a dream and Pat's speech is a false note.

<u>P. 39</u>   I thought she was worried about Breur—not her T.B. If so, this paragraph (the 2nd) is now misplaced.

<u>P. 41</u>   I liked Pat's lie about being feverish. People never blame women for social lies. It makes her more attractive taking the trouble to let him down gently.

<u>P. 42</u>   Again Pat's speech beginning "—if all I had" etc., isn't as good

---

[1]"He lit Daisy's cigarette from a trembling match, and sat down with her on a couch far across the room, where there was no light save what the gleaming floor bounced in from the hall."

[2]MGM producer.

as the original. People don't begin all sentences with <u>and, but, for</u> and <u>if</u>, do they? They simply break a thought in mid-paragraph, and in both <u>Gatsby</u> and <u>Farewell to Arms</u> the dialogue tends that way. Sticking in conjunctions makes a <u>monotonous</u> smoothness.

The next scene is all much much better but—

P. 46   Erich's speech too long at beginning. Erich's line about the bad smell spoils <u>her</u> line about spring smell.

P. 48   "Munchausen" is trite. Erich's speech—this repetition from first scene is distinctly self-pity.

I wired you about the flower scene. I remember when I wrote it, thinking whether it was a double love climax, and deciding it wasn't. The best test is that on the first couple of readings of my script <u>you didn't think so either</u>. It may not be George Pierce Baker[1] but it's right <u>instinctively</u> and I'm all for restoring it. I honestly don't mind when a scene of mine is cut but I think this one is terribly missed.

P. 49   Word "gunman" too American. Also "tried to strong-arm Riebling" would be a less obvious plant.

P. 51   Koster's tag not right. Suppose they both say, with different meanings, "You see?"

What I haven't mentioned, I think is distinctly improved.

New York is lousy this time of year.

Best always,

TO: *Joseph Mankiewicz*   *CC, 4 pp. Princeton University*
                       MGM stationery. Culver City, California

January 20, 1938

Dear Joe:

Well, I read the last part and I feel like a good many writers must have felt in the past. I gave you a drawing and you simply took a box of chalk and touched it up. Pat has now become a sentimental girl from Brooklyn, and I guess all these years I've been kidding myself about being a good writer.

Most of the movement is gone—action that was unexpected and diverting is slowed down to a key that will disturb nobody—and now they can focus directly on Pat's death, squirming slightly as they wait for the other picture on the programme.

To say I'm disillusioned is putting it mildly. For nineteen years, with two years out for sickness, I've written best-selling entertainment, and my dialogue is supposedly right up at the top. But I learn from the script that you've suddenly decided that it isn't good dialogue and you can take a few hours off and do much better.

[1]Professor of playwriting, Harvard and Yale.

I think you now have a flop on your hands—as thoroughly naive as "The Bride Wore Red" but utterly inexcusable because this time you <u>had</u> something and you have arbitrarily and carelessly torn it to pieces. To take out the manicurist and the balcony scene and then have space to put in that utter drool out of <u>True Romances</u> which Pat gets off on page 116 makes me think we don't talk the same language. God and "cool lip"'s, whatever they are, and lightning and elephantine play on words. The audience's feeling will be "Oh, go on and die." If Ted had written that scene you'd laugh it out of the window.

You are simply tired of the best scenes because you've read them too much and, having dropped the pilot, you're having the aforesaid pleasure of a child with a box of chalk. You are <u>or have</u> been a good writer, but this is a job you will be ashamed of before it's over. The little fluttering life of what's left of my lines and situations won't save the picture.

Example number 3000 is taking out the piano scene between Pat and Koster and substituting garage hammering. Pat the girl who hangs around the garage! And the re-casting of lines—I feel <u>somewhat outraged</u>.

Lenz and Bobby's scene on page 62 isn't even in the same category with my scene. It's dull and solemn, and Koster on page 44 is as uninteresting a plodder as I've avoided in a long life.

What does scene 116 mean? I can just hear the boys relaxing from tension and giving a cheer.

And Pat on page 72—"books and music—she's going to teach him." My God, Joe, you must see what you've done. This isn't Pat—it's a graduate of Pomona College or one of more bespectacled ladies in Mrs. Farrow's department. Books and music! Think, man! Pat is a lady—a cultured European—a charming woman. And Bobby playing soldier. And Pat's really <u>re</u>-fined talk about the flower garden. They do everything but play ring-around-a-rosie on their Staten Island honeymoon. Recognizable characters they simply are not, and cutting the worst lines here and there isn't going to restore what you've destroyed. It's all so inconsistent. I thought we'd decided long ago what we wanted Pat to be!

On page 74 we meet Mr. Sheriff again, and they say just the cutest merriest things and keep each other in gales of girlish laughter.

On page 93 God begins to come into the script with a vengeance, <u>but to say in detail what I think of these lines would take a book</u>. The last pages that everyone liked begin to creak from 116 on, and when I finished there were tears in my eyes, but not for Pat—for Margaret Sullavan.

My only hope is that you will <u>have a moment of clear thinking. That you'll ask some intelligent and disinterested</u> person to look at the two scripts. Some honest thinking would be much more valuable to the enterprise right now than an effort to convince people you've improved it. I am utterly miserable at seeing months of work and thought negated in one hasty week. I hope you're big enough to take this letter as it's meant—a desperate plea to restore the dialogue to its former quality—to put back the flower cart, the piano-moving, the balcony, the manicure girl—all those touches that were both natural and new. Oh, Joe, can't producers ever be wrong? I'm a good writer—honest. I thought you were going to play fair. Joan Crawford might as well play the part now, for the thing is as groggy with sentimentality as "The Bride Wore Red", but the true emotion is gone.[1]

TO: *Scottie Fitzgerald*   *Retyped copy, 1 p. Princeton University*
                                                    Hollywood, California

February 1938

Dearest Scottina;

So much has happened out here—and in the East, that a letter cant tell it.

Beginning at the end—Three Comrades went into production today and I started on the new Joan Crawford picture—as yet unnamed. I am half sick with work, overwhelmed with it and yet vaguely happier than I've been in months. The last part of a job is alwayss sad and very difficult but I'm proud of the year's output and havent much to complain of.

Your mother was better than ever I expected and our trip would have been fun except that I was tired. We went to Miami and Palm Beach, flew to Montgomery, all of which sounds very gay and glamorous but wasnt particularly. I flew back to New York intending to take you out with your friends Saturday but I discovered you were on bounds. My zero hour was Monday morning in California so there was nothing to do except fly back on Sunday afternoon. I didnt think you and I could cover much ground with the horses flying around the tan bark and steaming in Rosa Bonheur's steel engravibg on the wall.[2]

One time in Sophomore year at Princeton, Dean Wist got up and rolled out the great lines of Horace:

> "Integer Vitac, scelerisque pueris
> Non eget mauris, faculelnec arcu—"

—And I knew in my heart that I had missed something by being a poor latin scholar, like a blessed evening with a lovely girl. It was a great human experience I had rejected through laziness, through having sown no painful seed.

But when anything, latin or pig latin, was ever put up to me so immediately as your chance of entering Vassar next fall I could always rise to meet that. It is either Vassar or else the University of California here under my eye and the choice is so plain that I have no sympathy for your loafing. We

---

[1]Fitzgerald's original screenplay for *Three Comrades* was published by Southern Illinois University Press in 1978.

[2]Bonheur was a French painter known particularly for her animal pictures; Fitzgerald is describing the Ether Walker reception room.

are not even out of debt yet, you are still scholarship student and you might give them a break by making a graceful exit. They practically took you on your passport picture.

Baby, you're going on blind faith, as vain as Kitsy's beleif that she wouldnt grow a whisker,[1] when you assume that a small gift for people will get you through the world. It all begins with keeping faith with something that grows and changes as you go on. You have got to make all the right changes at the main corners—the price for losing your way once is years of unhappiness. You have not yet entirely missed a turning but failing to get somewhere with the latin will be just that. If you break faith with me I cannot feel the same towards you.

The Murphys, Nora, etc. asked after you. We will without fail go somewhere at Easter—your mother's going to make a stay in Montgomery with a companion and she'll meet us. Some New York gallery has taken some very expensive pictures of you—do you want any. I like them but my God they cost.

With Dearest Love always,
Daddy

TO: Harold Ober

TLS, 2 pp. Lilly Library
MGM stationery. Culver City,
California

February 9, 1938

Dear Harold:

I went on salary on the day I arrived, which was Monday, January 31st. The $200.00 is for the half week from Monday to Wednesday. The $400.00 is for the new week which will end today, February 9th. Beginning next week, I will be sending you $600.00 to bank $200.00 against taxes as we agreed.

I have two letters from you regarding Scottie and her expenses. I will take care of Scottie's expenses next week, or you can charge them against my general account.

It is all right about the dramatization of TENDER IS THE NIGHT, though I am returning the manuscript with some suggested changes. It seemed to me excellent. I am amazed at how much of the novel they got into it. My only fear is that there is perhaps a little too much of the novel in it, so that some of the dialogue has a Shavian voluminousness.[2]

I am writing Ann at length. Of course, every item of expense which she incurred in going to Hartford must go on my account. I must contribute at least that to the party which Scottie described as "perfectly wonderful".

---

[1] Presumably a reference to a children's story.
[2] The dramatization by Cora Jarrett and Kate Oglebay was not produced.

Sidney Skolsky, a columnist, says this week that: "The screen play of THREE COMRADES was written by F. Scott Fitzgerald and E. E. Paramore Jr., and there was grapevine news that it was one of the best scripts ever turned in at Metro." But though one is being given many compliments, the truth of the matter is that the heart is out of the script and it will not be a great picture, unless I am very much mistaken. Tracy has to go to the hospital and Franchot Tone plays his part, which is the final blow. I have been watching the taking of the mob scenes which ought to be excellent if they were about anything, now that the German Consul has had its say.

I am in the midst of one of those maddening weeks here where I am waiting to see Mr. Stromberg.[1] It seems odd to be paid for telephoning twice a day to see if I can get an appointment, but everyone says that I am lucky to be with him because when he works he goes directly to the point and is the best producer on the lot, if not in Hollywood.

I will be on the new Joan Crawford picture[2] and it looks at the moment as if I will have to write an original even though it will be founded on some play or story. There is no full length play or novel available that seems really suited for her, as she is the most difficult star to cast. Anyhow, that will be my assignment up to Easter, I think, and probably for some time afterwards.

I have a lot more to write you, but this will do for the present.

We had a terrible trip back, and the plane flew all over the South before it could buck through the winds up to Memphis, then it flew back and forth for three hours between Memphis and Nashville, trying to land. Then we got a tail-wind behind us and blew into Los Angeles only four hours late Monday morning.

I have not forgotten any of our conversations and shall try to follow your suggestions about money, work, etc.

Yours,
Scott

TO: Scottie Fitzgerald   *TLS, 1 p. Princeton University*
                                      MGM stationery. Culver City,
                                      California

Feb. 22, 1938.

Dearest Pie:

I never hear from you any more. Please drop me a line and tell me if all goes well.

I started my new picture which is after all a piece called INFIDELITY and will star Joan Crawford and I don't know who else. I will finish the first draft Easter and will come East to take you somewhere.

[1] Hunt Stromberg, MGM producer.
[2] "Infidelity"; the unproduced screenplay was published in *Esquire* (December 1973).

THREE COMRADES is halfway through. I have seen some of the shooting and some of the "rushes" (where they run off what they've shot that day), but you can't tell much from either. To my mind, the producer seriously hurt the script in rewriting it. It may be I am wrong.

People ask after you, but I am the most curious of all. May I be permitted to ask after you? I'd like a line about your health, your work, your morale, success or failure of the play and such affairs. If you will let me know when the play is, I will send you a message of congratulation or flowery tokens if you prefer.

I think of you always, darling, and will try to invent something very nice for Easter.

Just heard from Mrs. Turnbull who said you had three especial qualities—loyalty and ambition were two, the third I'll tell you later. She felt that would protect you from harm. I make no comment. She seemed very fond of you.

Also the Finneys have sent me the work of a musician to do something about, and I am taking the matter in hand.

With dearest love,

Daddy

TO: *Hunt Stromberg*   *CC, 2 pp. MGM stationery.*
Culver City, California

Feb. 22, 1938

Dear Mr. Stromberg:

Working out this somewhat unusual structure was harder than I thought, but it's at last on a solid basis. I began the actual writing yesterday.[1]

The first problem was whether, with a story which is over half told before we get up to the point at which we began, we had a solid dramatic form—in other words whether it would divide naturally into three increasingly interesting "acts" etc. The answer is yes—even though the audience knows from the mysterious indifference that the characters are headed toward trouble. They know before we go into the retrospect that the two characters are not finished or "accomplished," they know that the husband's love still lives and all is not lost. Even without the prologue the audience would know that the wife is going to find the guilty pair and their interest is in the way and how.

The second problem was that during the secretary-husband affair, which will require about twenty-five pages to do justice to, Joan is almost completely "off scene" and the audience's interest is in the other girl. I've turned the handicap into an asset by the following change:

At the point when the husband is being involuntarily drawn toward the

[1] "Infidelity."

old secretary, we dissolve to the wife in Europe with her mother. Her old sweetheart comes into the picture for the first time—in this episode she is not even faintly tempted—only disturbed—but disturbed enough so that she books a quicker passage to America. At this point we dissolve back to the secretary and the husband.

This point, her decision to sail, also marks the end of the "first act." The "second act" will take us through the seduction, the discovery, the two year time lapse and the return of the old sweetheart—will take us, in fact, up to the moment when Joan having weathered all this, is unpredictably jolted off her balance by a stranger. This is our high point—when matters seem utterly insoluble.

Our third act is Joan's recoil from a situation that is menacing, both materially and morally, and her reaction toward reconciliation with her husband.

So much for the story. Now, will the following schedule be agreeable to you? The script will be aimed at 130 pages. I will hand you the first "act"— about fifty pages—on March 11th, or two weeks from Friday. I will complete my first draft of the script on or about April 11th, totalling almost seven weeks. That is less time than I took on THREE COMRADES, and the fact that I understand the medium a little better now is offset by the fact that this is really an original with no great scenes to get out of a book. Will you let me know if this seems reasonable? My plan is to work about half the time at the studio but the more tense and difficult stuff I do better at home away from interruptions. Naturally I'll always be within call and at your disposal.

With best wishes,

TO: Dr. Robert S. Carroll[1] *CC, 2 pp. Princeton University*

Garden of Allah
8152 Sunset Boulevard
Hollywood, California
March 4th, 1938

Dear Dr. Carroll:

I have not heard from you as to when you think Zelda can make her tentative sortie into the world—though I gathered from our conversation in Greenville that you thought it would be about the end of March.

I am trying to arrange a week off here, so that I can see my daughter for the first time since September. (I got a glimpse of her at her school but, as you remember, they held me over here Christmas and New Year's.) The best time for me would be somewhere between March 23rd and 30th, and that would fit my daughter's vacation.

---

[1] Psychiatrist at Highland Hospital, Asheville, North Carolina.

If you have found a companion, Zelda could meet us somewhere, perhaps in Virginia. Otherwise, my daughter and I could come to Tryon, though there seem to be no children there my daughter's age, and we seem to have rather exhausted the place's possibilities.

My slip off the wagon lasted only three days. It was the reaction from a whole lot of things that preceded it and is not likely to recur because I have taken steps practically and mentally to prevent the set-up that caused it: the physical exhaustion and the emotional strain.

I have, of course, my eternal hope that a miracle will happen to Zelda, that in this new incarnation events may tend to stabilize her even more than you hope. With my shadow removed, perhaps she will find something in life to care for more than just formerly. Certainly the outworn pretense that we can ever come together again is better for being shed. There is simply too much of the past between us. When that mist falls—at a dinner table, or between two pillows—no knight errant can transverse its immense distance. The mainsprings are gone.

And if the aforesaid miracle should take place, I might again try to find a life of my own, as opposed to this casual existence of many rooms and many doors that are not mine. So long as she is helpless, I'd never leave her or ever let her have a sense that she was deserted.

Next week, I will begin clearing up the balance of what I owe you. The $500 a month[1] that we settled on for Zelda had best be sent her in weekly payments, through my agent—that is, sent to her companion, because Zelda has no idea whatsoever of money. I expect in another year to be completely out of debt and will make a more liberal allowance, though, of course, at your discretion, as you said you wanted her to live rather in the class of poor scholars than to return to the haunts of the rich.

Since seeing you, I have run into two of the most beautiful belles of my time—utterly ridden and ruined by drugs. I know scarcely a beautiful woman of Zelda's generation who has come up to 1938 unscathed.

For myself, I work hard and take care of myself. I had a scare a few months ago when, for a long stretch, tuberculosis showed signs of coming back—just portents—weakness, loss of appetite, sweating. I took an X-ray, lay very low for a few weeks, and the feeling passed.

I don't think I could keep up this work for more than two years at a stretch. It has a way of being very exhausting, especially when they put on the pressure. So what income I achieve here is not to be considered as an average. Zelda understands this and that my true career is as a novelist and she knows that at that time the squirrel must live on what nuts he has accumulated.

I wish you would let me know as soon as possible your time plans for Zelda. As I wrote Dr. Suitt,[2] I don't think she should go home to Montgom-

---

[1] This figure covered hospital expenses and Zelda's allowance.
[2] R. Burke Suitt, psychiatrist at Highland Hospital.

ery until she has had a definite period of adjustment to the companion because they might "gang up" against the companion. Mrs. Sayre, when it comes to Zelda, is an entirely irrational and conscienceless woman with the best intentions in the world.

Likewise, all I have told you should be spoken of vaguely in front of any of Zelda's family. If it ever comes to a point when a divorce should be in the picture, I think I would rather have you watch over Zelda's interests. As I told you in Greenville, you've been more than a father to her—doing a much more difficult job than Dr. Forel had in bringing her to this level of stability. Everything that you recommended for her has proved correct, and don't think I don't understand your theory of the danger to her of any toxic condition. I gave her a few cigarettes and a few glasses of sherry in the spirit of a wickedly indulgent grandfather, merely to turn her gratitude toward me for a few hours—and realized it should never be the regular thing for her.

Yours always, with deepest gratitude,

TO: *Anne Ober*   *TLS, 3 pp. Lilly Library*

8152 Sunset Boulevard
Hollywood, California
March 4th, 1938

Dear Anne:

I have just had a letter from "our" daughter, which I know I should laugh off as being merely the product of a mood. Even at that, I don't think she ought to have chosen her very gloomiest hour to write me. In it, there is not one word of cheer, hope or even a decent yielding to circumstances. One would suppose it to have emanated from some thoroughly brutalized child in an orphan asylum, who would shortly graduate from a woman's reformatory to her life's sentence in the prison of this world.

Among other points, I note that she is switching her allegiance from Vassar to Bryn Mawr. Now this might seem a slight thing, a mere vagary, but to a shrewd old diplomat like myself it has a different meaning. Bryn Mawr is an hour and a half by the clock from Baltimore, and Scotty has pictured college as a series of delightful weekends with the subdebutantes, in which she would find time of a Monday morning to slip back to Bryn Mawr to boast of her exploits. The distance of Vassar from Baltimore is a fair six hours. Moreover, in my opinion, it is safely insulated from the soft mellow breezes of the Southland and the scholars are actuated by the stern New England air—even though Poughkeepsie is just across the border.

So I wrote her that knowing her predilection for Baltimore, I was entering her—in case she failed to get into Vassar—in St. Timothy's School, so that she can be near her sacred city. St. Timothy's School happens to be a convent-like place, where the girls have to walk in twos on their Sunday outing, and patronized entirely by New Yorkers; and I'm afraid all she would ever see of Baltimore would be a few lights on the horizon at night.

The point is I am giving her her freedom proportionately as she will earn it by a serious attitude towards work. If she is going to college at sixteen, just as I went to college at sixteen, she could no more be kept in bib and tucker than I could have been kept from having a beer with my eighteen-year-old classmates. She will have earned her right to more freedom, with me praying that her judgment will keep pace with her precocity and keep her out of trouble. If, on the contrary, she is going to try to combine being a belle with getting an education, she had better stay under protection for another year. The idea is so simple that I should think she'd get it. But such phrases as "absurdly irrational" appear in her letters, applying to my attitude.

So I have become the heavy father again and lash into her. Her latest plaint is how can I expect her to get 80 in Latin when last term, doing some work, she got only 50. In other words, she has taken 50, her low mark, as a standard, instead of a passing point of 60.

I am taking off a week around the end of this month to try to establish communication with her again and see whether I have unknowingly begotten a monster of egotism, who writes me these letters.

She raved about the party. I had no idea that it was anything as elaborate as that. I thought merely it was a question of two or three girls and I would have gone utterly unprepared. But I suppose she was so indebted that she felt she had to entertain half the school to get square again. You were wonderful to her to do all that—much better than I ever could have done.

We will have to make a mass pilgrimage to her graduation this June. I am hoping her mother can come, too, and we will watch all the other little girls get diamond bracelets and Cord roadsters. I am going to a costumer's in New York and buy Scotty some phoney jewelry so she can pretend they are graduation presents. Otherwise, she will have to suffer the shame of being a poor girl in a rich girl's school. That was always my experience—a poor boy in a rich town; a poor boy in a rich boy's school; a poor boy in a rich man's club at Princeton. So I guess she can stand it. However, I have never been able to forgive the rich for being rich, and it has colored my entire life and works.

"Three Comrades" opens without Spencer Tracy, but with Margaret Sullavan doing a wonderful job. Shooting will be finished in twenty days, and the thing will be the most colossal disappointment of Metro's year. The producer wrote it over. The censors hacked at it. Finally, the German Government took a shot. So what we have left has very little to do with the script on which people still congratulate me. However, I get a screen credit out of it, good or bad, and you can always blame a failure on somebody else. This is simply to advise you stay away.

A good deal of the glow of Hollywood has worn off for me during the struggles with the first picture, but I would as soon be here as anywhere else. After forty, one's surroundings don't seem to matter as much.

Best to all of you.

> With devotion and gratitude,
> always,
> Scott

My God, What a garralous letter!

TO: *Maxwell Perkins*   *TLS, 2 pp. Princeton University*

> Garden of Allah
> 8152 Sunset Boulevard
> Hollywood, California
> March 4th, 1938

Dear Max:

Sorry I saw you for such a brief time while I was in New York and that we had really no time to talk.

My little binge lasted only three days, and I haven't had a drop since. There was one other in September, likewise three days. Save for that, I haven't had a drop since a year ago last January. Isn't it awful that we reformed alcoholics have to preface everything by explaining exactly how we stand on that question?

The enclosed letter is to supplement a conversation some time ago. It shows quite definitely how a whole lot of people interpreted Ernest's crack at me in "Snows of K." When I called him on it, he promised in a letter that he would not reprint it in book form. Of course, since then, it has been in O'Brien's collection,[1] but I gather he can't help that. If, however, you are publishing a collection of his this fall, do keep in mind that he has promised to make an elision of my name. It was a damned rotten thing to do, and with anybody but Ernest my tendency would be to crack back. Why did he think it would add to the strength of his story if I had become such a negligible figure? This is quite indefensible on any grounds.

No news here. I am writing a new Crawford picture, called "Infidelity." Though based on a magazine story, it is practically an original. I like the work and have a better producer than before—Hunt Stromberg—a sort of one-finger Thalberg, without Thalberg's scope, but with his intense power of work and his absorption in his job.

Meanwhile, I am filling a notebook with stuff that will be of more immediate interest to you, but please don't mention me ever as having any plans.

---

[1] Edward J. O'Brien's *The Best Short Stories 1937 and the Yearbook of the American Short Story* (1937).

"Tender Is the Night" hung over too long, and my next venture will be presented to you without preparation or fanfare.

I am sorry about the Tom Wolfe business.[1] I don't understand it. I am sorry for him, and, in another way, I am sorry for you for I know how fond of him you are

I may possibly see you around Easter.

Best to Louise.

Ever yours,
Scott

All this about the <u>Snows</u> is confidential

TO: *Zelda Fitzgerald* ALS, 2 pp.[2] *Bruccoli*
April 1938 *Hollywood, California*

I couldn't bring myself to write you last week—I was plenty sore with myself and also a good deal with you.[3] But as things settle down I can regard it all with some detachment. As I told you I was a sick man when I left California—had a beautiful little hemorage the end of March, the first in two years and a half—and I was carrying on only on the false exaltation of having done some really excellent work. I thought I'd just lie around in Norfolk and rest but it was a fantastic idea because I should have rested before undertaking the trip. There has been no drink out here, <u>not a drop of it</u>, but I am in an unfortunate rut of caffiene by day and chloral by night which is about as bad on the nerves. As I told you if I can finish one <u>excellent</u> picture to top <u>Three Comrades</u> I think I can bargain for better terms—more rest <u>and</u> more money.

These are a lot of "I"s to tell you I worry about you—my condition must have been a strain and I thought you had developed somewhat grandiose ideas of how to spend this money I am to earn which I consider as <u>capital</u>—this extravagant trip to the contrary. Dr. Carrol's feeling about money is simply that he wants to regulate your affairs for the time being and he can do so if you live on a modest scale and within call. He doesn't care personally whether you spend a hundred a month or ten thousand—doubtless for the latter you could travel in state with a private physician instead of a nurse. Here is the first problem you run up against trying to come back into the world + I hope you'll try to see with us and adjust yourself. You are not married to a rich millionaire of thirty but to a pretty broken and prematurely old man who hasn't a penny except what he can bring out of a weary mind and a sick body.

---

[1] Wolfe had left Charles Scribner's Sons.

[2] This letter may not have been sent.

[3] During the spring Fitzgerald had taken Zelda and Scottie on a disastrous trip to Virginia Beach and Norfolk, Virginia.

Any relations you want are all right with me but I have heard nothing from you and a word would be reassuring because I am always concerned about you

Scott

Oh, Zelda, this was to have been such a cold letter, but I dont feel that way about you. Once we were one person and always it will be a little that way.

TO: *Dr. Robert S. Carroll*   CC, *3 pp. Princeton University*
and Dr. R. Burke Suitt   *Hollywood, California*

April 7, 1938.

Dear Dr. Carroll or Dr. Suitt:

The first thing that struck me in regard to Zelda was her illusion or rather her exaggeration of what she is to do during these experimental trips away from the sanitarium that we talked of. How much I am to blame for this I don't know, but I know it is hard for you to tell at any exact point what she can do or what she can't. However, it seems to me that her <u>thinking</u> about it was more in proportion a few months ago than it is now.

The idea first took shape, as I remember, in a vague promise that she could go to her mother in the Spring. Around Christmas I began to be assured by letters from her mother and sister that she was to be discharged by then—I did not believe this was possible but dared to hope that some scheme of traveling with a companion, at the end of a radius with the clinic as its center, would be feasible.

When Dr. Carroll and I talked in Greenville last February, he even mentioned such locales as the Coast of Maine. With this as a foundation, however, Zelda has, I find, erected a bizarre edifice. To change the metaphor, she imagines herself as a sort of Red Scourge in golden heels, flitting East and West, back and forth across the ocean, munificently bicycling with Scottie through Provence etc., with a companion chosen by herself, now reduced to the status of a sort of lady's maid, who will allow her to do anything she wants. She even has one picked out, a former patient; and she intends to control the purse strings herself—her theory being that the hospital (and she should know that she was carried by the hospital at cost over very hard times) intends to profit greatly by the excursion. My part is to stay here and pay for this grandiose expedition, with no control over it.

The thing changes then in its aspect from a humble attempt at some gradual adjustment to a glorious jail break. Also in her gloomier moments she is going to exact from us all the last farthing in spiritual and financial payment for this long persecution.

To say I am disappointed is putting it mildly. The hope was that if the idea of her coming back to me were removed, as she has wanted it to be, it would give her more responsibility, make her walk with even more

355

guarded steps. The notion of her parading around irresponsibly, doing damage that might be irreparable, is as foreign to your ideas, I know, as to mine.

(After about two days of this rigmarole, I added to the general confusion by getting drunk, whereupon she adopted the course of telling all and sundry that I was a dangerous man and needed to be carefully watched. This made the whole trip one of the most annoying and aggravating experiences in my life. I had been physically run down and under a doctor's supervision for two months, working with the help of injections of calsium, sodium, iron and liver, living on too much caffeine by day and sleeping on clorol at night and <u>touching no liquor</u>; and I was looking forward to this as a much needed rest. In fact, the doctor who is apprehensive that the trouble in my lungs is about to flare up again, begged me to go to the country or someplace near here and rest for a week. But because I had been held here Christmas and New Years, I was anxious to see my daughter at least once. I think she was the only one on our corridor of the hotel that Zelda did not convince that I was a madman. Luckily I sent Scottie off to Baltimore before matters attained their final pitch of the ridiculous—on the boat coming up from Norfolk where I had some words with the idiotic trained nurse whom, by the way, Zelda had invited to accompany her on her exit into the world. All this isn't pretty on my part, but if I had been left alone, would have amounted to a two day batt—in fact, I sobered myself up the second I had gotten Zelda off for Carolina and caught the plane from Washington that night, arriving here Monday and reporting for work.)

One thing is apparent: that my present usefulness is over in the case. Living a vegetable life in Tryon, I got along with her all right; even had some <u>fairly</u> good times together—now our relations are about as bad as at any time in our lives—even worse on my part, for I am unable to feel any of the pity which usually ameliorated whatever she did. In the old days, I could interpose someone between her and our daughter; now, the rasp of temperament between the two simply makes me want to shut her up violently; makes daughter and I feel like conspirators when we can have a minute alone together away from the sing-song patronage which she thinks is the proper method of addressing children. The daughter in turn treats her like an individual, and over it all the well-meant hypocrisy of trying to pretend we are just a happy family, is hard to keep up. The daughter is sorry for her mother, but they are very different in temperament and if more than a few hours together, Mrs. Fitzgerald runs to me with her face red, talking about Scottie as if she were a potential criminal for not having exactly the same interests. To Zelda's mind, I have separated them—the fact is that life has done it beyond my power to add or detract by the tiniest fraction.

Beyond all this, Zelda made a concrete effort during all the mornings and most of the afternoons toward a sort of sweetness which, to me, seemed thin and which apparently my cousins in Norfolk found winning and quite normal. This was even exerted toward me at times, but toward the end I was so irritated that I was unable to judge whether it was sincere or a complete mask, because the moment its objects were out of sight, she had no good words for anyone in particular.

I am enclosing check for the bill received April 1st. I do not know how far this runs.

Meanwhile I await hearing from you, even a note as to what condition you feel she is in and what your plans for her are, so I will be able to estimate what the financial obligations will be. She considers the sum Dr. Carroll wanted her to have as ridiculously inadequate, not realizing the proportion of my salary, my only income, which is going back to pay former debts run up over these years of sickness and trouble. As I told you, at the very best, it will take me two years to be out of debt; and during the second of these years, I want also to put aside some sum which will give me a year off to write a novel. In case of her making trips, I should infinitely prefer you to regulate what she should spend, and I am sorry if these two extravagant flights, which were an attempt to make up for the long time apart from her, gave her any ideas of my scale of living. I am still driving a 1934 Ford and shall probably continue to drive it, as far as I can see ahead.

Sincerely,

TO: Scottie Fitzgerald   *Retyped copy, 1 p. Princeton University*
Spring 1938   *Hollywood, California*

Dearest;

I hope Mary Earle wont find the trip too expensive. It <u>is</u> if you are not going to Vassar, but if you are I think it will be such a worthwhile thing and I wish to God I could go over with you.

We have reached a censorship barrier in <u>Infidelity</u> to our infinite disappointment. It <u>wont</u> be Joan's next picture and we are setting it aside awhile till we think of a way of halfwitting halfwit Hayes and his legion of decency. Pictures needed cleaning up in 1932–33 (remember I didn't like you to see them?) but because they were suggestive and salacious. Of course the moralists now want to apply that to <u>all</u> strong themes—so the crop of the last two years is feeble and false, unless it deals with children. Anyhow we're starting a new story and a safe one.

About <u>adjectives</u>: all fine prose is based on the verbs carrying the sentences. They make sentences move. Probably the finest technical poem in English is Keats' <u>Eve of Saint Agnes</u>. A line like:

The Hare limped trembling through the frozen grass, is so alive that you race through it, scarcely noticing it, yet it has colored the whole poem with its movement—the limping, trembling, and freezing is going on before your own eyes. Would you read that poem for me, and report?

I'm having a controversy with the Highlands Hospital. They want to

357

keep your mothere there with only six weeks out a year and a few trips with Dr. and Mrs. Carroll. I cant see it—I think she should be out from one-fourth to one-half the time, using the hospital only as a base. If I insist, they threaten to realease her althogether to me which would be simply a catastrophe—I cant work and look after her. And she wouldnt obey any companion unless the hospital has authority back of the companion. Mrs. Sayre wants her to come and sit beside what will soon be a deathbed and I cant see that as promising any future (I dont mean Mrs. Sayre is sick but she is almost so) She (your mother) wants to come to your commencement with Newman and Rosalind—O.K. if it can be arranged for a nurse to take her to and from N.Y.

I dont dare at the moment to tell your mother about the Alice Lee Myers trip or the fact that I've taken a shack at the beach here (address Garden of Allah still). She would feel as if we were happy and she was in prison. If only old Carroll was less obstinate—however it should be solved within a few weeks—I _may_ have to go East but God forbid.

A letter from Miss Walker—never has my intuition so surely informed me of a thing than now, that you are walking on a most delicate line there. No matter how you feel I should play a "straight" role for five weeks, lest they mistake any action for a frivolous attitude. All through life there are such games to play—mine for instance, when I first came here, to keep away from any bars, even though I wasnt tempted to drink. The connection of "Bar-drunk" was too easy to establish in people's minds after my past performances. But dont tell your best friend that you are playing a sober role—such things travel fast and far. You will be smart in playing nun for the time being—five weeks will win you many months.

Dearest Love always.
Daddy

TO: *Maxwell Perkins*   *TLS, 4 pp. Princeton University*

Garden of Allah stationery.
Hollywood, California

PERSONAL AND CONFIDENTIAL

April 23, 1938

Dear Max:

I got both your letters and appreciate them and their fullness, as I feel very much the Californian at the moment and, consequently, out of touch with New York.

The Marjorie Rawlings' book[1] fascinated me. I thought it was even better than "South Moon Under" and I envy her the ease with which she does action scenes, such as the tremendously complicated hunt sequence, which

---

[1] *The Yearling* (Scribners, 1938).

For my darling Shielah
— after *such* a
bad time
from
Scott

THIS SIDE OF PARADISE

Fitzgerald inscribed this book for Sheilah Graham after an alcoholic episode in the fall of 1937 (Princeton University).

I would have to stake off in advance and which would probably turn out to be a stilted business in the end. Hers just simply flows; the characters keep thinking, talking, feeling and don't stop, and you think and talk and feel with them.

As to Ernest, I was fascinated by what you told me about the play, touched that he remembered me in his premonitory last word, and fascinated, as always, by the man's Byronic intensity. The Los Angeles Times printed a couple of his articles, but none the last three days, and I keep hoping a stray Krupp shell hasn't knocked off our currently most valuable citizen.

In the mail yesterday came a letter from that exquisitely tactful co-worker of yours, Whitney Darrow, or Darrow Whitney, or whatever his name is. I've never had much love for the man since he insisted on selling "This Side of Paradise" for a dollar fifty, and cost me around five thousand dollars; nor do I love him more when, as it happened the other day, I went into a house and saw someone reading the Modern Library's "Great Modern Short Stories" with a poor piece of mine called "Act Your Age"[1] side by side with Conrad's "Youth," Ernest's "The Killers" because Whitney Darrow was jealous of a copyright.

[1] "At Your Age."

His letter informs me that "This Side of Paradise" is now out of print. I am not surprised after eighteen years (looking it over, I think it is now one of the funniest books since "Dorian Gray" in its utter spuriousness—and then, here and there, I find a page that is very real and living), but I know to the younger generation it is a pretty remote business, reading about the battles that engrossed us then and the things that were startling. To hold them I would have to put in a couple of abortions to give it color (and probably would if I was that age and writing it again). However, I'd like to know what "out of print" means. Does it mean that I can make my own arrangements about it? That is, if any publisher was interested in reprinting it, could I go ahead, or would it immediately become a valuable property to Whitney again?

I once had an idea of getting Bennett Cerf to publish it in the Modern Library, with a new preface. But also I note in your letter a suggestion of publishing an omnibus book with "Paradise," "Gatsby" and "Tender." How remote is that idea, and why must we forget it? If I am to be out here two years longer, as seems probable, it certainly isn't advisable to let my name slip so out of sight as it did between "Gatsby" and "Tender," especially as I now will not be writing even the Saturday Evening Post stories.

I have again gone back to the idea of expanding the stories about Phillippe, the Dark Ages knight, but when I will find time for that, I don't know, as this amazing business has a way of whizzing you along at a terrific speed and then letting you wait in a dispirited, half-cocked mood when you don't feel like undertaking anything else, while it makes up its mind. It is a strange conglomeration of a few excellent over-tired men making the pictures, and as dismal a crowd of fakes and hacks at the bottom as you can imagine. The consequence is that every other man is a charlatan, nobody trusts anybody else, and an infinite amount of time is wasted from lack of confidence.

Relations have always been so pleasant, not only with you but with Harold and with Lorimer's Saturday Evening Post, that even working with the pleasantest people in the industry, Eddie Knopf and Hunt Stromberg, I feel this lack of confidence.

Hard times weed out many of the incompetents, but they swarm back—Herman Mankiewicz, a ruined man who hasn't written ten feet of continuity in two years, was finally dropped by Metro, but immediately picked up by Columbia! He is a nice fellow that everybody likes and has been brilliant, but he is being hired because everyone is sorry for his wife—which I think would make him rather an obstacle in the way of making good pictures. Utter toughness toward the helpless, combined with super-sentimentality—Jesus, what a combination!

I still feel in the dark about Tom Wolfe, rather frightened for him; I cannot quite see him going it alone, but neither can I see your sacrificing yourself in that constant struggle. What a time you've had with your sons, Max—Ernest gone to Spain, me gone to Hollywood, Tom Wolfe reverting to an artistic hill-billy.

Do let me know about "This Side of Paradise." Whitney Darrow's, or Darrow Whitney's letter was so subtly disagreeable that I felt he took rather personal pleasure in the book being out of print. It was all about buying up some second-hand copies. You might tell him to do so if he thinks best. I have a copy somewhere, but I'd like a couple of extras.

Affectionately always,
Scott

TO: *D. Mildred Thompson*[1]

CC, 2 pp. Princeton University
MGM stationery.
Culver City, California

June 12th, 1938

My dear Dean Thompson:

Some two years ago I wrote you entering my daughter for Vassar. One week ago, after her graduation from the Ethel Walker School, there occurred something in the nature of a catastrophe which you will have to examine before determining her qualifications for entrance. By now the school has probably written you—after the graduation week-end was over and the honor system put aside, my daughter and another girl went to New Haven in violation of the regulations, had dinner with two Yale students and were caught coming back at nine o'clock that night. One of the undergraduates was the "fiance" of the other girl—my daughter knew neither of them. The other girl telephoned to the fraternity house of her friend and they met in a restaurant, after which the boys immediately drove them back to Simsbury. The Walker School were particularly annoyed that they had "picked up a ride" to New Haven,—this was by no means the first time it had been done at the school, but it was the first time for my daughter and she was the first one caught. It was broad daylight and they chose a car with a single man in it, so they didn't feel it was risky—an adult has an entirely different reaction. Mrs. Smith telephoned me that she could not let my daughter remain for the rest of the Board preparations. I agreed and have no resentment whatever toward the school which had treated her with every kindness.

The picture at first glance is in perfect focus—the kind of a girl on whom a college education is wasted, probably boy-crazy, irresponsible, almost delinquent. Now compare it with this—a judgement of contemporaries, those who lived with her in the school for two years. A month ago her class of thirty-odd voted their likes and dislikes. Among them I copy these from the school paper:

Most likely to succeed . . . . Fitzgerald (1st)
Most entertaining . . . . Fitzgerald (1st)

---

[1] Dean of Vassar College.

Most artistic . . . . Fitzgerald (2nd)
Most original . . . . Fitzgerald (1st)
Frankest . . . . Fitzgerald (2nd)
In the choice for the composite "Most Perfect Girl" I find:
Personality . . . . Fitzgerald (1st)

The two pictures simply do not go together, for the above represents, I think, the sort of girl who <u>does</u> deserve a college education. Editing the school magazine and writing the school musical play took away from her marks somewhat this year but such things do indicate an active mind and a useful surplus of energy.

If I were able to take the blame for an act which the child herself is now trying desperately to understand, I would, but she is sixteen and must stand on her own feet. That she has been motherless for ten years and homeless for five is no explanation, for such a deprivation should make a girl more, not <u>less</u> mature. It is more to the point that this is only the second trouble she ever got into in her life—the other being a piece of insolence which culminated a long friction with a housemother at Miss Walker's.

But I'd like the two pictures to stand on their merits. Just as you now take more into account than the mere numerical aspect of a grade, so I wanted to present to you the other face of this coin. Because I don't know what one does in a case like this. To the majority of Walker girls the answer would be a debut in New York, but every arrow in this child points toward a career, points away from an idle, shiftless life. And at the very moment when school seems behind and the gates seem opening, she yields to this uncalculated impulse—something that a week later would have deserved no more than a strong rebuke from me. If this closes the gates where does all that talent and personality go from here? Only a month ago, she was "most likely to succeed." What is she now?

Sincerely,
F. Scott Fitzgerald

P.S. I need not add that she is not now the same child who did this rash thing, and will never be again.

TO: Scottie Fitzgerald   *Typed copy, 4 pp. Princeton University*
Hollywood, California

July 7th, 1938

Dearest Scottie:

I don't think I will be writing letters many more years and I wish you would read this letter twice—bitter as it may seem. You will reject it now, but at a later period some of it may come back to you as truth. When I'm talking to you, you think of me as an older person, an "authority," and when I speak of my own youth what I say becomes unreal to you—for the young can't believe in the youth of their fathers. But perhaps this little bit will be understandable if I put it in writing.

When I was your age I lived with a great dream. The dream grew and I learned how to speak of it and make people listen. Then the dream divided one day when I decided to marry your mother after all, even though I knew she was spoiled and meant no good to me. I was sorry immediately I had married her, but being patient in those days, made the best of it and got to love her in another way. You came along and for a long time we made quite a lot of happiness out of our lives. But I was a man divided—she wanted me to work too much for <u>her</u> and not enough for my dream. She realized too late that work was dignity and the only dignity and tried to atone for it by working herself but it was too late and she broke and is broken forever.

It was too late also for me to recoup the damage—I had spent most of my resources, spiritual and material, on her, but I struggled on for five years till my health collapsed, and all I cared about was drink and forgetting.

The mistake I made was in marrying her. We belonged to different worlds—she might have been happy with a kind simple man in a southern garden. She didn't have the strength for the big stage—sometimes she pretended, and pretended beautifully, but she didn't have it. She was soft when she should have been hard, and hard when she should have been yielding. She never knew how to use her energy—she's passed that failing on to you.

For a long time I hated <u>her</u> mother for giving her nothing in the line of good habit—nothing but "getting by" and conceit. I never wanted to see again in this world women who were brought up as idlers. And one of my chief desires in life was to keep you from being that kind of person, one who brings ruin to themselves and others. When you began to show disturbing signs at about fourteen, I comforted myself with the idea that you were too precocious socially and a strict school would fix things. But sometimes I think that idlers seem to be a special class for whom nothing can be planned, plead as one will with them—their only contribution to the human family is to warm a seat at the common table.

My reforming days are over, and if you are that way I don't want to change you. But I don't want to be upset by idlers inside my family or out. I want my energies and my earnings for people who talk my language.

I have begun to fear that you don't. You don't realize that what I am doing here is the last tired effort of a man who once did something finer and better. There is not enough energy, or call it money, to carry anyone who is dead weight and I am angry and resentful in my soul when I feel that I am doing this. People like Rosalind and your mother must be carried because their illness makes them useless. But it is a different story that <u>you</u> have spent two years doing no useful work at all, improving neither your body nor your mind, but only writing reams and reams of dreary letters to dreary people, with no possible object except obtaining invitations which you could not accept. Those letters go on, even in your sleep, so that I know your whole trip now is one long waiting for the post. It is like an old gossip who cannot still her tongue.

You have reached the age when one is of interest to an adult only insofar as one seems to have a future. The mind of a little child is fascinating, for it looks on old things with new eyes—but at about twelve this changes. The adolescent offers nothing, can do nothing, say nothing that the adult cannot do better. Living with you in Baltimore—(and you have told Harold that I alternated between strictness and neglect, by which I suppose you mean the times I was so inconsiderate as to have T.B., or to retire into myself to write, for I had little social life apart from you)—represented a rather too domestic duty forced on me by your mother's illness. But I endured your Top Hats and Telephones until the day you snubbed me at dancing school, less willingly after that. There began to be an unsympathetic side to you that alienated first Mrs. Owens, then your teachers at Bryn Mawr. The line of those who felt it runs pretty close to you—adults who saw you every day. Among them you have made scarcely a single close friend, with all your mastery of the exterior arts of friendliness. All of them have loved you, as I do, but all of them have had reservations, and important ones: they have felt that something in you wasn't willing to pull your weight, to do your part—for more than an hour.

This last year was a succession of information beginning as far back as December that you were being unfair to me, more frankly that you were cheating. The misinformation about your standing in your class, the failure to tutor at the Obers at Christmas, the unwillingness to help with your mother at Easter in golf or tennis, then the dingy outbreak in the infirmary at the people who were "on to you", who knew you had none of the scholar in you but lived in a babyish dream—of the dance favors of a provincial school. Finally the catastrophe which, as far as I am able to determine, had no effect except to scare you because you knew I wouldn't maintain you in the East without some purpose or reason.

If you did not have a charm and companionability, such a blow might have chastened you, but like my Uncle Phil you will always be able to find companions who will reassure you of your importance even though your accomplishment is a goose-egg. To the last day of his life Phil was a happy man, though he loafed always and dissipated a quarter of a million of his own and his sisters' money and left his wife in poverty and his son as you saw him. He had charm—great charm. He never liked me after I was grown, because once he lost his charm in front of me and I kicked his fat backside. Your charm must not have been in evidence on the day Mrs. Perry Smith figuratively did the same to you.

All this was the long preparation for the dispair I experienced ten days ago. That you did or did not know how I felt about Baltimore, that you thought I'd approve of your meeting a boy and driving back with him unchaperoned to New York by night, that you <u>honestly</u> thought I would have permitted that—well, tell it to Harold, who seems to be more gullible.

The clerk from the Garden of Allah woke me up with the telegram in which I mistook <u>Simmons</u> for <u>Finney</u> and I called the <u>Finneys</u>—to find them gone. The result was entirely a situation of your own making—if you had any real regret about the Walker episode you'd have respected my wishes for a single week.

To sum up: what you have done to please me or make me proud is practically negligible since the time you made yourself a good diver at camp (and now you are softer than you have ever been.) In your career as a "wild society girl", vintage of 1925, I'm not interested. I don't want any of it— it would bore me, like dining with the Ritz Brothers. When I do not feel you are "going somewhere", your company tends to depress me for the silly waste and triviality involved. On the other hand, when occasionally I see signs of life and intention in you, there is no company in the world I prefer. For there is no doubt that you have something in your belly, some real gusto for life—a real dream of your own—and my idea was to wed it to something solid before it was too late—as it was too late for your mother to learn anything when she got around to it. Once when you spoke French as a child it was enchanting with your odd bits of knowledge—now your conversation is as commonplace as if you'd spent the last two years in the Corn Hollow High School—what you saw in <u>Life</u> and read in <u>Sexy Romances</u>.

I shall come East in September to meet your boat—but this letter is a declaration that I am no longer interested in your promissory notes but only in what I see. I love you always but I am only interested by people who think and work as I do and it isn't likely that <u>I</u> shall change at my age. Whether you will—or want to—remains to be seen.

Daddy

P. S. If you keep the diary, please don't let it be the dry stuff I could buy in a ten-franc guide book. I'm not interested in dates and places, even the Battle of New Orleans, unless you have some unusual reaction to them. Don't try to be witty in the writing, unless it's natural—just true and real.

P.P.S. Will you please read this letter a second time—I wrote it over twice.

TO: *Scottie Fitzgerald*   *CC, 3 pp. Princeton University*
                              MGM stationery. Culver City, California

Sept. 19th
19 38

Dearest Pie:

Here are a few ideas that I didn't discuss with you and I'm sending this to reach you on your first day.

For heaven's sake don't make yourself conspicuous by rushing around inquiring which are the Farmington Girls, which are the Dobbs Girls, etc. You'll make an enemy of everyone who isn't. Thank heaven you're on an equal footing of brains at last—most of the eventual leaders will be high school girls and I'd hate to see you branded among them the first week as a snob—it's not worth a moment's thought. What is important is to go to the library and crack your first book—to be among the 5% who will do this and get that much start and freshness.

A chalk line is absolutely specified for you at present—because:

A. The Walker episode will necessarily remain for awhile in the Vassar authorities' minds. (It reached me for the first time last week in a rather garbled form.) But if there is no sequel it will die a natural death in six more months. Your bearing my name gives longevity to any such episodes whether they're grave or trifling—it makes them better morsels of gossip.

B. My second reason for the chalk line is allied with this last—beside the "cleverness" which you are vaguely supposed to have "inherited", people will be quick to deck you out with my sins. If I hear of you taking a drink before you're twenty, I shall feel entitled to begin my last and greatest non-stop binge, and the world also will have an interest in the matter of your behavior. It would like to be able to say, and would say on the slightest provocation: "There she goes—just like her papa and mama." Need I say that you can take this fact as a curse—or you can make of it a great advantage?

Remember that you're there for four years. It is a residential college and the butterfly will be resented. You should never boast to a soul that you're going to the Bachelors' Cotillion. I can't tell you how important this is. For one hour of vainglory you will create a different attitude about yourself. Nothing is as obnoxious as other people's luck. And while I'm on this: You will notice that there is a strongly organized left-wing movement there. I do not particularly want you to think about politics, but I do not want you to set yourself against this movement. I am known as a left-wing sympathizer and would be proud if you were. In any case, I should feel outraged if you identified yourself with Nazism or Red-baiting in any form. Some of those radical girls may not look like much now but in your lifetime they are liable to be high in the councils of the nation.

I think it would be wise to put on somewhat of an act in reference to your attitude to the upper classmen. In every college the class just ahead of you is of great importance. They approach you very critically, size you up and are in a position to help or hinder you in anything you try. I mean the class just ahead of you. A Sophomore class is usually conceited. They feel that they have been through the mill and have learned something. While this is very doubtful, it is part of wisdom to humor that vanity in them. It would pay dividends many times to treat them with an outward respect which you might not feel and I want you to be able to do such things at will, as it happens that all through life you may be in a position in which you will constantly have to assume a lowly rank in a very strict organization. If anybody had told me my last year at Princeton that I would stand up and take orders from an ex-policeman, I would have laughed. But such was the case because, as an army officer, he was several grades above me in rank and competence—and that is not the last time it has happened.

Here is something you can watch happen during your college course. Always at the beginning of the first term about half a dozen leaders arise. Of these at least two get so intoxicated with themselves that they don't last the first year, two survive as leaders and two are phonics who are found out within a year—and therefore discredited and rated even lower than before, with the resentment people feel for anyone who has fooled them.

Everything you are and do from fifteen to eighteen is what you are and will do through life. Two years are gone and half the indicators already point down—two years are left and you've got to pursue desperately the ones that point up!

I wish I were going to be with you the first day, and I hope the work has already started.

With dearest love,

TO: Harold Ober   ALS, 2 pp.
Received November 9, 1938   Encino, California

Dear Harold:
Back at work on a new job that may be something really good—Mme. Curie for Gretta Garbo. It was quite a plum and I'm delighted after the thankless months spent on fixing up leprous stories. Knopff said I could do my original if I wanted but he strongly advised this.

Im sorry my concern about Scottie overcast that day at your house—I think Mr Haas[1] thought it was all about a football game, which shames me for having shown in public my dismay about the child. There is nothing much to do except let it work itself out—but I must beg you again not to give her money. I know how you feel about it—that I am cruel and unjust but remember you've gotten all your ideas on the subject from Scottie. I am under the greatest obligation to you but, if I may say so, I think the

---

[1]Donald Haas of Random House was Ober's neighbor in Scarsdale, New York.

headmistress and teachers at Walkers, the Dean + professors at Vassar and I, who have been in constant communication with them and have concerned myself deeply with the child since she was seven—that we are in a better position to evaluate her character than you. I have to deal in results—points of stability and honor—you touch Scottie only on the superficial points of charm. So I ask you to let me have a fair chance by not giving her cash or credit—which she uses, specifically in the case of the evening dress—to come out into a frank defiance of me.

I do not want to bring her out here—I have written her a last letter asking for very simple concessions. We will see what we will see. So long as she lies it is all very difficult and tortuous from any point of view.

Ever Yours
Scott

TO: *Frances Turnbull*[1]   *CC, 2 pp. Princeton University*
                                             Encino, California

November 9, 1938

Dear Frances:

I've read the story carefully and, Frances, I'm afraid the price for doing professional work is a good deal higher than you are prepared to pay at present. You've got to sell your heart, your strongest reactions, not the little minor things that only touch you lightly, the little experiences that you might tell at dinner. This is especially true when you <u>begin</u> to write, when you have not yet developed the tricks of interesting people on paper, when you have none of the technique which it takes time to learn. When, in short, you have <u>only</u> your emotions to sell.

This is the experience of all writers. It was necessary for Dickens to put into Oliver Twist the child's passionate resentment at being abused and starved that had haunted his whole childhood. Ernest Hemingway's first stories "In Our Time" went right down to the bottom of all that he had ever felt and known. In "This Side of Paradise" I wrote about a love affair that was still bleeding as fresh as the skin wound on a haemophile.

The amateur, seeing how the professional having learned all that he'll ever learn about writing can take a trivial thing such as the most superficial reactions of three uncharacterized girls and make it witty and charming— the amateur thinks he or she can do the same. But the amateur can only realize his ability to transfer his emotions to another person by some such desperate and radical expedient as tearing your first tragic love story out of your heart and putting it on pages for people to see.

---

[1] Daughter of the Turnbull family from whom Fitzgerald had rented "La Paix"; at this time she was a Radcliffe sophomore.

That, anyhow, is the price of admission. Whether you are prepared to pay it or, whether it coincides or conflicts with your attitude on what is "nice" is something for you to decide. But literature, even light literature, will accept nothing less from the neophyte. It is one of those professions that want the "works". You wouldn't be interested in a soldier who was only a <u>little</u> brave.

In the light of this, it doesn't seem worth while to analyze why this story isn't saleable but I am too fond of you to kid you along about it, as one tends to do at my age. If you ever decide to tell <u>your</u> stories, no one would be more interested than,

Your old friend,
F. Scott Fitzgerald.

P.S. I might say that the writing is smooth and agreeable and some of the pages very apt and charming. You have talent—which is the equivalent of a soldier having the right physical qualifications for entering West Point.

TO: Scottie Fitzgerald   *CC, 3 pp. Princeton University*
                              MGM stationery. Culver City, California

November 11, 1938.

Dearest Scottie:—

I <u>still</u> believe you are swimming, protozoa-like, in the submerged third of your class, and I still think your chance of flunking out is all too rosy— two 'B' tests in your easiest subjects are absolutely no proof to the contrary. You would have to be a complete numbskull to write a lower test than that in French or English. As a freshman at Princeton we had to struggle with Plautus, Terrence, Sallust and Integral Calculus.

However, the point of this letter is that I am compelled at last by this telegraph matter to dock your allowance. I pay you almost as much as some stenographers on this lot get for a hard week—and you treat me to this childish monkey business! You see I put a tracer on that call and the telegraph company reports that <u>you</u> told them the telegram was received by your roommate. Your letter tells quite another story. On the basis of it I am claiming damage from the Company for non-delivery, which unless your conscience is clear may lead to some trouble in Poughkeepsie. If your conscience <u>isn't</u> clear you'd better come clean right away.

I'm habituated to the string of little lies (such as you telling Dorothy that you went to the Navy-Princeton game, telling me that Gordon Meacham was Captain of the Freshman football team) but this sort of thing can lead into a hellish mess. I once saw a pathological liar in police court, her face blazing with pimples, her blue eyes straight as a die, as she told the sargeant the most amazing circumstantial story about where her boy friend had been the night of the holdup. I knew that the sargeant had the proof of the guilt on his blotter but there was something admirable, even awe-inspiring, about the way the girl invented even though she must have been squirming inwardly. If you should happen to be there next term I want you to take music and continue making up your songs and plays, because I kept thinking how, if life had been a little kinder, that girl might have been a great creator of fiction.

Instead she got two years.

Anyhow, the allowance is definitely docked to $3.85 until you come clean on the following questions:

1. The telegram matter. I think it would be wiser to settle it with me instead of the Dean.

2. I wrote you a letter, unacknowledged, of which the purport was that I didn't want you to go to debutant affairs in New York this year. I still don't want you to go to them. That includes Dorothy Burns' tea. My reasons are manifold and I will be glad to go into them with you further

3. I want you to go to Baltimore this Thanksgiving, leaving on the first day of vacation and remaining until Sunday. It shames me, and you too, to have to say that I must put a check on this, and that if you let me down I will consider that there is no use keeping you at Vassar another day.

4. I have asked you to stay at Vassar the week-end after the Yale game.

5. You can certainly find time to read eighteen Elizabethan lyrics. If I could spare the time and trouble to try to fix up the matter of the English course, what do you do with your hours?

On another slip I have listed these questions. Until I get a clear answer on every one, together with an affirmation that you intend to play square with me and stop this line of opposition, you will have to get along with pin money.

I know that you must have worries of your own and I hate to add to them. What I ask seems so very little. This year of many liberties is something I gave you with money and care (do you remember the schedules at Bryn Mawr?) Do you think it's fair to use these privileges against _me_? I've made every sort of appeal to your more civilized instincts and all I get is the most insincere "Can't we be friends?"—in other words, can't we be friends on _your_ terms.

Friends!—we don't even speak the same language. I'll give you the same answer my father would have given to me—at seventeen, eighteen or nineteen or twenty. Either you can decide to make concessions to what I want in the East or you can come out here Thanksgiving and try something else.

Since you've finished the "Farewell To Arms" the second bit of reading includes only the following poems. The reference is to the index of first lines in either the Oxford book or the Golden Treasury.

Come Unto These	Shakespeare
Tell Me Where	"
Hark, Hark the Lark	"

Take Oh Take	"
Go Lovely Rose	Waller
Oh Western Wind	Anon
Art Thou Poor Yet	Dekker
Fear No More	Shakespeare
My True Love	Sidney
Who is Sylvia	Shakespeare

The question will be along about <u>Wednesday</u>. If you read these ten poems you can answer it in a flash.

TO: Scottie Fitzgerald   *RTLS, 2 pp.*[1] Princeton University
                                             MGM stationery. Culver City, California

November 18
1938

Dearest Scottie:

I'm certainly glad to catch a glimmer of wisdom in your attitude—even though you unveiled the story of the blow-away pink slip <u>after</u> the telegraph company had checked on you. And even though in one page of your letter you had intended to go to Baltimore from Thursday to Saturday, while in another part you hadn't intended to go at all.

[I'm sorry about ——'s tea. I've nothing against her except that she rather stuck her neck out about Vassar, which I suppose she is attending for the social prestige involved. She seemed very nice, quite transparent—a type that turned up all too frequently in the Cottage Club at Princeton. I do wish you would find some more interesting friends. To take the curse off your not going to her party I wrote a nice letter to her mother explaining my apparent tyranny in forbidding it. Same to the mother of ——.

In answering my questions you asked some yourself. The one about Baltimore can be answered from <u>Ecclesiastes</u>, "There is a time for weeping, a time for laughing," etc. Fourteen was simply not the time for you to run around on evening dates—at least Pete Finney and I thought not in our erroneous ways. The parents of —— and —— thought differently. Who is interested in a girl with her bloom worn off at sixteen? The one thing you still reproach me for is letting you go, against my better judgment, to the dance at St. Andrew's School.]

It is now perfectly sensible for you to go with college boys. (I didn't want you to stay in Baltimore this fall because I felt it would shoot you into Vassar with your mind full of gayety or love, which it apparently did, for your first month there was a flat bust. Also, I did not want you to start with a string of football games this fall.) If you are invited to the Yale or

---

[1] The Princeton University Library document is incomplete. Bracketed words have been supplied from Turnbull's text; his source is unknown.

Princeton Proms this winter or next spring by a reputable boy—and I'm entitled to the name, please—I'd have absolutely no objection to your going.[1] <u>The whole damn thing about going to the colleges is to keep it in proportion</u>. Did you ever hear of a college boy, unless he were an idiot, racing from Smith to Vassar to Wellesley? There are certain small sacrifices for a college education or there wouldn't be any honor in having gone to college.

But the New York thing is as wrong now as the auto date was at fourteen. I will quote you from a letter I wrote Harold Ober: "Those debutante parties in New York are the rendezvous of a gang of professional idlers, parasites, pansies, failures, the silliest type of sophomores, young customers' men from Wall Street and hangers-on—the very riff-raff of social New York who would exploit a child like Scottie with flattery and squeeze her out until she is a limp colorless rag. In one more year she can cope with them. In three more years it will be behind her. This year she is still puppy enough to be dazzled. She will be infinitely better off here with me than mixed up with that sort of people. I'd rather have an angry little girl on my hands for a few months than a broken neurotic for the rest of my life." But I don't have to tell you this—you probably read the <u>Life</u> article on the dim-witted Frazier girl and the razz on her in <u>The New Yorker</u>.

As to the money. Your full allowance for next Monday, $13.85, will reach you almost as soon as this does. I'm sorry you were inconvenienced at the loss of the $10.00, but it is a trifle compared to the inconvenience you have caused at this end. I will also send an additional $5.00, which will make $18.85 for the Baltimore trip, but that $5.00 will come off the following week's allowance. I want you to stay in Baltimore until Sunday, and I mean specifically in Baltimore, not at Vassar, not at Scarsdale. This money must <u>absolutely</u> take care of the Baltimore trip!

Yes, it <u>is</u> too bad you have to be checked up on like a girl of ten. I'd hoped you'd be rather different this year. If Peaches hadn't been with you that first day in Hollywood I would have squelched the idea of rooming with a debutante as I had meant to. I let it go because I didn't want to open her visit that way. I'm as sick of this bloody matter as you are. I can just see people pointing at you at New York dances and saying "That's Scott Fitzgerald's daughter. She likes her champagne young. Why doesn't he do something about it?"

Even if your aims are the most worldly, the road that I am pointing out is the right one. A great social success is a pretty girl who plays her cards as carefully as if she were plain.

With dearest love,
Daddy

P.S. <u>Please address all future correspondence to my new address, 5221 Amestoy Ave., Encino, Los Angeles, California</u>.

[1] If it doesn't come in an examination week.

TO: *Sidney Franklin*[1] CC, 1 p. *Princeton University*
MGM *memo. Culver City, California*

12/22/38

Dear Sidney:

Barring illness and (I have a sty as big as a Jefferson nickle—and less valuable) I will deliver you the stuff Tues. the 28th at midday. <u>So save Tuesday afternoon</u>! Singing! Dancing! Thorium! One of the Fitz Brothers in person! Soft-ball finals: Script vs. Sound!

I could give it to you Mon. the 26th at 11:45 P.M. but it would be an inferior script—hurried, careless and full of Christmas neckties. Wait till Tuesday for the genuine article.[2]

Ever yours,
F. Scott Fitzg.

P.S. Seriously I'm sorry it's taken five weeks—I didn't think it would be 75 pages.

TO: *Maxwell Perkins* TLS, 2 pp. *Princeton University*
MGM *stationery. Culver City, California*

December 24, 1938.

Dear Max:

Since the going-out-of-print of "Paradise" and the success (or is it one?) of the "Fifth Column" I have come to feel somewhat neglected. Isn't my reputation being allowed to let slip away? I mean what's left of it. I am still a figure to many people and the number of times I still see my name in <u>Time</u> and the <u>New Yorker</u> ect. make me wonder if it should be allowed to casually disappear— when there are memorial double deckers to such fellows as Farrel and Stienbeck.[3]

I think something ought to be published this Spring. You had a plan for the three novels and I have another plan, of which more hereafter, for another big book; the recession is over for awhile and I have the most natural ambition to see my stuff accessible to another generation. Bennet Cerf obviously isn't going to move about <u>Tender</u> and it seems to me things like that need a spark from a man's own publisher. It was not so long ago that "Tender" was among the dozen best of a bad season and had an offer from the Literary Guild—so I can't be such a long chance as say, Callaghan. Either of the two books I speak of might have an awfully good chance to pay their way. A whole generation now has never read "This Side of

---

[1] MGM producer.
[2] Fitzgerald's treatment for *Madame Curie* was rejected.
[3] Novelists James T. Farrell and John Steinbeck.

Paradise". (I've often thought that if Frank Bunn at Princeton had had a few dozen copies on his stands every September he could have sold them all by Christmas).

But I am especially concerned about <u>Tender</u>—that book is not dead. The <u>depth</u> of its appeal exists—I meet people constantly who have the same exclusive attachment to it as others had to <u>Gatsby</u> and <u>Paradise</u>, people who identified themselves with Dick Diver. It's great fault is that the <u>true</u> beginning—the young psychiatrist in Switzerland—is tucked away in the middle of the book. If pages 151–212 were taken from their present place and put at the start the improvement in appeal would be enormous. In fact the mistake was noted and suggested by a dozen reviewers. To shape up the ends of that change would, of course, require changes in half a dozen other pages. And as you suggested, an omnibus book should also have a preface or prefaces—besides my proposed glossary of absurdities and inaccuracies in <u>This Side of Paradise</u>. This last should attract some amused attention.

The other idea is this:

A Big collection of stories leading off with <u>Phillipe</u>—entirely rewritten and pulled together into a 30,000 word novelette. The Collection could consist of:

1. Phillipe
2. Pre-war (Basil & Josephine)
3. May Day
4. The Jazz Age (the dozen or so best Jazz Stories).
5. About a dozen others including Babylon.

The reason for using <u>Phillipe</u> is this: He is to some extent completed in the 4th story (which you have never read) and in spite of some muddled writing, he is one of the best characters I've ever "drawn". He should be a long book—but whether or not my M.G.M. contract is renewed I'm going to free-lance out here another year to lay by some money and then do my modern novel. So it would be literally <u>years</u> before I got to <u>Phillipe</u> again— if ever.

In my work here I can find time for such a rewrite of <u>Phillipe</u> as I contemplate—I could finish it by the first of February. The other stories would go in to the collection unchanged. Unlike Ernest I wouldn't want to put in <u>all</u> the stories from all four books but I'd like to add four or five never published before.

I am desperately keen on both these schemes—I think the novels should come first and, unless there are factors there you haven't told me about, I think it is a shame to put it off. It would not sell wildly at first but unless you make some gesture of confidence I see my reputation dieing on its feet from lack of nourishment. If you could see the cards for my books in the public libraries here in Los Angeles continually in demand even to this day, you would know I have never had wide distribution in some parts of the country. When <u>This Side of Paradise</u> stood first in the <u>Bookman's Monthly List</u> it didn't even appear in the score of the Western States.

You can imagine how distasteful it is to blow my own horn like this but it comes from a deep feeling that something could be done if it is done at once, about my literary standing—always admitting that I have any at all.

Ever your friend,
Scott

TO: Harold Ober   *Wire. Lilly Library*
December 26, 1938   *Van Nuys, California*

METRO NOT RENEWING TO MY GREAT PLEASURE BUT WILL FINISH CURIE THERES LOTS OF OTHER WORK OFFERED STOP HOWEVER PLEASE SAY NOTHING WHATEVER TO PERKINS OR TO SCOTTIE WHO WOULD NOT UNDERSTAND STOP AM WRITING SCOTT.

TO: Harold Ober   *ALS, 1 p. Lilly Library*
Received December 29, 1938   *Los Angeles, California*

Dear Harold:

As I wrote you the contract wasn't renewed. Why I dont know—but not on account of the work. It seems sort of funny—to entrust me alone with their biggest picture, + <u>continue</u> me on it with a "your services will not be required". Finally Eddie[1] said that when I finished it he hoped he'd have good contract for me. O.K. If <u>Curie</u> is a hit I'd go back for $2000 a week. Baby am I glad to get out! Ive hated the place ever since Monkeybitch rewrote 3 Comrades!

Glad Scottie was nice.

Shielah sends her best

Ever
Scott

TO: Maxwell Perkins   *TLS, 2 pp. Princeton University*
         MGM stationery. Culver City, California

January 4, 1939

Dear Max:

Your letter rather confused me. I had never clearly understood that it was the Modern Library who were considering doing my three books as a giant volume. I thought it was an enterprise of yours. If they show no special

---

[1] Edwin Knopf.

enthusiasm about bringing out Tender by itself, I don't see how they would be interested in doing a giant anyhow. You spoke of it last year as something only the recession kept you from doing.

What I don't like is the out-of-print element. In a second I'm going to discuss the Philippe business with you, but first let me say that I would rather have "This Side of Paradise" in print if only in that cheap American Mercury book edition than not in print at all. I see they have just done Elliot Paul's "Indelible".[1] How do you think they would feel about it? And what is your advice on the subject?

Now about Philippe. When I wrote you I had envisaged another year of steady work here. At present, while it is possible that I may be on the coast for another year, it is more likely that the work will be from picture to picture with the prospect of taking off three or four months in the year, perhaps even more, for literary work. Philippe interests me. I am afraid, though, it would have to be supported by something more substantial. I would have to write 10,000 or 15,000 more words on it to make it as big a book as "Gatsby" and I'm not at all sure that it would have a great unity. You will remember that the plan in the beginning was tremendously ambitious—there was to have been Philippe as a young man founding his fortunes—Philippe as a middle-aged man participating in the Captian founding of France as a nation—Philippe as an old man and the consolidation of the feudal system. It was to have covered a span of about sixty years from 880 A.D. to 950. The research required for the second two parts would be quite tremendous and the book would have been (or would be) a piece of great self-indulgence, though I admit self-indulgence often pays unexpected dividends.

Still, if periods of three or four months are going to be possible in the next year or so I would much rather do a modern novel. One of those novels that can only be written at the moment and when one is full of the idea—as "Tender" should have been written in its original conception, all laid on the Riviera. I think it would be a quicker job to write a novel like that between 50 and 60,000 words long than to do a thorough revision job with an addition of 15,000 words on "Philippe". In any case I'm going to decide within the next month and let you know.

Thanks for your letter. I wish you'd send me a copy of the Tom Wolfe article because I never see anything out here. John wrote about me in the Virginia Quarterly, too.

Ever your friend,

Scott

P.S. I hope Jane and Scottie see a lot of each other if Scottie stays in, but as I suspected, she has tendencies toward being a play-girl and has been put on probation. I hope she survives this February.

[1] 1922 novel.

TO: David O. Selznick[1]   *Typed memo, 1 p. Harry Ransom Humanities*
Research Center, University of Texas, Austin
Selznick International Pictures stationery. Culver City, California

January 10, 1939

"GONE WITH THE WIND"

Just a word about the beginning. To suggest the romance of the old South immediately I should suggest borrowing from the trailers. Under the turning pages of the book I'd like to see a two or three minute montage of the most beautiful pre-war shots imaginable and played over it I'd like to hear the Stephen Foster songs right off the bat. I'd like to see young men riding, negroes singing, long shots of the barbecue, shots of Tara and Twelve Oaks and carriages and gardens and happiness and gaiety.

Otherwise, we open on an actress in a hoopskirt and two unknown young men. The great expectancy would be both assuaged and whetted by such a montage. Then we could go into the story of disappointed love, betraying overseers, toiling niggers and quarreling girls necessary to the plot because they're just incidents against this background of beauty. It is against this background seen or remembered that we play the picture and what I missed from the very first was a sense of happiness.

TO: David O. Selznick   *Typed memo, 6 pp. Harry Ransom Humanities*
Research Center, University of Texas, Austin
Selznick International Pictures stationery. Culver City, California

January 10, 1939

"GONE WITH THE WIND"
SLIGHT CHANGES AND CUTS
(Scene numbers refer to
shooting script or
yellows)

SCENE 19:

Pork (addressing Ellen as she mounts
steps)
Miss Ellen—Mist' Gerald tuk on bad at you runnin' out ter hulp them Slatterys. Yo' dint eat yo' supper.

---

[1] During the last weeks of his MGM contract, Fitzgerald was loaned to producer Selznick to polish Oliver H. P. Garrett's revision of Sidney Howard's screenplay for *Gone With the Wind*. He was dismissed because relays of writers were being brought in to work on the screenplay.

Jonas Wilkerson steps out from the shadow, confronting her. He has some papers in his hands. He is nervously brushing his nose and sniffling—a characteristic gesture.

Wilkerson

Good evening, Mrs. O'Hara.

She stares at him—her expression hardening.

Wilkerson

The cotton reports are ready—when it's convenient for you, Ma'am.

— — — — — — — — —

SCENES 21 & 23:

It has no doubt occurred to you that Ellen's addressing Gerald as "Mr. O'Hara" is going to puzzle a lot of people outside of the deep South. My Alabama mother-in-law almost always referred to her husband as "Judge Sayre" in public, but often slipped to "Anthony." I can't imagine that she called him Judge Sayre in friendlier and more intimate moments. My suggestion is that in scene 21 Ellen calls him "Gerald" and that in scene 23, where the girls are running into the shot, she switches to the more formal "Mr. O'Hara." If we leave the audience in confusion for even a minute as to who Ellen is there in scene 21, they are liable not to hear the lines about dismissing the overseer.

— — — — — — — — —

SCENE 22:

Carreen

Mother, where've you been?

Scarlett

Mother, there's a lot of things—

Suellen

Mother, Scarlett's being selfish—

— — — — — — — — —

SCENE 25:

Scarlett

Mother, the lace is loose on my ball dress. Will you show me—

Suellen

Mother, can't I wear Scarlett's green? She said we'd change around.

Carreen

Mother, I'm quite old enough for the ball tomorrow night.

– – – – – – – – –

SCENE 26:

Pork

Miss Ellen, you kain't skip yo' meals like this—you come along.

– – – – – – – – –

SCENE 35:

Prissy is teetering on high-heel French slippers.

Prissy (proudly)

They use' b'long Miss Scarlett. They sho' does push a pusson fo'ward.

Suggest that Pork goes out of shot and Prissy either has an awful time on the first step or else takes them off and goes up barefooted.

– – – – – – – – –

SCENE 36:

After "I'll have to get a husband":

Prissy enters with a tray.

Mammy (gesturing where to put the
food)

You'll have to get that down with a shoe-horn.
(she laughs at her own joke)

Prissy (sets the tray down and stares
wide-eyed at the cutlery)

I didn't bring no shoe-horn.

– – – – – – – – –

SCENE 50:

I have your change in Cathleen's remark. Before I got it I had gone back to the book, as you suggested, and preserved the line, "He's not received." It is Scarlett who discovers later that Rhett is not a gentleman at heart, but at this point he is still a gentleman by birth although a fallen one.

– – – – – – – – –

SCENE 51:

I have interchanged Brent and Stuart in scene 51. Stuart, a little drunk, is more likely to rush away for dessert, while Brent can

379

cue the situation of Ashley and Melanie. Note that several birds are killed with one stone.

—————————

SCENES 51 & 52:

Scarlett's remark about why she chose the ottoman isn't funny coming from her—it makes her stick out her chin just a little too much, so I switched it to Rhett—it is just the sort of observation that he would make about Scarlett, something she thought, not said. He always knows what she is thinking.

As to John Wilkes' remark about her being hard-hearted—in the book it was said very laughingly in Scarlett's presence, not pronounced grimly and definitively by an old man. Old men like her.

—————————

SCENE 55:

Scene 55 is confused and contradictory. It is well planted that Scarlett is so full that she's had to belch, so how could she have already consumed a large dish of pork and encouraged her swains to bring her two more? I am substituting new lines.

—————————

SCENE 60:

Every once in a while Miss Mitchell slips though I admire her careful documentation. One of the places is scene 60. I refer to Ashley's Journey's-end-1925 brand of pacifism. It sounds like one of those feeble sops that Warner Brothers now put into their pictures. The grandson of those people who fought the Revolution believed passionately in righteous wars. What the more radical of them hated was Napoleonic militarism. Anyhow, the speech was better in its Margaret Mitchell form and I have restored it somewhat.

—————————

SCENE 67:

The scene between Ashley and Scarlett in the library has been badly tampered with. It is important that Scarlett goes into her dance at the very beginning and the evident intention of prolonging the suspense by the lines about "going upstairs and resting" doesn't come off.

Secondly, while I agree we should show her strong physical attraction for Ashley, I think that in his long speech which includes the line "passionately—with every fibre of my being," Ashley goes entirely out of character and completely wrecks the meaning and the spirit of it all. The entire sympathy for Ashley would be lost in that moment. A man who turns down a woman is always suspected as being a prig. For an unmarried man to turn down a woman whom he loves "passionately and with every fibre of his being" makes him simply unforgivable, inexplicable and heartless. Margaret Mitchell by having Ashley show admirable control has established a credible situation. Ashley has <u>never allowed</u> himself to love Scarlett "passionately and with every fibre of his being." That is the whole point of the scene. When he says "Yes, I care," he is really saying that he knows he <u>could</u> love her—no more, no less than that.

— — — — — — — — —

SCENE 71:

This scene should end with Rhett's laughter. Both these scripts seem to believe that Scarlett needs the exit line, but I think Margaret Mitchell's instinct was just right. We have a dissolve here and our imagination is quite capable of realizing what is going on inside Scarlett.

— — — — — — — — —

SCENE 75:

The expansion of Charles' proposal in scene 75 is rather decidedly inept. In the first place, "I love you" is never really effective on the screen. Usage has done something to it—killed it, warped it in some way so it is only an expression that leaves some audiences cold and makes others snicker. Now, shouldn't we follow Miss Mitchell's method here? All this building up of Scarlett's love and Scarlett's plan has made possible the short, sharp <u>denouements</u> in the library and in this scene. They are effective as they are. They are all prepared for and we are simply interested in the answers. Here, as in the library scene, the script writer has seen fit to blow it up and make it draggy.

The underlying truth here is that Scarlett's show-off has worked perfectly, but it has worked not for Ashley but for <u>Charles</u>, who was little more than a bystander. We don't have to sell his love to the audience—and more important, we don't even have to sell Scarlett's astounding decision.

I have taken the liberty of making many cuts and additions in this scene using the old dialogue.

Shouldn't there be a seat on the landing for Charles and Melanie in this scene?

———————

SCENE 74:

While the men are rushing away to war, I seem to hear the melody of "Goodnight, Ladies" played swiftly and satirically while Scarlett makes her arrangements with Charles Hamilton.

TO: Barbara Keon[1]   *Typed memo, 1 p. Harry Ransom Humanities Research Center, University of Texas, Austin Selznick International Pictures stationery. Culver City, California*

January 24, 1939

"GONE WITH THE WIND"
REASONS AGAINST
SCARLETT'S MISCARRIAGE
AT THE END.

It seems obvious to me that three such bitter doses as the death of a child, a miscarriage and the death of a woman in childbirth will leave a terribly bitter taste in the audiences' collective mouth at the end of the picture. Melanie's death was prepared for more adequately in the book than we can do it in the picture—and in the book the miscarriage seems a less of a disaster since Scarlett already had three children.

Most of all, the three events are necessary in such close juxtaposition in the picture, one scene crowding upon the other, that I think the miscarriage can certainly be spared. Mr. Selznick's scheme of having Melanie's talk with Rhett follow the night of the party seems to me infinitely superior.

If all three of these catastrophes are used there is not a reporter in the press who will not seize upon them and blame them for the impression of general unhappiness which the picture will leave. There is something about <u>three</u> gloomy things that is infinitely worse than two, and I do not believe that people are grateful for being harrowed in quite this way.

F. Scott Fitzg——

FSF: cf

[1]Scenario Assistant and Production Secretary, Selznick International Pictures.

TO: *Scottie Fitzgerald*   *Typed copy, 1 p. Princeton University*
January 1939   *Encino, California*

Dearest Pie:

Day of rest! After a wild all-night working on <u>Gone with the Wind</u> and more to come tomorrow. I read it—I mean really read it—it is a good novel—not very original, in fact leaning heavily on The Old Wives' Tale, Vanity Fair, and all that has been written on the Civil War. There are no new characters, new technique, new observations—none of the elements that make literature—especially no new examination into human emotions. But on the other hand it is interesting, surprisingly honest, consistent and workman like throughout, and I felt no contempt for it but only a certain pity for those who considered it the supreme achievement of the human mind. So much for that—I may be on it two weeks—or two months. I disagreed with everybody about how to do Madame Curie and they're trying it another way.

Your cold stirred certain gloomy reflections in me. Like me, you were subject to colds when young, deep chest colds near to pneumonia. I didn't begin to be a heavy smoker until I was a Sophomore but it took just one year to send me into tuberculosis and cast a shadow that has been extremely long. I wish there was something that would make you cut it out—the only pay off is that if you're run down by June to spend a summer in the open air, which is a pity with so much to do and learn. I don't want to bury you in your debut dress.

My own plans are uncertain. I am pretty disgusted with pictures after all that censorship trouble and want to break off for a while when I have another good credit (I wont get one on <u>The Women</u>.)—but <u>when</u>, I don't know.

Havent read <u>De Monarchia</u>.[1] Read several pieces by Cornelia Skinner[2] and found them thin and unamusing. Since you've undertaken the Dorian Grey I hope you make a success of it but I hope the professor knows what you're doing. She might not consider the rearrangement of someone else's words a literary composition, which would leave you out on a limb. Are you taking swimming?

Dearest love,

Daddy

P.S. Of course I do not care if you postpone Cynara, etc., though it's such a detail, and you must be in the library everyday. Your college work comes first—but I cant help wondering how, if time is reduced to such minuscules, you would ever have thought of trying out for a play. That of course is entirely out at present—last year should have taught you <u>that</u> lesson.

[1] Treatise on government by Dante Alighieri.
[2] Cornelia Otis Skinner, writer and actress.

TO: Scottie Fitzgerald   ALS, 5 pp. Princeton University
Winter 1939   Encino, California

Dearest Scottina: I know you looked first at the check, but it does <u>not</u> represent a business transaction. I am too tired at the moment to argue but your figures are wrong. However I'm having it all checked up by my secretary. I think there is a gift somewhere.

Sorry you got the impression that I'm quitting the movies—they are always there—I'm doing a two weeks rewrite for Paramount at the moment after finishing a short story. But I'm convinced that maybe they're not going to make me Czar of the Industry right away, as I thought 10 months ago. It's all right Baby—life has humbled me—Czar or not we'll survive. I am even willing to compromise for Assistant Czar!

Seriously, I expect to dip in and out of the pictures for the rest of my natural life, but it is not very soul-satisfying because it is a business of telling stories fit for children and this is only interesting up to a point. It is the greatest of all human mediums of communication and it is a pity that the censorship had to come along + do this, but there we are. <u>Only</u>—I will never again sign a contract which binds me to tell none other than children's stories for a year and a half!

Anyhow Im on the new Madeline Carrol[1] picture (go to see "Café Society"—it's pretty damn good, I think. This one is the same producer-director-stars combination) and anyhow the movies are a dull life and one hopes one will be able to transcend it.

You've let me down about the reading. I'm sorry you did because I'll have to bargain with you. Read <u>Moll Flanders</u>, for any favors asked. I mean this: skip <u>Tono Bungay</u> but if you don't care enough about my advice to do some fractional exploring in literature instead of skimming <u>Life</u> + <u>The New Yorker</u>—I'm going to get into one of those unsympathetic moods—if I'm not sorry for people's efforts there seems to be an icy and inhuman reaction. So please report on Moll Flanders immediately . . . meanwhile airmail me another travel folder on Mrs. Draper + her girls. Who is she and they? And who is Moll Flanders?

I hope you enjoy the Princeton Prom—please don't be overwhelmingly—but no, I am done with prophecies—make your own mistakes. Let me only say "Please don't be overwhelmingly anything!", and, if you are, don't give my name as the responsible parent! (And by the way never give out any interview to any newspaperman, formal or informal—this is a most definate and most advised plea. My name + you, bearing parts of it, is (are) still news in some quarters—and my current policy, for reasons too numerous to explain, is <u>silence</u>. Please do me this courtesy!)

I should like to meet you somewhere early in April—the 3d or 4th.

Your mother <u>is</u> in Florida—it seems to have been delayed.

[1] Madeleine Carroll, British actress.

Of course I'm glad + it warms me all over to know that even ungramatically "both your French English + history teachers" ect. Though you are pretty completely hatched + I can be little more than your most dependable friend your actions still have a most decided effect on me and at long range I can only observe you thru the eyes of Vassar. I have been amazed that you do not grasp a certain advantage that is within your hand—as definate as the two-headed Russian eagle—a girl who didn't <u>have</u> to have an education because she had the other women's gifts by accident—and who <u>took one anyhow</u>. Like Tommy Hitchcock who came back from England in 1919 already a newspaper hero in his escapes from Germany + the greatest polo player in the world—and went up to Harvard in the same year to become <u>a freshman</u>—because he had the humility to ask himself—"Do I know anything?" That combination is what forever will put him in my pantheon of heroes.

Go thou + do likewise.

Love
Daddy

TO: Budd Schulberg   ALS, 1 p. Schulberg

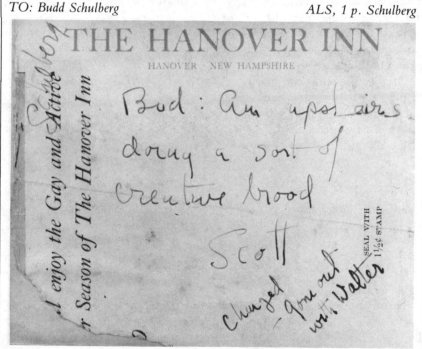

After the expiration of his MGM contract Fitzgerald went to the Dartmouth College Winter Carnival with Budd Schulberg to collaborate on the Winter Carnival screenplay for producer Walter Wanger. Fitzgerald got drunk and was fired. Schulberg later wrote a novel, The Disenchanted (1950), based on these events.

TO: *Budd Schulberg*   *CC, 1 p. Princeton University*

5521 Amestoy Avenue
Encino, California

February 28, 1939

Dear Budd:

I didn't send my Dartmouth impressions because I know that when one is once separated from a picture any advice is rather gratuitous—seems to come from a long and uninformed distance. However, if Walter still wants to use the Indian school for a prologue it would be very funny if the Indian students were being solemnly addressed by Ebenezer when you cut outside and pick up young squaws approaching on snow shoes, bursting into the school and dancing around with the young braves. From there you could dissolve to the station and the arrival of the girls.

Also your introduction of some character at the station might be a student smashing baggage, followed by a newly-arrived girl. And his turning suddenly, mutual recognition: the pay-off is his finding that he has picked up the baggage of his own girl.

On that same working-your-way-through basis, I got a kick from the student waiters going out of character and talking to the guests—like the man who hired himself out to do that sort of thing.

The picture seems temporarily very far away, and I am engrossed in work of my own. But I wish you well, and I won't forget the real pleasure of knowing you, and your patience as I got more and more out of hand under the strain. In retrospect, going East under those circumstances seems one of the silliest mistakes I ever made.

Always your friend,

TO: *Scottie Fitzgerald*   *CC, 2 pp. Princeton University*

March 11, 1939

5521 Amestoy Avenue
Encino, California

Dear Scottie:

Thanks for your long letter about your course of subjects.

Generally, I think that your election of French as a major is a wise decision. I imagine that there will be some competition for the Sorbonne but it might be something to aim at. Also, if you want to take one English course I think you have chosen wisely. Once again I concur about the History of Music if it pleases you. But I wish you would thoroughly reconsider the chemistry question. It is an extremely laborious subject—it requires the most meticulous care and accuracy during long laboratory hours. Moreover, unless your mathematics are at your fingertips—and you were never very good at mathematics—you will be continually re-doing experiments because of one small slip, and I just can't see it fitting in with hours of music practice and some regular exercise.

One suggestion is to take <u>preliminary</u> physics. I don't know whether, if you have already offered that as an entrance, they would allow it, but they might and it would be a fairly easy running over of it as a very essential and interesting subject. I do not mean that I advise a second year physics course because that would run into as much mathematics as chemistry. But if, God help us, they insist on a science I should advise you to consider them in the following order: botany, physiology, or child study. Think of the enormous pleasure amounting, almost, to the consolation for the tragedy of life, that flowers have been to your mother and your grandmother. Maybe you could be a landscape architect like LeNotre[1] but the personal element is equally important. I felt all my life the absence of hobbies except such for me as abstract and academic ones, as military tactics and football. Botany is such a definite thing. It has its feet on the ground. And after reading Thoreau I felt how much I have lost by leaving nature out of my life.

I am sorry about the philosophy. I should think that if anything your test questions will deal with the big key figures, and a certain concentration of work upon Plato, Aquinas, and Descartes would pay more dividends than trying to study over entirely the course from the beginning. Please don't give it up as a bad job. Are you sure that you entirely understand the great usages thru the ages of such terms as <u>nominalists</u> and <u>realists</u>? I want you to keep your interest at least as far as Hegel from whose stem all Marxian thinking flows; certainly you will agree that Marxism does not concern itself with vague sophistries but weds itself to the most practical mechanics of material revolution.

I should suggest that you go to Sea Island with the party and return by yourself, passing at least a full day with your mother in Ashville, and a day, if you like, in Baltimore; that is—I think the Finneys would be a little offended if you did not pay at least a courtesy visit. I shall try my best to be East by the second, and at least cross your path—perhaps in Ashville— but I have let myself be inveigled into another picture and it may possibly run on to the tenth of April; on the other hand it may blow up tomorrow. (It is the new Carroll-MacMurray picture.)

With dearest love.

P.S. Can you give me some sort of budget for your trip to Sea Island.
2nd P.S. You are not entirely right about the translations (poetry, of course, cannot be translated, but even there we have exceptions such as "The Rubai-yat"). Constance Garnet's Russian translations are excellent, while Scott-Moncrief's "Proust" is a masterpiece in itself.[2] And please do not leave

---

[1] André Lenôtre, seventeenth-century French landscape architect best known for his work at Versailles.
[2] Constance Garnett and C. K. Scott-Moncrieff.

good books half-finished, you spoil them for yourself. You shouldn't have started "War and Peace" which is a man's book and may interest you later. But you should finish both the Defore[1] and the Samuel Butler. Don't be so lavish as to ruin masterpieces for yourself. There are not enough of them!

TO: *John Biggs, Jr.*   *ALS, 10 pp. Princeton University*
Spring 1939   *Encino, California*

Dear John—

Your letter with its family chronicle facinated me. It was nice to catch up a little. I remember Baba as a wild fascinating little witch with a vague touch of Wuthering Heights about her as she wrestled with her brothers. One girl in a family of boys has her dangers—like one boy in a family of girls who inevitably has a touch of the milksop—anyhow I'm glad Baba has temperment + sorry you've had to send her to reform school so young. That's where I wanted to send Scottie when she was <u>fired</u> from Walkers last June.

That's a story in herself. Suffice to say it was nothing vicious—a surreptitious trip to a ball game in New Haven—it was after school had closed + some of the girls were sticking around for the Board exams. But it was plenty desturbing—the headmistress had to go up to Vassar and plead with the Dean not to strike her off the list of candidates.

However it ended luckily—if not quite well. That is she got into Vassar at 16 and is still there but I dont think it taught her much, or perhaps taught her the wrong thing. Instead of learning that a fool is one who makes the same mistake twice she learned that a clever person can usually squirm out of trouble—a most dangerous conclusion. She got herself on probation at Vassar in Dec + is only just off last week thank God. Maybe this is too black a picture to paint. She's very popular—was voted most popular + most attractive in her Walker class of 43—and did after all get a diploma from the school. She's coming out with her best friend "Peaches" Finney (do you remember <u>Eben</u> at Hill + Princeton) in Baltimore next Octtober. Pete's going to present her at the Bachellor's Cottillion. That sounds odd from an old solitary like me with anti-bourgeoise leanings but remember Karl Marx made every attempt to marry his daughters into the Brittish nobility.

As to sons—that's another question. I'd feel on a big spot if I were you. Tho you're not a worrier. With daughter I can feel sure she's about like me—very little of her mother save the good looks—like me with less positive artistic talent and much more natural social talent. She hasn't the <u>lonleness</u> of the artist—though one can't be sure that means anything. Ernest wasn't lonely superficially—what I mean is that in spite of the fact that

[1]Defoe.

Scottie edited her school paper + wrote the school play she doesn't <u>care</u>— doesn't care deeply + passionately so that she feels the nessessity to say. And its just as well. Nothing is more fatuous than the American habit of labeling one of their four children as the artist on a sort of family tap day as if the percentage of artists who made any kind of go of the lowsy business was one to four. It's much closer to 1 to 400,000. You've got to have the egotism of a maniac with the clear triple-thinking of a Flaubert. The amount of initial talent or let us say skill and facility is a very small element in the long struggle whose most happy can only be a mercifully swift exhaustion. Who'd want to live on like Kipling with a name one no longer owned— the empty shell of a gift long since accepted + consumed?

To go back. I wont discuss boys. They are incalculable. But I would like to sit around with you for hours discussing men in particular JB Jr. + F.S.F. I would make you read some of the stuff that's stirred me lately + append this list, culled from two years.

(a.) <u>Julius Caesar</u> by James Anthony Fronde.[1] Don't be appalled—it's as modern as Strachey[2] + I find from Max that Scribner never lets it go out of print.

(b.) <u>Flaubert and Madame Bovary</u>.[3] Absolute Tops.

(c.) <u>The Culture of Cities</u>[4] which you must have read.

(d.) <u>The Trial</u>—fantastic novel by the Czek Franz Kaffka which you may have to wait for but it is worth it—its an influence among the young comparable only to Joyce in 1920–25.

(e.) As for Americans there's only one—Jerome Weidman,[5] whose two books have been withdrawn as too perspicacious about the faults of his own race. He's a grand writer tho—only 25 and worth fifty of this Steinbeck who is cheap blatant imitation of D.H. Lawrence. A book club return of the public to its own vomit.

(f.) (I am now writing this letter for my files as well as to you) The best <u>individual</u> novel of the last five years is still Malraux <u>Man's Fate</u>.[6] I fought against reading it liking neither the scene nor what I thought was going to be the attitude—but <u>Jesus</u>, once I'd gotten into it—it's as absorbing as the <u>Farewell to Arms</u>. On the other hand <u>Man's Hope</u>[7] is hasty journalism— about as good as Ernests Spanish stuff. (He agrees with me about Steinbeck by the way—thinks he's a phoney like Farrel) You know how generous I feel toward new men if they have something and I hope you wont read

---

[1] *Caesar: A Sketch* (Scribners, 1937), by James Anthony Froude; first published by Scribners in 1880.

[2] Lytton Strachey, biographer and essayist.

[3] A 1939 study by Francis Steegmuller.

[4] 1938 study by Lewis Mumford.

[5] Simon & Schuster temporarily ceased printing Weidman's novel *I Can Get It for You Wholesale* (1937) because of its unflattering portrait of Jewish businessmen; the novel's sequel, *What's in It for Me?*, was published in 1938.

[6] *Man's Fate*, a novel about Communism in China, was first published in 1933.

[7] *Man's Hope*, a novel about the Spanish Civil War, was first published in 1937.

under this a jealousy of which I think I'm incapable. I keep waiting for Odets[1] to produce something fine.

For God's sake order these right away and for good jazz I append Guedalla's <u>Wellington</u>,[2] and Burns <u>Lee, Grant and Sherman</u>[3]—they'll kill a night of insomnia. Hayes book on Lincoln[4] neither brings us closer nor further away—ends by being a bore because he seems to have been conspicuously non-communicative about what we have now decided were the great moments. I guess Lincoln was just too busy to throw him his little crust of attention + he was out whoring somewhere.

I hope you'll be a better Judge than I've been a man of letters. I've worked here on the best jobs—<u>Madame Curie</u>, <u>Three Comrades</u>, <u>Gone with the Wind</u>, ect but it's an uphill business and the only great satisfaction Ive had has been paying off my debts—which amounted to <u>about $40,000</u> at the end of 1936. At that point, despite Becky Sharps[5] dictum that you can live on your debts for awhile people begin to distrust you—and someday in Dostoievskian manner I'm going to write about the great difference between how you highheartedly helped me over a hurdle and the heartburnings and humiliations I went thru in the process of approaching you. (That sentence is as full of "h's" as a passage in the later Swinburne.)

Anyhow we have always been great good friends to each other and that is a satisfaction as Gertrude Stien would say. I am glad for Bobby as only an old lunger can be glad (was she ever one). I only play ping-pong but if she ever condescends to that let her have a table ready at the point where our paths next cross.

Scott

TO: *Zelda Fitzgerald*   CC, 1 p. *Princeton University*
Encino, California

May
6
1939

Dearest Zelda:-

Excuse this being typewritten, but I am supposed to lie in bed for a week or so and look at the ceiling. I objected somewhat to that regime as being drastic, so I am allowed two hours of work every day.[6]

---

[1] Clifford Odets, proletarian playwright, whose work included *Waiting for Lefty* (1935), *Awake and Sing* (1935), and *Golden Boy* (1937).

[2] *Wellington* (1931), by Philip Guedalla.

[3] A 1938 study by Alfred Higgins Burne.

[4] *Lincoln and the Civil War in the Diaries and Letters of John Hay* (1939).

[5] Becky Sharp, Thackeray's unscrupulous heroine in *Vanity Fair*; one of the novel's chapters is entitled "How to Live Well on Nothing a Year."

[6] Fitzgerald's tuberculosis had become active.

You were a peach throughout the whole trip[1] and there isn't a minute of it when I don't think of you with all the old tenderness and with a consideration that I never understood that you had before. Because I can never remember anything else but consideration from you, so perhaps that sounds a little too much like a doctor or someone who knew you only when you were ill.

You are the finest, loveliest, tenderest, most beautiful person I have ever known, but even that is an understatement because the length that you went to there at the end would have tried anybody beyond endurance. Everything that I said and that we talked about during that time stands—I had a wire from daughter in regard to the little Vassar girl, telling me her name, and saying that the whole affair was washed out, but I don't feel at home with the business yet.

There was a sweet letter waiting here from you for me when I came. With dearest love.

TO: *Edmund Wilson*   *CC, 1 p. Yale University*

May
16
1939

Dear Bunny:-News that you and Mary[2] had a baby reached me rather late because I was out of California for several months. Hope he is now strong and crawling. Tell him if he grows up any bigger I shall be prepared to take him for a loop when he reaches twenty-one at which time I shall be sixty-three. I don't know any girl in the last several years with more charm than Mary. It was a delight to meet her and spend an evening with you all. If I had known about the news in time, I would have wired you.

I called up Louise Fort in San Diego, but couldn't get her number and imagine she had left before I came back to California. However, I am sending on your letter to Ted Paramore who may have more luck.

Believe me, Bunny, it meant more to me than it could possibly have meant to you to see you that evening. It seemed to renew old times learning about Franz Kafka and latter things that are going on in the world of poetry, because I am still the ignoramus that you and John Bishop wrote about at Princeton. Though my idea is now, to learn about a new life from Louis B. Mayer[3] who promises to teach me all about things if he ever gets around to it.

Ever your devoted friend,

5521 Amestoy Avenue
Encino, California

[1] In April Fitzgerald had met Zelda in Asheville and taken her to Cuba.
[2] Wilson had married writer Mary McCarthy in 1938.
[3] Head of MGM.

TO: *Maxwell Perkins*   *TLS, 1 p. Princeton University*

May
22
1939

Dear Max:-

Just had a letter from Charlie Scribner—a very nice letter and I appreciated it and will answer it. He seemed under the full conviction that the novel was about Hollywood[1] and I am in terror that this mis-information may have been disseminated to the literary columns. If I ever gave any such impression it is entirely false: I said that the novel was about some things that had happened to me in the last two years. It is distinctly not about Hollywood (and if it were it is the last impression that I would want to get about.)

It is, however, progressing nicely, except that I have been confined to bed for a few weeks with a slight return of my old malady. It was nice getting a glimpse of you, however brief—especially that last day. I caught the plane at half past four and had an uneventful trip West.

I have grown to like this particular corner of California where I shall undoubtedly stay all summer. Dates for a novel are as you know, uncertain, but I am blocking this out in a fashion so that, unlike "Tender", I may be able to put it aside for a month and pick it up again at the exact spot factually and emotionally where I left off.

Wish I had some news, but what I have seen lately is only what you can see outside a window. With very best to all—and please do correct that impression which Charlie seems to have.

> Ever your friend,

> > Scott

5521 Amestoy Avenue
Encino, California

TO: *Harold Ober*   *TLS, 2 pp. Lilly Library*

May 29 1939

Dear Harold:—

This letter is going to be full of information, some of which I may have let drop in New York or which you may have guessed. In the first place, as I suspected, I have been ill with a touch of the old malady from about the time I came off "Gone With the Wind". I knew I should not have taken on those last two pictures both of which were terrors and far beyond my

---

[1]Fitzgerald's novel in progress, *The Love of the Last Tycoon*, was, in fact, about Hollywood, but he feared that if his subject were known he would be denied employment by the studios.

strength at the time.[1] The sudden outburst of drink was a result of an attempt to keep up my strength for an effort of which I was not capable. After consultations here I have been condemned, in no uncertain terms, to a period at home some of which has to be spent in bed. This doesn't mean that I am not working—I am allowed three to four hours a day for that, but I have told Swanie[2] to sign me off any available list. (This Hitchcock from England seems to have had me first on the list to do "Rebecca") But Swanie evidently realized that I really wasn't up to anything (for observed on a list by Sheilah who happened to see it in Hitchcock's office at Selznick's was, "Unavailable—gone to Cuba.")

Well, "Unavailable—gone to Cuba" is as good as anything else. So to friends in the East I would rather not have it known that I was ill. Any story that I have gone away into the California mountains to write a novel will cover the situation because if I should want to go back to actual picture making next Fall, I would not want anyone to be able to say, "Well—that Fitzgerald, I understand he's been sick and we don't want anyone that's liable to break down on this picture." In other words, it would do me a damage here which it would not do in the East, as this is a hot bed of gossip. I even prefer Swanie to think that I am a bluffing hypochondriac than to know the whole truth. I think I told him that I had a little mild heart trouble. I am cut off here in Encino from anything and anybody who might disturb me, under the charge of an excellent doctor. There's no taint of alcoholism to confuse the issue and my only visitor is Shielah who comes out two or three times a week. We are friends again, even intimates—though we stick to our old resolution not to go back to the same basis as before.

Now, I wish you could airmail me the following information and please do not spare me in this, because my morale is high and I want to know the exact situation where I stand with the magazines—notably the Post. As in our previous discussions I told you that that five thousand word length is likely to be a terror for me and while I realize that Collier's has the right to see some stories still I cannot somehow see it as a permanent relation. I have planned my work in the following order:

First, I have blocked out my novel completely with a rough sketch of every episode and event and character so that under proper circumstances I could begin writing it tomorrow. It is a short novel about fifty thousand words long and should take me three to four months.

However, for reasons of income tax I feel I should be more secure before I launch into such a venture—but it will divide easily into five thousand word lengths and Collier's might take a chance on it where the Post would not. They might at least be promised a first look at it when it's finished— possibly some time late in the Fall. Secondly, I have hesitated between the idea of those picture originals which I discussed with you and the idea of

---

[1] Winter Carnival and Air Raid.
[2] H. N. Swanson.

doing some short stories and have decided on the second because since I haven't done a short story for over two years I feel rather full of material and rather enthusiastic about doing a few. What I want to know most is how much the <u>Post</u> would pay me. I want to know frankly from their contact man what is the opinion of the new editor of of my work and as specifically as possible the sum they would offer. After this long lapse—(it has now been four years since I was their prize boy)—I do not expect $4000., naturally, but if he suggested any such sum as $2000., it would lead me to believe that he did not especially like my work, or else felt that I had fallen off and gone Hollywood or wants to make a clean sweep of Lorimer's old authors. Whatever you cannot find out specifically, I wish you would write me the <u>feel</u> of.

Also in regard to other magazines. <u>The Pictorial Review</u> has not published those two Gwen stories. They weren't good stories—were written at a bad time, and I don't blame them. Perhaps later I can either revise those stories or send them another to go with them which will make it an interesting series. That, however, is out for the present as I feel that everything I wrote in '35 was all covered with a dust of gloom and illness. Likewise with Balmer whom I suppose has never forgiven me for the dilatory arrival of the Red Book stories. What does that leave as possible high-priced markets in New York? As I say, I feel I have from two to four short stories in me which will be in my own manner. And now let me repeat that if you could airmail me this information or as much of it as you can collect, it would be of inestimable value at this moment.

I warned you this would be a long letter. With warmest regards to you and Ann and the children.

Ever,
Scott Fitzg

5521 Amestoy Avenue
Encino, California

TO: S. J. Perelman[1]

CC, 1 p. Princeton University
Encino, California

June 7, 1939

Dear Sidney:

Seeing your apparently dead but only sleeping pan in the magazine, I was reminded to address you on several things. One is that while you once inherited a baby nurse from me I have now evened matters up by owning your 1937 Ford which gives excellent service. But the real purpose is this—

---

[1] Humorist and screenwriter.

that Laura's brother (Nathaniel West) sent me his book[1] and a very nice letter with it which has totally disappeared since a trip I made to Cuba and I don't know where to reach him to answer it.

The book though it puts Gogol's "The Lower Depth" in the class with "The Tale of Benjamin Bunny" certainly has scenes of extraordinary power—if that phrase is still in use. Especially I was impressed by the pathological crowd at the premiere, the character and handling of the aspirant actress and the uncanny almost medieval feeling of some of his Hollywood background, set off by those vividly drawn grotesques. The book bears an odd lopsided resemblance to Victor Hugo's "Notre Dame de Paris" except that the anonymous builders of the middle ages did a better job with their flying buttresses than Mannix, Katz and Company with their theory of the buttocks in place.[2]

Anyway, all good wishes to you. I'll be out of pictures at least till late Fall, working on a novel. Best to Laura.

Ever your friend,

TO: *Maxwell Perkins*   *Wire. Princeton University*
1939

ENCINO CALIF   JUL 3

HAVE BEEN WRITING IN BED WITH TUBERCULOSIS UNDER DOCTORS NURSES CARE SIS ARRIVING WEST. OBER HAS DECIDED NOT TO BACK ME THOUGH I PAID BACK EVERY PENNY AND EIGHT THOUSAND COMMISSION.[3] AM GOING TO WORK THURSDAY IN STUDIO AT FIFTEEN HUNDRED CAN YOU LEND ME SIX HUNDRED FOR ONE WEEK BY WIRE TO BANK AMERICA CULVERCITY. SCOTTIE HOSPITAL WITH APPENDIX AND AM ABSOLUTELY WITHOUT FUNDS. PLEASE DO NOT ASK OBERS COOPERATION

SCOTT
JUL 4   730A.

TO: *Harold Ober*   *Wire. Lilly Library*
July 13, 1939   *Van Nuys, California*

STILL FLABBERGASTED AT YOUR ABRUPT CHANGE IN POLICY AFTER 20 YEARS ESPECIALLY WITH STORY IN YOUR HANDS STOP MY COMMERCIAL VALUE CANT

---

[1] *The Day of the Locust* (1939), by Nathanael West.

[2] Eddie Mannix and Sam Katz were movie producers. Fitzgerald is referring to the Hollywood rule that viewers must be so interested in a movie that they are unaware of their numb posteriors.

[3] Ober had informed Fitzgerald that family obligations prevented him from making further advances or loans.

HAVE SUNK FROM 60 THOUSAND TO NOTHING BECAUSE OF A SLOW HEALING
LUNG CAVITY STOP AFTER 30 PICTURE OFFERS DURING THE MONTHS I WAS IN
BED SWANSON NOW PROMISES NOTHING FOR ANOTHER WEEK STOP CANT YOU
ARRANGE A FEW HUNDRED ADVANCE FROM A MAGAZINE SO I CAN EAT TODAY
AND TOMORROW STOP WONT YOU WIRE
    SCOTT

TO: *Arnold Gingrich*   ALS, 1 p. *Princeton University*
July 1939

Hide-out adress! Now that   {   5521 Amestoy Ave.
I've paid off 99/100 of my debts   {   Encino, Cal.
people want me to contract more

Dear Arnold:
    My account books are on their way out here and Ive forgotten what you
used to pay me for stories. Anyhow will you credit these[1] against my balance
and airmail me how much that leaves? (also whether you like the stories)?
    One more thing—and here I'm intruding into your province. Both these
stories depend on <u>surprise</u> as much as an old O. Henry did—and sometimes
your editors give away what used to be called the "jist" in the top caption.
I know for some pieces that's advisable—here it would be absolutely fatal.
Could you note this on the stories?
    With thanks and best wishes

                                   Scott Fitzgerald

Excuse pencil but this is one of those days. The stories are shorter than I
thought but I'd made a last cut.

TO: *Arnold Gingrich*   *Wire. University of Michigan*
July 17, 1939

BEEN SICK IN BED FOUR MONTHS AND WRITTEN AMONG OTHER THINGS TWO
GOOD SHORT STORIES ONE 2300 WORDS AND 1800 BOTH TYPED AND READY FOR
AIR MAIL STOP WOULD LIKE TO GIVE YOU FIRST LOOK AND AT SAME TIME TOUCH
YOU FOR 100 WIRED TO BANK OF AMERICA CULVERCITY CALIFORNIA STOP EVEN
IF ONLY ONE SUITED YOU I WOULD STILL BE FINANCIALLY ADVANCE IN YOUR
BOOKS PLEASE WIRE IMMEDIATELY 5521 AMESTOY AVENUE ENCINO CALIFORNIA
AS AM RETURNING STUDIO MONDAY MORNING
    THAT GHOST   SCOTT FITZGERALD.

---

[1] After two years of working on screenplays Fitzgerald resumed writing fiction and sent two
stories to *Esquire*—probably "Design in Plaster" and "The Lost Decade."

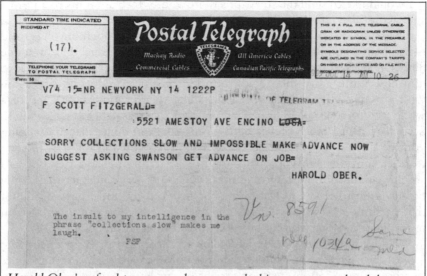

Harold Ober's refusal to resume advances resulted in a permanent break between Fitzgerald and his agent in 1939 (Princeton University).

TO: Kenneth Littauer[1]   TLS, 3 pp. New York Public Library

July
18
1939

Dear Kenneth: —

I was of course delighted to finish off the Civil War story[2] to your satisfaction at last—I may say to my satisfaction also, because the last version felt right. And after twenty months of moving pictures it was fun to be back at prose-writing again. That has been the one bright spot in a situation you may have heard of from Harold Ober: that I have been laid up and writing in bed since the first of May, and I am only just up and dressed.

As I told your Mr. Wilkinson when he telephoned, the first thing I did when I had to quit pictures for awhile was to block out my novel (a short one the size of Gatsby) and made the plan on a basis of 2500 word units. The block-out is to be sure that I can take it up or put it down in as much time as is allowed between picture work and short stories. I will never again sign a long picture contract, no matter what the inducement: most of the profit when one overworks goes to doctors and nurses.

Meanwhile I am finishing a 4500-word piece designed for your pages. It should go off to you airmail Saturday night because I am going back to the studios for a short repair job Monday.

[1] Colliers fiction editor.
[2] "The End of Hate," Colliers (June 22, 1940).

I would like to send the story <u>directly to you</u>, which amounts to a virtual split with Ober. This is regrettable after twenty years of association but it had better be masked under the anonymity of "one of those things." Harold is a fine man and has been a fine agent and the fault is mine. Through one illness he backed me with a substantial amount of money (all paid back to him now with Hollywood gold), but he is not prepared to do that again with growing boys to educate—and, failing this, I would rather act for a while as my own agent in the short story, just as I always have with Scribner's. But I much prefer, both for his sake and mine, that my sending you the story direct should be a matter <u>between you and me</u>. For the fact to reach him through your office might lead to an unpleasant cleavage of an old relationship. I am writing him <u>later in the week</u> making the formal break on terms that will be understood between us, and I have no doubt that in some ways he will probably welcome it. Relationships have an unfortunate way of wearing out, like most things in this world.

Would you be prepared, in return for an agreement or contract for <u>first look at the novel</u> and at <u>a specified number of short stories in a certain time</u>, to advance me $750, by wire on receipt of this letter—which will be even before the story reaches you Monday? This is a principal factor in the matter at the moment as these three months of illness have got me into a mess with income tax and insurance problems. When you get this, will you wire me Yes or No, because if you can't, I can probably start studio work Friday. This may be against your general principles—from my angle I am offering you rather a lot for no great sum.

Ever yours with best wishes,

Scott Fitzgerald

P.S. If this meets your favorable consideration the money should be wired to the Bank of America, Culver City. If not would you wire me an answer anyhow because my determination to handle my magazine relationship myself is quite final.

The novel will run just short of 50,000 words

5521 Amestoy Avenue
Encino, California

TO: Maxwell Perkins   *CC, 2 pp. Princeton University*

July
19
1939

Dear Max:—

I expected to go to work last Wednesday and have been offered two jobs and had to turn them down—though there is no connection with the old fairy tale of the man who always started looking for a certain kind of game immediately after it passed out of his sight. I can do any kind of work except (a) the kind with producers who work all night which the doctor says is absolutely out, and (b) stories of the Tarzan and Mark of Zorro persuasion which require the practically stationary brain. I am even strong enough to work within the studio walls now and it is a question of days until a romantic comedy or a boy-and-girl story shows up.

The main point of this letter is confidential for the most important reasons. Harold Ober and I are parting company. Whether he is throwing me over or me him may be a subject of controversy—but not on my part. I think he is doing it even if Madame Ober uses me for the rest of her life as an example of gross ingratitude. She was very kind in taking Scottie during many of the intervals between vacations from camp and school in '35 and '36 when I was so ill—I have always wanted to do something for her boys in return. Also I shall be forever grateful to Harold for his part of the help in backing me through that long illness, but his attitude has changed and I tell you this without any anger, but after a month's long and regretful consideration. He is a single-tracked man and the feeling that he once had of definite interest combined with forgiveness of my sins, has changed to a sort of general disapproval and a vague sense that I am through—this in spite of the fact that I paid him over ten thousand dollars in commissions in the last year-and-a half and refunded the whole thirteen thousand that I owed him.

I think something to do with it is the fact that almost every time I have come to New York lately I have just taken Zelda somewhere and have gone on more or less of a binge, and he has formed the idea that I am back in the mess of three years ago.

Anyhow, it is impossible to continue a relation which has become so strained and difficult. Even though there has been no spoken impoliteness there is a new fashion of discussing my stories as if he was a rather dissatisfied and cranky editor and of answering telegrams with delayed airmails and, most of all, completely changing his old policy of backing me up to the limit of what the next story will probably be sold for which makes it impossible to go on. He fairly earned the fifty thousand dollars or so of commissions that I've paid him and nothing snows one under quicker than a send of disbelief and disillusion in anyone close. The final touch was when I had to sell two stories to Esquire at $250., when I wanted cash quick—one of them was worth at least $1000., from Liberty if he could have given me enough advance to survive the wait.

So while I feel regret I have no moral compunction. This is a matter of survival. A man lost in the Arctic for the second time cannot sit waiting while a former rescuer refuses to send out another relief expedition. I would rather deal personally with the editors, as I deal always with you, and get opinions at the source. Harold's greatest help was when I lived in Europe. As you know we have never been very close either intellectually or emotionally (save for his kindness to Scottie). . . .[1] I stuck with him, of course, when he left Reynolds, but now he has many correct and conventional Agatha Christies, etc., on his list who never cause any inconvenience, so I doubt if I will be missed.

I thought you should know this—know also that he has always treated me fairly and generously and is above reproach as an agent. The blame which brought about this situation is entirely mine. But it is no such illogical step as the one which made Tom Wolfe leave Scribner's. A few weeks ago when three Fitzgeralds at once were in the hands of the medical profession he found it inconvenient to help and under the circumstances of the last year and a half the episode served to give me a great uncertainty as to his caring what becomes of me.

Above all things I wish you wouldn't discuss this with him. I have not, nor will ever say, nor could say anything against him either personally or professionally, but even the fact that I have discussed the matter with you might upset him and give him ideas that I had, and turn what should be a peaceful cleavage into an unpleasant affair.

I am better day by day and long only to make some picture money and get back to the novel.

                                                        Ever your friend,

5521 Amestoy Avenue
Encino, California

TO: Harold Ober   *TL (CC), 2 pp. Princeton University*

                                              July 19 1939

Dear Harold:—

This is not a request for any more backing—there will be no more requests. I am quite sure you would be as stubborn in any decision that I am through as you were up to 1934 about the value of my stories. Also I am writing this letter with, I hope, no touch of unpleasantness—simply from a feeling that perhaps you share, that I have depended too long on backing and had better find out at the source whether my products are considered deficient and why.

As I said in my telegram, the shock wasn't so much at your refusal to lend me a specific sum, because I know the demands on you and that you may not have felt able to do so at that time—it was rather "the manner of the doing", your sudden change of policy in not lending me up to the limit of what a story would sell for, a custom which had obtained between us for over a dozen years. The consequence here is of little interest now—I turned down several picture offers under the conviction that you could tide

---

[1]Twenty-three words omitted by the editor.

me over until I got through to a magazine (and this a few months after telling me there was no hurry about paying back that money and just after a year and a half during which I paid your firm over ten thousand dollars in commissions and you personally thirteen thousand dollars in advances.) Sick as I was I would have taken those offers rather than go along on two loans which melted immediately into medical bills and has left me most of the past seven weeks with bank balances of between eighty and fourteen dollars.

You were not here; long distance calls are unsatisfactory and telegrams suddenly did not deserve more than an airmail answer from you so I had no choice but to come to the conclusion that you were through with me in a big way. I repeat, I don't blame you. Every time I've come East I have gone on a binge, most often after a time with Zelda, and the last time I brought a good deal of inconvenience into your settled life. Though you were very nice and polite about it (and I can scarcely remember twice in our relations when there has been any harshness between us—certainly never any harsh feeling on my side) and my unwritten debt to you is terribly large and I shall always be terribly aware of it—your care and cherishing of Scottie during the intervals between school and camp in those awful sick years of '35 and '36. I have wanted someday to be able to repay that to your boys with the same instinct that made me want to give the little Finney girl a trip out here.

But Harold, I must never again let my morale become as shattered as it was in those black years—and the situation resolves itself into this: it is as if a man had once trekked up into the Arctic to save a partner and his load, and then when the partner became lost a second time, the backer was not able or willing to help him get out. It doesn't diminish the lost man's gratitude for former favors, but rather than perish, he must find his own way out—and quickly. I had to sell a 2400 word story to Esquire[1] that I think Liberty would have paid a thousand for because three Fitzgeralds needed surgeons, psychiatrists and T.B. doctors and medicines at the same time.

I feel less hesitation in saying this because it is probably what you wanted for some time. You now have plenty of authors who produce correctly and conduct their affairs in a business-like manner. On the contrary, I have a neurosis about anyone's uncertainty about my ability that has been a principal handicap in the picture business. And secondly, the semi-crippled state into which I seem to get myself sometimes (almost like the hero of my story "Financing Finnegan") fill me, in the long nights, with a resentment toward the absurd present which is not fair to you or to the past. Everything I have ever done or written is me, and who doesn't choose to accept the whole cannot but see the wisdom of a parting. One doesn't change at 42 though one can grow more tired and even more acquiescent—and I am very close

---

[1] "Design in Plaster."

to knowing how you feel about it all: I realize there is little place in this tortured world for any exhibition of shattered nerves or anything that illness makes people do.

So goodbye and I won't be ridiculous enough to thank you again. Nothing would ever make me forget your many kindnesses and the good times and laughs we have had together. With very best to Ann and the children.

Ever yours, gratefully,

P.S. I know you are not worrying about the $500., but I will pay you out of the first money I make, which probably won't be long now.

5521 Amestoy Avenue
Encino, California

TO: Kenneth Littauer   *CC, 1 p. Princeton University*
Late July? 1939

Dear Kenneth:—

Here's another Hollywood story. It is absolutely true to Hollywood as I see it. Asking you to read it I want to get two things clear. First, that it isn't particularly likely that I'll write a great many more stories about young love. I was tagged with that by my first writings up to 1925. Since then I have written stories about young love. They have been done with increasing difficulty and increasing insincerity. I would either be a miracle man or a hack if I could go on turning out an identical product for three decades.

I know that is what's expected of me, but in that direction the well is pretty dry and I think I am much wiser in not trying to strain for it but rather to open up a new well, a new vein. You see, I not only announced the birth of my young illusions in "This Side of Paradise" but pretty much the death of them in some of my last <u>Post</u> stories like "Babylon Revisited." Lorrimer seemed to understand this in a way. Nevertheless, an overwhelming number of editors continue to associate me with an absorbing interest in young girls—an interest that at my age would probably land me behind the bars.

I have a daughter. She is very smart; she is very pretty; she is very popular. Her problems seem to me to be utterly dull and her point of view completely uninteresting. In other words, she is exactly what I was once accused of being—callow. Moreover she belongs to a very overstimulated and not really adventurous generation—a generation that has been told the price of everything as well as its value. I once tried to write about her. I couldn't.

So you see I've made a sort of turn. My hope is that, like Tarkington, if I can no longer write "M. Beaucaire" and the "Gentleman from Indiana",

I can make people laugh instead as he did in "Seventeen" which is completely objective and unromantic.[1]

The second thing is my relation to Ober. It is completely vague. I've very seldom taken his advice on stories. I have regarded him as a mixture of friend, bill collector and for a couple of sick years as backer. So far as any editorial or financial dealing, I would much rather, as things are now, deal directly with an editor. For instance, if this sort of story is worth less to you than a story of young love, I would be perfectly willing to accept less. I would not want any agent to stand in my way in that regard. I think all the agents still act as if we were back in the 1920's in a steadily rising market.

So can I again ask you to deal telegraphically with me? I hope this story amuses you.

Ever yours,

TO: *Harold Ober*   *TLS, 2 pp. Lilly Library*

August 2 1939

Dear Harold:—

I have been and still am somewhat shocked by your sudden and most determined reversal of form. Only six months ago you were telling me "not to be in too much of a hurry to pay you back" but instead try to save some money. It was something of a counter-blast to find that my credit was now worth much less than I loaned Charles Warren and other young authors last year.

Your advice that I should have "taken on some movie work" with a lung cavity and a temperature of 102° was a new slant. The cavity evidently began to form about the time I started on "Air Raid", and your implication that I had been loafing must have been based on those two day binges in New York, several months apart. Anyhow, when the temperature was still a hundred and the cavity still crackling I was asking Swanie to get me work and meanwhile putting in five hours a day on a bed-desk.

Being in need, I make no apology for having sent the original of the enclosed[2] directly to the <u>Post</u>, with the request that they communicate by wire to me as well as by letter to you. I had a fifteen day wait on "Temperature"—it is hard to remember there was a time your cables reached me in North Africa. Sending a story direct may be bad policy but one doesn't consider that when one is living on money from a hocked Ford—every day counts, less in the material matter of eating than in the inestimable question of morale. Swanie turned down a dozen jobs for me when I was sick in bed—but there just haven't been any since the cavity began to heal.

[1]Novels by Booth Tarkington published respectively in 1900, 1899, and 1916.
[2]"Director's Special," published as "Discard," *Harper's Bazaar* (January 1948).

I don't have to explain that even though a man has once saved another from drowning, when he refuses to stretch out his arm a second time the victim has to act quickly and desperately to save himself. For change you did, Harold, and without warning—the custom of lending up to the probable yield of a next short story obtained between us for a dozen years. Certainly you haven't just discovered that I'm not any of the things a proper business man should be? And it wasn't even a run around—it was a walk-around that almost made me think the New York telegraph was closed. Finally I had to sell a pair of stories[1] to <u>Esquire</u> the longer one of which (2800 words) might have brought twice as much from <u>Liberty</u>.

Whatever I am supposed to guess, your way of doing it and the time you chose, was as dispiriting as could be. I have been all too hauntingly aware during these months of what you did from 1934 to 1937 to keep my head above water after the failure of <u>Tender</u>, Zelda's third collapse and the long illness. But you have made me sting none the less. Neither Swanson nor Sheilah nor Eddie Knopf have any idea but that I have labored conscientiously out here for twenty months and every studio (except Wanger, but including Metro!) asked for, according to Swanson, me at some time during April and May.

Your reasons for refusing to help me were all good, all praise-worthy, all sound—but wouldn't they have been equally so any time within the past fifteen years? And they followed a year and a half in which I fulfilled all my obligations.

If it is of any interest to you I haven't had a drink in two months but if I was full of champagne I couldn't be more confused about you than I am now.

Ever yours,
Scott

P.S. "Temperature" turned up yesterday at the Van Nuys Railway Express—and in case you think that's incredible I forward the evidence.

5521 Amestoy Avenue
Encino, California

TO: *Zelda Fitzgerald*　　　　　　　*AL (draft), 4 pp. Princeton University*
August 1939　　　　　　　　　　　　　　　*Encino, California*

Dearest
I know you're going to miss Scottie and I hope August passes quickly for you. It seems strange that it's here—this last month has been too much

---

[1] Probably "Design in Plaster," *Esquire* (November 1939), and "The Lost Decade" (December 1939).

of a hell for me to help much, but now I can see light at the end of the passage. It was like 1935–1936 when no one but Mrs Owens and I knew how bad things were and all my products were dirges and elegies. Sickness + no money are a wretched combination. But, as I told you, there has not at least been, an accumulation of debt + there are other blessings. I see that only the rich now can do the things you + I once did in Europe—it is a tourist class world—my salary out here during those frantic 20 months turned out to be an illusion once Ober + the governments of the U.S. and Canada was paid and the doctors began.

Keep well. I'm going to try to. I'm glad your mother's illness was a false alarm.

Have arranged for Scottie to have a piano near bye, tho not in this cottage. She seems to have had a happy time with you. I have written two long + two short stories and wait daily for Swanson to find me a studio job that wont be too much of a strain—no more 14 hour days at any price. By the time you get this I hope I'll be paying the small (not formidable) array of bills that have accumulated. Here is another check to be used most sparingly—not on presents but nessessitics of Scottie's departure, ect. Her tickets + traveling money will reach there Tuesday morning if all goes well. Her rail fare Round Trip is only 78.50 round trip, with 5.00 extra fare both ways.

Dearest Love,

Of course you can count on going South in September. We could even meet you there.

And the editorial comment about your paintings was a real thrill to me. We must do something about that soon.

TO: Arnold Gingrich　　　　　　　　　　*Wire. University of Michigan*
August 13, 1939　　　　　　　　　　　　*Van Nuys, California*

IF YOU LIKE QUOTE SALUTE UNQUOTE[1] DO YOU WANT A MORTGAGE ON ANOTHER TO BE WRITTEN MONDAY IF SO PLEASE TELEGRAPH IT TO BANK OF AMERICA CULVERCITY STOP KINDLY WIRE AS DOCTOR SAYS I CAN DEFINITELY RETURN STUDIO WORK TUESDAY OR WEDNESDAY STOP THIS WOULD MAKE SERIES OF FOUR =
　　SCOTT FITZGERALD.

---

[1]"Salute to Lucy and Elsie"—unpublished.

TO: *Harold Ober*   *TLS, 1 p. Lilly Library*

September 19 1939

Dear Harold:

The job at Goldwyn's lasted <u>one week</u>.[1] Goldwyn and Wood[2] had a fight on the set, and Wood said he'd quit if he had to rehearse the characters in new dialogue. Eddie Knopf told Swanson my stuff was grand and that he'll get me back some way.

Very encouraging. Almost as much fun as the war. I've had two picture offers since I began to walk again last July. Each for one week. The last one paid the income tax and left a cash balance of $38.00. I've never asked Swanie for money <u>unless</u> I was working—he told me in advance that he never lent money to writers. Once I used to write him pieces for <u>College Humor</u> as a favor. You always thought it was rather foolish. I guess you were right.

And so it goes. I can't possibly pay Scottie's Vassar tuition of $615.00. I'm working today on an Esquire story to get her back here. The situation is all so preposterous that I can't even discuss it any more. <u>Because</u> I made $68,000 last year, <u>because</u> Swanie won't offer me for less than fifteen hundred, I can't keep Scottie in school.

Ever yours,
Scott

5521 Amestoy Avenue
Encino, California

TO: *Scottie Fitzgerald*   *Wire. Princeton University*
September 21, 1939   *Encino, California*

YOU CAN REGISTER AT VASSAR STOP IT COST A HEMORRHAGE BUT I RAISED SOME MONEY FROM ESQUIRE AND ARRANGED WITH COMPTROLLER TO PAY OTHER HALF OCTOBER 15TH IF YOU DONT PLAY STRAIGHT THIS WILL BE ALL STOP FORGIVE ME IF UNJUSTLY CYNICAL REMEMBER HARMONY MORE PRACTICAL THAN MUSIC HISTORY ALSO OTHER CHANGE STOP RETURN ME FORMER CHECK AIR MAIL LOVE
   DADDY.

TO: *Gerald Murphy*   *Wire. Honoria Murphy Donnelly*
September 21, 1939   *Encino, California*

WAS TAKEN ILL OUT HERE LAST APRIL AND CONFINED TO BED FIVE MONTHS AND NOW UP AND WORKING BUT COMPLETELY CLEANED OUT FINANCIALLY WANT

[1] Fitzgerald was working on the film *Raffles*.
[2] Director Sam Wood.

DESPERATELY TO CONTINUE DAUGHTER AT VASSAR CAN YOU LEND 360 DOLLARS
FOR ONE MONTH IF THIS IS POSSIBLE PLEASE WIRE ME AT 5521 AMESTOY AVENUE
ENCINO CALIF
    SCOTT FITZGERALD

TO: Gerald and Sara Murphy   *ALS, 4 pp. Honoria Murphy Donnelly*
September 22, 1939   *Encino, California*

Gerald + Sara:
    What a strange thing that after asking every other conceivable favor of
you at one time or another I should be driven to turn to you for money!
The story is too foolish, too dreary to go in to—I was ill when I saw you
in February and for a week had been going along on drink. Like a fool—
for I had plenty of money then—I took two more jobs and worked myself
up to a daily temperature of 102° + then just broke + lay in bed four
months without much ability to do anything except lie to the world that I
was "fine." I couldn't even reduce costs—there were the doctors and the
government + the insurance, and the "face."
    Well, I'm up now. I've even worked two weeks + tomorrow may find
the financial crisis over—an idea at Metro—but the way all ones personal
prides + vanities melt down in the face of a situation like not being able to
continue a child's education is astonishing. Not having any credit, What a
thing! When credit was exactly what one thought one had.
    Last year for example I payed my Eastern agent $12,000 which he had
advanced me over two years plus 10% of my gains (of about $68,000).
Would he back me again—for $1000—$500? No—in spite of the $70,000
in commissions I've paid him in the past. All this may interest you, Gerald,
as an indication of the fluctuation of talent value—I can see Sara yawn + I
don't blame her. Anyhow it has been frightening and lost + strange. One's
own reaction was:—I couldn't call on the impecunious, and eternally so, to
whom I had "lent" or rather given many thousands—not only because they
didn't have it—but because some relation established at the time of the
lending forbade it. There were the bores I have tolerated because they have
been nice to Zelda or some such reason, but once in a faintly similar situation
years ago I sounded out one— + buttoned up my overcoat quickly at the
chill in the air.
    Then there were relatives + friends. My relatives are all poor now, except
my sister whom I detest, and, as Gerald once remarked, your friends are
the people you see. Forty-eight hours went into worry as to whether or not
to ask you to help me. And then I wired, knowing somehow that if you
were in America it would be all right, presuming on your grace. Next day
came your wire—telephoned, but I went down and got a copy of it.
    You had probably been going thru hell yourselves with Honoria on the
high seas. And how easy too, in these times, to have been irritated by the

intrusion of this preposterously personal problem—how can that Idiot, who has such abilities to be solvent, get himself in such a hole? Let it teach him a lesson!

You went a good deal further than that—you helped me perhaps because I would <u>never</u> learn—or "for help's sake itself," to paraphrase E. Browning. Anyhow it made me feel much too sentimental than is proper to one of our age + experience. And it is nice to know that when I send it back to you it will in time probably go to aid some other "unworthy case" (—do you remember Ernest's passage in "The Sun Also Rises" about being sorry for the wrong types, unsuccessful whores, ect.?)

You saved me—Scottie and me—in spite of our small deserts. I don't think I could have asked anyone else + kept what pride it is necessary to keep.

Scott

TO: *Kenneth Littauer*   *Incomplete CC, 4 pp. Princeton University*

5521 Amestoy Avenue
Encino, California
September 29, 1939

Dear Kenneth:—

This will be difficult for two reasons. First that there is one fact about my novel, which, if it were known, would be immediately and unscrupulously plagiarized by the George Kaufmans, etc.,[1] of this world. Second, that I live always in deadly fear that I will take the edge off an idea for myself by summarizing or talking about it in advance. But, with these limitations, here goes:

The novel will be fifty thousand words long. As I will have to write sixty thousand words to make room for cutting I have figured it as a four months job—three months for the writing—one month for revision. The thinking, according to my conscience and the evidence of sixty pages of outline and notes, <u>has already been done</u>. I would infinitely rather do it, now that I am well again, than take hack jobs out here.

★ ★ ★

The Story occurs during four or five months in the year 1935. It is told by Cecelia, the daughter of a producer named Bradogue[2] in Hollywood. Cecelia is a pretty, modern girl neither good nor bad, tremendously human. Her father is also an important character. A shrewd man, a gentile, and a scoundrel of the lowest variety. A self-made man, he has brought up Cecelia

---

[1] Fitzgerald thought that playwright George S. Kaufman had stolen the idea for *Of Thee I Sing* from Fitzgerald's play *The Vegetable*.
[2] Changed to Brady.

to be a princess, sent her East to college, made of her rather a snob, though, in the course of the story, her character evolves away from this. That is, she was twenty when the events that she tells occurred, but she is twenty-five when she tells about the events, and of course many of them appear to her in a different light.

Cecelia is the narrator because I think I know exactly how such a person would react to my story. She is of the movies but not in them. She probably was born the day "The Birth of a Nation" was previewed and Rudolf Valentino came to her fifth birthday party. So she is, all at once, intelligent, cynical but understanding and kindly toward the people, great or small, who are of Hollywood.

She focuses our attention upon two principal characters—Milton Stahr[1] (who is Irving Thalberg—and this is my great secret) and Thalia,[2] the girl he loves. Thalberg has always fascinated me. His peculiar charm, his extraordinary good looks, his bountiful success, the tragic end of his great adventure. The events I have built around him are fiction, but all of them are things which might very well have happened, and I am pretty sure that I saw deep enough into the character of the man so that his reactions are authentically what they would have been in life. So much so that he may be recognized—but it will also be recognized that no single fact is actually true. For example, in my story he is unmarried or a widower, leaving out completely any complication with Norma.[3]

In the beginning of the book I want to pour out my whole impression of this man Stahr as he is seen during an airplane trip from New York to the coast—of course, through Cecelia's eyes. She has been hopelessly in love with him for a long time. She is never going to win anything more from him than an affectionate regard, even that tainted by his dislike of her father (parallel the deadly dislike of each other between Thalberg and Louis B. Mayer). Stahr is over-worked and deathly tired, ruling with a radiance that is almost moribund in its phosphorescence. He has been warned that his health is undermined, but being afraid of nothing the warning is unheeded. He has had everything in life except the privilege of giving himself unselfishly to another human being. This he finds on the night of a semi-serious earthquake (like in 1935) a few days after the opening of the story.

It has been a very full day even for Stahr—the bursted water mains, which cover the whole ground space of the lot to the depth of several feet, seems to release something in him. Called over to the outer lot to supervise the salvation of the electrical plant (for like Thalberg, he has a finger in every pie of the vast bakery) he finds two women stranded on the roof of a property farmhouse and goes to their rescue.

---

[1] Changed to Monroe Stahr.
[2] Changed to Kathleen Moore.
[3] Actress Norma Shearer, Mrs. Irving Thalberg.

Thalia Taylor is a twenty-six year old widow, and my present conception of her should make her the most glamorous and sympathetic of my heroines. Glamorous in a new way because I am in secret agreement with the public in detesting the type of feminine arrogance that has been pushed into prominence in the case of Brenda Frazier, etc. People simply do not sympathize deeply with those who have had <u>all</u> the breaks, and I am going to dower this girl, like Rosalba in Thackeray's "Rose in the Ring" with "a little misfortune." She and the woman with her (to whom she is serving as companion) have come secretly on the lot through the other woman's curiousity. They have been caught there when the catastrophe occurred.

Now we have a love affair between Stahr and Thalia, an immediate, dynamic, unusual, physical love affair—and I will write it so that you can publish it. At the same time I will send you a copy of how it will appear in book form somewhat stronger in tone.

This love affair is the meat of the book—though I am going to treat it, remember, as it comes through to Cecelia. That is to say by making Cecelia at the moment of her telling the story, an intelligent and observant woman, I shall grant myself the privilege, as Conrad did, of letting her imagine the actions of the characters. Thus, I hope to get the verisimilitude of a first person narrative, combined with a Godlike knowledge of all events that happen to my characters.

Two events beside the love affair bulk large in the intermediary chapters. There is a definite plot on the part of Bradogue, Cecelia's father, to get Stahr out of the company. He has even actually and factually considered having him murdered. Bradogue is the monopolist at its worst—Stahr, in spite of the inevitable conservatism of the self-made man, is a paternalistic employer. Success came to him young, at twenty-three, and left certain idealisms of his youth unscarred. Moreover, he is a worker. Figuratively he takes off his coat and pitches in, while Bradogue is not interested in the making of pictures save as it will benefit his bank account.

The second incident is how young Cecelia herself, in her desperate love for Stahr, throws herself at his head. In her reaction at his indifference she gives herself to a man whom she does not love. This episode is not absolutely necessary to the serial. It could be tempered but it might be best to eliminate it altogether.

Back to the main theme, Stahr cannot bring himself to marry Thalia. It simply doesn't seem part of his life. He doesn't realize that she has become necessary to him. Previously his name has been associated with this or that well-known actress or society personality and Thalia is poor, unfortunate, and tagged with a middle class exterior which doesn't fit in with the grandeur Stahr demands of life. When she realizes this she leaves him temporarily, leaves him not because he has no legal intentions toward her but because of the hurt of it, the remainder of a vanity from which she had considered herself free.

Stahr is now plunged directly into the fight to keep control of the company. His health breaks down very suddenly while he is on a trip to New York to see the stockholders. He almost dies in New York and comes back to find that Bradogue has seized upon his absence to take steps which Stahr considers unthinkable. He plunges back into work again to straighten things out.

Now, realizing how much he needs Thalia, things are patched up between them. For a day or two they are ideally happy. They are going to marry, but he must make one more trip East to clinch the victory which he has conciliated in the affairs of the company.

Now occurs the final episode which should give the novel its quality—and its unusualness. Do you remember about 1933 when a transport plane was wrecked on a mountain-side in the Southwest, and a Senator was killed?[1] The thing that struck me about it was that the country people rifled the bodies of the dead. That is just what happens to this plane which is bearing Stahr from Hollywood. The angle is that of three children who, on a Sunday picnic, are the first to discover the wreckage. Among those killed in the accident besides Stahr are two other characters we have met. (I have not been able to go into the minor characters in this short summary.) Of the three children, two boys and a girl, who find the bodies, one boy rifles Stahr's possessions; another, the body of a ruined ex-producer; and the girl, those of a moving picture actress. The possessions which the children find, symbolically determine their attitude toward their act of theft. The possessions of the moving picture actress tend the young girl to a selfish possessiveness; those of the unsuccessful producer sway one of the boys toward an irresolute attitude; while the boy who finds Stahr's briefcase is the one who, after a week, saves and redeems all three by going to a local judge and making full confession.

The story swings once more back to Hollywood for its finale. During the story Thalia has never once been inside a studio. After Stahr's death as she stands in front of the great plant which he created, she realizes now that she never will. She knows only that he loved her and that he was a great man and that he died for what he believed in.

This is a novel—not even faintly of the propoganda type. Indeed, Thalberg's opinions were entirely different from mine in many respects that I will not go into. I've long chosen him for a hero (this has been in my mind for three years) because he is one of the half-dozen men I have known who were built on the grand scale. That it happens to coincide with a period in which the American Jews are somewhat uncertain in their morale, is for me merely a fortuitous coincidence. The racial angle shall scarcely be touched on at all. Certainly if Ziegfeld[2] could be made into an epic figure then what about Thalberg who was literally everything that Ziegfeld wasn't?

[1] In May 1935 Senator Bronson M. Cutting and others were killed in a Missouri plane crash. The wreckage was not plundered by local people.
[2] Broadway producer Florenz Ziegfeld.

There's nothing that worries me in the novel, nothing that seems uncertain. Unlike Tender is the Night it is not the story of deterioration—it is not depressing and not morbid in spite of the tragic ending. If one book could ever be "like" another I should say it is more "like" The Great Gatsby than any other of my books. But I hope it will be entirely different—I hope it will be something new, arouse new emotions perhaps even a new way of looking at certain phenomena. I have set it safely in a period of five years ago to obtain detachment, but now that Europe is tumbling about our ears this also seems to be for the best. It is an escape into a lavish, romantic past that perhaps will not come again into our time. It is certainly a novel I would like to read. Shall I write it?[1]

★ ★ ★

As I said, I would rather do this for a minimum price than continue this in-and-out business with the moving pictures where the rewards are great, but the satisfaction unsatisfactory and the income tax always mopping one up after the battle.

The minimum I would need to do this with peace of mind would be $15,000., payable $3000. in advance and $3000. on the first of November, the first of December, the first of January and the first of February, on delivery of the last installment. For this I would guarantee to do no other work, specifically pictures, to make any changes in the manuscript (but not to having them made for me) and to begin to deliver the copy the first of November, that is to give you fifteen thousand words by that date.

Unless these advances are compatible with your economy, Kenneth, the deal would be financially impossible for me under the present line up. Four months of sickness completely stripped me and until your telegram came I had counted on a buildup of many months work here before I could consider beginning the novel. Once again a telegram would help tremendously, as I am naturally on my toes and

TO: *Zelda Fitzgerald*   *CC, 1 p. Princeton University*

October
6
1939

Dearest Zelda:—

Living in the flotsam of the international situation as we all are,[2] work has been difficult. I am almost penniless—I've done stories for Esquire

---

[1]Fitzgerald's carbon copy of this letter has his note "Orig Sent thru here" after "Shall I write it?" The fragmentary continuation of the letter beginning "As I said" survives with the notes for *The Love of the Last Tycoon.*

[2]Germany had invaded Poland on September 1, 1939, leading Great Britain and France to declare war on Germany.

because I've had no time for anything else with $100. bank balances. You will remember it took me an average of six weeks to get the mood of a Saturday Evening Post story.

But everything may be all right tomorrow. As I wrote you—or did I—friends sent Scottie back to college. That seemed more important than any pleasure for you or me. There is still two hundred dollars owing on her tuition—and I think I will probably manage to find it somewhere.

After her, you are my next consideration; I was properly moved by your mother's attempt to send for you—but not enough to go overboard. For you to go on your first excursion <u>without</u> a nurse, <u>without</u> money, without even enough to pay your fare back, when Dr. Carroll is backing you, and when Scottie and I are almost equally as helpless in the press of circumstances as you—well, it is the ruse of a clever old lady whom I respect and admire and who loves you dearly but not wisely.

None of you are taking this very well. Rosalind and Newman who wouldn't lend Scottie a few hundred for Vassar entrance, when, in 1925, I lent him five hundred—and you and I were living on a bank margin of <u>less than I lent</u>! It would, according to Rosalind, behind whom he hid, inconvenience them. I <u>borrowed</u> to lend him the money when his life-insurance policy lapsed! Live and learn. Gerald and Sar <u>did</u> lend me the money!—and as gracefully as always.

I ask only this of you—leave me in peace with my hemorrhages and my hopes, and what eventually will fight through as the <u>right</u> to save you, the <u>permission</u> to give you a chance.

Your life has been a disappointment, as mine has been too. But we haven't gone through this sweat for nothing. Scottie has got to survive and this is the most important year of her life.

With Dearest Love Always,

5521 Amestoy Avenue
Encino, California

TO: *Harold Ober*   *TLS, 1 p. Lilly Library*

October 7 1939

Dear Harold:—

Thanks for your letter. Thanks for taking care of Scottie. And your saying that you had written me several letters and torn them up did something to clarify what I had begun to interpret as some sadistic desire to punish me. I sent the stories to Collier's for the simple reason that it seemed difficult to deal with someone who treats you with dead silence. Against silence you can do nothing but fret and wonder. Your disinclination to back me is, of course, your own business, but representing me without communication (such as returning a story to me without even an airmail stamp) is pretty close to saying you were through with me.

I communicated directly with Collier's and wrote a series of pieces for Esquire because we have to live and eat and nothing can interfere with that. Can't you regard this trouble as a question of a man who has had a bad break and leave out the moral problem as to whether or not, or how much it is his own fault? And if you think I can't write, read these stories. They brought just two hundred and fifty apiece from Esquire, because I couldn't wait to hear from you, because I had bank balances of five, ten and fifteen dollars.

Anyhow I have "lived dangerously" and I may quite possibly have to pay for it, but there are plenty of other people to tell me that and it doesn't seem as if it should be you.

I don't think there is any chance of fixing up that other story. It just isn't good.

Sincerely,
Scott

P.S. Could you mail me back these stories? I have no copies. Don't you agree that they are worth more than $250.? One of them was offered to Collier's in desperation—the first Pat Hobby story but Littauer wired that it "wasn't a story" Who's right?

5521 Amestoy Avenue
Encino, California

TO: Maxwell Perkins   *Wire. Princeton University*
October 1939   *Encinco, California*

PLEASE LUNCH IF YOU CAN WITH KENNETH LITTAUR OF COLLIERS IN RELATION TO SERIAL OF WHICH HE HAS THE OUTLINE. OBER TO BE ABSOLUTELY EXCLUDED FROM PRESENT STATE OF NEGOTIATIONS I HAD MY LAST DRINK LAST JUNE IF THAT MATTERS TELL LITTAUR THAT I FOOLISHLY TURNED DOWN LITERARY GUILD OFFER FOR TENDER. NIGHTLETTER ME IF YOU CAN. NOVEL OUTLINED ABSOLUTELY CON-FIDENTIAL AS EVEN A HINT OF IT WOULD BE PLAGIARIZED OUT HERE EVER YOURS =
     SCOTT FITZGERALD..

TO: Maxwell Perkins   *Wire. Princeton University*
October 14, 1939   *Van Nuys, California*

PLEASE DO GET IN TOUCH WITH LITTAUER HAVE OUTLINED EVERY SCENE AND SITUATION AND I THINK I CAN WRITE THIS BOOK AS IF IT WAS A BIOGRAPHY BECAUSE I KNOW THE CHARACTER OF THIS MAN EVER YOURS =
     SCOTT FITZGERALD.

TO: *Arnold Gingrich*   *TLS, 1 p. University of Michigan*

October
14
1939

Dear Arnold:
Again the old ache of money. Again will you wire me, if you like it.[1]
Again will you wire the money to my Maginot Line: The Bank of America,
Culver City.

Ever yours,
F Scott Fitzgerald

5521 Amestoy Avenue
Encino, California

TO: *Arnold Gingrich*   *Wire. University of Michigan*
October 16, 1939   *Encino, California*

THIS REQUEST SHOULD HAVE BEEN INCLOSED WITH PAT HOBBY'S CHRISTMAS
WISH WHICH IS THREE THOUSAND WORDS LONG IF YOU CANT GO UP BY $150 I
WILL HAVE TO SEND IT EAST I HATE TO SWITCH THIS SERIES BUT CANT AFFORD
TO LOSE SO MUCH PLEASE WIRE ME = [2]
    SCOTT.

TO: *Maxwell Perkins*   *TLS, 1 p. Princeton University*

October
20
1939

Dear Max:—
I have your telegram but meanwhile I found that Collier's proposition
was less liberal than I had expected. They want to pay $15,000. for the
serial. But (without taking such steps as reneging on my income tax, letting
go my life insurance for its surrender value, taking Scottie from college and
putting Zelda in a public asylum) I couldn't last four months on that. Certain
debts have been run up so that the larger part of the $15,000. has been, so
to speak, spent already. A contraction of my own living expenses to the

[1]"Pat Hobby's Christmas Wish," *Esquire* (January 1940).
[2]In an October 17 telegram Gingrich agreed to send Fitzgerald an extra $150 but advised
him "not to jeopardize old reliable instant payment market like this by use of strong arm
methods. . . ." In a second wire that day Gingrich, responding to an angry phone call from
Fitzgerald, apologized for the phrase "strong arm methods" and pledged his continued friendship and support.

barest minimum, that is to say a room in a boarding house, abandonment of all medical attention (I still see a doctor once a week) would still leave me at the end not merely penniless but even more in debt than I am now. Of course, I would have a property at the end, maybe. But I thought that I would have a property when I finished "Tender Is The Night"! On the other hand, if I, so to speak, go bankrupt, at least there will not be very much accumulating overhead.

However, if Collier's would pay more it would give the necessary margin of security and it would give me $2,000. in hand when I finish the novel in February. I feel quite sure that if I wasn't in such a tight spot Collier's would not figure that $20,000. was exorbitant for such a serial.

The further complication of money to get started with—to take me through the first ten thousand words, was something I hope you might be able to work out between you. Certainly there is no use approaching Harold with it in any way. I would have to pay the piper in the end by paying him a cut on a deal on which he has done nothing. He is a stupid hard-headed man and has a highly erroneous idea of how I live; moreover he has made it a noble duty to piously depress me at every possible opportunity. I don't want him to know <u>anything about the subject of the novel</u>.

Meanwhile I have sold in the last few months ten short stories to <u>Esquire</u>, at the munificent sum of $250. a piece. Only two of these were offered to another magazine because when you're poor you sell things for a quarter of their value to realize quickly—otherwise there wouldn't be any auctioneers.

Have you talked to Charlie Scribner or mulled over the question further? If you come to any decision which is possibly favorable, would you put it in the form of a night letter? I am enclosing a letter to Kenneth Littauer which will keep you up with the situation at present.

Ever yours,
Scott

5521 Amestoy Avenue
Encino, California

TO: Kenneth Littauer   *CC, 2 pp. Princeton University*

October
20
1939

Dear Kenneth:—

I was disappointed in our conversation the other day—I am no good on long distance and should have had notes in my hand.

I want to make plain how my proposition differs from yours. First there is the question of the <u>total</u> payment; second, the <u>terms</u> of payment, which would enable me to finish it in these straightened circumstances.

In any case I shall probably attack the novel. I have about decided to make a last liquidation of assets, put my wife in a public place, and my daughter to work and concentrate on it—simply take a furnished room and live on canned goods.

But writing it under such conditions I should want to market it with the chance of getting a higher price for it.

It was to avoid doing all this, that I took you up on the idea of writing it on installments. I too had figured on the same price per installment you had paid for a story, but I had no idea that you would want to pack more into an installment than your five thousand word maximum for a story. So the fifty thousand words at $2500. for each 5000 word installment would have come to $25,000. In addition, I had figured that a consecutive story is easier rather than harder to write than the same number of words divided into short stories because the characters and settings are determined in advance, so my idea had been to ask you $20,000. for the whole job. But $15,000.—that would be too marginal. It would be better to write the whole thing in poverty and freedom of movement with the finished product. Fifteen thousand would leave me in more debt than I am now.

On the question of the terms of payment, my proposition was to include the exact amount which you offer in your letter only I had divided it, so that the money would come in batches of $3000. every four weeks, or something like that.

When we had our first phone conversation the fact that I did not have enough to start on, further complicated the matter; I have hoped that perhaps that's where Scribner's would come in. A telegram from Max told me he was going to see you again but I've heard nothing further.

I hope that this will at least clear up any ambiguity. If the proposition is all off, I am very sorry. I regret now that I did not go on with the novel last April when I had some money, instead of floundering around with a lot of disassociated ideas that were half-heartedly attempted and did not really come to anything. I know you are really interested, and thank you for the trouble you have taken.

Ever Yours Gratefully

P.S. Whether the matter is dead or just dangling I still don't want Ober to have anything to do with the negotiation. For five years I feel he has been going around thinking of me as a lost soul, and conveying that impression to others. It makes me gloomy when I see his name on an envelope.

5521 Amestoy Avenue
Encino, California

TO: *Dr. Robert S. Carroll*   *TL, 2 pp.—draft with holograph revisions*
Princeton University

October
20
1939

Dear Dr. Carroll: (or Dr. Suitt)

I have been in bed for ten days with a slight flare-up of T.B. Regularly three mornings a week, come letters such as these from Zelda. I blew up the other day and wired her sister in Montgomery that Zelda could leave the hospital only on condition that I can not be responsible for setting loose a woman who, at any time may relapse into total insanity. A divorce would have to be obtained first.

It is the old story down there—that the only thing that counts is the peace of mind of an old lady of eighty. Unless you could assure me (and I know from your letters that you can't) that Zelda is 80% certain of holding her ground outside and not becoming a general menace or a private charge, I don't see how I can ask you to release her—except on the aforesaid basis of an agreed-upon divorce.

My daughter is of age now and can probably manage to keep out of her mother's way, so if the Sayres want to take over they are welcome. But I do not want a maniac at large with any legal claims upon me. She has cost me everything a woman can cost a man—his health, his work, his money. Mrs. Brinson and Mrs. Sayre have made fragmentary attempts to act impartially, but on the whole, have behaved badly, from the moment their first horrible accusation in 1932 that I put Zelda away for ulterior purposes. Mrs. Smith is simply a fool. I wish none of them any harm and I think Mrs Brinson has tried intermittently to execercise some of her Father's sense of justice but in these ten years I feel that every fragment of obligation on my part has been gradually washed out.

For me, life goes on without very much cheer, except my novel, but I think if there is any way to stop this continual nagging through Zelda it will be a help. I had every intention of sending her to Montgomery with a nurse this October, but there was no money. Of course, at present I am not in any mood to give her anything—even if I could afford it. After a few weeks in Montgomery, her first attempt would be to beg or borrow enough to get out here and hang herself around my neck—in which case a California State Asylum would be her last stop on this tragic journey.

All pretty black, isn't it? Please try to persuade her not to send me any more of those letters.

Ever yours, gratefully,

P.S. Of course I approve of what you've done about the room, ect. Scottie and I are living hard. A friend lent me enough to pay her first term in college. For better or worse Scottie + I form a structure—if that wormlike

418

convolusion in Montgomery is a family then lets go back to the age of snakes.

5521 Amestoy Avenue
Encino, California

TO: Scottie Fitzgerald   CC, 1 p. Princeton University
                                   Encino, California

October
31
1939

Scottina:—

(Do you know that isn't a nickname I invented but one that Gerald Murphy concocted on the Riviera years ago?) Look! I have begun to write something that is maybe great, and I'm going to be absorbed in it four or six months. It may not <u>make</u> us a cent but it will pay expenses and it is the first labor of love I've undertaken since the first part of "Infidelity" (—do you remember that half finished script the censor stopped that I showed you in Norfolk two years ago last Easter? You read it in the cabin of one of those Baltimore-Norfolk liners.)

Anyhow I am alive again—getting by that October did something—with all its strains and necessities and humiliations and struggles. I don't drink. I am not a great man, but sometimes I think the impersonal and objective quality of my talent and the sacrifices of it, in pieces, to preserve its essential value has some sort of epic grandeur. Anyhow after hours I nurse myself with delusions of that sort.

And I think when you read this book, which will encompass the time when you knew me as an adult, you will understand how intensively I knew your world—not <u>extensively</u> because I was so ill and unable to get about. If I live long enough I'll hear your side of things but I think your own instincts about your limitations as an artist are possibly best: you might experiment back and forth among the arts and find your nitch as I found mine—but I do not believe that so far you are a "natural".

So what? These are such valuable years. Let me watch over the development a little longer. What are the courses you are taking? Please list them. Please cater to me. Please do not ask me to rise to heights of nervous energy—in which I can usually discern the name of the dye on your instructor's hair at long distance or reconstruct the murder of March 1938 from a rag and a bone and a hank of hair. But give me some outlines.

a. What do Obers say about me? So sad?
b. What is this about my telling Mrs. Owens you were a heel?
c. What play are you in?
d. What proms and games? Let me at least renew my youth!

e. As a papa—not the made child of a mad genius—what do you do? and how?

f. What furniture? Do you still want etchings?

g. What did Rosalind write?

h. Do you want a test here?

i. Did you ever think of calling on the Murphys to make <u>them</u> happy— not to deprecate Honoria?

I'm glad you read Malreaux.[1] Did you get the driver's license? Is Mary Earle nice? I got an instant impression in Connecticut of a brave, lovely, impish person. And was [   ][2] somewhat slowed down in her inevitable dreary progress between the abortionist and the rest-cure? Don't answer that last. The name is still a sort of emetic to me.

TO: Sheilah Graham
November 9, 1939

Wire, 1 p. Princeton University
Encino, California

THE COUNTRY IS BEHIND YOU NOW STOP JUST RELAX AND DO YOUR HOUR[3] STOP NEWS JUST REACHED HERE ENGLAND IS AT WAR STOP IS DENIED AND AFFIRMED BY LOCAL PRESS SEEMS INCREDIBLE SIGNED CONSTANCE CAROL HEDDA STOP I STILL MISS YOU TERRIBLY =

SCOTT.

TO: Maxwell Perkins

TLS, 1 p. Princeton University

November
20
1939

Dear Max:—

A lot depends on this week. I've about decided to show him (Littauer) the first nine or ten thousand words and I think it's literally about fifty-fifty whether he'll want it or not. The material is definitely "strong". As soon as I hear anything from him I'll let you know.

Of course, if he will back me it will be a life-saver, but I am by no means sure that I will ever be a popular writer again. This much of the book, however, should be as fair a test as any. Thanks for your letter.

Ever yours,
F. Scott Fitzgerald

5521 Amestoy Avenue
Encino, California

[1] French novelist André Malraux.
[2] Name omitted by editor.
[3] Sheilah Graham was in Louisville, Kentucky, on a lecture tour. Fitzgerald was joking about the unreliability of Hollywood reporting.

TO: *Kenneth Littauer*   *Wire. New York Public Library*
November 28, 1939   *Encino, California*

NO HARD FEELINGS THERE HAS NEVER BEEN AN EDITOR WITH PANTS ON SINCE
GEORGE LORIMER
    SCOTT FITZGERALD.

TO: *Sheilah Graham*   *Wire, 1 p. Princeton University*
December 1, 1939   *Encino, California*

FINALLY WENT TO A FOOTBALL GAME TAKING MY ENTIRE STAFF STOP EVERY
TIME KENNY WASHINGTON[1] DID ANYTHING EXCEPTIONAL I THOUGHT OF YOU
SOMEWHERE IN THE STAND I AM GLAD WE WON AM AWFULLY SORRY FOR THE
HARSH THINGS THAT WERE SAID TODAY STOP I AM GOING TO BE AWAKE FOR AN
HOUR IF YOU COME IN DURING THAT TIME WILL YOU PLEASE CALL ME=
    SCOTT.

TO: *Sheilah Graham*   *TLS, 1 p. Princeton University*
                                               Encino, California

                                        December
                                             2
                                        1939

Dear Sheilah:
    I went berserk in your presence and hurt you and Jean Steffan.[2] That's
done.

But I said things too—awful things and they can to some extent be unsaid.
They come from the merest fraction of my mind, as you must know—they
represent nothing in my consciousness and very little in my subconscious.
About as important and significant as the quarrels we used to have about
England and America.

I don't think we're getting anywhere. I'm glad you no longer can think of
me with either respect or affection. People are either good for each other or
not, and obviously I am <u>horrible</u> for you. I loved with everything I had,
but something was terribly wrong. You don't have to look far for the
reason—I was it. Not fit for any human relation. I just <u>loved</u> you—you
brought me everything. And it was very fine and chivalrous-and you.

I want to die, Sheilah, and in my own way. I used to have my daughter
and my poor lost Zelda. Now for over two years your image is everywhere.

---

[1] Great UCLA halfback.
[2] A friend of Sheilah Graham.

Let me remember you up to the end which is very close. You are the finest. You are something all by yourself. You are too much something for a tubercular neurotic who can only be jealous and mean and perverse. I will have my last time with you, though you won't be here. It's not long now. I wish I could have left you more of myself. You can have the first chapter of the novel and the plan. I have no money but it might be worth something. Ask Hayward.[1] I love you utterly and completely.

I meant to send this longhand but I don't think it would be intelligible.

Scott

TO: *Sheilah Graham*   ALS, 2 pp.[2] *Princeton University*
Early December 1939   *Encino, California*

When I finally came to myself last Tuesday I found this,[3] which seems to be yours.

It is very quiet out here now. I went in your room this after noon and lay on your bed awhile, trying to see if you had left anything of yourself. There were some pencils and the electric pad that didn't work and the autumn out the window that won't ever be the same. Then I wrote down a lot of expressions of your face but one I cant bare to read, of the little girl who trusted me so and whom I loved more than anything in the world—and to whom I gave grief when I wanted to give joy. Some things should have told you I was extemporizing wildly—that anyone, including Scottie, should ever dare critizize you to me. It was all fever and liquor and sedatives—what nurses hear in any bad drunk case.

I'm glad you're rid of me. I hope you're happy and the last awful impression is fading a little till someday you'll say "he can't have been that black."

Goodbye, Shielo, I wont bother you any more.

Scott

TO: *Editors of* The Saturday Evening Post   CC, 1 p. *Princeton University*

December
6
1939

Dear Sirs:—

Another job prevented me from getting as far on with this revise as I had intended.[4] However, this additional thirteen hundred words introduces my

---

[1]Hollywood agent Leland Hayward.

[2]Possibly part of a longer letter.

[3]Unidentified.

[4]After Littauer declined to make an advance for *The Love of the Last Tycoon*, Fitzgerald offered it to *The Saturday Evening Post*; it was again declined.

422

Sheilah from Scott:

Frank Norris, after writing three great books died in 1902 at the age of just

1938
THE SUN DIAL PRESS, INC.

Thirty. He was our most promising man and might have gone further than Dreiser or the others. He claimed to be a disciple of Zola the naturalist, but in many ways he was better than Zola.

The time of the events is about 1880

The Octopus *was one of the books Fitzgerald assigned to Sheilah Graham in the "College of One" (Princeton University Library).*

heroine and should give you an idea of the "climate" of the story. The only thing I can think of is to push along with it little by little on Sundays until I have enough to enable you to make a tentative decision, but I felt I wanted you to get a glimpse at my leading girl.

Cecelia is a sort of juvenile in the old fashioned use of the term. She is my device for telling the story and though she has adventures of her own she is not one of the characters I am primarily interested in.

Please be discreet about the idea because I think it's one of those naturals that almost anybody could do only I'd like to be the one.

Sincerely

F. Scott Fitzgerald

5521 Amestoy Avenue
Encino, California

TO: Leland Hayward   *CC, 2 pp. Princeton University*

December

6

1939

Dear Leland:—

Here's the information you wanted[1]:

1. Metro—I worked there longest, a little over a year and a half. I was very fond of Edwin Knopf who I think likes my work very much. Joe Mankiewicz asked me to come back and work with him, but our relations were so definitely unpleasant after he decided to rewrite "Three Comrades" himself that I don't think I could do it. I worked with Sidney Franklin on "The Women" and on "Madame Curie." Whether he would be interested in having me work for him again I don't know. Anyhow his boss, Bernie Hyman, quite definitely doesn't like me. I don't know why because I've scarcely exchanged two words with him. Nor do I know Mayer, Mannix or Katz except that at some time I've shaken hands with all three of them. Hunt and I reached a dead end on "The Women." We wore each other out. He liked the first part of a picture called "Infidelity" that I wrote so intensely that when the whole thing flopped I think he held it against me that I had aroused his hope so much and then had not been able to finish it. It may have been my fault—it may have been the fault of the story but the damage is done. John Considine is an old friend and I believe asked for me in midsummer during the time I was so ill, but I believe he has kind of slowed down lately and I don't think I'd like to work for him. There's another producer I hardly know whose name I can't remember now, but he was a young man and was once Stromberg's assistant. I believe he was the pro-

---

[1] Fitzgerald was seeking freelance screenwriting assignments while working on *The Love of the Last Tycoon.*

ducer of "These Glamor Girls." Merian Cooper and I once talked over a story. We get along very well personally, but his reputation among authors is that he is never able to make up his mind and I imagine that he wouldn't be quite the man though I'd just as soon work for him if he knows pretty much what he wants when we start off. The other producers there, Cohn, etc., I don't even know by sight. King Vidor who is a personal friend several times asked me what I was doing and talked about a picture we were going to do together sometime.

2. Paramount—I worked for Jeff Lazarus. I've been told that he has been fired and I know that he is at present in Europe but I liked him very much and we got along in fine style always. On the same picture I worked with Griffith who has always wanted to do "The Great Gatsby" over again as a talkie. I do not know Mr. Le Baron or Mr. Hornblow. I know Tony Veiller slightly and he was interested in having me work on Safari but at the time I wasn't interested in pictures. This again goes back to last June and July. I don't think I know anybody else at Paramount.

3. Twentieth Century Fox—I met Harry Joe Brown. Don't think I know anyone else.

4. R.K.O. Radio—Don't think I know a soul.

5. Universal—Some producer asked for me one day when I was finishing a story but I've forgotten his name and the next day when I was ready to report to him and talk it over he had gone on vacation. My relations with Stahl were just a little too difficult so there's no use trying anything there.

6. United Artists—Wanger is out absolutely. Goldwyn I know nothing about. Sam Wood and I had always gotten along before, but during this week that I worked there on "Raffles" everything got a little strained and I don't think that he would welcome me as a collaborator. That seems to cover everyone I know at United Artists. Eddie Knopf and I have always been friends but I have no idea how much power he has there and my impression is that it is comparatively little. However, if such is not the case I think I'd rather work with him than any man I've met here.

7. Columbia—I don't know a soul except that I think that Sam Marx is there and I always thought of Sam as a rather dull fellow though very nice.

8. Selznick International—I find this studio the pleasantest studio that I have worked in (I was on Gone With the Wind about eight or nine days) but what Dave thinks of me I haven't any idea. I know that I was on the list of first choice writers on "Rebecca" but that may have been Hitchcock's doing. I think that Dave is probably under the impression that I am a novelist first and can't get the idea as to what pictures are about. This impression is still from back in 1921 when he wanted me to submit an original idea for Elaine Hammerstein.

9. Warner Bros.—The Warner Bros. I don't know personally though they once bought a picture right from me in the "Beautiful and Damned." I have talked to Bryan Foy on the telephone, but of course a quickie is exactly what I rather don't want to write.

Whatever company made "In Name Only" also asked for my services last July, but that was when I was sick and had to turn down offers.

I think that pretty well covers everything and, Leland, I would rather have $1000. or $750., without being rushed along and pushed around than go into a nervous breakdown at $1500.

Ever yours,

5521 Amestoy Avenue
Encino, California

TO: *Arnold Gingrich*   *Wire. University of Michigan*
December 18, 1939   *Encino, California*

THINGS HAVE BEEN A MESS HERE CAN YOU WIRE 50.00 TO MY BANK THE STORY WILL GO OFF TOMORROW NOON WITHOUT FAIL = [1]
    SCOTT.

TO: *Arnold Gingrich*   *TLS, 1 p.—with holograph final line*
                                              University of Michigan

December
19
1939

Dear Arnold:-
    You have already paid $150. for this. Frankly, I don't know how good it is. If you think it's worth $300., I could certainly use the balance and please remember by telegraph to the Bank of America, Culver City. At the same time wire me if you still want more Pat Hobby's. I can go on with them.
    On the other hand I have a couple of other short pieces in mind. I'd like to do two or three for you within the next week to cover me over Christmas as I've been sick in bed again and gotten way behind.
    Best wishes always,

Scott

P.S. I felt in spite of the title being appropriate to the season it was rather too bad to begin the Pat Hobby series with that story because it characterizes him in a rather less sympathetic way than most of the others. Of course, he's a complete rat but it seems to make him a little sinister which he

---

[1] "Pat Hobby's Christmas Wish."

essentially is not. Do you intend to use the other stories in approximately the order in which they were written?

Do <u>please</u> wire the money!

5521 Amestoy Avenue
Encino, California

TO: Maxwell Perkins   *TLS, 1 p. Princeton University*

December
19
1939

Dear Max:-

The opinion about the novel seems half good and half bad. In brief, about four or five people here like it immensely, Leland[1] likes it and you like it. Collier's, however, seems indifferent to it though they like the outline. My plan is to just go ahead and dig it out. If I could interest any magazine, of course it would be a tremendous help but today a letter from the Post seems to indicate that it is not their sort of material. The plan has changed a bit since I first wrote the outline, but it is essentially as you know it.

Your offering to loan me another thousand dollars was the kindest thing I have ever heard of. It certainly comes at the most opportune time. The first thing is this month's and last month's rent and I am going to take the liberty of giving my landlady a draft on you for $205., for January 2nd. This with the $150. that you have already sent me is $355. For the other $645., will you let me know when it is available?

I am not terribly in debt as I was in 1935–7, but uncomfortably so. I think though my health is getting definitely better and if I can do some intermittent work in the studios between each chapter of the novel instead of this un-profitable hacking for Esquire, I shall be able to get somewhere by spring.

Max, you are so kind. When Harold withdrew from the questionable honor of being my banker I felt completely numb financially and I suddenly wondered what money was and where it came from. There had always seemed a little more somewhere and now there wasn't.

Anyhow, thank you.

Ever your friend,
Scott

5521 Amestoy Avenue
Encino, California

---

[1] Leland Hayward.

TO: Arnold Gingrich
December 22, 1939

Wire. University of Michigan
Encino, California

THAT YOU WIRE A HUNDRED ADVANCE ON REALLY EXCELLENT STORY TO REACH
YOU TUESDAY SO I CAN BUY TURKEY IS PRESENT CHRISTMAS WISH OF=
PAT HOBBY FITZGERALD

TO: Arnold Gingrich

CC, 1 p. Princeton University

January
15
1940

Dear Arnold:-

I don't get a word from you except in telegrams. Please do take time to
answer this if you possibly can. You have one story of mine "Between
Planes"[1] which doesn't belong to the Pat Hobby series. It is a story that I
should hate to see held up for a long time. If your plans are to publish it
only at the end of the Pat Hobby series would you consider trading it back
to me for the next Pat Hobby story? I might be able to dispose of it
elsewhere. Otherwise I very strongly wish that you could schedule it at
least as early as to follow the first half dozen Pat Hobbys.

The weakest of the Hobby stories seem to me to have been "Two Old-
Timers" and "Mightier Than The Sword".[2] If you could hold those out of
type for a while I might be able either to improve them later or else send
others in their place. You remember I did this in the case of a story sent
you a few years ago.

Ever your friend,

5521 Amestoy Avenue
Encino, California

TO: Leland Hayward

CC, 2 pp. Princeton University

January
16
1940

Dear Leland:-

Another week having gone I make the assumption that the Kitty Foyle
deal is cold.[3] I am rather disappointed as I know there are three or four dull
jobs for every attractive one but thanks for trying. I am sufficiently acclimated to Hollywood to realize how uncertain anything is until a contract
is signed.

[1]"Three Hours Between Planes," *Esquire* (July 1941).
[2]*Esquire* (March and April 1941).
[3]Fitzgerald did not work on this movie.

Looking at it from a long view the essential mystery still remains, and you would be giving me the greatest help of all if you can find out why I am in the doghouse. Having dinner the other day at the Brown Derby I ran into Swanson and he began talking about jobs, mentioning that Kenneth McKenna had wanted me at Metro and why hadn't I answered his wire about it. I told him again that you were my agent now. That was all— nothing unpleasant. But it reminded me that both Knopf and McKenna who were my scenario heads for nine-tenths of the time that I have been employed in pictures seem to want me, yet when it comes to the question of a job there's always some barrier.

Once Bud Shulberg told me that, while the story of an official blacklist is a legend, there is a kind of cabal that goes on between producers around a backgammon table, and I have an idea that some such sinister finger is upon me. I know also that if a man stays away from pictures deliberately like I did from March to July he is forgotten, or else people think there's something the matter with him. And I know when that ball starts rolling badly, as it did in the case of Ted Paramore and a few other pinks, it can roll for a long time. But I have the feeling that there is some unfavorable word going around about me. I don't know whether a man like Edington would refer to Dave Selznick who thinks I should "write originals", or perhaps to Mannix who would say that I didn't come through for Hunt Stromberg, or to Bernie Hyman. I only know that I have a strong intuition that all is not well with my reputation and I'd like to know what is being said or not said. Swanson who is unpopular was unable to find out—but you can.

And if you do, wouldn't it be well when another offer comes up for you to tell the producer <u>directly</u> that certain people don't like me? That I didn't get along with some of the big boys at Metro? And refer them to people who <u>do</u> like me like Knopf, Sidney Franklin and I think, Jeff Lazarus. Isn't that better than having them start out with enthusiasm like Hempstead and then find out that in certain quarters I am considered a lame duck or hard to get along with. Or even that I drink, though there were only three days while I was on salary in pictures when I ever touched a drop. One of those was in New York and two were on Sundays.

In any case, it seems to me to be a necessity to find out what the underground says of me. I don't think we'll get anywhere till we <u>do</u> find out, and until you can steer any interested producers away from whoever doesn't believe in me and toward the few friends that I've made. This vague sense of competence unused and abilities unwanted is rather destructive to the morale. It would be much much better for me to give up pictures forever and leave Hollywood. When you've read this letter will you give me a ring and tell me what you think?

Ever your friend,

5521 Amestoy Avenue
Encino, California
STate 4-0578

TO: *Edwin Knopf*   *CC, 2 pp. Princeton University*

February
1
1940

Dear Eddie:-

An hour after I called you a letter came asking if McBride could use my sketch, "The Night before Chancellorsville" in an anthology. Armed with this coincidence I'll enlarge a little on my idea.

You may remember that the battles of Fredericksburg and Chancellorsville were fought respectively late in 1826 and early in 1863 and very nearly upon the same Virginia battlefield. I would begin my story with two girls who come South from Concord seeking the body of their brother who has been killed at Fredericksburg. They are sheltered puritanical girls used to the life of a small New England town. On the train going down they run into some ladies of the type pictured in my story. Moreover they encounter a charming Union cavalry captain with whom the gayer of the two Concord girls falls in love.

As in the story the train rides right into Jackson's surprise attack at Chancellorsville—the Union retreat and the Confederate advance. The girls are separated and their first task is to find each other. One of them meets a confederate private from Alabama who at first she dreads and dislikes. In a Union counter attack the Confederate private is captured. He is identified as a Mosby guerilla by a man who bears him a grudge and hung up by his thumbs. (This actually happened to a cousin of my father's in the Civil War and I have embodied the incident in another story called "When This Cruel War"[1] which Collier's bought last spring but has not yet published.) The northern girl cuts down the Confederate soldier and helps him to escape. The girl has begun by being impatient of her sister's gayety. During their time behind the Confederate lines she has conscientiously continued her search for her brother's grave. Now, after helping her enemy escape, and at the moment of a love scene between them she finds that they are only a few yards from her brother's grave. Entwined with the story of the two girls I would like to carry along the semi-comic character of one of those tarts, using her somewhat as Dudley Nichols used the tart in Stagecoach.[2]

There are two Civil Wars and there are two kinds of Civil War novels. So far, pictures have been made only from one of them—the romantic-chivalric-Sir-Walter-Scott story like "Gone With the Wind", "The Birth of a Nation", the books of Thomas Nelson Page and Mary Johnson.[3] But there is also the realistic type modelled primarily on Stendahl's great picture of Waterloo in "Le Chartreuse de Parme", Stephan Crane's "The Red Badge

---

[1] Published as "The End of Hate," *Collier's* (June 22, 1940).

[2] Nichols wrote the screenplay for the 1939 John Ford western.

[3] Page and Johnston wrote novels about the antebellum South.

of Courage" and the stories of Ambrose Bierce. This way of looking at war gives great scope for comedy without bringing in Stepin Fetchitt and Hattie McDaniels[1] as faithful negro slaves, because it shows how small the individual is in the face of great events, how comparatively little he <u>sees</u>, and how little he can do even to save himself. The Great War has been successfully treated like this—"Journey's End" and "All Quiet"—the Civil War never.

We can all see ourselves as waving swords or nursing the sick but it gets monotonous. A picture like this would have its great force from seeing ourselves as human beings who go on eating and loving and displaying our small vanities and follies in the midst of any catastrophe.

I would like to write this story, with any encouragement. What do you think?[2]

Ever your friend,
F. Scott Fitzgerald

5521 Amestoy Avenue
Encino, California

TO: *Zelda Fitzgerald*   *CC, 1 p. Princeton University*

February
16
1940

Dearest Zelda:-

I understand your attitude completely and sympathize with it to a great extent.[3] But the mood which considers any work beneath their talents doesn't especially appeal to me in other people, though I acknowledge being sometimes guilty of it myself. At the moment I am hoping for a job at Republic Studios, the lowest of the low, which would among other things help to pay your hospital bill. So the fact that anything you do can be applied on your bill instead of on our jaunt to the Isles of Greece doesn't seem so tough.

However, I am disappointed, with you, that the future Ruskins and Elie Faures and other anatomists of art will have to look at your windows instead of the mail hall. But something tells me that by the time this letter comes you will have changed your point of view. It is those people that have kept your talent alive when you willed it to sink into the dark abyss. Granted it's a delicate thing—mine is so scarred and buffeted that I am amazed that at times it still runs clear. (God, what a mess of similes) But the awful thing

[1] African-American character actors; Stepin Fetchit played comic, subservient types, and Hattie McDaniel played faithful servants, notably "Mammy" in *Gone With the Wind*, for which she won the first Academy Award presented to an African-American.

[2] Fitzgerald did not write this screenplay.

[3] Zelda had balked at painting decorations for Highland Hospital.

would have been some material catastrophe that would have made it unable to run at all.

Dearest love,

5521 Amestoy Avenue
Encino, California

TO: *Dr. Clarence Nelson*[1]   *CC, 1 p. Princeton University*

February
7
1940

Dear Dr. Nelson:-

Just to tell you I have not forgotten you nor what I owe you. Physically the situation is really miraculously improved. Financially it is still as bad as ever but I just don't see how it can go on being this bad. I have had no fever now for well over six weeks, feel no fatigue beyond what is normal, cough only a very little bit in the mornings and usually that is all for the whole day. In other words, as far as I can determine the disease is absolutely quiescent and if anything, I have been more active than at any time since I took to bed last March.

I suppose that my absolutely dry regime has something to do with it but not everything. Oddly enough the little aches around the elbows and shoulders return from time to time whenever I have had a great orgy of coco-cola's and coffee.

With very best wishes and hopes that soon I may be able to do something substantial about your bill.

Sincerely and gratefully,
F. Scott Fitzgerald

5521 Amestoy Avenue
Encino, California

TO: *Arnold Gingrich*   *TLS, 1 p. Princeton University*

February
7
1940

Dear Arnold:-

What would you think of this? You remember that about a week ago I wrote asking you about the publication of "Between Planes". You said that

[1] One of Fitzgerald's doctors in California.

you hadn't intended to publish it until after the Pat Hobby stories. Why don't you publish it under a pseudonym—say, John Darcy?[1] I'm awfully tired of being Scott Fitzgerald anyhow, as there doesn't seem to be so much money in it, and I'd like to find out if people read me just because I am Scott Fitzgerald or, what is more likely, don't read me for the same reason. In other words it would fascinate me to have one of my stories stand on its own merits completely and see if there is a response. I think it would be a shame to let that story stand over for such a long time now.

What do you think of this? While the story is not unlike me it is not particularly earmarked by my style as far as I know. At least I don't think so. If the idea interests you I might invent a fictitious personality for Mr. Darcy. My ambition would be to get a fan letter from my own daughter.

Ever your friend,
John Darcy
(F. Scott Fitzgerald)

5521 Amestoy Avenue
Encino, California

TO: Scottie Fitzgerald   *TLS, 1 p.—with holograph addition*
Princeton University

February
19
1940

Dearest Scottie:

Delighted that you're working on a play. In answer to a query in one of your past letters I do like Thomas Mann—in fact I had put his "Death in Venice" on that list I gave you last summer. Have sent your treasurer his check.

I was very interested to hear about Kilduff. Let me know what becomes of Andrew in the club elections. Things are still very vague here.

With dearest love,
F. S. Fitzg——

Have paid Peck + Peck + Peck + Peck + Peck.[2]

5521 Amestoy Avenue
Encino, California

---

[1] This pseudonym was not used.
[2] Peck & Peck, a fashionable New York women's clothing store, had a branch shop near the Vassar campus.

TO: *Arnold Gingrich*   *CC, 1 p. Princeton University*

February
23
1940

Dear Arnold:-

As you know Edward J. O'Brien wants "Design in Plaster" for his anthology.[1] Also Edward Everett Horton[2] has approached me with the idea of making the Pat Hobbys into a theatrical vehicle for him. So my stuff is getting a little attention.

I intended to write you before about my nom de plume, John Darcy.[3] My suggestion is that the first story be "Between Planes"; the next, the enclosed "Dearly Beloved"[4]; third "The Woman from 21"[5] and if you happen to like this poem, "Beloved Infidel",[6] and will seriously guard Mr. Darcy's identity, it might interest your readers. It has a touch of Ella Wheeler Wilcox about it and some shadows of Laurence Hope[7] and the early Kipling.

With best wishes always,

P.S. There will be another Pat Hobby on soon. I have written half of one but didn't like it. The enclosed story, "Dearly Beloeved" is so short you can have it for $200., but I wish you would wire the money.

5521 Amestoy Avenue
Encino, California

TO: *Phil Berg–Bert Allenberg Agency*[8]   *CC, 1 p. Princeton University*

February
23
1940

Messers Berg, Dozier and Allen

Following is the data I promised—from August 1937 when I arrived here on a six months Metro contract.

---

[1] *The Best Short Stories 1940* (1940).

[2] Character actor who was Fitzgerald's landlord at "Belly Acres" in Encino.

[3] One Fitzgerald story, "On an Ocean Wave," appeared posthumously under the pseudonym "Paul Elgin" in *Esquire* (February 1941).

[4] Gingrich declined "Dearly Beloved"; it was first published in the *Fitzgerald/Hemingway Annual 1969*.

[5] *Esquire* (June 1941).

[6] This poem addressed to Sheilah Graham was declined by *Esquire*; it was first published in *Beloved Infidel*, a memoir of Fitzgerald by Sheilah Graham and Gerold Frank (1958).

[7] Wilcox was a sentimental poet; Hope wrote romantic verse set in exotic locales.

[8] The Berg-Allenberg Agency represented Fitzgerald in Hollywood after he left the Swanson and Hayward agencies. William Dozier was head of the story department.

1. Two weeks on Yank at Oxford with Jack Conway and Michael Balcan. They used two scenes of mine.

2. Six months with Joe Mankiewicz on Three Comrades. Received the first credit. My contract was renewed with rise from $1000. to $1250.

3. Three months with Hunt Stromberg on "Infidelity" when we struck censorship problem and project was abandoned. Up to this point Hunt seemed highly pleased with my work and about then Joe Mankiewicz asked for me on another picture but I chose to stick with Hunt.

4. Five months with Stromberg on The Women, first working with Sidney Franklin and then with Don Stuart. Hunt was difficult to please on this and toward the end Don and I lost interest.

5. Three months with Sidney Franklin on Madame Curie. We were bucking Bernie Hyman's preconception of the thing as a love story. Hyman glanced at what we had done and shelved the whole project. Franklin had been very interested up to that time.

6. There had been many offers to borrow me by other studios. When Knopf told me that my contract was not to be renewed I went directly to Dave Selznick for G.W.T.W. Things were in a mess there and I went out after two or three weeks.

7. At this point I wanted to quit for a while—health bad and I was depressed about the Metro business. But Swanson argued me into a job with Wanger on Winter Carnival with a rise to $1500. This was a mistake. I blew up after a trip to Dartmouth and got flu and got drunk and walked out.

8. After a month's rest I took a job with Jeff Lazarus on Air Raid. We progressed for a month and then the picture was put aside for Honeymoon in Bali and I went to Cuba.

9. I found in the East, that I was sicker than I had thought and I came back here in May to lie around in bed till my health picked up. I had the refusal during these months of In Name Only, Rebecca and half a dozen others, but by July, when I wanted to work again, the offers seemed to stop. The first thing that came along was a week's job with Stahl on some vaguely projected original (at $1500.).

10. In September Eddie Knopf wanted me for Raffles. They were already shooting and I came in on a violent quarrel between Goldwyn and Wood. I refer you to Eddie Knopf on the matter. Somewhere around this time Harry Joe Brown called me over to Twentieth Century Fox on a Sonja Heine picture but it was apparently only for a day's pumping. Anyhow save for a nibble on the part of Hempstead for Kitty Foyle, no one has shown interest since then.

Such is the story of two and one half years.

5521 Amestoy Avenue
Encino, California

TO: Scottie Fitzgerald   *CC, 2 pp. Princeton University*

February
26
1940

Dearest Scottie:—

I am sorry you've got the February blues. Schoolmasters have told me that in small schools they look forward to February as a time of horror. I understand about the prom. Isn't it a question of your popularity turning on you—most people assume that a popular girl has surely been asked and are afraid to try. By this time you will either have gone or not gone and are no longer staying awake at night over it.

The Alumni Weekly has repercussions of the Princeton editorials. I have been very interested.[1]

With my own career at low ebb I have been hesitant to write you—because what at least carried financial pressure before hasn't that, much less any trace of authority. There are a couple of things though that have preyed in my mind come Maundy Thursday to wit: that the reason you missed the Messelaeni[2] is because you were a little Walker School about it. "I didn't know enough about politics" etc—what it really means is you are in the midst of a communist dominated student movement at Vassar which you do nothing about. The movement will go both up and down in the next few years. You can join it or let it simmer but you have never even considered it outside of classroom work—except to say, perhaps, that your father is rather far to the left. It would be foolish ever to make enemies of those girls. Silly and fanatical as they seem now some of them are going to be forces in the future of that section. You must have some politeness toward ideas. You can neither cut through, nor challenge nor beat the fact that there is an organized movement over the world before which you and I as individuals are less than the dust. Some time when you feel very brave and defiant and haven't been invited to one particular college function read the terrible chapter in Das Kapital on The Working Day, and see if you are ever quite the same.

I do not want you to lose your gayety ever—or ever your seriousness.

Do you know any lawyers? Ask somebody at the next Y.H.P. function who's gone on to law at Harvard. Then ask a law student who are the top prospects for the Editorship of the Harvard Law Review. Why not meet the lawyers. But for Christ's sake meet the people, meet the communists at Vassar and at least be politician enough to be absolutely dumb about politics and if you [   ] ake them on their side.[3]

---

[1] Articles on changing the Princeton club system in the *Princeton Alumni Weekly* (February 16 and 23, 1940).

[2] *The Vassar Miscellany.*

[3] The bottom of this page is torn off, removing words on the last line.

P.S. I can't accentuate this too much as you move in such varying worlds so at the risk of being a bore I beg you once more to consider politics as being a religion, something that you can only discuss freely among those of the same general attitude as your own. With other people you will find yourself in intolerable arguments—friendships are being made and broken over questions of policy, a state of things which is liable to increase month by month. It is all white hot and the long pinchers of tact can be very useful.

1403 N. Laurel Avenue[1]
Hollywood, California

TO: Dr. Robert S. Carroll   *CC, 1 p. Princeton University*

March
8
1940

Dear Dr. Carroll:

Your letter was a complete surprise, but of course I am delighted that you feel the way you do.[2] The news that she had been home alone in December was a complete surprise to me though as you know I would have been in agreement if you had ever thought before that a journey without a nurse was desirable. I have written Mrs. Sayre telling her of your letter and my agreement with it.

You have been magnificent about the whole thing and I am completely sensible of my financial and moral obligation to you. I may say privately that while I have always advocated her partial freedom my pleasure in this is qualified by an inevitable worry. Still one would rather have the worry than the continual sadness added to by her family's attitude. The attitude will continue but it will be on a different basis and easier to disregard.

I certainly hope that you will be able to write Mrs. Sayre at length about her responsibilities in the matter and about Zelda <u>doing</u> something. I still wish there was someone there a little keener and younger, but since I am utterly unprepared to take on the job again I suppose it is lucky that there is any sort of home where she will at least be loved and cherished. The possibility of dissipation frightens me more than anything else—which I suppose is poetic justice.

Again gratefully and sincerely yours,

5521 Amestoy Avenue
Encino, California

[1] This return address appears on the letter; the letters before and after it are from the Encino address.

[2] Zelda Fitzgerald was allowed a furlough from Highland Hospital and was planning to stay with her mother in Montgomery. This arrangement held until her death in 1948; she returned to the hospital voluntarily when she anticipated relapses.

TO: *Zelda Fitzgerald*   CC, *1 p. Princeton University*

March
8
1940

Dearest Zelda:—

It is wonderful to be able to write you this. Dr. Carroll has for the first time and at long last agreed that perhaps you shall try to make a place for yourself in the world. In other words, that you can go to Montgomery the first of April and remain there indefinitely or as long as you seem able to carry on under your own esteem.

So after four years of Dr. Carroll's regime interrupted by less than twenty scattered weeks away from the hospital, you will have the sense of being your own boss. Already I can share your joy and I know how Scottie will feel.

I am sorry your entrance will not be into a brighter world. I have no real finances yet and won't until I get a job. We have to live on those little pieces in Esquire and you know how little they pay. Scottie speaks of getting a job in Lord and Taylor's this summer but I do not want her to do that for all sorts of reasons. Maybe by the time you get home things will be brighter. So there we are.

With dearest love,

5521 Amestoy Avenue
Encino, California

TO: *Zelda Fitzgerald*   CC, *1 p. Princeton University*

March
19
1940

Dearest:-

It seems to me best not to hurry things.

(a) I'd like you to leave with the blessings of Dr. Carroll (you've con-sumed more of his working hours than one human deserves of another—you'd agree if you'd see his correspondence with me). Next to Forel he has been your eventual best friend—better even than Myer. (Though this is unfair to Myer who never claimed to be a clinician but only a diagnostician).

But to hell with all that, and with illness

(b) Also, you'd best wait because I will <u>certainly</u> have more money three weeks from now than at present, and

(c) <u>If</u> things develop fast Scottie can skip down and see you for a day during her vacation—otherwise you won't see her before summer. This is an <u>if</u>!

I don't think you fully realize the extent of what Scottie has done at Vassar. You wrote rather casually of two years being enough but it isn't. Her promise is unusual. Not only did she rise to the occasion and get in young but she has raised herself from a poor scholar to a very passable one; sold a professional story at eighteen; and moreover in very highbrow, at present very politically-minded Vassar she has introduced with some struggle a new note. She has written and produced a musical comedy and founded a club called the Omgim[1] to perpetuate the idea—almost the same thing that Tarkington did in 1893 when he founded the Triangle at Princeton. She did this against tough opposition—girls who wouldn't let her on the board of the daily paper because, though she could write, she wasn't "politically conscious".

We have every reason at this point to cheer for our baby. I would do anything rather than deny her the last two years of college which she has now earned. There is more than talent there—a real genius for organization.

Nothing has developed here. I write these "Pat Hobby" stories—and wait. I have a new idea now—a comedy series which will get me back into the big magazines—but my God I am a forgotten man. Gatsby had to be taken out of the Modern Library because it didn't sell, which was a blow.

With dearest love always

5521 Amestoy Avenue
Encino, California

TO: Scottie Fitzgerald   Retyped letter, 2 pp. Princeton University
                                                Encino, California

April

11

1940

Dearest Pie:-

Thanks for your letter. I'm writing this on a Sunday night, sans Françoise[2] and I hope you can read it. I go to cinema work tomorrow on a sort of half-pay, half "spec" (speculation) business on my own story Babylon Revisited.[3] Which is to say Columbia advances me living money while I work and if it goes over in installments with the producer, the company, the releasing people, I get an increasing sum. At bottom we eat—at top the deal is very promising.

[1] Oh My God, It's Monday.
[2] Frances Kroll, Fitzgerald's secretary.
[3] Producer Lester Cowan had bought movie rights to "Babylon Revisited" for $1,000 and hired Fitzgerald to write the screenplay for $500 a week.

Why I'm writing tonight is because I foresee three months of intensive toil (I feel like a criminal who has been in a hideout, been caught and has to go back to the big-house. I've been visited by my crooked doctor and my moll and Frances the Fence has protected me. Now the Big House again—Oh Jees them guards!)

To put you in a good humor for the ensuing gratuitous though friendly advice, let me say I got a letter from Andrew[1] today, out of two years silence, in which he "judges you objectively" as a very fine girl. I was pleased naturally and wish they hadn't counteracted the work I did on him by sending him to a school with a professional Holy-Joe for headmaster. His letter would make you very conceited—shall I send it? You seem to be a big shot down there.

The advice consists of this—Bobby Coleman's name bobs up in so many of your letters that I assume he plays a big part in your life, no matter how seldom you see him. I've naturally formed a picture of him—vaguely I associate it with my relation with Marie Hersey at about your time of life. I think she told herself that I was hers for the special effort. But they had become matter-of-fact to me—lesser girls would have rivalled them for new excitement and anyone who summed them up, or seemed to me like your mother, would simply have washed them out of my mind.

Supposing Bobby to be self-absorbed, charming, successful, and full of the same psychology I had—how definitely handicapped you might be in counting on him! By the very fact of old familiarity, old experience in common, it would be difficult, for men, if they're alive, are continually looking for the new. I mean, that he might so to speak meet the Queen of Abyssinia in his travels. And how can you rival her?

I'm not driving at the obvious answer of having many strings to your bow. I suppose you have. But haven't you taken Bobby as the only type? Women are capable of loving three or four types of masculine excellence like the women in Candida and Strange Interlude. You ought to have for example: as a cold intellectual—someone who's made the Harvard Law Review—you can find him with a little effort. He'll probably be taken already but it can be done. The point is that you have not exhausted any other type at its best except Bobby—you have only examined the second rate unproved man of other species (Kilduff, Naylor, etc.) You should know the young predatory business type, hard as hell, he will lick you maybe but you should know him. A lead at Princeton would be one of the Ivy boys—not Harvey but he might be a wedge—a boy inheriting a big business.

All the above is probably very obvious so froget it. Are any of the enclosed friends of yours?

Dearest love,

Daddy

P.S. Have paid The Wallace Co., $35. and Altman $40., on account.

[1] Turnbull.

The printed enclosure reminded me that if you have occasion to drive, I forgot to tell you that in the rain <u>don't depress the clutch</u>—use the break <u>only</u>. And on hills—go down in the gear in which you'd have come up.

I'm moving in town to be near my work, so will you address me care of my new agent, Phil Berg, 9484 Wilshire Boulevard, Beverly Hills or General Delivery, Encino, as they will also forward it. Will write you as soon as I have a permanent address.

TO: *Zelda Fitzgerald*   *CC, 1 p. Princeton University*
                                                      Encino, California

April
11
1940

Dearest Zelda:-

I got your wire today asking for $5. and simultaneously one came from Dr. Carroll saying you were coming out. I don't know what the rail fare to Montgomery is, but I am sending you herewith $60., which I hope will take care of your ticket, baggage, etc. You are leaving bills behind you, I know, which I will try to take care of as soon as I can. I have sent Jean West $25. on account. Moreover I have sent a check to your mother for your expenses when you get to Montgomery.

Now as to the general arrangement: I am starting to work on this "speculation" job. That is, they are giving me very little money but if the picture is resold when finished the deal will be somewhat better. I hesitated about accepting it but there have been absolutely no offers in many months and I did it on the advice of my new agent. It is a job that should be fun and suitable to my still uneven state of health. (Since yesterday I seem to be running a fever again) In any case we can't go on living indefinitely on those Esquire articles. So you will be a poor girl for awhile and there is nothing much to do about it. I can manage to send you $30., a week of which you should pay your mother about $15. for board, laundry, light, etc. The rest will be in checks of alternately $10. and $20.—that is, one week the whole sum will amount to $35., one week $25., etc. This is a sort of way of saving for you so that in alternate weeks you will have a larger lump sum in case you need clothes or something.

You will be cramped by this at first—moreso than in the hospital, but it is everything that I can send without putting Scottie to work which I absolutely refuse to do. I don't think you can promise a person an education and then snatch it away from them. If she quit Vassar I should feel like quitting all work and going to the free Veteran's Hospital where I probably belong.

The main thing is not to run up bills or wire me for extra funds. There simply aren't any and as you can imagine I am deeply in debt to the government and everyone else. As soon as anything turns up I will naturally increase your allowance so that you will have more mobility, clothes, etc.

I am moving in town to be near my work. For the present, will you address me care of my new agent, Phil Berg, 9484 Wilshire Boulevard, Beverly Hills, California. If you forget, "General Delivery, Encino" will be forwarded to me also. As soon as I have a new permanent address I will write you. I do hope this goes well. I wish you were going to brighter surroundings but this is certainly not the time to come to me and I can think of nowhere else for you to go in this dark and bloody world. I suppose a place is what you make it but I have grown to hate California and would give my life for three years in France.

So Bon Voyage and stay well.

Dearest love,

TO: Scottie Fitzgerald *TLS, 1 p. Princeton University*
Encino, California

April
12
1940

Dearest Scottie:

I'm sorry about the tone of the telegram I sent you this morning, but it represents a most terrific worry. You are doing exactly what I did at Princeton. I wore myself out on a musical comedy there for which I wrote book and lyrics, organized and mostly directed while the president played football. Result: I slipped way back in my work, got T.B., lost a year in college—and, irony of ironies, because of scholastic slip I wasn't allowed to take the presidency of the Triangle.

From your letter I guess that you are doing exactly the same thing and it just makes my stomach fall out to think of it. Amateur work is fun but the price for it is just simply tremendous. In the end you get "Thank you" and that's all. You give three performances which everybody promptly forgets and somebody has a breakdown—that somebody being the enthusiast.

Please, please, please delegate every bit of the work you can and keep your scholastic head above water. To see a mistake repeated twice in two generations would be just too much to bear. This is the most completely experienced advice I've ever given you. What about that science and the philosophy? You've got to find hours to do them even if you have to find a secret room where you can go and study.

Dearest love always.
Daddy

TO: S. J. and Laura Perelman   *CC, 1 p. Princeton University*

May
13
1940

Dear Sid and Laura:-

This is a love missive so do not be alarmed. I am not giving a tea for either the Princess Razzarascal or Two-ticker Forsite. <u>But</u> I am leaving this Elysian haunt in two weeks (the 29th to be exact) and sometime before that nonce I wish you two would dine or lunch. I know Sunday isn't a good day for you because of the dwarfs and Saturday next I'm going to Maurice Evans[1] and Sunday I'm engaged (now you know, girls, isn't it <u>wonderful</u>?)

—but any other day between now and the 28th would be fine. I <u>want</u> to see you and very specifically you, and for the most general and non-specific reasons. The days being at their longest it is no chore to find this place up to 7:30 and perhaps the best idea is dinner. We could either dine à quatre or add the Wests and some other couple—say the Mannerheims or Browders, and afterwards play with my model parachute troops. At any event, side arms will not be <u>de rigeur</u>.★ Sheilah will be with me just as merry as can be, to greet you on the porch with a julep. I have just re-read "Crime and Punishment" and the chapters on gang labor in "Capitalist Production" and am meek as a liberal bourgeoise lamb.

Call me up on the party line or drop me a note. The only acceptable excuse is that you're going on vacation or have empetigo because I want to see you.

With spontaneous affection,

★Outer boom or gaff on an old New England square-riggered ship.

5521 Amestoy Avenue
Encino, California
phone: STate 4-0578

TO: Zelda Fitzgerald   *CC, 1 p. Princeton University*

Encino, California

May
18
1940

Dearest Zelda:-

It's hard to explain about the Saturday Evening Post matter. It isn't that I haven't tried, but the trouble with them goes back to the time of Lorimer's

---

[1] British actor.

443

retirement in 1935. I wrote them three stories that year and sent them about three others which they didn't like. The last story they bought they published last in the issue and my friend, Adelaide Neil on the staff, implied to me that they didn't want to pay that big price for stories unless they could use them in the beginning of the issue. Well that was the time of my two year sickness, T.B., the shoulders, etc., and you were at a most crucial point and I was foolishly trying to take care of Scottie and for one reason or another I lost the knack of writing the particular kind of stories they wanted.

As you should know from your own attempts, high priced commercial writing for the magazines is a very definite trick. The rather special things that I brought to it, the intelligence and the good writing and even the radicalism all appealed to old Lorimer who had been a writer himself and liked style. The man who runs the magazine now is an up and coming young Republican who gives not a damn about literature and who publishes almost nothing except escape stories about the brave frontiersmen, etc., or fishing, or football captains—nothing that would even faintly shock or disturb the reactionary bourgeois. Well, I simply can't do it and, as I say, I've tried not once but twenty times.

As soon as I feel I am writing to a cheap specification my pen freezes and my talent vanishes over the hill and I honestly don't blame them for not taking the things that I've offered to them from time to time in the past three or four years. An explanation of their new attitude is that you no longer have a chance of selling a story with an unhappy ending (in the old days many of mine <u>did</u> have unhappy endings—if you remember.) In fact the standard of writing from the best movies, like Rebecca, is, believe it or not, much higher at present than that in the commercial magazines such as Colliers and the Post.

Thank you for your letter. California is a monotonous climate and already I am tired of the flat, scentless tone of the summer. It is fun to be working on something I like and maybe in another month I will get the promised bonus on it and be able to pay last year's income tax and raise our standard of living a little.

Love to you all and dearest love to you.

P.S. I am sending you the copy of the article you sent me about Scottie. You said something about giving it to Mrs. McKinney.

TO: *Maxwell Perkins*   *TLS, 2 pp. Princeton University*

c/o Phil Berg Agency
9484 Wilshire Blvd.
Beverly Hills, Calif.
May 20, 1940

Dear Max:-

I've owed you a decent letter for some months. First—the above is my best address though at the moment I'm hunting for a small apartment. I am in the last week of an eight week movie job for which I will receive $2300. I couldn't pay you anything from it, nor the government, but it was something, because it was my own picture <u>Babylon Revisited</u> and may lead to a new line up here. I just couldn't make the grade as a hack—that, like everything else, requires a certain practised excellence—

The radio has just announced the fall of St. Quentin! My God! What was the use of my wiring you that Andre Chamson has a hit when the war has now passed into a new stage making his book a chestnut of a bygone quiet era.

I wish I was in print. It will be odd a year or so from now when Scottie assures her friends I was an author and finds that no book is procurable. It is certainly no fault of yours. You (and one other man, Gerald Murphy) have been a friend through every dark time in these five years. It's funny what a friend is—Ernest's crack in <u>The Snows</u>, poor John Bishop's article in the Virginia Quarterly (a nice return for ten years of trying to set him up in a literary way)[1] and Harold's sudden desertion at the wrong time, have made them something less than friends. Once I believed in friendship, believed I <u>could</u> (if I didn't always) make people happy and it was more fun than anything. Now even that seems like a vaudevillian's cheap dream of heaven, a vast minstrel show in which one is the perpetual Bones.

Professionally, I know, the next move must come from me. Would the 25 cent press keep <u>Gatsby</u> in the public eye—or <u>is the book unpopular</u>. Has it <u>had</u> its chance? Would a popular reissue in that series with a preface <u>not</u> by me but by one of its admirers—I can maybe pick one—make it a favorite with class rooms, profs, lovers of English prose—anybody. But to die, so completely and unjustly after having given so much. Even now there is little published in American fiction that doesn't slightly bare my stamp— in a <u>small</u> way I was an original. I remember we had one of our few and trifling disagreements because I said that to anyone who loved "When Lilacs last—" Tom Wolfe couldn't be such a <u>great</u> original. Since then I have changed about him. I like "Only the Dead" and "Arthur, Garfield etc.", right up with the tops. And where are Tom and I and the rest when psychological Robespierres parade through American letters elevating such melo as "Christ in Concrete"[2] to the top, and the boys read Steinbeck like

[1]"The Missing All," *Virginia Quarterly Review* (Winter 1937).
[2]A 1939 novel by Pietro Di Donato.

they once read Mencken! I have not lost faith. People will <u>buy</u> my new book and I hope I shan't again make the many mistakes of <u>Tender</u>.

Tell me news if you have time. Where is Ernest and what doing? How about Elizabeth Lemmon, the lovely, & unembittered and sacrified virgin, the victim of what I gradually and depressingly found was the vanity of her family. How I disliked them—the heavily moustached Mrs. Doctor, the panting Virginian hausfrau sister who fancied herself an aristocrat, the Baltimore bond-salesman who will inherit. And, in the midst, the driven snow of Elizabeth. It was too sad to bear.

Love to all of you, of all generations.
Scott

TO: *Lester Cowan*   *CC, 1 p. Princeton University*

May
28
1940

Dear Lester:

My idea is to lie up in Santa Barbara or Carmel for a week or ten days. Bill Dozier will give you the addresses and when I have a permanent one I will wire it to you myself. I don't know how anybody can get away from anything these days and I'm even taking a radio. But just the idea of having the house off my back is a relief.

The picture was fun to write. The only snag was in the final Swiss Sequence. I found out that there is no trace of winter sport in Switzerland <u>before the middle of December</u> and the stockmarket crash occurred very definitely the <u>last part of October</u> so, instead of a routine based on bobsleds such as we talked about, I had to resort to an older device. I think this sequence carries the emotion of the others but it is the one with least originality of treatment, and audiences are more and more responding to originality after five years of double-feature warm-overs.

Sheilah has several times mentioned to me a little actress named Mary Todd (aged eight). She was the child who played the piano in "Intermezzo" and also did a touching scene in George Cukor's "Zaza"—when the child had to receive her father's mistress not understanding the situation at all. She is certainly somebody to keep in mind, though I can't seem to visualize her face at this moment.

Also the actor[1] who played the chief commissar in "Ninotchka" and the bookkeeper in "Shop Around the Corner", might be worthy of consideration for Pierre, though the types he has played so far are largely South European. And for this he would have to be a sprucer and more attractive man externally to match up with Marion.

[1] Felix Bressart.

75E

For Victoria Schulberg
    in memory of a
three day mountain-climbing
trip with her illustrious
father — who pulled me
out of crevices into which
I sank and away from
avalanches —
        with affection to you
both
            F Scott Fitzgerald
        Beverly Hills
    1940

Victoria was the newly born daughter of Budd Schulberg. Fitzgerald phoned Schulberg at Cedars of Lebanon Hospital after her birth and lectured him on the father-daughter relationship.

Lester, I'm terribly sorry that I didn't get around to reading the Hilton script. I did actually go through it quickly and enjoyed it—but not enough to give any constructive suggestions. I wish it the greatest success.

There are so many new things in our script that I thought it best to deliver it to Bob under seal. So many of the scenes are easily repeated in the most innocent way, and the ear of Hollywood is notoriously hungry. I think you will like the title.[1] It is an unusual name with a peculiarly sonorous quality and so many of the more popular pieces—Babbitt, Rebecca, David Copperfield—have been only names. I think it you sleep on it, it will grow on you.

Looking forward to seeing your face or hearing your voice. Best to Ann.

With warm personal regards

P.S. This of course, is the best and final version of the 1st draft.

Encino, California

TO: *Scottie Fitzgerald*   *TL, 3 pp. Princeton University*

> 1403 Laurel Avenue
> Hollywood
> California
> (new address)
> June 7, 1940

Dearest Scottie:

Thank you for your letter. Planning from week to week, I am not quite sure yet about anything, but go ahead about the Summer School, make reservations and so forth. I think it can be managed all right. I went to San Francisco with some friends for one day, and found it much too long to see that singularly second-rate and uninspired Fair—though they had some good Cranachs and El Grecos in the art exhibition.

Vassar's only fault to the outer world is the "Vassar manner"—which of course is founded on the sense of intellectual intensity that you mention. I found it particularly annoying in Margaret Culkin Banning's daughter in Tryon some years ago. She told me all about American literature in the first half hour I met her—I believe she had been editor-in-chief of the Miscellaeni, the year before. Of course it does not usually show itself like that, but, like the Harvard manner of 1900 which gave Harvard a country-wide unpopularity, makes itself known in a series of smug silences. Southern manners are better—especially the rather punctilious deference to older people. The

---

[1] The working title for the screenplay of "Babylon Revisited" was "Honoria," but Fitzgerald also considered calling it "Cosmopolitan." The movie was never made from Fitzgerald's screenplay, which was published by Carroll & Graf in 1993.

chances are that some toothless old codger who doesn't open his mouth may turn out to be the greatest authority in the world on some recondite subject, and you feel rather a fool when you have judged him and settled his hash with the glossy learning of a year or so. So be careful of it, especially this summer when you will meet many idiots, some in hysterical panic about the war and others too dumb to know what is going on.

You credit me with a gift of prophecy I don't have. I _did_ feel the war was coming in '39 and said so to a lot of people, but it was calculated by the time when Germany would have several new replacement classes to make up for the decreased birth-rate from 1915 to 1918. We all knew the German army wasn't beaten and Woodrow Wilson didn't want it to be beaten, not appreciating the utter helpless decadence of the English—something that has been apparent to even English intellectuals for twenty years. The intellectuals, those few who ever dabbled in military affairs, knew that the war was lost at Munich and that the Germans would tear the Allies to pieces, in Europe at least. And the American rich will try to betray America in exactly the same way as the British conservatives. A pogrom could be organized over-night against all the "subversive elements" (whose power is tremendously over estimated at the moment) but the rich will have to have the pants scared off them before they stop skulking in their tents and begin to get their boys safe jobs in the quarter-master department.

The Comrades out here are in a gloomy spot; Donald Stewart goes around groaning how "the Revolution will have to come the hard way," in other words the party line is to let National Socialism (Nazism) conquer us and then somehow milk Marxism out of Hitler's sterile teats! Stalin has pulled another boner just as he did in Finland. He had no intention of letting Hitler go this far.

With the situation changing as fast as it does now, it is difficult for Liberals to have a policy. The war may lead to anything from utter chaos to a non-Comintern American Revolution, but the world that I knew and that you have had eighteen years of will never exist again in our time. On the other hand I do not think it possible for the Germans to win the South American war against us. The native Yankee is still the most savage and intelligent fighter in the world. He plays the toughest, hardest games with a cooler head and it is simply unthinkable that an oppressed stock could be whooped up in one decade to conquer him. Still I think many of your friends will probably draw their last breaths in Paraguay or the forests of the Chaco. Did you see that Lehman has called for anti-aircraft defense for New York? What a cowardly panic! Next we will have Louis B. Mayer calling for anti-aircraft guns to defend Metro.

This letter has turned into gossip, and I have much to do. I finished the picture and am doing a short story. Had intended to rest for a week, but there wasn't a chance. Dear, I have had a very depressed letter from your mother and another from your grandmother—the second told me in cautious language that your mother had had a "toxic attack." I know what this means, only I expected her to hold out at least two months. She seems to be recovered from that, but her own letter shows a great deal of despair, and your grandmother's has a defeatism that I have never seen before. I don't know what is going to happen, but as this may be the last time you have a chance to see your mother in a sane period, <u>I want you to find ten days to spend with her this June</u>. This may bust hell out of your plans, but remember that for ten months you have lived for yourself and you owe this to me. I don't care when you go, except it is to be before Summer School opens, and not just three or four days.

The Harper's business is all right for me if you can fit it in with everything else. Will you tell me what you are going to take at Summer School? I think I wrote you that I thought your next year's Vassar course is fine, except for the <u>Greek Civilization and Literature</u>, which seems to me a profound waste of time. Your other three courses are so completely cultural that I wish that the fourth could be as practical a one as Vassar offers—I wish they had Business School—or else a supplementary French course or another language. <u>Greek Civilization and Literature</u> is something you cannot learn in nine months, and it seems to me a rather dilettantish way of wasting time.

I expect to hear in a day or so whether I am going back to work on my picture story—I told you once it was an old Saturday Evening Post story called "Babylon Revisited" that I wrote in 1931. You were one of the principal characters.
With dearest love,

Daddy

TO: *Scottie Fitzgerald*   *TLS, 2 pp.*[1] *Princeton University*

1403 North Laurel Avenue
Hollywood, California
June 12, 1940

Dearest Scottina:

Thanks for your nice full letter—it made me happy, and I don't doubt your sincerity about work. I think now you will always be a worker, and I'm glad. Your mother's utterly endless mulling and brooding over insolubles paved the way to her ruin. She had no education—not from lack of opportunity because she could have learned with me—but from some inner stubbornness. She was a great original in her way, with perhaps a more intense flame at its highest than I ever had, but she tried and is still trying to solve all ethical and moral problems on her own, without benefit of the thousands dead. Also she had nothing "kinetic", which, in physics, means internal driving force—she had to be led or driven. That was the

---

[1] The bracketed passage—not in the Princeton University copy—is transcribed from Turnbull.

tired element that all Judge Sayre's children inherited. And the old mother is still, at times, a ball of fire!

I could agree with you as opposed to Dean Thompson if you were getting "B's". Then I would say: As you're not going to be a teacher or a professional scholar, don't try for "A's"—don't take the things in which you can get "A", for you can learn them yourself. Try something hard and new, and try it hard, and take what marks you get. But you have no such margin of respectability, and this borderline business is a fret to you. Doubt and worry—you are as crippled by them as I am by my inability to handle money or my self-indulgences of the past. It is your Achilles' heel—and no Achilles' heel ever toughened by itself. It just gets more and more vulnerable. [What little I've accomplished has been by the most laborious and uphill work, and I wish now I'd never relaxed or looked back—but said at the end of The Great Gatsby: "I've found my line—from now on this comes first. This is my immediate duty—without this I am nothing.". . . .]

Please wire me what days you have chosen to go South so I can make financial arrangements.

Can't you tell some story down there that it's urgently necessary to go to summer school because you've been on the edge of flunking out? Otherwise they'll wonder why the money couldn't be spent for a seaside vacation for you all. I'm living in the smallest apartment here that will permit me not to look poor, which I can't afford to do in Hollywood. If the picture goes through, I will give your mother a trip in August. At the moment I am keeping her on a slender allowance, as for ten years she has absorbed the major proportion of the family income.

I did listen to the radio all through my trip. Jesus! What a battle!

Please at least go in to see Gerald Murphy at Mark Cross for five minutes in passing thru N.Y. this summer!

Send me the details about Harvard Summer School. Can I pay in installments?

Even as a construction man, Pinero was inferior to both Shaw and Ibsen. What purpose is served in teaching that second rate Noel Coward at Vassar?

The 'New Yorker' story might hamper you if you attach too much importance to it. The play was an accomplishment—I admit it with pride and pleasure. I'd like to see the story. Can't you send me a copy?

Reading over your letter, you don't sound like an introvert at all. You sound a little flushed and over-confident, but I'm not worried.

With Dearest Love,

Daddy

P.S. You want to go to summer school. I will have to do extra work for that, and I'll do it gladly. But I want you to spend ten days with your mother first. And please give me a full complete report on your mother's condition. Your request for $15.00 just came as I was putting this in an envelope. To get it to you (Frances is away) cost me my morning. You must not ask me to wire you money—it is much harder to get than last summer. I owe <u>thousands</u>. I couldn't have had this trip except that the Rogers were going + invited me. Sorry to close the letter this way but you must count your pennies.

TO: Zelda Fitzgerald   *CC, 1 p. Princeton University*

June
14
1940

Dearest Zelda:-

At the moment everything is rather tentative. Scottie is coming South about the 20th and after that wants to go to summer school at Harvard. If I can possibly afford it I want her to go. She wants an education and has recently shown that she has a right to it. You will find her very mature and well informed. My feeling is that we are in for a ten year war and that perhaps one more year at Vassar is all she will have—which is one reason why the summer school appeals to me. If I can manage that for a month, than perhaps I can manage the seashore for you in August—by which time you will have had a good deal of Montgomery weather. A lot depends on whether my producer is going to continue immediately with "Babylon Revisited"—or whether any other picture job turns up. Things are naturally shot to hell here with everybody running around in circles yet continuing to turn out two million dollar tripe like "All This and Heaven Too".

Twenty years ago "This Side of Paradise" was a best seller and we were settled in Westport. Ten years ago Paris was having almost its last great American season but we had quit the gay parade and you were gone to Switzerland. Five years ago I had my first bad stroke of illness and went to Asheville. Cards began falling badly for us much too early. The world has certainly caught up in the last four weeks. I hope the atmosphere in Montgomery is tranquil and not too full of war talk.

Love to all of you.

1403 N. Laurel Avenue
Hollywood, California

TO: Scottie Fitzgerald   *TLS, 1 p. Princeton University*

June
14
1940

Dearest Scottie:—

By my mistake the money was <u>not</u> sent to Mary Law. I wired you $15. care of Ober and here's another $15. The allowance for the week of June 17 will be sent you tomorrow and you can use it to get to Montgomery.

Things not so bright here.

Dearest love,
Daddy

P.S. Gloria[1] was a much more trivial and vulgar person than your mother. I can't really say there was any resemblance except in the beauty and certain terms of expression she used, and also I naturally used many circumstantial events of our early married life. However the emphases were entirely different. We had a much better time than Anthony and Gloria had.

1403 N. Laurel Avenue
Hollywood, California

TO: Scottie Fitzgerald   *TLS, 1 p. Princeton University*

June
15
1940

Dearest Scottie:

Here is your round trip fare to Montgomery. I'm sorry it can't be more but, while my picture <u>is</u> going to be done, the producer is going to <u>first</u> do one that has been made for the brave Laurence Olivier who will defend his country in Hollywood (though summoned back by the British Government). This affects the patriotic and unselfish Scott Fitzgerald to the extent that I receive no more money from that source until the company gets around to it; so will return to my old standby Esquire.

Meanwhile I have another plan which may yield a bonanza but will take a week to develop, so there's nothing to do for a week except try to cheer up your mother and derive what consolation you can in explaining the Spenglerian hypotheses to Miss Le Grand and her fellow feebs of the Confederacy. Maybe you can write something down there. It is a grotesquely pictorial country as I found out long ago, and as Mr. Faulkner has since abundantly demonstrated.

Anyhow they need you. I will dig you out in time for the summer school.

Love,
Daddy

[1] Gloria Patch of *The Beautiful and Damned.*

P.S. As I said, I am trying to give you $30. a week this summer, and when there is a lot of traveling to be done will increase this somewhat. For instance, I gave you $20. extra to get out of Vassar and there is $10. extra in this check which makes $30. and which will cover a good deal of transportation to date (including the round trip fare to Montgomery). Will send the next check there.

1403 N. Laurel Avenue
Hollywood, California

TO: *Arnold Gingrich*   *TLS, 1 p. University of Michigan*

July
15
1940

Dear Arnold:

My name is Paul Elgin and Paul will presently send you some contributions.

I see that your next scheduled story is "Pat Hobby Does His Bit"[1] and I hope that the one after that is "No Harm Trying".[2] It certainly seems to me next in order of merit. You didn't comment on "Fun in an Artist's Studio".[3] Perhaps if your secretary told me in which order the remaining stories are scheduled I might be able to make some changes in one or two of them before they go into type. There are a couple there that don't please me at all.

Thanks for your note. Best wishes.

Ever your friend,
Scott Fitzg

1403 N. Laurel Avenue
Hollywood, California

TO: *Scottie Fitzgerald*   *Retyped letter, 1 p. Princeton University*
                                   Hollywood, California

July
18
1940

Dearest Scottie:

This summer has shown among other things that your education to date is entirely theoretical. I have no general quarrel with this and I believe it is

---

[1] *Esquire* (September 1940).
[2] *Esquire* (November 1940).
[3] *Esquire* (February 1941).

as it should be in preparing for any sort of literary work. However the odds are against your having the type of talent that matures very quickly—most of my contemporaries did not get started at twenty-two, but usually at about twenty-seven to thirty or even later, filling in the interval with anything from journalism teaching sailing a tramp-schooner and going to wars. The talent that matures early is usually of the poetic, which mine was in large part. The prose talent depends on other factors—assimilation of material and careful selection of it, or more bluntly: having something to say and an interesting, highly developed way of saying it.

Looking at the problem from short range only, you see how difficult it was to get a job this summer. So let's see what Vassar's got. The first thing that occurs to me is Spanish, which is simply bound to be of enormous value in the next ten years. Every junior-high-school child in California gets a taste of it and could beat you out of a job in South America if we expand that way. It is enough like French so that you have few alphabetical troubles, is pronounced as written, and has a fairly interesting literature of its own. I mean it's not like studying Bulgarian or Chippewa or some strange dialect in which no one had ever had anything to say. Don't you think this would be a much wiser move than the Greek and Latin culture?— the which shocks me that Vassar has such a namby-pamby "course".

I wonder if you've read anything this summer—I mean any one good book like "The Brothers Karamazov" or "Ten Days That Shook the World" or Renan's "Life of Christ". You never speak of your reading except the excerpts you do in college, the little short bits that they must perforce give you. I know you have read a few of the books I gave you last summer— then I have heard nothing from you on the subject. Have you ever, for example, read "Pere Goriot" or "Crime and Punishment" or even "The Doll's House" or "St. Matthew" or "Sons and Lovers"? A good style simply doesn't form unless you absorb half a dozen top flight authors every year. Or rather it _forms_ but, instead of being a subconscious amalgam of all that you have admired, it is simply a reflection of the last writer you have read, a watered-down journaleese.

Don't be too hard on Princeton. Harvard produced John Reed[1] but they also produced Richard Whitney[2] who I like to believe would have been spotted as a punk at Princeton. The Honor System sometimes has a salutary effect on light-fingered gentry.

With dearest love,
Daddy

[1]Reed was a member of the American Communist Party, author of _Ten Days That Shook the World_ (1919), and the only American buried in the wall of the Kremlin.

[2]Whitney, a socially prominent stockbroker and head of the New York Stock Exchange, went to prison for embezzlement.

TO: Zelda Fitzgerald   *CC, 1 p. Princeton University*

July
29
1940

Dearest Zelda:—

The Temple[1] thing is this: she's too old to have a child's appeal and though they've put everything in her last pictures—song, dance, sleight of hand, etc.,—they fail to hold the crowd. In fact the very last is rather nauseous in its sentimentality.

So this "independent" producer Cowan, now of Columbia, shortly to be at Paramount, had the idea of a romantic drama for her and bought my <u>Babylon Revisited</u> last year for $900. for that purpose. I should have held out for more but the story had been nearly ten years published without a nibble. So then, in a beautifully avaricious way, knowing I'd been sick and was probably hard up, Mr. Cowan hired me to do the script on a percentage basis. He gives me—or <u>gave</u> me—what worked out to a few hundred a week to do a quick script.[2] Which I did and then took to bed to recuperate. Now he says he wants me to do another, and I'm supposed to be grateful because since I haven't done a movie for so long the conclusion is easy for this scum that I can't write. If you could see and talk for five minutes with the People I deal with you'd understand without words how difficult it is to master a bare politeness.

Anyhow I <u>think</u> it's been a good thing except for the health angle and if and when he sells Mrs. Temple and Paramount the script there'll be a little more money—if he doesn't think of a way to beat me out of it.

So that's the story. Tell me—did the watch come? You never mentioned it.

With Dearest Love,

1403 N. Laurel Avenue
Hollywood, California

TO: Scottie Fitzgerald   *TLS, 2 pp.*[3] *Princeton University*
                                          Hollywood, California

July 29, 1940

I am still on the Temple picture and will continue on if a very avaricious gent named Cowan will loosen up. If he doesn't, I will rest for a week, and can stand it as my cough has become a public nuisance.

[1]Cowan wanted Shirley Temple to play the role of Honoria in the movie version of "Babylon Revisited."
[2]Fitzgerald received a total of $5,000 for the rights to the story and his screenplay.
[3]The top portion of this letter is torn off.

I wonder who was the ex-Westover woman you met. I wasn't responsible for Ginevra getting fired but that's the way of a legend—it was some Yale boys.

This job has given me part of the money for your tuition and it's come so hard that I hate to see you spend it on a course like "English Prose since 1800." Anybody that can't read modern English prose by themselves is subnormal—and you know it. The chief fault in your style is its lack of distinction—something which is inclined to grow with the years. You had distinction once—there's some in your diary—and the only way to increase it is to cultivate your own garden. And the only thing that will help you is poetry which is the most concentrated form of style.

Example: You read Melantha which is practically poetry and sold a New Yorker story—you read ordinary novels and sink back to a Kitty-Foyle-Diary level of average performance.[1] The only sensible course for you at this moment is the one on English Poetry—Blake to Keats. (English 241). I don't care how clever the other professor is, one can't raise a discussion of modern prose to anything above teatable level. I'll tell you everything she knows about it in three hours and guarantee that what each of us tells you will be largely wrong, for it will be almost entirely conditioned by our responses to the subject matter. It is a course for clubwomen who want to continue on from Rebecca and Scarlett O'Hara.

Strange Interlude[2] is good. It was good the first time, when Shaw wrote it and called it Candida. On the other hand you don't pass an hour of your present life that isn't directly influenced by the devastating blast of light and air that came with Ibsen's Doll's House. Nora wasn't the only one who walked out of the Doll's House—all the women in Gene O'Neill walked out too. Only they wore fancier clothes.

Well, the old master wearies—the above is really good advice Pie, in a line where I know my stuff. Unless you can break down your prose a little it'll stay on the ill-paid journalistic level. And you can do better.

Love,
Daddy

P.S. Understand me, I think the poetry courses you took in school (and I read the booklets) were utterly sissified drool. But a real grasp of Blake, Keats, etc. will bring you something you haven't dreamed of. And it should come now.

---

[1] "Melanctha," one of the stories in Gertrude Stein's *Three Lives* (1909); *Kitty Foyle*, 1939 novel by Christopher Morley.
[2] 1928 play by Eugene O'Neill.

TO: *Gerald and Sara Murphy*   ALS, 5 pp. Honoria Murphy Donnelly
Summer 1940   *Hollywood, California*

Honey—that goes for Sara too:

I have written a dozen people since who mean nothing to me—writing you I was saving for good news. I suppose pride was concerned—in that personally and publicly dreary month of Sept. last about everything went to pieces all at once and it was a long uphill pull.

To summarize: I don't have to tell you anything about the awful lapses and sudden reverses and apparent cures and thorough poisoning effect of lung trouble. Suffice to say there were months with a high of 99.8, months at 99.6 and then up + down and a stabilization at 99.2 every afternoon when I could write in bed—and now for 2½ months and one short week that may have been grip—nothing at all. With it went a psychic depression over the finances and the effect on Scotty and Zelda. There was many a day when the fact that you and Sara did help me at a desperate moment (and remember it was the <u>first</u> time I'd ever borrowed money in my life except for business borrowings like Scribners) seemed the only pleasant human thing that had happened in a world where I felt prematurely passed by and forgotten. The thousands that I'd given and loaned—well, after the first attempts I didn't even worry about that. There seem to be the givers + the takers and that doesn't change. So you were never out of my mind—but even so no more present than always because this was only one of so many things.

In the land of the living again I function rather well. My great dreams about this place are shattered and I have written half a novel and a score of satiric pieces that are appearing in the current Esquires about it. After having to turn down a bunch of well paid jobs while I was ill there was a period when no one seemed to want me for duck soup—then a month ago a producer asked me to do a piece of my own for a small sum ($2000) and a share in the profits. The piece is <u>Babylon Revisited</u>, an old and not bad Post story of which the child heroine was named Honoria! I'm keeping the name.

It looks good. I have stopped being a prophet (3d attempt at spelling this) but I think I may be solvent in a month or so if the fever keeps subservient to what the doctors think is an exceptional resistance. Thank heaven I was able to keep Scottie at Vassar (She came twice to the New Weston to call but found you gone) because there was no other place for her. I think she will go on now for the four years.

Zelda is home since this week Tuesday—at her mothers in Montgomery. She has a poor pitiful life, reading the Bible in the old fashioned manner walking tight lipped and correct through a world she can no longer understand—playing with the pieces of old things as if a man a thousand years hence tried to reconstruct our civilization from a baroque cornice, a figurine from Trojans columns, an aeroplane wing and a page of Petrarch all picked up in the Roman forum. Part of her mind is washed clean + she is no one

I ever knew (—This is all from letters and observations of over a year ago—I haven't been East since Spring.)

So now you're up to date on me and it wont be so long again. I might say by way of counter reproach that there's no word of any of <u>you</u> in your letter. It is sad about Pauline.[1] Writing you today has brought back so much and I could weep very easily

With Dearest Love
Scott

TO: *Lester Cowan*　　　　　　　　　　*CC, 1 p. Princeton University*
c. August 1940　　　　　　　　　　　　　*Hollywood, California*

Monday night.

Dear Lester:

I phoned but you were gone. I saw the <u>Great McGinty</u>[2] and heard the crowd respond and I think your answer is there and not in this wretched star system. When you said you were not going to begin with the prologue and seemed to give credence to some director's wild statement that Petrie was the best character—I felt that you were discouraged about the venture and it was warping your judgment. If it is such a poor script that it can be so casually mutilated then how will it be improved with two slipping stars?

The virtue of the Great McGinty was one and singular—mark this—it had only the virtue of being told to an audience as it was conceived. It was inferior in pace, it was an old story—the audience loved it because they are desperately tired of s—— put up every week in new cans. It had not suffered from compromises, polish jobs, formulas and that familiarity which is so falsely consoling to producers—but read the last <u>Variety</u> (N.Y. edition) and what the average man gives as his reason for staying away. That scene of familiarity which seems to promise out here that old stuff has made money before, has become poison gas to those who have to take it as entertainment every night—boy meets girl, gang formula, silk-hat western. The writing on the wall is that <u>anybody</u> this year who brings in a good new story <u>intact</u> will make more reputation and even money, than those who struggle for a few stars. I would rather see new people in this picture than Gable and Temple. I think it would be a bigger and better thing for you.

Ever your Friend,

---

[1] Hemingway had been divorced from Pauline Pfeiffer Hemingway.
[2] 1940 movie written by Preston Sturges.

TO: Scottie Fitzgerald   TLS, 2 pp. Princeton University

August
3
1940

Dear Scottie:

Jane Perkins[1] passed through and happened to mention that she had taken that Blake-to-Keats course—I became less enthusiastic about it because she said they studied Amy Lowell's biography which is a saccharine job compared to Colvin's.[2] However, in the catalogue I see a course called #217 in verse writing. It says, "limited to twelve members—permission required" and it gives only one point. Is that at all practical? I imagine there would be some latitude in the poets that you would read. There is also that Shakespeare course (165) and one in French Poetry (240), one point. Some of the history and philosophical courses look good to me but—oh, hell I can't advise you from this distance. I'm just sorry you can't read some poetry.

It isn't something easy to get started on by yourself. You need, at the beginning, some enthusiast who also knows his way around—John Peale Bishop performed that office for me at Princeton. I had always dabbled in "verse" but he made me see, in the course of a couple of months, the difference between poetry and non-poetry. After that one of my first discoveries was that some of the professors who were teaching poetry really hated it and didn't know what it was about. I got in a series of endless scraps with them so that finally I dropped English altogether.

Poetry is either something that lives like fire inside you—like music to the musician or Marxism to the Communist—or else it is nothing, an empty, formalized bore around which pedants can endlessly drone their notes and explanations. The Grecian Urn is unbearably beautiful with every syllable as inevitable as the notes in Beethoven's Ninth Symphony or it's just something you don't understand. It is what it is because an extraordinary genius paused at that point in history and touched it. I suppose I've read it a hundred times. About the tenth time I began to know what it was about, and caught the chime in it and the exquisite inner mechanics. Likewise with The Nightingale which I can never read through without tears in my eyes; likewise the Pot of Basil with its great stanzas about the two brothers, "Why were they proud, etc."; and The Eve of St. Agnes, which has the richest, most sensuous imagery in English, not excepting Shakespeare. And finally his three or four great sonnets, Bright Star and the others.

Knowing those things very young and granted an ear, one could scarcely ever afterwards be unable to distinguish between gold and dross in what one read. In themselves those eight poems are a scale of workmanship for

[1]One of Maxwell Perkins's daughters.
[2]Lowell's *John Keats* was published in 1925; Sir Sidney Colvin published several books on Keats, among them *John Keats* (Scribners, 1917).

anybody who wants to know truly about words, their most utter value for evocation, persuasion or charm. For awhile after you quit Keats all other poetry seems to be only whistling or humming.

You still have that French typewriter in storage, haven't you? Would it be any good? We rent one here and it costs only $5. for three months. You threaten to send <u>me</u> money! If you have any extra, pay your bills in Poughkeepsie. My suggestion is that after you visit Miss Doyle, you go to Lake Forest and from there go South to Montgomery. I'm afraid the latter seems to be necessary. Your mother most particularly asked to see you again and the only alternative would be to send her North to see you, which means sending <u>two</u> people. I know it will be dull going into that hot little town early in September—but you are helping me. Even invalids like your mother have to have mileposts—things to look forward to and back upon. It gives her more pride there in Montgomery if you come to see her, something to talk about. Only think how empty her life is and you will see the importance of your going there. Will you figure out what the fare to Chicago will be?

You wrote me such a full letter that I haven't answered it all even now. When we get some breathing space here I'll have Frances figure how much you cost this year.

Dearest love.

Daddy

P.S. Be careful about showing my letters—I mean to your mother for instance. I write you very freely.

1403 N. Laurel Avenue
Hollywood, California

TO: Mrs. Richard Taylor   *TLS, 1 p. Princeton University*

August
14
1940

Dearest Ceci:

Aunt Elise's death was a shock to me. I was very fond of her always—I was fond of Aunt Annabel and Aunt Elise, who gave me almost my first tastes of discipline, in a peculiar way in which I wasn't fond of my mother who spoiled me. You were a great exception among mothers—managing by some magic of your own to preserve both your children's love and their respect. Too often one of the two things is sacrificed.

With Father, Uncle John and Aunt Elise a generation goes. I wonder how deep the Civil War was in them—that odd childhood on the border between the states with Grandmother and old Mrs. Scott and the shadow of Mrs.

Suratt.[1] What a sense of honor and duty—almost eighteenth century rather than Victoria. How lost they seemed in the changing world—my father and Aunt Elise struggling to keep their children in the haute bourgeoisie when their like were sinking into obscure farm life or being lost in the dark boarding houses of Georgetown.

I wrote Scottie to stop by and say hello to you on her way south to see her mother next month. I would so like to see you all myself. Gi-gi wrote me such a nice letter from Richmond.

With Dearest Love Always

Scott

1403 N. Laurel Avenue
Hollywood, California

TO: Gerald Murphy   *TLS, 1 p. Honoria Murphy Donnelly*
                                       Twentieth Century–Fox stationery.
                                       Hollywood, California

September
14
1940

Dear Gerald:

I suppose anybody our age suspects what is emphasized—so let it go. But I was flat in bed from April to July last year with day and night nurses. Anyhow as you see from the letterhead, I am now in official health.

I find, after a long time out here, that one develops new attitudes. It is, for example, such a slack soft place—even its pleasure lacking the fierceness or excitement of Provence—that withdrawal is practically a condition of safety. The sin is to upset anyone else, and much of what is known as "progress" is attained by more or less delicately poking and prodding other people. This is an unhealthy condition of affairs. Except for the stage-struck young girls people come here for negative reasons—all gold rushes are essentially negative—and the young girls soon join the vicious circle. There is no group, however small, interesting as such. Everywhere there is, after a moment, either corruption or indifference. The heroes are the great corruptionists or the supremely indifferent—by whom I mean the spoiled writers, Hecht, Nunnally Johnson, Dotty, Dash Hammet[2] etc. That Dotty has embraced the church and reads her office faithfully every day does not affect her indifference. She is one type of commy Malraux didn't list among his categories in Man's Hope—but nothing would disappoint her so vehemently as success.

---

[1] Mary Surratt was hanged for her participation in the assassination of Abraham Lincoln.

[2] Ben Hecht, Nunnally Johnson, Dorothy Parker, and Dashiell Hammett had enjoyed success in other genres before becoming Hollywood screenwriters.

I have a novel pretty well on the road. I think it will baffle and in some ways irritate what readers I have left. But it is as detached from me as <u>Gatsby</u> was, in intent anyhow. The new Armegeddon, far from making everything unimportant, gives me a certain lust for life again. This is undoubtedly an immature throw-back, but it's the truth. The gloom of all causes does not affect it—I feel a certain rebirth of kinetic impulses—however misdirected.

Zelda dozes—her letters are clear enough—she doesn't want to leave Montgomery for a year, so she says. Scottie continues at Vassar—she is nicer now than she has been since she was a little girl. I haven't seen her for a year but she writes long letters and I feel closer to her than I have since she was little.

I <u>would</u> like to have some days with you and Sara. I hear distant thunder about Ernest and Archie[1] and their doings but about you I know not a tenth of what I want to know.

With affection,
Scott

1403 N. Laurel Ave.
Hollywood, California

TO: Gerald and Sara Murphy   ALS, 1 p. Honoria Murphy Donnelly

September
14
1940

Dear Gerald and Sara—

I can't tell you how this has worried me. This is the first <u>personal</u> debt I've ever owed and I'm glad to be able to pay back $150 out of the $350.

Your generosity made me able to send Scottie back to Vassar last Fall. This year she is the Harper's Bazaar representative and has sold stories to various magazines and things are in every way easier. But she <u>was</u> the type to whom a higher education meant everything and it would have been heartbreaking not to give it to her.

With love to you both and so <u>much</u>
gratitude,

Scott

1403 N. Laurel Avenue
Hollywood, California

---

[1]Hemingway outfitted his fishing boat so that he could patrol the Caribbean for German submarines; MacLeish had been appointed Librarian of Congress in 1939 and organized several new departments in the U.S. government during the war years.

TO: Zelda Fitzgerald   *CC, 1 p. Princeton University*

September
14
1940

Dearest Zelda:-

Am sending you a small check next week which you should really spend on something which you need—a winter coat, for instance—or if you are equipped, to put it away for a trip when it gets colder. I can't quite see you doing this, however. Do you have extra bills, dentist's, doctors', etc., and, if so, they should be sent to me as I don't expect you to pay them out of the thirty dollars. And I certainly don't want your mother to be in for any extras. Is she?

This is the third week of my job and I'm holding up very well but so many jobs have started well and come to nothing that I keep my fingers crossed until the thing is in production. Paramount doesn't want to star Shirley Temple alone on the other picture and the producer can't find any big star who will play with her so we are temporarily held up.

As I wrote you, Scottie is now definitely committed to an education and I feel so strongly about it that if she wanted to go to work I would let her really do it by cutting off all allowance. What on earth is the use of having gone to so much time and trouble about a thing and then giving it up two years short of fulfillment. It is the last two years in college that count. I got nothing out of my first two years—in the last I got my passionate love for poetry and historical perspective and ideas in general (however superficially), it carried me full swing into my career. Her generation is liable to get only too big a share of raw life at first hand.

Write me what you do?

With dearest love,

P.S. Scottie may quite possibly marry within a year and then she is fairly permanently off my hands. I've spent so much time doing work that I didn't particularly want to do that what does one more year matter. They've let a certain writer here direct his own pictures and he has made such a go of it that there may be a different feeling about that soon. If I had that chance I would attain my real goal in coming here in the first place.

1403 N. Laurel Avenue
Hollywood, California

TO: *Scottie Fitzgerald*   *TLS, 2 pp. Princeton University*
Hollywood, California

October
5
1940

Dearest Scottie:

Glad you liked <u>Death in Venice</u>. I don't see any connection between that and <u>Dorian Gray</u> except that they both have an implied homosexuality. <u>Dorian Gray</u> is little more than a somewhat highly charged fairy tale which stimulates adolescents to intellectual activity at about seventeen (it did the same for you as it did for me). Sometime you will re-read it and see that it is essentially naive. It is in the lower ragged edge of "literature," just as <u>Gone with the Wind</u> is in the higher brackets of crowd entertainment. <u>Death in Venice</u>, on the other hand, is a work of art, of the school of Flaubert— yet not derivative at all. Wilde had two models for <u>Dorian Gray</u>: Balzac's "Le Peau de Chagrin" and Huysman's "A Rebours".

After which literary lecture I can only sympathize with the practically desolate state of Vassar and assure you that many of those that have left will lament through their lives that they didn't go on. In that connection, by the way, aren't there many transfers from other colleges in junior year? I should think after this past year everything would indeed be anti-climax. You've had almost everything you wanted—in Vassar, in Baltimore, and in general. But it's rather lucky that in life we don't go on repeating. Certainly you should have new objectives now—this of all years ought to be the time of awakening for that nascent mind of yours. [Once one is caught up into the material world not one person in ten thousand finds the time to form literary taste, to examine the validity of philosophic concepts for himself, or to form what, for lack of a better phrase, I might call the wise and tragic sense of life.

By this I mean the thing that lies behind all great careers, from Shakespeare's to Abraham Lincoln's, and as far back as there are books to read— the sense that life is essentially a cheat and its conditions are those of defeat, and that the redeeming things are not "happiness and pleasure" but the deeper satisfactions that come out of struggle. Having learned this in theory from the lives and conclusions of great men, you can get a hell of a lot more enjoyment out of whatever bright things come your way.][1]

You speak of how good your generation is, but I think they share with every generation since the Civil War in America the sense of being somehow about to inherit the earth. You've heard me say before that I think the faces of most American women over thirty are relief maps of petulant and bewildered unhappiness.

---

[1] The bracketed passage—not in the Princeton University copy—is transcribed from Turnbull.

Well, and fare the well. You never answer the specific questions in my letters. You tell me about your courses in general, but not in particular. And that was an important question about your literary name—I'm against your using <u>two</u> names of mine, like in the College Bazaar.[1]

With dearest love.

Daddy

TO: *Zelda Fitzgerald*   *CC, 1 p. Princeton University*

October
11
1940

Dearest Zelda:-

Another heat wave is here and reminds me of last year at the same time. The heat is terribly dry and not at all like Montgomery and is so unexpected. The people feel deeply offended, as if they were being bombed.

A letter from Gerald yesterday. He has no news except a general flavor of the past. To him, now, of course, the Riviera was the best time of all. Sara is interested in vegetables and gardens and all growing and living things.

I expect to be back on my novel any day and this time to finish, a two months' job. The months go so fast that even <u>Tender Is the Night</u> is six years' away. I think the nine years that intervened between <u>The Great Gatsby</u> and <u>Tender</u> hurt my reputation almost beyond repair because a whole generation grew up in the meanwhile to whom I was only a writer of Post stories. I don't suppose anyone will be much interested in what I have to say this time and it may be the last novel I'll ever write, but it must be done now because, after fifty one is different. One can't remember emotionally, I think except about childhood but I have a few more things left to say.

My health is better. It was a long business and at any time some extra waste of energy has to be paid for at a double price. Weeks of fever and coughing—but the constitution is an amazing thing and nothing quite kills it until the heart has run its entire race. I'd like to get East around Christmas-time this year. I don't know what the next three months will bring further, but if I get a credit on either of these last two efforts things will never again seem so black as they did a year ago when I felt that Hollywood had me down in its books as a ruined man—a label which I had done nothing to deserve.

With dearest love,

1403 N. Laurel Ave.
Hollywood, Calif.

[1] Scottie had published an article signed Frances Scott Fitzgerald in the college issue of *Harper's Bazaar.*

TO: *Zelda Fitzgerald*   *CC, 1 p. Princeton University*

October
19
1940

Dearest Zelda:-

I'm trying desperately to finish my novel by the middle of December and it's a little like working on "Tender is the Night" at the end—I think of nothing else. Still haven't heard from the Shirley Temple story but it would be a great relaxation of pressure if she decides to do it, though an announcement in the paper says that she is going to be teamed with Judy Garland in "Little Eva," which reminds me that I saw the two Duncan Sisters both grown enormously fat in the Brown Derby. Do you remember them on the boat with Viscount Bryce and their dogs?

My room is covered with charts like it used to be for "Tender is the Night" telling the different movements of the characters and their histories. However, this one is to be short, as I originally planned it two years ago, and more on the order of "Gatsby".

Dearest love,

1403 N. Laurel Avenue
Hollywood, Calif.

TO: *Zelda Fitzgerald*   *CC, 1 p. Princeton University*

October
23
1940

Dearest Zelda:-

Advising you about money at long distance would be silly but you feel we're both concerned in the Carrol matter. Still and all I would much rather you'd leave it to me and <u>keep</u> your money. I sent them a small payment last week. The thing is I have budgeted what I saved in the weeks at 20th to last until December 15th so I can go on with the novel with the hope of having a full draft by then. Naturally I will not realize anything at once (except on the very slim chance of a serial) and though I will try to make something immediately out of pictures or Esquire it may be a pretty slim Christmas. So my advice is to put the hundred and fifty away against that time.

I am deep in the novel, living in it, and it makes me happy. It is a <u>constructed</u> novel like <u>Gatsby</u>, with passages of poetic prose when it fits the action, but no ruminations or side-shows like <u>Tender</u>. Everything must contribute to the dramatic movement.

It's odd that my old talent for the short story vanished. It was partly that times changed, editors changed, but part of it was tied up somehow with you

TO: *Norma Shearer Thalberg*
c. 1940

Draft inscription for
The Love of the Last Tycoon.
Princeton University
Hollywood, California

To Write in Copy to Shearer

Dear Norma:
You told me you read little because of your eyes but I think this book will interest you — perhaps you could see it as an attempt to preserve something of Irving and though the story is purely imaginary and ~~He inspired~~ My own impression of him ~~about but I~~ shortly recorded but very dazzling in its effect on me, inspired the best part of the character of Stahr — though I have put in something drawn from much of other men and, inevitably, much of myself.

~~It is a tragic story~~ I invented a tragic story ~~because~~ and ~~Stahrs~~ Irving's life was, of course, not tragic except his struggle against ill health because no one has ever written a tragedy about Hollywood and often beautiful story (a Star is Born was a pathetic story but not a tragedy) and doomed and heroic things do happen here.
~~My~~ With old affection and Gratitude

|

Actress Norma Shearer was the widow of producer Irving Thalberg, the inspiration for Monroe Stahr in Fitzgerald's unfinished novel.

and me—the happy ending. Of course every third story had some other ending but essentially I got my public with stories of young love. I must have had a powerful imagination to project it so far and so often into the past.

Two thousand words today and all good.

With dearest love

1403 N. Laurel Ave.
Hollywood, Calif.

TO: *Scottie Fitzgerald*   *Retyped letter, 1 p. Princeton University*

November
2
1940

Dearest Scottina:—

Listening to the Harvard-Princeton game on the radio with the old songs reminds me of the past that I lived a quarter of a century ago and that you are living now. I picture you as there though I don't know whether you are or not.

I remember once a long time ago I had a daughter who used to write me letters but now I don't know where she is or what she is doing, so I sit here listening to Puccini—"Someday she'll write (<u>Pigliano edda ciano</u>)."[1]

With dearest love,

Daddy

1403 N. Laurel Avenue
Hollywood, California

TO: *Ernest Hemingway*   *CC, 1 p. Princeton University*
Hollywood, California

November 8, 1940

Dear Ernest:

It's a fine novel, better than anybody else writing could do. Thanks for thinking of me and for your dedication.[2] I read it with intense interest, participating in a lot of the writing problems as they came along and often quite unable to discover how you brought off some of the effects, but you always did. The massacre was magnificent and also the fight on the mountain and the actual dynamiting scene. Of the side shows I particularly liked the vignette of Karkov and Pilar's Sonata to death—and I had a personal interest in the Moseby guerilla stuff because of my own father. The scene in which the father says goodbye to his son is very powerful. I'm going to read the whole thing again.

[1] Fitzgerald was inventing an aria from Italian opera; Edda Ciano was Mussolini's daughter.
[2] Hemingway had inscribed a copy of *For Whom the Bell Tolls* (Scribners, 1940) to Fitzgerald: "To Scott with affection and esteem Ernest" (Bruccoli).

I never got to tell you how I liked <u>To Have and to Have Not</u> either. There is observation and writing in that that the boys will be imitating with a vengeance—paragraphs and pages that are right up with Dostoiefski in their undeflected intensity.

Congratulations too on your new book's great success. I envy you like hell and there is no irony in this. I always liked Dostoiefski with his wide appeal more than any other European—and I envy you the time it will give you to do what you want.

With Old Affection,

P.S. I came across an old article by John Bishop about how you lay four days under dead bodies at Caporetto and how I flunked out of Princeton (I left on a stretcher in November—you can't flunk out in November) and how I am an awful suck about the rich and a social climber. What I started to say was that I do know something about you on the Italian front, from a man who was in your unit—how you crawled some hellish distance pulling a wounded man with you and how the doctors stood over you wondering why you were alive with so many perforations. Don't worry— I won't tell anybody. Not even Allan Campbell[1] who called me up and gave me news of you the other day.

P.S. (2) I hear you are marrying one of the most beautiful people I have ever seen. Give her my best remembrance.[2]

TO: Zelda Fitzgerald   *CC, 1 p. Princeton University*

November
23
1940

Dearest Zelda:

Enclosed is Scottie's little story—she had just read Gertrude Stein's <u>Melanctha</u> on my recommendation and the influence is what you might call perceptible.

The odd thing is that it appeared in eastern copies of the New Yorker and not in the western, and I had some bad moments looking through the magazine she had designated and wondering if my eyesight had departed.

The editor of "Collier's" wants me to write for them (he's here in town), but I tell him I'm finishing my novel for myself and all I can promise him is a look at it. It will, at any rate, be nothing like anything else as I'm digging it out of myself like uranium—one ounce to the cubic ton of rejected ideas. It is a novel <u>a la Flaubert</u> without "ideas" but only people moved singly and in mass through what I hope are authentic moods.

[1]Screenwriter Alan Campbell was Dorothy Parker's husband.
[2]Hemingway married journalist and novelist Martha Gellhorn in 1940.

The resemblance is rather to "Gatsby" than to anything else I've written. I'm so glad you're well and reasonably happy.

With dearest love,

P.S. Please send Scottie's story back in your next letter—as it seems utterly impossible to get duplicates and I shall probably want to show it to authors and editors with paternal pride.

1403 N. Laurel Ave.
Hollywood, California

TO: *Edmund Wilson*   *CC, 1 p. Princeton University*

November
25
1940

Dear Bunny:

I've been reading your new essays with interest and if you expect (as Max Perkins hinted) to republish them sometime, I'd like to put you on to something about Steinbeck. He is a rather cagey cribber. Most of us begin as imitators but it is something else for a man of his years and reputation to steal a whole scene as he did in "Mice and Men". I'm sending you a marked copy of Norris' "McTeague" to show you what I mean. His debt to "The Octupus" is also enormous and his balls, when he uses them, are usually clipped from Lawrence's "Kangaroo". I've always encouraged young writers—I put Max Perkins on to Caldwell, Callaghan and God knows how many others but Steinbeck bothers me. I suppose he cribs for the glory of the party.

Two years after it was published I ran across an article by John Bishop in the Virginia Quarterly. His war story about Ernest under the corpses is pure crap. Also he says that I flunked out of Princeton, though in the year referred to I went to my last class November 28th, when it is somewhat unusual to flunk out. Also he reproached me with being a suck around the rich. I've had this before but nobody seems able to name these rich. I always thought my progress was in the other direction—Tommy Hitchcock and the two Murphys are not a long list of rich friends for one who, unlike John, grew up among nothing else but. I don't even know any of the people in "Cafe Society." It seems strange from John. I did more than anyone in Paris to help him finish his Civil War book and get it published. It can't be jealousy for there isn't much to be jealous of any more. Maybe it's conscience—nobody ever sold himself for as little gold as he did.

I think my novel is good. I've written it with difficulty. It is completely upstream in mood and will get a certain amount of abuse but is first hand and I am trying a little harder than I ever have to be. exact and honest emotionally. I honestly hoped somebody else would write it but nobody seems to be going to.

With best to you both,

P.S. This sounds like such a bitter letter—I'd rewrite it except for a horrible paucity of time. Not even time to be bitter.

1403 N. Laurel Ave.
Hollywood, California

TO: *Scottie Fitzgerald*

TLS, 2 pp. Princeton University

November 29, 1940

Dearest Scottie:

I started Tom Wolfe's book on your recommendation.[1] It seems better than Time and the River. He has a fine inclusive mind, can write like a streak, has a great deal of emotion, though a lot of it is maudlin and inaccurate, but his awful secret transpires at every crevice—he did not have anything particular to say! The stuff about the GREAT VITAL HEART OF AMERICA is just simply corny.

He recapitulates beautifully a great deal of what Walt Whitman said and Dostoevski said and Nietzsche said and Milton said, but he himself, unlike Joyce and T. S. Eliot and Ernest Hemingway, has nothing really new to add. All right—it's all a mess and it's too bad about the individual—so what? Most writers line themselves up along a solid gold bar like Ernest's courage, or Joseph Conrad's art, or D. H. Lawrence's intense cohabitations, but Wolfe is too "smart" for this and I mean smart in its most belittling and most modern sense. Smart like Fadiman in the New Yorker, smart like the critics whom he so pretends to despise. However, the book doesn't commit the cardinal sin: it doesn't fail to live. But I'd like you to think sometime how and in what way you think it is superior to such a piece of Zolaesque naturalism as Maugham's "Of Human Bondage" or if it is superior at all. Did you like the description of Max Perkins as "Foxhall?" I believe Max had mixed emotions.

I'm taking a day off from my novel to go to the dentist, the doctor, and my agent, to the latter in order to discuss picture business when and if I go back to it in February. And I have saved an hour to rush in where angels fear to tread. I don't know Bobby and have had to piece him together from what you have told me and from a letter you showed me and so forth. But it sounds to me as if he had a perceptible dash of lavender. I know exactly what you mean about the Dwight Fiske attitude—sometimes the Harvard manner approaches that deceptively as a pose—but when a man is tired of life at 21 it indicates that he is rather tired of something in himself. One

[1] *You Can't Go Home Again* (1940).

thing I'm sure of. There are plenty of absolutely first-rate men who will be within your range in the next two years. I remember that Lois Moran used to worry because all the attractive men she knew were married. She finally inverted it into the credo that if a man <u>wasn't</u> married and inaccessible, he wasn't a first-rate man. She gave herself a very bad time. The sea is still as full as ever of sharks, whales, trout and tuna. The real handicap for a girl like you would have been to have worn herself out emotionally at sixteen. I think we cut that by about two-thirds by keeping you comparatively busy in those two very crucial years. Life should be fun for you and there's plenty of time. All I care for is that you should marry someone who is not too much a part of the crowd.

Lanahan[1] is wrong about your disposition. You take adversity very well, but you are utterly dependent on sleep. Your extraordinary performance out here two years ago was directly attributable to the fact that you hadn't slept since getting off the boat, if you slept on board of it! It amounts almost to an idiosyncracy in you and you should never make important decisions when you are extremely tired.

With dearest love,
Daddy

P.S. It's O.K. about the Xmas money but go slow. The phone rang after I finished this letter and the doctor after seeing my cardiogram has confined me to the house.[2] So at this moment I <u>couldn't</u> go to the studios if I wanted to. Try to save your fare to Baltimore and back.

1403 N. Laurel Avenue
Hollywood, California

TO: Zelda Fitzgerald   *CC, 1 p. Princeton University*

December
6
1940

Dearest Zelda:

No news except that the novel progresses and I am angry that this little illness has slowed me up. I've had trouble with my heart before but never anything organic. This is not a major attack but seems to have come on gradually and luckily a cardiogram showed it up in time. I may have to move from the third to the first floor apartment but I'm quite able to work, etc., if I do not overtire myself.

---

[1] Samuel J. Lanahan, a Princetonian, whom Scottie married in 1943.
[2] Fitzgerald had suffered a heart attack at Schwab's drugstore on Sunset Boulevard, Hollywood.

Scottie tells me she is arriving South Xmas day. I envy you being together and I'll be thinking of you. Everything is my novel now—it has become of absorbing interest. I hope I'll be able to finish it by February.

With dearest love,

1403 N. Laurel Ave.
Hollywood, Calif.

TO: Maxwell Perkins

TLS, 1 p. Princeton University
Hollywood, California

December
13
1940

Dear Max:

Thanks for your letter. The novel progresses—in fact progresses fast. I'm not going to stop now till I finish a first draft which will be some time after the 15th of January. However, let's pretend that it doesn't exist until it's closer to completion. We don't want it to become—"a legend before it is written" which is what I believe Wheelock[1] said about "Tender Is the Night". Meanwhile will you send me back the chapters I sent you as they are all invalid now, must be completely rewritten etc. The essential idea is the same and it is still, as far as I can hope, a secret.

Bud Shulberg, a very nice, clever kid out here is publishing a Hollywood novel with Random House in January.[2] It's not bad but it doesn't cut into my material at all. I've read Ernest's novel and most of Tom Wolfe's and have been doing a lot of ruminating as to what this whole profession is about. Tom Wolfe's failure to really explain why you and he parted mars his book but there are great things in it. The portraits of the Jacks (who are they?) Emily Vanderbilt are magnificent.

No one points out how Saroyan has been influenced by Franz Kafka. Kafka was an extraordinary Czchoslovakian Jew who died in '36. He will never have a wide public but "The Trial" and "America" are two books that writers are never able to forget.

This is the first day off I have taken for many months and I just wanted to tell you the book is coming along and that comparatively speaking all is well.

Ever your friend,
Scott

P.S. How much will you sell the plates of "This Side of Paradise" for? I think it has a chance for a new life.

---

[1] Scribners editor John Hall Wheelock.
[2] *What Makes Sammy Run?* (1941).

TO: *Scottie Fitzgerald*[3]   ALS, *3 pp. Princeton University*
c. December 15, 1940   *Hollywood, California*

Dearest Scottie:

There has reached you by this time I hope, a little coat. It was an almost never worn coat of Shielah's that she wanted to send you. It seemed very nice to me—it may fill out your rather thin wardrobe. Frances Kroll's father is a furrier and he remade it—<u>without charge</u>!

So you must <u>at once please</u> write the following letters.

(1.) To Shielah, not stressing Mr. Kroll's contribution

(2) To Frances praising the style.

(3) To me (in the course of things) in such a way that I can show the letter to <u>Shielah</u> who will certainly ask me if you liked the coat.

You make things easier for me if you write these letters promptly. A giver gets no pleasure in a letter acknowledging a gift three weeks late even though it crawls with apologies—you will have stolen pleasure from one who has tried to give it to you. (Ecclesiases Fitzgerald)

Lastly drum up some story for Alabama that you bought the coat from some girl. Don't say it came through me.

For the rest I am still in bed—this time the result of twenty five years of cigarettes. You have got two beautiful bad examples of parents. Just do everything we didn't do and you will be perfectly safe. But be sweet to your mother at Xmas despite her early Chaldean rune-worship which she will undoubtedly inflict on you at Xmas. Her letters are tragically brilliant in all matters except those of central importance. How strange to have failed as a social creature—even criminals do not fail that way—they are the law's "Loyal Opposition", so to speak. But the insane are always mere guests on earth, eternal strangers carrying around broken decalogues that they cannot read.

I am still not through Tom Wolfe's novel + can't finally report it but the story of the fire is magnificent. Only Im afraid that after the grand character planting nothing is going to come of it all. The picture of "Amy Carleton" (Emily Davies Vanderbilt who used to come to our appartment in Paris—do you remember?) with the cracked grey eyes and the exactly reproduced speech, is just simply perfect. She tried hard to make Tom—<u>sans succes</u>—and finally ended by her own hand in Montana in 1934 in a lonely ranch house. The portrait of Mrs. Jack is grand too. I believe her absolutely.

With Dearest Love

Daddy

PS. In the name of Somerset Maughn, the <u>letter</u>![1]

---

[1] Last letter of Fitzgerald to Scottie Fitzgerald.

[2] Reference to Maugham's "The Letter."

Dear Scottie:

There has reached you by this time I hope, a little coat. It was an almost never worn coat of Shielah's that she wanted to send you. It seemed very nice to me — it may fill out your rather thin wardrobe. Frances Kroll's father is a furrier and he remade it without charge!

So you must at once please write the following letters.

(1.) To Shielah, not stressing her Kroll's contribution

(2.) To Frances praising the style.

(3.) To me (in the course of things) in such a way that I can show the letter to Shielah who will certainly ask me if you liked the coat.

You make things easier for me if you write these letters promptly. A giver gets no pleasure in a letter acknowledging a gift three weeks late even though it crawls with apologies — you will have stolen pleasure from one who

Fitzgerald's last letter to Scottie Fitzgerald (Princeton University).

has tried to give it to you. (Ecclesiastes Fitzgerald)

Lastly drum up some story for
Alabama that you bought the coal from
some ~~girl~~ girl. Don't say it came through
me.

For the rest I am still in bed — this
time the result of twentyfive years of cigarettes.
You have got two beautiful bad examples
for parents. Just do everything we didn't
do and you will be perfectly safe. But
be sweet to your mother at Xmas despite
her early Chaldean mnure-worship which she will
undoubtedly inflict on you at Xmas. Her letters
are tragically brilliant on all matters except
those of central importance. How strange to
have failed as a social creature — even
criminals do not fail that way — they are
the law's "Loyal Opposition", so to speak.
But the ~~insane are~~ always more guests
on earth, eternal strangers with a
carrying around broken decalogues that they cannot
read.

③

I am still not through Tom's world's ^novels — can't finally report it but the story of the fire is magnificent. Only I'm afraid that after all the grand character planting nothing is going to come of it all. The picture of "Amy Carleton" (Emily Davies Vanderbilt who used to come to our appartment in Paris — do you remember?) with the cracked grey eyes and the exactly reproduced speech, is just simply perfect. ~~She~~ tried hard to make Tom — sans succes — and finally ended ~~it~~ by her own hand in Montana in 1934 in a lonely ranch house. ~~The part~~ Mrs. Jack is grand too. I believe her absolutely.

With Dearest Love

Daddy.

P.S. Settle name of Somerset Maughan, the <u>letter</u> !

Biographical Notes

❖

John Biggs, Jr. (1895–1979) was Fitzgerald's roommate at Princeton; they edited the *Princeton Tiger* and collaborated on a Triangle Club show. Biggs wrote novels while practicing law. Scottie Fitzgerald wrote: " 'He left the estate of a pauper and the will of a millionaire,' Judge Biggs growled when Fitzgerald died after naming him his Executor. Then he proceeded for ten years to administer the virtually non-existent estate as a busy Judge on the United States Circuit Court, selflessly and devotedly—the very incarnation of the words, 'Family Friend.' " See Seymour I. Toll, *A Judge Uncommon* (Philadelphia: Legal Communications, 1993).

John Peale Bishop (1892–1944) was Fitzgerald's classmate at Princeton, and Fitzgerald credited Bishop with having taught him to understand poetry. Bishop became a respected poet and critic. Although Fitzgerald and Bishop maintained their friendship, their meetings became infrequent after Bishop married a wealthy woman the Fitzgeralds found uncongenial. See Elizabeth Carroll Spindler, *John Peale Bishop: A Biography* (Morgantown: West Virginia University Library, 1980).

Scottie Fitzgerald (1921–1986), the Fitzgeralds' only child, became a journalist and was active in the Democratic Party. Her gift of the Fitzgerald Papers to the Princeton University Library facilitated the extensive research and publication on her parents. Although she resisted publicity as what she referred to as "daughter of," she generously aided students and scholars. She edited (with Bruccoli and Joan P. Kerr) *The Romantic Egoists: A Pictorial Autobiography from the Scrapbooks and Albums of Scott and Zelda Fitzgerald* (New York: Scribners, 1974). Scottie Fitzgerald Lanahan Smith was much loved and admired.

Sheilah Graham (d. 1988) was a Hollywood columnist when she met Fitzgerald in the summer of 1937. They became lovers; when Fitzgerald learned about her deprived London childhood and her invented background, he undertook to educate her in his "College of One." Their relationship endured despite his alcoholism, and he died in her apartment at 1443 North Hayworth Avenue, Hollywood. Graham's books about Fitzgerald include *Beloved Infidel* (New York: Holt, Rinehart & Winston, 1958) and *College of One* (New York: Viking, 1967).

Ernest Hemingway (1899–1961) provided Fitzgerald's most intense literary friendship, which involved Fitzgerald's admiration for Hemingway and

479

Hemingway's rivalry with Fitzgerald. When they met in 1925 Hemingway had not yet published a book, and Fitzgerald worked to advance Hemingway's career, bringing him to Scribners. Fitzgerald later wrote of him that "a third contemporary had been an artistic conscience to me—I had not imitated his infectious style, because my own style, such as it is, was formed before he published anything, but there was an awful pull toward him when I was on a spot." See Bruccoli, *Scott and Ernest: The Authority of Failure and the Authority of Success* (New York: Random House, 1978).

Sir Shane Leslie (1885–1971) was an Anglo-Irish man of letters. Well connected (a first cousin of Winston Churchill) and well educated (a graduate of Eton College and Cambridge University), he was a convert to Catholicism. Through his friend, Monsignor Fay, he met Fitzgerald at the Newman School. Leslie encouraged Fitzgerald's literary ambitions and sent Fitzgerald's first novel, *The Romantic Egotist*, to Charles Scribner II. Reviewing Leslie's *The Oppidan* in 1922, Fitzgerald declared:

> He first came into my life as the most romantic figure I had ever known. He had sat at the feet of Tolstoy, he had gone swimming with Rupert Brooke, he had been a young Englishman of the governing classes when the sense of being one must have been, as Compton McKenzie says, like the sense of being a Roman citizen.
>
> Also, he was a convert to the church of my youth, and he and another [Fay], since dead, made of that church a dazzling, golden thing, dispelling its oppressive mugginess and giving the succession of days upon gray days, passing under its plaintive ritual, the romantic glamour of an adolescent dream.

H. L. Mencken (1880–1956) was the most influential literary and social critic in America during the 1920s. With George Jean Nathan he edited *The Smart Set*, the first magazine to pay for Fitzgerald's stories. Two of Fitzgerald's best stories, "May Day" and "The Diamond as Big as the Ritz," were published in *The Smart Set*. Mencken later published "Absolution" and "Crazy Sunday" in the *American Mercury*. In his 1921 review of Mencken's *Prejudices* Fitzgerald stated that "he has done more for the national letters than any man alive."

Gerald Murphy (1888–1964) and **Sara Murphy** (1883–1975) were an affluent expatriate American couple the Fitzgeralds met on the Riviera in 1924. Gerald painted, and the Murphys were involved in the arts. They were fabled hosts at their Villa America on Cap d'Antibes. Fitzgerald wrote of Murphy that "a fourth man had come to dictate my relations with other people when these relations were successful: how to do, what to say. How to make people at least momentarily happy. . . . This always confused me and made me want to go out and get drunk, but this man had seen the game, analyzed it and beaten it, and his word was good enough for me." *Tender Is the Night* is dedicated "To Gerald and Sara Many Fêtes." See

Honoria Murphy Donnelly with Richard N. Billings, *Sara & Gerald: Villa America and After* (New York: Times Books, 1982).

Harold Ober (1881–1959) was Fitzgerald's agent for magazine writings. Most of Fitzgerald's income came from the magazines, and through Ober's efforts *The Saturday Evening Post* paid Fitzgerald his peak price of $4,000 per story in 1929. Ober received a ten-percent fee. The Ober-Fitzgerald financial relationship was complex with Ober acting as Fitzgerald's banker, making interest-free loans against unsold and even unwritten stories. The Obers became Scottie's surrogate parents during her prep-school and Vassar years. Fitzgerald broke with Ober in 1939 over the agent's refusal to commence a new cycle of loans after Fitzgerald had paid his debts.

Maxwell E. Perkins (1884–1947), editorial director at Charles Scribner's Sons, was Fitzgerald's generous friend and closest literary adviser. He fought for the publication of Fitzgerald's first novel, *This Side of Paradise*, and thereafter provided encouragement and financial backing. At Scribners Perkins assembled a great stable of writers that included Ring Lardner, Ernest Hemingway, and Thomas Wolfe. His literary judgment and commitment to his writers have become legendary. See A. Scott Berg, *Max Perkins: Editor of Genius* (New York: Dutton/Congdon, 1978).

Charles Scribner's Sons. Founded by the first Charles Scribner in 1846, the firm achieved literary prestige under Charles Scribner II, president from 1879 to 1928. During the 1920s editor Maxwell Perkins altered the reputation of the House of Scribner from a conservative publisher to a firm receptive to innovative work. See Charles Scribner III, *A History of Charles Scribner's Sons* (Cleveland: Rowfant Club, 1985), and Charles Scribner, Jr., *In the Web of Ideas* (New York: Scribners, 1993).

Edmund Wilson (1895–1972) was a class ahead of Fitzgerald at Princeton and encouraged him to write for the *Nassau Literary Magazine*. Wilson became a distinguished literary and social critic, and Fitzgerald wrote of him that "For twenty years a certain man had been my intellectual conscience." Wilson played a key role in the reassessment of Fitzgerald, editing *The Last Tycoon* (1941) and *The Crack-Up* (1945). See Wilson, *The Twenties: From Notebooks and Diaries of the Period* (New York: Farrar, Straus & Giroux, 1945).

INDEX